UNDERSTAN̶̶ LAW OF TER̶̶̶SM

UNDERSTANDING THE LAW OF TERRORISM

Wayne McCormack
Professor of Law
University of Utah

Library of Congress Cataloging-in-Publication Data

McCormack, Wayne.
    Understanding the law of terrorism / Wayne McCormack.
    p. cm.
    Includes index.
    ISBN 978-1-4224-1775-1 (soft cover)
    1. Terrorism—United States. 2. Terrorism—United States—Prevention. 3. Law
enforcement—United States. 4. Terrorism—Prevention. I. Title.
KF9430.M33 2007
345.73'02—dc22

2007036694

NOTE TO USERS
To ensure that you are using the latest materials available in this area, please be sure to periodically check the LexisNexis Law School web site for downloadable updates and supplements at www.lexisnexis.com/lawschool

Editorial Offices
744 Broad Street, Newark, NJ 07102 (973) 820-2000
201 Mission St., San Francisco, CA 94105-1831 (415) 908-3200
701 East Water Street, Charlottesville, VA 22902-7587 (434) 972-7600
www.lexis.com

(Pub.03248)

PREFACE

Throughout the last quarter of the 20th Century, I was aware of terrorism probably in about the same fashion as most Americans. I saw the pictures and heard the news reports from the Munich Olympics and from a series of airplane hijackings. I read Robert Ludlum and Tom Clancy novels. As the century and millennium drew to their close, I became increasingly aware of violence in the Middle East. Nobody in the U.S. could fail to feel revulsion for the bombing of the Oklahoma City Federal Building with its day care center, nor fail to shudder at the images and reports of death at the Branch Davidian Compound in Waco. Like most Americans, I assumed that law enforcement would work with the advantages of American geography, mainly our physical distance from most of the world's hot spots, to allow us to walk about the streets of our cities with little more to fear than our home-grown domestic violence.

In 1997, I was asked to coordinate the involvement of the University of Utah with the 2002 Olympic Winter Games. The University had already agreed to host the Olympic Stadium and Olympic Village on our campus. Obviously, I needed much more knowledge and wisdom than I possessed at the time. Fortunately, my education was spurred by some very talented administrative staff within the University itself but also some extraordinarily talented professionals in state and local law enforcement, the Secret Service, and the Justice Department.

Among the many things they taught me, the first was the difference that existed at the time between security and law enforcement. Security was about prevention of incidents, and law enforcement was about incidents that were occurring or had occurred. Enhanced security means decreased access to facilities. This fact needed to be explained over and over to university constituents whose lives became a bit less convenient as the Games approached. But as the planning and operations teams did their work, they were constantly attentive to the need to keep disruptions of the university community to the minimum necessary to assure a reasonable level of safety for everyone involved.

At the University we had to walk a fine line comprised of demands by our constituents that their lives not be disrupted while they were kept safe from terrorist attacks. Some university faculty and staff wanted the Games to go away entirely, while at the other extreme some embraced their presence with enthusiasm. Most people in the middle were well aware that the Games would happen but they wanted to go on with their lives as smoothly as possible.

Then 9/11 happened, just five months before the 2002 Games. The American public were frightened and ready to throw vast resources at the problem of homeland security. In Salt Lake City, nothing changed. Our plans were in place, although we did obtain some more money and personnel that had been requested earlier.

I cannot say enough about the professionalism of the security planners with whom I dealt for this five-year period. They understood the demands of the University to keep the campus open and operating throughout the Games. They understood the desire of University constituents to prevent the campus from becoming an armed encampment. They understood the pressures to have minimum impact on the convenience of researchers, teachers, and students as they went about their academic pursuits. They understood and protected the interests of dissidents who wanted to use public fora for expression of their beliefs. But they also understood the fears and needs for planning to limit the ability of anyone to cause injury or damage during a major special event. My two sons have fond memories of watching the world's best at snowboarding and iceskating events in their home town, thanks to the efforts of all these professionals.

Things did change on 9/11. The major change is the blending of law enforcement and security so that investigators and prosecutors now have a prevention strategy at the front of their agendas. In addition, the military options were placed alongside prevention and law enforcement in the tools available for dealing with terrorism.

The three modes of response are not the same, each has benefits and limits, and it will be difficult to find the proper balance among them. This book is about balance. I have learned, painfully in some phases of my life, that the yin and yang are omnipresent, that the wisdom of the ages is all about balance and harmony, that in public life a balance needs to be struck between control and freedom.

Balance may not be a stirring, inspiring message that rouses patriotic fervor, but it is critically important at this stage of our history. If the US is to be a world leader in this or any other area, we need to demonstrate that our democratic systems work and that we are strong enough to be restrained in our approach to crisis. At times, we must be better than we want to be.

TABLE OF CONTENTS

———

Chapter 1

STRUCTURES & DEFINITIONS

§ 1.01   INTRODUCTION

This book is about institutional responses to terrorism. There are three available institutional responses that comprise governmental reaction to violence: prevention, prosecution, and military action. None of the three can work alone, and none of the three should be allowed to operate without controls. The terrorist needs to be stopped and society protected, but there is little point in doing so if the result were loss of the freedoms that define the society that we are trying to protect. Those freedoms exist through institutional limits and controls on government action, so our challenge is to provide a forceful institutional response to violence while controlling that response, a challenge that has occupied western democracies for at least the past 400 years. Terrorism is yet one more threat to social order that needs to be met in a controlled fashion.

Before we turn to the responses, it is necessary to gain some understanding of the problem — what is terrorism? why does it provoke such emotional responses? what are the values that it touches? The word "terrorism" evokes many images for each person who hears it. A single mention of the word might set my mind loose on a kaleidoscopic rampage from Munich Olympic Village, to the Achille Lauro, to a masked gunman in the cockpit of an airplane in Athens, to guerillas in the jungles of Colombia, to a sidewalk café bomb in Spain, and ultimately to fully loaded airplanes flying into the World Trade Center Towers.

The most obvious consistent theme is merely the violence of the images. Almost all that violence is directed toward civilians, and much of it is calculated for maximum insult, as if to say "in your face." Some other themes lurking in these incidents may be red herrings, and in fact it may be misleading to emphasize the commonalities over the differences. All but the last incident occurred outside the United States. Most in recent years involve Middle Eastern Islamist fundamentalists. Many were linked to demands for a Palestinian or Basque homeland, or a radical Colombian regime. A few involve people such as Timothy McVeigh who acted out of sheer malice or hatred of government but with no apparent political agenda.

When faced with abhorrent conduct to which we want to respond, the human mind naturally wants to define that conduct so that we can distinguish it from what is acceptable behavior. Most importantly, articulable definitions and distinctions are essential to the rule of law. To control and confine governmental actions requires defining the conduct to which government is allowed to respond. Yet searching for a definition within the chaotic nature of terrorism threatens to send us on a series of wild goose chases into a quagmire. (The mixing of metaphors in this sentence is intentional to emphasize that chaotic events can cause chaotic thinking, which can lead in turn to misguided or unintelligible responses.)

In the aftermath of 9/11, the United States public realized its vulnerability, but it seemed to believe that vulnerability to be curable. The American public, raised on stories of two centuries of successful uses of violence through military force to enhance our peacetime safety, believed two things: first, that for us to have become vulnerable, our government must have screwed up, and second, that if we responded vigorously (and violently), we could reestablish our public safety. Both beliefs are palpably wrong. Unfortunately, violence will always be with us, and our best efforts will only contain the scope of the problem.

Here are three truths and an observation to guide us the rest of the way:

    1.   The committed, resourceful terrorist can beat any security system.

We have a tendency to equate security with physical methods of intervention, such as locking doors, screening persons at entry points, deploying high-tech devices, and the like. Even with unlimited resources, physical security can never anticipate nor forestall the imaginative miscreant because the miscreant has the advantages of time and anonymity. Security planners must therefore deal with the reality of making a reasonable allocation of resources to security versus other public needs.

2. The more open the society, the weaker its security systems and the more vulnerable it is to violence.

Physical security measures limit the mobility and freedom of the populace. It is possible to have a community in which the ordinary citizen is reasonably protected from violence by other civilians, but only at the cost of giving over large measures of control to governmental units. In totalitarian regimes, the social order has merely traded some threats of violence for another.

3. Security, law enforcement, and military action are distinct functions that overlap in some areas.

Security planning uses a risk-threat formula to allocate available resources to a given situation. Risk refers to the potential for harm at a particular location (e.g., an event at a stadium, a nuclear reactor), and threat refers to likely attempts to cause harm. Threat analysis requires information about persons, groups, and political interests that are traditionally part of "protected" freedom.

Law enforcement most often seeks information about past wrongdoing, using sanctions for past wrongs as deterrence of future misconduct. Its connection to "protected" interests should be secondary. Only in rare instances, such as the Unabomber case, should inquiry into political agendas be necessary for solving past crimes. These also may be instances in which capturing a serial criminal directly prevents future crimes.

Military action is designed to achieve strategic objectives by application of force. Most often a successful military action achieves its objectives by applying greater force than the other party can defend, but "asymmetric" force may give the advantage to the smaller clandestine operative. Modern military planning thus requires intelligence to know what kinds of force to deploy and where.

4. Post-9/11, U.S. institutional priorities have shifted in ways that produce issues for civil liberties.

Prevention relies on information. Gathering of information threatens privacy and freedom of expression much more directly than the judicially controlled methods of law enforcement. Without a clear separation between security and law enforcement, government has employed tools that raise significant civil liberties issues.

§ 1.02 WHY TERRORISM?

Why is the public psyche so consumed with terrorism? In terms of loss of life, terrorism pales by comparison to traffic fatalities and gun deaths — even just counting U.S. fatalities in the latter two categories. The chart below depicts worldwide terrorism deaths for the year 2001 as reported by the U.S. State Department, including the 3,000 deaths on September 11.

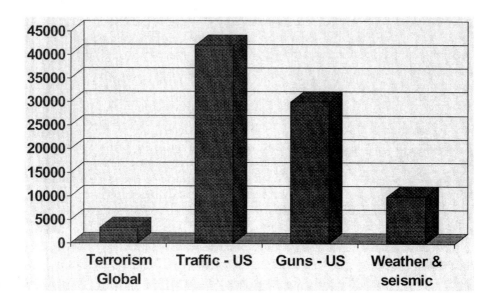

Traffic deaths in the U.S. recently have hovered at about 42,000 following a peak of almost 50,000 in the late 1980s. Deaths from guns in the U.S. divide into about 17,000 suicides, 11,000 homicides, and 1,000 accidents per year.[1] Deaths from weather and seismic incidents are much harder to quantify, and I have chosen to depict an estimated average for the past decade. Deaths and suffering from natural disasters impact thousands, almost always the poorer regions and persons of the globe.[2] Human trafficking enslaves hundreds of thousands of persons every year, most of them children exploited in sex markets but also many thousands of desperate immigrants and refugees.[3]

---

[1] *See* www.ojp.usdoj.gov/bjs/glance/tables/frmdth.htm.

[2] The year beginning in December 2004 was particularly devastating — 220,000 dead in the Christmas tsunami, 20,000 or more in the October 2005 earthquakes, thousands left homeless from a record-setting hurricane season in the U.S. and Caribbean. Predictions of the consequences of global warming are even more dire.

[3] Information about the extent of human trafficking is difficult to come by. The United Nations Office on Drugs and Crime describes the phenomenon and numbers this way:

> Trafficking in human beings is a crime in which victims are moved from poor environments to more affluent ones, with the profits flowing in the opposite direction, a pattern often repeated at the domestic, regional and global levels. It is believed to be growing fastest in Central and Eastern Europe and the former Soviet Union. In Asia, girls from villages in Nepal and Bangladesh — the majority of whom are under 18 — are sold to brothels in India for $1000. Trafficked women from Thailand and the Philippines are increasingly being joined by women from other countries in Southeast Asia. Europol estimates that the industry is now worth several billion dollars a year.

Terrorism and slavery may be linked in a number of ways. Terrorist tactics can be used to enslave a population, and enslaved populations can be trained in the ways of terrorism. In the modern world, human trafficking may provide both funds and camouflage for terrorist organizations. Both are linked in organized crime along with drug trafficking and piracy. The United Nations Office on Drugs and Crime deals primarily with terrorism, human trafficking, drugs, and corruption. The Law of the Sea Convention gives all nations jurisdiction over piracy. Organizationally, piracy is addressed by the International Maritime Bureau, an arm of the International Chamber of Commerce.[4]

Slavery became a subject of treaty law in the 1800s and some scholars believe it would have been considered a crime under international law by the middle of that century.[5] It was not until 1926, however, that the subject was mentioned in an international document. The Slavery Convention was proposed by the League of Nations in 1926. The International Labour Organization promulgated the Convention on Forced or Compulsory Labour in 1930, and the 1948 Universal Declaration of Human Rights included a broad proscription against slavery.[6] Finally, in 2003 a treaty committed most nations of the world to taking effective steps to stamp out trade in humans, placing a special emphasis on children and women. Protocol to Prevent, Suppress and Punish Trafficking in Persons, adopted as an adjunct to the Convention Against Transnational Organized Crime.[7]

> Trafficking in human beings is not confined to the sex industry. Children are trafficked to work in sweatshops as bonded labour and men work illegally in the "three D-jobs" — dirty, difficult and dangerous. A recent CIA report estimated that between 45,000 to 50,000 women and children are brought to the United States every year under false pretenses and are forced to work as prostitutes, abused labourers or servants. UNICEF estimates that more than 200,000 children are enslaved by cross-border smuggling in West and Central Africa. The children are often "sold" by unsuspecting parents who believe their children are going to be looked after, learn a trade or be educated.

U.N.O.D.C., Fact Sheet on Human Trafficking, *available at* www.unodc.org/unodc/ trafficking_victim_consents.html (last visited on June 21, 2007).

One credible author estimates that there are 27 million persons held in some form of forced labor today. KEVIN BALES, DISPOSABLE PEOPLE: NEW SLAVERY IN THE GLOBAL ECONOMY (1999).

[4] *See* U.N. Convention on the Law of the Sea, Part VII, December 10, 1982, *available at* www.un.org/Depts/los/convention_agreements/texts/unclos/unclos_e.pdf. *See generally* www.icc-ccs.org/prc/overview.php.

[5] The concepts of *jus cogens* (immutable rules) and *erga omnes* (applicable to all) were developed primarily to deal with piracy, so that a pirate was subject to universal jurisdiction and could be punished by any nation obtaining custody. Slavery may have been treated in similar fashion, but there was not the same level of consensus regarding it as there was regarding piracy. Part of the reason may have been that slavery was effectively stamped out in the domains of the European-American hegemony of the Colonial Era; its remnants in other parts of the world were then ignored by the major powers.

[6] For a very useful summary of the international agreements, see the website of the Human Rights Education Association, www.hrea.org/learn/guides/slavery.html (last visited June 21, 2007).

[7] *See* www.unodc.org/unodc/en/trafficking_protocol.html.

Despite universal revulsion toward slavery, there are many forms of forced labor still in practice, and international law retains some definitional issues to be resolved.

Terrorism, other than the genocidal practices of some recent civil wars, does not have the widespread impact of these phenomena, yet it captures the attention of the public in astonishing degrees. Why? The terrorist uses the tactic for the very reason that it will generate passion and fear. A little more detail will clarify why this is so.

[A] The Values Challenged

First, the act is "in your face"; it was never more dramatically so than on 9/11. The symbolism embodied in graphic television coverage of two towering structures collapsing in the heart of the capitalist West's financial center substantially exceeded the death toll itself. The symbolism oddly trivializes the pain and loss of the relatives of those who died, and the psychological effect goes far beyond the physical consequences. The psychological effect is designed not just to intimidate but also to demand retaliation; in the terrorist's ideal scenario, the victim will overreact and get drawn into an untenable position, such as invasion of another country.

Second, there is a deep primeval aspect to the terror inflicted by malicious unknowns on the purely innocent. There is nothing the victim has done to bring this evil about, and the evil comes out of the dark like an alien monster. The human inclination to light a fire to keep the dark at bay just doesn't work with this faceless evil.

Third, many terrorist acts are designed for the appearance of randomness — a bomb on a bus in the middle of the day or in a shopping area or a nightclub on a quiet evening creates the impression that death can stalk in the most mundane of circumstances. A fearful populace is a tense populace, and the terrorist's hope is that a tense populace eventually will yield to some demands just to ease the tension.

Fourth, the perpetrators fall into either of two camps, persons who appear to have the official imprimatur of the victim's own government or faceless unidentifiable persons who could be standing next to you on the next street corner. Because they are not uniformed personnel of another nation's military, there are no ready avenues for seeking them out or guarding against their next act.

Fifth, modern terrorism challenges the very legitimacy of government itself. To the extent that the terrorist can create the impression that government is helpless to protect its citizenry, the government loses not just credibility but authority itself.[8] This creates pressure for the government to overreact and enforce severe restrictions on its citizenry, further undermining confidence and trust between government and citizen. In the

---

[8] *See* BRUCE HOFFMAN, INSIDE TERRORISM 48 (2d ed. 2006) (quoting MENACHEM BEGIN, THE REVOLT: STORY OF THE IRGUN 52 (1977)).

internationalization of terrorism, the action and reaction also affect global opinion which can further undermine stability of the government.

[B] Values Involved in Responding

The "Global War on Terrorism" may be a tragic misnomer,[9] but it is also true that the normal processes of domestic criminal law enforcement may not be adequate to the task of confronting international terrorism. It has been said in many political settings that we are "confronting a new threat" or a "new type of enemy." That is simply not true. Terrorism, patterned violence against civilians for political ends, has been part of the human condition since people first started to gather in communities and maybe even before.

Is there something new about the internationalization or globalization of terrorism? Certainly, just as the communication, economic, and military capabilities of states have become global, so the capabilities and network structures of terrorist collectives have become globalized. But the threat of violence against civilian populations remains the same set of challenges regardless of the scale or complexity of their operations. Because of the globalized nature and loose-knit structure of terrorist operations today, there is a clear need for international cooperation in their pursuit and prosecution, but that does not mean that society should curtail or abandon any of its long-standing values under a threat that is no different in kind than what has been faced for centuries.

There is an interlocking set of "communities" devoted to public safety within government today. Similarly, there are interlocking legal controls or restraints that operate both on the individual or group who contemplates terrorist action and on the government agencies attempting to respond. The essence of the government framework is a tripod consisting of protective services, law enforcement, and the military. In the wake of a major event, whether large terrorist attack or natural disaster, the proper balance of the three functions is naturally called into question. Following 9/11, the U.S. has heavily emphasized the military option while European nations emphasized both prevention and law enforcement.

The choice of how to use each of the available resources and how much to allocate in each area depends on a calculus that is itself value-driven. For example, planning a major international event such as a World Cup soccer game starts with evaluating the likelihood of various risks and the degree of impact that would be felt if each were realized. Knowing that not all risk can be eliminated, the planner decides on a reasonable allocation of resources to meet the most likely levels and types of threat. At each stage, these calculations place a weight on human life and balance it against the resources available for protection.

---

[9] In mid-2005, the Administration began promoting the idea that the struggle with terrorism was a long-term ideological struggle rather than a war. Eric Schmitt & Thom Shanker, *U.S. Officials Retool Slogan for Terror War*, N.Y. TIMES, July 26, 2005. The revision in terminology seems to have been short-lived.

Each of the countermeasures carries costs that can be measured in terms of human values — impositions on privacy, on liberty to move around, or on freedom of expression are often called into play in the name of security. Countermeasures also present value choices in how they interact with cultural norms and values of other societies. Some of the most obvious blunders of the U.S. in the past five years have come from failures to understand or show concern for values inherent in Muslim or Arab culture, but this factor has also been present in some dealings with groups such as the IRA and FARC.

Thus, the interlocking network of contributive factors and countermeasures presents opportunities for identifying cultural and universal values at work in each level of choice or decision-making. Paying attention to what kinds of values are implicated with various policy choices will be critical in making the rational allocation of resources required by counter-terrorism planning.

§ 1.03 DEFINING TERRORISM

Defining terrorism is as important as it is difficult. It is important so that we can understand what new phenomenon we are asking government to address. It is difficult because there are so many variations and similarities to behavior than that should be addressed by ordinary processes.

The one consistent theme in terrorism is violence against civilians. But not all violence against civilians is considered terrorism, most is simply criminal conduct by one civilian against another. Three common elements can be isolated in most actions labeled as terrorism: the terrorist appears in civilian clothing, attacks civilian targets, and blends back into civilian populations. But many people classify state-uniformed "death squads" and the like as terrorist activities.[10] And many experts will not call an action terrorism unless the perpetrator has some kind of political motivation. Nor is an isolated incident of civilian violence considered terrorism, not even when committed by a person who kills more than once.[11]

What difference does it make whether we can define terrorism so long as we have the ability to prepare for and punish unjustified violence? Arriving at a coherent definition is important for several related reasons. First, the rule of law depends on reasonably clear definitions. Preventing arbitrary use of power demands that governmental actions, whether domestic or international, be taken according to articulated standards. Second, definitions may be critical to determining which among various available options will be pursued. There may be choices to be made among both domestic and international fora, and those choices must be intelligible if they are to have credibility. Third, definitions that are reliable will help

---

[10] CHRISTOPHER HARMON, TERRORISM TODAY 31-33 (2000).

[11] Thus, serial killers are not usually considered terrorists. This paradigm is being challenged in the prosecution of John Allen Muhammad in Virginia under the state terrorism statute. *See* Muhammad v. Commonwealth, 619 S.E.2d 16 (Va. 2005).

in controlling emotional responses to violent situations. If people know how to label an action, they will have more confidence that some appropriate response may be forthcoming. And finally, in keeping with our concern for controlling government action, definitions are critical to limiting governmental responses.

The U.S. Department of State is mandated by federal law to designate "foreign terrorist organizations" based on three criteria:

- that it is a foreign organization,
- that it engages in terrorist activity,
- and that its terrorist activity threatens the safety of U.S. nationals or the national security of the U.S.[12]

"Terrorist activity" in turn is defined with four elements (italicized here): "premeditated, *politically motivated violence* perpetrated against *noncombatant targets* by *subnational groups* or clandestine agents, usually *intended to influence* an audience."[13] The elements in this definition can be summarized most succinctly as:

1. violence
2. civilian targets
3. subnational or clandestine perpetrator
4. political motivation

The consequences of designation include blocking of the organization's financial assets in the U.S.,[14] prohibiting members of the organization from entering the U.S.,[15] and criminalizing provision of material support to the organization.[16] There are significant constitutional issues with regard to the process for designation[17] and the use of such a designation in criminal prosecutions[18] — issues that we will consider later. For now, however, the State Department's annual report is useful for its descriptions of the organizations that it tracks and monitors.

[A] Describing the Terrorist Groups

The most famous, or infamous, terrorist groups active in the world today are al Qaeda, Hezbollah and its related groups, FARC (Revolutionary Armed Forces of Colombia), ETA (Basque Fatherland and Liberty — Spain), and Aum Shinrikyo (Japan). The IRA (Irish Republican Army) and Shining

---

[12] 8 U.S.C. § 1189 (2007).

[13] 22 U.S.C. § 2656f (2007).

[14] 18 U.S.C. § 2339B(a)(2) (2007).

[15] 8 U.S.C. § 1182(a) (2007).

[16] 18 U.S.C. § 2339B (2007).

[17] *See* National Council of Resistance of Iran v. Dep't of State, 251 F.3d 192 (D.C. Cir. 2001); *see also* People's Mojahedin Org. of Iran v. United States Dep't of State [MEK], 182 F.3d 17 (D.C. Cir. 1999).

[18] United States v. Rahmani, 209 F. Supp. 2d 1045 (C.D. Cal. 2002).

Path (Peru) have cooled their level of activity over the past several years. Other groups come and go. The purely political ideologues of the 1960s and 1970s, such as the Red Brigade (Brigate Russo — Italy) and Baader-Meinhoff (Germany) have all but disappeared.

As of April 30, 2007, the State Department designated 42 "Foreign Terrorist Organizations" and provided background information on 43 "Other Groups of Concern." Roughly 2/3 of the designated groups have a Palestinian or Islamist focus, nine (not counting the Palestinian groups) are seeking separatist goals for some identifiable ethnic or cultural group, five are Marxist revolutionary groups, and one is a fringe Israeli Zionist group.

The "other" list appears to be composed of groups that meet the first two elements for designation (foreign organization that engages in terrorist activity) but does not represent a threat to the security of U.S. nationals or U.S. interests.

[1] Religious Motivations

Many observers have noted that terrorism took on particularly violent overtones in the 1990s with the heightening of religious tensions. But the connection between religious fanaticism and violence against civilians is hardly a recent phenomenon. Even in recent decades, some of the most violent attacks occurred in Northern Ireland where religion and cultural groupings were the prime distinguishing characteristics.

The Islamist connection with so many of the groups on both State Department lists deserves some special discussion. Obviously, the level of religious fervor and the avowed justifications of jihad based on Islamist rhetoric has grown exponentially in the past few decades. To most observers, including Islamic leaders, the preaching of jihad by terrorist groups is a perversion of Muslim beliefs. There is an argument to be made that the conditions of "just war" in Muslim teaching parallel the Western view that use of military force should only be defensive in nature, but even sympathetic scholars recognize a significant difference, namely that in Islamic law "there is no mechanism for recognizing a non-Muslim government as legitimate."[19]

Fundamentalism can be found in all three of the world's leading monotheistic religions,[20] but there is one distinction that makes it difficult for the three to communicate. Both Hebraic and Islamic traditions support a view of divine ordination of a government that is intertwined with religion (and in which religion could be intertwined with ethnicity and ethnicity with culture).[21] European-American attitudes toward religion historically flow

---

[19] Douglas E. Streusand, *What Does Jihad Mean?*, MIDDLE EAST Q., Sept. 1997, *available at* www.ict.org.il/articles/jihad.htm.

[20] *See generally* KAREN ARMSTRONG, THE BATTLE FOR GOD (2000).

[21] In some quarters of the Arab world, religion, culture, and ethnicity all commingle to form a basis for a special type of government, one that will fulfill the goals and missions of the

from Christian sources, which for the most part emphasized separation of church and state.[22] The need to come to an understanding of these traditions is important in today's violent world.[23]

[2] Separatism, Revolution, and Political Motivations

The nine designated groups with separatist objectives seek outcomes such as a Basque homeland from Spain or a Tamil enclave in Sri Lanka. A number of other groups, mostly Marxist, seek to overthrow the governments of their homelands in entirety. And the remnants of the IRA, now known as the "Real IRA," still pursue the objective of unifying Northern Ireland with the Catholic South. These groups have an identifiable political objective in the sense of territory that they seek to control and govern. As discussed below, the classic definitions of terrorism have sought to distinguish it from ordinary criminal behavior by looking at political objectives, but very few of the Islamic groups have genuine "political" objectives in the sense of controlling and governing definable territory. The Marxist groups may fantasize about taking power from the existing state, but it is doubtful that any of them except the drug-funded Colombian rebels have a serious agenda for seizing control of the political machinery of government.

Most of the Islamist groups wish to oust the foreign infidels from the Middle East or Indian subcontinent, or they want to see the establishment of a Palestinian homeland or both. The point here is that most of these groups have no definable political objective of their own ambition. This leads to the realization that there is no bargaining to be done with anything remotely resembling an insurgent force. The lack of a defined political goal is one of the aspects that make the ideological or religious terrorist acutely dangerous. Fatah and Hamas have been involved in various negotiations with apparent territorial objectives but the events of 2007 leave open questions about the actual motivations of many of the fighters. By contrast, the Colombian government has been in negotiation with the Marxist ELN and FARC for several years now with some prospect for success if sufficient accommodations can be reached. In the meanwhile, the negotiations and the recognized insurgent status of these groups offer some hope for reducing the level of violence toward civilians.

Christopher Harmon, a faculty member at the Marine Corps Command and Staff College, contends that "Terrorism is always political, even when

---

faith. The radical Islamists assert that the loyal Muslim must attempt to create Islamic governments and spread the power of Islam to any fertile ground. Ayatullah Morteza Mutahhari, *Jihad: The Holy War of Islam and Its Legitimacy in the Quran, available at* www.al-islam.org/short/jihad/.

[22] It is understandable that Christian dogma would have sought refuge in this position as a rationale for protection against the actions of potentially hostile governments starting with Rome, running through the Middle Ages, and eventually motivating many of the British colonials. It even serves as a sensible reaction to some of the excesses of Christianity's own state-sanctioned Inquisition.

[23] *See generally* MARY HABECK, KNOWING THE ENEMY: JIHADIST IDEOLOGY AND THE WAR OF TERROR (2006).

it also evinces other motives, such as the religious, the economic, or the social. . . . If terrorism is best defined by its calculated abuse of the innocent for political purposes, there is reason to survey the political objectives which prompt such actions by militants of the modern day."[24] He describes organizations with political agendas of anarchism, communism, neofascism, national separation, religion, and pro-state terrorism. With this variety of political motivations, can we even conclude that political objectives are a defining characteristic of terrorism? Harmon concedes that "Individual terrorists may find the clandestine struggle so appealing that it almost becomes an end in itself, a way of life. But while such nihilism is present by degrees in anyone willing to maim and murder the innocent, it is a mistake to think that nihilism, rather than purpose, is the essence of the typical contemporary terrorist organization."[25]

We will return to the question of motivation in a moment, as we explore the definition problem further.

[3] Funding

Understanding the methods of funding for terrorist organizations is particularly helpful to the preventive effort and is also a useful method for tracing illegal activity. "Follow the money" is a long-standing maxim of criminal enforcement. Funding for terrorism has come primarily from one or more of three sources: state sponsorship, donations, or illegal activities.

States have supported insurgent groups within other states for millenia, including the critical late-stage support of France for the American Revolution. The Soviet Union made this activity almost an art form by attempting to export revolution around the world, and the United States answered with support both for incumbent governments and insurgents of its own. The United States, of course, may have been there first with both open and clandestine support for coups and insurgencies in Latin America during the late 19th and early 20th Centuries, the era of the so-called banana republics. The critical factor in assessing the contribution of state support to terrorism, however, lies in how the rebel force uses violence. For "one person's freedom fighter" to be "another's terrorist," the insurgent must be violating rules of warfare not just by attacking without justification or identifying marks but also by attacking civilian targets. If the revolutionary group targets only military or government installations, then they may not be entitled to protections of the Geneva Conventions but they probably would not be saddled with the terminology of "terrorist." This is important in international law, which is now recognizing systematic attacks on civilians by insurgents as "crimes against humanity." An increasingly strong component of U.S. foreign policy over the past three decades has been efforts within the international community to thwart state-sponsored terrorism.

---

[24] HARMON, *supra* note 10, at 1.
[25] *Id.* at 45.

Private donations may be the most important source of start-up support for the fledgling guerilla force, but it is not clear how significant this source is for ongoing support of terrorist organizations. Britain was disturbed for decades by apparent lack of U.S. cooperation in stemming the flow of money from the U.S. to the IRA. Americans also contributed heavily to the "Zionist" movement before recognition of the State of Israel. Today, the U.S. is assiduously following money trails that lead to Islamist fundamentalist groups, and another strong component of U.S. policy is the freezing or forfeiture of assets destined for designated terrorist organizations.

Profits from illegal activities may be a source of funding for political or other illegal activities. The myth of Robin Hood expresses some popular sentiment for this mode of operation. Self-styled revolutionaries in the U.S. have turned frequently to bank robbery to fund their operations. Today, the "war on drugs" is being conflated with the "war on terrorism" because of the recognition that trafficking in drugs may yield exorbitant profits that can be turned to other criminal activity such as terrorism. Conversely, terrorist methods may support the criminal organizations involved in illicit drug trade. The prime examples of this connection in the current atmosphere are the Colombian revolutionary groups, but several Islamist groups are allegedly heavily involved in drug trafficking as well. This connection has led Senator Hatch to float the idea of declaring war on "narco-terrorism" on the one hand,[26] while Judge Posner has noted that cancelling the war on drugs could eliminate the exorbitant profits that can be used to support terrorism.[27]

[4] Organization

Understanding the internal structure of terrorist organizations is similarly helpful in choosing methods for combating their activities. The term "cell" was used for several decades to describe the bottom rung of communist organizations. It is now the standard term for terrorist groups. Although some organizations claim to have anarchic styles, most have attempted to follow a traditional management model that could be drawn on an ordinary organizational chart — each cell or squad has a leader who reports to the next level and so on up through a hierarchical pyramid. The pyramid model is like a traditional corporate organization chart.

Variations on this theme, however, abound for good reasons. Any clandestine organization will attempt to shield its operatives from knowledge of

---

[26] *Narco-Terrorism: International Drug Trafficking and Terrorism — A Dangerous Mix* (May 20, 2003) (statement of Sen. Orrin G. Hatch before the Senate Judiciary Committee).

[27] Richard Posner, *Security Versus Civil Liberties*, Atlantic Monthly, Dec. 2001, *available at* http://www.theatlantic.com/dec/200112/posner:

> The war on drugs has been a big flop; moreover, in light of what September 11 has taught us about the gravity of the terrorist threat to the United States, it becomes hard to take entirely seriously the threat to the nation that drug use is said to pose. Perhaps it is time to redirect law-enforcement resources from the investigation and apprehension of drug dealers to the investigation and apprehension of international terrorists.

each other to reduce the risk of information's getting out to unauthorized sources. One distinguishing factor among cells in a traditional structure would be whether a cell has an "action" or "infrastructure" mandate. A well-disciplined and cohesive terrorist organization might protect its action cells by having several cells with similar goals in place in any given locale, none of whom knows what the other is doing so that penetration of one by investigators would yield no information about the others. At the same time, the organization may organize other cells for other purposes.

The trial in the "embassy bombings" case laid out a scheme in which one cell would be responsible for target selection, another for weapons and finance, another for funding and travel documents, and so on.[28] This structure is reminiscent of industrial management, with separate departments for functions such as finance, manufacture, and sales. It provides efficiency in one cell's ability to supply several different operations with logistical support, but it carries the risk of opponents' dealing a major blow by "rolling up" the funding cell. Therefore, with a very large organization, some diffusion of responsibility will be expected.

The diffusion of responsibility in terrorist structures has evolved from the pyramidal structure through variations of "conspiracy" models and now to highly diffused models that are really more like unstructured networks of loosely affiliated or even unaffiliated bands.

In 1929, the British courts promulgated the metaphor of "wheels" and "chains" to describe two distinct types of conspiracy: "There may be one person . . . round whom the rest revolve. The metaphor is of the centre of a circle and the circumference. There may be a conspiracy of another kind, where the metaphor would be rather that of a chain; A communicates with B, B with C, C with D, and so on to the end of the line of conspirators."[29]

These images illustrate why it has been thought to be important to capture some of the key players for interrogation rather than simply taking military or clandestine action to kill the leaders. Even if some of the top leadership were killed, others in the organization could move into those positions of leadership and continue the movement. If enough information about the groups could be obtained, however, then it would be possible to "roll up" an entire organization.

Technological advances have modified the world in ways that have had a heavy influence on terrorist behavior. Communications and transportation advances mean that terrorist groups can be more mobile and more diffuse while also having more impact. A "group" may actually be a collection of unrelated individuals who communicate anonymously by

---

[28] United States v. Bin Laden, 92 F. Supp. 2d 225 (S.D.N.Y. 2000) (motion for bill of particulars).

[29] Rex v. Meyrick and Ribuffi, 21 CRIM. APP. R. 94 (1929); *see* Jerome Campane, *Chains, Wheels, and the Single Conspiracy, Pt. I*, FBI LAW ENFORCEMENT BULL., Aug. 1981, at 24 and Pt. II, Sept. 1981, at 24; Note, *Federal Treatment of Multiple Conspiracies*, 57 COLUM. L. REV. 387 (1975).

electronic methods or who don't even communicate directly but instead simply share ideas in cyber space. The result can range from a highly diffuse assortment of relatively autonomous actors to a tightly coordinated network. A depiction of an advanced coordinated network would look like this:

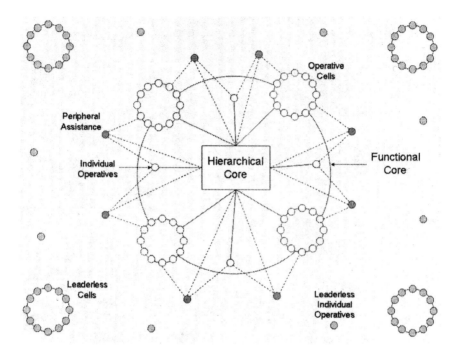

This diagram is provided by George Hepner and Richard Medina, who describe the structure as a composite of different types of groups and connections.[30]

---

[30] George Hepner & Richard Medina, *Geospatial Analysis of Dynamic Terrorist Networks*, to be published in VALUES & VIOLENCE: INTANGIBLE ASPECTS OF TERRORISM (forthcoming 2008):

> The network core contains the hierarchical core leadership, operative cells, and individual operatives, while the periphery contains peripheral assistance, and beyond the periphery are leaderless cells and individual operatives. It is assumed that the leaderless cells and operatives are not connected in the typical sense of connectivity between nodes in a network, but are connected by ideological-religious beliefs and/or purpose. . . . Weak ties in a social network typically refer to the connection between acquaintances. These ties can connect nodes in the network to nodes in the periphery, such that they are not operational actors in the network, but are functional in the sense that they offer recruitment assistance, shelter and safe havens, monetary support, as well as other types of assistance. . . . Depending on the organization, cells and operatives are more or less decentralized, and leaderless cells and operatives may or may not exist.

The complexity and diversity of networking make it difficult to generalize about the nature of terrorist structures today. It is also difficult to confront what is essentially a movement more than an organization. On the other hand, it is arguable that the internal organizational difficulties of a complex organization are no different for terrorists than for other complex structures and that these bureaucratic difficulties can be exploited to our advantage.[31] Whatever the reality of that argument with any particular group or movement, the essential point is that different structures call for different responses, which heightens the importance of good intelligence.

[B] Definitions and Motivation

Harmon defines terrorism as "the deliberate and systematic murder, maiming, and menacing of the innocent to inspire fear for political ends."[32] Caleb Carr, writing as a military historian, provides a perspective that shifts the focus to the language and usages of war: "terrorism . . . is simply the contemporary name given to, and the modern permutation of, warfare deliberately waged against civilians with the purpose of destroying their will to support either leaders or policies that the agents of such violence find objectionable."[33]

Harmon and Carr agree that political motivation is an essential factor in defining a terrorist, although it is interesting to think about what happens if the terrorist achieves his or her political objectives. Harmon claims that "when organizations dominated by terror rise to power, they remain antithetical to popular self-government."[34] Carr asserts that "the nation or faction that resorts to warfare against civilians most quickly, most often, and most viciously is the nation or faction that stands the greatest chance of seeing its interests frustrated and, in many cases, its existence terminated."[35] As we will see, there are some groups which, upon approaching their original goals, will escalate the goals to continue the justification for their way of life.

Philip Heymann employs the more traditional elements of a definition by describing terrorism as "violence conducted as a political strategy by a subnational group or secret agents of a foreign state."[36] This definition reflects most of the elements in the State Department definition and is similar to that found in other U.S. statutes. One such statute appears in the criminal code but does not define a crime; it is useful primarily as a prelude to civil liability of terrorist groups.[37] As the statute itself makes

---

[31] Mariano-Florentino Cuellar, *The Untold Story of al Qaeda's Administrative Law Dilemmas*, 91 MINN. L. REV. 1302 (2007).

[32] HARMON, *supra* note 10, at 1.

[33] CALEB CARR, THE LESSONS OF TERROR 6 (2003).

[34] HARMON, *supra* note 10, at 187.

[35] CARR, *supra* note 33, at 16-17.

[36] PHILIP HEYMANN, TERRORISM AND AMERICA 6 (1998).

[37] 18 U.S.C. § 2331. As used in this chapter [18 USC §§ 2331-2339C]

(1) the term "international terrorism" means activities that —

clear, the terrorist act is already a crime by the nature of the act without regard to the motivation. Yet another definition[38] is used to modify otherwise applicable statutes of limitations[39] and to enhance punishments under the Federal Sentencing Guidelines when the accused has been convicted of something that is a crime by virtue of another statute.[40]

Why do motivations matter unless the potential for harm depends upon them? One answer could be that motivation may distinguish the terrorist from the common criminal or serial killer. With this in mind, how should we characterize Theodore Kaczynski, the Unabomber? The Unabomber Manifesto decried technology and the industrial society, proposing a revolution that would smash the factories and even burn the books to prevent future regeneration of technology. This may represent a political motivation but the Manifesto made clear that he had no affirmative objectives for the future,[41] and his acts did not carry outside the domestic concerns of the U.S. Moreover, he acted alone, which reduces the likelihood of his actions being repeated after his capture. On the other hand, many authors consider Timothy McVeigh to be a terrorist because he acted out of malice for the government, but there is no known indication that he had an alternative in mind that would qualify as a political agenda nor any

(A) involve violent acts or acts dangerous to human life that are a violation of the criminal laws of the United States or of any State, or that would be a criminal violation if committed within the jurisdiction of the United States or of any State;

(B) appear to be intended

(i) to intimidate or coerce a civilian population;

(ii) to influence the policy of a government by intimidation or coercion; or

(iii) to affect the conduct of a government by mass destruction, assassination or kidnapping; and

(C) occur primarily outside the territorial jurisdiction of the United States, or transcend national boundaries in terms of the means by which they are accomplished, the persons they appear intended to intimidate or coerce, or the locale in which their perpetrators operate or seek asylum.

[38] 18 U.S.C. § 2332(b)(g)(5)(B): " 'Federal crime of terrorism' means an offense that (A) is calculated to influence or affect the conduct of government by intimidation or coercion, or to retaliate against government conduct; and (B) is a violation of [one of a list of 39 other criminal statutes]."

[39] 18 U.S.C. § 3286.

[40] 18 U.S.C. App. § 3A1.4 (2003).

[41] See Unabomber Manifesto ¶ 184, available at www.time.com/time/reports/unabomber/unifesto3.html#24:

To relieve the pressure on nature it is not necessary to create a special kind of social system, it is only necessary to get rid of industrial society. Granted, this will not solve all problems. Industrial society has already done tremendous damage to nature and it will take a very long time for the scars to heal. Besides, even pre-industrial societies can do significant damage to nature. Nevertheless, getting rid of industrial society will accomplish a great deal. It will relieve the worst of the pressure on nature so that the scars can begin to heal. It will remove the capacity of organized society to keep increasing its control over nature (including human nature). Whatever kind of society may exist after the demise of the industrial system, it is certain that most people will live close to nature, because in the absence of advanced technology there is not other way that people CAN live.

organization to carry the violence forward after his capture. Political motivation in these examples is not a key ingredient, and may be totally irrelevant, in deciding what to label as terrorism and what as "ordinary" crime.

Another reason for considering motivation is from the perspective of the victims and potential victims. If terrorism can be made to appear as if the power of the state is behind it, then the intimidation of civilian populations can be even more overwhelming than when the terrorist acts are clearly the work of renegade bands. But this factor depends on the appearance of state sanction or authorization, not on the motivations of the perpetrators.

Does motivation distinguish the "terrorist" from the ordinary street criminal, especially one with ties to an international criminal organization? Take, for instance, a murder committed on the streets of an American city by a drug dealer who knows in some vague way that his livelihood is linked to a well-organized and well-funded cartel in Colombia or Afghanistan and who intends the murder not just to eliminate an immediate problem but also to intimidate others into compliance with his edicts. Is this an act of terrorism? Is it an act of war? Is the U.S. justified in invading Colombia because there are organized criminals there who carry out violence on U.S. civilians? This has been the theme of at least two recent movies,[42] both carrying the message that U.S. involvement in Colombia would be permissible only with the permission of the Colombian government, certainly the correct answer under international law. Meanwhile, international law is creating cooperative efforts to deal with the transborder aspects of large criminal organizations without promoting intrusion into the internal affairs of any one nation.[43]

On the global stage, what distinguishes José Padilla from Timothy McVeigh? Assuming the facts as disclosed in press releases about Padilla, both were motivated by extreme hatred for the U.S. government, both were planning mass civilian casualties at governmental centers. Padilla was in league with foreign citizens, but what does this signify? How do we distinguish him from alleged Mafiosi, or drug dealers in league with Colombian cartels? The only distinguishing characteristic of Padilla is that he allegedly was working in concert with a far-reaching organization with the resources and ability to carry out an ongoing campaign of terror.

---

[42] CLEAR AND PRESENT DANGER (Paramount 1994) and COLLATERAL DAMAGE (Warner Bros. 2002).

[43] The United Nations Office on Drugs and Crime is charged with coordinating efforts with respect to organized crime and links closely with the Security Council's Counter-Terrorism Committee. ODC's principal mandate is the Convention Against Transnational Organized Crime.

> The recent increase in the scope, intensity and sophistication of crime around the world threatens the safety of citizens everywhere and hampers countries in their social, economic and cultural development. The dark side of globalization allows multinational criminal syndicates to broaden their range of operations from drug and arms trafficking to money laundering and trafficking in human beings.

www.unodc.org/unodc/en/crime_prevention.html.

This potential for definition confusion is presented in the state prosecution of John Allen Muhammad, the alleged Maryland-Virginia sniper. In addition to ordinary murder charges, he is charged under a Virginia statute aimed at terrorism, defined as an "act of violence . . . committed with the intent to (i) intimidate the civilian population at large; or (ii) influence the conduct or activities of the government of the United States, a state or locality through intimidation."[44] His attorneys argued for dismissal of the terrorism charge on the ground that all potential jurors were alleged victims of the crime. The prosecution countered with an agreement to a change of venue outside the area of killings.[45]

Let us grant that Harmon is correct that terrorism "is always political" but that does not mean that political objectives should be part of the defining characteristics of terrorism. The terrorist may be motivated by political events and perceived wrongs without having any identifiable political objective. Destroying the means of government or expelling foreign infidels hardly qualifies as a political objective. These are just statements of motivation or intent, not identifiable objectives. The difference is in thinking of motivation as impelling from the past rather than thinking of motivation as a goal for the future. Finally, there is no reason to think that political motivation is any indicator of the potential for harm, although the extent of resources or organization of a group may well be relevant to the potential for harm.

Seen in that fashion, it is difficult to see any reason why political motivation should play any role in the definition of terrorism. Both international and domestic U.S. law could benefit from reformulating the definition of terrorism to focus on the scale or impact of the organization rather than the motives of the actors.[46]

[C] International Attempts To Define

"One person's terrorist is another's freedom fighter." For many years, this deceptively ominous statement stalled the world's debates over outlawing terrorism. As numerous authors have pointed out, this is an almost silly argument because universal law criminalizes attacks on civilian populations without regard to the political motivations of the actor. The difficulty is not whether there could be justification for an attack on civilians because legally there cannot be. The difficulty is in determining by what process to respond to such an attack.

The United Nations Office on Drugs and Crime points out that the definition problem has plagued international cooperation for decades.

In order to cut through the Gordian definitional knot, terrorism expert A. Schmid suggested in 1992 in a report for the then U.N.

---

[44] VA. CODE ANN. § 18.2-46.4 (2002).

[45] *See* CNN News, *Prosecutors in Sniper Trial Willing to Support Change of Venue, available at* www.cnn.com/2003/LAW/07/11/sprj.dcsp.muhammad/index.html (July 11, 2003).

[46] *See* page 29 *infra.*

Crime Branch that it might be a good idea to take the existing consensus on what constitutes a "war crime" as a point of departure. If the core of war crimes — deliberate attacks on civilians, hostage taking and the killing of prisoners — is extended to peacetime, we could simply define acts of terrorism as "peacetime equivalents of war crimes."[47]

In 1996, India introduced a Draft Comprehensive Convention on Terrorism, which the General Assembly referred to an Ad Hoc Committee.[48] To date, the committee has produced a convention on terrorist bombings, one on nuclear terrorism, and one on terrorist financing but has yet to promulgate a proposed general convention.[49] The major problems are in determining whether terrorism encompasses only nonstate actors and whether to exempt actions against oppressive regimes:

> Some other delegations emphasized the importance of including, in the draft comprehensive convention, a legal definition of terrorism to distinguish it from the legitimate struggle of peoples for self-determination. In addition, other delegations expressed the view that State terrorism would have to be included in any comprehensive convention on international terrorism. It was reiterated that acts of State terrorism were of serious concern to the international community and that such acts only contributed to a vicious cycle of terrorism.[50]

During a crowded holiday travel period, an Egyptian expatriate in the United States opened fire at the El Al counter in Los Angeles Airport and killed three people. The U.S. and Israel disagreed over the question of whether he would be considered a terrorist.

> American and Israeli officials initially appeared to disagree on Thursday about whether Mr. Hadayet's rampage should be called a terrorist attack. But it became clear today that the difference was really over what constitutes terrorism. Yuval Rotem, Israel's consul general in Los Angeles, said that even a lone individual attacking an Israeli target like the El Al ticket counter should be considered a terrorist. But F.B.I. officials said that only if Mr. Hadayet was linked to a terrorist organization would American investigators call it that, rather than a hate crime.[51]

---

[47] www.unodc.org/unodc/terrorism_definitions.html.

[48] G.A. Res. 51/210 (1996).

[49] www.un.org/law/terrorism/index.html. For summations of the status of the effort, see Center for Nonproliferation Studies, Inventory of International Nonproliferation Organizations and Regimes, Aug. 11, 2006, *available at* cns.miis.edu/pubs/inven/pdfs/intlterr.pdf.

[50] Report of the Ad Hoc Committee established by General Assembly resolution 51/210 of 17 December 1996, Feb. 2007, *available at* daccessdds.un.org/doc/UNDOC/GEN/N07/242/89/PDF/N0724289.pdf?OpenElement.

[51] N.Y. TIMES, July 6, 2002, at U.N. Office on Drugs & Crime, *Conventions Against Terrorism.*

At the international level, there have been many attempts over the years to define terrorism. Thus far, all attempts have failed with one narrow exception. The United Nations Office for Drug Control and Crime Prevention lists 12 separate "Conventions Against Terrorism."[52] With the same single exception, however, the specific subjects of these conventions are not terrorism but aircraft crimes, protection of nuclear materials, hostage taking, and bombing. Each of the conventions commits signatory nations to define the offenses as crimes within their own law, which in turn leads to a commitment either to extradite or to place an apprehended accused on trial.

The Convention on Terrorist Bombings uses the word in its title but then not in the body of the document. It applies to "any person" who "unlawfully and intentionally delivers, places, discharges or detonates an explosive or other lethal device in, into or against a place of public use, a State or government facility, a public transportation system or an infrastructure facility"[53] except when "the offence is committed within a single State, the alleged offender and the victims are nationals of that State, the alleged offender is found in the territory of that State and no other State has a basis to exercise jurisdiction."[54]

The Convention on Financing of Terrorism is the only international document with anything that resembles a definition of terrorism. The Convention applies to "any person" who "wilfully provides or collects funds with the intention that they should be used or in the knowledge that they are to be used, in full or in part, in order to carry out" any "act intended to cause death or serious bodily injury to a civilian, or to any other person not taking an active part in the hostilities in a situation of armed conflict, when the purpose of such act, by its nature or context, is to intimidate a population, or to compel a Government or an international organization to do or to abstain from doing any act."[55]

U.N. Security Council Resolutions have called on member states to suppress terrorism without defining terrorism.[56] The Sixth Committee of the International Law Commission is working on a draft Declaration that would include a definition of terrorism that focuses on violence against civilians for political purposes.

Curiously, of all adopted documents at the international level, only the Convention on Financing refers to political motivations and is the only one that attempts to define terrorism. By contrast, the Convention on Terrorist

---

[52] www.unodc.org/unodc/terrorism_conventions.html (last visited June 21, 2007).

[53] International Convention for the Suppression of Terrorist Bombings, art. 2, U.N. DOC A/RES/52/I64 (Dec. 15, 1997).

[54] *Id.* art. 3.

[55] International Convention for the Suppression of the Financing of Terrorism, art. 2, U.N. DOC A/RES/54/109 (Feb. 25, 2000).

[56] Most notable of the Security Council Resolutions is S.C. Res. 1373 U.N.DOC. S/RES/373 (Sept. 28, 2001), which created a Counter-Terrorism Committee to work within the Security Council framework.

Bombings is very straightforward in condemning any bombing but excepting those that are purely domestic in impact.

"The African National Congress, Provisional Irish Republican Army, and the radical organizations of the Jewish settlers before the creation of Israel all engaged in attacks on civilian targets, and yet their leaders have been treated as heroes."[57] Heymann describes terrorism as combining elements of crime and armed combat. It is different from normal crime because of its purposes (crime is usually motivated by greed, jealousy, anger, or power) and different from legitimate combat because of its clandestine and unauthorized character. His view of terrorism thus is "an illegal form of clandestine warfare that is carried out by a sub-state group to change the policies, personnel, structure, or ideology of a government, or to influence the actions of another part of the population — one with enough self-identity to respond to selective violence."[58]

Coinciding with this theme of armed conflict, other scholars define terrorism as the "peacetime equivalent of war crimes: acts that would, if carried out by a government in war, violate the Geneva Convention."[59] Similarly, Harmon notes that "Terrorism is also sometimes used in conjunction with legitimate forms of political struggle. But alliance with legitimate methods cannot justify illegitimate ones; terrorism remains distinguishable from legitimate methods of political struggle."[60]

How would the conscientious, arguably heroic, freedom fighter differ from the condemnable terrorist? Here we move into the realm of international law. "International Law" is often derided as being no law at all but just what the strongest nations impose on the weaker. "To the victor go the spoils." Although there is some truth in this view, the total truth is very subtle and contains many elements of a somewhat enforceable set of rules for governing on the global stage. Customary international law is the expression of a consensus about what is permissible and thus affects the arguments that are made even in purely political contexts. At a relatively mundane level, international law may be the basis of criminal prosecutions. And eventually the rules of customary international law will shape the actions of nation-states as they conform to widely accepted norms. As the world has been shrunk by rapid communications and transportation, globalization of economies has produced and will continue to produce increasing levels of globalization of law.

International law as it relates to terrorism must begin with the rules of warfare considered in more detail in the next chapter. Briefly, the rules dealing with limits on the use of force are codified in the Hague Conventions of 1907, particularly the "Laws and Customs of War on Land." These rules were violated by use of poison gases during World War I, but were

---

[57] HEYMANN, *supra* note 36, at 7.

[58] *Id.* at 9.

[59] ALEX P. SCHMID & RONALD D. CRELINSTEN, WESTERN RESPONSES TO TERRORISM 13 (1993).

[60] HARMON, *supra* note 10, at 1.

nonetheless considered to be important elements guiding armed conflict in World War II (at least by the German and Allied forces, less so by the Japanese forces). The rules governing use of force and treatment of prisoners of war were recodified and elaborated in the Geneva Conventions of 1949. Meanwhile, the Treaty of London governed trials of accused Nazi war criminals at Nuremberg.

The founding of the United Nations in 1945 set the stage for what many hoped to become a "new world order." The U.N. Charter loosely incorporates all the previous Conventions by declaring that military force may be used only defensively, and holds out the threat of enforcement by collective action of all other member nations against a nation that violates this basic command. The Security Council is charged with determining whether violations have occurred and what response, from diplomatic or economic sanctions to military action, should be enforced.

International law, as found from custom as well as from the various conventions regarding use of force, has given rise to a heading of "universal jurisdiction" for any nation to prosecute offenses against the law of nations. This power was first used in relation to piracy and slave trade, but it could be a source of law with regard to terrorism as well.

In addition to these steps, the U.N. has been an integral part of prosecuting war crimes and genocide. It formed ad hoc tribunals for the trial of crimes committed in Rwanda and Yugoslavia. At the same time, it promoted the drafting and eventual adoption of the International Criminal Court, a multinational body asserting jurisdiction over offenses against the law of nations in the categories of war crimes, crimes against humanity, and genocide. These tribunals have begun to develop the theme that acts of terrorism within the context of a "widespread" or state-supported pattern could be considered crimes against humanity.[61] The ICC would not be expected to assert jurisdiction over an act of terrorism unless it formed part of a "widespread or systematic attack directed against any civilian population."[62]

Thus, international law is becoming an increasing presence in regard to the behavior of persons formally affiliated with a nation-state (a state actor) and is promoting cooperation and assistance among the nations for dealing with non-state-actors such as terrorists and drug lords. As we will see in Chapter 6, most of international law is moving toward dealing with terrorist acts under the heading of "crimes against humanity," in which the relevant criteria are not motivations but the "widespread, systematic, or continuous" nature of the conduct.

---

[61] *See* § 6.02[C] *infra*.

[62] Rome Statue of the International Criminal Ct, art. 7, U.N. DOC A/CONF 183/9 (as corrected Nov. 10, 1998 and July 12, 1999).

§ 1.04 SHARED EXPERIENCE: VIOLENCE IN OTHER STATES

In the early post-Civil War experience of the U.S., Congress acted to quell racial violence by first attempting to legislate directly. Concerned about its constitutional power to do so, it promulgated the Fourteenth Amendment with its familiar Due Process, Equal Protection, and Privileges and Immunities Clauses. Unfortunately, the Amendment only acted against the States and seemed to give Congress no authority over the behavior of non-state actors. Similarly, in the early days of international law, nations believed that their only authority was to act against each other, that they had no authority over the behavior of nonstate actors. Just as the U.S. ultimately came to grips with the debilitating effects of private racial violence, the international community came to deal with crimes against humanity.

Now the international community is struggling to agree on a definition of terrorism that will match its frequently expressed consensus that terrorism is to be condemned. The problem is — what is it that we have condemned? The most common way to define an activity to be proscribed is to ask why the institution wants to eliminate it. In other words, why does one state care about violent behavior within another state?

From the review of both international and U.S. law above, there are at least four interests that might be affected by patterned violence against persons in other states. These are state action, denial of rights, inadequacy of state response, and group animus. The first three are all related to the state's willingness or ability to protect the rights of persons within its territory while the fourth relates to the psyche of the perpetrator.

[A] The State Action Interest

Both the very tangible U.S. federal government and the intangible international community share a concern for the autonomy of their constituent units. California does not want Alabama interfering in its affairs and so is reluctant to intrude into how Alabama deals with its own citizens. France does not want Sudan (or anyone else) meddling in its affairs and so it is reluctant to intrude into how Sudan deals with its own citizens. That reluctance can also have a more mundane pragmatic source based on assessments of the likelihood of success and the risks to the intervener.

Official violence undermines the legitimacy of all governments. It destabilizes the state, and destabilizing one state may cause the citizens of another state to question the legitimacy of their own government.[63] A failed state creates conditions that foster increased levels of violence within the state,

---

[63] This is exemplified by the 1960s slogans "Don't trust anyone over 30" and "Down with the pigs." These anarchic responses to perceived police brutality may seem silly at this distance, but they seemed very real to their adherents at the time.

and it promotes exporting of violence to other states.[64] In addition, the resulting power vacuum might be filled by a brutal regime that becomes more likely to be an aggressor against other nations.[65] California may not want Alabama to interfere in its affairs, but the citizens of California want assurance that if their government ever turns against them, then all the states of the U.S. will help, and California does not want Alabama's violence spilling over to affect it directly.

Finally, official violence against citizens is just plain wrong. The basic fundamental rights of personhood recognized by both the federal government in this country and the international community include at minimum rights to personal autonomy and freedom from official violence. These are guaranteed by the due process of Anglo-American law and by numerous provisions of international law.

[B] Denial of Rights

Closely related to the supra-state interest in state action is the interest in denial of rights. Once a supra-state institution has defined something to be a basic fundamental right, then the institution should have some interest in protecting that right from encroachment. In terms of the U.S. Constitution, a great deal of anxiety and energy have gone into the question of whether anyone but the state itself can "deny equal protection of the laws" to another person.[66]

There is a simple conundrum that expresses this aspect of the problem. If I prevent someone from exercising a right, can it be said that the other person no longer has that right? Or is it not more accurate to say that the right still exists, but that I have violated the right by failing to discharge my duty to that person? Under precepts of the rule of law, the latter is the better way of conceptualizing a right, which makes it apparent that only the state can "deny" a right — nonstate actors only "violate" the right.[67]

---

[64] Daniel Thürer, *The "Failed State" and International Law*, INTERNATIONAL REVIEW OF THE RED CROSS No. 836, 731 (Dec. 1999), *available at* www.icrc.org/Web/eng/siteeng0.nsf/iwpList314/438B7C44BDEAC7A3C1256B66005DCAAB.

[65] Liberia's experience under Charles Taylor or Uganda's with Idi Amin are modern examples.

[66] The Supreme Court's involvement with this issue stems from the Civil Rights Cases, 109 U.S. 3 (1883). There was a time in the 1960s when it seemed that the state action requirement had been substantially reduced if not eliminated; *see* Jerre Williams, *The Twilight of State Action*, 41 TEX. L. REV. 346 (1963). That apparent development ended with the Rehnquist Court. *See* Jackson v. Metropolitan Edison Co., 419 U.S. 345 (1974); *see also* Moose Lodge No. 107 v. Irvis, 407 U.S. 163 (1972). For a recent exchange on the state's role in addressing so-called "positive rights," *see* Mark Tushnet, *State Action, Social Welfare Rights, and the Judicial Role: Some Comparative Observations*, 3 CHI. J. INT'L L. 435 (2002); *see also* Cass Sunstein, *State Action is Always Present*, 3 CHI. J. INT'L L. 465 (2002).

[67] This is the conceptual basis of the Civil Rights Cases, which created the doctrine of state action in U.S. law. *See Civil Rights Cases*, 109 U.S. at 17:

[C]ivil rights, such as are guaranteed by the Constitution against State aggression, cannot be impaired by the wrongful acts of individuals, unsupported by State

At the same time, the state has an interest in vindicating the right because otherwise the state looks derelict or inept, another form of threat to the legitimacy of the state.[68]

Therefore, the state attempts not only to define rights but to create mechanisms for their enforcement and vindication. The nub of the supra-state interest in violence is how to define a crime that does not swallow all violence.[69] The right to personal physical integrity theoretically would be violated by even the most minor instance of assault, but surely not every schoolyard fight is going to become the subject of an international criminal tribunal. Therefore, the international community will find it necessary to subdivide its recognized rights into two subclasses, one consisting of those rights that will be protected by international enforcement institutions and one for those which the nations agree to enforce themselves. Thus far, the first subclass consists only of war crimes, crimes against humanity, and genocide.[70] The second subclass, those to be enforced by the nations themselves without an international tribunal, consists of slavery,[71] piracy,[72] hostage taking,[73] torture,[74] terrorist financing,[75] and a few others defined by international convention.[76]

Common among these crimes calling for international support are factors such as the use of international means, or effects on international systems, or the likelihood that an act of violence will affect multiple interests. These

---

authority in the shape of laws, customs, or judicial or executive proceedings. The wrongful act of an individual, unsupported by any such authority, is simply a private wrong, or a crime of that individual; an invasion of the rights of the injured party, it is true, whether they affect his person, his property, or his reputation; but if not sanctioned in some way by the State, or not done under State authority, his rights remain in full force, and may presumably be vindicated by resort to the laws of the State for redress. An individual cannot deprive a man of his right to vote, to hold property, to buy and sell, to sue in the courts, or to be a witness or a juror; he may, by force or fraud, interfere with the enjoyment of the right in a particular case.

[68] If the state wants to keep its monopoly on the use of force, then it must be perceived as having the will and ability to protect individual rights. Otherwise, people turn to self-help and the state's monopoly on force dissipates.

[69] In striking down the Gun-Free School Zones Act, the Court commented that "if we were to accept the Government's arguments, we are hard-pressed to posit any activity by an individual that Congress is without power to regulate." United States v. Lopez, 514 U.S. 549, 564 (1994).

[70] ICC Statute of Rome. There is a separate crime of aggression that is folded into war crimes here for convenience.

[71] *See* ICCPR art. 8; UDHR art. 4.

[72] *See* U.N. Convention on the Law of the Sea, *supra* note 4.

[73] *See* ICCPR art. 9.

[74] *See* ICCPR art. 7, UDHR art. 5.

[75] *See* U.N. International Convention for the Suppression of the Financing of Terrorism, G.A. Res. 54/109 (Dec. 9, 1999).

[76] For example, narcotics trafficking is covered by three principal conventions and a United Nations Commission to facilitate cooperation. *See* www.unodc.org/unodc/en/drug_and_crime_conventions.html.

are similar to the reasons why some denial of rights within a state of the United States will trigger federal law while others do not.

[C] Group Animus

A third reason for supra-state concern, in addition to the "under color of law" and "protected rights" concerns, has been the "discrimination" rationale. In U.S. law, the question usually has been whether the defendant acted out of a "class-based" hostility.[77] The most recent criminal statute applies to action taken against any person "because of his race, color, religion or national origin."[78] But mere discrimination alone is not enough to trigger federal authority because the "state action" phenomenon acts as a limit on Congress' power.[79] Therefore, in addition to discrimination there must be an additional layer of federal concern, such as use of the instrumentalities of interstate commerce, or participation in governmental activities such as voting or access to public facilities.

For example, John Paul Franklin was prosecuted under federal law for shooting two African-American joggers in a public park.[80] Based on multiple statements of his own, it was easy enough to infer that he picked them out because of their race and particularly because they were jogging with two white women.[81] But the racial motivation would not have been enough without the added element of their use of public facilities. This may seem a silly nuance — surely racial violence should be punishable regardless of whether it takes place in a city park or in a private home. The key question should be whether an incident rises to the level of notice for the federal government. Why should California care what happens in a Utah park?

Franklin actually illustrates well why there would be interstate interest in some acts of racial violence. Franklin picked out two strangers in a public setting based purely on their race, thus triggering the likelihood of instilling fear and intimidation into a discrete segment of the populace. Moreover, that fear is set in the context of using public facilities, an important right for minority ethnic groups that may be in doubt about full participation in the life of the community.

On the other hand, the public facility aspect is almost a tautology. Doesn't every murder interfere with the victim's ability to use public facilities? Indeed, if the defendant intended to kill, then isn't it a reasonable inference that the defendant intended to deprive the victim of the ability to use public facilities, or anything else for that matter, regardless of where the victim happened to be located at the time? Among the many thousands of murders that take place in the U.S. every year, some are racially motivated but are

---

[77] *See generally* Griffin v. Breckenridge, 403 U.S. 88 (1971).

[78] 18 U.S.C. § 245 (2004).

[79] *See generally* Moose Lodge v. Irvis, 407 U.S. 163 (1972).

[80] United States v. Franklin, 704 F.2d 1183, 1188 (10th Cir. 1983).

[81] *Franklin*, 704 F.2d at 1187.

handled in the ordinary course of state prosecution because they do not take place in or on public facilities.

With genocide, the international jurisdictional element is "intent to destroy, in whole or in part, a national, ethnical, racial or religious group."[82] With respect to crimes against humanity, the jurisdictional element is "when committed as part of a widespread or systematic attack against any civilian population on national, political, ethnic, racial or religious grounds."[83] The discriminatory motivation is almost the same with both crimes, although widespread violence against a political group would be a crime against humanity without becoming genocide.

The principal difference is "widespread or systematic" in the definition of crimes against humanity, which does not appear in the definition of genocide. But the two crimes should be roughly equivalent because it is doubtful that a single or even a number of related incidents of racial violence would amount to attempted genocide unless they are part of a "widespread or systematic" pattern of violence. A single perpetrator could engage in a pattern of racial violence, as when John Paul Franklin and John Allen Muhammad each shot several people because of their race. But those actions probably would not amount to either genocide or crimes against humanity under international law simply because they are not sufficiently pervasive to trigger international concern.

[D] Reluctance or Inability of the State

Implicit throughout all this discussion is that supra-state bodies take an interest in a violent situation when the local state is either unwilling or unable to quell the situation. That factor explains the ICTY and ICTR experiences rather directly. As described above, violence against civilians perpetrated or condoned by state officials draws into question the legitimacy of the state itself. And when a state ceases to have the ability to monopolize the use of force within its borders, it becomes a failed state and a threat to the rest of the global community.

The U.S. designates nation-states that support terrorism and prohibits transactions with those nations.[84] The state's lack of enforcement will be a factor in the likelihood of criminal behavior, and it may well be a factor in the degree to which other states are motivated to intervene, but there is no need to evaluate the state's behavior as an element of a criminal offense itself. Thus, in considering international definitions of terrorism, the role of states is largely irrelevant.

---

[82] *See* ICC Statute of Rome art. 6.

[83] *Id.* art. 7.

[84] As of July 2007, there were five nations on this list: Cuba, Iran, North Korea, Syria, and Sudan. This authority is exercised under section 6(j) of the Export Administration Act of 1979, 50 U.S.C. App. § 2405 (2007). *See* Dep't of Treasury, Office of Foreign Asset Control (OFAC) information, *available at* www.treasury.gov/offices/enforcement/ofac/programs/terror/terror.shtml (last visited July 31, 2007).

§ 1.05 TOWARD AN INTERNATIONAL DEFINITION

The similarities between U.S. federalism concerns and global sovereignty concerns reflect a common interest in addressing some levels of violence by use of supra-state law. The next step is to identify the factors that go into this interest so as to create a test for international terrorism from such precedents as the "widespread and systematic" test of international law and U.S. law's "color of state law" and "class-based animus" tests.

An international definition built on the likelihood of transnational action or the appearance of state action would avoid the idelogoical issues raised by definitions that focus on political motivation.[85]

An international definition of terrorism is needed for several reasons: delineation of universal jurisdiction, eventual inclusion within the framework of the ICC, treaties and informal arrangements for cooperative law enforcement. Some of these steps might take place with traditional concepts of murder, but the killing that triggers international concern is targeted killing of civilians by members of a group that has the capability to carry out a systematic campaign. That is the definition of terrorism that ought to be adopted by the international community.[86]

An international crime paradigm is emerging as a result of supra-state concern over mass murder and abuse. The concepts of genocide and crimes against humanity share one quintessential element with terrorism: ongoing violence against civilians. Genocide is distinguished by the attempt to eliminate a group presence defined by ethnic, culture, or religion. Crimes against humanity are distinguished by "widespread or systematic" violence. Terrorism falls into a similar setting as ongoing violence against civilian populations and is distinguished by the clandestine nature of the perpetrators.

§ 1.06 UNDERSTANDING TERRORISTS

"Who Becomes a Terrorist and Why" is the name of a study conducted by the staff of the Library of Congress in 1999 attempting to determine from the available literature whether a psychological profile could be built of the typical terrorist.[87] Although some gross generalizations were available, the basic conclusion was that profiling a terrorist would not make it possible to pick out the terrorist from a crowd. Other significant questions concern whether there are factors which can be identified and used to turn potential terrorists into more acceptable channels of behavior, or to guide societal responses to different groups, or to assist in apprehension and

---

[85] *See* § 6.03[B] *infra.*

[86] Jeff Breinholt & Wayne McCormack, *Defining Terrorism: Perfection as Enemy of the Possible*, International Assessment and Strategy Center, *available at* www.strategycenter.net/research/pubID.141/pub_detail.asp (Jan. 17, 2007).

[87] The LC STUDY was published in book form by Lyons Press without a publication date but sometime after 9/11. REX A. HUDSON, WHO BECOMES A TERRORIST AND WHY (Lyons Press).

prosecution after an incident.[88] A number of recent publications explore the phenomenon of violence in religion generally or Islamist fundamentalism specifically.[89]

Terrorist foot-soldiers tend to be in their 20s while the leaders are somewhat older (nothing surprising in that),[90] about 80% are male,[91] and most feel that they have a political (perhaps ethnic or religious) injury to redress.[92] Obviously there are millions of oppressed males in their 20s who do not turn to terrorism, so the next question is what psychological forces can combine to produce the violence of terrorism.

From a psychological standpoint, there are a number of reasons why someone turns to terrorism. Richardson describes the "Three R's: Revenge, Renown, Reaction."[93] Similarly, the LC Study described frustration-aggression, negative identity, and narcissistic rage.[94] Simplistically, an individual with either very low self-esteem or highly inflated views of self (and often these are found in the same person) may be so frustrated with his/her place in society that violence seems the only method of releasing the pressure on his/her psyche.

All authors caution against making too much of this type of oversimplified psycho-profile.[95] Nevertheless, it is possible to generalize that terrorist groups attract persons who are "action-oriented, aggressive persons who are stimulus-hungry and seek excitement." This description could apply to many persons who go into law enforcement; there are even people who enter more sedentary professions and seek their adrenaline rushes from rock climbing or snowboarding.

One factor that is often emphasized is the religious fanaticism of many recent terrorists. Some authors link this with the increasing fatality levels of the past two decades. In the 1970s and 1980s, the prevailing belief was

---

[88] *See* Martha Crenshaw, *Questions To Be Answered, Research To Be Done, Knowledge To Be Applied, in* WALTER REICH, ORIGINS OF TERRORISM 247-60 (1998) (first published in 1990); FATHALI MODHADDAM & ANTHONY MARSELLA, UNDERSTANDING TERRORISM (2004); LOUISE RICHARDSON, WHAT TERRORISTS WANT (2006).

[89] MARY HABECK, KNOWING THE ENEMY (2006); CHARLES KIMBALL, WHEN RELIGION BECOMES EVIL (2002); MICHAEL SHEUER, THROUGH OUR ENEMIES' EYES (2d ed. 2006); JESSICA STERN, TERROR IN THE NAME OF GOD (2003).

[90] LC STUDY, *supra* note 87, at 73.

[91] *Id.* at 81-90; *But see* Marilyn Friedman, *Female Terrorists: Martyrdom and Gender Equality, in* VALUES & VIOLENCE: INTANGIBLE ASPECTS OF TERRORISM (forthcoming 2008).

[92] LC STUDY, *supra* note 87, at 33-35.

[93] RICHARDSON, *supra* note 88, at 71.

[94] *Id.* at 29-33.

[95] LC STUDY, *supra* note 87, at 91:

> [T]he terrorist is not diagnosably psychopathic or mentally sick. Contrary to the stereotype that the terrorist is a psychopath or otherwise mentally disturbed, the terrorist is actually quite sane, although deluded by an ideological or religious way of viewing the world. . . . A member who exhibits traits of psychopathy or any noticeable degree of mental illness would only be a liability for the group.

that "Terrorists want a lot of people watching, not a lot of people dead."[96] That quite obviously is no longer the case.[97] It is possible that the strength of religion-based interpretations of reality ease the leaders' ability to instill fervor and lack of remorse in their followers.

An orderly and systematic analysis of terrorist motivation can provide valuable clues about strategies for responding to terrorism in terms of both protection and mitigation activities (antiterrorism) and for direct action involving preemption, interdiction, or retribution (counterterrorism).[98] The terrorist's background and personal makeup can be combined to think of the "psychosocial" setting of the terrorist's worldview. This permits analyzing the worldview itself for a number of purposes. For example, to consider the likelihood that a terrorist organization may negotiate, Hoffman suggested categorizing terrorists into rational, psychological, and cultural types.[99]

In this framework, the rational terrorists with specific political objectives may "sound a lot like legitimate military authorities planning an operation or even business executives developing an advertising campaign"[100] except that they choose illegal means of targeting civilian populations to accomplish their goals. One might expect to be able to negotiate compromises with such a group because the weighing of costs and benefits is part of the formulation of their strategy, and obtaining partial benefits at reduced costs may look attractive.

For Hoffman's "psychological" terrorist with a personal orientation to the world "the impetus to commit acts of violence is often related to a profound sense of failure or inadequacy for which the perpetrator may seek redress through revenge."[101] This person may possess elements of what many of us would think of as psychosis.[102] This may be the category in which we could differentiate most cleanly between the terrorist and the criminal. The "lone wolf" seeking to ameliorate some deep personal pain does not easily fit the common-sense definition of terrorist because he or she is not acting pursuant to the direction of, or in complicity with, an organized group. Timothy McVeigh to many people is a terrorist, but without a group identity he does not represent an ongoing threat that will continue after his capture. The psychological terrorist may, on the other hand, be part of a group that represents a significant threat.[103]

---

[96] Brian Jenkins, High Technology Terrorism and Surrogate Warfare 15 (1975).

[97] Kimball, *supra* note 89, at 4.

[98] *See* Thomas Ditzler, *Malevolent Minds: The Teleology of Terrorism*, *in* APA 188.

[99] Bruce Hoffman, *"Holy Terror"*: The Implications of Terrorism Motivated by a Religious Imperative (1993).

[100] Ditzler, *supra* note 98, at 200.

[101] *Id.* at 202.

[102] *See* Jerold Post, *Terrorist Psycho-Logic: Terrorist Behavior as a Product of Psychological Forces*, *in* Reich, *supra* note 88, at 25.

[103] Hoffman noted that if these groups achieve any meaningful progress toward their espoused goals, they often adopt increasingly radicalized positions characterized by increas-

The third category is the "culturally motivated" terrorist with a strong "group" identity. According to Hoffman, "the motivation for these groups to commit violent acts typically derives from an almost primordial fear of cultural extermination or the loss of cultural identity." Ditzler concentrates on religious fundamentalists in this category and finds again an extreme lack of ability or willingness to negotiate. "In this worldview, the failure to respond to the utmost of one's ability would be tantamount to an acceptance of damnation."[104] "In a world of absolute truth . . . there is no room for dissent and no room for theological doubt."[105] Racial/ethnic/cultural groups without the overlay of religion could be viewed in similar light — examples range from Nazi Germany through the atrocities in Kosovo and Rwanda. Any use of cultural/ethnic/religious identification in crafting either sanctions or accommodations would raise very significant issues of discrimination and potential violations of international human rights law, and there are many pitfalls for a government that treads such a path.

A psychological understanding of terrorism should yield several benefits. One is the realization that not all responses to terrorism should be the same. Different responses could yield results with different types of groups possessing different motivations. A second use of the analysis would be to realize that the motivation is not the same as the goal. Definitions that depend on "political motivation" may be addressing either impetus or goals and as a result be ambiguous.

§ 1.07 CONCLUSION

This chapter has presented several themes that will recur throughout the chapters that follow:

1. The three modes of responding to violence (prevention, prosecution, predominance) need to be balanced, each limited within its own sphere and controlled by its own traditions.

2. Definitions of terrorism need to be constructed in light of the purposes for which the definition is constructed, i.e., with due regard for the responses that may be triggered by a definition.

3. Understanding terrorism is important to delineating appropriate responses.

Subsequent chapters will explore international law, U.S. criminal law, civil liberties, intelligence gathering, and uses of military power. The effort in this volume is to delineate what measures are appropriate for what actions and what controls are appropriate on each measure. The recurring

---

ingly nonachievable goals. The development of these goals may become necessary for the organization, because the attainment of true success would threaten their continuing need to exist. Ditzler *supra*, note 98, at 202.

[104] Ditzler, *supra* note 98, at 204.

[105] A. Sullivan, *This Is a Religious War*, N.Y. Times (Magazine), Oct. 7, 2001, at 46.

theme of this book is a very conservative approach to law: there are traditions that have been built around the rule of law for good reasons and they are not lightly to be abandoned.

Chapter 2

CHOICES OF RESPONSE

§ 2.01   THE INSTITUTIONAL RESPONSES TO VIOLENCE

Western society, if not all societies, has formulated three primary institutional responses to threats and acts of violence:

1. Prevention — combination of protective devices and persuasion

2. Prosecution — traditional civilian criminal processes

3. Military action — use of lethal force to subdue and control

Each of these modes of response carries its own limitations to ensure adequate controls on government action. Each was part of the U.S. bag of tools in 2001, but for a variety of reasons the media and politicians chose to emphasize the military option and to blend prevention with prosecution. All three routes are still available and should be used, but there are open questions about whether they should be blended or confined each to its own arena with its own limitations.

It could be a mistake to combine these functions just as it is a mistake to combine other functions of government. Each response is subject to controls that have developed over extended periods of time, controls evolved from reasons and traditions that are not lightly to be set aside. That there are points of intersection and overlap among the three does not mean that some degree of separation is not desirable. For example, a long-standing statute of the U.S., known as the *posse comitatus* provision, bars the military from engaging in domestic law enforcement. Similarly, court orders allowing wiretaps on telephones were, and could be again, based on different standards for preventive or prosecutorial uses.

To promote safety while limiting the intrusion of government into our lives, we need to understand the framework of responses available to us. There is an interlocking set of "communities" devoted to public safety within government today. Similarly, there are interlocking legal controls or restraints that operate both on the individual or group who contemplates terrorist action and on the government agencies attempting to respond.

The U.S. government, more than most governments in history or even in the world today, has divided and separated various units that deal with different aspects of public safety. The three principal divisions which deal with violence are intelligence, law enforcement, and the military.[1] In a rather loose sense, their functions could be thought to form a spectrum of prevention, prosecution, and warfare. There are many other agencies involved in public safety, primarily those that deal with public health and response to emergencies.

The division of public safety into different units could be analogized to how individuals deal with their own home safety. Think about the steps you take to guard against intrusions on your own space. First, you lock your doors. This is a phenomenon of relatively recent vintage, and there are many societies in the world today that still do not have locking doors. If this is not enough, and you have the money, you install an electronic security system, and perhaps you have that system wired to call armed guards at a signal of intrusion, or maybe you even go so far as to build a gated community with guards at the entrance. All these are progressive steps of increasingly aggressive preventive measures that you can take on your own or in conjunction with immediate neighbors.

Second, if you have been the subject of an intrusion, you may want to apprehend and punish the intruder. In early stages of society, this might have been done by the individual acting alone or by a family group, but for many centuries this function has been turned over to more or less formalized community representatives and most recently to law enforcement agencies. Whether the purpose is to disable the specific intruder or to deter others, punishment is the province of communal groups.

Finally, if the community feels threatened as a group by some outside group, we move to the level of armed conflict between politically defined groups. Again, in more "primitive" societies these conflicts were often less deadly and widespread than is likely to be the case today, but the concept of an organized military response that operates across more or less defined borders between recognized political groups is ancient.

These three steps reflect roughly the three divisions of prevention, enforcement, and military action. Each stage carries not only its own culture and modes of operation, but is also constrained by a set of limiting rules. The civil liberties implications of prevention (such as limits on demonstrations or searching persons entering an airport) may differ somewhat from the civil liberties aspects of criminal law enforcement. The limitations on military action are among the most elusive of legal concepts

---

[1] I am not ignoring the other aspects of public safety, such as fire and emergency medical services, but those are not addressed to suppression of violent behavior as are the three under consideration.

because they arise rather infrequently and because the enforcement mechanisms for those limits themselves are somewhat tenuous.

The three modes interact with each other to form something like a tripod on which public safety rests. The tripod would not stand as well without all three, and the strength of each depends not only on its own structure but on the controls that keep it in place.

Prior to 9/11, the Department of Justice and related agencies had been pursuing the prosecutorial option for years and were beginning to respond to terrorism just as effectively as we can respond to domestic violence, sexual assaults, or any other form of socially promulgated violence — that is to say, not to anyone's genuine satisfaction but with enough commitment to protect some potential victims.[2] The Departments of State[3] and Treasury[4] with their related agencies had been engaged in preventive measures such as interception of illegal imports, tracking of illicit financial transactions, participation in international law conferences, funding of economic development in beleaguered areas of the world — again, not a completely satisfactory response but one with some promise of long-term gains. Meanwhile, the Department of Defense and its related agencies had been gathering intelligence and placing assets in hot spots to be prepared for some military involvement as needed.

Each response carries its own limitations, both legal and practical. Ordinary criminal law enforcement is widely perceived to be an inadequate

---

[2] Prior to 9/11, prosecutions of terrorist acts with international overtones were carried out in the U.S. Attorney's Offices, mostly in the District of Columbia or Southern District of New York. Now, prosecutions are controlled more directly out of the Washington National Office. The Counterterrorism Section of the National Security Division at the Department of Justice "is responsible for the design, implementation, and support of law enforcement efforts, legislative initiatives, policies and strategies relating to combating international and domestic terrorism. The Section seeks to assist in preventing and disrupting acts of terrorism which may occur anywhere in the world which impact on significant United States interests and persons through investigation and prosecution." Affiliated with the Section is an Antiterrorism Task Force with Regional Coordinators and representatives from various agencies. *See* U.S. Department of Justice Counterterrorism Section, *available at* www.usdoj.gov/nsd/counter_terrorism.htm (last visited June 21, 2007).

[3] The State Department's Counterterrorism Office works with other governments to curtail terrorism, designates foreign terrorist organizations, and helps develop U.S. policy regarding responses to terrorism. *See* U.S. Department of State Office of the Coordinator for Counterterrorism, *available at* www.state.gov/s/ct (last visited June 21, 2007).

[4] The Treasury Department's Executive Office of Terrorist Financing and Financial Crimes describes its mission this way:

> EOTF/FC develops and implements U.S. government strategies to combat terrorist financing domestically and internationally, develops and implements the National Money Laundering Strategy as well as other policies and programs to fight financial crimes, participates in the Department's development and implementation of U.S. government policies and regulations in support of the Bank Secrecy Act and the USA Patriot Act, represents the United States at focused international bodies dedicated to fighting terrorist financing and financial crimes; and develops U.S. government policies relating to financial crimes.

See USinfo.state.gov, *U.S. Treasury Creates New Unit to Combat Terrorist Financing*, *available at* usinfo.state.gov/ei/Archive/2004/Jan/07-179876.html (last visited June 21, 2007).

response to international terrorism for a number of reasons. A nation's jurisdiction to prescribe criminal sanctions for an action depends on either a nexus with that action or *jus cogens* (*erga omnes*). Pursuit and capture in another state can create enormous diplomatic issues. Medium-scale, long-term operations raise stakes above ordinary crime. The public expects interdiction more than post-hoc punishment. A terrorist group can be infiltrated only at great risk.

Military action is constrained by the law of war, now more often known as the law of armed conflict (LOAC). With military action, the "war" metaphor overreaches for a number of reasons and the language just does not fit the situation — there is no cohesive enemy, no territorial objective, no single peace resolution available. And if terrorist operatives were enemy combatants, then it could be asserted that actions they take against military targets would be legitimate and not punishable. On the other hand, there certainly are appropriate uses of military force in pursuit of terrorists. The idea of a limited military engagement or "military operation other than war" (MOOTW) is more appropriate than the language of war.

Prevention through the use of intelligence information relies on government information about private persons, which raises secrecy and privacy concerns. Use of that information for either detention or other punitive measures also raises due process problems.

[A] The Intelligence Community

By both Executive Order and statute, the Intelligence Community is defined as consisting of the CIA, the eight intelligence agencies within the Department of Defense (DIA, NSA, NRO, NIMA, and the intelligence agencies (IAs) of the four uniformed services), and portions of five executive departments (State, Treasury, Homeland Security, Energy, and FBI).[5]

Until recently, under the National Security Act,[6] the CIA was formally the lead agency for coordination of all intelligence. Amendments to the IC structure in 2004, including creation of a Director of National Intelligence, may or may not affect the actual operation of the IC.

There are many interesting assessments available on the internet of the U.S. intelligence effort. In 1996, there was a presidential review of intelligence operations that resulted in enhancing the role of the Defense Department.[7]

---

[5] 50 U.S.C. § 401a (4) (2007).

[6] 50 U.S.C. § 401 et seq.

[7] Commission on the Roles and Capabilities of the United States Intelligence Community, Preparing for the 21st Century: An Appraisal of U.S. Intelligence (March 1, 1996), *available at* www.gpoaccess.gov/int/report.html (last visited July 31, 2007). The Federation of American Scientists did an analysis of the IC budget following the 1996 review. Although the details of the number of personnel and actual dollar amounts are secret, FAS extrapolated from public information to reach some estimates for each agency. www.fas.org/irp/commission/budget.htm; *see also* Federation of American Scientists, *Intelligence Agency Budgets: Commission Recommends No Release but Releases Them Anyway, available at* www.fas.org/irp/commission/budget.htm (last visited July 23, 2007).

About 80% of the total intelligence budget of the U.S. is in the Defense Department, which first emphasized technological intelligence to track and identify military targets and then shifted that technology to monitoring communications traffic. That factor, plus budget cuts at the end of the Cold War, plus the fact that most CIA personnel were trained in the ways of Soviet intelligence rather than the distinctly different culture of terrorist organizations, all combined by the late 1990s to leave the U.S. less than adequately prepared to infiltrate or monitor terrorist organizations.[8] The National Commission on Terrorist Attacks Upon the United States (9/11 Commission) put it this way:

> During the Cold War, intelligence agencies did not depend on seamless integration to track and count the thousands of military targets — such as tanks and missiles — fielded by the Soviet Union and other adversary states. Each agency concentrated on its special mission, acquiring its own information and sharing it via formal, finished reports. The Department of Defense had given birth to and dominated the main agencies for technical collection of intelligence.[9]

The Commission commented that the end of the Cold War also meant budget cuts, that the CIA had become highly risk averse and had no personnel trained for infiltrating terrorist organizations, and that the "intelligence community's confederated structure left open the question of who really was in charge of the entire U.S. intelligence effort."[10]

The Commission made specific recommendations addressing the structure of the Intelligence Community:

> The United States has the resources and the people. The government should combine them more effectively, achieving unity of effort. We offer five major recommendations to do that:
>
> - unifying strategic intelligence and operational planning against Islamist terrorists across the foreign-domestic divide with a National Counterterrorism Center;
>
> - unifying the intelligence community with a new National Intelligence Director;
>
> - unifying the many participants in the counterterrorism effort and their knowledge in a network-based information-sharing system that transcends traditional governmental boundaries;
>
> - unifying and strengthening congressional oversight to improve quality and accountability; and
>
> - strengthening the FBI and homeland defenders.[11]

---

[8] *See* 9/11 COMMISSION REPORT 86-91, *available at* www.9-11commission.gov.

[9] *Id.* at 407.

[10] *Id.* at 93.

[11] *Id.* at 399-400.

When bills were introduced in Congress to implement these recommendations, political controversy arose over whether the new NID would have full
budgetary and personnel control over the existing units within the Department of Defense. The Commission's recommendation for a Director of
National Intelligence to sit above the Director of Central Intelligence was
designed to relieve the DCI of some of the office's conflicting job descriptions
by assuming overall coordination of the Intelligence Community. On
December 17, 2004, Congress passed a bill incorporating most elements of
the Commission recommendations. The DNI is to have some degree of
involvement with the funding and deployment of intelligence resources in
the Department of Defense, and also to have consultation authority with
domestic agencies such as the FBI.[12]

On a more substantive plane, the Commission's recommendation to "unify
across the foreign-domestic divide" runs counter to the mandate of EO
12,333 issued by President Ronald Reagan on December 4, 1981.[13] Unifying
raises two concerns, each of which has both policy and value dimensions.
EO 12,333 was based on some of the work of the so-called "Church
Commission," which held hearings and issued reports from 1973-1976
primarily on the activities of the CIA. Although a major focus of the
recommendation for a foreign-domestic divide was the protection of civil
liberties of U.S. persons, another aspect was the belief that the accumulation of too much power in one place could make that agency inefficient by
reducing the need for it to justify its actions to other agencies.

Second, and related to the first, the unification of all intelligence gathering would eliminate competition within the government for attention and
resources. Not all competition is good, but Judge Posner makes a strong
argument that it would be a good thing in this context.[14]

These are critical issues for the structure and control of intelligence gathering, which will in turn dictate legal arguments over the validity of
investigatory techniques. The prevention leg of our tripod involves protecting the homefront through various devices, ranging from ordinary locks to
ultra-sophisticated biotechnology. The major problem with this approach
is that security relies on information, and information means invasion of
privacy. The tension between security and privacy leads to First-Amendment-
based limits on the degree to which government can intervene into a
terrorist plot before harm occurs.

---

[12] National Security Intelligence Reform Act of 2004, Pub. L. 108-458 (2004).

[13] Exec. Order No. 12,333, 46 Fed. Reg. 59, 941 (Dec. 4, 1981). The key elements of the
"foreign-domestic divide" were summarized in this statement of the CIA:

> Collection within the United States of foreign intelligence not otherwise obtainable
> shall be undertaken by the FBI or, when significant foreign intelligence is sought,
> by other authorized agencies of the Intelligence Community, provided that no foreign
> intelligence collection by such agencies may be undertaken for the purpose of
> acquiring information concerning the domestic activities of United States persons.

www.cia.gov/about-cia/eo12333.html.

[14] RICHARD POSNER, PREVENTING SURPRISE ATTACKS (2005).

A second problem with the prevention strategy is that to be most effective, it should include attempts to engage the issues that are enraging the terrorist. Ideally, the terrorist would yield to the logic and compassionate persuasion of violence avoidance, but the very statement of the problem assumes that moral suasion has been tried and failed. To engage the terrorists' issues on their merits, a tightrope must be walked, not appearing to reward terrorism by yielding to the terrorists' demands while defusing the hatred by recognizing and acceding to their legitimate demands.

Prevention is directed obviously to the future. It consists primarily of gathering and analyzing intelligence data to determine who is about to commit what kind of harm. The prevention step itself may consist of an arrest in the nature of a conspiracy charge or unlawful possession charges, which is where prevention and prosecution overlap, or it may consist instead of mere warnings or even attempts to "turn" a conspirator to become an informant. Thus, when prevention services successfully "break a terrorist cell," they may prosecute, make a public statement that a threat has been eliminated, or secretly leave the cell in place for future monitoring.

[B]   The Law Enforcement Approach

The U.S. had successfully prosecuted a number of terrorism cases prior to 9/11. Among the most famous were the first World Trade Center cases and the conspiracy case against Sheikh Rahman and some of his followers. The WTC prosecution resulted in conviction of four conspirators.[15] Although the alleged mastermind Ramzi Yousef fled the country, he was later apprehended in Pakistan and prosecuted for other crimes. In a separate prosecution, Sheikh Rahman and nine of his followers were prosecuted for conspiracy to blow up tunnels and bridges in the New York area.[16]

In the year 2000, there was a pending indictment in the Southern District of New York against Osama bin Laden and a number of others for the bombing of the Embassies in Kenya and Tanzania.[17] Several defendants in the embassy bombing case eventually pleaded guilty, offered differing levels of cooperation, and were sentenced to various terms in prison. El-Hage and three other defendants were convicted after trial and sentenced to life imprisonment. In failing to come to a unanimous recommendation for the death penalty, the jury noted that some of its members believed that life imprisonment was a worse punishment than death.

Other successful prosecutions of terrorists had included Fawaz Yunis, who hijacked Royal Jordanian Flight 402 in 1985 and blew up the plane after letting the passengers go.[18] The only apparent connection between this incident and the U.S. was that two American citizens were on board

---

[15] *See generally* United States v. Salameh, 152 F.3d 88 (2d Cir. 1998).

[16] *See generally* United States v. Rahman, 189 F.3d 88 (2d Cir. 1999).

[17] United States v. Bin Laden, 109 F. Supp. 2d 211 (S.D.N.Y. 2000).

[18] United States v. Yunis, 924 F.2d 1086 (D.C. Cir. 1991).

the plane and thus were held hostage for a period of time during the incident.

More directly related to U.S. interests was the prosecution of Omar Rezaq for aircraft piracy. In the words of the D.C. Circuit:

> In 1985, Rezaq hijacked an Air Egypt flight shortly after takeoff from Athens, and ordered it to fly to Malta. On arrival, Rezaq shot a number of passengers, killing two of them, before he was apprehended. Rezaq pleaded guilty to murder charges in Malta, served seven years in prison, and was released in February 1993. Shortly afterwards, he was taken into custody in Nigeria by United States authorities and brought to the United States for trial.[19]

Although one of the murdered passengers was American, Rezaq was not prosecuted for murder of United States nationals but was charged with air piracy in which death resulted, a potential capital offense.

Ramzi Yousef was involved in the first World Trade Center bombing, indeed was probably the mastermind of the operation, but was arrested in Pakistan after attempting to orchestrate a bombing of several airplanes in the Philippines. He was brought by U.S. authorities to the U.S. and charged with conspiracy to destroy U.S. commercial airliners as well as one count of completed bombing of a Philippines Airline craft bound for Tokyo.[20]

Despite this history of successful prosecutions and the presence of well-trained prosecutorial teams within the U.S. Justice Department, the Administration has chosen to emphasize the military option and the President's role as Commander-in-Chief of the armed forces. One study says that the number of terrorism prosecutions spiked after 9/11 but has since declined.[21] What might explain a decline in prosecution of terrorism cases in the U.S.? a lack of interest? movement of resources and personnel to other matters? that there have been no terrorist acts in the U.S. to prosecute? that suspected terrorists have been the subject of rendition to other countries? that federal priority has shifted dramatically to military action? Perhaps a combination of all of these factors, and others unknown, has been

---

[19] United States v. Rezaq, 134 F.3d 1121, 1125 (D.C. Cir. 1998).

[20] United States v. Yousef, 927 F. Supp. 673 (S.D.N.Y. 1996).

[21] The Transactional Records Access Clearinghouse (TRAC) monitors investigatory reports and prosecutions by the federal government in a number of fields. In 2006, TRAC issued a report containing these observations:

> In the twelve months immediately after 9/11, the prosecution of individuals the government classified as international terrorists surged sharply higher than in the previous year. But timely data show that five years later, in the latest available period, the total number of these prosecutions has returned to roughly what they were just before the attacks. Given the widely accepted belief that the threat of terrorism in all parts of the world is much larger today than it was six or seven years ago, the extent of the recent decline in prosecutions is unexpected.

TRAC Reports, *Criminal Terrorism Enforcement in the U.S. During the Five Years since the 9/11/01 Attacks, available at* trac.syr.edu/tracreports/terrorism/169/ (last visited June 21, 2007).

at work. The important question is whether the criminal justice system is prepared to deal with prosecution of terrorist plots.

It is often said in the Anglo-American legal system that it is better that a guilty person go free than that an innocent person go to prison. The entire structure of our system is loaded to protect the accused against government over-reaching. This tilt starts with the burden of proof (beyond a reasonable doubt), extends through the manifold procedural protections of trial (right to counsel, confrontation of witnesses, right against self-incrimination, right to a jury, double jeopardy), includes some more substantive protections (protection against *ex post facto* legislation, freedom of expression), and is subsumed under the general heading of due process of law. There is an interesting debate that can be had over the question of the degree to which the single phrase "due process" subsumes all the other specific guarantees of the Bill of Rights, but for present purposes it is enough to emphasize that due process is the expression of a tradition stretching back to the Magna Carta.

The principal values emphasized in all western criminal justice systems and now finding their way internationally through documents such as the Universal Declaration of Human Rights and the International Convention on Civil and Political Rights include:

- presumption of innocence
- public trial
- trial rights, such as
  - confrontation of witnesses
  - right to counsel
- rule of law precepts such as the ban on *ex past facto* laws
- protection of liberal values such as freedom of expression
- resistance to inchoate crimes

All of these values are weighted toward protection of the accused, making it difficult for the state to be unduly repressive. The basic difference between a "police state" and an "open society" lies in the processes of the criminal justice system.

The prosecution (or law enforcement) option uses the most traditional modes of Western governmental response to anti-social behavior. Counter-terrorism sections within most of the Western governments follow a multi-pronged but not overly complicated strategy: informants or open sources provide some clues to active terrorist cells, unusual behaviors or money flowing from illegal activities can be traced to active plots, while surveil-lance and gathering of physical evidence at incident scenes can produce evidence on which to base a prosecution.[22]

---

[22] For a brief description of investigative strategies in the context of terrorist bombings, see RICHARD HEYMANN, TERRORISM AND AMERICA 105-110 (1998).

Prosecution is directed to past events. The principal law enforcement agencies in the U.S. federal system are the FBI and the Justice Department. These correspond roughly to the police and prosecution offices at the state and local levels. Of course, the growth of federal government agencies following the New Deal and World War II means that there are enforcement investigators and lawyers in a wide variety of federal agencies. Some have their own litigation authority while others can go to court only under the auspices of the Justice Department. While criminal prosecutions are thought to have a deterrent effect on the behavior of others, or at least on the behavior of the particular defendant, they are addressed solely to past wrongdoing. That wrongdoing may be in the form of a conspiracy to initiate an action in the future, but for reasons that are rooted in the history of freedom of expression, a conspiracy may not be prosecuted until at least one overt act in furtherance of the plan has been committed.

Controls to prevent abuse of the prosecutorial authority are expressed in the traditions of criminal procedure, many of which in the United States are incorporated in or elaborated by constitutional protections. These norms of control are now finding their way into international law, both by custom and by specific treaty obligations.

[C] The Military Option

The immediate response to 9/11 from the Bush administration was to declare "War on Terrorism." Although some seasoned professionals cautioned that this was not a proper or wise use of the term "war,"[23] the glamor and power of the imagery prevailed over prudence and the U.S. embarked on a massive war-like effort. That effort has taken its toll on U.S. resources, credibility, and domestic civil rights.[24] Nevertheless, there are appropriate uses of military options in addressing terrorism, including primarily a role for the military in enforcing international norms of law.

The appropriate use of, and controls on, military force will be one of the principal focal points in any study of terrorism for two reasons. One is that the terrorist act is often conceptualized as an illegal act of war, and the other is that military force may be called into play as one immediate response to a terrorist act. A critical aspect of the relationship of the military to our other two communities, however, is that the military is not to be used in law enforcement. Military intelligence intersects with other intelligence agencies, it can feed information to law enforcement, and it can use information from either community in planning its strategy for military response.

---

[23] *See* CNN.com, *Powell battles Pentagon over response strategy, available at* www.cnn.com/2001/US/09/20/ret.powell.divisions/index.html (last visited June 21, 2007).

[24] Although my distaste for this response is obvious, and I do not attempt to hide it, my goal with this book is not to criticize so much as to lay out the availability of other options. The position that it is legally impossible to be "at war" with a nonterritorial group is well stated in Jordan Paust, *War and Enemy Status After 9/11: Attacks on the Laws of War*, 28 YALE J. INT'L. L. 325 (2003).

Although military force is a part of the formula, good sense and military practice indicate the limited utility of sending uniformed and organized groups into conflict with clandestine operatives who hide within civilian populations. Part of the reason is implicit in the statement of the issue, the military units are easily identifiable and their movements relatively predictable while the terrorist is hidden within residents many of whom are sympathetic and willing to provide assistance. Because the military units, if following the rules of war, are not allowed to attack civilian targets, the terrorist essentially has thrown up an impregnable shield to military force. A related concept is that of "asymmetrical" warfare, in which a smaller group using more mobile weapons can travel faster and hide more easily than can the larger force, particularly one which is dependent on and trained in large-scale technology. Of course, modern military units have trained on equipment and with methods that can be more rapidly deployed than in the past, but unless they are willing to engage civilian populations, the military unit is hampered by the tactics of the terrorist who is not so constrained.

The controls on excesses of military force may at first glance seem minimal, that the nation inclined to engage in aggressive military action does so at risk only of military response. But the world community has now demanded that abuse of military force be subject to criminal prosecution, and the norms of international law are expanding the number of countries who may become involved in responding to an abuse of military power. Moreover, on the domestic scene, the political controls on military force, as expressed through acts of Congress or elections, are guided by legal arguments. So the controls on this leg of our tripod have legal as well as political content.

The international law of armed conflict (LOAC), often still known by the older name of "law of war," is relevant to the study of terrorism for three reasons:

1. LOAC sets the terms of armed conflict between two cognizable entities, and terrorist tactics are a violation of LOAC when it applies,

2. some observers, including the Bush administration, have improperly treated terrorist tactics as violations of LOAC regardless of the character of the perpetrator, and

3. LOAC provides, through the concept of crimes against humanity, useful analogies for crafting an international legal regime applicable to terrorism.

American policy following 9/11 has seemed to be driven by a sharp distinction between the concepts of war and the concepts of crime, as if we had only two choices for an appropriate response. It has been argued that if the only two options for categorizing terrorism are war or crime, then law creates the following "asymmetry" or "disconnect" problem: "In crime, one generally cannot kill until after capture, but at that point, cold-blooded execution is legally permissible. In war, one may kill almost at will before surrender and capture, but after capture, the prisoner cannot be killed or otherwise sanctioned."[25]

That disconnect is not as significant in many instances as it might at first seem. If, as the Bush administration has insisted, al Qaeda operatives are enemy combatants, then it might seem that actions they take against military targets (such as the USS Cole) would be legitimate and not punishable. But the "clandestine" operative will violate the requirement to "have a fixed distinctive emblem recognizable at a distance,"[26] and most "terrorist" actions will be taken against civilian targets and thus violate basic norms of warfare.

One place where the disconnect becomes acute is with regard to the use of deadly force in the pursuit or pre-capture stage. U.S. intelligence managed to pinpoint the identity and location of Abu Ali, "chief suspect" in the USS Cole bombing, to the point of being able to target his automobile with a drone missile and kill him along with five other "suspected al Qaeda members."[27] How is it legal to seek out and kill someone who is not at the moment "carrying arms" against the U.S.? Israeli Mossad agents hunted down and killed in Sweden someone who they believed had been responsible for the Munich Olympic incident, but it turned out that they got the wrong person. Ahmad Salameh, who probably was the mastermind of Munich, later was killed in a car-bombing in Lebanon. Sweden sentenced the first group to relatively short prison terms and Israel agreed to pay compensation to the victim's family.[28]

A similar way in which the disconnect is troublesome is in the justifications for use of military force to root out alleged terrorist cells. When the U.S. invaded Afghanistan, the justification was that Afghanistan had "harbored" al Qaeda; in fact, there was a symbiotic relationship in which al Qaeda had provided substantial support to the Taliban regime. Although "harboring" may be a stretch as justification for invasion, there is a powerful argument that the actions of al Qaeda could be "attributed" to the Taliban and thus have constituted acts of war justifying invasion. On the other hand, there was no such showing with respect to Iraq. The support of the world community for the invasion of Afghanistan and the lack of support for invasion of Iraq demonstrate this difference (although certainly other factors enter into the support or lack thereof in those events).

---

[25] Noah Feldman, *Choices of Law, Choices of War*, 25 HARV. J.L. & PUB. POL'Y 457, 458 (2002).

[26] Hague Convention on the Laws and Customs of War on Land, Annex art. I(2) (Oct. 18, 1907).

[27] CNN.com, *Sources: U.S. Kills Cole Suspect, available at* www.cnn.com/2002/WORLD/meast/11/04/yemen.blast/index.html (last visited June 21, 2007).

[28] See AARON J. KLEIN, STRIKING BACK: THE 1972 MUNICH OLYMPICS MASSACRE AND ISRAEL'S DEADLY RESPONSE (2005); *Mossad: The Institute for Intelligence and Special Tasks, available at* www.globalsecurity.org/intell/world/israel/mossad.htm (last visited July 31, 2007); *Norway Solves Riddle of Mossad Killing,* THE GUARDIAN, March 2, 2000, *available at* www.guardian.co.uk/israel/Story/0,2763,193475,00.html.

The nexus between terrorism and warfare is subtle but it does not justify equating terrorism with warfare. The nexus certainly is not as direct as this bumper sticker proclaims: "War is Terrorism with a Bigger Budget." And it is not true that "one person's freedom fighter is another person's terrorist." Some war fighters will use terror as a tactic, but the deliberate targeting of civilians is illegal by both the law of war and international humanitarian law. Another nexus is that the terrorist uses the language of war, primarily for motivation and emotional appeal but also in attempted justification. It is important that the effort to justify terror actions in the language of warfare not be allowed to succeed — the terrorist is not a war fighter. The terrorist often uses tools of warfare, such as weapons or explosives, but uses them on the wrong targets. The terrorist may have training and discipline similar to those of military forces and may employ some of the same tactics. Indeed, the terrorist often has been trained by the very society that he targets. The Romans trained the Germanic tribes, the French trained many Algerians, and the U.S. trained the mujahadeen who became al Qaeda. [29] But none of those groups then became legitimate war fighters, and none of them should be honored with the language of warfare.

Terrorism by subnational groups does not fit within the war paradigm and is not adequately addressed by the existing law enforcement paradigm. Rather than contorting the traditions of either existing paradigm, it would be better to come up with a third paradigm, one that reflects the concerns of an emerging supra-state body of law. International criminal law that is developing around offenses of genocide and crimes against humanity offers an attractive option for a paradigm in which to place terrorism.

[D]   Separation of Functions

The idea of separating the modes of response to terrorism is similar, but far from identical, to the idea of separation of powers among legislative, executive, and judicial branches. Some of the same principles of control to prevent governmental abuse apply in both situations, but the nature of interactions will be quite different. At the top level, "separation of powers" stems from Montesquieu [30] as elaborated for the American states by James Madison:

> The great security against a gradual concentration of the several powers in the same department consists in giving to those who administer each department the necessary constitutional means and personal motive to resist encroachment on the others. Ambition must be made to counteract ambition. [31]

---

[29] *See generally* CALEB CARR, THE LESSONS OF TERROR (2003); JOHN COOLEY, UNHOLY WARS (2002); ROHAN GUNARATNA, INSIDE AL QAEDA (2002).

[30] THE SPIRIT OF LAWS (1748).

[31] FEDERALIST No. 51.

To accomplish the setting of "ambition against ambition," the U.S. Constitution did not create rigid "separation" but employed a system of "checks and balances" in which each branch has some ability to intervene in, or counteract, the actions of the other branches. The result has been aptly described as "a government of separated institutions sharing powers."[32] There are some aspects of governmental practice that can be made more efficient by separation of powers among the branches, as when the legislative branch is freed from having to enforce the law or the judicial branch is freed from engaging in elections or partisan political debates, but for the most part separation runs counter to the goals of efficiency:

> The doctrine of the separation of powers was adopted by the Convention of 1787, not to promote efficiency, but to preclude the exercise of arbitrary power. The purpose was, not to avoid friction, but, by means of the inevitable friction incident to the distribution of the governmental powers among three departments, to save the people from autocracy.[33]

When the New Deal brought an expanded bureaucracy with quasi-legislative (rulemaking) and quasi-judicial (adjudicatory) functions, the first step was to determine whether these functions could be placed in the executive branch. The Supreme Court acceded to the need for shared functions so long as Congress did the essential lawmaking by giving the agency an "intelligible principle" to apply.[34] The scope of "delegation" of legislative power to the executive branch remains contentious precisely because it involves a sharing of a power once thought to be separated, but "lawmaking" is not so easily compartmentalized and courts have recognized the pragmatic need for at least interpretive powers in the executive branch.[35] In the first instance, it is up to the political processes to control the extent of delegation to agencies, although the courts could weigh in if a delegation contained no guidance.

At the level of administrative agencies, the concept of "separation of functions" operates to create a form of tripartite division within each agency, so that investigators, adjudicators, and policy makers are usually somewhat separated.[36] But separation in this context is not constitutionally required and differs markedly from the separation among security, law enforcement, and military action.

By contrast, I am describing three modes of response to violence without arguing for a constitutional requirement that the three be separated or even

---

[32] RICHARD E. NEUSTADT, PRESIDENTIAL POWER 33 (1960).

[33] Myers v. United States, 272 U.S. 52, 293 (1926) (Brandeis, J., dissenting). Although this particular language appears in a dissenting opinion, it expresses a universally accepted principle.

[34] Mistretta v. United States, 488 U.S. 361 (1989); J.W. Hampton Jr. & Co. v. United States, 276 U.S. 394, 406 (1928).

[35] See Whitman v. American Trucking Ass'n, 531 U.S. 457 (2001) (EPA required to set air quality standards "the attainment and maintenance of which are requisite to protect the public health").

[36] Administrative Procedure Act § 5(c), 5 U.S.C. § 1004(c), (2000).

arguing that they could be separated in any stringent degree. What I am asserting is that the constitutional controls that are in place with respect to each will be more difficult to apply if the functions are merged. This raises nonconstitutional public policy arguments in favor of relatively more separation rather than less.

All three options involve some degree of gathering information. Military strategists need intelligence to know what to plan, against whom, and with what resources. Protection of the homefront demands information about what groups might be planning to attack what event or facility. And prosecution requires assembling information that may or may not ultimately be relevant in a court of law. Obviously, all intelligence gathering will produce accumulations of data about responsible law-abiding persons, whether citizens or aliens.

The official American dogma of distrust for government must be factored in at this point.[37] Investigation and prosecution of criminal behavior demands confrontation of witnesses,[38] proof by credible evidence,[39] public trials (for the most part),[40] as well as numerous criminal procedure details such as privileges, juries and representation by counsel that are not necessarily grounded in constitutional language. All of this flows from the oft-stated desire to prevent tyrannical instincts of the moment from overwhelming the individual rights of the populace. At the same time, accumulation of information itself presents a number of civil liberties issues because of citizen mistrust of government agencies to handle information responsibly.[41] And investigation of ethnic-or religious-based terrorism, whether for preventive or apprehension purposes, can easily produce difficulties with discriminatory application of government power.[42]

---

[37] See Whitney v. California, 274 U.S. 357, 375 (1927) (Brandeis, J. concurring):

> Those who won our independence . . . knew that order cannot be secured merely through fear of punishment for its infraction; that fear breeds repression; that repression breeds hate; that hate menaces stable government; that the path of safety lies in the opportunity to discuss freely supposed grievances and proposed remedies; and that the fitting remedy for evil counsels is good ones. . . . Recognizing the occasional tyrannies of governing majorities, they amended the Constitution so that free speech and assembly should be protected.

See also United States v. United States Dist. Ct. (Keith, J.), 407 U.S. 297, 314 (1972):

> History abundantly documents the tendency of Government — however benevolent and benign its motives — to view with suspicion those who most fervently dispute its policies. Fourth Amendment protections become the more necessary when the targets of official surveillance may be those suspected of unorthodoxy in their political beliefs.

[38] U.S. CONST. Amend. VI.

[39] U.S. CONST. Amend. V (due process).

[40] U.S. CONST. Amend. VI. Some minor exceptions have been made for excluding the public when classified information is to be presented. See § 7.03[E] infra.

[41] See generally DAVID COLE & JAMES DEMPSEY, TERRORISM AND THE CONSTITUTION (2002); PHILLIP MELANSON, SECRECY WARS (2001); STEPHEN SCHULHOFER, THE ENEMY WITHIN (2002).

[42] The Department of Justice guidelines regarding racial profiling are discussed in § 10.03[A] infra.

Thus, vigorous pursuit of terrorism through either prevention or prosecution raises the hackles of civil liberties advocates. One consequence of the post-9/11 U.S. response was a shift in emphasis from prosecution to prevention, and many agencies such as the Department of Justice are struggling with the shift. At the same time, the military option has obvious difficulties of its own. Our task is to assess the risks and benefits of the three types of response to impel government into the best possible balance of the three.

§ 2.02 DETENTIONS WITHOUT TRIAL

There is one more device that can be considered for the immobilization of suspected terrorists — imprisonment without trial. Stated in this bald fashion, it seems unthinkable that a western nation would resort to such an outmoded notion as imprisonment without due process, yet that is exactly what almost every nation has tried in one form or another. In the U.S., there are basically four types of detentions that have been attempted:

1. detention of aliens accused of immigration violations;

2. material witness warrants;

3. detention overseas; and

4. executive detention of "enemy combatants."

Detention of suspected terrorists in undisclosed overseas locations will be considered in Chapter 4. Detention in military facilities of suspected terrorists will be considered in Chapter 9. The first two types, deportation candidates and material witnesses will be considered here.

[A] Aliens and Visa Violations

Permission to enter and remain in the U.S. is open to non-citizens only by what is known as the "plenary" authority of Congress. This language expresses the idea that the ability of an alien to be in the U.S. is meant to be purely a matter of largesse to be allocated according to statutory classifications and thus not reviewable or enforceable by the courts. Yet when a person has lawfully entered the U.S., there is at least some degree of due process protection attached to questions of whether he or she has violated the conditions of entry. This due process concern is carried out by the administrative procedures of Immigrations and Customs Enforcement (ICE, formerly INS) that require notice and a hearing prior to deportation.

One aspect of the USA PATRIOT Act that received vociferous critique was section 412, which authorized the Attorney General hold aliens suspected of terrorist connections for up to six months in renewable increments.[43] Justice Department states that it has not used the section

---

[43] 8 U.S.C. § 1226a(a)(6) (2007):

> An alien detained [for suspicion of terrorist or espionage activity] and whose removal is unlikely in the reasonably foreseeable future, may be detained for additional periods of up to six months only if the release of the alien will threaten the national security of the United States or the safety of the community or any person.

412 authorization because it had sufficient authority under existing law to hold aliens considered for deportation without bond.[44]

The Office of Detention and Removal housed over 22,000 aliens per day during 2004. It has announced that it is so overwhelmed with mandated detentions, fueled by pressure not to release anyone who might be a threat to public safety for any reason, that it is embarking on aggressive alternatives to detention.[45] A February 2007 study by the Office of Inspector General in Homeland Security provides a great degree of detail about the detention of aliens under threat of deportation.[46]

Just prior to 9/11 and the PATRIOT Act, the Supreme Court decided in *Zadvydas v. Davis*[47] that an alien who was subject to a removal order (deportation) but who had nowhere to go could be held in detention, according to the immigration statutes, only pursuant to the attempt to remove. Therefore, a detained alien would be entitled by due process to a hearing to determine whether removal was possible. "Freedom from imprisonment — from government custody, detention, or other forms of restraint — lies at the heart of the liberty" protected by due process.[48] The Court implicitly held that release into the U.S. would be required at some point because "an alien may be held in confinement until it has been determined that there is no significant likelihood of removal in the reasonably foreseeable future."[49] The British and Canadian courts have invalidated indefinite detention of aliens suspected of terrorist connections in post-9/11 cases.[50]

In the wake of 9/11, the FBI questioned many immigrants of Arab descent. Some were detained on probable visa violations. Information about these detainees was kept from the public, and in many instances even from their families. The Department of Justice's Office of Inspector General undertook a review of these detentions and the conditions of confinement. The

---

[44] www.lifeandliberty.gov/subs/add_myths.htm#s412 (last visited July 25, 2007):

As of February 2004, the Attorney General had not used section 412. Numerous aliens who could have been considered have been detained since the enactment of the USA PATRIOT Act. But it has not proven necessary to use section 412 in these particular cases because traditional administrative bond proceedings have been sufficient to detain these individuals without bond. The Department believes that this authority should be retained for use in appropriate situations.

[45] www.ice.gov/graphics/news/factsheets/061704detFS2.htm.

[46] Homeland Security Office of Inspector General, *ICE's Compliance With Detention Limits for Aliens With a Final Order of Removal From the United States*, available at www.dhs.gov/xoig/assets/mgmtrpts/OIG_07-28_Feb07.pdf.

[47] 533 U.S. 678 (2001).

[48] *Id.* at 690.

[49] Internal tensions within the *Zadvydas* opinion, the difficulties it leaves for dealing with removable aliens who have nowhere to go, and the implications for detention of those with suspected terrorist connections are discussed in T. Alexander Aleinikoff, *Detaining Plenary Power: The Meaning and Impact of* Zadvydas v. Davis, 16 Geo. Immig. L.J. 365 (2002).

[50] *See* § 10.04 *infra*.

IG concluded that some detentions were not justified beyond a few days and that some of the detainees were badly treated while in custody.[51]

Attorney General Ashcroft responded to the OIG Report with a statement that emphasized that the detentions were authorized by existing law based on visa violations and that the Department was fully justified in its actions. The Department's Office of Legal Counsel also argued that detentions were within the statutory authority of the AG and that it was appropriate to "use all legal tools available to protect the American people from additional terrorist attacks." After reviewing the responses of the AG and INS, the DOJ Inspector General provided a follow-up analysis, which reported progress in improving the agencies' handling of the situation.[52]

Some complaints regarding the handling of alien detainees in the aftermath of 9/11 has been the agencies' refusal to provide information to the public about those detained. Several groups attempted to obtain information under the Freedom of Information Act but were rebuffed by the D.C. Circuit.[53] The groups were seeking for all persons detained in relation to the 9/11 investigation "their names, their attorneys, dates of arrest and release, locations of arrest and detention, and reasons for detention." The detainees in question were in three categories: those detained on visa violations, those detained for arraignment on criminal charges, and those detained on material witness warrants. The court applied FOIA's exemption for "records or information compiled for law enforcement purposes, but only to the extent that the production of such law enforcement records or information . . . could reasonably be expected to interfere with enforcement proceedings."[54]

In light of the deference mandated by the separation of powers and Supreme Court precedent, we hold that the government's

---

[51] Dep't of Justice, Office of the Inspector General, *The September 11 Detainees: A Review of the Treatment of Aliens Held on Immigration Charges in Connection with the Investigation of the September 11 Attacks*, June 2003, *available at* www.usdoj.gov/oig/special/0306/index.htm:

> With regard to allegations of abuse, the evidence indicates a pattern of physical and verbal abuse by some correctional officers at the MDC [Manhattan Detention Center] against some September 11 detainees, particularly during the first months after the attacks. Although most correctional officers denied any such physical or verbal abuse, our interviews and investigation of specific complaints developed evidence that abuse had occurred.
>
> In sum, while the chaotic situation and the uncertainties surrounding the detainees' connections to terrorism explain some of these problems, they do not explain them all. We believe the Department should carefully consider and address the issues described in this report, and we therefore offered a series of recommendations regarding the systemic problems we identified in our review.

[52] Dep't of Justice, Office of the Inspector General, *Analysis of the Second Response by the Department of Justice to Recommendations in the Office of the Inspector General's June 2003 Report on the Treatment of September 11 Detainees*, Jan. 2004, *available at* www.usdoj.gov/oig/special/0401/index.htm.

[53] Center for Nat'l Security Studies v. U.S. Dep't of Justice, 331 F.3d 918 (D.C. Cir. 2003).

[54] *Id.* at 922 (citing 5 U.S.C. § 552(b)(7) (2000)).

expectation that disclosure of the detainees' names would enable al Qaeda or other terrorist groups to map the course of the investigation and thus develop the means to impede it is reasonable. A complete list of names informing terrorists of every suspect detained by the government at any point during the September 11 investigation would give terrorist organizations a composite picture of the government investigation, and since these organizations would generally know the activities and locations of its members on or about September 11, disclosure would inform terrorists of both the substantive and geographic focus of the investigation. Moreover, disclosure would inform terrorists which of their members were compromised by the investigation, and which were not. This information could allow terrorists to better evade the ongoing investigation and more easily formulate or revise counter-efforts.[55]

Against this assertion of deference to executive fears, the dissenting judge insisted that the statute required the government to convince the court of the likelihood of harm to investigative efforts:

The only argument that could conceivably support withholding innocent detainees' names is the assertion that disclosure of the names "may reveal details about the focus and scope of the investigation and thereby allow terrorists to counteract it." That Reynolds believes these harms may result from disclosure is hardly surprising — anything is possible. But before accepting the government's argument, this court must insist on knowing whether these harms "could reasonably be expected to" result from disclosure — the standard Congress prescribed for exemption under 7(A). Nothing in Reynolds's declaration suggests that these harms are in fact reasonably likely to occur.[56]

A citizen watchdog group ordinarily does not have "standing" to sue the government just because it doesn't like something government is doing.[57] FOIA, however, gives anyone a statutory right to see information in government files unless the information fits within one of the defined exemptions. Nevertheless, identifying the interest that the complainants might have in knowing these names could affect a court's perception of the reasonableness of the government's fear that disclosure would interfere with law enforcement efforts. Presumably, the interest groups wanted to track the degree to which detentions were based on mere ethnicity rather than reasonable suspicions of individual ties to terrorist activities.

The DOJ Inspector General Report criticized a failure to distinguish between suspected terrorists and mere immigration violators. Why is this significant? Ted Bundy was stopped three times for traffic violations which

---

[55] *Id.* at 928.

[56] *Id.* at 942.

[57] *See, e.g.,* Lujan v. Defenders of Wildlife, 504 U.S. 555 (1992); Allen v. Wright, 468 U.S. 737 (1984).

led to his arrests for serial rape and murder. Other serial killers have been apprehended for similar violations. Criminal conspirators often commit minor violations in the course of their bigger conspiracies. If police are searching for a bank robber, shouldn't they be particularly alert to anyone driving oddly, waving a pistol around, or wearing a mask on the street? What is wrong with picking up immigration violators to see if there is a terrorist lurking in their midst? The difference is that focusing on immigration violations necessarily targets groups on the basis of national origin, which will lead to the use of ethnicity as the basis for initial contact. The concern of the IG may have been the same as the concern of the interest groups seeking information: that immigration violations could be used as a subterfuge for ethnicity-based detentions similar to *Korematsu*.[58]

The Report also criticizes failure to provide access to lawyers or relatives. AG Ashcroft's statement and the government's position before the D.C. Circuit claim that secrecy was necessary to prevent terrorists from passing information to each other. The dissenting judge points out that fear of a possibility is different from the reasonable apprehension demanded by FOIA. Moreover, even if a mere possibility were adequate justification for government secrecy in normal circumstances, the rationale becomes more attenuated when a plausible claim of racial or ethnic differentiation is at stake. The degree of likely harm may be difficult to assess but if ethnic distinctions are the only basis of differential treatment, then *Korematsu* would demand strict scrutiny, not just a mere possibility of harm.

All these considerations involve the question of whether there are reasons for using ethnicity or national origin as the basis for differential treatment of persons. Attempting to penetrate the secrecy in detention and interrogation would have been the first step in challenging the basis of selection of detainees. The Report does not address the issue of ethnic or religious profiling implicit in the roundup of Arabic or Muslim males. The issue of ethnic profiling is considered further in Chapter 10.

[B] Material Witness Warrants

Material witness warrants are an important tool of criminal procedure that are mostly beyond the scope of this course, but which along with grand jury subpoenas make some of the more controversial aspects of PATRIOT virtually irrelevant. A material witness warrant is issued by a judge or magistrate under conditions similar to an arrest warrant but the purpose is to secure that person's testimony rather than to hold the person for trial.

The Justice Department stated to Congress in May 2003 that less than 50 persons had been detained on material witness warrants "in the course of the September 11 investigation." Of those, all but about 5 were "detained for 90 days or less."

In the FOIA case[59] the D.C. Circuit said that even material witness

---

[58] Korematsu v. United States, 323 U.S. 214 (1944).

[59] Center for National Security Studies v. U.S. Department of Justice, 331 F.3d 918 (D.C. Cir. 2003).

warrants allow the detainee to contact the press. That assumes, of course, that their custodians provide the mechanism to do so. The court notes that two former material witnesses were being held at that time "for alleged terrorist activity." José Padilla was held incommunicado for almost four years, initially as a material witness then as an enemy combatant, before charges were finally filed against him.[60] Ali al-Marri was originally charged with perjury, then detained as an enemy combatant, for a total detention of four years before the Fourth Circuit finally held that he must be released or tried.[61] Because the Government has refused to detail the number of persons held on material witness warrants and the length of time held, on the ground that grand jury proceedings are secret for several reasons, there are a number of advocacy groups expressing deep suspicion about abuse of the material witness warrant in this context.

In *United States v. Awadallah*,[62] Osama Awadallah was taken into custody in Los Angeles after his name and phone number were found on a gum wrapper in the car of one of the 9/11 hijackers. He was detained on a material witness warrant and flown to New York where he testified twice before a grand jury over the course of several weeks. He admitted knowing one of the hijackers but first denied knowing a second one whom he later remembered. Charged with perjury for the first statement, he moved to dismiss the indictment for abuse of the material witness statute. The district judge held that "no Congress has granted the government the authority to imprison an innocent person in order to guarantee that he will testify before a grand jury conducting a criminal investigation. Because Awadallah was unlawfully detained, his grand jury testimony must be suppressed. The indictment is therefore dismissed." The Second Circuit reversed, holding that obtaining grand jury testimony would be an appropriate use of the material witness statute:

> The district court noted (and we agree) that it would be improper for the government to use § 3144 for other ends, such as the detention of persons suspected of criminal activity for which probable cause has not yet been established. However, the district court made no finding (and we see no evidence to suggest) that the government arrested Awadallah for any purpose other than to secure information material to a grand jury investigation. Moreover, that grand jury was investigating the September 11 terrorist attacks. The particular governmental interests at stake therefore were the indictment and successful prosecution of terrorists whose attack, if committed by a sovereign, would have been tantamount to war, and the discovery of the conspirators' means, contacts, and operations in order to forestall future attacks.[63]

---

[60] The Fourth Circuit upheld his detention but when his attorneys filed for certiorari, the Government decided to try him in civilian criminal court. Hanft v. Padilla, 546 U.S. 1084 (2006).

[61] Al-Marri v. Wright, 487 F.3d 160 (4th Cir. 2007).

[62] 349 F.3d 42 (2d Cir. 2003).

[63] *Id.* at 59.

Chapter 3

U.S. STATUTES & JURISDICTION

SYNOPSIS

§ 3.01   U.S. Statutes Related to Terrorism
§ 3.02   Extraterritorial Application of U.S. Law
§ 3.03   Foreign Capture and Treatment of Suspects
    [A]   Abduction for Trial
    [B]   Mistreatment of Prisoners on Foreign Soil
    [C]   Extraordinary Renditions and Interrogation
§ 3.04   Private Actions Against Terrorist Activity
    [A]   Alien Tort Claims and International Law
    [B]   State Sponsors of Terrorism
    [C]   Claims Against Nonstate Actors

Terrorism is hardly a new phenomenon. Some historians claim that it has always been a part of human attempts to subdue a population.[1] The character and frequency of terrorist activity adapted in the late 20th Century to take advantage of mass media and instant global communications, but the basic phenomenon is no different than it was 3,000 years ago and is not likely to be any different in the next millennium.[2]

Certainly, there is no reason to believe that it can be eliminated from common experience, no more than can be other crimes of violence or other activities on which governments have "declared war" such as drug trafficking. It should be apparent by now that when politicians declare war on drugs or poverty or terrorism, they are not using "war" as a term of art. It is just a statement of seriousness of intent, not appropriately used as a calling into play of specific tools. One reality that must be borne in mind is that clandestine organizations are not amenable to brute force. In fact, the "war" on terrorism has splintered groups and made new converts to an increasingly diffuse and disconnected collection of terrorism adherents, requiring that the forces of law and order themselves respond with clandestine and cunning.[3]

---

[1] Caleb Carr traces the phenomenon back to pre-history and points out that the Roman Republic even had a name for it — "punitive war." CALEB CARR, THE LESSONS OF TERROR 31 (2002).

[2] *See generally* CHRISTOPHER C. HARMON, TERRORISM TODAY (2000).

[3] *See al-Qaida Recruiting Made Web of Militants*, ASSOCIATED PRESS, March 16, 2004: "Al-Qaida is now 'separate and loose groups' bound only by an ideology, but working independently. They know the general guidelines and they know what is required to do."

Taking the metaphorical language of warfare out of the terrorism discussion, it might be helpful to review what the ordinary mechanisms of public safety and law enforcement offer in the way of prevention and control of terrorist activity. This article reviews the tools available both to security planners and prosecutors in the struggle against terrorism.

The story of U.S. involvement with terrorism really begins with the post-Civil War statutes aimed at the Ku Klux Klan, but the story of domestic terrorism is slightly different from the prosecutions and statutes involving "international terrorism." As a subset of U.S. law, international terrorism begins with response to airplane hijackings in the 1970s.

§ 3.01   U.S. STATUTES RELATED TO TERRORISM

There is no criminal offense of terrorism in U.S. federal law. U.S. statutes do contain several definitions of terrorism, the impacts of which are either procedural, investigation authorization, or punishment enhancement. On the other hand, like many nations, the U.S. has dozens of statutes that address specific actions that might be taken by terrorists, such as use of explosives, murder, and the like. The U.S., also like many other nations, has statutes that criminalize conduct covered by several international conventions.

The U.S. passed the Aircraft Piracy[4] and Hostage Taking[5] statutes in response to treaty obligations entered into during the 1970s. Of particular interest is that under both statutes, if the offense results in the death of another person, U.S. law provides for imposition of the death penalty. This runs counter to the attitudes of most Western nations and makes it difficult for the U.S. to obtain extradition of persons from countries that object to the death penalty.[6]

The Omnibus Diplomatic Security and Antiterrorism Act of 1986 produced what is now 18 U.S.C. § 2332, which sets penalties for murder or manslaughter in the case of anyone who "kills a national of the United States, while such national is outside the United States." The statute goes on to state that

> [n]o prosecution for any offense described in this section shall be undertaken by the United States except on written certification of the Attorney General or the highest ranking subordinate of the Attorney General with responsibility for criminal prosecutions that,

---

[4] 49 U.S.C. § 46502 (2006).

[5] 18 U.S.C. § 1203 (2006).

[6] Richard C. Dieter, *International Perspectives on the Death Penalty: A Costly Isolation for the U.S.*, Death Penalty Info. Ctr., (1999), *available at* deathpenaltyinfo.org/article.php?scid = 45&did = 536.

The U.K., while signing a new extradition treaty with the U.S. in April 2003, announced that it would not send a suspect to the U.S. without assurance that the suspect would not be subject to the death penalty. BBC News, *UK Rules out Death Penalty Extradition, available at* news.bbc.co.uk/1/hi/uk_politics/2920563.stm (last visited March 11, 2004).

in the judgment of the certifying official, such offense was intended to coerce, intimidate, or retaliate against a government or a civilian population.[7]

This provision raises a host of questions. What is the point of the limitation to murder committed for the purpose of coercion, intimidation, or retaliation? And if the concern was over diplomatic officials, why apply it to any U.S. national? For that matter, why the need for a special statute applying to homicide of a U.S. national in the first place?

The last question sets up some of the other issues. For reasons unique to federalism, the U.S. could not have a general homicide statute.[8]

Therefore, a statute applying to acts committed outside the U.S. makes sense, and there is nothing in international law to prevent the U.S. from asserting adjudicative jurisdiction over the murder of a U.S. national by a foreign national in a foreign country.[9] But in that situation, an extradition treaty typically would not require the foreign country to deliver up their national for trial in a U.S. court because extradition treaties often exempt nationals of the requested nation or at least acknowledge discretion to refuse delivery. Even extradition pursuant to international conventions on specific offenses such as aircraft hijacking or torture will give the requested nation an option of extraditing or placing the suspect on trial in its own courts. If the U.S. could obtain custody of the defendant on the high seas or in a third country, then extradition would not be an issue. And if the U.S. could obtain custody and transport the defendant to the U.S. from within that person's domicile nation (jurisdiction by abduction), then the question would be whether an existing treaty prevented abduction of a national from that country.[10]

What the special statute provides is a basis for being clear that the crime is covered by U.S. law and triggers rights of the U.S. to obtain extradition under the Convention on the Prevention and Punishment of Crimes Against Internationally Protected Persons.[11] In return, the U.S. must criminalize attacks on internationally protected persons of other countries while on U.S. soil.[12] Perhaps the U.S. chose to cover any U.S. national simply to avoid

---

[7] 18 U.S.C. § 2332(d) (2007).

[8] *See* United States v. Morrison, 529 U.S. 598 (2000) (noneconomic incident of violence not within Congress' commerce power).

[9] *See* United States v. Yunis, 924 F.2d 1086, 1090 (2d Cir. 1991).

[10] *See* § 3.03[A] *infra*.

[11] The Convention defines internationally protected person as a Head of State and his or her entourage plus "any representative or official of a State or any official or other agent of an international organization of an intergovernmental character who, at the time when and in the place where a crime against him, his official premises, his private accommodation or his means of transport is committed, is entitled pursuant to international law to special protection from any attack on his person, freedom or dignity, as well as members of his family forming part of his household." Convention on the Prevention and Punishment of Crimes Against Internationally Protected Persons, art. 1(1)(b), Feb. 20, 1977, 1035 U.N.T.S. 167.

[12] This obligation is carried out in 18 U.S.C. § 112 (2007).

a potential difficulty of showing the requisite jurisdictional facts in a given case.

That still leaves the question of why require the Attorney General's certification of a political motivation for the crime. A separate statute already applies the same penalties to anyone who commits murder or manslaughter of an officer or employee of the U.S. government while in the course of his or her duties.[13] Prosecutors always prefer the ability to charge multiple crimes from the same acts for a variety of reasons having to do with negotiation strategy, enhancement of sentences, and the like, but the certification acts to limit that discretion.[14] The legislative history of this provision shows that the certification is designed to prevent the statute's application to "ordinary" crime.[15] In the extradition context, it also provides assurance to the requested country that extradition is not sought lightly, that the suspect is believed to be part of a larger scheme or organization.

The Antiterrorism and Effective Death Penalty Act of 1996 was the next major statutory enactment of the U.S. in this field. It produced what is now 18 U.S.C. § 2332b, "Acts of terrorism transcending national boundaries." This statute has the appearance of being the quintessential statement of U.S. criminal policy toward terrorism, but it contains a very curious anomaly. There is a specific definition of "Federal Crime of Terrorism" that does not have any effect on the definition of a crime.[16] Other portions of section 2332b make it an offense to engage in violence under any of several circumstances that would trigger U.S. extraterritorial jurisdiction without regard to whether there is any political motivation element in the defendant's conduct. Section 2339A (providing material support to terrorists) proscribes provision of goods and services "knowing or intending that they

---

[13] 18 U.S.C. § 1113 (2007).

[14] *See* United States v. Yousef, 327 F.3d 56, 116 (2d Cir. 2003).

[15] "The committee of conference does not intend [§ 2332] reach nonterrorist violence inflicted upon American victims. Simple barroom brawls or normal street crime, for example, are not intended to be covered by this provision." H.R. Rep. No. 99-783, at 87-88 (1986) (conf. Rep.).

[16] The definition in § 2332b reads:

the term "Federal crime of terrorism" means an offense that

(A) is calculated to influence or affect the conduct of government by intimidation or coercian, or to retaliate against government conduct; and

(B) is a violation of [listed federal crimes such as arson, murder, hostage taking, use of chemical or biological weapons, bombing public buildings, etc]

This definition is similar but not identical to 18 U.S.C. § 2331(1):

the term "international terrorism" means activities that

(A) involve violent acts dangerous to human life that are a violation of the criminal laws of the United States or of any State, or that would be a criminal violations in committed within the jurisdiction of the United States or of any State;

(B) appear to be intended

(i) to intimidate or coerce a civilian population;

(ii) to influence the policy of a government by intimidation or coercion;

(iii) to affect the conduct of a government by mass destruction, assassination, or kidnaping.

are to be used" in the commission of specified crimes, none of which is itself dependent on the definition in 2332b. Section 2339B (providing material support to designated foreign terrorist organization) proscribes provision of goods or services to any organization designated by the Secretary of State under 8 U.S.C. § 1189, which refers in turn to this succinct definition used for the purpose of designating terrorist organizations:

> the term "terrorism" means premeditated, politically motivated violence perpetrated against noncombatant targets by subnational groups or clandestine agents.[17]

The State Department definition (§ 2656) is probably the easiest to apply, consisting as it does of four discrete elements: violence, civilian targets, clandestine perpetrator, and political motivation. Setting aside the relevance of political motivation for the moment, the point remains that the § 2656 definition is picked up in only one criminal statute (§ 2339B) and there only indirectly as the mechanism for designation of an organization by the Secretary of State.

So what is the point of the definition in § 2332b? It defines a category of offense over which the "Attorney General shall have primary investigative responsibility," but its only other use is in the Sentencing Guidelines promulgated by the Federal Sentencing Commission. There we find that the sentence upon conviction of an offense under some other provision of federal law will be enhanced if the judge determines that the predicate offense "involved, or was intended to promote" a "federal crime of terrorism."[18] The courts of appeals are uniform in holding that if the defendant's conduct has the effect of promoting a "federal crime of terrorism," then sentencing enhancement is warranted even though the defendant pleaded to a different charge.[19]

Given the lack of statutory use of the § 2332b definition, what statutory definitions of offenses do apply? As indicated above, there are the "providing support" statutes (§ 2339A and § 2339B), there are a wealth of federal statutes that do not depend in any degree on political motivation or other elements of terrorism (all those dealing with air piracy, explosives, kidnaping, chemical weapons, and the like that are listed in § 2332b), and there is one statute dealing with torture which applies to any U.S. national or person found in the U.S. who committed the defined offense of torture while outside the U.S.[20]

---

[17] 22 U.S.C. § 2656(f)(d)(2) (2005).

[18] U.S. Sentencing Guidelines Manual § 3A1.4 (2007):

> (a) If the offense is a felony that involved, or was intended to promote, a federal crime of terrorism, increase by 12 levels; but if the resulting offense level is less than level 32, increase to level 32.

[19] United States v. Arnaout, 431 F.3d 994 (7th Cir. 2005); United States v. Mandhai, 375 F.3d 1243, 1247 (11th Cir. 2004); United States v. Graham, 275 F.3d 490 (6th Cir. 2001).

[20] 18 U.S.C. § 2340 (2007). Definitions

> (1) "torture" means an act committed by a person acting under the color of law specifically intended to inflict severe physical or mental pain or suffering (other than

The truth of the matter is that, except for the two statutes dealing with providing support to terrorists or terrorist organizations, U.S. law does not depend on the definition of terrorism. U.S. law deals with offenses of violence without regard to the motivation or the type of organization involved. In most instances, this is a perfectly acceptable position. The U.S. jurisdictional statutes that apply to crimes of violence depend instead upon use of interstate commerce or threats to U.S. interests.[21]

There are very limited reasons why we should have any interest in defining "terrorism" as an offense separate and apart from the crimes of violence that are already framed in federal law. One would be to invoke "universal" jurisdiction if the international regime were to settle on a definition of terrorism that equated it with piracy or slavery for that purpose,[22] but the U.S. extraterritorial jurisdiction statutes already provide rather ample bases of jurisdiction. A second reason in federal law is to provide for a variety of noncriminal sanctions, such as freezing or forfeiture of assets. There are two less technical and more "political" reasons for settling on a definition, to promote international prosecution of terrorism and to distinguish terrorist actions from "ordinary" mass or serial killers.[23]

---

pain or suffering incidental to lawful sanctions) upon another person within his custody or physical control;

(2) "severe mental pain or suffering" means the prolonged mental harm caused by or resulting from—

(A) the intentional infliction or threatened infliction of severe physical pain or suffering;

(B) the administration or application, or threatened administration or application, of mind-altering substances or other procedures calculated to disrupt profoundly the senses or the personality;

(C) the threat of imminent death; or

(D) the threat that another person will imminently be subjected to death, severe physical pain or suffering, or the administration or application of mind-altering substances or other procedures calculated to disrupt profoundly the senses or personality; and

(3) "United States" includes all areas under the jurisdiction of the United States including any of the places described in sections 5 and 7 of this title and section 46501(2) of title 49.

18 U.S.C. § 2340A. Torture

(a) Offense. Whoever outside the United States commits or attempts to commit torture shall be fined under this title or imprisoned not more than 20 years, or both, and if death results to any person from conduct prohibited by this subsection, shall be punished by death or imprisoned for any term of years or for life.

(b) Jurisdiction. There is jurisdiction over the activity prohibited in subsection (a) if—

(1) the alleged offender is a national of the United States; or

(2) the alleged offender is present in the United States, irrespective of the nationality of the victim or alleged offender.

[21] *See, e.g.,* 18 U.S.C. § 7 (2007); 18 U.S.C. § 2332 (2007).

[22] *See Yousef,* 927 F. Supp. at 681-82.

[23] The federal government has blurred this distinction by invoking the terrorism enhancement provision of the Sentencing Guidelines with McVeigh and Nichols. *See* United States v. Nichols, 169 F.3d 1255 (10th Cir. 1999).

§ 3.02   EXTRATERRITORIAL APPLICATION OF U.S. LAW

United States v. Yunis[24] appears to be the earliest reported appellate decision in which the United States pursued and prosecuted an incident of international terrorism. Yunis was acting as part of a rogue Lebanese organization calling itself the Amal Militia, which objected to the presence of Palestinian refugees in Lebanon. He and four colleagues hijacked a Royal Jordanian Airlines flight out of Beirut in 1985 and tried to fly to Tunis to draw attention to their issues at a meeting of the Arab League. They were blocked from landing in Tunis, then refueled in Palermo, tried again to land in Tunis, stopped again in Cyprus, and returned to Beirut, where more militia members came aboard. The plane then took off for Syria but was turned away and went back to Beirut. "There, the hijackers released the passengers, held a press conference reiterating their demand that Palestinians leave Lebanon, blew up the plane, and fled from the airport."[25]

The FBI identified Yunis as the ringleader, lured him to a yacht in the Mediterranean with a bogus drug deal, flew him back to the U.S., and put him on trial. He was convicted of conspiracy, aircraft piracy, and hostage-taking. He admitted his role in the incident. His principal contentions on appeal were lack of extraterritorial jurisdiction and that the circumstances of his apprehension constituted a denial of due process.

With regard to extraterritoriality, the Hostage-Taking Act specifically applied to conduct outside the U.S. if either the hostage or the offender were a U.S. citizen. Because two U.S. citizens were on the flight, the statutory elements were satisfied but Yunis argued that international law required that the hostages be taken *because of* their citizenship. The court did not pause to determine the truth of that statement because it did not believe that international law would prevail in any event.

> Yunis seeks to portray international law as a self-executing code that trumps domestic law whenever the two conflict. That effort misconceives the role of judges as appliers of international law and as participants in the federal system. Our duty is to enforce the Constitution, laws, and treaties of the United States, not to conform the law of the land to norms of customary international law. . . . To be sure, courts should hesitate to give penal statutes extraterritorial effect absent a clear congressional directive. Similarly, courts will not blind themselves to potential violations of international law where legislative intent is ambiguous. But the statute in question reflects an unmistakable congressional intent, consistent with treaty obligations of the United States, to authorize prosecution of those who take Americans hostage abroad no matter where the offense occurs or where the offender is found.[26]

---

[24] 924 F.2d 1086 (D.C. Cir. 1991).

[25] *Id.* at 1089.

[26] *Id.* at 1091.

Similarly, Yunis argued that both the Hostage-Taking and Hijacking statutes applied only if the offender were "found in" the United States and not if he were "brought to" the United States specifically for the purpose of trial. The court rejected this argument because neither statute contained language precluding extraterritorial apprehension, while also noting that at least air piracy and perhaps hostage-taking as well may be recognized internationally as crimes of universal jurisdiction.[27]

The *Yunis* court did not engage in an extensive discussion of extraterritorial jurisdiction. It relied on the U.S. nationality of victims, what is sometimes alliteratively called the "passive personality principle" but more descriptively would be "victim nationality," as well as on the more controversial concept of "universal jurisdiction."

"Victim nationality" raises the question of whether "ordinary" violence against a U.S. national abroad will be subject to the extraterritorial jurisdiction of a U.S. court, the issue to which the prosecutorial limitation of § 2332 is addressed. Consistently with some commentary in the Restatement, the Ninth Circuit read "victim nationality" rather narrowly in dictum while upholding jurisdiction over defendants who were prosecuted for a drug-related murder of a U.S. citizen in Mexico.[28] The same court then explained that more than victim nationality will be at stake when elements of the "general and maritime jurisdiction" statute are met, because then there will be effects on either the territory or the interests of the U.S.[29]

Universal jurisdiction is hinged on the thought that some crimes are so heinous or so established as offenses against all peoples (*erga omnes*), that any nation acquiring power over the offender can punish the offense. The idea of universal jurisdiction is closely related to the emerging notion of

---

[27] *Id.* at 1091-92.

[28] *See* United States v. Vasquez-Velasco, 15 F.3d 833, 841 n.7 (9th Cir. 1994):

> Extraterritorial application of [18 U.S.C.] § 1959 [murder in the course of racketeering] to the random murder of tourists abroad would be inappropriate because such extraterritorial application would rely completely on the fact that an American citizen was murdered. Thus, extraterritoriality would be based solely on the passive personality principle, under which jurisdiction is asserted based on the nationality of the victim. In general, this principle has not been accepted as a sufficient basis for extraterritorial jurisdiction for ordinary torts and crimes. *See* Restatement § 402 comment g. *See also* Restatement (Second) of Foreign Relations Law of the United States § 30(2) (1965) (stating that "[a] state does not have jurisdiction to prescribe a rule of law attaching legal consequences to conduct of an alien outside its territory merely on the ground that the conduct affects one of its nationals"). More recently, the passive personality principle has become increasingly accepted as an appropriate basis for extraterritoriality when applied to terrorist activities and organized attacks on a state's nationals because of the victim's nationality. Moreover, the passive personality principle serves as the basis of a recent United States statute directed at acts of terrorism overseas. *See* Omnibus Diplomatic Security and Antiterrorism Act of 1986 § 1202, 18 U.S.C. § 2231. However, a random murder of an American tourist is unlikely to qualify as terrorist activity or an organized attack, indicating that extraterritoriality would be inappropriate even under this standard.

[29] *See* United States v. Neil, 312 F.3d 419, 423 (9th Cir. 2002).

"international crimes" and has not yet received wide acceptance outside the domain of treaty law defining specific crimes that all member nations are required to criminalize.[30]

The basic concepts are reasonably well-established in U.S. law, although there are nuances of difference in some of the authorities' description of them. Courts have described five different bases of extraterritorial jurisdiction;[31] in addition to universal and victim nationality (the two in *Yunis*), criminal jurisdiction could be based on the nationality of the offender, effects felt within the prosecuting nation, or "protective jurisdiction" to address harms to interests or possessions of the prosecuting nation.

There is a rather different approach to the issue in RESTATEMENT (THIRD) OF FOREIGN RELATIONS LAW OF THE UNITED STATES § 402:

> Subject to § 403, a state has jurisdiction to prescribe law with respect to:
>
> (1) (a) conduct that, wholly or in substantial part, takes place within its territory;
>
> (b) the status of persons, or interests in things, present within its territory;
>
> (c) conduct outside its territory that has or is intended to have substantial effect within its territory;
>
> (2) the activities, interests, status, or relations of its nationals outside as well as within its territory; and
>
> (3) certain conduct outside its territory by persons not its nationals that is directed against the security of the state or against a limited class of other state interests.

Section 403 exempts offenses that would otherwise be subject to extraterritorial jurisdiction but whose prosecution would be "unreasonable" in light of such factors as expectations in the international community or interference with the interests of another state.

The Restatement does not seem to authorize "universal" jurisdiction, and the other four headings of extraterritorial jurisdiction are framed by the Restatement in slightly different terms than they are by the courts, but the total effect is similar: actions within the territory or having an effect within the territory, actions that affect national interests, actions by or against nationals. Similarly, 18 USC § 7 defines "special maritime and territorial jurisdiction of the United States" to include such areas as the high seas, vessels and vehicles registered in the U.S. or owned by U.S.

---

[30] Alfred P. Rubin, *Piracy*, *in* III ENCYCLOPEDIA OF PUB. INT'L L. 1039 (1997).

[31] *See* United States v. Vasquez-Velasco, 15 F.3d 833 (9th Cir. 2002); United States v. Felix-Gutierrez, 940 F.2d 1200, 1204 (9th Cir. 1991).

citizens, military installations within the U.S., and diplomatic or consular properties overseas. It also includes

> (7) Any place outside the jurisdiction of any nation with respect to an offense by or against a national of the United States.

> (8) To the extent permitted by international law, any foreign vessel during a voyage having a scheduled departure from or arrival in the United States with respect to an offense committed by or against a national of the United States.

Subsection 8 is the only provision limited by the language "to the extent permitted by international law." Although some of the special statutes related to terrorism refer back to 18 USC § 7, most of them also carry their own jurisdictional statements. The combination can make for very confusing efforts to parse the statutes.

"Special maritime and territorial jurisdiction" is an awkward phrase for a statute that describes "extraterritorial jurisdiction" and which could be applied to hundreds of criminal statutes. It would be a good idea to rewrite the entire statute to focus on extraterritorial jurisdiction and pare the categories down to the five commonly cited ones. There could be any number of subcategories and descriptions, and there could be "special" provisions in individual statutes that seemed to need them, but a leaner general list would make for less confusion. It would also provide an opportunity for Congress to endorse "universal" jurisdiction for the special offenses of piracy, slavery, and terrorism.[32]

§ 3.03 FOREIGN CAPTURE AND TREATMENT OF SUSPECTS

Yunis also made an argument that he could not be subject to a U.S. prosecution because of the circumstances of his capture and treatment abroad. On an early appeal by the Government from an order suppressing his confession (*Yunis I*),[33] the court described his capture this way:

> Yunis was arrested by means of a "take down": agents on either side of Yunis grabbed his arms and kicked his feet out from under him, so that he ended up face down on the deck of the boat. He was [transferred to] the USS Butte [and] taken to a small room that was to be his living quarters for the next four days, as the Butte made its way westward across the Mediterranean. The room was small — eight by ten feet — and poorly ventilated, as a malfunctioning vent evidently blew hot air into the room; the room's estimated

---

[32] War crimes, crimes against humanity, and genocide might also be thought to be proper subjects of universal jurisdiction except that the international community has gone in the direction of creating a special institutional regime for these offenses through creation of the International Criminal Court. Unfortunately, the U.S. withdrew its signature for the Charter of the ICC, leaving it unclear what role the U.S. will take in pursuit of these offenses.

[33] United States v. Yunis, 859 F.2d 953 (D.C. Cir. 1988).

temperature was 85 degrees. Although there were no windows, a hatch door (which at all times remained open) gave out onto a deck area, with some exposure to the ocean. In this room, a naval doctor examined Yunis and found him to be in good health, aside from his seasickness. During the examination, an FBI agent who was fluent in Arabic served as interpreter, since Yunis speaks very little English. The doctor did not notice any problem with Yunis' wrists, and Yunis did not complain about them at this time. However, it was later established by x-rays (after Yunis reached the United States) that both wrists had been fractured, apparently when the FBI agents first arrested him by means of the "take down."

He signed a form recognizing that he was being accorded *Miranda* rights and then interrogated. After about 12 hours of questioning spread over three days, he provided a written statement with details not only of the hijacking but other events as well.[34] The court of appeals held that his confession was admissible over his objections based on physical discomfort at the time of his waiver.[35]

There are a number of jurisdictional-type issues involved in this type of case. One is whether U.S. agents can enter foreign territory to apprehend a suspect and forcibly remove him to the U.S. Another is whether alleged mistreatment of a prisoner can be grounds for dismissal of a prosecution. The application of *Miranda* to a captive held overseas is yet another.

[A] Abduction for Trial

The first question, apprehension of suspects overseas, has been the subject of two rather inflammatory incidents, one involving Panama and the other Mexico. The one with the most publicly visible repercussions was the apprehension of Manuel Noriega by invasion of Panama in 1989.[36] Prior to the invasion, Noriega had been indicted in a U.S. federal court on drug trafficking charges to which he responded by attempting to seize political control of Panama and declaring that a state of war existed between Panama and the U.S. The first President Bush stated that the purposes of the invasion were "safeguarding American lives, restoring democracy, preserving the Panama Canal treaties, and seizing Noriega to face federal drug charges in the United States." After his apprehension, he was brought to the U.S. for trial and convicted. On appeal, Noriega objected that a military invasion violated the extradition treaty between the U.S. and Panama and also amounted to a violation of standards of decency embedded in the due process clause. The Eleventh Circuit rejected this argument in reliance on Supreme Court rulings.

---

[34] *Id.* at 955-57.

[35] *Id.* at 966.

[36] United States v. Noriega, 117 F.3d 1206 (11th Cir. 1997).

Abduction for trial is generally covered by what is known as the *Ker-Frisbie* doctrine,[37] under which the Supreme Court has stated that "the power of a court to try a person for crime is not impaired by the fact that he had been brought within the court's jurisdiction by reason of a forcible abduction."[38]

The Supreme Court applied this doctrine to the treaty issue in *United States v. Alvarez-Machain*,[39] the second of our two infamous incidents. Dr. Alvarez was abducted from Mexico by DEA agents without seeking any cooperation of the Mexican government. He was accused of participating in the particularly brutal torture and murder of DEA agent Enrique Camarena. The Court reiterated the general rule that "forcible abduction is no sufficient reason why the party should not answer when brought within the jurisdiction of the court which has the right to try him . . . and presents no valid objection to his trial in such court."[40] By contrast, when a defendant is brought within the jurisdiction by extradition, he "can only be tried for . . . the offence with which he is charged in the proceedings for his extradition, until a reasonable time and opportunity have been given him, after his release or trial upon such charge, to return to the country from whose asylum he had been forcibly taken under those proceedings."[41]

The combination of the doctrines on forcible abduction and extradition would seem to make a game of extraterritorial apprehension. If you use the extradition treaty and want to try the defendant for something else, then you should let him go and follow him back to the host country, at which point you can then forcibly abduct him and try him for anything you like. The reason for this apparent anomaly has to do with relations with the other government, not with any sense of fairness to the individual. The host government might complain of prosecution for an offense for which it did not extradite, but may not complain of abduction unless the abduction itself violates the extradition treaty or constitutes a violation of sovereignty under international law.

Thus in *Alvarez-Machain*, the Court stated that the crucial question in an abduction is whether an existing extradition treaty between the two countries prohibited abductions. According to the Fifth Circuit in *Noriega*, the Supreme Court held that "precedent and practice" would allow forcible abductions unless the extant treaty "expressly" prohibited abductions, an

---

[37] Ker v. Illinois, 119 U.S. 436 (1886); Frisbie v. Collins, 342 U.S. 519 (1952). Both cases involved forcible abductions from another jurisdiction, Ker from Peru to Illinois and Frisbie from Illinois to Michigan. The Court distinguished another case decided the same day as *Ker*, United States v. Rauscher, 119 U.S. 407 (1886), in which the Court reversed a conviction for a crime other than that for which the defendant had been extradited to the U.S. In the *Rauscher* situation, the prosecution violated the extradition treaty, whereas in the other cases, the abductions did not depend in any way on the existence of a treaty.

[38] *Frisbie*, 342 U.S. at 522.

[39] 504 U.S. 655 (1992).

[40] *Ker*, 119 U.S. at 444.

[41] United States v. Rauscher, 119 U.S. 407, 430 (1886).

unlikely occurrence.[42] Although the Supreme Court did not use the term "expressly," its rejection of Alvarez' argument that the treaty "impliedly" banned abduction makes the Fifth Circuit's characterization reasonable.

With regard to Mexico's position, the Mexican government indeed had complained of Alvarez' abduction through diplomatic channels, but the Court stated that the decision whether to respond to this protest by sending Alvarez back was a decision for the Executive, as the nation's representative in foreign affairs.[43] With regard to Alvarez' argument that international law prohibited incursion by one nation into the territory of another nation, the Court conceded that the abduction "may be in violation of general international law principles," but because it did not violate the treaty with Mexico then there was nothing to "prohibit his trial in a court in the United States for violations of the criminal laws of the United States."[44]

A rare example of pure universal jurisdiction and forcible abduction is *United States v. Rezaq*.[45] Rezaq hijacked an Air Egypt flight out of Athens, ordered the pilot to fly to Malta, then "shot a number of passengers, killing two of them, before he was apprehended." He pleaded guilty to murder in Malta and served seven years, after which he was released and traveled to Nigeria. He was then apprehended by U.S. agents in Nigeria and brought to the U.S. for trial. There was no basis for jurisdiction in the U.S. other than "universal jurisdiction" arising from the Anti-Hijacking Treaty. He argued that the hijacking statute's application to one who is "found in the United States" must mean something other than brought before the court involuntarily because that would make the provision a nullity. The court said that requiring the defendant to be present before the court is not meaningless because "at a minimum, it confirms the rule, issuing from the Confrontation Clause of the Sixth Amendment and from the Due Process Clause, that a defendant ordinarily may not be tried in absentia."[46]

[B] Mistreatment of Prisoners on Foreign Soil

The second issue raised by Yunis was that his treatment in custody was so outrageous as to require dismissal of the prosecution. The Second Circuit noted that it had earlier held, in *United States v. Toscanino*,[47] that "due process requires courts to divest themselves of personal jurisdiction acquired through 'the government's deliberate, unnecessary and unreasonable invasion of the accused's constitutional rights.'" The *Yunis* court expressed some doubts about the vitality of *Toscanino* and pointed out that

---

[42] *Noriega*, 117 F.3d at 1213.

[43] *Alvarez-Machain*, 504 U.S. at 669.

[44] *Id.*

[45] 134 F.3d 1121 (D.C. Cir. 1998).

[46] *Id.* at 1132. FED. R. CRIM. P. 43 provides for removal of a persistently unruly defendant and for completion of a trial when the defendant voluntarily absents himself after trial has begun.

[47] 500 F.2d 267 (2d Cir. 1974).

it had been limited to instances of "torture, brutality, and similar outrageous conduct."[48] Yunis was found to have suffered only trickery and the discomfort of being interrogated while seasick.

The Fifth Circuit in *Noriega* also expressed doubts about the *Toscanino* "unconscionable conduct" exception to *Ker-Frisbie*. Assume that U.S. agents savagely beat a person in their custody while overseas, either attempting to get information about additional suspects or just because they are angry. What should a court do about this? Government agents acting on U.S. soil are subject to due process constraints of which *Miranda* interrogation limits are only a part. Are U.S. agents held to the same levels of propriety while acting abroad that they should be while on home soil? Should there be different standards for dealing with suspected terrorists?

Ramzi Ahmed Yousef presented an example of both extraterritorial jurisdiction and alleged mistreatment. Although Yousef was originally indicted as a participant and key player in the first World Trade Center bombing,[49] he was convicted both for participation in that conspiracy and for participation in a series of bombings of aircraft in the Phillipines. He was arrested in Pakistan and asserted that he was kept in confinement for a period of almost three months prior to being turned over to U.S. agents.

> Yousef maintains that a United States official was present during a period of his interrogation when he was taken to a desert jail cell in Pakistan some days after his alleged abduction, but before his arrest and surrender to United States officials in Islamabad on February 8, 1995. According to Yousef, the torture which he suffered while in the desert consisted of forced intake of drugs to keep him awake and the denial of rest except at meal times. Yousef does not claim that he was tortured or otherwise mistreated during his period of custody in Islamabad, from February 7 to February 8, 1995, or after his transfer to United States agents.[50]

The trial court simply did not believe Yousef's allegations. Other evidence rebutted his primary assertion that he was held in long captivity, and he did not have any credible evidence of U.S. agents' involvement even if he were tortured by Pakistani officials.

Several factors, including media attention and U.S. disclosures in the military custody cases before the Supreme Court, have brought interrogation practices of alleged terrorists to public attention. U.S. officials have told the courts in the military custody cases[51] that they wanted to hold

---

[48] United States *ex rel.* Lujan v. Gengler, 510 F.2d 62, 65 (2d Cir. 1975).

[49] United States of America v. Salameh, 152 F.3d 88 (2d Cir. 1998). Yousef successfully fled the country after the World Trade Center bombing but then was captured in Pakistan and delivered to U.S. agents.

[50] United States v. Yousef, 927 F. Supp. 673, 677 (S.D.N.Y. 1996), *aff'd*, 327 F.3d 56 (2d Cir. 2003).

[51] Padilla v. Rumsfeld, 352 F.3d 695, 2003 (2d Cir. 2003), *cert. granted*, 540 U.S. 1173 (2004), *rev'd*, 542 U.S. 426 (2004); Hamdi v. Rumsfeld, 316 F.3d 450 (4th Cir. 2003), *cert. granted*, 540 U.S. 507, *vacated*, 542 U.S. 507 (2004); Al Odah v. United States, 321 F.3d 1134 (D.C. Cir. 2003), *cert. granted*, Rasul v. Bush, 540 U.S. 1003 (2003), *rev'd*, Rasul v. Bush, 542 U.S. 466 (2004). *See also* Gherebi v. Bush, 352 F.3d 1278 (9th Cir. 2003).

these prisoners in isolation without access to counsel to exert psychological pressure and create a feeling of dependency on the interrogators, thus increasing the likelihood of getting them to talk. Some rumors of more aggressive treatment, such as sleep deprivation and being forced to remain in painful positions, have appeared in the press with respect to the Guantánamo detainees.[52]

Modern coercive interrogation techniques were brought to world judicial attention when Ireland accused Great Britain of engaging in "torture" of a number of suspected IRA sympathizers, documenting a number of practices such as sleep deprivation and being forced to maintain painful postures for extended periods. The European Court of Human Rights determined that these practices did not amount to "torture" although they could be considered "inhuman or degrading" treatment.[53] The difference is that torture is a crime while the lesser category would be merely a violation of human rights conventions.

A thorough journalistic review of interrogation techniques by both Israeli and U.S. agents discussed many of the more questionable practices of interrogators.[54] Techniques include sleep deprivation, emotional pain by threats to loved ones, tainted food, severe cold or damp without clothing, and being forced to remain in extremely painful positions for hours at a time.

The Israeli Government has responded to United Nations inquiries regarding harsh interrogation practices, and the Israeli Supreme Court has stated that some such measures are illegal. The U.S. Government has engaged in several internal disputes over interrogation practices and has been exposed to severe public criticism for the experiences of Guantánamo and Abu Ghraib. All of this is explored further in Chapter 10. For the moment, we will deal with the less widely known practice of incarceration and interrogation in secrecy.

[C]   Extraordinary Renditions and Interrogation

The practice of "extraordinary rendition" has been widely publicized and criticized. In ordinary rendition, Country A can arrest someone within its borders and hand that person over to Country B without going through the formalities of extradition. Under the extraordinary version, Country C (such as the U.S.) might capture a suspect in Country A, spirit that person out of the territory and hand him over to Country B for whatever treatment lies in store. There have been widespread allegations that the U.S. has engaged in extraordinary rendition with countries that are known to mistreat, allegedly even torture, persons in their custody.[55] The Convention

---

[52] ABC.net, *Claims of Torture in Guantánamo Bay, available at* www.abc.net.au/am/content/2003/s962052.htm (last visited June 21, 2007).

[53] Republic of Ireland v. United Kingdom, 2 Eur. Ct. H.R. (Ser. A) at 25 (1980).

[54] Mark Bowden, *The Dark Art of Interrogation*, Atlantic Monthly, Oct. 2003, *available at* http://www.theatlantic.com/200310/bowden.

[55] *See, e.g.*, Jane Mayer, *Outsourcing Torture*, New Yorker, Feb. 14, 2005, *available at*

Against Torture specifically prohibits transfer of a prisoner to a country "where there are substantial grounds for believing that he would be in danger of being subjected to torture."[56]

Maher Arar is a Syrian-born Canadian citizen who traveled to Tunisia on vacation. His return flight to Canada took him through Kennedy Airport where he was detained by U.S. authorities on the basis of a tip from Canadian authorities. He was allegedly transported to Syria, where he was imprisoned and beaten for over a year before finally being released and returned to Canada. Canada has apologized and provided a settlement of $10.5 million for its part in the situation.[57]

Arar sued various U.S. officials but all his claims were dismissed for various reasons.[58] The claims based on his being tortured were dismissed because the federal statutes on torture apply only to those who are acting under color of law of a foreign nation,[59] his common-law claims of unconstitutional treatment were dismissed in deference to government appeals to foreign policy and national security interests,[60] and his due process claims

---

www.newyorker.com/archive/2005/02/14/050214fa_fact6; Human Rights Watch, *Black Hole: The Fate of Islamists Rendered to Egypt, available at* www.hrw.org/reports/2005/egypt0505/ (Human Rights Watch has an extensive list of press releases and publications on various aspects of the practice).

[56] Convention Against Torture and Other Cruel, Inhuman or Degrading Treatment or Punishment art. 3. Article 3 is implemented in the U.S. by the Foreign Affairs Reform and Restructuring Act of 1988 ("FARRA"), Pub. L. No. 105-277 (codified as Note to 8 U.S.C. § 1231), which provides that "it shall be the policy of the United States not to expel, extradite, or otherwise effect the involuntary return of any person to a country in which there are substantial grounds for believing the person would be in danger of being subjected to torture."

[57] Prime Minister Stephen Harper, *Prime Minister releases letter of apology to Maher Arar*, Jan. 26, 2007, *available at* www.pm.gc.ca/eng/media.asp?id = 1510 (last visited July 28, 2007).

[58] Arar v. Ashcroft, 414 F. Supp. 2d 250 (E.D.N.Y. 2005).

[59] *Id*. at 266. Arar relied on the Torture Victim Protection Act (TVPA), Pub. L. No. 102-256 (codified as Note to 28 U.S.C. § 1350), as to which the court stated:

> The decision by Congress not to provide a private cause of action under FARRA for individuals improperly removed to countries practicing torture militates against creating one in this case under the Torture Victim Protection Act. Moreover, the color of "foreign law" requirement, combined with the intent by Congress to use the Torture Victim Protection Act as a remedy for U.S. citizens subjected to torts committed overseas, strongly supports defendants' claim that the Torture Victim Protection Act does not apply here. In conclusion, plaintiff does not meet the statutory requirements of the Torture Victim Protection Act, and, accordingly, Count 1 of the complaint is dismissed.

[60] *Arar*, 414 F. Supp. 2d at 281:

> [T]his case raises crucial national-security and foreign policy considerations, implicating "the complicated multilateral negotiations concerning efforts to halt international terrorism." The propriety of these considerations, including supposed agreements between the United States and foreign governments regarding intelligence-gathering in the context of the efforts to combat terrorism, are most appropriately reserved to the Executive and Legislative branches of government. Moreover, the need for much secrecy can hardly be doubted. One need not have much imagination to contemplate the negative effect on our relations with Canada if discovery were to proceed in this case and were it to turn out that certain high

based on detention in the U.S. were dismissed for lack of specificity. With regard to the latter claims, the court stated that "plaintiff must replead those claims without regard to any rendition claim and name those defendants that were personally involved in the alleged unconstitutional treatment."[61] Oddly, a later motion to certify the torture-based claims for immediate appeal was denied by the district court on the basis that those claims might be related to the due process claim as to which the plaintiff still had the option to replead.[62]

In *El-Masri v. United States*,[63] Khalid el-Masri sued the Director of Central Intelligence, three corporations, and 20 unnamed employees of those entities. He asserted that he was a German citizen traveling in Macedonia when he was picked up by Macedonian authorities, handed over to the CIA, flown to a detention center near Kabul, interrogated and mistreated for about five months, and finally released in a remote area of Albania.[64] The United States intervened and submitted both a classified and an unclassified declaration from the Director of Central Intelligence setting out the reasons why the action should be dismissed because of the impossibility of litigating without classified information. Both the district court and the court of appeals agreed that the action should be dismissed:

> If El-Masri's civil action were to proceed, the facts central to its resolution would be the roles, if any, that the defendants played in the events he alleges. To establish a prima facie case, he would be obliged to produce admissible evidence not only that he was detained and interrogated, but that the defendants were involved in his detention and interrogation in a manner that renders them personally liable to him. Such a showing could be made only with evidence that exposes how the CIA organizes, staffs, and supervises its most sensitive intelligence operations. With regard to Director Tenet, for example, El-Masri would be obliged to show in detail how the head of the CIA participates in such operations, and how information concerning their progress is relayed to him.[65]

Canadian officials had, despite public denials, acquiesced in Arar's removal to Syria. More generally, governments that do not wish to acknowledge publicly that they are assisting us would certainly hesitate to do so if our judicial discovery process could compromise them. Hence, extending a *Bivens* remedy "could significantly disrupt the ability of the political branches to respond to foreign situations involving our national interest."

[61] *Id.* at 287.

[62] Arar v. Ashcroft, 2006 U.S. Dist. LEXIS 45550 (E.D.N.Y. 2006).

[63] 479 F.3d 296 (4th Cir. 2006), *aff'g* El-Masri v. Tenet, 437 F. Supp. 2d 530 (E.D. Va. 2006).

[64] The initial detention apparently was based on the similarity of his name with that of Khalid al-Masri, a shadowy figure who may have been a recruiter for the Hamburg cell involved in the 9/11 plot. A third similar name is Abu Hamza al-Masri, who has since been convicted in Britain of incitement to murder and racial hatred. *Cleric Convicted of Stirring Hate*, N.Y. Times, Feb. 8, 2006, *available at* select.nytimes.com/search/restricted/article?res=F60612FD3F5A0C7B8CDDAB0894DE404482.

[65] *El-Masri*, 479 F.3d at 309.

The court of appeals was particularly concerned about the difficulties involved in the defendants' ability to present their side of the story.[66]

An Egyptian Muslim cleric, Hassan Mustafa Osama Nasr, claims to have been abducted by CIA agents and taken to Egypt where he was imprisoned and tortured before being released three years later. Italian authorities have indicted a number of American agents, none of whom is still in Italy,[67] and the case may involve complicity of some Italian officials.[68]

In addition to rendering prisoners to other countries, the U.S. has operated some secret prisons in undisclosed locations. President Bush acknowledged the existence of the program on September 6, 2006. The Parliament of the European Union appointed a "Temporary Committee on the Alleged Use of European Countries by the CIA for the Transportation

---

[66] *Id.* at 309-10:

Furthermore, if El-Masri were somehow able to make out a prima facie case despite the unavailability of state secrets, the defendants could not properly defend themselves without using privileged evidence. The main avenues of defense available in this matter are to show that El-Masri was not subject to the treatment that he alleges; that, if he was subject to such treatment, the defendants were not involved in it; or that, if they were involved, the nature of their involvement does not give rise to liability. Any of those three showings would require disclosure of information regarding the means and methods by which the CIA gathers intelligence. If, for example, the truth is that El-Masri was detained by the CIA but his description of his treatment is inaccurate, that fact could be established only by disclosure of the actual circumstances of his detention, and its proof would require testimony by the personnel involved. Or, if El-Masri was in fact detained as he describes, but the operation was conducted by some governmental entity other than the CIA, or another government entirely, that information would be privileged. Alternatively, if the CIA detained El-Masri, but did so without Director Tenet's active involvement, effective proof thereof would require a detailed explanation of how CIA operations are supervised. Similarly, although an individual CIA officer might demonstrate his lack of involvement in a given operation by disclosing that he was actually performing some other function at the time in question, establishing his alibi would likely require him to reveal privileged information.

Moreover, proof of the involvement — or lack thereof — of particular CIA officers in a given operation would provide significant information on how the CIA makes its personnel assignments. Similar concerns would attach to evidence produced in defense of the corporate defendants and their unnamed employees. And, like El-Masri's prima facie case, any of the possible defenses suggested above would require the production of witnesses whose identities are confidential and evidence the very existence of which is a state secret. We do not, of course, mean to suggest that any of these hypothetical defenses represents the true state of affairs in this matter, but they illustrate that virtually any conceivable response to El-Masri's allegations would disclose privileged information.

[67] Ian Fisher, *Italy Indicts 26 Americans in C.I.A. Abduction Case*, N.Y. TIMES, Feb. 16, 2007.

[68] National Public Radio reported on July 6, 2006 that two Italian intelligence officials were arrested for complicity in the abduction. www.npr.org/templates/story/story.php?storyId=5537551. The Italian courts are weighing difficulties of evidentiary problems in light of claims of state secrecy. Anthony DiPaola & Chiara Remondini, *Italian Judge Slows CIA Abduction Trial to Await Court Ruling*, BLOOMBERG, June 18, 2007, *available at* www.bloomberg.com/apps/news?pid=20601085&sid=ahXq5lHtj8oc&refer=europe.

and Illegal Detention of Prisoners" which reported in February 2007.[69] In response to the report, the EU Parliament adopted a resolution stating that it:

> 2. Considers that after 11 September 2001, the so-called "war on terror" — in its excesses — has produced a serious and dangerous erosion of human rights and fundamental freedoms.

> 39. Condemns extraordinary rendition as an illegal instrument used by the United States in the fight against terrorism; condemns, further, the condoning and concealing of the practice, on several occasions, by the secret services and governmental authorities of certain European countries.[70]

On July 20, 2007, President Bush reasserted the position that the Geneva Conventions do not apply to suspected terrorists and authorized the CIA to continue detaining and interrogating suspects in undisclosed locations.[71] The order purports to limit interrogation methods to those that are not cruel, inhumane, or degrading.

§ 3.04   PRIVATE ACTIONS AGAINST TERRORIST ACTIVITY

There are four principal statutes under which injured persons can bring civil actions against state sponsors of terrorism or against private individuals. The Torture Victims Protection Act (TVPA) is codified as a note to the Alien Tort Claims Act (ATCA).[72] The civil version of the criminal "material support" statutes is generally known as the Anti Terrorism Act (ATA).[73] The Foreign Sovereign Immunity Act (FSIA) withholds sovereign immunity for acts committed by designated terrorist states and for torts committed within the U.S.[74]

Although it is tempting to downplay the role of civil lawsuits in light of the extensive action of the past decade in criminal law enforcement, bear in mind that some of the most severe blows struck at the Ku Klux Klan was a series of lawsuits by which the Klan and its supporters lost most of their assets and thus much of their ability to function. The website of

---

[69] www.europarl.europa.eu/comparl/tempcom/tdip/final_report_en.pdf.

[70] European Parliament Resolution on the Alleged Use of European Countries by the Cia for the Transportation and Illegal Detention of Prisoners (2006/2200(INI)), *available at* www.europarl.europa.eu/comparl/tempcom/tdip/final_ep_resolution_en.pdf (last visited July 28, 2007).

[71] Executive Order: Interpretation of the Geneva Conventions Common Article 3 as Applied to a Program of Detention and Interrogation Operated by the Central Intelligence Agency (July 20, 2007), *available at* www.whitehouse.gov/news/releases/2007/07/20070720-4.html (last visited July 28, 2007).

[72] 28 U.S.C. § 1350 (2007).

[73] 18 U.S.C. § 2333 (2007).

[74] 28 U.S.C. § 1605 (2007).

the Southern Poverty Law Center describes the evolution of its "Klanwatch" program into its current "Intelligence Project."[75]

[A] Alien Tort Claims and International Law

Prior to the 1990s, there was a serious question about the ability of an alien to sue another alien in U.S. courts for violations of humanitarian law. In *Filartiga v. Pena-Irala*,[76] the plaintiff citizens of Paraguay sued a Paraguayan official for torturing and killing their son and brother. The ATCA provided jurisdiction over suits "by an alien for a tort only, committed in violation of the law of nations or a treaty of the United States." Because Article III does not provide for diversity jurisdiction between two aliens, the statute would not be valid unless it applies to a suit that "arises under" federal law. Treaty law would be such law but treaties very seldom create private rights of action. Therefore, the question was whether the "law of nations" was federal law that would support subject matter jurisdiction. The Second Circuit in *Filartiga* held that "an act of torture committed by a state official against one held in detention violates established norms of the international law of human rights, and hence the law of nations."[77]

Tel-Oren v. Libyan Arab Republic[78] produced a badly splintered court in what Judge Edwards called "an area of the law that cries out for clarification by the Supreme Court." The *Tel-Oren* case was brought by survivors and representatives of victims of an attack on a bus in Israel in 1978. Two of the many defendants were Libya and the PLO, who were alleged to have acted in complicity in carrying out the attack. The three judges on the panel could agree on only a terse *per curiam* statement affirming the dismissal of the action by the district court. Each wrote a separate concurring opinion.

Judge Edwards argued that international law could supply the rule of decision for a claim of torture but not for murder.[79] Libya was not alleged to have tortured anyone and would have enjoyed sovereign immunity at the time. The PLO was "not a recognized member of the community of nations" and thus was not subject to the rules and conventions on torture.[80]

---

[75] *See* www.splcenter.org/intel.

[76] 630 F.2d 876 (2d Cir. 1980).

[77] *Id.* at 880.

[78] 726 F.2d 774 (D.C. Cir. 1984).

[79] *Id.* at 781:

> Judge Kaufman characterized the torturer in *Filartiga* as follows: "Indeed, for purposes of civil liability, the torturer has become — like the pirate and slave trader before him — *hostis humani generis*, an enemy of all mankind." *Filartiga*, 630 F.2d at 890. The reference to piracy and slave-trading is not fortuitous. Historically these offenses held a special place in the law of nations: their perpetrators, dubbed enemies of all mankind, were susceptible to prosecution by any nation capturing them.

[80] *Id.* at 796:

> While I have little doubt that the trend in international law is toward a more expansive allocation of rights and obligations to entities other than states, I decline to read section 1350 to cover torture by non-state actors, absent guidance from the Supreme Court on the statute's usage of the term "law of nations."

Nor did Judge Edwards think that international law at the time uniformly condemned acts of terrorism.[81]

Judge Bork insisted that international law did not recognize a private right of action for either torture or murder. Thus, unless Congress created a right of action, none would exist as a matter of federal law. Judge Edwards' response to this argument was that international law states the norms but leaves to each nation the methods of protection, whether through civil suit or otherwise.

Judge Robb would have declared the whole dispute to be a political question lacking in judicially manageable standards.

The Supreme Court did not accept Judge Edwards' plea for clarification, but Congress did. The Torture Victims Protection Act (TVPA)[82] in 1991 explicitly created a civil action for official torture or "extrajudicial killing" but only when the action is taken "under color of law of a foreign nation." The civil remedy usually known as the Anti-Terrorism Act,[83] was added in 1992. In 1996, Congress adopted amendments to the Foreign Sovereign Immunity Act (FSIA) which takes away sovereign immunity from designated foreign state sponsors of terrorism for acts of torture, extrajudicial killing, aircraft sabotage, hostage taking, or material support of terrorist acts.[84] These are the principal statutes that form the basis for the civil suits in the following cases.

[B]   State Sponsors of Terrorism

Price v. Socialist People's Libyan Arab Jamahiriya[85] was an action by two American citizens against the Socialist People's Libyan Arab Jamahiriya ("Libya") for torture and hostage taking. The plaintiffs were employed by a Libyan company but were arrested for taking photos and were imprisoned in Libya and mistreated for three months before being released. The D.C. Circuit held that they were not hostages because Libya sought nothing in return for their release, that they might be able to state a claim for torture if they amended their complaint, and that Libya is not a person within the meaning of the due process clause so that there is no personal jurisdiction problem with suing the state in a U.S. court.[86]

---

[81] *Id.*:

I cannot conclude that the law of nations — which, we must recall, is defined as the principles and rules that states feel themselves bound to observe, and do commonly observe — outlaws politically motivated terrorism, no matter how repugnant it might be to our own legal system.

[82] Codified as a note to 18 U.S.C. § 1350 (2007).

[83] 18 U.S.C. § 2333 (2007).

[84] 28 U.S.C. § 1605(a)(7) (2007).

[85] 352 U.S. App. D.C. 284, 294 F.3d 82 (D.C. Cir. 2002).

[86] The court also noted several cases that were precursors to the FSIA amendments, pointing out the need for some remedy against state violations of rights under international law. Smith v. Socialist People's Libyan Arab Jamahiriya, 101 F.3d 239 (2d Cir. 1996) (holding that Libya retained its sovereign immunity for the bombing of Pam Am 103 over Lockerbie, Scotland);

The court noted that there was a

> question, however, whether the FSIA creates a federal cause of action for torture and hostage taking *against foreign states*.[87] The "Flatow Amendment" to the FSIA confers a right of action for torture and hostage taking against an "official, employee, or agent of a foreign state,"[88] but the amendment does not list "foreign states" among the parties against whom such an action may be brought. While it is possible that such an action could be brought under the "international terrorism" statute,[89] no such claim has been raised in this case. [citations by the court converted to footnotes]

The "Flatow Amendment" problem arises because of the distinction between subject matter jurisdiction and a cause of action, a rather esoteric problem of federal procedure created by the limited subject matter jurisdiction of federal courts. Although § 1605(a)(7) provides subject matter jurisdiction, the question is whether there is a source of law for a claim.

The D.C. Circuit in *Price* left open the question, and on remand the district court interpreted the Flatow Amendment to provide a cause of action against foreign states for any act that would provide a court with jurisdiction under the statute.[90] The same question also was answered in the affirmative by the district court in *Pugh v. Socialist People's Libyan Arab Jamahiriya*.[91] That incident involved bombing of a UTA airliner bound from the Congo to Paris in which seven U.S. citizens were killed.

This question should not deter the courts from proceeding because it would be silly for Congress to provide jurisdiction for a claim without a source of law; it certainly should be easy to infer the private right of action when the jurisdiction is so clearly spelled out.

Rein v. Socialist People's Libyan Arab Jamahiriya[92] was the second try for representatives of the victims of the Pan Am Lockerbie bombing, which killed 259 persons, many of them U.S. citizens. The first suit brought in 1994 was dismissed for lack of subject matter jurisdiction and the Second Circuit affirmed. After the FSIA was amended in 1996, the plaintiffs tried

---

Princz v. Fed. Republic of Germany, 307 U.S. App. D.C. 102, 26 F.3d 1166 (D.C. Cir. 1994) (holding that plaintiff could not recover for slave labor performed at Nazi concentration camps, because Germany's conduct was not commercial activity causing a "direct effect in the United States" and did not constitute an implied waiver of sovereign immunity); Siderman de Blake v. Republic of Argentina, 965 F.2d 699 (9th Cir. 1992) (holding that Argentina was immune from liability for acts of torture committed by the ruling junta); Tel-Oren v. Libyan Arab Republic, 233 U.S. App. D.C. 384, 726 F.2d 774, 775 n.1 (D.C. Cir. 1984) (Edwards J., concurring) (FSIA precludes jurisdiction over Libya for armed attack on civilian bus in Israel).

[87] *See* Roeder v. Islamic Republic of Iran, 195 F. Supp. 2d 140, 171-73 (D.D.C. 2002).

[88] *See* Flatow v. Islamic Republic of Iran, 999 F. Supp. 1, 12-13 (D.D.C. 1998).

[89] 18 U.S.C. § 2333(a).

[90] Price v. Socialist People's Libyan Arab Jamahiriya, 274 F. Supp. 2d 20 (D.D.C. 2003).

[91] 290 F. Supp. 2d 54 (D.D.C. 2003).

[92] 162 F.3d 748 (2d Cir. 1998).

again and Libya argued that the provision was unconstitutional as a bill of attainder and as an ex post facto law. The Second Circuit responded that those provisions apply only to criminal sanctions and do not invalidate a retroactive civil action. The court also dealt with an argument by Libya that Congress unconstitutionally delegated power to the Executive through the assignment of liability premised on designation of foreign states as sponsors of terrorism. Because the designation fell within an area of traditional executive discretion in foreign affairs, the delegation was not invalid even though it affected the subject matter jurisdiction of the federal judiciary.

Before turning to actions against "private" entities, it is worth emphasizing that the TVPA and FSIA provide claims only against persons acting "under color of law" or states that are designated as sponsors of terrorism.

[C] Claims Against Nonstate Actors

Boim v. Quranic Literacy Institute [93] was an action by the parents of a "young United States citizen murdered in Israel by Hamas terrorists" [94] against several individuals and organizations alleged to have supported Hamas violence.

Applying basic principles of tort law to the first question, the Seventh Circuit held that the statutes did not create a form of "strict liability."

> In the very least, the plaintiffs must be able to show that murder was a reasonably foreseeable result of making a donation. Thus, the Boims' first theory of liability under section 2333, funding *simpliciter* of a terrorist organization, is insufficient because it sets too vague a standard, and because it does not require a showing of proximate cause. [95]

The court did, however, hold that provision of material support within the meaning of sections 2339A or 2339B would support civil liability "so long as knowledge and intent are also shown." Ultimately, the civil liability

---

[93] 291 F.3d 1000 (7th Cir. 2002).

[94] *Id.* at 1002:

> David Boim was the son of Joyce and Stanley Boim, who are United States citizens. David held dual citizenship in the United States and Israel. In 1996, the Boims were living in Israel, where seventeen-year-old David was studying at a yeshiva. On May 13, 1996, David was murdered as he waited with other students at a bus stop near Beit El in the West Bank. He was struck by bullets fired from a passing car, and was pronounced dead within an hour of the shooting. His two attackers were later identified as Amjad Hinawi and Khalil Tawfiq Al-Sharif. The Palestinian Authority apprehended Hinawi and Al-Sharif, and temporarily imprisoned them in early 1997. They were released shortly thereafter, apparently pending trial. Al-Sharif subsequently killed himself and five civilians and injured 192 other people in a suicide bombing in Jerusalem on September 4, 1997. Two other suicide bombers joined him in this action. Hinawi, who confessed to participating in the shooting of David Boim, was eventually tried for David's murder by a Palestinian Authority court and was sentenced to ten years' imprisonment on February 17, 1998.

[95] *Id.* at 1012.

is premised on showing that the defendants "aided and abetted terrorist acts," so the plaintiffs must "prove that the defendants knew of Hamas' illegal activities, that they desired to help those activities succeed, and they engaged in some act of helping the illegal activities."[96]

A troubling issue for many plaintiffs will be that of personal jurisdiction in a U.S. court over the foreign defendants. In *Pugh v. Socialist People's Libyan Arab Jamahiriya*,[97] Libya was a defendant along with seven individual defendants in wrongful death actions arising from the bombing of a UTA flight over Africa in which seven U.S. citizens were killed. The State was subject to personal jurisdiction under the reasoning of *Price*, but the individual defendants claimed they had no contacts with the U.S. The district court responded:

> Taking the factual allegations of the complaint as true for present purposes, the individual defendants in the instant action conspired to sabotage and succeeded in destroying a civilian commercial aircraft filled to capacity with innocent and unsuspecting passengers while in flight. As the plane they chose to destroy was on an international flight and expected to stop in several nations before reaching its final destination, the individual defendants could and should have reasonably postulated that passengers of many nationalities would be on board, from which they could also expect they might be haled into the courts of those nations whose citizens would die. Given the number of passengers on UTA Flight 772, and the international nature of the flight, it was also altogether foreseeable that some Americans would be aboard the plane, whose lives would be lost, and that the individual defendants would have to answer in some fashion in American courts for the consequences of their actions if their identities were ever discovered. . . . And because they should have anticipated as much, this Court concludes that it may constitutionally exercise personal jurisdiction over the individual defendants in their personal capacities without offending any "traditional notions of fair play and substantial justice."[98]

Probably the most massive litigation in the terrorism arena is *In re Terrorist Attacks on September 11, 2001*,[99] consolidating numerous cases brought by injured survivors, representatives and insurers of those killed on 9/11. There are over 200 defendants, including several princes of the royal family of Saud, banks and investment companies alleged to have ties with Osama bin Laden, and charities that may have funneled money to terrorist organizations. The court thus far has dealt with a number of motions to dismiss and has reached the following conclusions:

1. the Princes of the royal family are immune when acting in their governmental capacity but may be liable for private donations

---

[96] *Id.* at 1023.

[97] 290 F. Supp. 2d 54 (D.D.C. 2003).

[98] *Id.* at 59-60.

[99] 392 F. Supp. 2d 539 (S.D.N.Y. 2006); 349 F. Supp. 2d 765 (S.D.N.Y. 2005).

from their own funds but only if they had knowledge of the wrongful intent or activities of the organization to which they were donating,

2. banks that are carrying out functions of the Saudi Arabia government are also immune (there is no torture allegation, so the analysis of Judge Edwards in *Tel-Oren* regarding state entities is applicable),

3. banks providing "routine banking services" with no knowledge of the illegal activities of their customers are not liable under a material support theory,

4. to obtain personal jurisdiction, plaintiffs will have to show that an individual defendant "purposefully directed his activities at this forum by donating to charities that he knew at the time supported international terrorism,"

5. for substantive theories of liability, the federal statutes are deemed to incorporate basic principles of tort law including the idea of conspiracy or aiding and abetting. "To be liable under either conspiracy or aiding and abetting, however, the defendant must know the wrongful nature of the primary actor s conduct, and the conduct must be tied to a substantive cause of action."[100]

A number of cases are pursuing the theory that banks may be liable for failing to curtail the flow of money to terrorist organizations. For example, in *Weiss v. Nat'l Westminster Bank*,[101] various plaintiffs are suing a London bank through which subsidiaries of Hamas allegedly funnel their funds. The bank relied on the holding in *In re Terrorist Attacks* that provision of "routine banking services" does not violate the federal statutes. The court has denied motions to dismiss, explaining:

> In holding that there could be no liability on the basis of "routine banking business" that court did not mean that the provision of basic banking services could never give rise to bank liability. Rather the court relied on the routine nature of the banking services to conclude that the defendant bank had no knowledge of the client's terrorist activities.[102]

The plaintiffs will also be required to show that the provision of services was a proximate cause of their losses. This is different from the criminal provisions, as will be seen in Chapter 5, because Congress can declare an act to be criminal so long as it has a sufficient propensity to cause harm.

---

[100] 349 F. Supp. 2d at 826.

[101] 453 F. Supp. 2d 609 (S.D.N.Y. 2006).

[102] *Id.* at 625.

In the civil liability context, however, compensatory damages are tied to the causing of the harm.[103] The concept of proximate cause in this context, of course, is no more free of difficulty than in other contexts:

> Defendant argues that plaintiffs cannot prevail merely by showing that defendant provided material assistance or funding to the terrorist organization responsible for perpetrating the attacks which injured the plaintiffs. Rather, defendants argue, plaintiffs must allege, for example, that the funds supplied by the defendant were used to buy the specific weapons and train the specific men who killed or injured the plaintiffs. However, taking into account the legislative history of these statutes and the purpose behind them, proximate cause is not so limited. Congress intended these provisions to impose "liability at any point along the causal chain of terrorism."[104]

> While the lapse of time may factor into the proximate cause inquiry, given the fungible nature of money and the fact that it is difficult to say when the particular dollar given to a terrorist is actually used, I cannot conclude as a matter of law that NatWest's transaction in 2000 could not be the proximate cause of an attack that occurred less than two years later in 2002. While defendant is correct that a transaction which occurred after a terrorist attack cannot be the proximate cause of that attack, because each attack was preceded by at least one relevant transaction by NatWest, plaintiffs have sufficiently alleged that each attack was proximately caused by NatWest.[105]

The liability of banks is also affected by a criminal statute dealing specifically with financing of terrorism, applying to one who "unlawfully and willfully provides or collects funds with the intention that such funds be used, or with the knowledge that such funds are to be used, in full or in part, in order to carry out" a terrorist act.[106] This section, however, clearly depends upon knowledge and intent to support terrorist activity.[107]

---

[103] Section 2333 applies to injuries occurring "by reason of" acts of terrorism.

[104] *Weiss*, 453 F. Supp. 2d at 631.

[105] *Id.* at 632.

[106] 18 U.S.C. § 2339C (2007).

[107] Linde v. Arab Bank, PLC, 384 F. Supp. 2d 571, 588 (E.D.N.Y. 2005):

> [P]laintiffs allege both that the Bank plays a central role in a well-publicized plan to reward terrorists killed and injured in Palestinian suicide attacks in Israel and that the Bank knows that the groups to which it provides services are engaged in terrorist activities. The very groups that the Bank is alleged to support are the same groups alleged to be responsible for the terrorist attacks that injured the plaintiffs. Nothing in the complaints suggests that Arab Bank is a mere unknowing conduit for the unlawful acts of others, about whose aims the Bank is ignorant.

Chapter 4

CONSPIRACIES AND INCITEMENT

A distinguishing feature of Anglo-American criminal law is the concept of "conspiracy." Conspiracy principles allow prosecution of an agreement to commit an offense before the harm occurs, as well as punishment of inactive co-conspirators. European law may punish one person for "incitement" of another to commit an offense, but until recently the concept of incitement was premised on a completed offense.[1] Other systems, most notably those of Asian and Islamic origin, punish only active participants in completed offenses.

Conspiracy cases consistently refer to the principle of vicarious liability known as the Pinkerton Doctrine. *Pinkerton v. United States*[2] established

---

[1] The European Court of Human Rights dealt with a prosecution for "incitement to hatred and hostility" a bit differently from how British or U.S. courts probably would have handled it, although with a similar result. *See* Ceylon v. Turkey, 30 E.H.R.R. 73 (2000). The majority looked primarily at the nature of the statements themselves, while the concurring judge looked at context to apply the Holmes "clear and present danger" test. These issues are discussed further at § 4.03 *infra*.

[2] 328 U.S. 640 (1946).

several propositions regarding the law of conspiracy. One of the most important is the proposition that a person may be convicted of conspiracy without knowing the details of what others are planning to do. Agreement to commit a *category* of offense may produce liability for all members of the conspiracy when any one of the members commits an overt act of the type contemplated. "An overt act of one partner may be the act of all without any new agreement specifically directed to that act."[3]

Pinkerton also confirms that conspiracy is an offense separate and apart from the "substantive" crimes contemplated. Thus, there is no double jeopardy involved in prosecution for the agreement as well as for the criminal act. And, thirdly, conspiracy is an inchoate offense that is punishable even if no physical harm ever occurs to a victim. "For two or more to confederate and combine together to commit or cause to be committed a breach of the criminal laws, is an offense of the gravest character, sometimes quite outweighing, in injury to the public, the mere commission of the contemplated crime. It involves deliberate plotting to subvert the laws, educating and preparing the conspirators for further and habitual criminal practices. And it is characterized by secrecy, rendering it difficult of detection, requiring more time for its discovery, and adding to the importance of punishing it when discovered."[4]

§ 4.01   THE TERRORIST CONSPIRACY

[A]   World Trade Center I and Embassy Bombings

Al Qaeda took center stage in U.S. terrorism concerns almost a decade before 9/11. The first bombing of the World Trade Center occurred in February 1993 and bombings of the U.S. embassies in Kenya and Tanzania occurred on August 7, 1998.[5]

World Trade Center I resulted in two separate prosecutions which illustrate some of the issues of conspiracy prosecutions.[6] The four defendants in the *Salameh* case were tried for various levels of involvement in a conspiracy to bomb structures used in interstate commerce and related charges.[7] Sheikh Abdel Rahman and a number of others were then prosecuted for somewhat more peripheral connections to this incident and for a more broad-reaching charge of "seditious conspiracy" consisting of "making war against the United States."[8]

---

[3] *Id.* at 646-47 (quoting United States v. Kissel, 218 U.S. 601, 608 (1910)).

[4] *Id.* at 644.

[5] Al Qaeda was also credited with attacks on U.S. troops in Somalia in 1993 and for the bombing of the USS Cole in 1997.

[6] Yousef, the alleged mastermind of the WTC incident, was brought back after capture in Pakistan for trial in the United States on charges of aircraft piracy. United States v. Yousef, 927 F. Supp. 673 (S.D.N.Y. 1996).

[7] United States v. Salameh, 152 F.3d 88 (2d Cir. 1998).

[8] United States v. Rahman, 189 F.3d 88, 103 (2d Cir. 1999).

United States v. Salameh [9] involved four of the six "active" participants in World Trade Center I. The trial took nine months, during which a complex set of facts was laid out before the jury. The appellate court's two-page summary alone shows how complicated the investigation of an incident of this type must be. The plot also shows how even careless and occasionally inept terrorists can easily circumvent the security arrangements of an open society.

The alleged mastermind, Yousef, trained at an Afghan terrorist camp with one Ajaj. When the two flew back into the U.S. with a plan to bomb the WTC and other structures, Ajaj used a forged passport and carried a "terrorist kit" consisting of bomb manuals and the like. Ajaj was imprisoned but still managed to communicate with Yousef while the latter recruited and worked with the four other conspirators. One person, an engineer with a chemical company, acquired materials and equipment. Another rented an apartment where the explosives were assembled. Salameh rented a van and storage facility. And the fourth acquired smokeless powder and helped assemble the explosive charge.

After the bomb exploded, Yousef and two of the others fled the country. Salameh had planned to flee but was arrested when he went back to the rental agency to attempt to obtain a refund of the rental deposit on the van that was blown up in the explosion. Without this critical error, "ludicrous" in the words of the appellate court, the investigation would have been more difficult but rifts were already occurring in the structure of the plotters, as the *Rahman* case below shows.

This was the straightforward part of the case. All the prosecution had to show was participation by each of the four defendants in the assembling of the explosive device. Given that there could have been no lawful purpose for such a device, any defendant who participated would have had a difficult time of convincing the jury that he was not guilty of at least conspiring to commit some illegal act. With respect to at least one of the conspirators, the appellate court pointed out that it was not necessary to show that he knew what building was to be bombed. "To convict a defendant on a conspiracy charge, the government must prove that the defendant agreed to the 'essential nature of the plan'. . . and on the 'kind of criminal conduct . . . in fact contemplated.'"[10] The conspiracy concept thus allows some lack of specificity in knowledge on the part of a defendant who would not be an accomplice without knowledge of which particular building was to be targeted.

The Government then brought ten additional conspirators to trial on a variety of charges which raised greater difficulties with conspiracy law. *United States v. Rahman* [11] involved convictions for "seditious conspiracy and other offenses arising out of a wide-ranging plot to conduct a campaign of urban terrorism." The Second Circuit listed the convictions as follows:

[9] 152 F.3d 88 (2d Cir. 1998).

[10] *Id.* at 147 (quoting United States v. Gleason, 616 F.2d 2, 16 (2d Cir. 1979)).

[11] 189 F.3d 88 (2d Cir. 1999).

The defendants were convicted of the following: seditious conspiracy (all defendants); soliciting the murder of Egyptian President Hosni Mubarak and soliciting an attack on American military installations (Rahman); conspiracy to murder Mubarak (Rahman); bombing conspiracy (all defendants found guilty except Nosair and El-Gabrowny); attempted bombing (Hampton-El, Amir, Fadil, Khallafalla, Elhassan, Saleh, and Alvarez); two counts of attempted murder and one count of murder in furtherance of a racketeering enterprise (Nosair); attempted murder of a federal officer (Nosair); three counts of use of a firearm in relation to a crime of violence (Nosair); possession of a firearm with an obliterated serial number (Nosair); facilitating the bombing conspiracy by shipping a firearm in interstate commerce and using and carrying a firearm in relation to a crime of violence (Alvarez); two counts of assault on a federal officer (El-Gabrowny); assault impeding the execution of a search warrant (El-Gabrowny); five counts of possession of a fraudulent foreign passport, and one count of possession with intent to transfer false identification documents (El-Gabrowny).[12]

Obviously, there are many rather tenuously connected behaviors charged in this single case. This runs the risk of having evidence of wrongdoing before the jury that would not be admissible were it not for the allegation of an overall plan. But what was the plan? To wreak havoc in the U.S.?

Some of these actions constituted completed crimes. Others were attempts. And yet others were mere plans or schemes. The court opinion reviews the evidence of each conviction and finds it sufficient to support each verdict. Evidence of all these various offenses was introduced in a single trial because they allegedly formed part of a single plan. Again we ask, what was the plan?[13]

The key to the scheme here is in the conviction of all the defendants for "seditious conspiracy to levy war against the United States." El-Gabrowny was convicted of a number of offenses on his own but was acquitted on the bombing conspiracy. Meanwhile, Nosair could not be charged on many of the offenses because he was in jail for the murder of Rabbi Kahane. What linked El-Gabrowny and Nosair was the overall seditious conspiracy, which the prosecution defined as "levying war against the U.S.," a very broad and general outline of a plan.

Al Qaeda made the task of the Government easier when it "declared war" on the U.S. in the form of calling for "jihad" and the killing of Americans. If the defendants themselves declare a wide range of activities to be part of a single plan, then who are we as judges and jurors to question their intentions? At the time of WTC I, however, the Rahman group and al Qaeda

---

[12] *Id.* at 103-04.

[13] *Id.* at 111-12.

were, at least to some degree, separate entities. The court in *Rahman* does not indicate that Sheikh Rahman himself was explicit about the scope and nature of "jihad":

> According to his speeches and writings, Rahman perceives the United States as the primary oppressor of Muslims worldwide, active in assisting Israel to gain power in the Middle East, and largely under the control of the Jewish lobby. Rahman also considers the secular Egyptian government of Mubarak to be an oppressor because it has abided Jewish migration to Israel while seeking to decrease Muslim births. Holding these views, Rahman believes that jihad against Egypt and the United States is mandated by the Qur'an. Formation of a jihad army made up of small "divisions" and "battalions" to carry out this jihad was therefore necessary, according to Rahman, in order to beat back these oppressors of Islam including the United States.[14]

At this point, we come close to the point at which a conspiracy prosecution could be based on speech normally considered protected under the First Amendment. As prevailing doctrine on advocacy and the right of association shows,[15] a defendant can cross the line from protected advocacy to criminal conspiracy with the first overt act toward a substantive harm. But here we have a plethora of offenses charged in a single conspiracy because of statements by one member of the conspiracy. This person is the "hub" of the conspiracy wheel while other "conspirators" constitute the "spokes" of the wheel. In the next section, we will see that the Supreme Court has required that there be some element making up the "rim" to tie all the disparate elements together. Without that, persons could be charged and convicted under a conspiracy theory for activity in which they had no role and no intention of furthering.

[B] Defining the Terrorist Conspiracy

Conspiracy classically is defined as "a combination of two or more persons to achieve an unlawful object or to achieve a lawful object by unlawful means."[16] In the context of terrorism, this definition raises intriguing possibilities right from the start.

The most successful terrorist organizations carefully hide the "cells" from each other. For comparison, consider a normal business-style organization chart. In the classic business enterprise, members of the various departments feed information to their managers who then share it with the CEO and other managers to make the entire enterprise flow as smoothly as possible. The employees in a department will know as much or as little about the activities of employees in other departments as their managers

---

[14] *Id.* at 104.

[15] Brandenburg v. Ohio, 395 U.S. 444 (1969) (holding criminal conspiracy statute invalid for punishing advocacy).

[16] WAYNE LAFAVE, CRIMINAL LAW 615 (4th ed. 2003).

have time or inclination to share, plus whatever information is shared in informal settings such as meetings, social occasions, or rumor mill. If an investigator, say a journalist doing a story on the company, asks questions about how an employee's work fits into the overall business plan, the employee may draw upon both fact and rumor to provide as complete a picture as possible. Typically, each employee will know at least something of the work of other departments because that knowledge feeds the "team spirit" of the company in pursuit of their common objectives.

In a clandestine operation, it becomes important that the members of each "department," usually known as "cells," know as little as possible about each other. This is so that an investigator who manages to capture or "turn" one cell member will not thereby be able to learn anything about the other cells. Everyone who has ever read a spy novel will recognize that the lieutenants (cell "managers") may even insulate themselves from the cell members by a series of "cutouts," anonymous or pseudonymous individuals who themselves know little or nothing of either the cells or the lieutenants. In a highly sophisticated operation such as al Qaeda or the Medellin Cartel of the 1980s, only the ruling elite or inner circle will know each other.

Now suppose that Cell 1 has been successful in carrying out a terrorist act while Cells 3 and 5 attempted similar actions but did not bring them to completion. Can the members of the other cells be prosecuted for conspiracy along with the members of Cell 1 as to whose existence they had no knowledge?

The metaphor of a "chain" conspiracy refers to links in a single line, while the "wheel" model refers to an inner core around which unconnected spokes revolve.[17] In the wheel model, the question is whether each of the spokes of the wheel may be involved in a single conspiracy with each other even though they do not know each other's identity. In the chain, persons far removed from each other because of the presence of intermediaries may similarly be engaged in a single conspiracy. The element of secrecy in clandestine schemes was recognized by the U.S. Supreme Court when it declared that "the law rightly gives room for allowing the conviction of those discovered upon showing sufficiently the essential nature of the plan and their connections with it, without requiring evidence of knowledge of all its details or the participation of others."[18]

There are limits, both constitutional and otherwise, on the application of these models. In *Kotteakos v. United States*,[19] the hub of the conspiracy dealt with each of the spokes separately. The Supreme Court acknowledged that the person at the hub may have thought of the entire enterprise as

---

[17] Rex v. Meyrick, 21 Crim. App. R. 94 (1929). *See also Campane, Chains, Wheels, and the Single Conspiracy*, Pts. I & II, FBI LAW ENFORCEMENT BULL., Aug. 1981, at 24, FBI LAW ENFORCEMENT BULL., Sept. 1981, at 24; Note, *Federal Treatment of Multiple Conspiracies*, 57 COLUM. L. REV. 387 (1957).

[18] Blumenthal v. United States, 332 U.S. 539, 551 (1947).

[19] 328 U.S. 750 (1946).

a single scheme, but without something more to tie the individual transactions together (a rim around the spokes), "there was no drawing of all together in a single, overall comprehensive scheme."[20]

A wheel may have spokes each of which itself is a chain (the "chain-wheel"). In *United States v. Perez*,[21] the defendants were involved in multiple instances of fake traffic accidents in which doctors and lawyers concocted fraudulent reports for submission to insurance companies. Each chain included several persons (one driver and a pedestrian, or two drivers and a passenger, plus a doctor, a lawyer, and a "recruiter" who set up each accident), and each chain reported back to the central organizer. The court considered that none of the participants could rationally have believed that the scheme would work if there were not others out doing the same thing because otherwise the risks would not be worth the payoff to professionals such as the doctors and lawyers. This inference of knowledge was sufficient to form a rim around the spokes to complete the wheel.

Only slightly tongue in cheek, we can now imagine bringing every gangbanger in Los Angeles to trial for "conspiracy to intimidate the population of Los Angeles and thus to interfere with their rights to use public thoroughfares." It might make us more comfortable if we had a better idea of what constitutes a single plan. It is obvious that a single plan does not have to be limited to a single act of violence. But at the other extreme, a single plan surely could not be made out by showing that the defendants were all committed to acts of violence within the United States without some link to tie those acts together. *Rahman* pushed the envelope by permitting definition of a conspiracy to destroy bridges, tunnels, and buildings in New York.

The key in the wheel-chain model analogy is to find a single link that ties the various acts together. In the case of a terrorist network, even if it were possible to tie all members of every cell back to a central organizer, the members of one cell should not have any knowledge about the plans or perhaps even the existence of the other cells, so they could not be charged with the acts of the other cells. If they knew in general terms that there was a coherence in which their plans were coordinated with the plans of other cells, then every conspirator could be charged with complicity in the acts of every other conspirator. There could even be instances when nobody outside the particular cell, even the linkages back along the chained spoke, knew what the members of that cell were planning. In that case, the links to other cells and back along the chained spoke to the hub may well have been broken. This does not mean that the conspiracy could not be charged among those who did know what was going on, but just that the breadth of the conspiracy may be limited.

---

[20] *Blumenthal*, 332 U.S. at 558.

[21] 489 F.2d 51 (5th Cir. 1973).

[C] When to Intervene

As with many conspiracy investigations, one crucial question for law enforcement officials will be when to intervene and make arrests. Agents who have information about impending criminal acts will naturally be inclined to let the conspiracy run long enough to shore up their criminal case without letting it run long enough to permit harm to innocent victims. The terrorism examples of this phenomenon can be particularly nerve-wracking because of the sudden and literally explosive nature of the plans laid during the conspiracy.

United States v. Sarkissian [22] was the first reported case in which a Foreign Intelligence Surveillance Act (FISA) [23] wiretap resulted in a criminal prosecution. The frightening aspects of *Sarkissian*, showing the dilemma of conspiracy investigators, are that even with the wiretap the plotters succeeded in getting dynamite on board a U.S. commercial airliner, and that the government agents came close to losing their prosecution by failing to get a search warrant at the critical moment.

A group of Armenian dissidents in Los Angeles came under the scrutiny of the FBI. With a wiretap order from the FISA Court, FBI agents learned that they were planning to bomb the Armenian Consulate in Philadelphia. Continuing to monitor the telephone conversations, agents learned that parts of a bomb were being carried from Los Angeles to Boston. They deduced the probable flight and probable identity of the courier, and notified the Boston FBI Office, which sent 50 agents to Logan Airport to intercept the courier. Using dogs and x-ray as luggage was unloaded from the plane, Boston agents detected sticks of dynamite in a suitcase and eventually arrested the person who had checked the suitcase. [24]

After conviction, the first issue on appeal was suppression of fruits of the search of the luggage at the airport. The Ninth Circuit determined that the danger to the public in the airport constituted "exigent circumstances" justifying a warrantless search of the luggage. The FBI agents in Boston were completely occupied with finding the dynamite and preventing violence, but the Los Angeles agents had all the information and were not so engaged in the on-the-ground action. "Although the investigation preoccupied Maples [the L.A. agent] throughout the early morning hours, after 10:00 a.m. EDT he did little but wait to 'see what happened.' [He] never considered trying to get a telephonic warrant. Though we find that troubling, we affirm." [25]

---

[22] 841 F.2d 959 (9th Cir. 1988).

[23] *See* § 7.02 *infra*.

[24] In more detail, the agents at the airport located the suitcase with the dynamite, returned the dynamite to the suitcase and allowed the suitcase to be placed on the baggage claim carousel. The suspect, however, became nervous with the level of activity around the baggage claim area and fled, only to be arrested later. Although the court questioned the judgment of the L.A. agents in not obtaining a warrant while the plane was in the air, it did not comment on the wisdom of leaving dynamite in a suitcase in a public area of the airport.

[25] *Sarkissian*, 841 F.2d at 963.

Sarkissian presents a classic example of the difficulty of knowing when to intervene. Can government agents create "exigent circumstances" for a warrantless search merely by waiting for the conspiracy to unfold until it reaches a danger point? The Court says that probable cause for a search arose about three hours before the plane landed when the L.A. agents identified the courier with the luggage. Probable cause may have existed earlier as soon as the field agents became convinced that a conspiracy with some overt acts had been triggered, perhaps a couple of days earlier. Could the FBI be faulted for not moving on the house before a suitcase full of dynamite was checked into the luggage hold of a public passenger plane bound from Los Angeles to Boston?

Even granting that early movement would have resulted in a tenuous conspiracy prosecution, there is a lost opportunity here for investigator-prosecutor cooperation. A somewhat optimistic version of investigative practice prior to 9/11 would have had a prosecutor from the U.S. Attorney's Office in Los Angeles involved as soon as the FBI agents learned of an active plot to use explosives. An affidavit could be drafted and amended as new information became available so that it was ready to go by fax from L.A. to Boston at a moment's notice. The Boston U.S. Attorney's Office could be prepared to take the affidavit to a magistrate, obtain a signature, and telephone or radio the authorization for search to the agents in the field. With this procedure in place, the warrant could have been issued well before the plane touched down in Boston, allowing special handling of all the luggage on the plane, and thus eliminating much of the danger to the public that the court finds to create exigent circumstances. After 9/11, the investigation would be coordinated out of Washington,[26] but the rest of the scenario remains the same.

This scenario would allow for an effective prosecution while decreasing some of the risk to the public. But, obviously, a procedure of this type entails time and expense, not to mention bureaucratic crossing of turf from FBI to Justice Department lawyers. From a prosecutor's standpoint, this scenario raises two concerns: 1) Will a court accept the justification for a warrantless search? 2) Are agents flirting with danger by delaying intervention? And overlaying these questions is the degree of expense that the public is willing to bear in occupying the time of agents and prosecutors in such degree.

Having reviewed some of the "ordinary" incidents of law enforcement and prosecution as they relate to terrorism, we need to add the unusual issues raised by the need for secrecy and the special problems of international terrorism. The classic terrorism case will involve government surveillance (wiretaps and other electronic surveillance) carried out under the Foreign Intelligence Surveillance Act,[27] seizure of dangerous material and arrest

---

[26] The re-authorization of the PATRIOT Act in 2006 created the Counterterrorism Section of the National Security Division of the Department of Justice.

[27] 50 U.S.C. §§ 1801-1862 (2005).

of the defendants (quite possibly without warrant under exigent circumstances), and the defendants' desire to obtain or introduce into evidence information that the government considers secret and subject to the Classified Information Procedures Act.[28] These complications will be covered in Chapter 7 in dealing with intelligence information.

[D]   Examples of Conspiracy Prosecutions

United States v. Lavasseur[29] is an example from domestic terrorism that more closely resembles the post-hoc prosecution format than the prevention mode in which law enforcement is now trying to operate. The Second Circuit described the background of the United Freedom Front this way:

> Appellants . . . were the subjects of a decade-long, nationwide search prior to their arrests in 1984 and 1985. They were suspects in a variety of crimes for which several underground organizations with which appellants were allegedly affiliated took credit. Among those crimes were eight Boston-area bombings occurring between 1976 and 1979, the murder of a New Jersey State Trooper and the attempted murder of a Massachusetts State Trooper, several other assaults on law enforcement officers, and several armed bank robberies.[30]

None of those offenses was charged, however, when the defendants were arrested in 1984. Instead, they were charged with 10 bombings that occurred in 1982 and 1983 when they called themselves the UFF. This is an example of a limited conspiracy charge in which the conspiracy only covered the buildings on which a plan or agreement to bomb was actually launched. If agents had information about the plan before any bomb had been placed, then we would have the more preventive type of case.

The ease of prosecuting *Lavasseur* compared with the difficulty of intervention in *Sarkissian* illustrates the very different world in which U.S. law enforcement has found itself with the terrorism threat. Attempting to use traditional models of investigation and evidence-gathering for preventive purposes while then also using the same information for prosecution blends the different functions. This blending raises significant constitutional issues surrounding probable cause for search warrants (see the FISA discussion below), as well as the due process concern over breadth of conspiracy charges.

One issue that will arise in prosecuting plotters on the international scene is that an individual may be conspiring with others whose identities remain secret. The Supreme Court has been quite clear that a conspiracy

---

[28] 18 U.S.C. app. §§ 1-16 (2007).

[29] 816 F.2d 37 (2d Cir. 1987).

[30] *Id.* at 39.

conviction against one person can stand without knowing the other conspirators.[31]

It is equally clear that a conspiracy need not have specific targets in mind. It is enough for § 2339A that terrorist acts be contemplated and enough for § 956 (conspiring to kill, kidnap, maim, and injure persons and to damage and destroy property in a foreign country) that the plan include the requisite violent intent.[32]

Another related issue is whether the accused must have a direct connection with the person who carries out the act. In Anglo-American law, this issue has long been settled with the proposition that a tacit understanding of the mutual enterprise is sufficient. In international law, it has given rise to the notion of "joint criminal enterprise" and has produced some extensive discussions in the International Criminal Tribunals for Yugoslavia and Rwanda. In short, the Appeals Chamber of the ICTY has ruled that it is not necessary that the person who is to carry out the act even be aware of the common purpose.[33] Thus, the plotter who is able to make use of a distant unknown perpetrator is guilty without a showing of agreement or understanding with that actor — all that is required is that the crime be part of the common purpose.

The prosecution of Sami al-Arian highlights a potentially confusing aspect of conspiracy prosecutions when combined with charges of material support for a terrorist organization. The material support issues will be covered in Chapter 5 — in essence, that crime consists of providing money, goods, or services to a designated organization regardless of knowledge of the organization's activities or intent to further those wrongs. By contrast, a conspiracy charge requires some guilty intent.

Al-Arian was an Assistant Professor at the University of South Florida from 1986 until his dismissal in December 2001.[34] He was an outspoken Palestinian supporter and was indicted in 2003 for both conspiracy to commit murder of civilians in Israel and providing material support to a designated terrorist organization. The heart of the government's case was that al-Arian had personally collected funds for transfer to Palestinian Islamic Jihad, some of whose followers were engaged in bombings in Israel and which was designated as a terrorist organization in 1995.

Following a 6-month trial, al-Arian was acquitted on the conspiracy charges and the jury was hung on the material support charges.[35]

---

[31] Rogers v. United States, 340 U.S. 367, 375 (1951) ("[A]t least two persons are required to constitute a conspiracy, but the identity of the other members of the conspiracy is not needed, inasmuch as one person can be convicted of conspiring with persons whose names are unknown."); United States v. Rey, 923 F.2d 1217, 1222 (6th Cir. 1991) ("[I]t is not essential that a conspirator know all other conspirators.").

[32] United States v. Sattar, 314 F. Supp. 2d 279 (S.D.N.Y. 2004).

[33] *Radoslav Brdjanin*, ¶¶ 362-4ICTY (IT-99-36) (April 3, 2007).

[34] The United Faculty of Florida maintains an extensive website devoted to the al-Arian matter, see w3.usf.edu/~uff/AlArian/index.html.

[35] *No Guilty Verdicts In Al-Arian Trial*, ST. PETERSBURG TIMES TAMPA BAY ONLINE, Dec. 6, 2005, *available at* news.tbo.com/news/MGBAT3MOWGE.html.

Conviction on the conspiracy counts would have required showing that he had knowledge that the organization to which he was providing funds was engaged in criminal activity. To make matters more confusing, the trial judge instructed the jury that conviction on the material support charges would also require an intent to further the violent aims of the organization, a position that has been rejected by other courts.[36] The al-Arian jury apparently believed that the conspiracy charges had not been proved because the evidence did not show that particular funds went to further particular criminal acts.[37]

Following the jury verdicts, al-Arian pleaded guilty to one count of conspiracy to provide material support and was sentenced to 57 months, 39 of which he had already served. The plea agreement also called for his being deported as soon as he finished his 18 months in prison. In February 2007, however, he was held in contempt of court for refusing to testify in a Virginia prosecution and is being held on that basis so that his sentence does not run. As of June 2007, he was on a hunger strike in prison.

By contrast to the government's difficulty in proving a conspiracy case against al-Arian, Ali al-Timimi was convicted in June 2005 of crimes that essentially amounted to inducing others to conspire to aid the Taliban.[38] He was a lecturer at Dar Al Hijrah Islamic Center in Falls Church, Virginia, teaching about the history and culture of Islam. The specifics by which he induced others to engage in criminal conspiracies consisted primarily of (1) a meeting at another person's house on September 16, 2001, at which he "told [others] that the time had come for them to go abroad to join the mujahideen engaged in violent jihad in Afghanistan," and at which he "advised" two persons "how to reach [a] training camp undetected,"[39] and (2) a session at his own home in October at which he "told . . . others that they were obligated to help the Taliban in the face of an attack by the United States." In addition, he promulgated some highly inflammatory language about the wrongdoing of the U.S. to his followers.[40] These overt acts

---

[36] *See* § 5.01[D] *infra*.

[37] *Case Too Complex to Get a Conviction*, ST. PETERSBURG TIMES TAMPA BAY ONLINE, Dec. 8, 2005, *available at* www.sptimes.com/2005/12/08/Tampabay/Case_too_complex_to_g.shtml.

[38] He was convicted on all ten counts with which he was charged, which were:

Count 1: Inducing Others to Conspire to Use Firearms

Count 2: Soliciting Others to Levy War

Count 3: Inducing Others to Conspire to Levy War

Count 4: Attempting to Contribute Services to the Taliban

Count 5: Inducing Others to Aid the Taliban

Count 6: Inducing Others to Conspire to Violate the Neutrality Act

Counts 7-8: Inducing Others to Use Firearms

Counts 9-10: Inducing Others to Carry Explosives

[39] The indictment alleged that they discussed a training camp run by the LET [Lashkar-e-Taiba], a "designated foreign terrorist organization" (FTO) first allied with the Taliban and then engaged in opposition to the government of India.

[40] In the words of the indictment,

were taken in the context of his knowledge that some of his audience owned assault-type weapons and were seriously considering going to paramilitary training camps in Pakistan to train as mujahadeen fighters in Islamist organizations.

In the culture clash between religious fundamentalism and the rest of the world, al-Timimi is on the wrong side. His words certainly encouraged young Muslim men to violence and contributed to the atmosphere of hate and fear that permeates religious fundamentalist paranoia.[41] But by

---

On February 1, 2003, Ali Al-Timimi provided the following message to his followers:

This morning, the world heard news about the crash of the space shuttle. There is no doubt that Muslims were overjoyed because of the adversity that befell their greatest enemy. Upon hearing the news, my heart felt certain good omens that I liked to spread to my brothers.

First: The Name of the Shuttle: "Columbia" is the name of the shuttle, called after the name of "Columbus," the sailor who discovered the American Continent in 1492 after the fall of Grenada, the last Islamic stronghold in Andalusia. Historians know that, after discovering the two American Continents, the Romans (the Christians of Europe) exploited their wealth in order to be able to control the Islamic World. The Columbia crash made me feel, and God is the only One to know, that this is a strong signal that Western supremacy (especially that of America) that began 500 years ago is coming to a quick end, God Willing, as occurred to the shuttle.

Second: The Shuttle Crew: The Israeli Ambassador to the U.N. described the Israeli astronaut as someone carrying all the hopes and ambitions of the Israeli people. And so, God Willing, all these hopes and ambitions were burnt with the crash and the burning of the shuttle and one of its astronauts, the Israeli.

Third: The Crash Location: As soon as CNN announced the crash of the space shuttle nearby the city of Palestine, in Texas, I said to myself "God is Great." This way, God Willing, America will fall and disappear (nearby Palestine). The State of Texas is also the state of the foolish, obeyed President Bush the son. And so we hope, God Willing, similar to the crash of the shuttle on his state, his nation would fall upon his head due to his foolish policy.

Fourth: The President's Condolences to the American People: In the words that President Bush used to console his people, he referred to the Book of Isiah where there is a praise to God's creation, His stars and planets. I said to myself, Praise the Lord, in this same Book of Isiah there are news about the coming of Prophet Muhammad and a warning of the destruction of the Jews at the end of time. [A citation from the Koran follows.]

And so, there are other signs that would take a long time to recount. For example, every time the Americans believe that they control the whole earth and the skies, and act as they wish, there comes a sign that reminds us that God, Almighty, is greater than his creatures, sitting on His Chair, handling everything, and that His angels act according to His commands. And so, he whoever will try to raise the Jews, who are a nation that God covered with humiliation and deserved God's wrath, will be afflicted with divine humiliation and wrath as much as he supports them. As I mentioned earlier, these are all ideas that came to me when I heard of the accident, and hopes that I wish God would fulfill, and God is the only One to know.

[41] Islamists clearly did not invent either fundamentalism or the use of violence to pursue a religious ideal. The world's three major monotheistic religions have each had their share of the experience. *See generally* KAREN ARMSTRONG, THE BATTLE FOR GOD (2000). The term, itself, however, is usually dated from the early 20th Century as a response by American Christians to the eroding influence of their own position in public life. *See* Religious Movements, *Fundamentalism, available at* religiousmovements.lib.virginia.edu/nrms/fund.html (last visited June 22, 2007). The Fundamentalism Project of the University of

human rights standards consistent with liberal values, did he commit a crime? Western liberalism has struggled for centuries with trying to forestall violent or other harmful conduct while permitting maximum play of individual freedom. This tension has been played out in two areas of Anglo-American law related to inchoate crime: the limits of conspiracy law and protection for advocacy as part of freedom of expression.

Conspiracy law has not been overtly tied to freedom of expression, but the requirement of an agreement along with, usually, an "overt act" serves to prevent punishment of desires that fall short of a live threat.[42] Even when an agreement alone would constitute a crime, the watchword for U.S. law with regard to when advocacy can be punished has been "imminent," reflecting how close the advocacy must be to producing a substantive harm.[43] That word is now matched in the customary international law of the International Criminal Tribunals in defining the crime of "incitement" to prohibited conduct.[44]

§ 4.02 TREASON, ASSOCIATION, AND CONSPIRACY

The law of treason has not been widely studied in a very long time, but it may offer us some interesting insights. The *Salameh* case included charges of seditious conspiracy, which sounds much like treason, and Sheikh Rahman raised First Amendment defenses that sound much like

---

Chicago, funded by the American Academy of Arts and Sciences, produced a series of volumes devoted to the subject. *See The Fundamentalism Project, available at* www.press.uchicago.edu/ Complete/Series/FP.html (last visited June 22, 2007). For purposes of the study of terrorism, fundamentalism is marked by a vision of a cosmic struggle between good and evil that characterizes all nonbelievers as evil, thus justifying elimination of those on the other side. *See generally* GABRIEL A. ALMOND, R. SCOTT APPLEBY, & EMMANUEL SIVAN, STRONG RELIGION: THE RISE OF FUNDAMENTALISMS AROUND THE WORLD (2002).

Unfortunately, politicians occasionally fall into the fundamentalist trap by responding in the vein of "If you're not with us, you're against us." Even worse can be the use of buzzwords that play directly into the fundamentalist view of history:

> President Bush's reference to a "crusade" against terrorism, which passed almost unnoticed by Americans, rang alarm bells in Europe. It raised fears that the terrorist attacks could spark a "clash of civilizations" between Christians and Muslims, sowing fresh winds of hatred and mistrust. "We have to avoid a clash of civilizations at all costs," French foreign minister Hubert Vedrine said on Sunday. "One has to avoid falling into this huge trap, this monstrous trap" which he said had been "conceived by the instigators of the assault."

Peter Ford, *Europe Cringes at Bush "Crusade" Against Terrorists*, CHRISTIAN SCI. MONITOR, Sept. 19, 2001, *available at* www.csmonitor.com/2001/0919/p12s2-woeu.html.

[42] The Supreme Court has said that the "function of the overt act in a conspiracy prosecution is simply to manifest 'that the conspiracy is at work.'" Yates v. United States, 354 U.S. 298, 334 (1957). The Court has held that Congress can eliminate the over act requirement and make the "criminal agreement itself . . . the *actus reus*." United States v. Shabani, 513 U.S. 10, 15 (1994) (conspiracy to distribute drugs). *See also* Singer v. United States, 323 U.S. 338 (1945) (Selective Service Act); Nash v. United States, 229 U.S. 373 (1913) (antitrust). *See generally* WAYNE LAFAVE, CRIMINAL LAW 626-28 (2003).

[43] *See* § 4.03[A] *infra.*

[44] *See* § 4.03[B] *infra.*

the concerns of the Framers with regard to treason itself. The Second Circuit pointed out that treason is a crime which applies only to those who have a duty of allegiance to the United States.[45] The court also intimated that there could be a variety of other crimes with similar elements going by different names and questioned whether the constitutional restraints on treason prosecutions (such as two witnesses to the same overt act) would apply to those crimes.

To understand the dispute over the terms "training" and "personnel," a bit of background on the concepts of treason and political association should be helpful.

[A] Treason and Political Freedom

In dealing with the "seditious conspiracy" charges in *Rahman*, the Second Circuit engaged in an extended discussion of the constitutional restrictions on prosecutions for treason.

> In the late colonial period, as today, the charge of treason carried a "peculiar intimidation and stigma" with considerable "potentialities . . . as a political epithet."[46] At the time of the drafting of the Constitution, furthermore, treason was punishable not only by death, but by an exceptionally cruel method of execution designed to enhance the suffering of the traitor. *See* 4 WILLIAM BLACKSTONE, COMMENTARIES *92 (observing that the punishment for treason is "terrible" in that the traitor is "hanged by the neck, then cut down alive," that "his entrails [are then] taken out, and burned, while he is yet alive," "that his head [is] cut off," and that his "body [is then] divided into four parts."). In contrast, lesser subversive offenses were penalized by noncapital punishments or less brutal modes of execution. *See id.* at *94-*126. The Framers may have intended to limit the applicability of the most severe penalties — or simply the applicability of capital punishment for alleged subversion — to instances of levying war against, or adhering to enemies of, the United States. Today treason continues to be punishable by death, while seditious conspiracy commands a maximum penalty of twenty years imprisonment.[47]

The Framers were so concerned about the potential misuses of treason charges that this is the only "crime" which is given special treatment in the Constitution. Article III, section 3 provides:

> Treason against the United States, shall consist only in levying War against them, or in adhering to their Enemies, giving them Aid and Comfort. No Person shall be convicted of Treason unless on the

---

[45] *Rahman*, 189 F.3d at 112.

[46] William Hurst, *Treason in the United States (Pt. II)*, 58 HARV. L. REV. 395, 424-25 (1945).

[47] *Rahman*, 189 F.3d at 112.

Testimony of two Witnesses to the same overt Act, or on Confession in open Court.[48]

The Treason Clause builds extremely high barricades against prosecution for this "heinous" crime, so the question becomes whether those barricades can be circumvented by creating other crimes, or by calling the traitor something else such as an "enemy combatant." To be flippant, could we avoid restrictions on prosecution for treason by calling it jaywalking?

Article III's "peculiar phraseology observable in the definition" of treason, and "the equally stringent feature" requiring two eyewitness' testimony of the same overt act, have been said to flow from the Framers' discomfort with "abuses . . . under the tyrannical reigns of the Tudors and the Stuarts."[49] In particular, the Framers were reacting to the concept of "constructive treason" by which anyone who spoke in support of, or was friendly with, those who promoted resistance to policies of the Crown could be accused of treason.[50]

The Treason Clause creates two categories of treason: levying war against the United States, and providing aid and comfort to the enemy. In the first there must be an armed assemblage and the second requires an enemy. Chief Justice Marshall gave us our first instruction in the operation of the Treason Clause in *Ex parte Bollman*,[51] dealing with some of the alleged conspirators in the Burr escapade. Marshall distinguished strongly between treason and conspiracy, emphasizing that treason requires that "war must be actually levied against the United States" but that the legislature could define other crimes such as conspiracy.[52] It must be remembered, however,

---

[48] U.S. CONST. art. III, § 3.

[49] *In re* Charge to Grand Jury, 30 F. Cas. 1034, 1035 (C.C.N.Y. 1861) (No. 18, 271).

[50] *See* J. HURST, THE LAW OF THE TREASON IN THE UNITED STATES 152-53 (1971).

[51] 8 U.S. (4 Cranch) 75 (1807).

[52] *Id.* at 126:

> To constitute that specific crime for which the prisoners now before the court have been committed, war must be actually levied against the United States. . . . To conspire to levy war, and actually to levy war, are distinct offences. [I]f war be actually levied, that is, if a body of men be actually assembled for the purpose of effecting by force a treasonable purpose, all those who perform any part, however minute, or however remote from the scene of action, and who are actually leagued in the general conspiracy, are to be considered as traitors. But there must be an actual assembling of men for the treasonable purpose, to constitute a levying of war.
>
> Crimes so atrocious as those which have for their object the subversion by violence of those laws and those institutions which have been ordained in order to secure the peace and happiness of society, are not to escape punishment because they have not ripened into treason. The wisdom of the legislature is competent to provide for the case; and the framers of our constitution, . . . must have conceived it more safe that punishment in such cases should be ordained by general laws, . . . than that it should be inflicted under the influence of those passions which . . . a flexible definition of the crime, or a construction which would render it flexible, might bring into operation. It is therefore more safe as well as more consonant to the principles of our constitution, . . . that crimes not clearly within the constitutional definition, should receive such punishment as the legislature in its wisdom may provide.

that the Burr escapade did not involve a foreign enemy, so there was no occasion for him to deal with the offense of providing aid and comfort to the enemy.

In a number of cases stemming from the Civil War, the judges expanded Marshall's view of conspiracy to state that there could be no such concept as an accessory to treason because an act was either treason or not.[53] They consistently recognized the differences between the two kinds of treason, the first depending on whether the defendant has taken up arms, the second consisting of providing material support to a recognized enemy. It is familiar ground that President Lincoln attempted to use the military courts for prosecution of Southern sympathizers, leading eventually to the opinion in *Ex parte Milligan*.[54]

After the War, the Court dealt with the question of whether debts payable in Confederate currency were still valid as between two individuals (and, thus, payable in U.S. currency after the war ended).[55] Chief Justice Chase distinguished among different levels of *de facto* governments. At one extreme would be a solidly established actual government such that "adherents to it in war against the government *de jure* do not incur the penalties of treason."[56] The government of the Confederacy, he said, was sufficiently established that it obtained "actual supremacy, however unlawfully gained, in all matters of government within its military lines."

> That supremacy did not justify acts of hostility to the United States. How far it should excuse them must be left to the lawful government upon the re-establishment of its authority. But it [Confederate hegemony] made obedience to its authority, in civil and local matters, not only a necessity but a duty. Without such obedience, civil order was impossible.[57]

By this language, Chase was implying that there could be no prosecution for providing aid and comfort to the enemy by a person residing within the military control of the Confederacy. As we know, there were no such prosecutions.

World War I produced the seminal case for all of First Amendment law, *Schenck v. United States*.[58] Schenck and his cohorts were convicted of conspiracy to violate the Espionage Act of 1917, which made it unlawful to "cause insubordination . . . in the military and naval forces of the United States, and to obstruct the recruiting and enlistment service of the United States."[59] Justice Holmes' famous opinion for the Court, after using the

---

[53] *See, e.g.*, United States v. Greathouse, 26 Fed. Cas. No. 18 (C.C. Cal. 1863) (No. 15,254). There are a number of similar cases in the same volume.

[54] 71 U.S. (4 Wall.) 2 (1866).

[55] Thorington v. Smith, 75 U.S. (8 Wall.) 1 (1869).

[56] *Id.* at 8.

[57] *Id.* at 11.

[58] 249 U.S. 47 (1919).

[59] *Id.* at 49.

analogy of "falsely shouting fire in a crowded theater," stated:

> The question in every case is whether the words used are used in such circumstances and are of such a nature as to create a clear and present danger that they will bring about the substantive evils that Congress has a right to prevent. It is a question of proximity and degree. When a nation is at war many things that might be said in time of peace are such a hindrance to its effort that their utterance will not be endured so long as men fight and that no Court could regard them as protected by any constitutional right. It seems to be admitted that if an actual obstruction of the recruiting service were proved, liability for words that produced that effect might be enforced. The statute of 1917 in § 4 punishes conspiracies to obstruct as well as actual obstruction. If the act, (speaking, or circulating a paper,) its tendency and the intent with which it is done are the same, we perceive no ground for saying that success alone warrants making the act a crime. [60]

By the time *Schenck* was decided, Congress had already responded to the emerging level of dissension regarding U.S. entry into the war in Europe by passing the 1918 amendments to the Espionage Act. Under the amendments, it was unlawful to "urge, incite, or advocate" actions that could disrupt the war In *Abrams v. United States*, [61] the majority of the Court found that an intent to disrupt the war effort was sufficient to uphold conviction under the statute. Justice Holmes, joined by Justice Brandeis, dissented with the famous "marketplace of ideas" metaphor. [62] The combination of opinions sounds as if the majority were treating the statute as if it were a finding by Congress of "clear and present danger." The interesting point for our purposes is that nobody questioned whether Congress could define crimes that came very close to "providing aid and comfort to the enemy" without requiring two witnesses to the same overt act. It seems that in this stage, Congress and the Court had accepted Chief Justice Marshall's invitation to Congress to define non-treason offenses.

The only World War II case in the Supreme Court on the subject of treason was *Cramer v. United States*, [63] a follow-up to *Ex parte Quirin*, the notorious case of the eight German saboteurs who landed by submarine and were tried for violation of the law of war. [64] One of the eight saboteurs, Thiel, had a friend in the U.S. named Cramer, who was German by birth and a naturalized U.S. citizen. Thiel contacted Cramer in New York, met with him twice in public places, and gave Cramer some money to hold for him. Cramer testified that he suspected Thiel was here as a propagandist for the German government, but there was no evidence that Cramer

---

[60] *Id.* at 52.

[61] 250 U.S. 616 (1919).

[62] *Id.* at 630.

[63] 325 U.S. 1 (1945).

[64] 317 U.S. 1 (1942).

suspected anything of the violent intentions of the saboteurs.[65] Cramer was convicted of treason. The basic question presented to the Supreme Court was whether an overt act in furtherance of treason needed to be done with intent by the defendant of furthering enemy action against the government, or whether an innocent overt act could be treasonous because of its role in the enemy's plan.

Justice Jackson's majority opinion in *Cramer* canvassed the history of treason prosecutions from English law through the colonial era, pointing out that much of the turbulence of those periods could lead to a citizen's being caught between competing loyalties and thus subject to treason from two different sides. The Framers built protections against treason prosecutions to guard against two dangers: "(1) perversion by established authority to repress peaceful political opposition; and (2) conviction of the innocent as a result of perjury, passion or inadequate evidence."[66] The critical passage for definition of criminal behavior is this:

> Thus the crime of treason consists of two elements: adherence to the enemy; and rendering him aid and comfort. A citizen intellectually or emotionally may favor the enemy and harbor sympathies or convictions disloyal to this country's policy or interest, but so long as he commits no act of aid and comfort to the enemy, there is no treason. On the other hand, a citizen may take actions which do aid and comfort the enemy — making a speech critical of the government or opposing its measures, profiteering, striking in defense plants or essential work, and the hundred other things which impair our cohesion and diminish our strength — but if there is no adherence to the enemy in this, if there is no intent to betray, there is no treason.[67]

Applying these thoughts to the evidence, Jackson pointed out that the prosecution had "withdrawn" the safekeeping of money as an overt act to be submitted to the jury. That left only the two meetings with Thiel that were corroborated by eyewitness testimony. These could not be said to have shown furtherance of a scheme sufficient to prove either aid or adherence to the enemy. By contrast, the money transaction, if proved by the requisite testimony, would have made "a quite different case." Finally, Justice Jackson addressed the Government's arguments for relaxing the standards related to treason:

> The Government has urged that our initial interpretation of the treason clause should be less exacting, lest treason be too hard to prove and the Government disabled from adequately combating the techniques of modern warfare. But the treason offense is not the only nor can it well serve as the principal legal weapon to vindicate our national cohesion and security. In debating this provision,

---

[65] *Id.* at 3.

[66] *Id.* at 27.

[67] *Id.* at 29.

Rufus King observed to the Convention that the "controversy relating to Treason might be of less magnitude than was supposed; as the legislature might punish capitally under other names than Treason." His statement holds good today. Of course we do not intimate that Congress could dispense with the two-witness rule merely by giving the same offense another name. But the power of Congress is in no way limited to enact prohibitions of specified acts thought detrimental to our wartime safety.[68]

Congress, with the assistance of many subsequent administrations, has accepted this invitation by enacting many statutes that relate to providing aid and comfort to those who threaten the public safety of the United States. Perhaps the most directly relevant are those that criminalize "providing material support to terrorists" (§ 2339A) and "providing material support or resources to designated terrorist organizations" (§ 2339B).[69] There are also crimes, such as that to which John Walker Lindh pleaded guilty, defined as violations of Presidential directives blocking trading with, or providing services to, regimes designated in time of national emergency, most of which are punishable under IEEPA. Given the history of the Treason Clause, and particularly Justices Marshall's and Jackson's invitations to Congress, there can be little doubt about the validity of these statutes, except insofar as they might in some situations be subject to First Amendment restrictions.

[B] The Communist Conspiracy and the Right of Association

Prior to the Terrorism Scare, the U.S. confronted the Red Scare. Starting with the anarchists of the late 19th Century and moving through the Bolshevik Revolution into the Communist International era of the 1920s, both state and federal governments reacted to what was perceived to be a threat to the social and political order of the West by attempting to criminalize groups that advocated overthrow of governments.

In *Whitney v. California*,[70] Ms. Whitney was convicted under a state statute of "knowingly becom[ing] a member of an organization, society, group or assemblage of persons organized or assembled to advocate, teach or aid and abet criminal syndicalism." Criminal syndicalism was defined "as any doctrine, advocating [or] teaching unlawful methods of terrorism as a means of accomplishing a change in industrial ownership or control, or effecting any political change." Although Whitney was a delegate to the state Communist Labor Party convention, at which most members favored violence as a means of securing political change, she argued that she did not favor violence and in fact had attempted to forestall violence as a method of political change. The Supreme Court said that she was raising

---

[68] *Id.* at 45.

[69] 18 U.S.C. §§ 2339A, 2338B (2005).

[70] 274 U.S. 357 (1927).

issues of fact which had been found against her and which an appellate court could not reconsider.[71] The Court also reiterated the familiar formula that acting in concert was a greater threat to the public order than the expressions or acts of individuals acting separately.[72]

Justices Brandeis and Holmes concurred on the basis that she had failed to raise her constitutional claims in the state courts but added a warning thought contrary to the views of the majority:

> The wide difference between advocacy and incitement, between preparation and attempt, between assembling and conspiracy, must be borne in mind. In order to support a finding of clear and present danger it must be shown either that immediate serious violence was to be expected or was advocated, or that the past conduct furnished reason to believe that such advocacy was then contemplated.

> If there be time to expose through discussion the falsehood and fallacies, to avert the evil by the processes of education, the remedy to be applied is more speech, not enforced silence. Only an emergency can justify repression.[73]

Justice Brandeis' warning did not save the organizers of the Communist Party from prosecution under federal law. In *Dennis v. United States*,[74] several leaders of the American Communist Party were convicted of violating the federal Smith Act, which was essentially the same as the California Criminal Syndicalism statute. The majority opinion for the Supreme Court stated that it accepted the "clear and present danger" test as amplified by Brandeis and Holmes in *Whitney* but found that the circumstances of the U.S. in the 1940s met the test because "we cannot bind the Government to wait" until an attempt to act is imminent.[75]

---

[71] *Id.* at 367.

[72] *Id.* at 372.

[73] *Id.* at 375-77.

[74] 341 U.S. 494 (1951).

[75] *Id.* at 509-11:

> If Government is aware that a group aiming at its overthrow is attempting to indoctrinate its members and to commit them to a course whereby they will strike when the leaders feel the circumstances permit, action by the Government is required. Certainly an attempt to overthrow the Government by force, even though doomed from the outset because of inadequate numbers or power of the revolutionists, is a sufficient evil for Congress to prevent. The damage which such attempts create both physically and politically to a nation makes it impossible to measure the validity in terms of the probability of success, or the immediacy of a successful attempt. In the instant case the trial judge charged the jury that they could not convict unless they found that petitioners intended to overthrow the Government "as speedily as circumstances would permit." This does not mean, and could not properly mean, that they would not strike until there was certainty of success. What was meant was that the revolutionists would strike when they thought the time was ripe. We must therefore reject the contention that success or probability of success is the criterion.

> The mere fact that from the period 1945 to 1948 petitioners' activities did not result in an attempt to overthrow the Government by force and violence is of course no

Justice Jackson concurred on this basis that the "basic rationale of the law of conspiracy is that a conspiracy may be an evil in itself, independently of any other evil it seeks to accomplish."[76] Justice Frankfurter concurred on the ground that it was up to Congress to decide if an emergency existed sufficient to justify suppression of speech.[77]

Justices Black and Douglas dissented, arguing that the convictions were based on pure suppression of speech without any connection to a conspiracy to commit substantive harms.

Following *Dennis*, the government attempted a few more prosecutions for violation of the Smith Act and found essentially that the Court was not so receptive as it was initially. In *Yates v. United States*,[78] Justice Harlan recast the holding of *Dennis*:

> The essence of the *Dennis* holding was that indoctrination of a group in preparation for future violent action, as well as exhortation to immediate action, by advocacy found to be directed to "action for the accomplishment" of forcible overthrow, to violence "as a rule or principle of action," and employing "language of incitement," is not constitutionally protected when the group is of sufficient size and cohesiveness, is sufficiently oriented towards action, and other circumstances are such as reasonable to justify apprehension that action will occur.[79]

Scales v. United States[80] further limited the Smith Act in ways that will be relevant in the cases below, implying that the limitations were required by the First Amendment. The Court held that "active" participation in a group with "guilty knowledge and intent" could be punished but not "merely

---

answer to the fact that there was a group that was ready to make the attempt. The formation by petitioners of such a highly organized conspiracy, with rigidly disciplined members subject to call when the leaders, these petitioners, felt that the time had come for action, coupled with the inflammable nature of world conditions, similar uprisings in other countries, and the touch-and-go nature of our relations with countries with whom petitioners were in the very least ideologically attuned, convince us that their convictions were justified on this score. And this analysis disposes of the contention that a conspiracy to advocate, as distinguished from the advocacy itself, cannot be constitutionally restrained, because it comprises only the preparation. It is the existence of the conspiracy which creates the danger. If the ingredients of the reaction are present, we cannot bind the Government to wait until the catalyst is added.

[76] *Id.* at 572.

[77] *Id.* at 550-51:

It is not for us to decide how we would adjust the clash of interests which this case presents were the primary responsibility for reconciling it ours. Congress has determined that the danger created by advocacy of overthrow justifies the ensuing restriction on freedom of speech. The determination was made after due deliberation, and the seriousness of the congressional purpose is attested by the volume of legislation passed to effectuate the same ends.

[78] 354 U.S. 298 (1957).

[79] *Id.* at 324.

[80] 367 U.S. 203 (1961).

an expression of sympathy with the alleged criminal enterprise, unaccompanied by any significant action in its support or any commitment to undertake such action."[81] The companion case of *Noto v. United States*[82] essentially spelled the end of prosecutions under the Smith Act by insisting that the government prove in each case that the defendant was engaged in current advocacy of violent acts.[83]

McCarthyism died of the weight of its own intolerance and the misdeeds of its namesake.[84] Nevertheless, the "red scare" continued to occupy a central place in the politics of the United States throughout much of the Cold War era despite the lack of prosecutions for criminal advocacy or syndicalism. The Supreme Court then found that it was a threat from another quarter, ironically a home-grown terrorist organization, that would cause it to rethink much of its First Amendment lore.

Brandenburg v. Ohio[85] was a prosecution under the Ohio version of the same criminal syndicalism statute as was involved in *Whitney*, but this time the defendant was a leader of a Ku Klux Klan group. Referring to the Communist cases from *Dennis* to *Scales* and *Noto*, the Court stated:

> These later decisions have fashioned the principle that the constitutional guarantees of free speech and free press do not permit a State to forbid or proscribe advocacy of the use of force or of law violation except where such advocacy is directed to inciting or producing imminent lawless action and is likely to incite or produce such actions. A statute which fails to draw this distinction impermissibly intrudes upon the freedoms guaranteed by the First and Fourteenth Amendments. It sweeps within its condemnation speech which our Constitution has immunized from governmental control.[86]

Whitney was overruled. *Brandenburg* then became the sole referent needed for invalidating statutes that purported to punish advocacy as opposed to a conspiracy to commit a criminal act. But what about the person who belongs to an organization which has members who are committing or have committed proscribable acts? Even prior to *Brandenburg*, the Court had recognized a First Amendment claim of association based on the right of peaceable assembly. *NAACP v. Alabama ex rel. Patterson*[87] unanimously declared that the state could not seek membership lists because disclosure would negatively impact the right of association. Through the 1980s and

---

[81] *Id.* at 228.

[82] 367 U.S. 290 (1961).

[83] *Id.* at 298. Justice Harlan concluded that "there is no evidence that such acts of sabotage were presently advocated; and it is *present* advocacy, and not an intent to advocate in the future or a conspiracy to advocate in the future once a groundwork has been laid, which is an element of the crime under the membership clause."

[84] Senator McCarthy was censured by the Senate in 1954 and died in 1957.

[85] 395 U.S. 444 (1969).

[86] *Id.* at 447-48.

[87] 357 U.S. 449 (1958).

1990s, the Court elaborated on the right of association in a number of situations dealing with regulation of political parties and the electoral process.[88] The scope of constitutional protection for election campaign giving, campaign reforms, and the like are all beyond the scope of the discussion here, but it is safe to say that the right of association is now firmly entrenched in the First Amendment.

The final case in this sequence deals with a state attempt to impose liability on the organization and some of its members on the basis of wrongful acts by a few. *NAACP v. Claiborne Hardware*[89] is cited frequently in the cases below on material support of terrorism. The Court overturned a state court judgment against the NAACP on behalf of merchants who had been damaged by a boycott of their businesses. Although some aspects of the boycott may have been unlawful, neither the organization nor its members could be held liable without a showing of direct participation in the unlawful activity. "Civil liability may not be imposed merely because an individual belonged to a group, some members of which committed acts of violence. For liability to be imposed by reason of association alone, it is necessary to establish that the group itself possessed unlawful goals and that the individual held a specific intent to further those illegal goals."[90]

§ 4.03   HOW IMMINENT IS IMMINENT?

[A]   U.S. — Threats and Incitements

The *al-Timimi* case unquestionably pushes the envelope of incitement law because his speech was several steps removed from actual violence.

In the Holmes formulation, speech can be punished only if there is a "clear and imminent danger that it will bring about forthwith certain substantive evils that the United States constitutionally may seek to prevent." The

---

[88] Buckley v. Valeo, 424 U.S. 1 (1976), dealt with the validity of the Federal Election Campaign Act of 1971. Among other things, FECA limited individual contributions to federal campaigns and attempted to limit campaign expenditures by individuals or groups, as well as expenditures by candidates themselves. The Supreme Court started with the proposition that all these activities carried First Amendment protection as part of the political process and under the right of association. "In a republic where the people are sovereign, the ability of the citizenry to make informed choices among candidates for office is essential. The expenditure limitations were struck down on that basis. With regard to the contribution limitations, the Court found that the claim of freedom of expression was lessened: "A contribution serves as a general expression of support for the candidate and his views, but does not communicate the underlying basis for the support." The Court went on to hold that, although the contribution limits "impinge on protected associational freedoms," they were warranted by a "sufficiently important interest" in "limit[ing] the actuality and appearance of corruption resulting from large individual financial contributions." These basic propositions were revalidated in *McConnell v. FEC*, 540 U.S. 93 (2003), while also recognizing that some expenditures could actually be counted as contributions toward a particular campaign when the expenditures were closely coordinated with the campaign itself.

[89] 458 U.S. 886 (1982).

[90] *Id.* at 920.

Brandeis gloss added that "there must be reasonable ground to fear that serious evil will result if free speech is practiced" and that "enactment of the statute cannot alone establish the facts which are essential to its validity." If Congress can "constitutionally seek to prevent" activity that is precursor to a physical harm, then incitement to the precursor behavior would literally fit within the Holmes formulation. But in the Brandeis formulation, the precursor activity would have to be itself a "serious evil" because Congress could not "establish the facts" by mere "enactment of the statute" (i.e., could not criminalize incitement to a precursor offense).

More recently, the Supreme Court has added the category of "true threats" to the proscribable area. In *Virginia v. Black*,[91] allowing criminalization of cross-burning "with intent to intimidate," the Court explained its view of threats and intimidation this way:

> "True threats" encompass those statements where the speaker means to communicate a serious expression of an intent to commit an act of unlawful violence to a particular individual or group of individuals. The speaker need not actually intend to carry out the threat. Rather, a prohibition on true threats "protects individuals from the fear of violence" and "from the disruption that fear engenders," in addition to protecting people "from the possibility that the threatened violence will occur." Intimidation in the constitutionally proscribable sense of the word is a type of true threat, where a speaker directs a threat to a person or group of persons with the intent of placing the victim in fear of bodily harm or death.[92]

By itself, *Black* might not appear to have much impact on speech such as *al-Timimi*'s because he did not himself communicate a threat to anyone. *Black* may have a significant impact, however, in its recognition that fear is a harm that government is permitted to deter and its statement that the speaker may not intend to carry out the threat but could still be responsible for "the possibility that the threatened violence will occur" (presumably by someone other than the speaker).

[B]　International Standards of Incitement

Black has been read in a rather expansive fashion in an important decision from the International Criminal Tribunal for Rwanda. The ICTR dealt with the crime of "incitement to genocide" in its *Nahimana* judgment.[93] The two directors of the national radio and television along with the publisher of a newspaper were charged with genocide, incitement to genocide, conspiracy to commit genocide, and complicity in genocide. The broadcasts and publications on which the charges were based extended so far as publication of the names of Tutsis along with messages that implied if not stated that it would be desirable to "exterminate" the enemies.

---

[91] 538 U.S. 343 (2003).

[92] *Id.* at 359-60.

[93] Prosecutor v. Nahimana, ICTR-99-52-T (2003).

The incitement charge prompted the most elaborate legal analysis. The genocide and complicity charges could be approached with reasonably traditional notions of *mens rea* and *actus reus* in the commission of completed crimes. Conspiracy, of course, is an inchoate crime that would need evidence of at least a tacit agreement. But incitement runs directly into norms protecting freedom of expression, norms that now find explicit recognition as rights in international conventions and customary law. The Tribunal framed its task as "assessment of criminal accountability for direct and public incitement to genocide, in light of the fundamental right of freedom of expression."[94]

International declarations and conventions include promises of both freedom of expression and protection from discrimination.[95] As the Tribunal saw it, these are "two fundamental rights, which in certain contexts may be seen to conflict, requiring some mediation."[96] The International Covenant on Civil and Political Rights requires of signatory nations that "advocacy of national, racial or religious hatred that constitutes incitement to discrimination, hostility or violence shall be prohibited by law."[97] Under an Optional Protocol, a signatory nation may authorize the U.N. Committee on Human Rights to issue advisory opinions in matters brought to the committee by aggrieved individuals. The ICTR referred to several of these cases to illustrate how far the protection against incitement might extend. A Canadian school teacher was disciplined for having "denigrated the faiths and beliefs of Jews,"[98] another Canadian was "precluded from using public telephone services after using them to circulate messages warning of the dangers of international Jewry,"[99] and a French citizen was convicted "for publishing his view doubting the existence of gas chambers for extermination purposes at Auschwitz and other Nazi concentration camps."[100]

The school teacher case might have come out the same way in the U.S. because of the special position of school teachers in educational settings, although it is far from certain.[101] The other two almost certainly would

---

[94] *Id.* at ¶ 980.

[95] *See* Universal Declaration of Human Rights, G.A. Res. 217 A, art. 7, U.N. GAOR, 3d Sess., 1st plen, mtg., U.N. DOC A/810 (Dec. 12, 1948): "[a]ll are entitled to equal protection against any discrimination" and in article 19 that "[e]veryone has the right to freedom of opinion and expression."

[96] *Nahimana, supra* note 93, at ¶ 983.

[97] The United States ratified with this reservation: "That article 20 does not authorize or require legislation or other action by the United States that would restrict the right of free speech and association protected by the Constitution and laws of the United States."

[98] Ross v. Canada, UN Human Rights Comm., Communication No. 763-1997, U.N. DOC. A/56/40 vol. 2 (Oct. 18, 2000).

[99] J.R.T. and the W.G. Party v. Canada, UN Human Rights Comm., Communication No. 104/1981, U.N. DOC. CCPR/C/OP/2 at 25 (1984).

[100] Robert Faurisson v. France, UN Human Rights Comm., Communication No. 550/1993, U.N. DOC. 550/1993, U.N. DOC CCPR/C/58/D/550/1993 (1996).

[101] Although teachers have First Amendment protection for their views on "matters of public concern," the school district would likewise have an interest in protecting its students and the educational environment. As Justice O'Connor explained in *Waters v. Churchill*, 511 U.S.

have triggered First Amendment protection in U.S. courts. Of special interest is the opinion of the Human Rights Committee in the French case to the effect that "restriction on publication of these views . . . was necessary under" the ICCPR. On this view, the government of a signatory nation is not just permitted but required to penalize assertion of views that would almost certainly be protected under U.S. First Amendment law.

The Tribunal also explored decisions of the European Court of Human Rights, acting under the European Covenant on Human Rights. That Court's opinions showed a marked tendency to restrain abusive or discriminatory speech, even just barely overturning the conviction of a Danish journalist who interviewed several youthful members of a racist group without aggressively disavowing the racist views of those interviewed.[102] The Court also upheld the conviction of a Turkish city mayor who stated that he "supported the PKK" while condemning their killing of women and children.[103]

Faced with these sources of law appearing to value nondiscrimination over free expression, the defendants in *Nahimana* urged the Tribunal "that United States law, as the most speech-protective, should be used as a standard, to ensure the universal acceptance and legitimacy of the Tribunal's jurisprudence." The Tribunal's response was twofold: first, that "evolving universal standards" of international law rather than the widely varying standards of domestic law should be its "point of reference;" and second, that even U.S. law would allow prosecution of various forms of expression including some "hate speech" and incitement to violence.[104]

The principal themes of the Tribunal's discussion were "the importance of taking context into account when considering the potential impact of expression," and that protection of minorities is part of the rationale for freedom of expression.

> The dangers of censorship have often been associated in particular with the suppression of political or other minorities, or opposition to the government. . . . The special protections for this kind of speech should accordingly be adapted, in the Chamber's view, so that ethnically specific expression would be more rather than less

---

661, 675 (1994), "The government cannot restrict the speech of the public at large just in the name of efficiency. But where the government is employing someone for the very purpose of effectively achieving its goals, such restrictions may well be appropriate."

[102] Jersild v. Denmark, Eur. Ct. H.R. (ECHR) (22 Aug. 1994).

[103] Zana v. Turkey, ECHR, (25 Nov. 1997).

[104] *Nahimana, supra* note 93, at ¶ 1010:

> The Chamber notes that the jurisprudence of the United States also accepts the fundamental principles set forth in international law and has recognized in its domestic law that incitement to violence, threats, libel, false advertising obscenity, and child pornography are among those forms of expression that fall outside the scope of freedom of speech protection. In *Virginia v. Black* [538 U.S. 343 (2003)], the United States Supreme Court recently interpreted the free speech guarantee of the First Amendment of the Constitution to permit a ban on cross burning with intent to intimidate.

carefully scrutinized to ensure that minorities without equal means of defence are not endangered.[105]

Setting aside for the moment the thought that minorities are entitled to more protection than majorities, this language is still important for the sense that the international community reads U.S. law as allowing the criminalization of hate speech and for the view that a government may be obligated to do so under international law.

The discussion implying that hate speech alone should be criminalized, however, must be read in light of the Tribunal's insistence on "the importance of taking context into account when considering the potential impact of expression." This language takes us back to considering how close is too close. It implies that speech will not be penalized unless it carries a propensity to produce actual violent results, again emphasizing the concept of "imminent" action.

[C]   Other Nations

[1]   United Kingdom[106]

The Terrorism Act of 2000 adopted an approach similar to that of the U.S. in designating certain organizations[107] and criminalizing assistance to those organizations. The 2000 statute applied to those who "belong to," "invites support for," or addresses a meeting of" a proscribed organization. An organization can be proscribed if it is "concerned in terrorism."[108] The British system allows a proscribed organization to petition for delisting and provides for review by a Proscribed Organizations Appeal Commission. A very interesting feature of the system is its periodic review of terrorism measures by an independent member of the House of Lords.[109]

The Terrorism Act of 2006[110] added provisions prohibiting "encouragement of terrorism," "distribution of terrorist publications," and "training for

---

[105] *Id.* at ¶ 1008.

[106] *See generally* CLIVE WALKER, BLACKSTONE'S GUIDE TO THE ANTI-TERRORISM LEISLATION (2002).

[107] There are currently 44 groups listed by the Home Secretary, see *www.homeoffice.gov.uk / security / terrorism-and-the-law / terrorism-act / proscribed-groups.* Schedule 2 of the 2000 Act originally designated 14 organizations that operated in Northern Ireland. The Home Secretary immediately added 21 more, most of which were Islamist militant groups.

[108] Terrorism Act of 2000, § 3(5):

[A]n organisation is concerned in terrorism if it—

(a) commits or participates in acts of terrorism,

(b) prepares for terrorism,

(c) promotes or encourages terrorism, or

(d) is otherwise concerned in terrorism.

[109] *See* Home Office, *Checks on Terrorism Laws,* *available at* www.homeoffice.gov.uk/ security/terrorism-and-the-law/checks-on-laws2/.

[110] *See* Office of Public Safety Information, *Terrorism Act of 2006,* *available at* www.opsi.gov.uk/acts/acts2006/20060011.htm.

terrorism." Encouraging is criminal if the speaker "intends" or "is reckless" in relation to "inducing" another to "commit, prepare, or instigate" an act of terrorism. A statement is criminal if it is "likely to be understood by some or all of the members of the public to whom it is published as a direct or indirect encouragement or other inducement to them to the commission, preparation or instigation of acts of terrorism." Statements are conclusively within the proscription if they "glorify acts of terrorism" or if a reasonable person would understand that terrorism is "being glorified as conduct that should be emulated by them in existing circumstances."

The British prosecution pushing the furthest into advocacy and speech was that of Abu Hamza al-Masri, the Imam of a very radical North London mosque who has also been indicted in the U.S. on material support charges and is wanted in Yemen on charges related to attacks on tourists there in 2004. Al-Masri was convicted on six counts of soliciting murder and two counts of "using threatening, abusive or insulting words or behaviour with the intention of stirring up racial hatred." The solicitation counts sound as if they related to specific acts of violence but in fact the prosecution identified no specific targets of violence and the charges depended completely on general incitement principles.[111] The racial hatred counts would be difficult to sustain in the U.S. despite the recognition in *Virginia v. Black* that threats may lie outside the protection of the First Amendment.

The rants of al-Masri were very much like those of al-Timimi, who was convicted in the U.S. of "inducing others to conspire to aid the Taliban" among other inducement charges. Both of these cases push the envelope of incitement law. The al-Timimi prosecution was made easier by the fact that two people in his audience in fact traveled to Afghanistan to join Taliban forces. Similarly, al-Masri's mosque produced Richard Reid, the shoe-bomber, and Zacarias Moussaoui, the alleged 20th hijacker. Without actual attempts at violence by some members of the speaker's audience, it is highly doubtful that an incitement prosecution could stand.

[2] Germany

The Bundesrepublik Deutschland is a federation of 16 states (*Länder*) with a structure similar to that of the U.S. The national government has exclusive responsibility for defense, foreign affairs, immigration, transportation, communications, and currency standards.[112]

Traditional wisdom in the U.S. has been that continental legal systems do not contain the concept of "conspiracy" as it exists in the Anglo-American system. The German law on "attempt to participate," however, is virtually

---

[111] *Cleric Convicted of Stirring Hate*, N.Y. TIMES, Feb. 8, 2006.

[112] The federal and Land governments have concurrent authority in a number of areas such as land management and public health. Library of Congress, Country Studies, Germany, see lcweb2.loc.gov/frd/cs/detoc.html#de0122.

the same as Anglo conspiracy law in punishing one who "agrees with another to commit or incite the commission of a serious criminal offense."[113]

Section 129 of the German Penal Code states that "whoever forms an organization, the objectives or activity of which are directed towards the commission of crimes, or whoever participates in such an organization as a member, recruits for it or supports it" is guilty of a crime.[114] This provision is much broader than RICO, its counterpart in U.S. law, which only criminalizes the use of money acquired by racketeering means.[115]

Section 129a is the German counterpart to U.S. material support statutes. It is labeled "Formation of Terrorist Organization" and describes an "organization, the objectives or activity of which are directed towards the commission of . . . murder, manslaughter or genocide" or other specified crimes of violence. Whoever forms, recruits for, or supports such an organization is guilty of a crime.

In contrast to the U.S. and British provisions, the German system does not contemplate designation of proscribed organizations. Therefore, the prosecution will have to prove in any individual case that the defendant was providing support to an organization with the proscribed objectives. It might seem that this leaves prosecutors subject to the varying whims of different fact-finders, but remember that the German system does not use juries but panels of judges. So long as the judges bring similar backgrounds to bear on cases and are aware of rulings by their colleagues, there should be little risk of conflicting rulings on terrorist organizations.

[3] Netherlands

The Netherlands has been particularly assertive in dealing with terrorism. According to the Ministry of Interior, "recruiting for the jihad is now an offence, (activities of) terrorist organizations may be prohibited and information of the General Intelligence and Security Service may be used in criminal cases."[116] The Crimes of Terrorism Act criminalizes conspiracy to commit a terrorist crime, recruiting for an armed struggle, and

---

[113] German Penal Code Section 30. Attempted Participation

   (1) Whoever attempts to induce or incite another to commit a serious criminal offense shall be punished according to the provisions governing serious criminal offense attempt. However the punishment shall be mitigated pursuant to Section 49 subsection (1). Section 23 subsection (3) shall apply accordingly.

   (2) Whoever declares his willingness, whoever accepts the offer of another, or whoever agrees with another to commit or incite the commission of a serious criminal offense, shall be similarly punished.

[114] A rather amusing aspect of the statute is that it exempts "a political party, which the Federal Constitutional Court has not declared to be unconstitutional." *See* http://www.iuscomp.org/gla/statutes/stgb.htm#129.

[115] Racketeer Influenced and Corrupt Organizations, 18 U.S.C. § 1962 (2006).

[116] *See* Ministerie van Binnenlandse Zaken en Konikrijksrelaties, *Public Safety*, *available at* www.minbzk.nl/bzk2006uk/subjects/public-safety/fight_against.

participating in an organisation with the objective of committing terrorist crimes.[117]

The National Coordinator for CounterTerrorism (NCTb) coordinates the efforts of the police and intelligence services while providing policy analysis.[118] The NCTb is housed within the Ministry of Justice, which gives it some opportunity to interact with the prosecutor services. The Dutch, however, maintain a strict wall of separation between intelligence and law enforcement, which insulates the prosecution from knowledge of classified information that the intelligence agencies want to keep from defendants.

[4] France

French Penal Code § 421-1 contains a list of violent acts and possession of proscribed weapons which become "terrorist acts" when "the purpose of which is seriously to disturb public order through intimidation or terror." The Code goes on to provide that "participation in any group formed or association established with a view to the preparation, marked by one or more material actions, of any of the acts of terrorism provided for under the previous articles shall in addition be an act of terrorism."[119] Another very interesting provision is one that criminalizes "being unable to account for resources corresponding to one's lifestyle when habitually in close contact with a person or persons who engage in one or more of the activities" listed as a terrorist act.[120]

[5] Australia

Australia provides that an organization may be deemed to be a terrorist organization either from listing by regulation of the Attorney General or by adjudication that it meets the statutory definition.[121] An organization can be listed if it is planning or fostering a terrorist act regardless of whether a terrorist act occurs.[122]

---

[117] *See* National Coordinator for Counterterrorism, *Legislation*, *available at* english.nctb.nl/Preventing_terrorism/Legislation/Nationaal/Crimes_of_terrorism_act.asp.

[118] *Id.* About the NCTB, english.nctb.nl/about_the_nctb/.

[119] French Penal Code § 421-2-1.

[120] France Penal Code § 421-2-3.

[121] The Australian Government has a single website devoted to counterterrorism. *See* www.nationalsecurity.gov.au/agd/www/nationalsecurity.nsf/AllDocs/95FB057CA3DECF30CA256FAB001F7FBD?OpenDocument.

[122] Australian Criminal Code of 1995 § 102.1:

terrorist organisation means:

  (a) an organisation that is directly or indirectly engaged in, preparing, planning, assisting in or fostering the doing of a terrorist act (whether or not the terrorist act occurs); or

  (c) an organisation that is specified by the regulations for the purposes of this paragraph.

www.comlaw.gov.au/comlaw/Legislation/Act1.nsf/framelodgmentattachments/411BBAB62B4D9F0BCA25722D0007253C.

§ 4.04 CONCLUSION

Islamist terrorism presents a culture clash between religious fundamentalism and the rest of the world. One view of the clash is that it is a battle between a peculiarly Arab perversion of Islam and the West. Another view is that it is a clash between the descendants of colonial regimes and their perceived oppressors. Whatever the sources and dimensions of the clash, it is a violent pattern that will play itself out over the next few decades at the same time that international tribunals are attempting to implement values of freedom embodied in human rights documents and conventions.

To some degree, the human rights values of emerging international law are articulated from Western heritage. But the international community promotes those values as universal, and indeed it should be possible to find at least some variation of those values in every society. It just happens that it is from Western sources that the written form of those principles has been drawn.

By these values, whether Western or universal, when does a person commit a crime by urging action in pursuit of his or her side of a culture clash? Western liberalism has struggled for centuries with trying to forestall violent or other harmful conduct while permitting maximum play of individual freedom. This tension is inherent in attempts to penalize inchoate crime. Limits on conspiracy law can be found in the due process notion that a person is not to be punished for thoughts without producing an actual threat. Limits on precursor crimes such as incitement or material support can be found in the related values of free expression. All of these values point to the same difficulty: a person is responsible for "incitement to imminent lawless action." No better phrasing of the test has yet been suggested.

If imminence remains the touchstone for First Amendment protection, then it is important to be clear about who decides this critical fact question. First Amendment law frequently relies on "constitutional facts" such as whether allegedly obscene material contains serious value. With a fact of this character, language can go only so far in delineating the precise criteria for decision. Ultimately, the fact-finder must decide with very little guidance other than what has gone before or how society should be ordered. Under these circumstances, perhaps the best we can say is that the government bears the burden of proof and that both judge and jury must be convinced. The fact of imminence will be determined by judges and juries with whatever individual and community values they can bring to bear on this critical factual question. The jury must be persuaded beyond a reasonable doubt (using whatever personal or community values the jurors bring to a fact question) while the judge must be persuaded that First Amendment values are not transgressed.

Chapter 5

MATERIAL SUPPORT OF TERRORISM

The United States now has a series of statutes that make it an offense to provide material support for terrorist activity[1] or to an organization designated by the Secretary of State as a terrorist organization.[2] "Material support" is defined in the statutes in a manner that focuses sufficiently on concrete goods and services that the First Amendment's protection of speech and press should not be directly implicated. The most problematic elements of the definition are provision of financial services, lodging, or training, each of which could be a service connected in some degree with a group committed to violence but undertaken without specific intent to assist in a specific act of violence.

The statutes appear to require specific knowledge or intent and should not be used to reach so far down the chain of service providers as to sweep in people who were mere sympathizers of the group. But there is always the prospect of coupling the "material support" statute with a general conspiracy charge so as to reach further down the chain of causation, thus posing some indirect threat to rights of association. A "conspiracy to provide material support" charge stretches the limits, but it is not out of the realm of possibility.[3]

What must the government prove to make out a conspiracy case while avoiding impact on the freedom of association? Providing material support

---

[1] 18 U.S.C. § 2339A (2007).

[2] 18 U.S.C. § 2339B (2007).

[3] *See* Eric Lichtblau, *Statute Becomes Justice Department's Weapon of Choice*, N.Y. TIMES, Apr. 6, 2003, *available at* http://select.nytimes.com/search/restricted/article?res = F40610FC39C0C758CDDAD0894DB404482.

"knowing or intending that they are to be used in preparation for, or in carrying out, a violation of" a specified statute (§ 2339A) differs from providing material support to a "foreign terrorist organization" designated by the Secretary of State (§ 2339B).[4] The designation places everyone on notice that mere support of this organization is unlawful, but does that really change the impact on the right of association? In other words, does the Constitution require knowledge of imminent violent or fraudulent behavior before we can punish support of an organization?

In the climate of Islamist fundamentalism and its relation to terrorist organizations, it is worth pointing out that Shari'ah mandates that Muslims practice the giving of alms, known as "zakat." Zakat is to be calculated not on the basis of income, as is tithing in most Christian denominations, but instead on the basis of accumulated wealth. It is usually calculated at 2.5% per year of cash, jewelry, and similar assets over a minimum value.[5] The effect of zakat practiced around the world is to generate billions of dollars per year for charitable purposes. The giving of money to groups that represent their objectives to be humanitarian aid therefore becomes a hot-button issue in the tracking of Islamist fundamentalist groups.

The courts struggled initially to resolve some of the conflict between First Amendment values and public safety interests represented in the material support statutes. The pattern has been similar to patterns that have been observable in other times of crisis. The first Supreme Court pronouncements with respect to freedom of speech under the First Amendment did not occur until World War I when the federal government encountered significant resistance to the war effort. From the first prosecutions under the Espionage Act through the communist conspiracy cases of the 1940s and 1950s, the emphasis was on criminalization of speech that could threaten interests unique to the government itself. It was not until prosecution of KKK members in the 1960s that the Court faced a First Amendment challenge to a governmental regulation designed to protect interests among individual citizens. From that point on, the Supreme Court was asked to delineate the point at which protected advocacy could be distinguished from proscribable conspiracy.

Similarly, with the worldwide attention paid to terrorism after the 1972 Olympic tragedy, governments began attempting to define criminal conduct that would allow intervention before a violent act could occur. Over the last 30 years, law enforcement has shifted attention from punishment to prevention.

§ 5.01 MATERIAL SUPPORT AND ASSOCIATION

Material support prosecutions raise constitutional issues of the right of association, vagueness and overbreadth of the statutes, and due process regarding the methods for designation of foreign terrorist organizations.

---

[4] 18 U.S.C. §§ 2339A, 2339B (2005).

[5] For A succinct description of the practice and calculations, see ISLAMICITY, *Zakat, available at* www.islamicity.com/mosque/Zakat/ (last visited July 20, 2007).

[A] Prohibiting Material Support

There are basically two statutory schemes for prohibiting material support to terrorists or terrorist organizations. One is the IEEPA system which has been administered by the Treasury Department's Office of Foreign Asset Control (OFAC) and which was the basis for Lindh's guilty plea for providing assistance to the Taliban regime. The other is the "§ 2339B" system sometimes known for its genesis in the Antiterrorism and Effective Death Penalty Act of 1996 (AEDPA).

In the IEEPA system, the President may name an entity a Specially Designated Terrorist (SDT) and subject it to the same embargo restrictions as a nation-state that has been deemed a threat to U.S. national security. Those restrictions are enforced by 50 U.S.C. § 1705, which makes it a crime to "violate, any license, order, or regulation issued under this title." IEEPA provides extreme flexibility to issue regulations prohibiting a variety of transactions with foreign states or organizations.

In the AEDPA system, the State Department may designate a group as a Foreign Terrorist Organizations (FTO) "if the Secretary finds that (A) the organization is a foreign organization; (B) the organization engages in terrorist activity . . .; and (C) the terrorist activity of the organization threatens the security of United States nationals or the national security of the United States."[6] Under 18 U.S.C. § 2339B, it is a crime to "knowingly provide material support" to a designated FTO; material support is defined to include a wide array of money, goods, or services. Prior to December 21, 2004, the list of support items included "training" and "personnel,"[7] which gave rise to questions similar to those in *Whitney* and *Noto* about the level of involvement that might be protected by the right of association, questions about vagueness for due process purposes, and even the possibility of unconstitutional vicarious liability similar to the *Claiborne Hardware* problem.

Humanitarian Law Project v. Reno[8] was a direct challenge to § 2339B and the designation system by persons who wanted to assist "only the nonviolent humanitarian and political activities of the Kurdistan Workers' Party ("PKK") and the Liberation Tigers of Tamil Eelam ("LTTE"). The

---

[6] 8 U.S.C. § 1189(a)(1) (2007).

[7] The prior version read:

> In this section, the term "material support or resources" means currency or other financial securities, financial services, lodging, training, safehouses, false documentation or identification, communications equipment, facilities, weapons, lethal substances, explosives, personnel, transportation, and other physical assets, except medicine or religious materials.

18 U.S.C. § 2339B (2004).

[8] 205 F.3d 1130 (9th Cir. 2000) (*HLP II*). In my casebook, Legal Responses to Terrorism (Matthew Bender 2005), I adopted a numbering system for these cases based on only the court of appeals decisions. Although the Ninth Circuit numbered them differently, other courts used the same numbering system that I adopted. But now in hopes of easing the confusion, I am recanting and adopting the Ninth Circuit's numbering system. My apologies to students who will have to work with different numbers in the casebook for a while.

challenge came in three parts. First, they contended that they were fearful that they could be prosecuted under § 2339B and sought the protection of *Claiborne Hardware*'s statement that "for liability to be imposed by reason of association alone, it is necessary to establish that the group itself possessed unlawful goals and that the individual held a specific intent to further those illegal aims." Second, the claimed that the designation process violated due process norms and intruded on the right of association. Third, they claimed that some of the "material support" provisions were unconstitutionally vague.

These three arguments run throughout a series of cases involving the material support statutes: (1) that support for political or humanitarian activities of the organization is protected regardless of the other activities of the organization, (2) that a contributor should be able to challenge the designation of the organization on due process grounds, and (3) that some of the items listed as material support are unconstitutionally vague. Although the latter two do not depend directly on associational interests of the contributor, the three arguments became blurred and confused when the government argued before the Ninth Circuit in a later appeal that the statutes did not contain a specific intent requirement and would be satisfied when a contributor knew that he or she was giving money regardless of any knowledge about the nature of the organization.[9] How this line of cases developed and Congress' modification of the statutes to meet the problem will be instructive for future prosecutions and regulatory measures. The questions in these cases harken back to the "driving with an open container of alcohol in the car" scenario — how far from the substantive harm can government reach before intruding on socially useful behavior?

The Ninth Circuit answered the association claim by pointing out that the contributor would not be punished "by reason of association alone" but for the furnishing of goods and services that could be used in support of terrorist activities. "What AEDPA prohibits is the act of giving material support, and there is no constitutional right to facilitate terrorism by giving terrorists the weapons and explosives with which to carry out their grisly missions. Nor, of course, is there a right to provide resources with which terrorists can buy weapons and explosives."[10]

The plaintiffs asserted that they should be able to contribute to the political and humanitarian aspects of an FTO by comparing these contributions to the expressive interests of campaign contributions recognized in cases such as *Buckley v. Valeo*.[11] *Buckley*, however, also recognized that money is more than just expression and can be regulated for its nonexpressive component so long as the control is no more than necessary to carry out an important governmental objective.[12] This leads to the critical issue with

---

[9] 352 F.3d 382 (9th Cir. 2003) (*HLP III*).

[10] *HLP II*, 205 F.3d at 1133.

[11] 424 U.S. 1 (1976).

[12] *Id.* at 21.

the material support statutes: can a contributor earmark funds for political or other nonviolent uses and claim First Amendment protection? The argument from *Brandenburg* and *Claiborne Hardware* is that a person's affiliation with, and support of, a subversive organization can be penalized only if the supporter has a "specific intent to further [the] illegal aims" of the organization.[13]

The Ninth Circuit agreed with the government's argument that "money is fungible; giving support intended to aid an organization's peaceful activities frees up resources that can be used for terrorist acts."[14] This holding is critical to further developments, although there are still the other two arguments to track before we come back to the *mens rea* problem.

With regard to the due process claim, the Ninth Circuit answered that the Secretary of State's decision would be based on the organization's activities ("terrorist acts" as defined in the statute) and that the decision was subject to judicial review in the United States Court of Appeals for the District of Columbia Circuit. "Although plaintiffs complain that the review is ineffectual because of the degree of deference accorded to the Secretary's decision, that is a necessary concomitant of the foreign affairs power. In any event, that challenge must be raised in an appeal from a decision to designate a particular organization."[15] This argument will come up again in the later sequence of cases.

The third set of arguments did produce a partial victory for the plaintiffs. The court found that two of the items of material support were vague in the context of the First Amendment interests asserted by supporters. "Training" and "personnel" both could be read to include the provision of political activities, such as providing one's own person to train other members of the group in effective advocacy. Because there is an expressive component to these activities, a prohibition would need to be especially clear, remembering that "advocacy is pure speech protected by the First Amendment. In order to keep the statute from trenching on such advocacy, the government urges that we read into it a requirement that the activity prohibited be performed 'under the direction or control' of the foreign terrorist organization." The court responded that the government position amounted to rewriting the statute, a job for Congress rather than the judiciary.[16]

On remand, the district court entered a permanent injunction against enforcement of the "personnel" and "training" provisions.[17] The case returned to the Ninth Circuit as *HLP III*.[18] First, the Government argued

---

[13] American-Arab Anti-Discrimination Comm. v. Reno, 70 F.3d 1045 (9th Cir. 1995).

[14] *HLP II*, 205 F.3d at 1136.

[15] *Id.* at 1137.

[16] *Id.* at 1138.

[17] 2001 U.S. Dist. LEXIS 16729 (N.D. Cal. 2001).

[18] 352 F.3d 382 (9th Cir. 2003) (see explanation of numbering at note 8 *supra*).

against the permanent injunction on vagueness but the Ninth Circuit held that those issues were foreclosed by its prior opinion.[19]

In *HLP III*, additional arguments were presented by both the plaintiffs and the government. HLP added an argument that due process would not allow conviction of its supporters without a showing of intent to further unlawful purposes, to which we will return below.

The government's additional argument was that "it could convict a person under § 2339B if he or she donates support to a designated organization *even if he or she does not know the organization is so designated.*"[20] The court answered that "to attribute the intent to commit unlawful acts punishable by life imprisonment to persons who acted with innocent intent — in this context, without critical information about the relevant organization — contravenes the Fifth Amendment's requirement of 'personal guilt.' "[21]

The court discussed *Scales*, *Yates*, and *Noto*, concluding that these cases stood for the proposition that punishing mere support of an organization without intent to promote its unlawful purposes would violate due process. The question then became whether to construe the statute as the government wished and then declare it unconstitutional or to construe the statue so that the word "knowingly" referred to the designation or unlawful activities of the organization. The court thought the latter construction was supported not only by the text but by the legislative history.[22] Of importance to the later cases, the Ninth Circuit considered that the *mens rea* requirement, knowledge of either the designation or the unlawful activities, was necessary to prevent penalization of innocent contributions to organizations that purport to provide such services as support for orphans or refugees in areas of civil unrest such as Kurdish or Tamil regions.

[B] Vagueness of "Training" and "Personnel"

There are three related arguments in the material support cases, the association claim, the designation claim, and the vagueness claim. Taking the latter first, what did John Walker Lindh provide to the Taliban? "personnel" in the form of himself? "Training" in the sense that he received training? The Statement of Facts in the *Lindh* case recited that he "willfully and unlawfully supplied and attempted to supply services to the Taliban."

---

[19] *Id.* at 393.

[20] *Id.* at 397 (emphasis added).

[21] *Id.*

[22] *Id.* at 402:

> In introducing the Senate Conference Report to the Senate, Senator Hatch stated: "this bill also includes provisions making it a crime to *knowingly provide material support to the terrorist functions* of foreign groups designated by a Presidential finding to be engaged in terrorist activities. I am convinced we have crafted a narrow but effective designation provision which meets these obligations while safeguarding the freedom to associate, which none of us would willingly give up." 142 CONG. REC. S3354 (daily ed. Apr. 16, 1996) (statement of Sen. Hatch) (*emphasis added*).

In responding to the defendant's motion to dismiss the indictment, the *Lindh* court stated:

> the plain meaning of "personnel" is such that it requires, in the context of Section 2339B, an employment or employment-like relationship between the persons in question and the terrorist organization. The Ninth Circuit's vagueness holding in *Humanitarian Law Project* is neither persuasive nor controlling. The term is aimed at denying the provision of human resources to proscribed terrorist organizations, and not at the mere independent advocacy of an organization's interests or agenda. Thus, the term "personnel" in Section 2339B gives fair notice to the public of what is prohibited and the provision is therefore not unconstitutionally vague.[23]

According to CNN,

> Three members of what government prosecutors called a "Virginia jihad network" were sentenced [to] 11 1/2 years each for travelling to Pakistan and seeking military training at a terrorist training camp. U.S. District Judge Leonie Brinkema rejected a government argument for stiffer sentences for both men. The judge said that she disagreed that their effort to obtain training constituted providing military services, as the prosecution contended. She said they were "absorbing resources, not providing them." She noted they gave no money or other materials to the cause.[24]

If the defendants were "absorbing resources, not providing them," then of what were they guilty? Apparently, they intended to fight with the Taliban against U.S. forces but were captured before they got the chance.

In *United States v. Khan*,[25] Judge Brinkema dealt with some of the remaining defendants who had gone to trial after the guilty plea above. She found that training could be a violation of the material support statute under active circumstances. The charges in *Khan* included provision of material support on the basis of supplying personnel who received training. Noting the *HLP II* holding, the court pointed out that the government had since interpreted the statute to apply only when the training went toward supplying personnel who would act on behalf of the organization in a directed capacity.

> The conspiracy alleged in Count 5 was not to provide "personnel" who would speak on behalf of LET, or provide moral support, or simply receive training, but to provide personnel who, after receiving training, would serve that organization as soldiers, recruiters, and procurers of supplies. Indeed, the evidence shows that the conspirators did much more than just receive training from LET

---

[23] United States v. Lindh, 212 F. Supp. 2d 541, 574 (E.D. Va. 2002).

[24] Terry Frieden, *Three sentenced in Virginia "Jihad" Case*, CNN.com, Nov. 7, 2003, *available at* www.cnn.com/2003/LAW/11/07/virginia.jihad.

[25] 309 F. Supp. 2d 789 (E.D. Va. 2004).

— they returned to the United States, recruited co-conspirators, and purchased technology for LET to use in its attacks on India.[26]

In recently enacted 18 U.S.C. § 2339D, Congress has now specifically criminalized the receipt of training from a designated terrorist organization. This solves the vagueness problem, but it would give rise to a more direct First Amendment association problem if it could include training in the provision of humanitarian relief or in political advocacy. The new statute specifically applies only to "military-type training" defined to mean instruction in the means of lethal force.[27] Moreover, the new statute also addresses the *mens rea* issue by limiting prosecutions to those who know of the designation or the illegal aims of the organization.[28]

In the final act of the "Virginia Jihad" sequence, as described in the opening paragraph of this article, al-Timimi was convicted of inducing others to conspire to aid the Taliban. Did he incite anyone to "imminent lawless action?" If his words contributed to others' decisions to receive military-style training, then surely he did. But the "lawless action" itself was an inchoate crime (a conspiracy) to commit a precursor crime (material support), thus at least two steps removed from physical violence. He essentially has been convicted of incitement to conspire. This raises the question of "how imminent is imminent," or how close the incitement must be to actions negatively impacting victims, and will be the subject of the concluding section of this article.

One more vagueness challenge is worth noting. Sheikh Rahman's lawyer and their interpreter were charged with violating prison regulations and also violating § 2339B by using their consultations with the Sheikh to pass messages to and from the Islamic Group.[29] They moved to dismiss the indictment for many of the same reasons covered by the Ninth Circuit in *HLP*. Specifically, they challenged the portion of the statute that prohibits provision of "communication devices" and the court agreed that their use of telephones could not be the basis of a criminal charge. "[B]y criminalizing the mere use of phones and other means of communication the statute provides neither notice nor standards for its application such that it is unconstitutionally vague as applied."

---

[26] *Id.* at 823.

[27] 18 U.S.C. § 2339D(c)(1) (2005):

[t]he term "military-type training" includes training in means or methods that can cause death or serious bodily injury, destroy or damage property, or disrupt services to critical infrastructure, or training on the use, storage, production, or assembly of any explosive, firearm or other weapon, including any weapon of mass destruction.

[28] 18 U.S.C. § 2339D(a):

To violate this subsection, a person must have knowledge that the organization is a designated terrorist organization, that the organization has engaged or engages in terrorist activity, or that the organization has engaged or engages in terrorism.

[29] United States v. Sattar, 272 F. Supp. 2d 348 (S.D.N.Y. 2003).

[C] The Designation Process

There are two somewhat separate due process claims with respect to the procedures and criteria for designation of foreign terrorist organizations. First is the organization's claim that it is entitled to a fair administrative hearing and to judicial review to be sure that the criteria are properly applied. Second is the claim of the individual contributor who wants to challenge the designation when prosecuted for providing material support. The second is the easier with which to deal and sets up a basis for understanding the due process claims of the organizations.

The individual at first glance appears to have a strong argument. She is being prosecuted for a criminal offense that can lead to life imprisonment, so it seems sensible that she be entitled to challenge each element of the offense. But her claim that the designation was improper does not attack an element of the offense. The defendants in *United States v. Afshari*[30] had persuaded the district court[31] that the procedures by which the designation of MEK[32] had been accomplished were unconstitutional. The district court dismissed the indictment and the government appealed. Without using the language of standing, the Ninth Circuit agreed with the government that the defendants could not "collaterally attack" the designation. Analogizing to a controlled substance offense, the court pointed out that "showing that the drug possessed by the individual defendant has a detrimental effect on the general welfare [is not] an element of the offense."[33]

The collateral attack language came into play in *Afshari* because the defendants attempted to rely on cases challenging prior proceedings when used as a predicate for a new offense. One case involved a charge of firearm possession by a convicted felon[34] and the other was a prosecution for illegal reentry by a prior deportee.[35] In the weapons case, the defendant asserted that the prior conviction was secured in violation of his right to counsel, but the Supreme Court held that he was not allowed to challenge the conviction in the context of the weapons charge because he could have challenged it prior to taking possession of the weapon. The *Afshari* defendants pointed out that they were not allowed by statute to challenge the FTO designation earlier and thus should be allowed to challenge it when prosecuted. To this, the Ninth Circuit responded that the MEK had ample opportunity to obtain judicial review of the designation and in fact had done so. This answer is not completely satisfactory, although the result is appropriate. A more complete answer would be to complete the analogy to

---

[30] 392 F.3d 1031 (9th Cir. 2004).

[31] United States v. Rahmani, 209 F. Supp. 2d 1045 (C.D. Cal. 2002).

[32] MEK (Mujahedin-e Khalq) is another name used by the People's Mojahedin Organization of Iran (PMOI). *See* § 5.02 *infra*.

[33] *Afshari*, 392 F.3d at 1037 (quoting Spawr Optical Research v. Baldrige, 649 F. Supp. 1366, 1372 n.10 (D.D.C. 1986)). *See also* United States v. Hammoud, 381 F.3d 316, 331 (4th Cir. 2004).

[34] Lewis v. United States, 445 U.S. 55 (1980).

[35] United States v. Mendoza-Lopez, 481 U.S. 828 (1987).

the weapons case by pointing out that the defendants could have sought a declaratory judgment of invalid designation prior to soliciting the funds for MEK. If they had done so, they certainly would have lost because of the preclusive effect of the judicial review brought by MEK itself but they would have had their day in court prior to entering into the forbidden transaction.

The illegal reentry case was a bit stronger for the defendants. In that one, the defendant was prosecuted for illegally reentering the country after deportation and wanted to challenge the prior deportation. The Supreme Court stated that "where a determination made in an administrative hearing is to play a critical role in the subsequent imposition of a criminal sanction, there must be some meaningful review of the administrative proceeding."[36] To this argument, the Ninth Circuit in *Ashfari* responded that the Supreme Court had not required that the judicial "review be had by the defendant in the subsequent criminal proceeding."[37] Apparently recognizing the weakness of this response, the court went on to point out that the defendant in that case was the same person who had been party to the prior proceeding while in *Afshari* it was MEK who had the responsibility to seek judicial review of the designation.

This brought the Ninth Circuit to a blend of standing and preclusion doctrines. The court asserted that "the defendants' rights were not directly violated in the earlier designation proceeding. The predicate designation was against the MEK, not the defendants." Because MEK had challenged the designation, "due process does not require another review of the predicate."[38] The statement about whose rights were at stake, like all standing decisions, is a mere conclusion, not an argument. If the court allowed the defendants to challenge the designation, then the rights at stake would belong to them.[39] By contrast, the preclusion-based point, that MEK had challenged the designation and lost, is perfectly consistent with the law of preclusion.[40]

In light of this analysis, the next question is what happens when a defendant is prosecuted for providing material support to a designated FTO but the FTO itself had never challenged the designation. In this situation, the preclusion-like holding of the weapons case still operates. The defendant could have brought a declaratory judgment action prior to contributing the funds. That she would have lost for "lack of standing" (*i.e.*, she has no

---

[36] *Mendoza-Lopez*, 481 U.S. at 838.

[37] *Afshari*, 392 F.3d at 1036.

[38] *Id.* at 1037.

[39] *See* Wayne McCormack, *The Justiciability Myth and the Concept of Law*, 14 HAST. CON. L.Q. 595, 608 (1987).

[40] The party most affected had already litigated the issue. If the plaintiffs were in privity with MEK, which could be inferred from their desire to contribute, then ordinary preclusion doctrine would apply to them as well as MEK. If the two parties were not in privity, the new plaintiffs would be entitled to their day in court despite the modern abandonment of the mutuality principle. Given the closeness of the plaintiffs' desired conduct to the claims litigated by MEK, application of privity to this situation would be completely justifiable.

associational right to contribute funds to a foreign organization) is merely illustrative of why the defendant loses — she has no right to enforce — not a reason to allow the challenge at the prosecution stage. As the Ninth Circuit put it, the validity of the designation is no more an element of the offense than is the validity of the drug classification in a controlled substance case.

So why does a person not have an associational right to contribute funds to a designated FTO? This takes us to the due process claims of the organizations themselves. The MEK's alter ego, PMOI, has been before the D.C. Circuit at least three times,[41] once in the company of the Tamil Tigers. In their first appearance, the D.C. Circuit held that a "foreign entity without property or *presence in* this country has no constitutional rights under the due process clause."[42] That holding, even assuming its accuracy, does not carry very far because the government's objective is to cut off the flow of funds to foreign organizations. To do so, it will assert that the organization has an "interest" in money as soon as it is collected for the organization's benefit and will attempt to "freeze" any asset in which that level of beneficial interest can be found. Thus, to be an effective sanction, the statute must reach "property" that is likely to flow to the organization and thus there will be due process rights to be asserted by almost any designated FTO. It would hardly be worth bothering with the designation if the Secretary did not have reason to believe that the organization was collecting funds from within the U.S.

When the Secretary designated not just PMOI but its alter ego NCRI, the D.C. Circuit saw things differently:

> Whereas [PMOI] did not have property or presence in the United States and was therefore not entitled to assert due process rights under the Constitution, . . . the National Council did have such presence or property and was therefore entitled to assert that claim. We therefore considered the merits of the due process claim. We held that the statute, as applied by the Secretary, did not provide "the fundamental requirement of due process," that is, "the opportunity to be heard at a meaningful time and in a meaningful manner."[43]

---

[41] People's Mojahedin Org. of Iran v. Dep't. of State, 182 F.3d 17 (D.C. Cir. 1999) (*PMOI I*); Nat'l Council of Resistance of Iran v. Dep't. of State, 346 U.S. App. D.C. 131, 251 F.3d 192 (D.C. Cir. 2001) (*NCRI*); People's Mojahedin Org. of Iran v. Dept of State, 327 F.3d 1238 (D.C. Cir. 2003) (*PMOI II*).

[42] *PMOI I*, 182 F.3d at 22:

"Aliens receive constitutional protections [only] when they have come within the territory of the United States and developed substantial connections with this country." United States v. Verdugo-Urquidez, 494 U.S. 259, 271 (1990). No one would suppose that a foreign nation had a due process right to notice and a hearing before the Executive imposed an embargo on it for the purpose of coercing a change in policy. *See* Regan v. Wald, 468 U.S. 222 (1984).

[43] *PMOI II*, 327 F.3d at 1241.

The Court held that the Secretary was required to allow the organization "to file responses to the nonclassified evidence against them, to file evidence in support of their allegations that they are not terrorist organizations," and provide "an opportunity to be meaningfully heard." Having done so, the Secretary renewed the designation and PMOI once again filed for review in the D.C. Circuit. PMOI renewed its claim that the Secretary could not rely on classified information in making a determination that would have such a major impact on the organization and its First Amendment rights. In due process terms, the argument relied on language from a visa denial case: "It is . . . the firmly held main rule that a court may not dispose of the merits of a case on the basis of *ex parte, in camera* submissions."[44] The court responded that the organization had received all the process that was "due under the circumstances of this sensitive matter of classified intelligence in the effort to combat foreign terrorism."[45]

POMI II is a sufficient answer to the designation argument only because the publicly available evidence was sufficient to support a finding that the organization was involved in terrorist activity. What happens when that is not the case, when the finding would need support of undisclosed classified information? Does the ordinary citizen have a claim of associational right to contribute to such an organization? The Ninth Circuit says no, because the giving of money is not as strong an interest as stating support through pure speech or expressive activity. Consider the following examples of what someone in Ashfari's position might have done or might still want to do:

    a.   encourage others in the U.S. to donate money to MEK without collecting the funds himself. (Is he guilty of conspiracy or does *Brandenburg* control?)

    b.   encourage people in other countries to donate money to MEK. (Does it matter whether those other countries are signatories to the Convention on Terrorist Financing?)

    c.   receive messages from MEK leaders in other countries and pass them on through the internet. (Is this a "providing of communication devices" punishable under § 2339B?)

    d.   discuss with MEK leaders in other countries methods by which the organization could get itself off the designation list. (Is this a providing of services that falls within *Lindh* or is it subject to the associational interests that prompted the holding in *HLP*?)

The use of classified information in a criminal proceeding would be subject to the Confrontation Clause. At this point, it is important to realize that the impact of using secret information is limited to the designation, which has the effect of curtailing funding. This is a significant First Amendment interest but it does not by itself result in anyone's going to prison. The potential contributor still has the choice of whether to give the funds.

---

[44] Abourezk v. Reagan, 785 F.2d 1043, 1061 (D.C. Cir. 1986).

[45] *PMOI II*, 327 F.3d at 1242-43.

This is not to say that the First Amendment concerns are minimal — the D.C. Circuit recited its agreement with the Ninth Circuit that "there is no constitutional right to facilitate terrorism by giving terrorists the weapons and explosives with which to carry out their grisly missions." This is hardly a response to the claim that the determination of terrorist activity has been made on the basis of secret information to which the organization would not be able to reply.

In *PMOI II*, the D.C. Circuit relented a bit and pointed out that there was ample evidence in the public domain on which to base a determination that it and its alter egos were regularly engaged in terrorist activity.[46] Given the vast quantities of public information available about terrorist organizations (on the internet among other sources), it is doubtful that any of the 40 or so designated FTOs could make a plausible argument that there is inadequate information in the public record on which to base the designation.

The more difficult problem would occur if an innocuous charitable name were used, such as the "Committee for Human Rights" under which MEK, itself a surrogate for PMOI and NCRI, solicited the funds at stake in *Afshari*. In this instance, the use of secret informers might be necessary to show that the innocuous name was actually a channel through which funds were being funneled to the designated organization. This problem will arise when the solicitors are prosecuted — it will not result in designation of every innocuously titled unincorporated nonentity to which members of the public are importuned to contribute. In the instance of a prosecution, ultimately the government will be put to the choice of disclosing its information to the fact-finder or dropping the prosecution.

The D.C. Circuit indicated in these cases its agreement with the basic proposition that the "Executive Branch has control and responsibility over access to classified information and has 'compelling interest' in withholding national security information from unauthorized persons in the course of executive business."[47] That opens the question of what constitutes "the course of executive business." Surely, the trial of an accused in the judicial system would require the disclosure of evidence pursuant to the Sixth Amendment right to confrontation.[48]

---

[46] *Id.* at 1243-44.

[47] *Id.* at 1242.

[48] *See Abourezk*, 785 F.2d at 1062. In *Abourezk*, the D.C. Circuit alluded to three instances of the use of *ex parte* information to "decide the merits of a dispute." One was when the dispute itself was over the question of whether a privilege existed. Another was "statutory" restrictions such as in a FOIA case to determine if the information could be disclosed. The third was described this way:

> Only in the most extraordinary circumstances does our precedent countenance court reliance upon ex parte evidence to decide the merits of a dispute. Our one case in point, *Molerio v. Federal Bureau of Investigation*, 242 U.S. App. D.C. 137, 749 F.2d 815 (D.C. Cir. 1984), involved the state secrets privilege, a privilege not invoked in this case. The government pressed acute national security concerns in *Molerio*, and we recognized a large risk that an unjust result would eventuate if the case proceeded

One more twist on this line of cases was presented by the district court opinion that led to *Afshari*.[49] Shortly after the D.C. Circuit's second opinion (what it called *NCOR*),[50] the district court in California dismissed an indictment against several fund-raisers for the MEK after answering "this somewhat provocative question:"

> If the procedure whereby an organization is designated by the Secretary of State as "terrorist" violates the Due Process Clause of the United States Constitution, may such *designation nevertheless be utilized as a predicate in a criminal prosecution against individuals* for providing material support to that designated terrorist organization?

The court answered the government's arguments on this point:

> The government also cites numerous cases where the Supreme Court found statutes unconstitutional but, nevertheless, upheld actions that occurred under the unconstitutional scheme. The government seems to be saying that the result in *NCRI [NCOR]*, wherein the D.C. Circuit found the MEK's designation unconstitutional but, nevertheless, upheld such designation, is legally supportable. The cases cited by the government are distinguishable from the instant case in one critical respect — they are all civil cases. Where, as here, a criminal defendant is charged with crimes that could result in as much as 15 years imprisonment or more, this court will not abdicate its duty to ensure that the prosecution of such charges comports with due process.[51]

Finally, with regard to the designation process, there has been one important challenge to the analogous process used by OFAC in Treasury to designate SDT's under IEEPA. The Holy Land Foundation was designated as a result of its close connections to Hamas and sought review in the D.C. Circuit.[52] Although Treasury did not claim to rely on secret or

---

without the privileged material. *See id.* at 825. While we allowed court recourse to the confidential information in *Molerio*, we based that allowance upon proper invocation of the privilege; a demonstration of compelling national security concerns; and public disclosure by the government, prior to any in camera examination, of as much of the material as it could divulge without compromising the privilege. In addition, the plaintiff in *Molerio* had been accorded considerable discovery of non-privileged materials.

Molerio was an employment discrimination claim against the FBI in which the defense was that the applicant could not obtain a security clearance because of secret information regarding his father. The court allowed the classified information to be reviewed *in camera*. Despite some misgivings that could be expressed about this result, it still does not involve conviction of an accused in violation of the Confrontation Clause.

[49] United States v. Rahmani, 209 F. Supp. 2d 1045 (C.D. Cal. 2002), *rev'd sub nom.* United States v. Ashfari, 392 F.3d 1031 (9th Cir. 2004).

[50] 251 F.3d 192 (D.C. Cir. 2001).

[51] *Rahman*, 209 F. Supp. 2d at 1058.

[52] Holy Land Foundation v. Ashcroft, 333 F.3d 156 (D.C. Cir. 2003).

classified information, it did rely on hearsay. The court was not particularly troubled by this aspect of the case because hearsay evidence is quite often used in administrative proceedings that do not have all the formality of a judicial proceeding. Were hearsay to be the basis of a criminal conviction, then there would be a Confrontation Clause problem, but once again the elements of the criminal offense of providing material support do not include the validity of the designation.

If a criminal defendant cannot be convicted on the basis of unknown evidence, then deprivation of property through an administrative designation would seem to be subject to the same due process requirements (even if it were only a temporary deprivation by freezing of assets). Moreover, if the information is accurate, then it is already known to the organization's representatives and superficially it would seem that there is no reason to withhold it from them. Yet the government's asserted interest in withholding secret information from the organization is the same as the claim of need for secrecy of intelligence results during wartime. "If I tell you what I know about you, then you will know how I learned it and can then change your operations to keep future information away from me." This leads to the perfectly understandable desire on the part of anti-and counter-terrorism specialists to use information acquired through incredibly difficult, and dangerous, methods to shut down terrorist organizations without destroying the intelligence networks by which the information was acquired.

But is proceeding by secret evidence an acceptable practice in a free and open society? That is the heart of several of the civil liberties issues presented in counter-terrorism. In criminal cases subject to the Classified Information Procedure Act, the fact-finder would not get the classified information unless the trial were closed to the public and the defendant also received the information. In the designation process, however, neither the organization nor the potential donor knows what the classified information is. One possible outcome of this line of development will be that the CIPA procedure will become the minimum requirements of due process for the designation stage.

[D] *Mens Rea* of Material Support

Sami al-Arian has been an Assistant Professor at the University of South Florida since 1986, participating actively in conferences and courses dealing with Arab or Middle Eastern Studies. He was instrumental in formation of a group known as World and Islamic Studies Enterprise (WISE), with which USF co-sponsored several conferences. In November 1994, a PBS documentary alleged that al-Arian was the "head of the Islamic Jihad terrorist group's domestic support network." From that point on, al-Arian and USF have been embroiled in political and legal disputes over his employment, including an investigation of academic freedom charges by the American Association of University Professors (AAUP). Finally, the

Department of Justice indicted Al-Arian along with a number of others.[53] Answering several motions to dismiss portions of the indictment, the district court held that the government would have to prove specific intent to further violent illegal activities of the organization, not just that the defendants knew of the designation.

Using the Ninth Circuit's vagueness example on "training," the statute could likewise punish other innocent conduct, such as where a person in New York City (where the United Nations is located) gave a FTO member a ride from the airport to the United Nations before the member petitioned the United Nations. Such conduct could be punished as providing "transportation" to a FTO under § 2339B. The end result of the Ninth Circuit's statutory construction in *HLP II* is to render a substantial portion of § 2339B unconstitutionally vague.[54]

This Court concludes that it is more consistent with Congress's intent, which was to prohibit material support from FTOs to the "fullest possible basis," to imply a *mens rea* requirement to the "material support" element of § 2339B(a)(1). Therefore, this Court concludes that to convict a defendant under § 2339B(a)(1) the government must prove beyond a reasonable doubt that the defendant knew that: (a) the organization was a FTO or had committed unlawful activities that caused it to be so designated; and (b) what he was furnishing was "material support." To avoid Fifth Amendment personal guilt problems, this Court concludes that the government must show more than a defendant knew something was within a category of "material support" in order to meet (b). In order to meet (b), the government must show that the defendant knew (had a specific intent) that the support would further the illegal activities of a FTO.[55]

---

[53] United States v. al-Arian, 308 F. Supp. 2d 1322 (M.D. Fla. 2004).

[54] *Id.* at 1338 n.31:

Other examples of innocent conduct that could be prohibited include the same person allowing the FTO member to spend the night at his house, cashing a check, loaning the member a cell phone for use during the stay, or allowing the member to use the fax machine or laptop computer in preparing the petition. And, the additional phrase "expert advice or assistance" added by the Patriot Act in 2002 could also fail as unconstitutionally vague.

[55] *Id.* at 1339 n.33:

This Court's conclusion is consistent with the Seventh Circuit's decision in *Boim v. Quranic Literacy Inst.*, 291 F.3d 1000 (7th Cir. 2002). In *Boim*, the Seventh Circuit considered whether a violation of § 2339B could serve as a basis for civil liability under Section 2333. The Seventh Circuit held that to succeed on a Section 2333 claim, plaintiff must prove that the defendant knew about the unlawful activities of the FTO and intended to help in those unlawful activities. This Court's construction of § 2339B avoids the anomaly of civil liability being more narrow than criminal liability based on the same statutory language.

In response to the government's argument that money is fungible and even the donation of money for charitable or humanitarian reasons should be criminalized, the court said:

> This Court does not believe this burden is that great in the typical case. Often, such an intent will be easily inferred. For example, a jury could infer a specific intent to further the illegal activities of a FTO when a defendant knowingly provides weapons, explosives, or lethal substances to an organization that he knows is a FTO because of the nature of the support. Likewise, a jury could infer a specific intent when a defendant knows that the organization continues to commit illegal acts and the defendant provides funds to that organization knowing that money is fungible and, once received, the donee can use the funds for any purpose it chooses. That is, by its nature, money carries an inherent danger for furthering the illegal aims of an organization. Congress said as much when it found that FTOs were "so tainted by their criminal conduct that any contribution to such an organization facilitates that conduct."[56]

Another case raising the *mens rea* argument dealt with a cigarette smuggling scheme in which some of the proceeds went to support Hizballah.[57] The Fourth Circuit reviewed the same associational, vagueness, and due process claims as had the D.C. and Ninth Circuits and found them wanting for the same reasons. The case is interesting because of the dissent by Judge Gregory, who stated

> I do not believe that these constitutional infirmities can be cured by reading the statutory term "knowingly" as a scienter require-ment meaning only that the defendant had knowledge of the organization's designation as a foreign terrorist organization ("FTO"), or that he or she knew of the organization's unlawful activities that caused it to be so designated.

> Instead, I would follow the reasoning of *United States v. al-Arian*, and conclude that to save the statute, one must apply the mens rea requirement to the entire "material support" provision such that the government must prove that the defendant (1) knew the organi-zation was a FTO or knew of the organization's unlawful activities that caused it to be so designated and (2) knew what he or she was providing was "material support," i.e., the government must show that the defendant had a specific intent that the support would further the FTO's illegal activities.[58]

---

[56] *Id.* at 1339 (citing Pub. L. No. 104-132 § 301(a)(7)).

[57] United States v. Hammoud, 381 F.3d 316 (4th Cir. 2004) (en banc).

[58] *Id.* at 371-72.

[E] The 2004 Material Support Amendments

The Ninth Circuit enjoined the "training" and "personnel" portions of the statute but then agreed to hear the case en banc.[59] Congress then added § 2339D in December 2004 to provide that

1. "personnel" consists of "1 or more individuals who may be or include oneself,"

2. "training" is "instruction or teaching . . . a specific skill, as opposed to general knowledge,"

3. "provision of personnel" means working directly with the organization and does not include "acting independently of the [FTO] to advance its goals or objectives,"[60]

4. mens rea with respect to a designated FTO can be either knowledge of the designation or knowledge that the organization has engaged in terrorism or terrorist activity,[61]

5. receiving "military-type training from or on behalf of" a designated FTO is a separate offense.

The Ninth Circuit then vacated its order for rehearing en banc, vacated the injunction, and remanded for "further proceedings if appropriate."[62] As a result of the amendments, there has been little further dispute over the *mens rea* requirement. To conclude our review of the material support statutes, there is virtual unanimity on these essential points:

1. Although a person has a First Amendment interest in supporting political and charitable organizations, there is no right to provide material support to a designated FTO.

2. The First Amendment and the Due Process clause require a *mens rea* that the defendant be shown to know either (a) that the organization is a designated FTO or SDT, or (b) that the organization engages in unlawful activity.

3. The vagueness of "training" and "personnel" in the original statute have been addressed by amendments to the statute.

4. Due process is satisfied in the designation by a meaningful opportunity to be heard on the conclusions of the agency, at least so long as there is sufficient evidence in the public domain on which to conclude that the organization engages in terrorist activities.

There is not yet unanimity on these points:

1. Two judges have held that the defendant must be shown to have had a specific intent to further the unlawful aims of the

---

[59] Humanitarian Law Project v. United States DOJ, 382 F.3d 1154 (9th Cir. 2004).

[60] 18 U.S.C. § 2339B(h) (2007).

[61] Engaging in terrorism and engaging in terrorist activity differ by reference to the statutes defining the two concepts.

[62] Humanitarian Law Project v. United States DOJ, 393 F.3d 902 (9th Cir. 2004) (*HLP IV*).

organization, although one recognized that the fungibility of money should make this an easy requirement for the government to meet.

2.   There has not yet been a test of whether designation is justifiable when the public record does not contain sufficient evidence on which to conclude that it engages in terrorist activities.

§ 5.02 TRADING WITH THE ENEMY

In the Anti-Terrorism and Effective Death Penalty Act of 1996 (AEDPA), Congress created the offenses of "material support" for terrorists[63] or for designated terrorist organizations.[64] These offenses raise similar First Amendment concerns to those of treason and conspiracy. There are subtle differences among material support, conspiracy, and aiding and abetting an attempt. One way to understand the statutes, which also bears on the approach of the courts to the First Amendment interests, is to focus on the scienter elements in the statutes.

The material support statutes are a logical outgrowth of statutes that prohibit "trading with the enemy."[65] In modern times, that concept has been extended to doing business with countries on designated embargo lists. The International Emergency Economic Powers Act (IEEPA),[66] authorizes the President to exercise broad powers to "deal with any unusual and extraordinary threat, which has its source in whole or substantial part outside the United States, to the national security, foreign policy, or economy of the United States, if the President declares a national emergency with respect to such threat."[67] Specific requirements and prohibitions apply to each nation so designated. Although the statute requires a finding of national emergency, prohibitions on trade may last for extended periods, as is the case with Cuba. Willful violations of regulatory orders under this statute are punishable as crimes.[68]

The material support statutes are closely linked to statutes outlawing money laundering[69] and structuring transactions to evade currency reporting requirements.[70] Money laundering and structuring statutes criminalize apparently benign conduct that could be either a precursor to a known

---

[63] 18 U.S.C. § 2339A (2005).

[64] 18 U.S.C. § 2339B (2005).

[65] The Trading With the Enemy Act (TWEA) of 1917 has been codified as 50 U.S.C. App. § 1-44 (2005). Although its literal terms applied to World War I and the Axis nations, it has never been repealed and can be applied during any state of war. *See* Propper v. Clark, 337 U.S. 47 (1949). The Uniform Code of Military Justice equivalent is "aiding the enemy" and is codified at 10 U.S.C. § 904 (2005).

[66] 50 U.S.C. §§ 1701-07 (2005).

[67] 18 U.S.C. § 1701(a) (2005).

[68] 50 U.S.C. § 1705 (2005).

[69] 18 U.S.C. § 1957; 31 U.S.C. §§ 5313-5316 (2005).

[70] 18 U.S.C. § 1956; 31 U.S.C. § 5324 (2005).

mischief (usually drug trafficking) or a method of covering up a completed offense. In similar fashion, the material support statutes represent an effort to enhance the preventive effectiveness of law enforcement by providing mechanisms to intercede in terrorist planning before an actual attack occurs. Government lawyers describe them as rough corollaries to laws against driving with an open container of alcohol in the car.[71] The progression is something like this: Society wants to minimize automobile fatalities, so we make it a crime to kill someone with an automobile while intoxicated. To make that even more unlikely, we make it a crime to drive while intoxicated whether anyone is injured or not. This gives law enforcement power to prosecute actions that could lead to harm before the substantive harm occurs. To extend out even further, most states prohibit driving with an open container of alcohol in the car. That is about the limit to which we can go because driving with a sealed container has sufficient social value that people are unwilling to outlaw that act.

In the "alcohol in the car scenario," all observers recognize that not every drunk driver would kill someone. Further, not everyone with an open container in the car will drive while intoxicated. Yet, in both instances, the precursor conduct is criminalized because the risk of harm outweighs the social utility of the precursor conduct. Another striking example is presented by statutes and ordinances that limit the sale of pseudophedrine and other active ingredients that are precursors for making methamphetamine.[72]

Similarly, prosecution of completed terrorist acts is not deemed sufficient to address the problem. When a completed crime occurs, then investigators will (as happened in the U.S. after 9/11 and England after 7/11) start tracing backward from that crime to find who supplied the money or other support and thus formed part of the conspiracy. To permit a chain of investigation to occur before the completed harm, the material support statutes create a precursor crime so that tracking and reporting requirements can be triggered at an earlier stage. Money laundering and financial reporting statutes move yet one more step out from completed harm.[73]

A major difference between the material support statutes and the alcohol-in-the-car scenario is that the social utility argument will be encountered much earlier when we are talking about interests of privacy and association.

---

[71] This analogy has been used by Jeff Breinholt, of the Justice Department's Counter-Terrorism Section, in public presentations. In his written analyses, he emphasizes the connection with drug trafficking. *See* Jeffrey Breinholt, *Reaching the White Collar Terrorist: Operational Challenges* (paper for the Int'l Monetary Fund, Sept. 2004), *available at* www.imf.org/external/np/leg/sem/2004/cdmfl/eng/breinh.pdf.

[72] Several states and local communities have moved to place pseudophedrine behind pharmacy counters and to prevent the sale of pseudophedrine in combination with substances that contain acids, such as some fertilizers. For more information, see PEA, *Methamphetamine*, www.dea.gov/concern/meth_factsheet.html (last visited June 22, 2007).

[73] Breinholt, *supra* note 71, at 6, points out that financial reporting requirements are a kind of self-created precursor conduct because only the person with something to hide would bother violating the requirement.

Particularly given the social interest in promoting charitable giving and political activism, there will be constitutional arguments to be made in almost every prosecution of this type.

By comparison, some proposed legislation reacting to the activities of animal rights groups would go very far from the predicate harm and could raise issues of the rights of privacy or association.[74] One example is a proposed Texas bill that reportedly would define an "animal rights or ecological terrorist organization as two or more persons organized for the purpose of supporting any politically motivated activity intended to obstruct or deter any person from participating in any activity involving animals."[75] Another set of proposals would criminalize the photographing or videotaping of animal facilities. These examples illustrate that the further a prohibition gets from the proscribable harm, the more likely the prohibition is to encounter First Amendment difficulties.

[A] Training and Trading with the Enemy

John Walker Lindh (the "American Taliban" as he came to be known in the press) was a U.S. citizen who left his Marin County home to join up with the "freedom fighters" of the mujahedin in Afghanistan, who had become al Qaeda by the time he arrived for training.[76] Unfortunately, he arrived too late to be of service in the cause against the U.S.S.R. and ended up fighting with the Taliban and al Qaeda against the war lords of the Northern Alliance.[77] When U.S. forces invaded Afghanistan, he surrendered to the Northern Alliance in the same area as Yaser Hamdi and both

---

[74] STEVEN BEST & ANTHONY NOCELLA II, TERRORISTS OR FREEDOM FIGHTERS?: REFLECTIONS ON THE LIBERATION OF ANIMALS (2004).

[75] STEVEN BEST, *It's War! The Escalating Battle Between Activists and the Corporate-State Complex, in* TERRORISTS OR FREEDOM FIGHTERS 300, 314 (2004).

[76] United States v. Lindh, 212 F. Supp. 2d 541 (E.D. Va. 2002).

[77] The District Court described his military career this way:

> Lindh, together with approximately 150 non-Afghani fighters, traveled from Kabul to the front line at Takhar, located in Northeastern Afghanistan, where the entire unit was placed under the command of an Iraqi named Abdul Hady. Lindh's group was eventually divided into smaller groups that fought in shifts against Northern Alliance troops in the Takhar trenches, rotating every one to two weeks. During this period, Lindh "carried various weapons with him, including the AKM rifle, an RPK rifle he was issued after the AKM rifle malfunctioned, and at least two grenades." He remained with his fighting group following the September 11, 2001 terrorist attacks, "despite having been told that Bin Laden had ordered the [September 11] attacks, that additional terrorist attacks were planned, and that additional al Qaeda personnel were being sent from the front lines to protect Bin Laden and defend against an anticipated military response from the United States." Indeed, it is specifically alleged that Lindh remained with his fighting group from October to December 2001, "after learning that United States military forces and United States nationals had become directly engaged in support of the Northern Alliance in its military conflict with Taliban and al Qaeda forces."

Id. at 546. In the Agreed Statement of Facts that accompanied his guilty plea, there is no mention of having carried arms in contemplation of facing U.S. forces.

were turned over to U.S. forces.[78] Hamdi was transferred to Guantánamo before it was discovered that he was a U.S. citizen and then transferred to a Navy brig in South Carolina. Lindh was turned over to the Justice Department upon his arrival at Andrews Air Force Base and was indicted for prosecution in the Eastern District of Virginia.

The charges against him were in roughly three categories: conspiracy to murder U.S. nationals (based on allegations that he continued with his unit after notice that they would be opposing U.S. forces), providing material support to designated terrorist organizations (al Qaeda and HUM), and providing material support to a regime subject to embargo orders by the Treasury Department (the Taliban). The Taliban charges were brought under IEEPA, while the al Qaeda charges were based on the "material support" provisions of § 2339B. The primary difference between the two statutes is that IEEPA deals with countries, entities, or persons designated by the Treasury Department[79] while AEDPA deals with groups designated by the State Department under somewhat tighter criteria defining a "foreign terrorist organization."[80]

Lindh ultimately pleaded guilty to carrying an explosive in the course of providing material support to an embargoed regime under IEEPA. Prior to that, however, he challenged each of the counts of the indictment and triggered a conflict among various federal courts over proper interpretation and constitutionality of § 2339B.

With respect to the charge of conspiracy to murder U.S. nationals, Lindh claimed that as a soldier for the Taliban regime, he was entitled to combat immunity. The district court provided a succinct statement of the law of armed conflict as it pertains to individuals[81] and held that the

---

[78] Both Lindh and Hamdi were in the Qala-e-Jangi Prison when an uprising occurred among the inmates resulting in the deaths of CIA agent Michael Spann and as many as 500 inmates. Lindh and Hamdi survived and were transported out of the country. Adam Liptak, *John Walker Lindh's Buyer's Remorse*, N.Y. TIMES, Apr. 23, 2007, *available at* http://select.nytimes.com/search/restricted/article?res = F3071FFB3C5A0C708EDDAD0894DF404482.

[79] Although IEEPA appears to deal only with countries, its reach has been expanded by Executive Orders to designated terrorist groups. Treasury's Office of Foreign Assets Control (OFAC) lists Specially Designated Global Terrorists (SDGT) pursuant to Exec. Order 13224. *See* 15 C.F.R. § 744.12 (2005). In addition, OFAC lists Specially Designated Terrorist (SDT) pursuant to Exec. Order 12947, which "prohibits transactions by U.S. persons with terrorists who threaten to disrupt the Middle East peace process." *See* 15 C.F.R. § 744.13 (2005).

[80] 8 U.S.C. § 1189 (2005) sets out the procedure by which an FTO is designated. The definition of "terrorism" for that purpose is "premeditated, politically motivated violence perpetrated against noncombatant targets by subnational groups or clandestine agents." 22 U.S.C. § 2256f(d) (2005).

[81] *Lindh*, 212 F. Supp. 2d at 553:

Lawful combatant immunity, a doctrine rooted in the customary international law of war, forbids prosecution of soldiers for their lawful belligerent acts committed during the course of armed conflicts against legitimate military targets. Belligerent acts committed in armed conflict by enemy members of the armed forces may be punished as crimes under a belligerent's municipal law only to the extent that they violate international humanitarian law or are unrelated to the armed conflict. This doctrine has a long history, which is reflected in part in various early international

requirements of the Geneva Convention for qualifying as a prisoner of war (GPW) also defined the circumstances under which one could claim combat immunity. With regard to the Taliban, the court concluded that combat immunity did not protect a combatant who was neither a regular member of the armed forces of a nation nor appearing in uniform.[82] These holdings, critical to understanding the confusion that later surrounded the Guantá-namo detainees, simply left Lindh amenable to the ordinary criminal processes of the civilian courts.[83]

Lindh's principal arguments were based on First Amendment claims of freedom of association. With regard to the basic associational claim, the district court stated rather tersely that Lindh was not "accused of merely associating with a disfavored or subversive group whose activities are limited to circulating inflammatory political or religious material exhorting opposition to the government" but with conspiracy in groups that actually carried out "acts of terror, violence, and murder."[84] Quoting and agreeing with the Ninth Circuit's earlier statement in *Humanitarian Law Project v. Reno* (*HLP II*)[85] that "there is no constitutional right to facilitate terrorism," the court distinguished sharply between advocacy and criminal conduct.

Lindh made a related argument based on overbreadth or vagueness with regard to the term "personnel" in the material support statute, an argument

---

conventions, statutes and documents. But more pertinent, indeed controlling, here is that the doctrine also finds expression in the Geneva Convention Relative to the Treatment of Prisoners of War ("GPW"), to which the United States is a signatory. Significantly, Article 87 of the GPW admonishes that combatants "may not be sentenced . . . to any penalties except those provided for in respect of members of the armed forces of the said Power who have committed the same acts." Similarly, Article 99 provides that "no prisoner of war may be tried or sentenced for an act which is not forbidden by the law of the Detaining Power or by international law, in force at the time the said act was committed." These Articles, when read together, make clear that a belligerent in a war cannot prosecute the soldiers of its foes for the soldiers' lawful acts of war.

[82] The court also pointed out that the Taliban militia members failed to have a coherent command structure and committed numerous violations of the law of war, each of which would also disqualify a militia member from POW status or combat immunity. Those factors, however, being generic to the militia and not specific to Lindh, are a bit more doubtful than the membership and uniform requirements that he violated on his own. *Id.* at 557 n.35.

[83] The GPW as interpreted in *Lindh* could have meant that a person who failed to qualify for combat immunity was either prosecuted or detained pursuant to exigencies of the battlefield and then released as a civilian entitled to protection under Geneva IV for Protection of Civilian Persons (GC). The confusion that later erupted arose because the Bush administration decided that there was a middle ground in which a person was entitled to no protection under any of the rules of war as exemplified in the Geneva Conventions. In this middle ground, they claimed, a person could be declared an "unlawful combatant" and treated as if no law applied whatsoever. The heart of the problem that this created for the Supreme Court was that the argument flies in the face of the basic assumption of the "rule of law" that government cannot take action against any person without some authority traceable to a provision of law. *See generally* Hamdi v. Rumsfeld, 542 U.S. 507 (2004).

[84] *Lindh*, 212 F. Supp. 2d at 569.

[85] *HLP II*, 205 F.3d at 1133.

that had been accepted by the Ninth Circuit.[86] He argued that criminalizing the provision of personnel could reach so far as sanctioning advocacy because joining a group and lending one's support could fall under the definition of providing personnel. The court responded that an appropriate narrowing construction was readily available in that provision of personnel should be read to mean "a body of persons usually employed (as in a factory, office, or organization)," or "a body of persons employed in some service."[87]

> The Ninth Circuit's vagueness holding in *Humanitarian Law Project* is neither persuasive nor controlling. The term is aimed at denying the provision of human resources to proscribed terrorist organizations, and not at the mere *independent* advocacy of an organization's interests or agenda.[88]

The disagreement between the district court in *Lindh* and the Ninth Circuit in *HLP* set the stage for a series of cases focusing on two separate issues — the alleged vagueness of the terms "personnel" and "training" and the *mens rea* required to prove a violation of the statute within constitutional restraints of the right of association.

In another unrelated case, the "training" concept produced a prosecution under yet another statute, the somewhat arcane Neutrality Act,[89] and also raised the issue of the connection between the Taliban and al Qaeda. A number of defendants were accused of multiple preparations for "violent jihad" by using paintball and toy car remote controls in their preparation and training in the hills of Virginia.[90] The defendants were preparing to assist, and some went to train with, the Lashkar-e-Taiba (LET or LT), a group warring against India in the Kashmir. This constituted a conspiracy to violate the Neutrality Act even though they never got to engage in action. In addition, some were charged with preparing to assist the Taliban and by inference al Qaeda. The judge disagreed with the inference of assistance to al Qaeda. "Although Khan's fighting on behalf of the Al Qaeda's protector,

---

[86] The Ninth Circuit's view was that "it is easy to see how someone could be unsure about what AEDPA prohibits with the use of the term 'personnel,' as it blurs the line between protected expression and unprotected conduct." An advocate for an FTO "could be seen as supplying them with personnel," given that "having an independent advocate frees up members to engage in terrorist activities instead of advocacy." *Id.* at 1137.

[87] *Lindh*, 212 F. Supp. 2d at 574:

> One who is merely present with other members of the organization, but is not under the organization's direction and control, is not part of the organization's "personnel." This distinction is sound; one can become a member of a political party without also becoming part of its "personnel;" one can visit an organization's training center, or actively espouse its cause, without thereby becoming "personnel." Simply put, the term "personnel" does not extend to independent actors. Rather, it describes employees or employee-like operatives who serve the designated group and work at its command or, in Lindh's case, who provide themselves to serve the organization.

[88] *Id.*

[89] 18 U.S.C. § 960.

[90] United States v. Khan, 309 F. Supp. 2d 789 (E.D. Va. 2004).

the Taliban, would certainly benefit Al Qaeda, such assistance does not fit the statutory definition of material support or resources."[91]

John Walker Lindh was the first person brought to trial following 9/11. He was taken into custody in Afghanistan during the U.S. military action against the Taliban regime. He was taken first to Guantánamo Bay in Cuba and then brought to the U.S. for trial in the Eastern District of Virginia.

The story of "the American Taliban" is reasonably familiar but little has been written about his judicial experience. Lindh eventually pleaded to the modern equivalent of "trading with the enemy" by providing services in violation of presidential orders declaring the Taliban off-limits for economic support. The Agreed Statement of Facts accompanying his guilty plea recited that the Taliban government had been embargoed since 1999 because of their support for al Qaeda, that Lindh traveled to Afghanistan to receive training, and then carried arms on behalf of the Taliban in November 2001 when he was captured.[92]

Why was Lindh not charged with treason? The plea agreement carefully avoids saying that Lindh carried arms against U.S. troops. Taking a cue from *Cramer*, Congress has provided ample other heads of criminality and there is no particular reason why the government should bother with the proof requirements of the treason clause.

The Lackawanna Six and Portland Five were two alleged al Qaeda sleeper cells "broken up" in the year following 9/11. A few terrorist cells in Europe were raided and found with sufficient hard evidence such as explosives to make a basis for prosecution on conspiracy to commit specific crimes. Apparently, however, in neither the Lackawanna nor Portland cases were authorities able to find plans or materials for specific acts of violence in this country. The Portland Indictment alleged that members of the cell had trained with al Qaeda and were preparing to travel through Hong Kong to Afghanistan to take up arms on behalf of the Taliban against the U.S. The Lackawanna Complaint alleged only that members of the cell had trained in Al-Farooq and stayed at an al Qaeda safe house. There is nothing in the affidavit accompanying the charges that indicates any future plans other than the statement that two uncharged co-conspirators had communicated by e-mail with "information which law enforcement personnel interpret as referring to possible terrorist activity."

Some defense attorneys complained that guilty pleas in the *Lindh* and Lackawanna cases were coercively tainted by the threat that the defendants could be subject to the "enemy combatant" designation that could be used to deprive them of a trial. In the wake of 9/11, federal agencies were

---

[91] *Id.* at 821. In sentencing some of the conspirators who pleaded guilty and had neither provided physical goods nor trained others, Judge Brinkema reportedly commented that the sentences would be somewhat lighter than the government desired because in receiving training, they were "absorbing resources, not providing them." *See* text accompanying note 24, *supra*.

[92] United. States v. Lindh, Statement of Facts, *available at* www.usdoj.gov/ap/statementoffacts.htm.

subjected to harsh criticism for failing to prevent the attacks. Breaking up terrorist cells would seem to be what the public and politicians want. But how does a federal agency "break up a cell"? Should there be some proof that the Lackawanna defendants planned to do something?

[B] Designated Terrorist Organizations

Prior to *Brandenburg*, the Court had already declared in a number of cases that mere membership in the Communist Party could not be penalized. In the process, there developed a distinct First Amendment "right of association." *Scales v. United States*[93] upheld a conviction for membership in the Communist Party only upon a finding of specific intent to engage in illegal action. *Noto v. United States*[94] overturned a similar conviction in which the specific intent was lacking. Both cases read the statute's criminalizing of membership as if it included an element of intent to act.

NAACP v. Claiborne Hardware[95] established strict requirements of both *actus reus* and *mens rea* for associational liability. "For liability to be imposed by reason of association alone, it is necessary to establish that the group itself possessed unlawful goals and that the individual held a specific intent to further those illegal goals." The question in the material support cases is how far the government can reach into an individual's private associations to find support for illegal activity.

The designation of a "foreign terrorist organization" by the Secretary of State places everyone on notice that mere support of this organization is unlawful, but does that really change the import of the right of association? In other words, doesn't the Constitution require knowledge of imminent violent or fraudulent behavior before we can punish support of an organization? An additional issueis whether the designation itself is valid. A sequence of cases in the D.C. and Ninth Circuits address both the designation and the mens rea requirements of the material support statutes.

The first step was challenging the basic premises of the statutes. The Humanitarian Law Project brought a suit on behalf of persons and groups wanting to support two designated organizations, the Kurdistan Workers' Party (PKK) and the Liberation Tigers of Tamil Eelam (LTTE). They claimed that the statute unconstitutionally criminalized their support of these designated organizations even though they themselves wished to support only the nonviolent humanitarian aspects of the organizations, that the statute intruded upon their associational rights and ability to express political positions through donations, and that the statute was not sufficiently narrowly drawn to prohibit only support of unlawful violence. The district court answered that association did not protect the advancement of violent action through the giving of money, but did hold that the terms "personnel" and "training" were vague and invalid.[96]

---

[93] 367 U.S. 203 (1961).

[94] 367 U.S. 290 (1961).

[95] 458 U.S. 886 (1982). *See* § 4.02[B] *supra*.

[96] *Humanitarian Law Project v. Reno (HLP I)*, 9 F. Supp. 2d 1176, 1205 (C.D. Cal. 1998).

In *Humanitarian Law Project v. Reno (HLP II)*,[97] the Ninth Circuit provided a response to the first argument that ran throughout its responses to the other arguments:

> Material support given to a terrorist organization can be used to promote the organization's unlawful activities, regardless of donor intent. Once the support is given, the donor has no control over how it is used.[98]

This is known as the "money is fungible" response. Because the money could be used for unlawful activities, government was entitled to prohibit donations even though this would also have spillover effect on political interests of both donors and the designated organizations. Moreover, even if this particular dollar could be limited to humanitarian purposes, that frees up another dollar that the organization can use for violent purposes. So, because money is fungible, the donor in fact is supporting unlawful activity regardless of his or her benevolent motives.

A separate line of argument, however, was presented with regard to the content of some of the prohibited means of support. Supplying "training" and "personnel" were both held to be unconstitutionally vague in relation to the potential for deterring protected advocacy:

> It is easy to see how someone could be unsure about what AEDPA prohibits with the use of the term "personnel," as it blurs the line between protected expression and unprotected conduct. Someone who advocates the cause of the PKK could be seen as supplying them with personnel; it even fits under the government's rubric of freeing up resources, since having an independent advocate frees up members to engage in terrorist activities instead of advocacy. But advocacy is pure speech protected by the First Amendment.[99]

> . . . The term "training" fares little better. Again, it is easy to imagine protected expression that falls within the bounds of this term. For example, a plaintiff who wishes to instruct members of a designated group on how to petition the United Nations to give aid to their group could plausibly decide that such protected expression falls within the scope of the term "training." The government insists that the term is best understood to forbid the imparting of skills to foreign terrorist organizations through training. Yet, presumably, this definition would encompass teaching international law to members of designated organizations. The result would be different if the term "training" were qualified to include only military training or training in terrorist activities.[100]

---

[97] 205 F.3d 1130 (9th Cir. 2000) (see explanation of numbering at note 8 *supra*).

[98] *Id.* at 1134.

[99] *Id.* at 1137.

[100] *Id.* at 1138.

On remand, the district court entered a permanent injunction against enforcement of the "personnel" and "training" provisions.[101] The Government appealed but the Ninth Circuit held that those issues were foreclosed by its prior opinion.[102] Meanwhile, HLP added an argument that due process would not allow conviction of its supporters without a showing of intent to further the unlawful purposes of the organization. The Government argued that the individual could be convicted for providing funds regardless even of knowledge that the organization was designated. To this, the court responded that the Government's position would yield an unconstitutional statute punishing people with no notice of illegality, while the plaintiffs' reading would make the statute useless. Therefore, the court settled on the middle ground that

> to sustain a conviction under § 2339B, the government must prove beyond a reasonable doubt that the donor had knowledge that the organization was designated by the Secretary as a foreign terrorist organization or that the donor had knowledge of the organization's unlawful activities that caused it to be so designated.[103]

At that point, Congress amended the statute to (1) add a scienter requirement conforming to the Ninth Circuit's view (knowledge of either the designation or the unlawful activities),[104] (2) limit the prohibition on providing personnel to providing one's services under the direction of the FTO,[105] and (3) add a section defining "training" as the receipt of "military-type" training with a scienter requirement.[106] The Ninth Circuit then vacated all its prior opinions and remanded to the district court.[107]

The D.C. Circuit then took up the process by which FTOs were designated by the State Department. In *Nat'l. Council of Resistance of Iran (NCRI) v. Dept. of State*,[108] the D.C. court held that designation without any notice or hearing violated the rights of organizations to procedural due process. The court required State to provide at least notice that designation was being considered, a summary of the non-classified information on which it was relying, and an opportunity to rebut the assertion that it engaged in terrorist activity. Following this decision, State then provided the necessary opportunities to designated organizations and reaffirmed the designations.

That was not the end of the story, however, because then a district judge in California decided that the whole scheme was unconstitutional. In *United*

---

[101] Humanitarian Law Project v. Reno, 2001 U.S. Dist. LEXIS 16729 (C.D. Cal. 2001) (*HLP II.5*).

[102] Humanitarian Law Project v. United States DOJ (*HLP III*), 352 F.3d 382 (9th Cir. 2003), *vacated at* 393 F.3d 902 (9th Cir. 2004) (*HLP IV*).

[103] *HLP III*, 352 F.3d at 402.

[104] 18 U.S.C. § 2339B(a)(1) (2007).

[105] 18 U.S.C. § 2339B(h) (2007).

[106] 18 U.S.C. § 2339D (2007).

[107] 393 F.3d 902 (9th Cir. 2004).

[108] 251 F.3d 192 (D.C. Cir. 2001).

States v. Rahmani[109] the district court dismissed the indictment in a "material support" case. The court held that the designation statute was unconstitutional on its face because it did not allow the organization to see the administrative record on which the decision was based and thus did not provide for effective judicial review even during a criminal prosecution. "[D]efendants, upon a successful Section [2339B] prosecution, are deprived of their liberty based on an unconstitutional designation they could never challenge."[110]

The Southern District of New York disagreed in *United States v. Sattar*.[111] For the New York court, the validity of the designation was simply irrelevant to whether the organization was in fact designated and the defendant thereafter contributed material support. "The statute is . . . explicit that a defendant in a criminal action may not raise any question of the validity of the designation as a defense or objection at any trial or hearing."[112]

> The designation of IG as an FTO had no effect on the defendants. While the defendants can challenge the allegation that they violated § 2339B by providing material support to an FTO or could contest that IG was, in fact, designated as an FTO, they cannot assert the due process claims of the FTO and challenge the underlying designation. The element at issue in this case is simply whether IG was designated as an FTO, and the defendants thereafter knowingly provided, or conspired to provide, material support or assistance to it, not whether the Secretary of State correctly designated IG as an FTO.[113]

In *NCRI*, the D.C. Circuit considered the question of whether the due process violation warranted setting aside the designations:

> We recognize that a strict and immediate application of the principles of law which we have set forth herein could be taken to require a revocation of the designations before us. However, we also recognize the realities of the foreign policy and national security concerns asserted by the Secretary in support of those designations. We further recognize the timeline against which all are operating: the two-year designations before us expire in October of this year. We therefore do not order the vacation of the existing designations, but rather remand the questions to the Secretary with instructions that the petitioners be afforded the opportunity to file responses to the nonclassified evidence against them, to file evidence in support of their allegations that they are not terrorist organizations,

---

[109] 209 F. Supp. 2d 1045 (C.D. Cal. 2002), *rev'd sub nom.* United States v. Ashfari, 392 F.3d 1031 (9th Cir. 2004).

[110] *Id.* at 1055.

[111] 272 F. Supp. 2d 348 (S.D.N.Y. 2002).

[112] *Id.* at 364.

[113] *Id.* at 364-65.

and that they be afforded an opportunity to be meaningfully heard by the Secretary upon the relevant findings. While not within our current order, we expect that the Secretary will afford due process rights to these and other similarly situated entities in the course of future designations.[114]

After remand and reconsideration, the organizations came back with arguments that the Secretary had relied on classified information not disclosed to them. The D.C. Circuit held that the organizations involved had displayed sufficient illegal behavior in public that they could be designated on the basis of public information.[115]

§ 5.03 MATERIAL SUPPORT — DESIGNATED FTOs

The three most widely known prosecutions for material support are those of Sami al-Arian, Mohammed Hammoud, and Lynne Stewart.

Al-Arian has been discussed above. His fund-raising on behalf of PIJ was well-documented, but the documented activity had occurred before the 1996 designation of PIJ as an FTO,[116] and the jury was unwilling to draw the inference that it had continued after designation.[117] The jury also seems to have had difficulty with the distinction between intangible adherence and material support.[118] The judge instructed the jury that belief in the

---

[114] *NCRI*, 251 F.3d at 209.

[115] People's Mojahedin Org. of Iran v. Dep't of State, 356 U.S. App. D.C. 101, 327 F.3d 1238 (D.C. Cir. 2003). "Were there no classified information in the file, we could hardly find that the Secretary's determination that the Petitioner engaged in terrorist activities is 'lacking substantial support in the administrative record taken as a whole,' even without repairing to the classified information submitted to the court." *Id.* at 1244.

[116] Meg Laughlin, Jennifer Liberto and Justin George, *8 Times, al-Arian Hears Not Guilty*, St. Petersburg Times, Dec. 7, 2005, *available at* http://www.sptimes.com/2005/12/07/ 8_times_ _al_arian_hea.shtml:

> While they knew that Al-Arian had phone conversations with PIJ leadership, jurors said, they still had trouble finding proof of illegal acts, since his conversations occurred before the PIJ was declared a Foreign Terrorist Organization, making association illegal.

Two videotapes in which he was shown extolling Islamist revolution and action against Israel were also made before the designation.

[117] *Id.*:

> There was much discussion among jurors over what prosecutors considered one of their best pieces of evidence: a 1995 letter Al-Arian wrote to a Kuwaiti legislator requesting money so actions, similar to a suicide bombing in Gaza, "could continue." The letter was found in Al-Arian's house during an FBI search, and prosecutors frequently mentioned it as proof of Al-Arian's criminal intent. But Ron, the juror, noted the original was found in Al-Arian's house, meaning it could not have been sent. And no government witnesses ever testified that it was sent.

[118] *Id.*

> Jurors say they were strongly affected by the jury instructions. In particular, they kept returning to these words: "Our law does not criminalize beliefs or mere membership in an organization. A person who is in sympathy with the legitimate aim of an organization but does not intend to accomplish that aim by a resort to illegal activity is not punished for adherence to lawful purposes of speech."

goals or membership in an organization is protected by the First Amendment, which it certainly is, but it is not clear to what extent the jury understood that contributing money is an action that is not protected by the First Amendment.

In pretrial motions, the trial judge had stated that a person could not be convicted of material support without proof that "the defendant knew (had a specific intent) that the support would further the illegal activities of a FTO." As an illustration of what the judge meant by this, he referred to the "innocent" transaction of a New York cabdriver taking a representative of an FTO to the United Nations for peace negotiations. Under this theory, a donation restricted to "humanitarian" purposes such as education or clothing could also be protected. The judge went on to assert that "a jury could infer a specific intent when a defendant knows that the organization continues to commit illegal acts and the defendant provides funds to that organization knowing that money is fungible and, once received, the donee can use the funds for any purpose it chooses."

The problem with this analysis is that it relies on crafting exceptions to the statute that then make the statute vague and potentially confusing to a jury. The judge implies that the defendant is not responsible for the fungible nature of money if the organization makes a credible representation that the money will not be used for any but humanitarian purposes.[119] Congress specifically made the donation criminal regardless of the purpose, so the question is whether there is a First Amendment right to donate. The trial judge treated this as a Fifth Amendment vagueness issue, but there is no vagueness if there are no exceptions. The exceptions that the judge wanted for protection of "innocent conduct" are only innocent if their provision does not further the violent purposes of the organization, a judgment with which Congress could rationally disagree. The cab driver and hotel clerk examples are instances in which Congress has spoken clearly and any *de minimis* exceptions should be created by prosecutorial discretion rather than rewriting of the statute.

Mohammed Hammoud engaged in cigarette smuggling operation, running cigarettes from North Carolina to Michigan and selling them without paying the Michigan tax. Much of the profits from these untaxed sales then were transmitted to representatives of Hizballah (the Fourth Circuit's spelling).[120] Hammoud's argument on appeal of his conviction was similar to that of the trial judge in *al-Arian* — that criminalizing support for the

---

[119] In fact, the judge stated that:

> Other examples of innocent conduct that could be prohibited include the same person allowing the FTO member to spend the night at his house, cashing a check, loaning the member a cell phone for use during the stay, or allowing the member to use the fax machine or laptop computer in preparing the petition. And, the additional phrase "expert advice or assistance" added by the Patriot Act in 2002 could also fail as unconstitutionally vague.

Id. at n.31.

[120] United States v. Hammoud, 381 F.3d 316 (4th Cir. 2004) (en banc).

humanitarian prongs of an organization would violate the First Amendment and that the statute thus was overbroad and vague. The Fourth Circuit met the overbreadth argument by saying that "Hammoud has utterly failed to demonstrate, however, that any overbreadth is substantial in relation to the legitimate ends of § 2339B." This response essentially weighs the difficulty of crafting *de minimis* exceptions for First Amendment purposes against the need for sanctioning donations of money, particularly given the fungibility of cash, and gives the nod to law enforcement. Once the overbreadth is dealt with in this fashion, the vagueness argument disappears because, as the court said, "There is nothing at all vague about the term 'currency.'"[121]

One dissenting judge in *Hammoud* adopted the reasoning of the trial court in *al-Arian*.[122] The judge pointed out that lack of a "specific intent" requirement would mean that "the statute would apply to a citizen who sent a human rights or constitutional law treatise to Hizballah to urge it to respect human rights and desist from committing terrorist acts."[123] It is not easy to see how the statute produces this result — written material arguing against violence could hardly be supportive of the organization. But even assuming that the statute could be so read, this argument is still simply the overbreadth argument to which the majority answered that the *de minimis* applications were not fatal to the legitimate purposes and reach of the statute.

Thus, the arguments over material support boil down to this: when the legislature criminalizes precursor conduct, how much innocent conduct should it be allowed to sweep in? If the Second Amendment were repealed and legislatures decided that stopping murders would be substantially advanced by banning handguns, then some people would argue that the legislation has gone too far by criminalizing the defensive possession of handguns. To this argument, the proponents of the ban would argue that we can't be sure that a handgun in a nice person's possession wouldn't end up being used for wrongful purposes and it's better to forestall the "innocent" possession that take a chance on a violent use. In this kind of argument, the issue is at what point does society decide that the precursor conduct is sufficiently socially desirable that we should allow it to continue despite its possibility of producing harm in extreme situations.

Stewart is the third of our noteworthy material support prosecutions.[124] Sheikh Rahman's lawyer, Lynne Stewart, and their interpreter were charged with violating prison regulations and also violating § 2339B by using their consultations with the Sheikh to pass messages to and from the Islamic Group. They moved to dismiss the indictment including a challenge to that portion of the statute prohibiting provision of "communication devices," and the court agreed that their use of telephones could not

---

[121] *Id.* at 331.

[122] *Id.* at 371 (Gregory, J., dissenting).

[123] *Id.* at 376.

[124] United States v. Sattar, 272 F. Supp. 2d 348 (S.D.N.Y. 2003).

be the basis of a criminal charge. "[B]y criminalizing the mere use of phones and other means of communication the statute provides neither notice nor standards for its application such that it is unconstitutionally vague as applied." The court agreed with the Ninth Circuit that the "personnel" provision was also unconstitutionally vague. The 2004 amendments to the statute included clarification that provision of services consists of providing "individuals (who may be or include himself) to work under that terrorist organization's direction or control."[125]

In *United States v. Khan*,[126] the trial judge found that training could be a violation of the material support statute under active circumstances. The charges in *Khan* included provision of material support on the basis of supplying personnel who received training. Noting the *HLP II* holding, the court pointed out that the government had since interpreted the statute to apply only when the training went toward supplying personnel who would act on behalf of the organization in a directed capacity.

> The conspiracy alleged in Count 5 was not to provide 'personnel' who would speak on behalf of LET, or provide moral support, or simply receive training, but to provide personnel who, after receiving training, would serve that organization as soldiers, recruiters, and procurers of supplies. Indeed, the evidence shows that the conspirators did much more than just receive training from LET — they returned to the United States, recruited co-conspirators, and purchased technology for LET to use in its attacks on India.[127]

Hamid Hayat was convicted of violation of § 2339B on the basis of having attended a terrorist training camp.[128]

The self-proclaimed largest Muslim charity in the U.S. was the Holy Land Foundation, whose assets were frozen upon its designation as an SDGT in December 2001, an action that was upheld by the D.C. Circuit.[129] The Government then brought criminal charges under § 2339B against HLF and five individuals affiliated with HLF based on funneling money to Hamas through various cutouts. The defendants' motions to dismiss on the ground of vagueness were denied by the trial court.[130]

> The defendants contend that if their donations to alleged subsidiaries of Hamas violated the statute, then § 2339B is unconstitutional because "[n]othing in the language of the statute gives a

---

[125] 18 U.S.C. § 2339B(h) (2007). In what must be a masterpiece of redundancy, the statute goes on to provide that "Individuals who act entirely independently of the foreign terrorist organization to advance its goals or objectives shall not be considered to be working under the foreign organization's direction and control."

[126] 309 F. Supp. 2d 789 (E.D. Va. 2004), *aff'd*, 461 F.3d 477 (4th Cir. 2006).

[127] *Khan*, 309 F. Supp. 2d at 822.

[128] United States v. Hayat, 2007 U.S. Dist. LEXIS 40157 (2007).

[129] Holy Land Foundation v. Ashcroft, 333 F.3d 156 (D.C. Cir. 2003).

[130] United States v. Holy Land Foundation for Relief & Dev., 2007 U.S. Dist. LEXIS 37464 (N.D. Tex. 2007).

person of common intelligence notice that he or she may be found guilty of violating that statute by providing humanitarian aid through organizations alleged (although not designated) to be associated with" a foreign terrorist organization. The defendants give insufficient credit to people of "common intelligence." It requires no extraordinary acumen to realize that funneling money to an organization operated by or on behalf of a specially designated terrorist organization with the intent that the money be passed on to the designated terrorist group would, at the very least, constitute an attempt to provide support or resources to the terrorist organization in contravention of § 2339B. The statute would be unconstitutional in its application to the defendants only if it sought to punish them for innocently giving money to organizations which they later learned were affiliated with Hamas. However, if the government is unable to prove that the defendants knew the groups to whom they gave money were affiliated with Hamas when they provided support, then the defendants cannot be found guilty under the terms of the statute.[131]

Meanwhile, civil plaintiffs who obtained a $116,000,000 default judgment against Hamas[132] have sought to levy on the assets of HLF, but those assets are currently frozen by the federal government.[133]

An unusual twist on the material support theme was the corporate guilty plea entered by Chiquita Banana on March 19, 2007, for providing material support to the United Self-Defense Forces of Colombia (AUC).[134] The company made payments after the AUC was designated in 2001 but believed those payments were necessary to protect its personnel and property from harm — in other words, the company executive believed the company was a victim of extortion. Counsel advised the company executives to disclose the payments, which they did in communications to the U.S. Department of Justice, but the payments still continued. In announcing the plea agreement, DOJ emphasized its view that extortion is no excuse for the making of illegal payments.

Another conviction that pushes the envelope of conspiracy is that of Rafiq Sabir, a doctor who got caught up in the zeal of Islamist brotherhood. He was convicted of conspiring and attempting to provide material support to al Qaeda when most of what he did was talk. According to the U.S. Attorney's press release, his only overt acts were that he pledged loyalty to al Qaeda and that he "wrote down his telephone numbers in code, and gave them to the [undercover agent] for the UC to provide to the "brothers" in

---

[131] *Id.* at *6-7.

[132] Estates of Ungar *ex rel.* Strachman v. Palestinian Auth., 304 F. Supp. 2d 232, 238, 242 (D.R.I. 2004).

[133] *Holy Land Foundation*, 2007 U.S. App. LEXIS at 17135 (on behalf of Ungars).

[134] U.S. Dep't Justice Press Release, *Chiquita Brands International Pleads Guilty to Making Payments to a Designated Terrorist Organization And Agrees to Pay $25 Million Fine*, available *at* www.usdoj.gov/opa/pr/2007/March/07_nsd_161.html (3/19/07).

Saudi Arabia, inviting them to call him and expressing his desire to meet them."[135]

§ 5.04 MATERIAL SUPPORT — NO DESIGNATED FTO

A rare example of a successful prosecution under § 2339A (material support in aid of a terrorist act) is *United States v. Awan*.[136] Awan was arrested and pleaded guilty on credit card fraud charges. While serving that sentence, he was indicted for provision of material support and conspiracy to commit murder. The evidence consisted primarily of his own admissions and statements to the effect that he had provided money to a "leader of the Khalistan Commando Force ("KCF") and that the KCF was involved in killing people in India." In post-trial motions, he argued that there was no "meeting of the minds" regarding a conspiracy in India to murder, kidnap or maim. His statements, however, indicated full awareness that the KCF was involved in killings and plots to assassinate the Prime Minister of India. He admitted providing money and the court ruled that there was ample basis for the jury to infer that the money was intended for use in furthering the objective of killing in India.

Another interesting example under § 2339A is *United States v. Lakhani*,[137] who was convicted of conspiring to provide material support when he attempted to peddle a fake missile which had been concocted by U.S. and Russian authorities.[138] The episode resulting in his arrest

---

[135] Press Release, *Florida Doctor Convicted of Conspiring and Attempting to Support al Qaeda* (May 21, 2007), *available at* www.usdoj.gov/usao/nys/pressreleases/May07/sabirconvictionpr.pdf:

> The evidence at trial proved that Sabir conspired with his good friend, Tarik Shah, to provide martial arts training and medical assistance to al Qaeda, through a man whom they believed to be a recruiter for the terrorist organization. The recruiter was in fact an FBI agent, acting undercover, who recorded numerous conversations involving Sabir and Shah, including the May 2005 ceremony in the Bronx. During that meeting, Sabir and Shah pledged "bayat," or allegiance, to Osama bin Laden and al Qaeda, and agreed to provide Sabir's medical expertise and Shah's martial arts expertise to train al Qaeda fighters.
>
> From September 2003 through May 2005, Shah engaged in multiple meetings and conversations, first with a confidential source (the "CS") and later with the FBI undercover agent (the"UC"). In these conversations, the vast majority of which were recorded, Shah discussed his desire and intent to aid al Qaeda, and repeatedly discussed his friend, who was a doctor, as being someone who shared his desire.

[136] 2007 U.S. Dist. LEXIS 16063 (2007).

[137] 480 F.3d 171 (3d Cir. 2007).

[138] The court was almost amused by both the defendant and the key informant ("As we reviewed the twelve-volume record in this case, we increasingly agreed with one of the foreign witnesses who remarked at one point, '[M]uch of this has become incomprehensible even more.'" *Id*. at 175 n.4).

> Lakhani, now 71 years old, was born in India but resided in London. He was a trader (i.e., a "middleman") and didn't limit himself in scope — groceries, rice, textiles, oil. In addition to these benign commodities, Lakhani also traded in weapons, which had become his primary business in recent years. Though arms

involved a paid informant who negotiated to purchase a shoulder-fired Russian missile. FBI and Russian agents supplied an operational missile filled with sand rather than explosives. Lakhani's principal arguments on appeal were entrapment and violations of due process through the involvement of government agents, arguments that were answered by a sufficient showing of "predisposition" on Lakhani's part.

Predisposition negatives the idea of entrapment and can be shown by "(1) an existing course of criminal conduct similar to the crime for which the defendant is charged, (2) an already formed design on the part of the accused to commit the crime for which he is charged, or (3) a willingness to commit the crime for which he is charged as evidenced by the accused's ready response to the inducement."[139]

---

trading carries sinister connotations, it can be a legitimate business. And indeed, Lakhani had previously engaged in legal arms transactions. In this case, however, he didn't discriminate among customers, illegality notwithstanding.

    Muhammad Habib Ur Rehman is a native of Pakistan and a professional informant. He began his informing career by working for the Pakistani government as it combated that country's drug trade. Eventually, Rehman was introduced to the U.S. Drug Enforcement Agency and then served as one of its informants on international drug trading and terrorism. Along the way, Rehman informed on one-too-many people, and his U.S. handlers were forced to extract him and his family from Pakistan. In the United States, where Rehman received asylum, he continued working as an informant for the DEA and, then, the Federal Bureau of Investigation. Rehman estimates that he has received about $400,000 from the Government in his 19 years of informing. For reasons unclear, Rehman was deemed "untrustworthy" in July 2001 and let go from Government service.

Id. at 174.

[139] *Id*. at 179.

Chapter 6

INTERNATIONAL LEGAL ACTION

SYNOPSIS

International action to control violence comes in two forms. First is cooperation among states, traditionally consisting of extradition of alleged offenders by one state for trial in another, and in recent years emerging as codified agreements to cooperate in the detection, apprehension, and prosecution of offenders. The second, and much more recent, phenomenon is collective action in the form of supranational tribunals. American law students will find familiar themes in the difference between trial of an offender under state law compared with definition and prosecution of crimes by the federal government. Thus far, however, the only international tribunals are for war crimes, crimes against humanity, and genocide. That leaves terrorism to be prosecuted in domestic courts despite the strong international interest in suppressing it.

One state may wish to enlist the help of other states because perpetrators have fled their borders,[1] because the perpetrators have support systems beyond those borders,[2] or because the incident took place against the state's interests but outside its borders.[3] In these instances, the state is interested in international sanctions and assistance to redress an incident or to avoid

---

[1] *See generally* United States v. Yousef, 327 F.3d 56 (2003).

[2] The U.S. has sought rendition of a number of alleged al Qaeda operatives and has cooperated with other nations both in secret and in public renditions.

[3] *See generally* United States v. Yunis, 924 F.2d 1086 (1991).

a future threat to the state represented. But the interest in cooperative suppression of terrorism extends beyond those basic pragmatic concerns. Nations have seen counter-terrorism to be within their mutual interest because of the very nature of the interests affected.

The right to personal physical integrity theoretically would be violated by even the most minor instance of assault, but surely not every schoolyard fight is going to become the subject of an international criminal tribunal. Therefore, the international community will find it necessary to subdivide its recognized rights into two subclasses, one consisting of those rights that will be protected by international enforcement institutions and one for those which the nations agree to enforce themselves. Thus far, the first subclass consists only of war crimes, crimes against humanity, and genocide.[4] The second subclass, those to be enforced by the nations themselves without an international tribunal, consists of slavery,[5] piracy,[6] hostage taking,[7] torture,[8] terrorist financing,[9] and a few others defined by international convention.[10]

There is a further subclass to this second subclass of rights, those that cry out for enforcement under an international legal regime and those that can be left to enforcement under the municipal law of a state with a sufficient connection. The first subclass consists of crimes condemned by *jus cogens* (law of nations that is peremptorily binding) and consisting of *erga omnes* (among all) offenses.[11] Not all offenses condemned by conventions and customary law will be *erga omnes*. For example, despite prohibitions on racial discrimination in human rights covenants,[12] it is not likely

---

[4] International Criminal Court, Statute of Rome (ICC). There is a separate crime of aggression that is folded into war crimes here for convenience.

[5] *See* International Covenant on Civil and Political Rights (ICCPR) art. 8; Universal Declaration of Human Rights (UDHR) art. 4.

[6] *See* Convention on the Law of the Sea.

[7] *See* ICCPR art. 9.

[8] *See* ICCPR art. 7, UDHR art. 5.

[9] *See* International Convention for the Suppression of the Financing of Terrorism, G.A. Res. 54/109 (Dec. 9, 1999).

[10] For example, narcotics trafficking is covered by three principal conventions and a United Nations Commission to facilitate cooperation. *See* www.unodc.org/unodc/en/drug_and_crime_conventions.html.

[11] The basis for and scope of the term *erga omnes* was discussed by the ICJ in the *Barcelona Traction* case in these terms:

> In view of the importance of the rights involved, all States can be held to have a legal interest in their protection; they are obligations erga omnes. Such obligations derive, for example in contemporary international law, from the outlawing of acts of aggression, and of genocide, as also from the principles and rules concerning the basic rights of the human person, including protection from slavery and racial discrimination.

Case concerning the Barcelona Traction, Light & Power Co., Ltd., 1970 I.C.J. 3, ¶¶ 33-34; *see* MAURIZIO RAGAZZI, THE CONCEPT OF INTERNATIONAL OBLIGATIONS *ERGA OMNES* (1997).

[12] UDHR arts. 2, 7, 26.

that private sporadic racial epithets are going to be the subject of a criminal prosecution under international law anytime soon.

Slavery and piracy are in the *erga omnes* category because they are difficult to accomplish without international or non-national (high seas) components. Absent those cross-border aspects, they amount only to false imprisonment and theft, matters that can be addressed by the state in which they occur. But with the cross-border aspects, they become especially difficult for any one nation to address adequately and become a threat to all nations — hence the universal jurisdiction.

Similarly, torture is actionable if accomplished with state action, and otherwise is personal assault, battery, and mayhem. Thus, state-condoned torture is an offense *erga omnes* while personal torture is not.[13] Hostage-taking and terrorist financing are criminal only in the context of international traffic. For example, a hostage situation in a purely domestic incident, such as a local bank robbery or marital dispute, does not rise to the level of international concern.

§ 6.01 CRIMINAL LAW WITH COOPERATION

[A] International Conventions Related to Terrorism

The United Nations Office for Drug Control and Crime Prevention (ODCCP) lists 12 separate Conventions Against Terrorism. The principal headings are aircraft crimes, protection of nuclear materials, hostage taking, and the most recent on financing of terrorism.

International concern over terrorism started with airplane hijackings in the 1960s. Although many of those incidents were just attempts by desperate persons to get "home" or conversely to flee to a perceived safer environment, some created dangerous situations as pilots were forced to divert their aircraft.[14] These incidents also occasioned significant expense for the companies and countries involved. Even when the receiving country could make political mileage of the incident, it could prove costly.

For example, there were 19 hijackings of U.S. planes to Cuba in 1968 and 77 in 1969, at a time when pilots of all U.S. commercial flights carried landing instructions for Havana and were instructed to cooperate. When a hijacker diverted a plane from the U.S. to Cuba, the Cuban government probably realized some political gains from the attendant publicity of people desperate to get to Cuba, but Cuba would have incurred expenses in

---

[13] *See Ex parte* Pinochet Ugarte (No. 3), [2000] 1 AC 147, [1999] 2 All ER 97 (HL 1999).

[14] Wikipedia, *Aircraft Hijacking, available at* http://en2.wikipedia.org/wiki/Aircraft_hijacking (last visited June 21, 2007):

> Since 1947, 60% of hijackings have been refugee escapes. In 1968-69 there was a massive rise in the number of hijacking. In 1968 there were 27 hijackings and attempted hijackings to Cuba. In 1969 there were 82 recorded hijack attempts worldwide, more than twice the total attempts for the whole period 1947-67.

landing, refueling, and sending the plane on its way before it even experienced the political costs associated with harboring someone who had committed what most countries would consider the crime of piracy. So, even in this early stage of posturing, there were motivations on the part of all nations to curtail the incidence of aircraft hijacking.

The attitude of the international community changed with the campaign of Palestinian hijackings beginning with an El Al flight in 1968 and continuing through 1972 with hijackings of U.S. and British flag carriers. In some of those incidents, passengers and crew were killed. In most the hijackers were set free as part of negotiated deals, and in some instances the planes were blown up at the end of their usefulness.

The first extortionate or terrorist hijacking was on July 23, 1968, when an El Al flight was diverted to Algiers. After negotiations between Algiers and Israel, several PFLP members were released by Israel in return for release of the plane, crew, and passengers. This incident is generally regarded as the only successful hijacking of an El Al flight. On September 6, 1970, two U.S. planes and one Swiss plane were hijacked by PFLP members; a British plane was taken the next day. Three ended up in Jordan and one in Cairo before all four were blown up.

As the hijacking phenomenon unfolded, western nations enacted specific statutes criminalizing the offense of air piracy and attempted to extradite perpetrators. The host country, however, might be unwilling to extradite because it had promised safe haven to the hijacker as part of a deal in which the plane was allowed to land and the hijacker freed the crew and passengers. Reneging on that promise would then cause difficulties in future negotiations with hijackers.

The first international convention dealing with the issue attempted to meet the threat head-on by authorizing the pilot ("aircraft commander") to subdue any person who threatened the safety of a flight.[15] It also created an obligation on the part of a state in which an aircraft landed to restore control of the aircraft to its crew and to send it on its way. Notably, however, the treaty specifically stated that "nothing in this Convention shall be deemed to create an obligation to grant extradition."[16]

A major shift in international opinion, and international law, occurred when consensus formed around the obligation to extradite hijackers for criminal prosecution. The 1970 Hague Convention[17] dealing with aircraft hijacking and the 1971 Montreal Convention[18] dealing with placing explosives on an airplane attempted to establish two central themes: signatory countries agreed to punish the proscribed offenses with "severe penalties"

---

[15] Tokyo Convention on Offences and Certain Other Acts Committed on Board Aircraft (Sept. 14, 1963).

[16] Id. Art. 16(2).

[17] Convention for the Suppression of Unlawful Seizure of Aircraft (Dec. 16, 1970).

[18] Convention for the Suppression of Unlawful Acts Against the Safety of Civil Aviation (Sept. 23, 1971).

and a country having custody of an offender was required either to extradite or prosecute.

The 1972 Munich Olympics saw the kidnaping of the Israeli wrestling team and the botched rescue attempt at the Munich airport; the final outcome of this incident was 9 Israeli dead, 3 terrorists shot and three terrorists imprisoned for a brief period. Then came the Achille Lauro, with the cold-blooded murder of a U.S. citizen in a wheelchair, and a series of kidnapings and murders of western diplomats in various African and Middle East countries. The 1970s were most notable for the rise of the Palestinian-oriented terrorist movements, although some leftist groups continued to operate in various places around the world. The initial shock of Palestinian attacks in Europe may have been amplified by European countries' kid-glove treatment of terrorists who happened to be captured during that time.[19] Bruce Hoffman lends some support for this view by pointing out that "a handful of Palestinian terrorists had overcome a quarter-century of neglect and obscurity" and that "the number of organizations engaged in international terrorism grew from only eleven in 1968 . . . to an astonishing fifty-five in 1978."[20]

The 1980s were most notable for the collapse of the Soviet Union, which left Muslim freedom fighters trained and equipped by the U.S. with no target for their frustration and rage except for the West in general and the U.S. in specific.[21] The bombing of Pan Am 103 over Lockerbie, Scotland was the first significant event to touch U.S. interests or soil, but it was rather clearly a state-sanctioned act that was met with both military and diplomatic sanctions against Libya. The two key events that triggered U.S. involvement in counter-terrorism were the first bombing of the World Trade Center[22] and the bombings of U.S. embassies in Africa, for which a number of associates of Osama bin Laden were convicted and bin Laden himself was indicted.[23] By the 1990s, the leftist groups were more or less moribund, the IRA had entered into peace accords, and ethnic-religious conflict took center stage. The transition from the second to the third millennium was accompanied by the campaign of suicide bombings in Israel, widespread terrorism across the sub-Asian islands and Africa, the ethnic bloodbaths of Yugoslavia and Rwanda, and then came 9/11.

Meanwhile, the diplomatic wheels were grinding out more Conventions: taking of hostages, piracy against maritime shipping, acts involving airports, control of nuclear devices and plastic explosives. Each of the conventions commits a signatory nation to define the offenses as crimes within

---

[19] ALAN DERSHOWITZ, WHY TERRORISM WORKS (2002).

[20] BRUCE HOFFMAN, INSIDE TERRORISM 75 (1998).

[21] JOHN COOLEY, UNHOLY WARS (2002).

[22] United States v. Rahman, 189 F.3d 88 (2d Cir. 1999).

[23] United States v. Bin Laden, 92 F. Supp. 2d 225 (S.D.N.Y. 2000).

its own law,[24] which in turn leads to a commitment either to extradite or to place the accused on trial.[25]

No convention prior to the "Financing of Terrorism" in 1999 attempted to define terrorism. Instead, the conventions described "offenses" and committed signatory nations to criminalize those offenses. In many instances, there were exceptions to the description of offenses such as that the offense of placing an explosive on an aircraft did not apply to military or police aircraft.[26] Another notable exception was that exploding a device in a public place did not constitute an offense under the convention if the perpetrator and victims were nationals of the same nation in which the acts occurred.[27] It was only in these backhanded fashions that the international community addressed the phenomenon known as "terrorism" by excluding from international sanctions some actions that would be criminal under domestic law but not of concern to other nations.[28]

---

[24] A typical example is the Convention Against the Taking of Hostages (Dec. 18, 1979):
Article 1:

> Any person who seizes or detains and threatens to kill, to injure or to continue to detain another person (hereinafter referred to as the "hostage") in order to compel a third party, namely, a State, an international intergovernmental organization, a natural or juridical person, or a group of persons, to do or abstain from doing any act as an explicit or implicit condition for the release of the hostage commits the offence of taking of hostages ("hostage-taking") within the meaning of this Convention.

Article 2:

> Each State Party shall make the offences set forth in article 1 punishable by appropriate penalties which take into account the grave nature of those offences.

[25] *Id.* art. 8:

> The State Party in the territory of which the alleged offender is found shall, if it does not extradite him, be obliged, without exception whatsoever and whether or not the offence was committed in its territory, to submit the case to its competent authorities for the purpose of prosecution, through proceedings in accordance with the laws of that State.

[26] Convention for the Suppression of Unlawful Acts Against the Safety of Civil Aviation, art. 4(1).

[27] Convention for the Suppression of Terrorist Bombings, art. 3 (Jan. 12, 1998).

[28] One of the oddest provisions in all these Conventions is the one that raises the "freedom fighter" issue in the Convention Against the Taking of Hostages, article 12, which excepts actions "in which peoples are fighting against colonial domination and alien occupation and against racist regimes in the exercise of their right of self-determination." This provision is ambiguous. It might simply refer incidents that occur in an "armed conflict" to the appropriate Geneva Convention and accompanying laws of war or it might be read to exclude hostage taking from any sanctions if done in pursuit of resistance to colonialism or oppression.

In the Convention for the Suppression of Financing of Terrorism, it finally became necessary to define what the international community conceived to be terrorism:

Article 2

1. Any person commits an offence within the meaning of this Convention if that person by any means, directly or indirectly, unlawfully and wilfully, provides or collects funds with the intention that they should be used or in the knowledge that they are to be used, in full or in part, in order to carry out:

(a) An act which constitutes an offence within the scope of and as defined in one of the treaties listed in the annex; or

(b) Any other act intended to cause death or serious bodily injury to a civilian, or to any other person not taking an active part in the hostilities in a situation of armed conflict, when the purpose of such act, by its nature or context, is to intimidate a population, or to compel a Government or an international organization to do or to abstain from doing any act.

The Convention exempts violence against persons engaged in a "situation of armed conflict" to place those persons under the various rules and conventions governing warfare. This is not to say that any person engaged in armed conflict can kill or be killed with impunity but that the rules are to be found elsewhere.

The purpose requirement (to intimidate a population or coerce a government) contains a host of interesting questions. For example: what is the point of the mens rea requirement? what is a population? what does it mean to measure an act "by its nature or context?"

One reason for the purpose requirement may be to distinguish terrorism from ordinary criminal behavior. If a drug dealer shoots an informer on the streets of Los Angeles, that is criminal behavior which would not ordinarily trigger thoughts of any connection to international terrorism. But if the drug dealer lets it be known that his "troops" will conduct drive-by shootings in any neighborhood in which a snitch or informer might be living, this would be terrorism within the terms of the Convention because the purpose of the action is to intimidate a population. The Convention would then apply to someone who is contributing funds and would require that person's host country to cooperate and extradite the contributor to the country where the terrorist actions occur.

Our drug-dealing terrorist scenario may seem a bit far-fetched but it really isn't. The frightening aspect of terrorism is that it is organized violence. To be organized requires funding, and the link between drug trafficking and terrorism has been widely reported over the past several decades. If drug money is being used to promote violence and fear within another country, then it seems a perfectly appropriate subject of international cooperation to intervene.

What may be more critical in this scenario than the "purpose to intimidate" is whether the violence is promoted by an organization capable of reaching across borders to create "widespread or systematic" violence against civilians. The size and strength of the organization, its ability to plan an attack, and its level of international resources make the terrorist organization an appropriate subject of international criminal law. The purpose is really irrelevant except that it is part of the criminal scheme.

If intimidation were the sole purpose of a conspiracy, then it would be a psychopathic act, perhaps undertaken just for the mere enjoyment of watching other people suffer. Psychopathic behavior has not been the hallmark of terrorism because the psychopath tends to work alone and eventually triggers his own demise.[29] We may be legitimately frightened of psychopaths, and they can wreak enormous damage before imploding or being captured. Certainly, there is every reason to take aggressive action to apprehend serial killers. But terrorism is a concern of the international community because of the organization that it entails, the ability to bring in new recruits to the cause, and the crossing of international borders with resources to carry out violence.

With regard to the funding provision itself, do I commit an offense if I contribute money to an organization that is often described in the popular press as "having ties" or being the "political arm" of a group that does use violence, such as Sinn Fein and the IRA? Or what about all the various factions of the PLO? The U.S. Supreme Court held in *Buckley v. Valeo*[30] that contributing money to an election campaign is protected by the free expression clause of the First Amendment to the U.S. Constitution. In subsequent cases, this protection was extended to contributions to campaigns for political agenda other than partisan elections,[31] but with some

---

[29] *See* LIBRARY OF CONGRESS, WHO BECOMES A TERRORIST AND WHY 47 (2002):

> The selectivity with which terrorist groups recruit new members helps to explain why so few pathologically ill individuals are found within their ranks. Candidates who appear to be potentially dangerous to the terrorist group's survival are screened out. Candidates with unpredictable or uncontrolled behavior lack the personal attributes that the terrorist recruiter is looking for.

See also CHRISTOPHER HARMON, TERRORISM TODAY 201 (2000):

> It is mostly on the surface that terrorism appears to be madness, or mindless. Behind the screaming and the blood there lies a controlling purpose, a motive, usually based in politics or something close to it, such as a drive for political and social change inspired by religion.

These assessments slightly obscure, but are still consistent with, the realization of the psychological profession that many psychopaths are capable of highly organized strategic or tactical planning in pursuit of their desires. A more complete picture would look at the factors that impel individuals to engage in widespread bloodshed free of moral strictures or thoughts for their victims. *See* Albert Bandura, *The Role of Selective Moral Disengagement in Terrorism and Counterterrorism*, *in* UNDERSTANDING TERRORISM 121 (2004); Donald M. Taylor & Winnifred Louis, *Terrorism and the Quest for Identity*, *in* UNDERSTANDING TERRORISM 169 (2004).

[30] 424 U.S. 1 (1976).

[31] First Nat'l Bank v. Bellotti, 435 U.S. 765 (1978).

important qualifiers.[32] The Court has also protected the freedom of association by which persons join organizations to carry out political objectives,[33] while leaving intact a holding that a state could require registration of Ku Klux Klan members on the ground that the KKK is devoted to unlawful terrorist activities.[34] Is there an argument that some of activity could fall within the definition in the Convention yet also be protected by the U.S. Constitution? These are questions worth exploring at another time because they bear on the validity of U.S. statutes that prohibit material support of terrorists[35] and terrorist organizations.[36]

[B] Extradition and Universal Jurisdiction

The International Conventions all proceed on the following structure: state parties agree to criminalize certain behavior, to cooperate in the apprehension of persons who commit that behavior, and then either to extradite or prosecute an accused person. Extradition arises only by operation of treaties and not by operation of general customary international law, although there is some reason to expect this to change under increasing pressure of international regimes.

One reason that it is important for states to agree to criminalize the defined behavior is that extradition hinges on the principle of "dual criminality," which permits extradition only if the alleged conduct would be criminal in both the requesting and requested states. Dual criminality does not require identity of all elements of the crime or of procedures for adjudication; it requires only that the specific alleged conduct would be criminal in both jurisdictions.

In this regard, there is at least one puzzling aspect of the handling by the British House of Lords of the request for extradition of Pinochet to Spain.[37] Pinochet was the former President of Chile who was accused of torture and murder during his tenure as head of state. When he went to Great Britain for medical treatment, the Spanish Government moved to extradite him to Spain to stand trial for criminal offenses under the heading of universal jurisdiction. Spain and Britain were both parties to the International Convention on Torture, which required extradition to a requesting country and required all parties to criminalize torture. Britain in 1988 adopted a statute (section 134) designed to carry out the Convention

---

[32] *See* Nixon v. Shrink Missouri Gov't PAC, 528 U.S. 377 (2000). *See also* Austin v. Michigan Chamber of Commerce, 494 U.S. 652 (1990). *See generally* Richard Briffault, *Issue Advocacy: Redrawing the Elections/Politics Line*, 77 Tex. L. Rev. 1751 (1999).

[33] NAACP v. Alabama *ex rel.* Patterson, 357 U.S. 449 (1958).

[34] Bryant v. Zimmerman, 278 U.S. 63 (1928).

[35] 18 U.S.C. § 2339A (2004).

[36] 18 U.S.C. § 2339B (2004). *See* Humanitarian Law Project v. United States Dep't. of Justice, 352 F.3d 382 (9th Cir. 2003) (*HLP III*) (holding parts of prior § 2339B to be unconstitutionally vague).

[37] *Ex parte* Pinochet Ugarte (No. 3), 2 All Eng. Rep. 97 (HL 1999).

by making it a crime under British law to commit torture in another country.

The House of Lords put considerable effort into determining whether Pinochet was extraditable for offenses committed before the Convention and before the adoption of section 134. Lord Browne-Wilkinson stated: "No one has suggested that before section 134 came into effect torture committed outside the United Kingdom was a crime under United Kingdom law." Why not? Surely torture and murder were crimes in the United Kingdom long before 1988. And dual criminality does not require that the requested nation assert extraterritorial jurisdiction over the alleged misconduct. Indeed, most often extradition will occur precisely because the crime was committed in another nation and the requested nation would not claim jurisdiction over it. So what is the point of requiring that the requested nation criminalize conduct committed outside its borders?

Maybe the real issue in *Pinochet* was not so much whether the acts would have been a crime under English law, as whether the particular crime would have been triable by Spain. Murder and assault would not have been criminal under international *jus cogens* and thus not subject to universal jurisdiction, but Torture (with a capital T) would be, so the question was whether there was an offense of Torture in England on which Spain could then base its extradition request.

Viewed in this fashion, the efficacy of international conventions requires either adoption into the criminal code of each nation a crime *as defined by the Convention*, or recognition of the offense as being against the universal norms of international law known as *jus cogens*. To rely on *jus cogens* and universal jurisdiction, it would not be necesary that the rendering state has a crime with many of the same elements because all states would have jurisdiction to enforce the universal norm.

International law essentially consists of three categories in ascending order of the degree to which a state is free to modify or ignore the rule: treaty law, customary law, and *jus cogens*.

> Viewed from the perspective of international law as understood in the first part of the 20th century, *jus cogens* seemed hardly conceivable, since at that time the will of States was taken as paramount: States could, between themselves, abrogate any of the rules of customary international law. . . . After World War II the international community became conscious of the necessity for any legal order to be based on some consensus concerning fundamental values which were not at the disposal of the subjects of this legal order. . . . These obligations are seen as fundamentally different from those existing vis-a-vis another State in the field of diplomatic protection.[38]

---

[38] Jochen Abr. Frowein, *Jus Cogens, in* III ENCYCLOPEDIA OF PUB. INT'L L. 66 (1997).

Another factor in this area is the relatively recent application of international law to individuals.[39] The earliest aspects of international law applied to individuals were general proscriptions against piracy and slave trading, but these were "crimes" that for the most part were committed on the high seas. In some instances, when a pirate was captured and punished (or killed without benefit of capture), there was little need for concern with international law because the municipal law of the nation was sufficient to punish offenses against its own nationals or its own shipping.[40] From early days, however, Gentili and Grotius asserted that every nation could punish piracy, eventually leading to both a universalist position and a position that the pirate had committed an offense against each nation that operated on the high seas.[41]

Following World War II, it has become possible to speak of crimes against universally applicable international law, *jus cogens*, such as war crimes, crimes against humanity, genocide, and probably slavery and piracy.[42] "Violations of *jus cogens* will in most cases also be violations of obligations *erga omnes*. . . . It has been recognized that in such cases third States may legitimately have recourse to some sort of response."[43]

The International Criminal Tribunal for Yugoslavia discussed some of this history in these terms:

> There exists today universal revulsion against torture: as a USA Court put it in *Filartiga v. Pena-Irala*, "the torturer has become, like the pirate and the slave trader before him, *hostis humani generis*, an enemy of all mankind." This revulsion, as well as the importance States attach to the eradication of torture, has led to the cluster of treaty and customary rules on torture acquiring a particularly high status in the international normative system, a status similar to that of principles such as those prohibiting genocide, slavery, racial discrimination, aggression, the acquisition of

---

[39] Michael Byers, *The Law and Politics of the Pinochet Case*, 10 DUKE J. COMP. & INT'L L. 415, 417-18 (2000):

> According to the traditional view, only states can be relevant actors in international law. States are sovereign and theoretically equal; it follows that one state cannot be impugned before the courts of another and, inexorably, that a head of state (or a former head of state) is entitled to claim absolute immunity from the jurisdiction of national courts, whether in criminal or civil proceedings.

> Traditional international law has changed profoundly since the Second World War. An alternative view has emerged, positing that the international community comprises not only states, but individuals, peoples, inter-governmental organizations, non-governmental organizations, and corporations. These entities have emerged as international actors engaged in international discourse and, in some areas, they have been granted important rights, such as the right of individuals not to be tortured.

[40] United States v. Wiltburger, 18 U.S. (5 Wheaton) 76 (1820); United States v. Klintock, 18 U.S. (5 Wheaton) 144 (1820).

[41] Alfred P. Rubin, *Piracy*, in III ENCYCLOPEDIA OF PUB. INT'L L. 1036-37 (1997).

[42] The Barcelona Traction Case, 1970 I.C.J. Reports 3.

[43] Frowein, *supra* note 38, at 68.

territory by force and the forcible suppression of the right of peoples to self-determination. [44]

The ICTY may be overreaching a bit in stating that racial discrimination and offenses against self-determination stand on the same footing as genocide or torture, but the Tribunal is probably correct in stating that torture has followed piracy and slaving in the international pantheon of universally proscribed offenses "against all mankind." The significance of that statement is that the individual who violates the "law of nations" may then be prosecuted wherever found, without regard to where the offenses occurred. As the cases in the Yugoslav and Rwanda tribunals have unfolded, genocide, war crimes, and atrocities have become the focal points of prosecutions by supranational bodies, which is the topic explored in the next section. What these developments are leading to is the question of whether terrorism itself may become such an internationally proscribed offense. If so, then a definition of the offense will be required.

§ 6.02 MULTINATIONAL CRIMINAL PROCEEDINGS

In addition to reliance on national courts, the last half of the 20th Century saw the beginnings of law enforcement through international criminal processes, starting with violations of the law of war. It is not likely that international tribunals will be established in the near future for dealing on a regular basis with terrorism, but some terrorist acts could be of such a scale to qualify as violations of the law of nations or the law of war. Moreover, the patterns of international tribunals will provide models and lessons to follow in dealing with the international phenomenon of terrorism. In a very real sense, terrorism touches more nations than do acts of war and could be seen as a concern of the total world community.

Starting with Nuremberg, the international community began to impose individual criminal sanctions for serious violations of the law of war, genocide, and crimes against humanity. The first effort of this type under United Nations auspices was establishment of the International Criminal Tribunal for the Former Yugoslavia in 1993, followed closely by the International Criminal Tribunal for Rwanda in 1994. Meanwhile, the U.N. was working through its International Law Commission on drafting a convention that would create a permanent international tribunal for prosecution of crimes against the law of war, genocide, and crimes against humanity.

[A] International Criminal Court

The Statute of the International Criminal Court went into effect on 1 July 2002 with 139 signatory nations. [45] The statute creates a court for prosecution of individuals who commit crimes in four categories: aggression,

---

[44] Prosecutor v. Furundzija, Case No. ICTY 95-17, Judgment, ¶ 147 (Dec. 10 1998).

[45] The official website of the Court is at www.icc-cpi.int/.

genocide, crimes against humanity, or war crimes. There are definitional elaborations for each of these categories except for the crime of aggression. The applicable law is stated to be the Statute itself, plus "applicable treaties and the principles and rules of international law, including the established principles of the international law of armed conflict" and "general principles of law derived by the Court from national laws."[46] The United States initially signed the document on 31 December 2000 (during the last weeks of the Clinton administration) and then withdrew its consent during the Bush administration.[47]

The ICC Prosecutor recently initiated its first case, proceeding against two senior officials of the Sudanese government and requesting cooperating nations to arrest the defendants.[48] The ICC is also following hot spots such as the Congo and Liberia in which allegations of atrocity in the course of civil wars have become almost commonplace.

Whether an act of terrorism might be prosecuted before the ICC depends not only on the definitions of crimes within its charter but also on the degree of power that the Court may obtain. As the statute now stands, there is a serious question whether the tribunal is capable of apprehending and prosecuting an alleged terrorist. The Statute creates a supranational body with investigatory power within the borders of any State Party but only through the "cooperation" and within the mechanisms of that state.[49] The cooperative approach, of course, recognized the "sovereign" status of nation-states and was central to obtaining ratification by many States that would not have consented to an external police force's operating within its borders.

When the U.N. Security Council created the International Criminal Tribunals for Yugoslavia and Rwanda, it provided the Prosecutors with somewhat more independent investigatory powers. "The Prosecutor shall have the power to question suspects, victims and witnesses, to collect evidence and to conduct on-site investigations. In carrying out these tasks, the Prosecutor may, as appropriate, seek the assistance of the State authorities concerned." In both the ICC and the ICT's, the Prosecutor is something of a hybrid between the executive prosecutor of the Anglo-American system and the investigating magistrate of the continental

---

[46] Rome Statute of the Int'l Criminal Ct., art. 21, U.N. Doc A/Conf 183/9* (as corrected Nov. 10, 1998 and July 12, 1999) (hereafter Rome Statute), *available at* www.icc-cpi.int/library/about/officialjournal/Rome_Statute_English.pdf.

[47] The U.S. government sent the following communique to the U.N. on May 6, 2002:

> This is to inform you, in connection with the Rome Statute of the International Criminal Court adopted on July 17, 1998, that the United States does not intend to become a party to the treaty. Accordingly, the United States has no legal obligations arising from its signature on December 31, 2000. The United States requests that its intention not to become a party, as expressed in this letter, be reflected in the depositary's status lists relating to this treaty.

[48] Prosecutor v. Ahmad Harun and Ali Kushayb, ICC-02/05-01/07, *available at* www.icc-cpi.int/library/cases/ICC-02-05-01-07-1_English.pdf (last visited April 27, 2007).

[49] Rome Statute art. 54.

system.[50] The prosecutor is not completely independent because of the supervision of the Pre-Trial Chamber but the assembling of evidence is not designed to be such a neutral judicial function as in the continental system.

There are some subtle differences among the three tribunals that will affect the ability of the prosecutors to investigate and assemble evidence of criminal activity. The power of the ICC Prosecutor to conduct "independent" investigations was a hot issue in the debates leading to the ICC but does not seem to have generated as much controversy in the ICTY and ICTR drafting because the Security Council functioned as a supra-national body enforcing a collective demand. As a practical matter, the ICT Prosecutors have a bit more force behind their investigatory powers because of the presence of U.N. peacekeeping forces on the ground, or the potential for forceful intervention.

In none of the three tribunals, however, is there provision for an independent police force. To analogize to federalism, it would be as if the U.S. Executive were not given authority to execute the laws itself but only the ability to call on the states for cooperation.[51] The ultimate stumbling block for the three tribunals is that none of them has independent arrest powers.[52] Regardless of how much cooperation the prosecutor obtains in investigating, and with the ICC that could turn out to be rather slight, the evidence will be worth very little if there is no power over the accused. If states look upon requests for "surrender" in the same fashion as they do extradition of their own nationals, then obtaining the person of an accused will be little more than a political exercise. Although the tribunals' statutes attempt to draw a distinction between surrender to the tribunal and extradition to another state,[53] the asylum state still may have very little incentive, and certainly will feel no compulsion, to deliver up one of its own nationals for a criminal trial.[54] Even with the greater force of the Security Council behind it, the ICTY has not been able to obtain the person of either Radovan Karadzic or Ratko Mladic to stand trial.[55]

Eventually, it should become true that an international tribunal such as the ICC will have coercive force behind it, and it should be hoped that it will not take a cataclysmic event on the order of the American Civil War to bring about realization of the need for states to yield a portion of their sovereignty to the whole. The action of the U.S. in withdrawing from the ICC was a major blow, not just to the existing regime but to any prospect of long-term development of coercive power.

---

[50] WILLIAM A. SCHABAS, AN INTRODUCTION TO THE INTERNATIONAL CRIMINAL COURT 94-96 (2001).

[51] The lack of an executive under the Articles of Confederation is widely cited as one of the principal motivations for drafting of the U.S. Constitution.

[52] LYAL S. SUNGA, THE EMERGING SYSTEM OF INTERNATIONAL CRIMINAL LAW 301-03 (1997).

[53] Rome Statute art. 102.

[54] SCHABAS, supra note 50, at 110-111.

[55] The U.S. has been the subject of criticism for tardiness in delivering suspects to the tribunals. Robert Kushen & Kenneth J. Harris, Surrender of Fugitives by the United States to the War Crimes Tribunals for Yugoslavia and Rwanda, 90 AMER. J. INT'L L. 254 (1996).

With regard to the definitions of crime and terrorism, there are certainly some possibilities. In the first place, the crime of "aggression" is not defined in the Statute at all. Because terrorists act without any authority, the terrorist attack is necessarily aggressive. But can an individual with no national authority commit the crime of aggression? The answer may turn on the question of the extent of state sponsorship behind the attack. One premise of the ICC, flowing from the international tribunal experience of Nuremberg and its progeny, is to make individuals responsible for producing unjustified wars, thus modifying the historic thrust of the law of war to curb the power of sovereigns and nations. But without inter-nation hostility, the crime would not seem to involve external concerns. If the terrorist is a national of the state in which violence occurs, then ordinarily the matter should be treated as an issue of domestic criminal activity. If the terrorist is supported or sponsored by another state, however, then the international community becomes involved. This issue is taken up first in the *Nicaragua* case and then in the ICTY analysis of state involvement.

One major impediment to ICC assertion of jurisdiction over acts of terrorism is simply that the Statute does not specify that authority with sufficient clarity to survive arguments of due process and fair notice. The ICC is not built for the purpose of internationalizing every aggressive act by an individual or organization against a signatory nation. Aggression in this sense almost certainly be limited to groups with at least the status of insurgents, if not belligerents, and acts that carry support from another state to the point that they might be deemed attributable to that state.

Aggression is different from other headings of offenses cognizable before the ICC. Attacking and murdering civilians is a component of a number of offenses under the general headings of "crimes against humanity," "genocide," and "war crimes," which may not carry the same connotation of involvement with a foreign state as would the concept of "aggression." The jurisdictional element of crimes against humanity is "part of a widespread or systematic attack directed against any civilian population." Similarly, the heading of "war crimes" applies to many types of acts but only when "part of a plan or policy or as part of a large-scale commission of such crimes" and perhaps only when there is an "armed conflict" whether international or not. These issues are considered in connection with the two ICT cases below, but first we should lay the groundwork with the WWII cases.

[B]   From Nuremberg to Fundamental Rights

The International Military Tribunal created for the purpose of trying Nazi war criminals by the victorious parties after World War II was governed by a Charter adopted through the Treaty of London.[56] The Charter

---

[56] The Avalon Project of Yale Law School provides extensive coverage of the documents and transcripts from the Nuremberg and related trials. *See* www.yale.edu/lawweb/avalon/imt/imt.htm (last visited June 21, 2007).

listed three categories of crimes: crimes of aggression, war crimes, and crimes against humanity. In what became known as the Trial of the Major War Criminals (or simply the Nuremberg Trial), twenty-two persons were indicted and tried by the tribunal (two more were indicted but not tried because one committed suicide and the other was too frail). Twelve were sentenced to death, three to life imprisonment, four to prison ranging from 10 to 20 years, and three were acquitted. Ten of the twelve sentenced to death were hanged on October 16, 1946. (Hermann Göring committed suicide just three hours before the hanging. Martin Bormann was tried in absentia and sentenced to death but it was later discovered that he had died.) Rudolf Hess was the controversial deputy to Hitler who flew to England in 1944, ostensibly to negotiate a peace without Hitler's approval; he was sentenced to life in prison and for decades was the only inmate of Spandau Prison in Berlin until his death at the age of 93 in 1987. The three persons acquitted at Nuremberg were sentenced by other courts to work camps. Conversely, Alfred Jodl was hanged but posthumously found by a German court to be not guilty of violating international law.

The Nuremberg Judgment of the Major War Criminals is something of a primer on customary international law and its application to individual defendants. The first issue was whether the Charter constituted an *ex post facto* law, to which the IMT responded:

> It was submitted that ex post facto punishment is abhorrent to the law of all civilised nations, that no sovereign power had made aggressive war a crime at the time the alleged criminal acts were committed, that no statute had defined aggressive war, that no penalty had been fixed for its commission, and no court had been created to try and punish offenders.

> In the first place, it is to be observed that the maxim *nullum crimen sine lege* is not a limitation of sovereignty, but is in general a principle of justice. To assert that it is unjust to punish those who in defiance of treaties and assurances have attacked neighbouring states without warning is obviously untrue, for in such circum-stances the attacker must know that he is doing wrong, and so far from it being unjust to punish him, it would be unjust if his wrong were allowed to go unpunished. Occupying the positions they did in the government of Germany, the defendants, or at least some of them must have known of the treaties signed by Germany, outlawing recourse to war for the settlement of international disputes; they must have known that they were acting in defiance of all international law when in complete deliberation they carried out the designs of invasion and aggression.[57]

With regard to war crimes, there was no *ex post facto* discussion because the various international conventions, such as the Hague Conventions of 1907, had sufficiently delineated the principles of individual responsibility

---

[57] *Id.* IMT Judgment, *The Law of the Charter.*

for illegal conduct during time of war. The defense asserted that there was no war in the occupied territories of the Reich once they were conquered, but the Tribunal answered merely that the occupation itself was illegal as an act of aggression, so this issue was not addressed further.

In the international arena, these concerns started with war crimes and "crimes against humanity." The latter were generally understood to refer to the atrocities of the Nazi regime, death camps, human experimentation, and brutality on a mass scale. With regard to war crimes, the IMT summed up its reactions this way:

> The truth remains that war crimes were committed on a vast scale, never before seen in the history of war. They were perpetrated in all the countries occupied by Germany, and on the High Seas, and were attended by every conceivable circumstance of cruelty and horror. There can be no doubt that the majority of them arose from the Nazi conception of "total war," with which the aggressive wars were waged. For in this conception of "total war," the moral ideas underlying the conventions which seek to make war more humane are no longer regarded as having force or validity. Everything is made subordinate to the overmastering dictates of war. Rules, regulations, assurances and treaties all alike are of no moment, and so, freed from the restraining influence of international law, the aggressive war is conducted by the Nazi leaders in the most barbaric way. Accordingly, war crimes were committed when and wherever the Fuehrer and his close associates thought them to be advantageous. [58]

With regard to "crimes against humanity," however, the IMT encountered the difficulty that the only statutory basis of criminality was contained in the Charter of the Tribunal itself, which referred to "inhumane acts committed against any civilian population, before or during the war, or persecutions on political, racial or religious grounds in execution of or in connection with any crime within the jurisdiction of the Tribunal." The Tribunal distinguished acts within its mandate this way:

> With regard to crimes against humanity, there is no doubt whatever that political opponents were murdered in Germany before the war, and that many of them were kept in concentration camps in circumstances of great horror and cruelty. The policy of terror was certainly carried out on a vast scale, and in many cases was organised and systematic. The policy of persecution, repression and murder of civilians in Germany before the war of 1939, who were likely to be hostile to the Government, was most ruthlessly carried out. The persecution of Jews during the same period is established beyond all doubt. To constitute crimes against humanity, the acts relied on before the outbreak of war must have been in execution of, or in connection with, any crime within the jurisdiction of the Tribunal. The Tribunal is of the opinion that revolting

---

[58] *Id.* IMT Judgment, *War Crimes and Crimes Against Humanity: General.*

and horrible as many of these crimes were, it has not been satisfactorily proved that they were done in execution of, or in connection with, any such crime. The Tribunal therefore cannot make a general declaration that the acts before 1939 were crimes against humanity within the meaning of the Charter, but from the beginning of the war in 1939 war crimes were committed on a vast scale, which were also crimes against humanity; and insofar as the inhumane acts charged in the Indictment, and committed after the beginning of the war, did not constitute war crimes, they were all committed in execution of, or in connection with, the aggressive war, and therefore constituted crimes against humanity. [59]

This statement is a bit puzzling because it seems to qualify the Charter's first clause of "inhumane acts committed against any civilian population, *before* or during the war" with the same limitations as the second clause dealing with "persecution . . . in execution of or in connection with any crime within the jurisdiction of the Tribunal." There is little explanation of the Tribunal's interpretation, but it is not terribly difficult to glean the impression that the Tribunal accepted some part of the defense argument that how Germany chose to treat its own citizens before the outbreak of war was no business of the international community but was instead a matter of internal policy. Respect for the sovereign decisions of the nation-state prior to the outbreak of war at that time still remained a hallmark of international law. Once Germany crossed its own borders, however, then its treatment of civilian populations at home could become a matter of concern for the international community.

The view that other nations have no jurisdiction within the internal affairs of one nation until that nation crosses its own borders, began to shift immediately after World War II. The U.N. General Assembly adopted the Universal Declaration of Human Rights in 1948. The first product of the Council of Europe was the European Covenant on Human Rights in 1950, which attempted to assure fair treatment of its own nationals by each signatory nation. At that time, this was an act of sovereignty by the signatory, not an application of extraterritorial will by other nations or by the international community. Given the economic devastation of Europe at the time, why was the ECHR adopted even before Conventions on economic matters?

Why did the international community become involved with Nazi treatment of its own civilians during time of war? Obviously, the coldly calculated attempt at genocide of the Jewish population colors the entire proceedings. This population included those with friends and relatives in many parts of the world. Secondly, even without the genocidal aspects, humane treatment of civilians during time of war had been a part of international concerns as exemplified in Common Article 3 of the Geneva Conventions. Finally, it is quite likely that the international community was convinced that Germany could not have engaged in the level of

---

[59] *Id.* IMT Judgment, *The Law Relating to War Crimes and Crimes Against Humanity.*

aggression it did without first being able to subjugate its own population. Regardless of the motivations, it is instructive that supranational involvement with human rights was very high, if not paramount, on the agenda of what Winston Churchill called the movement toward a "United States of Europe."

The immediate post-WWII actions of the international community are instructive for more than just the IMT. The first significant action of the United Nations was the Universal Declaration of Human Rights. It reflected a feeling that supra-national organizations would be concerned about a state's treatment of its own civilians even in peacetime. Eschewing the gross categories of war crimes, crimes against humanity, and genocide, the UDHR set out many of the same basic protections as the American concepts protecting "life, liberty, and property without due process of law," plus certain fundamental rights such as freedom of expression, religion, and marriage, and goes even further to establish "rights" to economic well-being. Of course, the Declaration is just a statement of principles by the General Assembly and is not considered legally binding in the sense that it will not serve by itself as the basis for a criminal prosecution against a violator.

The first Convention adopted by the new Council of Europe was not one dealing with economic rebuilding of Europe but was the European Convention on Human Rights. Later, the International Covenant on Civil and Political Rights was promulgated for adoption by the nations of the world. Both of these documents deal with the basics of protection from state action without attempting to guarantee minimum conditions of economic well-being, which were dealt with even later by the International Covenant on Economic, Social and Cultural Rights.

These post-WWII actions of the international community mirror the post-Civil War actions of the United States. By defining human rights that a state may not contravene within its own population, the supra-state bodies express their intolerance for subjugation of the state's own population.

The Universal Declaration and ECHR were followed by Conventions and Declarations addressing various forms of discrimination, "economic, social, and cultural rights," and "civil and political rights." In pursuing control of violence without regard to transnational activities, Conventions and Declarations were addressed to the status of refugees and torture, while the U.N. Security Council and NATO took increasingly active interest in what came to be known as "humanitarian" issues of the internal affairs of nations. All these developments bore on the development of customary international law condemning crimes against humanity, which have now been articulated as matters of international enforcement through the Tribunals dealing with Yugoslavia and Rwanda.

[C] International Criminal Tribunals

The first ad hoc International Criminal Tribunals were established to deal with atrocities from Yugoslavia and Rwanda. Since then, a Special

Court has been created jointly by Sierra Leone and the U.N. Security Council, and another by agreement between the United Nations and Cambodia.

The Sierra Leone court is a hybrid for which prosecutors and judges were chosen by Sierra Leone and the U.N. Secretary-General.[60] The funding for the court is to be provided by "voluntary contributions from the international community" and there is a management committee established from among the donors. The court has authority "to prosecute persons who bear the greatest responsibility for serious violations of international humanitarian law and Sierra Leonean law committed in the territory of Sierra Leone since 30 November 1996." As of summer 2007, the court has indicted eleven defendants but has not reached a judgment in any of the cases.

The Cambodia court is the outcome of a decade of negotiations among a number of nations including Cambodia. The process began in 1997 with a request for assistance from the Cambodian government.[61] A proposal for an international court was rejected by Cambodia and an agreement was reached initially for a "mixed" court of international and domestic partners. The King of Cambodia, however, promulgated a law in 2001 creating a special court within the Cambodian system for the prosecution of Khmer Rouge war crimes.[62] In March 2003, the U.N. and Cambodia came to agreement on a combination of domestic and international judges and prosecutors to staff the special court.

[1]   ICTY — Yugoslavia

The International Criminal Tribunal for Yugoslavia was established in 1993 by Security Council Resolution 827 in response to widespread allegations of atrocities in the republics that made up the former Yugoslavia. The Statute of the Tribunal adopted in the same resolution sets out four categories of offenses over which the Tribunal has authority:

3.   Grave breaches of the 1949 Geneva Conventions;

4.   Violations of the laws or customs of war;

5.   Genocide; and

6.   Crimes against humanity.

The Nuremberg Charter's lack of a separate category for genocide left it to be dealt with as a subcategory of war crimes or crimes against humanity, resulting in the Nuremberg Tribunal's holding that genocidal acts occurring before the outbreak of war in 1939 was not a violation of international law. By placing genocide in its own category, the Security Council is stating that genocide is a violation of international law without

---

[60] The website of the Sierra Leone court is at www.sc-sl.org/about.html.

[61] Columbia Law School, Human and Constitutional Rights Project, *UN and Cambodia Agree on Court to Try Khmer Rouge, available at* www.hrcr.org/hottopics/UNKhmer.html (last visited July 24, 2007).

[62] *Law on the Establishment of the Extraordinary Chambers in the Courts of Cambodia for the Prosecution of Crimes Committed during the Period of Democratic Kampuchea, available at* www.genocidewatch.org/CambodianTribunalLaw.htm (last visited July 24, 2007).

regard to whether it occurs in the context of armed conflict. The ICTY expended considerable effort elaborating the scope of internationally enforceable standards of individual responsibility for genocide.

The first case to be fully tried in the ICTY was that of Dusko Tadic,[63] a relatively obscure Serbian resident of Bosnia who was convicted of participating in brutalities as his Muslim and Croat neighbors were rounded up, imprisoned, and eventually either killed or expelled from the region. The major "ethnic" groups of the Balkan region are all in some degree Slav but subdivide into Slovenian, Croatian, Serbian, and Muslim. Yugoslavia after WWII was composed of constituent units identified as Slovenia, Croatia, Serbia, Bosnia-Herzegovina, Kosovo, and Montenegro. Following the breakup of the Soviet Union, Yugoslavia began to disintegrate into its component parts as Slovenia and Croatia declared their independence. As Yugoslav Serbian forces withdrew from Croatia, they attempted to solidify northern Bosnia to the remains of Yugoslavia composed of Serbia and Montenegro as part of the general campaign of creating a Greater Serbia. Serbian domination of whatever provinces would be part of Greater Serbia included "ethnic cleansing" of some regions to impose Serbian dominance.

Dusko Tadic was a Serbian shopowner in northern Bosnia. Chaos reigned as Serbian military and paramilitary forces destroyed Muslim and Croatian homes and businesses, killing many people in street fighting, then began rounding up Muslim and Croatian residents for execution or internment. In the "camps," both soldiers and civilian thugs were allowed to commit atrocities including beating, rape, sexual mutilation, and execution. Tadic was known to a few of the camp inhabitants and was alleged to have committed or been present at some of these incidents. His story was that he had a small political role in the community, was dragooned into the local traffic police, resisted conscription into the military, and eventually escaped to Germany. To assess his criminal responsibility, the ICTY Trial Chamber had to sort through conflicting testimony to determine whether he was a reluctant bystander in the atrocities or an active participant, deciding with regard to several incidents that he was actively involved.

Because *Tadic* was the first opinion of a tribunal instigated by the United Nations for criminal sanctions, both the Trial Chamber and the Appeals Chamber engaged in extensive analysis of questions regarding customary international law and individual criminal responsibility for atrocities against civilian populations. This background and analysis is part of what may become international criminal responsibility for terrorism, as it sets the stage for finding that targeting of civilians by an organized group, whether affiliated with a government or not, is a subject of customary international law and thus enforceable either by international tribunals or under the universal jurisdiction of individual states.

---

[63] Prosecutor v. Tadic, Case No. IT-94-I-T (July 15, 1999), *available at* www.un.org/icty/tadic/appeal/judgement/index.htm.

The Trial Chamber decided that the Geneva Conventions did not apply to protect nationals of Bosnia who were subject to atrocities by Bosnian Serbs, as opposed to those who were in the hands of the Yugoslav National Army controlled by Serbia. Although there was an "international armed conflict" occurring between Serbian Yugoslav forces and Bosnian resistance groups, the Bosnian Serbs such as Tadic were dealing with their own nationals. Thus, their victims did not fall within the protection of the Geneva Conventions:

> The consequence of this finding, as far as this trial is concerned, is that, since Article 2 of the Statute is applicable only to acts committed against "protected persons" within the meaning of the Geneva Conventions, and since it cannot be said that any of the victims, all of whom were civilians, were at any relevant time in the hands of a party to the conflict of which they were not nationals, the accused must be found not guilty of the counts which rely upon that Article.

The Prosecutor appealed from this ruling on the ground that the conflict was international in scope because the Bosnian Serb militias had a "demonstrable link" to the forces of Yugoslavia. It might seem a bit surreal to be asking whether Yugoslavia was involved in the conflict in Bosnia because international humanitarian law should condemn the mistreatment of civilians in any event, and indeed the ICTY Statute defined "crimes against humanity" as occurring during "armed conflict, whether international or internal." One might also have thought that convictions for crimes against humanity would make the acquittals for "grave breaches" of the Conventions immaterial or at most relate only to the length of sentence. In the view of the Prosecutor and Tribunal, however, establishing the criteria for application of the Conventions was important in itself.

One problem was that without the presence of a Party to the Conventions, such as Yugoslavia, there might be no basis for applying the Conventions. The Appeals Chamber approached this question by asking whether the Bosnian Serbs might be considered "lawful combatants" in the sense of the Convention on Prisoners of War. Under that Convention,

> militias or paramilitary groups or units may be regarded as legitimate combatants if they form "part of [the] armed forces" of a Party to the conflict or "belong" to a Party to the conflict and satisfy the other four requirements . . . . It is clear that this provision is primarily directed toward establishing the requirements for the status of lawful combatants. Nevertheless, one of its logical consequences is that if, in an armed conflict, paramilitary units "belong" to a State other than the one against which they are fighting, the conflict is international and therefore serious violations of the Geneva Conventions may be classified as "grave breaches."

This approach heightens the sense of surrealism by seeming to make the paramilitary groups subject to the controls of the Convention only if they can be termed "lawful combatants," which in turn depends on their satisfying the criteria, which include "that of conducting their operations in accordance with the laws and customs of war." This logic would lead to the conclusion that a paramilitary group could avoid application of the Convention to them by violating the laws and customs of war.

After creating this apparent conundrum, however, the Tribunal explained that what it was seeking was a mechanism by which to hold states accountable for the actions of irregulars even if they would prefer not to be.[64] The Appeals Chamber finally got down to business by asking whether the Bosnian Serbs had acted in collusion with the Serbian Yugoslav forces.

> 167. In the instant case the Bosnian Serbs, including the Appellant, arguably had the same nationality as the victims, that is, they were nationals of Bosnia and Herzegovina. However, it has been shown above that the Bosnian Serb forces acted as de facto organs of another State, namely, the FRY. Thus the requirements set out in Article 4 of Geneva Convention IV are met: the victims were "protected persons" as they found themselves in the hands of armed forces of a State of which they were not nationals.

Both the Trial Chamber and the Appeals Chamber seem to have been under the impression that the argument was whether the acts of Tadic could be "attributed" to Yugoslavia so that the other state would be

---

[64] *Id.* at ¶ 94-97:

> 94. States have in practice accepted that belligerents may use paramilitary units and other irregulars in the conduct of hostilities only on the condition that those belligerents are prepared to take responsibility for any infringements committed by such forces. In order for irregulars to qualify as lawful combatants, it appears that international rules and State practice therefore require control over them by a Party to an international armed conflict and, by the same token, a relationship of dependence and allegiance of these irregulars vis-à-vis that Party to the conflict. These then may be regarded as the ingredients of the term "belonging to a Party to the conflict."

> 95. The Appeals Chamber thus considers that the Third Geneva Convention, by providing in Article 4 the requirement of "belonging to a Party to the conflict", implicitly refers to a test of control.

> 96. This conclusion, based on the letter and the spirit of the Geneva Conventions, is borne out by the entire logic of international humanitarian law. This body of law is not grounded on formalistic postulates. It is not based on the notion that only those who have the formal status of State organs, i.e., are members of the armed forces of a State, are duty bound both to refrain from engaging in violations of humanitarian law as well as — if they are in a position of authority — to prevent or punish the commission of such crimes. Rather, it is a realistic body of law, grounded on the notion of effectiveness and inspired by the aim of deterring deviation from its standards to the maximum extent possible. It follows, amongst other things, that humanitarian law holds accountable not only those having formal positions of authority but also those who wield de facto power as well as those who exercise control over perpetrators of serious violations of international humanitarian law. Hence, in cases such as that currently under discussion, what is required for criminal responsibility to arise is some measure of control by a Party to the conflict over the perpetrators.

responsible for his actions. This leads to the conundrum that the Geneva Conventions apply to paramilitary units if they are under some degree of control by a state belligerent and do not apply if those persons are acting on their own. The Prosecutor attempted to get the Tribunal to focus on the reverse question of whether the defendant had triggered international concerns by acting as if he were a state official.[65] The Appeals Chamber stated that was not the issue in which it was interested — it insisted that the relevant issue was whether the defendant was acting as a de facto organ of a state.[66]

In this view, then, a paramilitary group acting outside the control of any state is not violating the Geneva Conventions. That does not mean that they are not violating some law — they may be in violation of any number of domestic laws as well as international humanitarian law — their crimes are just not to be found under the Geneva Conventions. This is relevant to the later discussion of U.S. military detentions. If a conflict is not an armed conflict within the meaning of the Geneva Conventions, then it is difficult to see how the private actors become "combatants" subject to the law of war.

The U.S. experience with the same issue is similar, albeit slightly different. Whether an individual has acted "under color of state law" for purposes of federal statutes is not premised on holding the state responsible for those actions. Instead, the question is whether the individual is clothed

---

[65] *Id.* at ¶ 103:

> 103. First, with a view to limiting the scope of the test at issue, the Prosecution has contended that the criterion for ascertaining State responsibility is different from that necessary for establishing individual criminal responsibility. In the former case one would have to decide whether serious violations of international humanitarian law by private individuals may be attributed to a State because those individuals acted as de facto State officials. In the latter case, one would have instead to establish whether a private individual may be held criminally responsible for serious violations of international humanitarian law amounting to "grave breaches." Consequently, it has been asserted, the Nicaragua test, while valid within the context of State responsibility, is immaterial to the issue of individual criminal responsibility for "grave breaches." The Appeals Chamber, with respect, does not share this view.

[66] *Id.* at ¶ 104:

> 104. What is at issue is not the distinction between the two classes of responsibility. What is at issue is a preliminary question: that of the conditions on which under international law an individual may be held to act as a *de facto* organ of a State. Logically these conditions must be the same both in the case: (i) where the court's task is to ascertain whether an act performed by an individual may be attributed to a State, thereby generating the international responsibility of that State; and (ii) where the court must instead determine whether individuals are acting as *de facto* State officials, thereby rendering the conflict international and thus setting the necessary precondition for the "grave breaches" regime to apply. In both cases, what is at issue is not the distinction between State responsibility and individual criminal responsibility. Rather, the question is that of establishing the criteria for the legal imputability to a State of acts performed by individuals not having the status of State officials. In the one case these acts, if they prove to be attributable to a State, will give rise to the international responsibility of that State; in the other case, they will ensure that the armed conflict must be classified as international.

with an appearance of state authority[67] or has acted in explicit or tacit concert with state officials.[68] In other U.S. statutes, individual criminal responsibility does not depend on "state action" but on impacts on federal interests such as effects on interstate commerce.

Nevertheless, the Tribunal's line of argument finally approaches some sense of realism in that the Geneva Conventions apply to *international* armed conflicts, not to internal conflicts. If two rival gangs in Los Angeles are engaged in bloodshed without following the laws and customs of war, that is no business of the international community but is a problem to be dealt with by local authorities. If the United States Government is engaged in bloodshed against its own civilians, there may be sources of international humanitarian law that apply but not the Geneva Conventions (unless the situation rises to the level of a "Common Article 3" situation as discussed in the Rwanda Tribunal later). In between these extremes, there is the possibility that one of the rival gangs is acting, as U.S. statutes put it, "under color of state law," in which case the federal government, but not the international community, takes an interest. An example in which the international community slowly came to take an interest without direct intervention was the Duvalier death squads known as Tontons Macoutes.

The Tribunal went to great pains to demonstrate that in its view the Geneva Conventions apply to the behavior of a paramilitary group only if it is "under control" of or is organized by a State Party. The entire discussion, however, was cast in terms of whether international law makes the State responsible for the actions of those units, not in response to the Prosecutor's argument that the question should be whether international law makes those units responsible for violations of the law and custom of war.

> 123. [I]nternational law renders any State responsible for acts in breach of international law performed (i) by individuals having the formal status of organs of a State (and this occurs even when these organs act *ultra vires* or *contra legem*), or (ii) by individuals who make up organised groups subject to the State's control. International law does so regardless of whether or not the State has issued *specific instructions* to those individuals. Clearly, the rationale behind this legal regulation is that otherwise, States might easily shelter behind, or use as a pretext, their internal legal system or the lack of any specific instructions in order to disclaim international responsibility.

If a rebel group is not playing by the rules, then perhaps the international community should leave them to the tender mercies of the government under attack and not take an interest in their behavior, at least insofar as the Geneva Conventions are concerned. Conversely, if the rebel group

---

[67] Monroe v. Pape, 365 U.S. 167 (1961); *see also* Wayne McCormack, *Federalism and Section 1983: Part I*, 60 Va. L. Rev. 5-10 (1974).

[68] Adickes v. S.H. Kress & Co., 398 U.S. 144 (1970).

is not playing by the rules, then the government need not be concerned about application of the Geneva Conventions to its treatment of the rebels.

The complication in Bosnia was that the "rebel" group was not actually a rebel group but was supported by what remnants of civil authority remained. They were accused of crimes against civilians of their own nationality, not against the state. In those circumstances, it should not matter whether they carried the authority of another state or simply were acting in concert with their own state. Even under the Tribunal's strained analysis, the focus could have been on attribution of their activities to Bosnia, not attribution to Serbia.

All of this, however, is limited to application of those Conventions that depend upon the existence of a state of "armed conflict." At least the government forces are still subject to Conventions such as those dealing with torture.

The next question is whether crimes against humanity and genocide have been sufficiently incorporated into customary international law that they can be applied to non-state actors. Two additional grounds of appeal by the Prosecutor dealt with the Trial Chamber's reading of the Statute's definition of "crimes against humanity" to exclude both purely personal pursuits and actions not tinged with discrimination on the basis of race, sex, religion, or similar criteria.

The Trial Chamber held that a person does not commit a "crime against humanity" when acting for purely personal reasons separated from any "armed conflict" during which those actions occur. This is not exactly the same as a "color of law" argument, because it recognizes that even private persons are subject to the rules against commission of crimes against humanity. Although Tadic had been convicted for these crimes and thus the ruling had no bearing on the outcome, the Appeals Chamber nevertheless took up this issue as an "matter of general significance for the Tribunal's jurisprudence."

The Appeals Chamber decided that personal motivation is irrelevant to crimes against humanity.[69] The U.S. has faced this issue in its KKK statutes that criminalize conspiracies to deprive persons of civil rights[70]

---

[69] 271. The Trial Chamber correctly recognised that crimes which are unrelated to widespread or systematic attacks on a civilian population should not be prosecuted as crimes against humanity. Crimes against humanity are crimes of a special nature to which a greater degree of moral turpitude attaches than to an ordinary crime. Thus to convict an accused of crimes against humanity, it must be proved that the crimes were related to the attack on a civilian population (occurring during an armed conflict) and that the accused knew that his crimes were so related.

272. [T]he Appeals Chamber does not consider it necessary to further require, as a substantive element of *mens rea*, a nexus between the specific acts allegedly committed by the accused and the armed conflict, or to require proof of the accused's motives. Consequently, in the opinion of the Appeals Chamber, the requirement that an act must not have been carried out for the purely personal motives of the perpetrator does not form part of the prerequisites necessary for conduct to fall within the definition of a crime against humanity under Article 5 of the Tribunal's Statute.

[70] 18 U.S.C. § 243 (2004).

and has imposed a group-based discriminatory intent requirement.[71] The ICTY decision, however, must be read in light of the particular wording of its statute, which criminalizes certain actions when taken "in armed conflict . . . and directed against a civilian population."

Could Tadic have been considered a terrorist? Was he engaged in "armed conflict" subject to the laws and customs of war? or was he a civilian engaged in violence against fellow civilians? Should particularly egregious street thugs be subject to the processes of international criminal law? In the context of widespread civil unrest and bloodshed, perhaps so.

[2] ICTR — Rwanda

Both the Geneva Convention issue and the crimes against humanity issues were addressed by the Security Council in creating the Statute of the International Tribunal for Rwanda. The ICTR is integrated with the ICTY in some degree. The Appellate Chamber and Prosecutor are the same for both Tribunals, but the staffs and Trial Chambers are separate entities. The Tribunal's authority, set out in the Statute adopted as part of Security Council Resolution 955 in 1994,[72] extends to genocide, crimes against humanity, and violations of "Common Article 3 of the Geneva Conventions of 1949."

Common article 3 prohibits mistreatment of civilians during "armed conflict not of an international character" (i.e., during times of civil war or insurrection). It places obligations on "Parties to the conflict" but certainly did not, as of 1949, appear to contemplate international intervention to punish atrocities wholly contained within a "sovereign state." Application of common article 3 to civil war now shows how far the international community has come in taking concern over the internal affairs of nation-states.

In similar fashion to the ICTY, the first fully adjudicated case of the ICTR involved a local government official, although one with significantly more political influence than Tadic. The emphasis in this case is more on delineating the differences among war crimes, crimes against humanity, and genocide.[73]

Jean-Paul Akayesu was a school teacher in Rwanda who in 1992 became the "bourgmester" of his province, a position similar to mayor or governor exercising chief executive functions. By all accounts, he was a reasonable and compassionate official until the events of April 18, 1994. Rwanda was first a German colony and then a Belgian colony from 1917 to about 1959. Its pre-colonial history included a nobility or ruling class known as the Tutsis and the rest of the population known as Hutus. It is generally accepted that these were classes more than ethnic groups, and history

---

[71] Griffin v. Breckenridge, 403 U.S. 88 (1971).

[72] S.C. Res. 955, U.N. Doc. S/RES/955 (Nov. 8, 1994).

[73] Prosecutor v. Akayesu, Case No. ICTR-96-4-T (Sept. 2, 1998), *available at* http:// 69.94.11.53/ENGLISH/cases/Akayesu/judgment/akay001.htm.

indicates that there was some mobility between the two classes. When the Belgians issued identity cards, however, they placed one of these two categories on each person's card and the identification became inheritable, so that it took on something of the nature of an ethnic grouping.

Following the withdrawal of Belgian colonial rule and independence of the state, elections resulted in a lopsided victory for the majority Hutus. From there, things went predictably downhill against the backdrop of violence and repression that existed within the historic relationships of the two groups. Some Tutsis organized a resistance movement and found support from neighboring Uganda (Idi Amin's regime). Hutu extremists capitalized on the fears of their supporters to portray the Tutsis as responsible for attacks on Hutus (which probably were fostered by the Hutu extremists themselves). As the Tutsi forces moved to attack government forces, widespread violence against Tutsi civilians broke out, resulting in what some reports indicate may have been as many as 800,000 deaths in the months of April and May 1994.

Akayesu initially may have asked for government help in suppressing the violence against Tutsis, but all accounts portray him as becoming frustrated and lashing out against the Tutsis himself after an incident in which a Tutsi schoolteacher was killed and a mob then killed one of the Hutu suspects. At least, the evidence tended to show that he turned a blind eye to Hutu atrocities in his province and he may even have promoted and fostered some of the beatings, rapes, and killings that took place.

The Prosecutor charged Akayesu with war crimes under the Geneva Convention, crimes against humanity, genocide, and also with violation of "common Article 3 of the Geneva Conventions." The major legal issues in the case had to do with application of the Geneva Conventions to something other than an "international armed conflict." As in *Tadic*, the ICTR Trial Chamber held that most of the Geneva Conventions did not apply to this situation because none of the victims could be considered a "protected person" under the Conventions in the absence of armed conflict between nations. On the other hand, both genocide and crimes against humanity trigger international criminal sanctions regardless of whether the conflict is international in character. In between these two positions was the application of Article 3, which is identical in all four Geneva Conventions, and which applies to "armed conflict not of an international character."[74]

---

[74] 601. The four 1949 Geneva Conventions and the 1977 Additional Protocol I thereto generally apply to international armed conflicts only, whereas Article 3 common to the Geneva Conventions extends a minimum threshold of humanitarian protection as well to all persons affected by a non-international conflict, a protection which was further developed and enhanced in the 1977 Additional Protocol II. In the field of international humanitarian law, a clear distinction as to the thresholds of application has been made between situations of international armed conflicts, in which the law of armed conflicts is applicable as a whole, situations of non-international (internal) armed conflicts, where Common Article 3 and Additional Protocol II are applicable, and non-international armed conflicts where only Common Article 3 is applicable. Situations of internal disturbances are not covered by international humanitarian law.

With regard to genocide and crimes against humanity, the Trial Chamber held that these offenses were crimes "regardless of whether they are committed in an armed conflict, international or internal in character."[75] Lest it be thought that the entire body of state criminal law has now been converted to matters of international interest, remember that the Statute creating the Tribunal provided jurisdictional elements for each offense. With genocide, the jurisdictional element is "intent to destroy, in whole or in part, a national, ethnical, racial or religious group." Granted, this is not much of a jurisdictional hurdle and certainly could apply to any act of racial violence because the intent to "destroy, in part, a group" could be found in the killing or serious injury of any member of the group. Thus, could genocide be triggered by what is known in the U.S. as a "hate crime" and thus become punishable internationally?

With respect to crimes against humanity, the jurisdictional element is "when committed as part of a widespread or systematic attack against any civilian population on national, political, ethnic, racial or religious grounds." Because the discriminatory motivation is the same with both crimes, the difference is "widespread or systematic" in the definition of crimes against humanity, which does not appear in the definition of genocide but ought to be implied. Without a widespread or systematic attack, the individual hate crime hardly seems to rise to the level of international concern at this point in history. It may some day, but that would be a giant second step that could occur only after the presence of the basic rule against genocide is firmly established.

With regard to "common Article 3," the Trial Chamber referred to the Appeals Chamber decision in *Tadic* "that an armed conflict exists whenever there is . . . protracted armed violence between governmental authorities and organized armed groups or between such groups within a State. International humanitarian law applies from the initiation of such armed conflicts and extends beyond the cessation of hostilities until . . . in the case of internal conflicts, a peaceful settlement is reached."[76] Given that there was a sufficiently well-organized Tutsi rebel force to create an "armed conflict," the question was whether Akayesu was to be held responsible criminally in an international tribunal. The Trial Chamber stated that the law mandated "imposition of individual criminal liability for war crimes on civilians where they have a link or connection with a Party to the conflict."

The Prosecutor appealed this ruling on the basis that a civilian should be held to the same standard regardless of whether he or she has a "special relationship" to one of the contending sides in an armed conflict. The Appeals Chamber agreed:

> 443. The Appeals Chamber is of the view that the minimum protection provided for victims under common Article 3 implies necessarily effective punishment on persons who violate it. Now, such

---

[75] *Akayesu, supra* note 73, at ¶ 565.

[76] *Akayesu, supra* note 73, at ¶ 619.

punishment must be applicable to everyone without discrimination, as required by the principles governing individual criminal responsibility as laid down by the Nuremberg Tribunal in particular. The Appeals Chamber is therefore of the opinion that international humanitarian law would be lessened and called into question if it were to be admitted that certain persons be exonerated from individual criminal responsibility for a violation of common Article 3 under the pretext that they did not belong to a specific category.

444. In paragraph 630 of the Judgment, the Trial Chamber found that the four Conventions "were adopted primarily to protect the victims as well as potential victims of armed conflicts." It went on to hold that "[t]he category of persons to be held accountable in this respect then, would in most cases be limited to commanders, combatants and other members of the armed forces." Such a finding is prima facie not without reason. In actuality authors of violations of common Article 3 will likely fall into one of these categories. This stems from the fact that common Article 3 requires a close nexus between violations and the armed conflict. This nexus between violations and the armed conflict implies that, in most cases, the perpetrator of the crime will probably have a special relationship with one party to the conflict. However, such a special relationship is not a condition precedent to the application of common Article 3 and, hence of Article 4 of the Statute. In the opinion of the Appeals Chamber, the Trial Chamber erred in requiring that a special relationship should be a separate condition for triggering criminal responsibility for a violation of Article 4 of the Statute.

With *Akayesu*, the ICT Appeals Chamber has rather solidly declared that any acts of violence by any individual during an "armed conflict" (meaning one in which there are identifiable contending groups) are criminal if they either (a) amount to genocide or (b) are part of a "widespread and systematic" attack with discriminatory intent. This position definitely pushes international law well into the internal affairs of many states, and for our purposes it promotes the view that acts of terrorism may be cognizable in international law without regard to sponsorship by another state.

There are a host of questions that probe at the limits of international interest in domestic violence. If "widespread and systematic" violence by civilians against fellow civilians is already criminal under international law, perhaps there is no need for a separate definition of terrorism? Perhaps all we need is recognition that "systematic and organized violence," as distinguished from violence that should be left to the domestic criminal law of the state in which it is occurring, is of sufficient concern internationally that it is a violation of customary international law.

[3] Joint Criminal Enterprise

The International Tribunals have developed a concept of criminal responsibility that may include responsibility of one person for the acts of another.

The concept of "joint criminal enterprise" (JCE) differs a bit from the Anglo-American concept of conspiracy.

The most complete explanation of JCE is in the ICTY Appeals Chamber opinion in the *Brdjanin* case.[77] The prosecution in Brdjanin appealed from some statements made by the Trial Chamber regarding the need to show an agreement between the accused and the persons who physically committed a wrong. Although the outcome of the argument would have no bearing on the case, the Chamber decided the issues because they were "of considerable significance to the Tribunal's jurisprudence."[78]

The Tribunal first pointed out that the post-World War II Tribunals dealing with Nazi war criminals had developed an approach that held individual officials responsible for the acts of others who carried out their wishes even when the underlings had no inclination to be involved in a "conspiracy" or any "common plan." Judges who sentenced persons to death and officers who directed the selection of persons for concentration camps were part of a common plan of genocide and crimes against humanity even though the actions were carried out by unknown functionaries who had no part in the common plan.[79]

From this starting point, the Tribunal has recognized three different kinds of joint criminal enterprise: the basic, the systemic, and the extended enterprise.[80] For all three types, the completed crime consists of three

---

[77] Prosecutor v. Radoslav Brdjanin, ICTY IT-99-36 (Appeals Chamber Apr. 27, 2007).

[78] *Id.* at ¶ 361. Obviously, the defendant would have little interest in an argument that would not affect his case, but the court received an amicus brief from the Association of Defense Counsel.

[79] *Id.* at ¶ 404:

[The] post-World War II jurisprudence: (1) recognizes the imposition of liability upon an accused for his participation in a common criminal purpose, where the conduct that comprises the criminal *actus reus* is perpetrated by persons who do not share the common purpose; and (2) does not require proof that there was an understanding or an agreement between the accused and the principal perpetrator of the crime to commit that particular crime.

[80] *Vasiljevic* at ¶¶ 97-99:

97. The first category is a "basic" form of joint criminal enterprise. It is represented by cases where all co-perpetrators, acting pursuant to a common purpose, possess the same criminal intention. An example is a plan formulated by the participants in the joint criminal enterprise to kill where, although each of the participants may carry out a different role, each of them has the intent to kill.

98. The second category is a "systemic" form of joint criminal enterprise. It is a variant of the basic form, characterised by the existence of an organised system of ill-treatment. An example is extermination or concentration camps, in which the prisoners are killed or mistreated pursuant to the joint criminal enterprise.

99. The third category is an "extended" form of joint criminal enterprise. It concerns cases involving a common purpose to commit a crime where one of the perpetrators commits an act which, while outside the common purpose, is nevertheless a natural and foreseeable consequence of the effecting of that common purpose. An example is a common purpose or plan on the part of a group to forcibly remove at gun-point members of one ethnicity from their town, village or region (to effect "ethnic cleansing") with the consequence that, in the course of doing so, one or more of the

elements:[81] multiple persons, a common purpose (not plan), and participation by the accused (not necessarily an overt act).[82]

The basic JCE is the garden variety understanding between two or more perpetrators to do an illegal act — each may have separate roles and neither may be involved in all aspects of the action. The systemic enterprise consists of organized violence such as concentration camps or pogroms as in Rwanda. The common purpose is evident in the nature of the undertaking. The extended enterprise occurs when the planner is distant from the actor, who may have had no knowledge or intent to engage in the common purpose. The example given by the Tribunal is that of removing people from a locality when it is foreseeable that violence will occur — if an agent shoots someone, then the JCE would include the death even though the agent had no role in formulating the common purpose.

The "extended" JCE also means that the defendant may be convicted without having any agreement or understanding with the person who pulls the principal perpetrator.[83] Although this seems jarring to the Anglo-American mind trained on the idea that conspiracy requires at least a "tacit" understanding, the context is such that eliminating an understanding between planner and perpetrator makes sense. These are crimes in which the jurisdictional starting point is "widespread and systematic" — without that, there is no crime against humanity or war crime. When the crimes are widespread and systematic, the element of common purpose is ample for individual responsibility and a requirement of a "meeting of the minds" would be overkill.

[4] Implications for Terrorism from ICTY and ICTR Law

The interplay between freedom of expression and incitement to genocide[84] indicates that at least state-sponsored or state-condoned "terrorism"

---

victims is shot and killed. While murder may not have been explicitly acknowledged to be part of the common purpose, it was nevertheless foreseeable that the forcible removal of civilians at gunpoint might well result in the deaths of one or more of those civilians.

[81] *Id.* at ¶ 100:

100. The actus reus of the participant in a joint criminal enterprise is common to each of the three above categories and comprises the following three elements: First, a plurality of persons is required. They need not be organised in a military, political or administrative structure. Second, the existence of a common purpose which amounts to or involves the commission of a crime provided for in the Statute is required. There is no necessity for this purpose to have been previously arranged or formulated. It may materialise extemporaneously and be inferred from the facts. Third, the participation of the accused in the common purpose is required, which involves the perpetration of one of the crimes provided for in the Statute. This participation need not involve commission of a specific crime under one of the provisions (for example murder, extermination, torture or rape), but may take the form of assistance in, or contribution to, the execution of the common purpose.

[82] *Brdjanin, supra* note 77, at ¶ 364.

[83] *Id* at ¶ 419.

[84] *See* § 4.03[B] *supra*.

aimed at ethnic minorities would constitute genocide. Under the Rome Statute of the International Criminal Court, there is not even a requirement of state sanction or degree, so that any killing or serious bodily harm will constitute genocide if "committed with intent to destroy, in whole or in part, a national, ethnical, racial or religious group."

The ICTY and ICTR Chambers have genocide within their jurisdiction when actions constitute "serious violations of international humanitarian law." Although neither tribunal has yet worried about the meaning of "serious" in this context, it is difficult to imagine what racially motivated killing would not be serious. Perhaps the word should be taken to connote "widespread or systematic" atrocities against definable groups, thus equating the threshold for prosecutions of genocide with that of crimes against humanity.

A number of terrorist groups could be accused of genocide. For example, the IRA's targeting of Protestants, the ETA's targeting of Spanish civilians, and al Qaeda's targeting of Americans (a national group) or even al Qaeda's targeting of all Westerners could qualify as genocide. To prevent international law from completely occupying the field of domestic criminal law, however, it will be natural for the international tribunals to seek some limitation on the scope of their authority.

International tribunals will seek limitations on their own authority for the same reasons that federal law in the U.S. has been limited so as not to occupy or preempt the roles of the states in addressing violence against civilians.[85] In the U.S. system, the states need to have some relative autonomy in the operation of their criminal justice systems and in the definition of crimes, although this autonomy is limited by procedural requirements of the Constitution, substantive limits gleaned from Constitutional protections of individual liberties, and preemption in some instances by federal law. With all these limitations, however, federalism has worked reasonably well to preserve some level of autonomy closer to where the people live. That autonomy serves to enhance the perception, if not the reality, of accountability of government to the populace.

At the international level, nation-states have been accustomed to independent sovereign status. The inroads on that status have begun with statements of international criminal responsibility for acts of state. As individual criminal responsibility expands, the autonomy of the nation-state will be reduced to the extent that it cannot immunize its nationals for conduct that the international community proscribes. In return, the international community will almost certainly be alert to encroachments on state autonomy because all international actors are, to some extent, also nationals of a nation-state themselves. In this sphere, the pressures for nation-state autonomy are identical to the pressures for autonomy of the states in the U.S. federal system.

---

[85] *See* United States v. Morrison, 529 U.S. 598 (2000); *see also* United States v. Lopez, 514 U.S. 549 (1995).

The development of internationally enforceable criminal law thus is relevant to our terrorism inquiry on several levels. First, it illustrates the inexorable shift of power away from local to supranational levels. Second, it sets out some of the definitional elements of criminal law as well as limitations on it, such as protections for freedom of expression. Third, by attempting to define those levels of anti-social behavior that will be subject to international authority, it assists in ascertaining what aspects of terrorism might be subject to international authority.

Determining what aspects of terrorism should be subject to international authority requires distinguishing those that could be left to domestic criminal processes, which once again shows the necessity of defining different levels or types of terrorism. Now we will turn to the U.S. experience to see what lessons might be gleaned.

§ 6.03 INTERSTATE CRIMINALITY

[A] The American KKK Experience

The experience of the U.S. with the KKK statutes enacted after the Civil War is of potential interest on the overall issue of what will make a non-state actor criminally responsible in supra-state or external courts for violence inflicted on fellow citizens.

In the Reconstruction of the South, federal interests were challenged by racial violence. When Congress debated enactment of criminal penalties, it was concerned about how to distinguish the violence that affected federal interests from ordinary, day-to-day criminal activity. The adopted formulas included a dual mechanism that ultimately resulted in some confusion as to what was covered:

18 U.S.C. § 242:

> Whoever, under color of any law, statute, . . . or custom, willfully subjects any person to the deprivation of any rights . . . secured by the Constitution or laws of the United States . . . shall be fined or imprisoned . . . .

18 U.S.C. § 241:

> If two or more persons conspire to injure, oppress, threaten, or intimidate any person . . . in the free exercise of enjoyment of any right or privilege secured to him by the Constitution or laws of the United States . . . or

> If two or more persons go in disguise on the highway . . . with intent to prevent or hinder . . . free exercise or enjoyment of any right or privilege so secured . . . .

> They shall be fined or imprisoned . . . .

These formulations deal with two elements of crime: (1) the actor and (2) the harm. The actors were subdivided into those who acted "under color of law" and those engaged in a "conspiracy." Either mechanism was sufficient to bring the actor within the scope of federal interests. With regard to the harms, however, the statutes did not criminalize all violence but instead focused on "rights secured by federal law." This produced the following conundrum: how could federal law, which at the time operated only on the states, be implicated in the actions of private persons or non-state actors? This is too similar to the questions of the ICT to avoid taking a brief look at the U.S. history.

The easiest answer to the question came in those instances in which the actor was "clothed with state authority" and was thus acting "under color of law." The Supreme Court's landmark case of *United States v. Classic*,[86] echoed in a civil damages action by *Monroe v. Pape*,[87] settled this issue while leaving some lingering questions. In these cases of police abuse, the actor was purporting to exercise the authority of the state as to which federal law applied as a direct control. Even though the actor may have been violating state law and thus was acting outside the authority of the state, it was the appearance of state authority that made the actions particularly intimidating and gave rise to legitimate demands that federal authority should be used to control the misuse of state authority. "Midnight raids and brutality by police officers generate fear among citizens that the power of the state is being used to repress elements which are politically or socially dissident. In short, the alleged conduct of the officers in *Monroe* was terrorism with a political impact, and so long as the officers set forth a 'pretense' of state authority, their acts conjure up the spectre of state repression."[88] Similarly, in the international arena, misuse of state authority should trigger the application of supranational law, a concept with which the ICT has had little difficulty in the cases of both *Tadic* and *Akayesu*.

But what about the non-state actor? In *Griffin v. Breckenridge*,[89] a civil action for damages under the corollary statute to § 241, the Supreme Court considered an incident of private hoodlums' stopping a car and harassing its occupants, allegedly violating their right to travel. Because defendants were motivated by racial prejudice and mistakenly believed that one of the occupants of the car was a civil rights worker, the Court held that they had displayed a sufficient "race or class-based animus" to trigger federal protections. It was the specter of roving bands of highwaymen intimidating the populace without adequate state responsiveness to protect the public, that prompted passage of the statute, and the federal government's interest in preventing the appearance of state approval of these actions satisfied the constitutional demand for a federal interest. In a corollary criminal case, *United States v. Guest*,[90] the Court similarly upheld convictions of private individuals engaged in a conspiracy to murder for race-based reasons.

---

[86] 313 U.S. 299 (1941).

[87] 365 U.S. 167 (1961).

[88] Wayne McCormack, *Federalism and Section 1983, Pt. I*, 60 Va. L. Rev. 1, 6-7 (1974).

[89] 403 U.S. 88 (1971).

[90] 383 U.S. 745 (1966).

In 1968, Congress addressed non-state actors further in 18 U.S.C. § 245:

(b) Whoever, whether or not acting under color of law, by force or threat of force willfully injures, intimidates or interferes with, or attempts to injure, intimidate or interfere with—

(1) any person because he is or has been [voting, participating in federally funded activities, or serving in a federal capacity] or

(2) any person because of his race, color, religion or national origin and because he is or has been [enrolling in any public school or college; participating in any state-funded activity, traveling in or using any facility of interstate commerce, or being a patron of a place of public accommodation].

Although § 245 is addressed to non-state actors, the threshold coverage requirements are addressed both to activities of the victim that raise federal concerns and to the state of mind of the perpetrator. The statute is in two parts. One protects anyone involved in specified federal activities. The second part deals with person who are targeted for racial or religious reasons and because using either state governmental facilities, channels of interstate commerce, or places of public accommodation. In light of the racial tensions in the United States over the past three decades, it may be a bit surprising that there have been rather few prosecutions under this statute. LexisNexis shows only 10 to 12 reported decisions under § 245.

Two notable cases that show the scope of the statute are *United States v. Franklin*[91] and *United States v. Nelson.*[92] Franklin, a white man, was convicted of shooting and killing two black men who were jogging in a public park with two white women. Through statements he had made in various settings, Franklin's motivation was shown to include a desire to strike at interracial socializing. Nelson, a black man, was convicted of killing a Jewish man who happened to be in the vicinity of an automobile accident in which two African-American children were injured by a Jewish driver; racial-ethnic motivation was shown from statements made to and by the mob at the scene. *Nelson* is particularly instructive on the uses of the statute because Nelson was previously acquitted of murder in a New York state court before the federal prosecution was brought.

Because there have been so few cases under this statute during a time in which the American consciousness has been particularly attuned to hate crimes may be attributable to the very phenomenon to which the statute was addressed: namely, that because the state prosecutors and courts have adequately addressed racially motivated violence, there has been little need for federal intervention. Another explanation may be that the proof requirements focusing on the defendant's state of mind set up significant hurdles for the prosecution.

---

[91] 704 F.2d 1183 (10th Cir. 1983).

[92] 277 F.3d 164 (2d Cir. 2002) (conviction reversed on the ground of bias in empaneling of the jury).

These cases illustrate, without fully explaining, how an upstream governmental entity acquires an interest in sanctioning private conduct that does not carry any overt message of state involvement. If a discrete segment of the population can be brought to believe that their safety is at risk and that the state is unwilling or unable to protect them, then this population can be intimidated into forgoing exercise of their rights. This draws into question the validity of government generally and threatens the integrity of all states. Thus arises the interest of other states, acting through a suprastate entity (the federal government in the U.S., or international tribunals on the global scale), in intervening to restore civilian confidence in the processes of government. New York is threatened by terrorism of the Ku Klux Klan in Alabama, so it acts through the federal government to intervene. France is threatened by terrorism of the Hutus in Rwanda, so it acts through the United Nations to intervene.

Now, with these similarities in mind, can we identify the factors that go into this interest so as to create better tests than the "widespread and systematic" test of international law or the "class-based animus" of U.S. law? Here are some factors to consider:

1. *links or connections to official state actors*

U.S. law applies to one who acts "under color of state law," of which the best definition may be that the defendant created the "appearance" of acting for the state. The ICT Appeals Chamber rejected this test but noted that many persons who meet the "widespread and systematic" test will have some link to state actors.

2. *widespread and systematic*

This jurisdictional nexus for "crimes against humanity" is found in the statutes of all three tribunals, ICTY, ICTR, and ICC. Something of the sort could be a sensible jurisdictional nexus for genocide as well because of the need to distinguish "serious violations of international humanitarian law" from sporadic incidents of hate crime. The corollary in U.S. law is the conspiracy statute (§ 242). Each of these tests focuses on the scope of the action rather than the intent of the actor. Intent of the actor, however, comes into the crime of genocide in the question of whether the action is taken to "destroy, in whole or in part," a group.

3. *class-based animus*

This test under the U.S. conspiracy statutes is closer to the "persecution" standard and the genocide crime than it is to the "widespread and systematic" test. The difference with genocide is that the U.S. conspiracy law may apply without an intent to "destroy," just an intent to "deprive of rights."

4. *extent of power to act*

A very important consideration could be the degree of harm available to the actor. U.S. law uses "two or more" as a bright-line test to identify those persons who are likely to create harm.

The concerns that have led to criminal sanctions at the international level and federal levels within the U.S. are similar. Both can be referred to as "suprastate" criminality. International organizations such as the U.N. are suprastate in relation to nation-states and the federal government is suprastate in relation to the states of the U.S.

The reason for supra-state intervention by international organizations into the affairs of a nation-state is the same as the reason for supra-state intervention by the U.S. federal government into the affairs of a U.S. state. It is the presence of an organization (whether recognized as the state or not) with sufficient resources to carry out violent actions against a civilian population without the state's being willing or able to control it. The terrorism organization acting within the U.S. becomes the concern of the federal government when either (a) it operates across state borders or has interstate connections that make it difficult for a single state to control it, or (b) it is able to create the appearance that the state condones its action. A terrorism organization becomes the concern of international organizations when either (a) it operates across national boundaries or has international connections that make it difficult for a single nation to control it, or (b) it is able to create the appearance that a nation condones its action.

What does all this have to do with terrorism? The progression is simply this: controlling state-sanctioned violence leads to interstate action to control those who, by either organization or resources, can either transcend state boundaries or allow them to create the appearance that the state condones their actions. Thus, the international concern with terrorism ought to abandon its emphasis on intent to intimidate a population or coerce a government and focus instead on what is really at stake, the organization and resources to carry out acts across national boundaries or to create the appearance that a nation-state condones the actions.

To complicate life a bit, it is not axiomatic that the definition of terrorism for domestic U.S. law must be the same as the international definition. U.S. law uses the concept of terrorism (with the element of political motivation) as punishment enhancement for existing crimes. There is no separate crime of terrorism in U.S. law. What the lawyers dealing with terrorism need are separate definitions for the different levels of terrorism, just as U.S. law needed a concept of "civil rights violations" for dealing with the KKK and related organizations.

Domestic law is adequately served with basic definitions of murder without any separate category for terrorism. Indeed, even punishment enhancement should be sufficiently covered with provisions for multiple deaths rather than using the awkward concept of political motivation. International law needs a definition that emphasizes the ability to act across borders or in a systematic campaign by nonstate actors.

Some will object that even governmental actors may employ terror as a tool. True enough, but not all uses of terror should be part of the definition of the crime of terrorism. Just as homicide includes a variety of killings other than murder, some of which are also unlawful, terror encompasses a variety of actions other than the crime of terrorism. We have adequate existing mechanisms for dealing with governmental abuse of power through definitions of war crimes, crimes against humanity, and genocide. The term terrorism should be reserved for actions of subnational groups that meet the threshold elements suggested here.

[B] A Paradigm of International Criminality

The paradigm of war does not work very well for dealing with terrorists. The "asymmetrical" confrontation of small clandestine groups by a large militarized force is likely to be ineffective, result in civilian casualties, invade the "sovereign" territory of another state, and ultimately create more resentment and violence than it deters.

The paradigm of crime is better than that of war but still not fully adequate for dealing with terrorism. Investigation across national borders is difficult, extradition may be problematic for any number of reasons while abduction leads to friction, enforcement of domestic criminal law does not authorize any degree of military incursion into the territory of another nation, and it completely excludes the possibility (unusual as it probably should be) of using deadly force against a known terrorist without prior hearing.

There may be a middle ground emerging in international law as a result of supra-state concern over mass murder and abuse. The concepts of genocide and crimes against humanity share one quintessential element with terrorism: ongoing violence against civilians. Genocide is distinguished by the attempt to eliminate a group presence defined by ethnic, culture, or religion. Crimes against humanity are distinguished by "widespread or systematic" violence. Terrorism falls into a similar setting as ongoing violence against civilian populations and is distinguished by the clandestine nature of the perpetrators.

If the ICC could not obtain independent investigative authority, even less likely is there to be, in the foreseeable future, legal recognition of the rights of one state to investigate within the borders of another state. Thus, even under an international criminality regime, the investigation, pursuit, and arrest are all likely to be contingent upon either the resident state's consent, action of the U.N. Security Council, or simple exertion of force by the investigating state. In this latter instance, the legal regime is a long way from recognizing a "right" of the aggrieved state to intervene on the territory of the resident state. In other words, it is not by legal claim of right, but by sheer force of ability, that one state may carry on investigations within another state.

Even if investigation must be clandestine, once evidence of wrongdoing by a person to be found within the borders of a resident state is obtained, the aggrieved state obtains a number of rights against the resident state. Conventions mandating cooperation operate with the premise of "extradite or prosecute." As international criminality develops, it eventually may be recognized that the aggrieved state may make a limited military incursion into the territory of another state that is "harboring" a terrorist organization or persons who have committed crimes against humanity or genocide.

This is a limited authorization, however, and would not be justification for "total war" or complete supplanting of the government of the invaded nation unless that government resists with its own military force. In other words, "military necessity and proportionality" would be defined by reference to the objective of capturing or disabling the perpetrators. In this fashion, an international criminality of genocide, terrorism, and crimes against humanity would supplement the choices of extradition and abduction by providing for a regularized, open, and visible incursion by military force.

An instructive historic experience with interstate criminalization of terrorism was the post-Civil War experience of the U.S. with the Ku Klux Klan, which did not reach fruition until after WWII. The effects of the Klan on the values of the collective whole, effects on the economies of other states, the ability of the Klan to organize and mobilize resources beyond the capacity or will of local law enforcement, all prompted federal action to deal with a problem that was not being adequately addressed by the states in which Klan activity was occurring. This is the identical problem with terrorism today. It means that the most salient defining characteristic of terrorism is not the purpose of the terrorist but the organization that lies behind the terrorist. It also means that terrorism will not be effectively combated until there is an international counter-terrorism task force, complete with transnational police power to operate within the territory of any nation.

Chapter 7

INTELLIGENCE INFORMATION

SYNOPSIS

Following 9/11, all the governments of the western world (and many of the rest of the world as well) shifted their emphasis from prosecution to prevention in regard to terrorist activity. In essence, this has meant that "stop the act" has become more important than "gather the evidence." But stopping the act depends on information and information can also be evidence in a criminal proceeding. There are two related tensions inherent in the way in which the professional intelligence community interacts with the prosecutorial community —

- tension between the two professions, each of which may zealously, and appropriately, wish to guard its way of doing business

- tension between the gathering of information and the civil liberties of the populace

§ 7.01 INTELLIGENCE AND SECRECY

These tensions are played out in various legal issues. Serious value questions arise from the sheer difficulty of gathering reliable intelligence about terrorist groups and their actions. Obviously, gathering information about clandestine operations requires clandestine investigation techniques, which leads to three fundamental problems:

1. The liberal democratic principles of the western world presume a level of open government operations. Keeping secrets in government cuts against the principle that the citizenry controls the government.

2. Secret investigation techniques can easily violate citizen privacy. The principle of judicial review embedded in warrant requirements protects against invasion of private domains.

3. Secrecy in government can easily lead to abuses and collection of data that can be misused.

Much of the controversy about the Bush Administration's domestic responses to terrorism has focused on the USA PATRIOT Act.[1] PATRIOT is almost a smokescreen because the vast bulk of it would be subject to only mild debate were it not that the administration made it the focal point of its domestic "war on terror," thus making it also the lightning rod for critics. In a sense, PATRIOT came to stand for other policies such as executive detentions, harsh interrogation, and extraordinary renditions, none of which is based in PATRIOT.

More recently, challenges to the policies of the Bush administration have also focused on the use of two investigative techniques — National Security Letters (NSLs) and the Terrorist Surveillance Program (TSP). The TSP is considered below[2] while the NSL issue illustrates the intelligence gathering problem and serves as a good introduction to the issues.

In *Doe v. Ashcroft*,[3] the district court held that FBI issuance of NSLs was unconstitutional. An NSL seeks to obtain information about a third party, in this instance information from electronic communications providers about subscribers and their billing records (phone numbers they have called, for example). At the time, NSLs were authorized by a statute that required the Director of the FBI to certify that the records were "relevant to an authorized investigation to protect against international terrorism or clandestine intelligence activities."[4]

A key issue in the case was what effect could be given to an NSL. Although the statute said the FBI could "request" subscriber information, it also said that the provider "shall comply" with a request. The statute

---

[1] Unifying and Strengthening America by Providing Appropriate Tools Required to Intercept and Obstruct Terrorism, Pub. L. 107-56 (Oct. 26, 2001).

[2] *See* § 7.02[B].

[3] 334 F. Supp. 2d 471 (S.D.N.Y.).

[4] 18 U.S.C. § 2709 (2004).

and letter went on to say that the recipient of the letter could not disclose to anyone the receipt of the letter. The court believed that this combination of factors meant that the recipient was led to believe that she had a legally enforceable obligation to turn over the information without even being allowed to consult with an attorney or to challenge the order in court. Read in that fashion, the NSL amounted to a judicially unreviewable search and seizure that violated the Fourth Amendment. Secondly, the court found First Amendment violations in the use of NSLs to acquire electronic communications while preventing the recipient from disclosing its receipt of the "request."[5]

While the appeal in *Doe* was pending, Congress amended the statutes to allow the recipient to seek judicial review of the order before complying[6] and to allow consultation with an attorney. The Second Circuit vacated and remanded in light of the changes to the statute.[7]

On remand, the district court in New York held that there were still First Amendment problems with the statute because it allowed the FBI to stifle expression by the recipient unless a reviewing court found "no reason to believe" that disclosure would produce national security harms and required the court to accept a government assertion of national security interest absent a showing of bad faith.[8] The court found separation of powers problems in the new procedure:

> [W]hile the "no reason to believe" standard impermissibly constrains the Court's First Amendment review, the requirement that the Court credit the government's invocation of national security as conclusive absent evidence of bad faith eviscerates any meaningful judicial review, as it clearly equates to an uncritical acceptance of the government's insistence of the need for secrecy. In requiring the Court to accept the government's certification as conclusive, § 3511(b) effectively allows the government to determine the constitutionality of its own actions, leaving only the difficult to prove and narrow issue of the existence of "bad faith" to the judiciary.[9]

This sequence of decisions illustrates well the values at stake in attempting to prevent clandestine violence. Prevention requires information that the holder wants to keep private. The more information government acquires, the more likely it can prevent violence before it occurs. But the intrusion into our lives at some point becomes intolerable to an open society.

---

[5] The New York judge hinted at First Amendment rights of the subscriber but relied specifically on First Amendment implications from the "gag order" provision applied to the recipient record holder. The District Court in Connecticut also found the non-disclosure provision to be an infringement of First Amendment rights of the recipient. Doe v. Gonzales, 386 F. Supp. 2d 66 (D. Conn. 2005).

[6] USA PATRIOT Improvement and Reauthorization Act of 2005, Pub. L. No. 109-177, 120 Stat. 192 (2006).

[7] Doe I v. Gonzales, 449 F.3d 415 (2d Cir. 2006).

[8] 18 U.S.C. § 3511(b) (2007).

[9] Doe v. Gonzales, 2007 U.S. Dist. LEXIS 65879, *105 (Sept 6, 2007).

Absent judicial review, investigators could allow record keepers to believe that they were compelled to hand over information about their customers. Further, in a truly clandestine investigation, agents may be expected to use deceit (e.g., informers and undercover agents) to obtain information, and these techniques lead to the proverbial slippery slope on which an open society does not want its government officials to step.

The paradigm of these problems may be found in the TSP. As revealed in some degree to this stage, the NSA was recording communications in violation of statutory authority while claiming national security justifications. We are now told that a judge of the FISA Court has approved the practices but the Government still does not disclose the scope of the program. Thus, the public does not know whether its laws are being followed or avoided.[10]

In addition, prevention requires interference with our freedom of movement. During the security planning for the 2002 Olympic Winter Games in Salt Lake, the University of Utah was preparing to host the Olympic Village and Olympic Stadium on our campus. Many faculty and staff were insistent that they wanted extreme measures taken for their safety — and that they wanted no interference with their ease of access to their places of work. That is impossible — safety limits access.

Finally, prevention implies a great deal of secrecy on the part of government. The Freedom of Information Act and the related "right to know" concepts embedded in the First Amendment reflect an understanding that the citizenry needs information about the government as much or more than government needs information about us. Every demand for governmental secrecy, legitimate and reasonably appearing as each might be in its own context, threatens the long-term credibility of government. Stack up too much government secrecy and we have a government in which no citizen can trust and ultimately one which few citizens will support.

The tension between prosecution and intelligence can be expressed as the need of the prosecutor to disclose information and the need of the intelligence community to protect information. Traditional western evidentiary standards mean that an individual cannot be imprisoned without the opportunity to have a fair trial, to confront the evidence against him or her. Disclosure of clandestinely acquired information, however, puts at risk the sources and methods by which that information was gathered. At its most rudimentary level, this concern has been understood by police the world over as meaning that government protects its snitches because otherwise they will be killed. At more sophisticated levels, protection of some information is necessary to avoid disclosure of the methods by which agencies operate (which businesses were asked to provide leads to which contacts). Thus, the constant theme in the Intelligence Community is protection of "sources and methods."

The resulting emphasis on secrecy is at odds with the transparency of judicial prosecution models. Therein lies the nub of the civil liberties

---

[10] See § 7.02[B] *infra*

controversies generated by terrorism investigations. The issues will be explored in this chapter by reference to two U.S. statutes, FISA and CIPA, and then we will take a quick look at the difficulties of interacting with the intelligence agencies of other countries.

[A] Sources and Methods — The Mosaic Problem

The overriding concern of intelligence professionals is protection of their "sources and methods." They will guard against disclosure of even the most mundane piece of information because of their fear that what seems innocuous to one person may be the key to a puzzle in the hands of a miscreant. This is known as the "mosaic" problem — that any given piece of information may fit into a mosaic that makes sense only to the bad guy.

The mosaic problem figured prominently in two cases involving closed deportation hearings. A bit of background on deportation is necessary for understanding these cases.

Exacerbating the fears that flow from lack of review is that the government has taken the position that information about the use of these techniques, even frequency of their use, is classified and need not be disclosed to the public. The aura of secrecy that has always been part of law enforcement is thus heightened substantially as part of the shift toward prevention of terrorist activity. Two cases dealing with closure of deportation proceedings to the press and public resulted in conflicting holdings.

Shortly after 9/11, the INS issued a memorandum known as the "Creppy Directive," asserting that deportation proceedings in "special interest" cases should be closed and information provided only to the alien's attorney or representative. When the government moved to deport Rabbi Haddad, a well-known Muslim activist in the Detroit area, the hearing was declared closed and newspapers sought to obtain access to the proceedings by way of an injunction from the federal court. The district court denied the request, citing the "plenary" authority of the government over deportation, but the Sixth Circuit reversed.[11]

The Sixth Circuit acknowledged that the government had a compelling interest in keeping some information out of the public eye. The court quoted from an affidavit filed by James Reynolds, Chief of the Terrorism and Violent Crimes Section of the Justice Department, to explain the reasons for preventing public disclosure of even the names of those detained:

1. "Disclosing the names of 'special interest' detainees . . . could lead to public identification of individuals associated with them, other investigative sources, and potential witnesses . . . and terrorist organizations . . . could subject them to intimidation or harm . . . ."

2. "Divulging the detainees' identities may deter them from cooperating [and] . . . terrorist organizations with whom they have

---

[11] Detroit Free Press v. Ashcroft, 303 F.3d 681 (6th Cir. 2002).

connection may refuse to deal further with them, . . ." thereby eliminating valuable sources of information for the Government and impairing its ability to infiltrate terrorist organizations.

3.   "Releasing the names of the detainees . . . would reveal the direction and progress of the investigation . . ." and "official verification that a member [of a terrorist organization] has been detained and therefore can no longer carry out the plans of his terrorist organization may enable the organization to find a substitute who can achieve its goals . . . ."

4.   "Public release of names, and place and date of arrest . . . could allow terrorist organizations and others to interfere with the pending proceedings by creating false or misleading evidence."

5.   "The closure directive is justified by the need to avoid stigmatizing 'special interest' detainees, who may ultimately be found to have no connection to terrorism . . . ."[12]

The Reynolds Affidavit went on to point out that revealing information about suspected terrorists would disclose to that person's colleagues some of the government's methods of acquiring information, thus allowing them to revise their practices to avoid detection. Moreover, disclosure could reveal what the government *does not know* about a particular person and thus alert co-conspirators that their plans have not yet been discovered.

The Sixth Circuit acknowledged the importance of all these concerns but held that they did not justify a blanket closure of all proceedings in light of the importance of the First Amendment interests in the public's right to know. The court held that the immigration judge would be required to make "specific findings on the record so that a reviewing court can determine whether closure was proper and whether less restrictive alternatives exist." The court acknowledged that the Supreme Court had indicated in *Zadvydas v. Davis*[13] that

it might be deferential in situations involving terrorism. However, nothing in *Zadvydas* indicates that given such a situation, the Court would defer to the political branches' determination of who belongs in that "small segment of particularly dangerous individuals" without judicial review of the individual circumstances of each case, something that the Creppy directive strikingly lacks.[14]

But judicial review of individual circumstances is precisely what the Government argues would create the "mosaic" problem described in the Reynolds Affidavit. "Bits and pieces of information that may appear innocuous in isolation" lie at the heart of the mosaic problem. So the Sixth Circuit's requirement of detailed findings regarding information to be protected runs directly counter to the whole point of the mosaic argument.

---

[12] *Id.* at 705-06.

[13] 533 U.S. 678 (2001).

[14] *Id.* at 692.

Presented with the same set of arguments in a similar case, the Third Circuit stated flatly that "we find ourselves in disagreement with the Sixth Circuit."[15]

The Sixth Circuit stated, "The Government could use its 'mosaic intelligence' argument as a justification to close any public hearing completely and categorically, including criminal proceedings."[16] The Third Circuit disagreed on the ground that a criminal proceeding would be subject to different standards than a deportation proceeding for reasons of tradition.[17]

The Sixth Circuit also responded point by point to each of the Government claims for secrecy and found that information was already available to the public through the detainee himself. That point was made in a Freedom of Information Act (FOIA) case in which several organizations sought information about who had been detained, for what period of time, and who his or her counsel was.[18] The D.C. Circuit in the FOIA case relied heavily on the proposition that the detainee himself was free to communicate with whomever he or she might choose. The Sixth Circuit thought that a detainee's ability to communicate with the public was a good reason for opening deportation hearings. The D.C. Circuit thinks that the same ability is an argument for not requiring government disclosure of information to the public. The difference apparently lies in the manner in which information would become available pursuant to a FOIA request: "even if terrorist organizations know about some of their members who were detained, a complete list of detainees could still have great value in confirming the status of their members. For example, an organization may be unaware of a member who was detained briefly and then released, but remains subject to continuing government surveillance."[19]

Judge Tatel dissented with a discussion of "deference" in the context of terrorism investigations. The heart of the difference was Judge Tatel's view that "requiring agencies to make the detailed showing FOIA requires is not second-guessing their judgment about matters within their expertise."[20] But it is a detailed showing that the Government says would be harmful to matters within its expertise. This is very similar to the disagreement between the Sixth and Third Circuits over the question of making individualized decisions on closing deportation hearings. Thus, the dilemma of how to monitor critical aspects of government behavior in a free society while still protecting the public from unknown risks is highlighted again by these differences of opinion.

---

[15] North Jersey Media Group, Inc. v. Ashcroft, 308 F.3d 198 (3d Cir. 2002).

[16] Zadvydas, 303 F.3d at 709.

[17] North Jersey Media Group, 308 F.3d at 212-13.

[18] Center for National Security Studies v. U.S. Dep't of Justice, 331 F.3d 918 (D.C. Cir. 2003).

[19] Id. at 930.

[20] Id. at 939.

[B] Intelligence, Investigations, and Privacy

Prevention means government accumulation of information. Government accumulation of information means loss of individual privacy. The more information government acquires, the more safe we can feel and the less privacy we will have in our daily lives. So how safe do we want to be? This is a good point at which to posit some basic premises in security planning:

    1.   The committed, resourceful terrorist can beat any security system.

We have a tendency to equate security with physical methods of intervention, such as locking doors, screening persons at entry points, deploying high-tech devices, and the like. Even with unlimited resources, physical security can never anticipate nor forestall the imaginative miscreant because the miscreant has the advantages of time and anonymity. Security planners must therefore deal with the reality of making a reasonable allocation of resources to security versus other public needs.

    2.   The more open the society, the weaker its security systems and the more vulnerable it is to violence.

Physical security measures limit the mobility and freedom of the populace. It is possible to have a community in which the ordinary citizen is reasonably protected from civilian violence, but only at the cost of giving over large measures of control to governmental units. In totalitarian regimes, the social order has merely traded some threats of violence for another.

    3.   Security, law enforcement, and military action are distinct functions that overlap in some areas.

Security planning uses a risk-threat formula to allocate available resources to a given situation. Risk refers to the potential for harm at a particular location (e.g., an event at a stadium, a nuclear reactor), and threat refers to likely attempts to cause harm. Threat analysis requires information about persons, groups, and political interests that are traditionally part of "protected" freedom.

Law enforcement most often seeks information about past wrongdoing, using sanctions for past wrongs as deterrence of future misconduct. Its connection to "protected" interests should be secondary. Only in rare instances, such as the Unabomber case, should inquiry into political agendas be necessary for solving past crimes.

Military action is designed to achieve strategic objectives by application of force. Most often a successful military action achieves its objectives by applying greater force than the other party can defend, but "asymmetric" force may give the advantage to the smaller clandestine operative. Modern military planning thus requires intelligence to know what kinds of force to deploy and where.

    4.   Post 9/11, U.S. institutional responses have shifted priorities in some troubling ways.

Prevention relies on information. Information threatens privacy and freedom of expression much more directly than traditional law enforcement. Without a clear separation between security and law enforcement, however, law enforcement is being expected to wield tools that intensify civil liberties issues.

[1] Criminal and Intelligence Investigations

The typical criminal investigation with which most of us are familiar begins with a civilian's lodging a complaint with a police officer. When your bicycle is stolen, the insurance company wants to know the "case number" assigned when you report it to the police. More serious crimes become the subject of investigation because a child is reported kidnaped, or a body is found under suspicious circumstances, or a white collar crime is suspected because someone has lost money. Once the "case" is initiated, investigating officers search for clues to what happened with regard to that incident by assembling a profile of the victim, searching for motives and opportunities for the crime, marshaling physical evidence at the scene, and the like. All of these aspects of an investigation have the objective of assembling a virtually complete picture of what happened at some point in the past. Only in the situation of an active serial criminal (e.g., Hillside Strangler, Son of Sam, Unabomber, Maryland sniper), are the investigators concerned about gathering information to prevent a reasonably certain future crime.

The investigation of a reported crime may produce "probable cause" to believe that a certain person committed the crime, so that search warrants can be issued to for that person's house or other premises. In some situations, there might even be probable cause to conduct electronic surveillance (such as a wiretap on the suspect's telephone) because evidence of the past crime might be transmitted either as part of evading detection or planning a future similar crime. Probable cause showings in the typical investigation, thus, are focused on information related to past events.

By contrast, the emphasis in most terrorism investigations is on preventing future crimes on the basis of a suspicion that a certain group of persons is contemplating violent action. This suspicion will not be based on evidence gathered in the context of a past crime but instead on the basis of rumors, reports from members of the public about their neighbors or friends, or just something an investigator reads in the newspaper. A search warrant or wiretap warrant would not even be possible until the "conspiracy" has been cemented through some overt act in furtherance of the conspiracy.

Launching a foreign intelligence investigation does not depend on a crime's having been committed or even contemplated; all that is required is indication that a person is connected to, or acting as an agent of, a foreign entity.[21] A domestic intelligence investigations would be based on the

---

[21] Being an agent of a foreign government without registering as such would be a crime, 18 U.S.C. § 951, but "foreign power" under FISA is much broader than that.

target's link to a group that appears to be involved in a crime and would proceed according to traditional law enforcement techniques. In short, the "no-crime" intelligence investigation is limited to suspected foreign agents within the U.S.

The Foreign Intelligence Surveillance Act (FISA)[22] was passed in 1978 to create a special court of designated federal judges (the FISA Court) who can issue surveillance orders for wiretap or other invasive surveillance, including clandestine searches and seizures, at the application of the Justice Department. The difference between a FISA order and an ordinary wiretap or search warrant under "Title III"[23] is that the FISA Court only requires probable cause to believe that the target is an "agent of a foreign power,"[24] which can include a foreign political organization,[25] while an ordinary warrant requires probable cause related to a crime. A few examples of prosecuted terrorist-type plots will show how a field investigation can lead to both prevention of harm and a prosecution.

United States v. Sarkissian[26] involved an investigation of Armenian radicals who were suspected of terrorist plotting. With a wiretap order from the FISA Court, FBI agents learned that they were planning to bomb the Armenian Consulate in Philadelphia. Continuing to monitor the telephone conversations, agents learned that parts of a bomb were being carried from Los Angeles to Boston. They deduced the probable flight and probable identity of the courier, and notified the Boston FBI Office, which sent 50 agents to Logan Airport to intercept the courier. Using dogs and x-ray as luggage was unloaded from the plane, Boston agents detected sticks of dynamite in a suitcase and eventually arrested the person who had checked the suitcase.[27] A subsequent prosecution for conspiracy to bomb, transportation of explosive materials, and possession of an unregistered firearm resulted.

Sarkissian presents the pre-9/11 pattern of a FISA investigation turned into a prosecution. (Incidentally, it also shows some ineptitude on the part of the plotters who used the same telephone repeatedly for making their plans. Skillful plotters are much more difficult to intercept.) The initial wiretap was obtained by court order from the FISA Court.[28]

---

22 50 U.S.C. §§ 1801-62 (2007).

23 18 U.S.C. § 2516 (2007).

24 50 U.S.C. § 1805(a)(3)(A) (2007).

25 50 U.S.C. § 1801(a)(5) (2007).

26 841 F.2d 959 (9th Cir. 1988).

27 In more detail, the agents at the airport located the suitcase with the dynamite, returned the dynamite to the suitcase and allowed the suitcase to be placed on the baggage claim carousel. The suspect, however, became nervous with the level of activity around the baggage claim area and fled, only to be arrested later. Although the court questioned the judgment of the Los Angeles agents in not obtaining a warrant while the plane was in the air, it did not comment on the wisdom of leaving dynamite in a suitcase in a public area of the airport.

28 No court order would have been required if there had been "no substantial likelihood that the surveillance would acquire the contents of any communication to which a United States person is a party." 50 U.S.C. § 1802(a)(1)(B) (2007). A "United States person" means a citizen, permanent resident alien, or a similar association or U.S. corporation. In the case

In cases such as *Sarkissian*, the actions of the surveilled persons themselves moved beyond conspiracy into criminal attempt and prompted an arrest and prosecution. Some difficult judgments are required in this type of setting to know when to interdict the conspiracy. Could the FBI have been faulted in this case for allowing the conspiracy to proceed so far that a suitcase containing dynamite was loaded onto a passenger airplane? If agents had moved in earlier, prosecution would have been much more difficult and it probably would have been difficult even to count the incident as a "prevention." What would the agents have done? walk up to Hosvepian's door and say "We know what you are planning so just be advised that we are watching?" Newspaper coverage of the "breakup" of a terrorist cell would be less than front-page news for one day. Under these circumstances, there is strong motivation for agents to wait and monitor the conspirators until they commit a crime of sufficient magnitude to land them in jail for an extended period and to get substantial news coverage.

The FBI agents in *Sarkissian* could be faulted for not moving in before dynamite was placed in a suitcase and checked as luggage onto an airplane, or at least for putting the suitcase with dynamite on the luggage carousel at its destination. But how realistic would such complaints be? How did the agents even have knowledge that the conspiracy was under way before there was probable cause to believe that a crime had been committed? It would have been difficult to obtain a search warrant prior to the dynamite's being packed in the suitcase and, by that time, as Sherlock Holmes would have said, "the game was afoot."

Another feature of intelligence gathering is that it most often works by assembling massive amounts of information, each piece of which may be seemingly innocent, until a malevolent pattern emerges. Modern high-tech artwork offers analogies that might be helpful in understanding the process. Think of the pictures, usually in children's books, that ask you to "find the _____" buried in an elaborate drawing. In this instance, all the irrelevant information is masking the one piece of critical information. The converse can be produced by taking hundreds or thousands of utterly innocent pictures, reducing them to miniature scale, and reassembling them into a pattern that produces an image totally unrelated to the component pictures. In this instance, the critical piece of information exists only as a pattern produced by assembling all the innocent images.

The art analogies are not perfect examples, but they reflect the very real difficulty of assembling information about various persons or events to put together a pattern that could alert officials to something nefarious. The 9/11 Commission Report describes how an FBI agent in Phoenix, three CIA analysts, and the Minneapolis FBI field office all had pieces of the puzzle

---

of a residential telephone, it would be virtually impossible to conclude that there is no substantial likelihood of acquiring communications from some U.S. person. If nothing else, the surveillance would pick up telephone solicitations. Only in the case of surveillance of a facility used exclusively by a foreign entity should this provision be used. This is the issue on which the controversial "NSA surveillance" plan turned. *See* § 7.02 *infra*.

but no means of assembling the pieces together.[29] How many other odd patterns had agents noticed which turned out to be patterns that were no more nefarious than their component parts? How many thousands of suspicions can government investigate without destroying the essence of a free society and thus doing what the terrorists seek?

The Supreme Court noticed this difficulty during the lull between the turbulence of the 1960s and the beginning of the terrorism expansion in the 1970s:

> National security cases . . . often reflect a convergence of First and Fourth Amendment values not present in cases of "ordinary" crime. Though the investigative duty of the executive may be stronger in such cases, so also is there greater jeopardy to constitutionally protected speech. . . . Fourth Amendment protections become the more necessary when the targets of official surveillance may be those suspected of unorthodoxy in their political beliefs. The danger to political dissent is acute where the Government attempts to act under so vague a concept as the power to protect "domestic security."

> [S]ecurity surveillance may involve different policy and practical considerations from the surveillance of "ordinary crime." The gathering of security intelligence is often long range and involves the interrelation of various sources and types of information. . . . Often, too, the emphasis of domestic intelligence gathering is on the prevention of unlawful activity or the enhancement of the Government's preparedness for some possible future crisis or emergency. Thus, the focus of domestic surveillance may be less precise than that directed against more conventional types of crime.[30]

In addition to the mere difficulty of intervention, there are very real political dynamics at work. The unfulfilled conspiracy will not result in very much of a prison sentence, so the conspirators can be back out and at work in relatively short order. Moreover, the headlines for arrests in an inchoate conspiracy will be smaller and of shorter duration than the headlines announcing arrests in a completed act of violence. Finally, prevention, as we have said before, operates on information. Acquiring information about politically-motivated conspiracies may produce massive amounts of information about "protected" political expression, something that the public and many law enforcement agencies are reluctant to countenance.

These are some of the factors that make prevention a more delicate exercise than enforcement investigation. Nevertheless, the public has demanded that a shift in strategy be made so that greater assurance of efforts toward prevention can be given.

---

[29] 9/11 REPORT at 268-76.

[30] United States v. U.S. Dist. Ct., 407 U.S. 297, 322 (1972) (Keith, J.).

With all these considerations in mind, we will expect to see challenges to government action as encroachments on civil liberties in at least these areas:

- Fourth Amendment challenges to surveillance operations;

- Fourth Amendment challenges to searches and seizures;

- General privacy challenges to government accumulation of information;

- First Amendment challenges to prosecutions for "material support";

- First Amendment challenges to restrictions at public events; and

- Due process challenges to detentions (e.g., material witness detentions)

[2] FISA and PATRIOT

The provision of PATRIOT that has been subjected to the most serious constitutional challenge is section 215, the provision dealing with FISA Court approval for seizure of third party records.[31] Most of the privacy issues in PATRIOT occur as amendments to FISA, making changes to existing law that in some instances raise genuine concerns about privacy but not as a matter of constitutional law.

PATRIOT tinkered with several aspects of FISA. The Justice Department argues that some elements are mere extensions of existing criminal practice in other areas to counterterrorism[32] — one allowing for "roving" wiretaps targeted at the person rather than a specific telephone[33] and one permitting "sneak and peek" search warrants under which notice of the warrant could be delayed by court order.[34] Another change, stating that acquisition of foreign intelligence information must be *a significant* purpose,[35] rather than the purpose of the surveillance or search, clarified some doubts that had arisen in the lower courts.[36]

---

[31] 50 U.S.C. § 1861 (2007).

[32] *See* Dep't of Justice, *USA PATRIOT Act: Myth vs. Reality, available at* www.lifeandliberty.gov/subs/add_myths.htm (last visited July 26, 2007).

[33] PATRIOT § 201, amending 18 U.S.C. § 2516(1).

[34] Section 213 of PATRIOT amended 18 U.S.C. § 3103a, which deals not with FISA orders but with ordinary search warrants.

[35] 50 U.S.C. § 1804(7)(B), § 1823(7)(B).

[36] The Fourth Circuit held that FISA satisfied the Fourth Amendment "only when the surveillance is conducted 'primarily' for foreign intelligence reasons." *United States v. Truong Dinh Hung*, 629 F.2d 908 (4th Cir. 1980). The Second Circuit stated that acquisition of foreign intelligence information must be the primary purpose of the surveillance but then went on to hold that there was nothing wrong with also having a law enforcement purpose. *United States v. Duggan*, 743 F.2d 59 (2d Cir. 1984). In *Sarkissian*, the Ninth Circuit held that it need not decide the issue because foreign intelligence was the primary purpose of the surveillance, even though the surveillance focused on a plot to blow up a consulate in Philadelphia. *See Sarkissian*, 841 F.2d 959.

Arguably the most important changes were provisions allowing for sharing of information between law enforcement and intelligence gathering offices.[37]

Finally, the amendment to FISA that is most problematic allows acquisition of a FISA court order to a third party for production of records in that party's possession. The basis for such an order again is the possibility of acquiring "foreign intelligence information" or "information related to terrorism." Advocates have argued that this provision is unconstitutional because it allows intrusion into third-party records on showing of a limited probable cause, and without any opportunity for the target of the investigation to be informed of the acquisition of personal data.[38] On the other hand, as the Justice department has correctly pointed out, an investigator could accomplish the same thing without any judicial review through the mechanism of a grand jury subpoena.[39] The key distinction, however, in the original statute was that the recipient of the FISA order was specifically enjoined from challenging the order or letting anyone know of the order. The ACLU had challenged section 215 in a wide-ranging lawsuit on behalf of a number of organizations before the statute was amended in March 2006 so that the recipient can now go to court to challenge the order.[40] In September 2006, the district court held that the organizations had standing to bring their action and allowed the plaintiffs to amend their pleadings in light of the amendments to the statute.[41]

Many advocacy groups in this field, in addition to the traditional civil rights groups, are principally concerned about electronic privacy but their

---

[37] Prior to PATRIOT, a variety of measures made it difficult for FBI agents and others engaged in intelligence work domestically to exchange information with CIA and other agents engaged in intelligence work abroad or even with agents involved in prosecution of criminal activity. 50 U.S.C. § 1806(b) permitted disclosure for law enforcement purposes only by express authorization of the Attorney General or Deputy Attorney General. This provision was read to erect a barrier between officers engaged in intelligence and those involved in obtaining information for prosecutions. PATRIOT began the process of breaking down these walls by permitting "consultation" between intelligence and law enforcement officers. 50 U.S.C. § 1806(k). PATRIOT did not, by itself, do anything to break down the barriers among the various agencies within the "Intelligence Community," many of which exist by operation of both the National Security Act and Executive Order 12333.

[38] See Electronic Privacy Information Center (EPIC), *available at* www.epic.org/privacy/terrorism/usapatriot/ (last visited July 26,2007):

> [Section 215], which overrides state library confidentiality laws, permits the FBI to compel production of business records, medical records, educational records and library records without a showing of "probable cause" (the existence of specific facts to support the belief that a crime has been committed or that the items sought are evidence of a crime). Instead, the government only needs to claim that the records may be related to an ongoing investigation related to terrorism or intelligence activities. Individuals served with a search warrant issued under FISA rules may not disclose, under penalty of law, the existence [sic] of the warrant or the facts that records were provided to the government.

[39] See www.lifeandliberty.gov/subs/add_myths.htm#s215.

[40] 50 U.S.C. § 1861(f) (2007).

[41] Muslim Community Ass'n v. Ashcroft, 459 F. Supp. 2d 592 (E.D. Mich. 2006).

attacks on the Patriot Act address many of its provisions. The analysis of the Electronic Privacy Information Center is a leading example.

A wiretap warrant can collect the content of a phone conversation. Similarly, a FISA order can be used to collect the content of e-mail communications. A telephone can be subject to "pen registers" and "trap and trace" devices that merely record the phone numbers called or the phones calling a targeted phone. EPIC objects to extension of these devices to computers on the ground that an innocent user may access any number of websites without having any connection to any of those sites.[42] In essence, the argument is that the user should have a reasonable expectation of privacy in surfing the web.

Reasonableness is a subjective factor — it is in the eye of the beholder. For example, the user who accesses a public website knows that the website is not private but might reasonably expect that his or her access to it is as private as reading a newspaper. By using these devices on computer websites, government acquires information about the user who accesses the website. EPIC and the government are in a debate over what should be the "reasonable expectations" of privacy in the computer age. The government's position is that if we can get the information, then nobody should have a reasonable expectation of privacy. EPIC's position is that if we can shield information from the government, then we should have a reasonable expectation of privacy. In other words, the legal standard is a judgment call on reasonableness more than an exercise in technology.

[3]　Concerns Over Collection of Intelligence

Why are we concerned about government's acquisition and storing of information about us? If we have nothing to hide, then why not let the government know all our secrets?

Most of the debate over the historical purposes of the Fourth Amendment has centered on whether the search and seizure rules were designed to protect the guilty or just the innocent. Arnold Loewy's classic hypothetical of the police department's perfect divining rod posits that if it were possible for law enforcement to target only evidence of illegal acts without disturbing any innocent person's belongings (or even a guilty person's innocent belongings), we would be happy to have this technology. In the absence of perfect technology, "the Fourth Amendment serves as an imperfect divining rod."[43]

---

[42] EPIC, *Pen Registers, the Internet and Carnivore, available at* www.epic.org/privacy/terrorism/usapatriot (last visited July 26, 2007):

> Because Carnivore provides the FBI with access to the communications of all subscribers of a monitored Internet Service Provider (and not just those of the court-designated target), it raises substantial privacy issues for millions of law-abiding American citizens.

[43] Arnold Loewy, *The Fourth Amendment as a Device for Protecting the Innocent*, 81 MICH. L. REV. 1229, 1244-45 (1983):

The Loewy example goes on to make an important point about the relationship between privacy and definition of substantive harms. In the example, there is a student whose locker has been searched and it contains a pejorative statement about the school principal.[44] Loewy contends that the Fourth Amendment's role as an imperfect divining rod prevents having this "innocent" expression detected by authorities who could misuse it or allow public embarrassment. But what makes this expression innocent? The student is actually "guilty" of saying bad things about the principal, even though the First Amendment would prevent the imposition of official punishment for her statements. In this sense, the Fourth Amendment stands as more than an "imperfect divining rod" to protect the innocent but also as a procedural mechanism to protect those who are guilty of something that we think worth protecting.

Some privacy advocates also complain that government intelligence gathering could be filtered for use by an irresponsible official. The opposite concern is that inefficiency could result in circulation of misleading information with an unwarranted appearance of authenticity, no trail to show exactly what its source might have been, and thus not easily subject to challenge.

These concerns can be grouped into four rather fuzzy and often overlapping categories:

    a.   Substantive abuse

    b.   Methods — harassment

    c.   Methods — deceit and secrecy lead to mistrust of government

---

In a Utopian society, each policeman would be equipped with an evidence-detecting divining rod. He would walk up and down the streets and whenever the divining rod detected evidence of crime, it would locate the evidence. First, it would single out the house, then it would point to the room, then the drawer, and finally the evidence itself. Thus, all evidence of crime would be uncovered in the most efficient possible manner, and no innocent person would be subject to a search. In a real society (such as ours), the Fourth Amendment serves as an imperfect divining rod.

[44] *Id.* at 1244:

Consider the following hypothetical: Principal X of Y High School, because of a hunch that students A, B, and C each have marijuana in their respective lockers, opens the lockers with a passkey. In A's locker, he finds marijuana, which is subsequently given to the police and used to convict A of possession of marijuana, for which A receives a year's imprisonment. In B's locker he finds a picture of his (Principal X's) head attached to the rear end of a horse with the caption: "X is a Horse's Ass." In C's locker, he finds a picture of C's mother with the caption: "Mom."

Assuming that these searches were unlawful, conventional wisdom suggests that A's rights were violated more than the others since only he suffered a criminal conviction by virtue of the search. Yet B's and C's legitimate privacy interests were more seriously intruded upon. B had a fourth (and probably a first) amendment right to keep his opinion of the principal to himself. His belief that the principal's prying eyes would not see his crude, but arguably cute, caricature is a reasonable one which ought to be protected. Similarly, C's hanging his mother's picture in his locker (though along with apple pie and the flag, the paradigmatic affirmation of true-blue American values) could be a source of embarrassment if made known to the public.

d.　Mistakes and factual errors

[a]　Substantive Abuse of Information

The two most widely reported abuses of information by government in the United States each spawned its own terminology — witch-hunts and McCarthyism. Some contemporary commentators have compared recent antiterrorism measures to McCarthyism.[45] As unlikely as deliberate abuse of information about private individuals may be, the possibility does exist.

Despite Chief Justice Burger's assurances in *Laird v. Tatum*[46] that the courts would intervene in the event of actual abuse of information, it is not entirely clear how a judicial remedy would be available, particularly in light of the citizen's reluctance to go to court and expose the information. Ruling out the likelihood of judicial relief leaves only preventing acquisition of the information as an effective defense against substantive abuse. Although limiting government accumulation of information is not in itself a constitutional requirement, as *Laird* illustrates, one of the most significant aspects of American political culture has been our resistance to government snooping.

In this sense, control of information is a civil liberty even though it is not constitutionally protected. Obviously, as a right that relies on political will for enforcement, it will be much more fragile in times of national emergency.

[b]　Methods — Harassment

The substantive misuse of information by government officials is closely linked to abuse in the methods of acquisition. Indeed, in the most famous examples of recent decades, harassment came in the form of both intrusive methods and veiled threats of misuse,[47] and it would have been difficult for the target to distinguish between the two. The only reason for making the distinction here is to clarify the nature of civil liberties issues involved.

Harassment is more likely than information abuse to be uncovered before it has run its course. Groups under investigation will cry "foul" often at the drop of a hat. Some of them will obtain public attention to their cause. Perhaps development of a general prohibition on harassment would be useful as a means of obtaining judicial review over the purposes of investigations, although the mere presence of such a judicial review check could easily be abused by target groups and individuals, thus hampering legitimate investigations. On balance, perhaps the political check that exists today is about as much as we can expect.

---

[45] HAYNES JOHNSON, THE AGE OF ANXIETY: MCCARTHYISM TO TERRORISM (2005); David Cole, *National Security State*, THE NATION, Dec. 17, 2001.

[46] 408 U.S. 1 (1972).

[47] PHILIP MELANSON, SECRECY WARS 72-76 (2001) (FBI pursuit of Martin Luther King, Jr., and CIA pursuit of Harry Belafonte).

[c]　Methods — Deceit and Secrecy

The third problem with intelligence gathering is that deceit and secrecy breed mistrust of government. The use of electronic surveillance may require a warrant depending on whether the target is in a private place or speaking in a public setting because the Fourth Amendment is designed to protect communications with an expectation of privacy. But eavesdropping and recording of even public conversations can be damaging to public trust and confidence. Even sending informants to public gatherings, while perfectly legal, raises hackles among large segments of the public and is limited by Justice Department guidelines.[48]

Likewise, obtaining information by trickery, as through use of undercover agents or informants for example, is perfectly legal so long as investigators do not cross the line of entrapment. But extensive use of trickery and deceit would be anathema to the American culture of open government when the targets have an element of political motivation in their activities. The American legal culture encourages a *healthy* level of distrust of government for the very reason that we want the public to keep government from moving too far in the direction of deceit and secrecy. A policy that openly fostered extensive deceit and secrecy would be unbearable to democratic premises of open government.

[d]　Mistakes and Factual Errors

The final difficulty with stored and retrievable information is that it can be based on or produce false data. Once the inaccurate information circulates beyond its original source, it has a tendency to grow and multiply. Everyone has heard of, if not participated in, the apocryphal parlor game in which a piece of information is whispered to one person and then repeated around the room until it bears no resemblance to the original statement. Mistakes in government files have the ability to destroy credit ratings and reputations, if not entire careers, especially given the sensitivity of innuendo in areas such as sexual harassment or child abuse.

Technology has brought us the concept of "data mining," which describes a variety of data gathering and processing projects, some fanciful and some quite real, which attempt to make links among data from different sources to find a suspicious pattern.[49] Some data mining projects have been

---

[48] USDOJ, *The Attorney General's Guidelines on General Crimes, Racketeering Enterprise and Terrorism Enterprise Investigations* 22:

> For the purpose of detecting or preventing terrorist activities, the FBI is authorized to visit any place and attend any event that is open to the public, on the same terms and conditions as members of the public generally. No information obtained from such visits shall be retained unless it relates to potential criminal or terrorist activity.

www.usdoj.gov/olp/generalcrimes2.pdf.

[49] *See* David Isenberg, *Multitude of Databases Complicates Information Sharing, available at* www.cdi.org/terrorism/inforsharing-pr.cgm. This report for the Center for Defense Information lists 16 databases including NSEERS (National Security Entry-Exit Registration System) and TIPS (Terrorism Information and Prefention System), both of which were instituted post-9/11 to collect and track information on aliens and suspicious persons.

prohibited by Congress following th epublic outcrey over DARPA's proposed Total Information Awareness program.[50] Until early 2007, the FBI used government databases along with NSLs to communication service providers to find patterns of suspicious activity.[51] At the state level, a project known as MATRIX promised to link many sources of publicly available information to a searvch engine that could produce names of persons who meet profiles of suspects in identified crimes. This effort was squelched in response to heavy public protest.[52]

There are two related problems with this kind of information accumulation, the sheer overwhelming volume of information collected and its susceptibility to corruption. While databases will continue to proliferate and their amenability to "fuzzy" search engines will increase, the limits on government manipulation of data are most likely to be political rather then judicially controlled.

[C] Intelligence and Multiplicity of Agencies

Roughly speaking, there have been essentially three communities of intelligence agencies operating within the United States Government: domestic, foreign, and military. Although 1996 statutory revisions placed the Director of Central Intelligence in charge of what is now called the "national intelligence community," the CIA itself since its inception has been debarred from operating on U.S. soil, while the FBI is charged with investigating foreign government activity within the U.S., and the Defense Intelligence Agency coordinates gathering of military intelligence both at home and abroad. This division of responsibility (along with human nature) has spawned jealousy, turf wars, and barriers among the various agencies in the domestic and foreign intelligence communities. Meanwhile, FISA was interpreted for many years as prohibiting intelligence-gathering arms of law enforcement form sharing information obtained by surveillance with their colleagues involved in gathering evidence for criminal prosecutions. A Reagan-era Executive Order prohibited the CIA and military intelligence from conducting intelligence operations within the U.S. except in coordination with the FBI.[53]

In the wake of national finger-pointing after 9/11, much of which was focused on whether we should have known the attack was coming, the PATRIOT Act attempted to alter the landscape of intelligence sharing. There were two major information-sharing changes made by PATRIOT.

---

[50] Jeffrey Seifert, *Data mining and Homeland Security: an Overview* 5-7 (Congressional Research Service Report, June 5, 2007).

[51] Eric Lichtblau, *F.B.I. Data Mining Reached Beyond Initial Targets*, N.Y. TIMES, Sept. 9, 2007, *available at* www.nytimes.com/2007/09/09/washington/ 09fbi.htm?ex = 1346990400&en = e0b585b2f0f51aa5&ei = 5088&partner = rssnyt&emc = rss.

[52] *See* ACLU, *Matrix, available at* www.aclu.org/privacy/spying/15701res20050308.html.

[53] EO 12333, 46 Fed. Reg. 59941 (Dec. 4, 1981): "The collection of foreign intelligence or counterintelligence within the United States shall be coordinated with the FBI as required by procedures agreed upon by the Director of Central Intelligence and the Attorney General."

One was to require the CIA to coordinate sharing of information across all agencies, including information obtained by the FBI under FISA.[54] The second was to break down the barriers within the Justice Department between "intelligence" and "law enforcement" information.[55] Later, the 9/11 Commission recommended bringing all the intelligence agencies of the U.S. under one head with both budgetary and personnel responsibility. In the Intelligence Reform Act of 2004, Congress created the Office of the Director of National Intelligence.[56]

The basic distinction between "intelligence" and "evidence" relates to the difference between prevention and prosecution, although they are not identical corollaries. Foreign intelligence is defined in the National Security Act as "information relating to the capabilities, intentions, or activities of foreign governments . . . or international terrorist activities."[57]

Prevention means gathering information. Gathering information means invasion of privacy. There are any number of persons and organizations concerned about the tendency of government to gather information. But should we be concerned enough to create legal and constitutional constraints on government? Yes, but it is difficult to know how to go about the task.

In *Laird v. Tatum*,[58] a number of plaintiffs brought suit to challenge practices of Army Intelligence that involved gathering and storing information. The plaintiffs described Army practices as "surveillance of lawful and peaceful civilian political activity." The Army described their activities as "gathering by lawful means . . . [and] maintaining and using in their intelligence activities . . . information relating to potential or actual civil disturbances [or] street demonstrations." The gathering of data about civilian political activity stemmed from riots following the assassination of Martin Luther King and criticism that the military was unprepared to assist civilian law enforcement in maintaining public safety. The Army launched a program of surveillance and processing of information about radical political groups to be better prepared in the event of another civil disturbance. As a result, military computers contained significant amounts of information about targeted groups and individuals.[59] The Supreme Court saw no constitutional harm in the program:

---

[54] PATRIOT § 902, 50 U.S.C. 403-3(c)(6) (2007).

[55] 50 U.S.C. § 1806(k) (2007).

[56] PUB. L. 108-458 (2004), codified at 50 U.S.C. § 403-04 (2007).

[57] 50 U.S.C. § 401a(2) (2007).

[58] 408 U.S. 1 (1972).

[59] *Id.* at 7:

The system put into operation as a result of the Army's 1967 experience consisted essentially of the collection of information about public activities that were thought to have at least some potential for civil disorder, the reporting of that information to Army Intelligence headquarters at Fort Holabird, Maryland, the dissemination of these reports from headquarters to major Army posts around the country, and the storage of the reported information in a computer data bank located at Fort Holabird. The information itself was collected by a variety of means, but it is

[Plaintiffs'] claim, simply stated, is . . . that the very existence of the Army's data-gathering system produces a constitutionally impermissible chilling effect upon the exercise of their First Amendment rights. That alleged "chilling" effect may perhaps be seen as arising from respondents' very perception of the system as inappropriate to the Army's role under our form of government, or as arising from respondents' beliefs that it is inherently dangerous for the military to be concerned with activities in the civilian sector, or as arising from respondents' less generalized yet speculative apprehensiveness that the Army may at some future date misuse the information in some way that would cause direct harm to respondents. Allegations of a subjective "chill" are not an adequate substitute for a claim of specific present objective harm or a threat of specific future harm.[60]

In other words, the Court found the Army's domestic intelligence operations to be within whatever constitutional boundaries might be placed upon it. Interestingly enough, however, Chief Justice Burger's opinion elaborated at some length that there are dangers from extensive military collaboration with civilian authorities, seemed to counsel the desirability of the "political" branches' reining in the program in question, and promised that in the event of actual harm the courts would not hesitate to intervene.[61]

Of course, as a practical matter, when it comes to challenges of military judgment the courts do hesitate to intervene. Probably the best that can be said of government intelligence gathering is that it will occur, that watchdog groups will attempt to persuade political leaders to "minimize"

---

significant that the principal sources of information were the news media and publications in general circulation. Some of the information came from Army Intelligence agents who attended meetings that were open to the public and who wrote field reports describing the meetings, giving such data as the name of the sponsoring organization, the identity of speakers, the approximate number of persons in attendance, and an indication of whether any disorder occurred. And still other information was provided to the Army by civilian law enforcement agencies.

[60] *Id.* at 13-14.

[61] *Id.* at 15-16:

The concerns of the Executive and Legislative Branches in response to disclosure of the Army surveillance activities — and indeed the claims alleged in the complaint — reflect a traditional and strong resistance of Americans to any military intrusion into civilian affairs. That tradition has deep roots in our history and found early expression, for example, in the Third Amendment's explicit prohibition against quartering soldiers in private homes without consent and in the constitutional provisions for civilian control of the military. Those prohibitions are not directly presented by this case, but their philosophical underpinnings explain our traditional insistence on limitations on military operations in peacetime. Indeed, when presented with claims of judicially cognizable injury resulting from military intrusion into the civilian sector, federal courts are fully empowered to consider claims of those asserting such injury; there is nothing in our Nation's history or in this Court's decided cases, including our holding today, that can properly be seen as giving any indication that actual or threatened injury by reason of unlawful activities of the military would go unnoticed or unremedied.

data gathering about civilian activities, and that the whole issue will ebb and flow with public perceptions of public need.

The flip side of a concern about abuse by government information gatherers is the fear that too many agencies will be running around gathering information and guarding their turf. The result could be such a lack of coordination that different agencies will be in possession of different pieces of information with no ability to fit the pieces together into a coherent picture. This is the fear that led to calls for reform of the intelligence community and which prompted investigations of 9/11.

Congress has taken three recent steps toward coordination of intelligence. The first was a statutory codification of intelligence structures in 1996 and the other was the reorganization resulting in the Department of Homeland Security. The 1996 rewriting of the National Security Act essentially codified most of what had been Executive Order 12333 promulgated during the Reagan administration. The resulting statutory structure placed the Director of Central Intelligence at the head of what is formally known as the Intelligence Community (IC). "An IC member is a federal government agency, service, bureau, or other organization within the executive branch that plays a role in the business of national intelligence."[62] The Intelligence Community comprises 14 such organizations, eight of them within the Department of Defense (DoD), which receives about 85 percent of the intelligence budget. The others include the Central Intelligence Agency and portions of five other executive branch organizations.

Until 2004, the Director of Central Intelligence was the primary link from the Intelligence Community to the President, which is now the function of the Director of National Intelligence.[63] It is difficult to see how a mere statutory exhortation for coordination will change the turf battles that exist in the intelligence world as in any other governmental field of endeavor.

Judge Posner argues that a healthy level of competition among agencies would be healthy for each agency, and would also alleviate the problem of "group think" that can creep in when coordination gives everyone at the table the feeling that they should support the existing conclusions.[64] He has gone further and suggested that there should be another agency outside the FBI involved in domestic intelligence with no law enforcement responsibilities.

§ 7.02 FOREIGN INTELLIGENCE SURVEILLANCE ACT

Following World War II, as the U.S. and USSR faced off across the espionage divide, and as technology began to open new channels of information gathering, the U.S. Executive branch began routinely to claim the power to conduct electronic surveillance "in the interest of national security." Meanwhile, the Supreme Court in two cases[65] held essentially that "wiretaps"

---

[62] www.intelligence.gov/1-members.shtml.

[63] 50 U.S.C. § 403 (2007).

[64] RICHARD POSNER, PREVENTING SURPRISE ATTACKS 121 (2005).

[65] Katz v. United States, 389 U.S. 347 (1967); Berger v. New York, 388 U.S. 41 (1967).

and similar intrusions into zones of privacy were subject to the Fourth Amendment requirements of warrants based on probable cause. The Court also held that Congress had not modified the warrant requirements for wiretaps based on "national security" but provided broad hints that the Fourth Amendment could be satisfied more easily in the case of security surveillance than in the investigation of "ordinary crime."[66] Congress responded in 1978 with FISA, setting out some procedures and standards to be met in conducting "foreign intelligence surveillance." The heart of the statutory scheme is the special court consisting of sitting district judges designated by the Chief Justice[67] to review applications for surveillance of foreign agents.[68] In this scheme, the Fourth Amendment is satisfied by a showing of probable cause to believe that the target is a foreign agent.[69]

[A] The Basics of FISA

Agents do not even need a court order to engage in electronic surveillance of foreign powers if the Attorney General certifies that there is "no substantial likelihood that the surveillance will acquire the contents of any communication to which a United States person is a party."[70] To obtain a court order authorizing electronic surveillance of foreign agents, it is not necessary for the investigator to allege probable cause of a criminal violation; it is enough that there is probable cause to believe that the "target of the surveillance is a foreign power or agent of a foreign power," that "the purpose [now changed to read 'a significant purpose'] of the surveillance is to obtain" information helpful for protection of national security, and that

---

[66] United States v. United States District Court, 407 U.S. 297 (1972) (Keith, J.).

[D]omestic security surveillance may involve different policy and practical considerations from the surveillance of "ordinary crime." The gathering of security intelligence is often long range and involves the interrelation of various sources and types of information. The exact targets of such surveillance may be more difficult to identify than in surveillance operations against many types of crime specified in Title III. Often, too, the emphasis of domestic intelligence gathering is on the prevention of unlawful activity or the enhancement of the Government's preparedness for some possible future crisis or emergency. Thus, the focus of domestic surveillance may be less precise than that directed against more conventional types of crime.

Different standards [for surveillance involving domestic security] may be compatible with the Fourth Amendment if they are reasonable both in relation to the legitimate need of Government for intelligence information and the protected rights of our citizens. For the warrant application may vary according to the governmental interest to be enforced and the nature of citizen rights deserving protection.

[67] 50 U.S.C. § 1803 (2007).

[68] 50 U.S.C. § 1804 (electronic surveillance); 50 U.S.C. § 1823 (physical searches). The target of surveillance or a search must be a "foreign power or an agent of a foreign power." "Foreign power" includes foreign governments, "faction of a foreign nation," a "group engaged in international terrorism," and even a "foreign-based political organization, not substantially composed of United States persons."

[69] *Sarkissian*, 841 F.2d 959; United States v. Duggan, 743 F.2d 59 (2d Cir. 1984).

[70] 50 U.S.C. § 1802(a)(1) (2007).

acceptable "minimization procedures" are in place.[71] Similar provisions apply to applications for orders for physical searches.[72]

So how does FISA become involved when the target is a group of disaffected Armenians living in the U.S.?[73] "Foreign power" includes "a group engaged in international terrorism or activities in preparation therefor" and even "a foreign-based political organization, not substantially composed of United States persons."[74] That the target of investigation is a foreign power (such as a foreign-based terrorist or political organization) satisfies the constitutional probable cause requirement, but the application also must certify the applying officer's belief that the information sought is "foreign intelligence information,"[75] which means information that "relates to . . . the ability of the United States to protect against" activities such as "international terrorism" or "clandestine intelligence activities."[76]

The FISA court order is not a warrant. The difference is that the probable cause showing relates only to the status of the target. There is no requirement of probable cause to believe that a crime has been or is about to be committed. Instead, the applying officer states a belief that information to be obtained "relates to" protection and prevention. In pre-9/11 parlance, the Justice Department operated under "minimization" guidelines that required a "wall" between intelligence activities and prosecution. Only by receiving approval from the Office of Intelligence Policy and Review (OIPR), whose activities were subject to monitoring by the FISA Court, could information from a FISA surveillance be "thrown over the wall" to a prosecution team.[77]

Prior to USA PATRIOT, information developed under FISA could be shared with prosecutors only by formal decision of the Office of Intelligence Policy in the Department of Justice. Now the "minimization guidelines" can provide for sharing and the statute explicitly calls for coordination and consultation between intelligence and law enforcement agents.[78] If information acquired in a FISA surveillance or search is subsequently used in a criminal prosecution, the defendant may make a motion to suppress on the basis that the information was not lawfully acquired or that the surveillance did not conform to the court order.[79] In this instance, the government may provide the court *ex parte* and *in camera* with "such materials relating to the surveillance as may be necessary to determine whether the surveillance was lawfully authorized and conducted."[80]

---

[71] 50 U.S.C. § 1805(a) (2007).

[72] 50 U.S.C. § 1824(a) (2007).

[73] *Sarkissian*, 841 F.2d 959.

[74] 50 U.S.C. § 1801(a)(5) (2007).

[75] 50 U.S.C. § 1804(a)(7) (2007).

[76] 50 U.S.C. § 1801(e) (2007).

[77] *See In Re* Sealed Case No. 02-001, 310 F.3d 717 (FIS Ct. Rev. 2002).

[78] 50 U.S.C. §§ 1806(k), 1825(k) (2007).

[79] 50 U.S.C. §§ 1806(e), 1825(f) (2007).

[80] 50 U.S.C. §§ 1806(f), 1825(g) (2007).

The most extensive discussion of the background and constitutionality of FISA is found in a Second Circuit case, *United States v. Duggan*.[81] The case involved some adherents of the Provisional Irish Republican Army who tried to buy missiles and explosives from an FBI informant in Boston. The negotiations and transactions were recorded and videotaped pursuant to approvals from FISC.

> Prior to the enactment of FISA, virtually every court that had addressed the issue had concluded that the President had the inherent power to conduct warrantless electronic surveillance to collect foreign intelligence information, and that such surveillances constituted an exception to the warrant requirement of the Fourth Amendment. [discussion of Keith, quoted below]
>
> [The] Act requires that the FISA Judge find probable cause to believe that the target is a foreign power or an agent of a foreign power, and that the place at which the electronic surveillance is to be directed is being used or is about to be used by a foreign power or an agent of a foreign power; and it requires him to find that the application meets the requirements of the Act. These requirements make it reasonable to dispense with a requirement that the FISA Judge find probable cause to believe that surveillance will in fact lead to the gathering of foreign intelligence information. Further, if the target is a United States person, the Act requires the FISA Judge to determine that the executive branch's certifications pursuant to § 1804(a)(7) are not clearly erroneous in light of the application as a whole, and to find that the application properly proposes, as required by § 1801(h), to minimize the intrusion upon the target's privacy.[82]

With respect to the differing treatment of nonresident aliens, the court had this to say:

> Although both the Fourth Amendment and the Equal Protection Clause afford protection to all aliens, nothing in either provision prevents Congress from adopting standards and procedures that are more beneficial to United States citizens and resident aliens than to nonresident aliens, so long as the differences are reasonable.[83]

The Supreme Court discussion in *Keith* led directly to FISA by this very significant dictum:

> The gathering of security intelligence is often long range and involves the interrelation of various sources and types of information. The exact targets of such surveillance may be more difficult to identify than in surveillance operations against many types of crime specified in Title III. Often, too, the emphasis of domestic

---

[81] 743 F.2d 59 (2d Cir. 1984) (2007).

[82] *Id.* at 74.

[83] *Id.* at 75.

intelligence gathering is on the prevention of unlawful activity or the enhancement of the Government's preparedness for some possible future crisis or emergency. Thus, the focus of domestic surveillance may be less precise than that directed against more conventional types of crime.

. . . Different standards [for surveillance involving domestic security] may be compatible with the Fourth Amendment if they are reasonable both in relation to the legitimate need of Government for intelligence information and the protected rights of our citizens. For the warrant application may vary according to the governmental interest to be enforced and the nature of citizen rights deserving protection.[84]

A cynic could conclude from these comments that the whole rationale for FISA is something like, "It is difficult to describe what we're looking for, so we shouldn't have to." Maybe nobody has a big problem with that when the target is a foreign agent or foreign power, but the *Keith* dictum sweeps extremely broadly to take in "domestic security," and FISA as amended by PATRIOT is inching out in that direction.

Prior to the USA PATRIOT Act, passed in October 2001, the "purpose" language required that "the purpose" of the surveillance be acquisition of foreign intelligence information. In ruling on motions to suppress, trial courts frequently had to assess whether the purpose of the surveillance was truly for intelligence purposes rather than to obtain evidence for a prosecution. Under the minimization guidelines of the Justice Department, a "wall" was erected between intelligence and prosecution so that the transfer of information from an intelligence operation to prosecution required approval of higher officials. As the courts struggled with this issue, they were split on whether "the purpose" meant "primary purpose,"[85] or "a purpose."[86] The 2001 amendment to "a significant purpose" was designed to resolve this controversy.

Sarkissian was a typical case of this type. The Ninth Circuit saw no problem in bypassing the Fourth Amendment warrant requirement so long as there was a "foreign intelligence" basis for the initial surveillance.

Regardless of whether the test is one of purpose or primary purpose, our review of the government's FISA materials convinces us that it is met in this case. It follows then that defendants were not entitled to a hearing. *See United States v. Belfield*, 223 U.S. App. D.C. 417, 692 F.2d 141, 147 (D.C. Cir. 1982) ("Disclosure and an adversary hearing are the exception, occurring only when necessary."); 50 U.S.C. § 1806(f) (providing for *ex parte in camera* review).

We refuse to draw too fine a distinction between criminal and intelligence investigations. "International terrorism," by definition,

---

[84] *Keith*, 407 U.S. at 323.

[85] United States v. Truong Dinh Hung, 629 F.2d 908 (4th Cir. 1980).

[86] United States v. Falvey, 540 F. Supp. 1306, 1313-14 (E.D.N.Y. 1982).

requires the investigation of activities that constitute crimes. That the government may later choose to prosecute is irrelevant. FISA contemplates prosecution based on evidence gathered through surveillance. "Surveillances . . . need not stop once conclusive evidence of a crime is obtained, but instead may be extended longer where protective measures other than arrest and prosecution are more appropriate."[87]

The change to "a significant purpose" and the courts' unwillingness to probe into the point at which an "intelligence" investigation becomes a "criminal" investigation should prompt renewed inquiry into the underlying constitutionality of the statutory scheme. In brief, if a court is never in a position to inquire into the reasons for electronic surveillance beyond the certification that there is a connection between the targets and foreign powers, the argument arises that this is a circumvention of the Fourth Amendment requirement for a search warrant.

The *Keith* rationale for this entire structure is that intelligence gathering cannot be premised on "criminal" probable cause because agents may not know what they are looking for until after they have found it but that this is not troublesome when dealing with agents of foreign powers. Intelligence gathering consists of monitoring the activities and conversations of persons to find out if either (a) they are doing something detrimental to the interests of the U.S., or (b) they have information that would be valuable to the U.S. In neither instance would it be possible to state in advance that agents have probable cause to believe that a crime has been committed, let alone by whom.

When "agent of a foreign power" is read broadly to include persons who might be working with foreign political organizations, this rationale specifi- cally contravenes the Fourth Amendment. Before turning to the "NSA surveillance" dispute of 2006, it is worth remembering the full discussion and actual holding of *Keith*, which was that the Executive has no inherent authority to bypass the demands of the Fourth Amendment when dealing with matters of national security.

> Thus, we conclude that the Government's concerns do not justify departure in this case from the customary Fourth Amendment requirement of judicial approval prior to initiation of a search or surveillance. Although some added burden will be imposed upon the Attorney General, this inconvenience is justified in a free society to protect constitutional values.[88]

---

[87] *Sarkissian*, 841 F.2d at 965, (quoting S. Rep. No. 701, 95th Cong., 2d Sess. 11, *reprinted in* 1978 U.S. CODE CONG. & ADMIN. NEWS 3973, 3980).

[88] *Keith*, 407 U.S. at 321:

> [A] recognition of these elementary truths does not make the employment by Government of electronic surveillance a welcome development — even when employed with restraint and under judicial supervision. There is, understandably, a deep-seated uneasiness and apprehension that this capability will be used to

As the Court went on to emphasize that its holding did not concern the issue of surveillance on "foreign powers or their agents," it opened the door for FISA. Then when the Administration wanted to throw a widespread net over international electronic communication, it decided that even the relatively lenient provisions of FISA were too cumbersome.

[B]   The Secret NSA Program

In December 2005, the press reported the existence of what has now become known as the Terrorist Surveillance Program. President Bush confirmed the existence of the program the next day in his radio address.[89] The Government attempted to justify the program on the basis that it did not target U.S. conversations:

> First, our international activities strictly target al Qaeda and their known affiliates. Al Qaeda is our enemy, and we want to know their plans. Second, the government does not listen to domestic phone calls without court approval. Third, the intelligence activities I authorized are lawful and have been briefed to appropriate members of Congress, both Republican and Democrat. Fourth, the privacy of ordinary Americans is fiercely protected in all our activities. We're not mining or trolling through the personal lives of millions of innocent Americans.[90]

The precise dimensions of the program remain classified. In a press briefing, Attorney General Gonzales stated that it consists of "intercepts of

---

intrude upon cherished privacy of law-abiding citizens. We look to the Bill of Rights to safeguard this privacy.

National security cases, moreover, often reflect a convergence of First and Fourth Amendment values not present in cases of "ordinary" crime. Though the investigative duty of the executive may be stronger in such cases, so also is there greater jeopardy to constitutionally protected speech. . . . The danger to political dissent is acute where the Government attempts to act under so vague a concept as the power to protect "domestic security."

We cannot accept the Government's argument that internal security matters are too subtle and complex for judicial evaluation. Courts regularly deal with the most difficult issues of our society. There is no reason to believe that federal judges will be insensitive to or uncomprehending of the issues involved in domestic security cases. Certainly courts can recognize that domestic security surveillance involves different considerations from the surveillance of "ordinary crime." If the threat is too subtle or complex for our senior law enforcement officers to convey its significance to a court, one may question whether there is probable cause for surveillance.

89 President's Radio Address of Dec. 17, 2005:

In the weeks following the terrorist attacks on our Nation, I authorized the National Security Agency, consistent with U.S. law and the Constitution, to intercept the international communications of people with known links to al Qaeda and related terrorist organizations. Before we intercept these communications, the Government must have information that establishes a clear link to these terrorist networks.

www.whitehouse.gov/news/releases/2005/12/print/20051217.html (last visited July 27, 2007).

90 *President Bush Discusses NSA Surveillance Program,* May 11, 2006, *available at* www.whitehouse.gov/news/releases/2006/05/20060511-1.html (last visited July 27, 2007).

contents of communications where one . . . party to the communication is outside the United States" and agents have "a reasonable basis to conclude that one party to the communication is a member of al Qaeda, affiliated with al Qaeda, or a member of an organization affiliated with al Qaeda, or working in support of al Qaeda."[91]

The Department of Justice stated the Administration's position in a memorandum released in January 2006:

> The NSA activities are supported by the President's well-recognized inherent constitutional authority as Commander in Chief and sole organ for the Nation in foreign affairs to conduct warrantless surveillance of enemy forces for intelligence purposes to detect and disrupt armed attacks on the United States.[92]

As this sentence indicates, the memorandum relied heavily on a portrayal of terrorists as constituting "enemy forces" engaged in "armed attacks" as if they were a nation subject to the principles of armed conflict. The memorandum also relied on the Authorization for Use of Military Force, which authorized "all necessary and appropriate force" against the 9/11 perpetrators.[93]

The Congressional Research Service provided an exhaustive analysis that began with the *Steel Seizure Case*,[94] an instance in which a President had similarly relied on "wartime exigencies" to take unusual measures impacting domestic interests. The CRS concluded that

> it appears unlikely that a court would hold that Congress has expressly or impliedly authorized the NSA electronic surveillance operations here under discussion, and it would likewise appear that, to the extent that those surveillances fall within the definition of "electronic surveillance" within the meaning of FISA or any activity regulated under Title III, Congress intended to cover the entire field with these statutes. To the extent that the NSA activity is not permitted by some reading of Title III or FISA, it may represent an exercise of presidential power at its lowest ebb, in which case exclusive presidential control is sustainable only by "disabling Congress from acting upon the subject."[95]

In January 2007, the Attorney General announced that "a Judge of the Foreign Intelligence Surveillance Court issued orders authorizing the

---

[91] White House, *Press Briefing by Attorney General Alberto Gonzales and General Michael Hayden, Principal Deputy Director for National Intelligence*, Dec. 19, 2005, *available at* www.whitehouse.gov/news/releases/2005/12/20051219-1.html (last visited July 27, 2007).

[92] Dep't of Justice, *Legal Authorities Supporting the Activities of the National Security Agency Described by the President*, Jan. 17, 2006, *available at* www.usdoj.gov/opa/whitepaperonnsalegalauthorities.pdf (last visited July 27, 2007).

[93] Pub. L. 107-40 § 2(a) (Sept. 18, 2001).

[94] Youngstown Sheet and Tube Co. v. Sawyer, 343 U.S. 579 (1952).

[95] CRS, *Presidential Authority to Conduct Warrantless Electronic Surveillance to Gather Foreign Intelligence Information*, Jan. 5, 2006, *available at* www.law.utah.edu/faculty/bios/mccormackw/website/Terrorism/book_update/index.htm.

Government to target for collection communications into or out of the United States where there is probable cause to believe that one of the communicants is a member or agent of al Qaeda or an affiliated terrorist organization."[96] It is not clear from the letter, and to date there has been no public announcement, whether this means that each interception must be authorized by individual court order or whether there is blanket permission now in place for all NSA intercepts.

A number of lawsuits were filed challenging the NSA program. One suit by the ACLU first obtained an injunction against the program by the district court in Michigan.[97] On appeal, the Sixth Circuit decided that none of the plaintiffs had standing to bring the action because they could not show that any particular conversation had been intercepted.[98] The Government successfully invoked the "state secrets" doctrine to prevent discovery of whether the individual plaintiffs had been surveilled, but the district court held there was sufficient likelihood that some of them had been surveilled that the plaintiffs presented a *prima facie* case of harm and it was up to the Government whether to disclose facts to rebut that showing.[99] The Sixth Circuit disagreed with the findings of the district court regarding the harm to plaintiffs' personal interests, holding that (1) an invasion of privacy had not occurred because the plaintiffs refrained from conversations that could be monitored, and (2) their decision not to communicate with clients was not protected by the First Amendment.[100]

Meanwhile, another lawsuit alleges that telephone service providers have violated their customers' rights by cooperating and assisting the NSA in surveillance of their phones.[101] The district court there has denied motions to dismiss, holding that the plaintiffs could state a prima facie claim and that the service provider could not establish a qualified immunity on the basis of the pleadings. The court has asked the parties for briefing on the question of whether to appoint a special master to "assist the court in

---

[96] Letter from Attorney General Gonzales to Senate Judiciary Committee, Jan. 17, 2007, *available at* www.law.utah.edu/faculty/bios/mccormackw/website/Terrorism/book_update/index.htm.

[97] ACLU v. Nat'l Sec. Agency, 438 F. Supp. 2d 754 (E.D. Mich. 2006).

[98] ACLU v. NSA, 2007 U.S. App. LEXIS 16149 (6th Cir. 2007).

[99] The plaintiffs included people who regularly communicated for professional reasons with persons in other countries who were likely to fall under suspicion of terrorist activity. *ACLU*, 438 F. Supp. 2d at 765.

[100] ACLU v. NSA, 2007 U.S. App. LEXIS 16149, at 29-30:

> By refraining from communications (i.e., the potentially harmful conduct), the plaintiffs have negated any possibility that the NSA will ever actually intercept their communications and thereby avoided the anticipated harm — this is typical of declaratory judgment and perfectly permissible. But, by proposing only injuries that result from this refusal to engage in communications (e.g., the inability to conduct their professions without added burden and expense), they attempt to supplant an insufficient, speculative injury with an injury that appears sufficiently imminent and concrete, but is only incidental to the alleged wrong (i.e., the NSA's conduct).

[101] Hepting v. AT&T Corp., 439 F. Supp. 2d 974 (N.D. Cal. 2007).

determining whether disclosing particular evidence would create a 'reasonable danger' of harming national security."[102]

§ 7.03 CLASSIFIED INFORMATION PROCEDURES ACT

Investigation of terrorist plots will often involve information that the government does not wish disclosed. In tension with that need are judicial proceedings in which information is needed for a full and fair hearing. Among the possibilities are the following:

Informants. The courts have long recognized an "informer's privilege" so that government may be able to keep secret the identity of an informant who is lodged within a criminal scheme. Some of the best information leading to prosecutions of mafiosi, drug rings, and paramilitary groups (e.g., KKK) has come from insiders. The informer's privilege may be invoked when the defendant challenges probable cause for a search or attempts to discover information that might shed light on the background of the investigation. It does not mean that government may introduce anonymous testimony at trial.

Hardware specifications. Terrorists may get their hands on explosives, military equipment, or related hardware that the government does not want described in detail during trial.

Technology and investigative techniques. High-tech industries have developed, often with government funding, some rather amazing abilities over the past few decades. The combination of sophisticated software to go with micro electronic devices allows eavesdropping on conversations in ways that most of us can only imagine. Satellites can pick up millions of telephone conversations while software filters those conversations for voice patterns or key words to isolate and record conversations that are of interest to an investigation. Other devices can monitor and record conversations taking place at great distances inside buildings and other structures. Infrared and similar devices can monitor human movements. Computers can break most codes, although concepts such as "one-time pads" and insider jargon may still baffle cryptography programs until behavior confirms what was communicated. Exactly how good all these devices are and what they can accomplish in many instances remain government-protected secrets.

Government planning and foreign relations. The earliest recognition of government secrets came in the form of the courts' noting that the executive branch should be allowed to keep secrets about other governments and about its own plans.[103]

---

[102] *Id.* at 1010.

[103] United States v. Curtiss-Wright Export Corp., 299 U.S. 304, 57 (1936):

> [The President] has his confidential sources of information. He has his agents in the form of diplomatic, consular, and other officials. Secrecy in respect of information gathered by them may be highly necessary, and the premature disclosure of it productive of harmful results. Indeed, so clearly is this true that the first President

[A]   The Problem of Secret Evidence

At the outset, it is important to realize that very little will allow the government to rely on secret information in presenting its own evidence in a prosecution. The Sixth Amendment's right to confront witnesses will allow hearsay testimony or summaries of secret information to be used in lieu of cross-examination of the most knowledgeable person only in recognized exceptions to the hearsay rule. Government secrecy may sometimes curtail the production of evidence and result in an acquittal, but that is just the price of protecting against government overreaching.[104] In a few rare instances, the right to a public trial may be compromised so that the public could be excluded from a portion of the trial in which secret information is placed before the factfinder.

One prosecution that shows the potential for problems in allowing unconfronted testimony to substitute for secret information is *United States v. Wilson*.[105] Edwin Wilson was a former CIA employee who was charged with various offenses related to attempting to provide weapons and explosives to Libya in 1980 after he left CIA employment. Allegedly realizing that he was under suspicion, he fled to Libya but was lured by U.S. agents to the Dominican Republic in 1982, apprehended and brought back to the U.S. for trial in two different cases. His conviction on firearms offenses was affirmed on appeal by the Fourth Circuit.[106] He then was prosecuted and convicted in the Southern District of Texas of attempting to ship 20 tons of C-4 explosives to Libya, and that conviction was also affirmed on appeal by the Fifth Circuit.[107] "After that, a court in the Southern District of New York sentenced him to twenty-five years — to run consecutively with his Virginia and Texas sentences — for attempted murder, criminal solicitation, obstruction of justice, tampering with witnesses, and retaliating against witnesses."[108]

Twenty years later, Wilson moved to vacate his sentence in the C-4 case, alleging that prosecution witnesses had testified falsely. This is how the trial judge saw the case:

refused to accede to a request to lay before the House of Representatives the instructions, correspondence and documents relating to the negotiation of the Jay Treaty — a refusal the wisdom of which was recognized by the House itself and has never since been doubted.

[104] The U.S. has been criticized in a number of quarters for not making evidence available because it chooses to hold key witnesses in secrecy. One effect has been dismissals in German courts of cases against Mounier el-Motassadeq and Abdelghani Mzoudi, both alleged conspirators in 9/11, on the basis of missing evidence in the person of Ramzi bin al-Shibh, who is in U.S. custody. *See* Joanne Mariner, *Witness Unavailable: How the U.S. Hinders Terrorism Prosecutions Abroad*, FINDLAW, Mar. 17, 2004, *available at* http://writ.news.findlaw.com/mariner/20040317.html.

[105] 289 F. Supp. 2d 801 (S.D. Tex. 2003).

[106] United States v. Wilson, 721 F.2d 967 (4th Cir. 1983).

[107] United States v. Wilson, 732 F.2d 404 (5th Cir. 1983).

[108] *Wilson*, 289 F. Supp. 2d at 803.

[Wilson's] defense was simple. He said he was still working for the Company. The government refused to disclose records of his continued association with the agency. When he presented witnesses to his contacts after the end of his formal employment, the government convinced the judge to admit an affidavit from a principal CIA official to the effect that there were, with one minor exception, none — zero. There were, in fact, over 80 contacts, including actions parallel to those in the charges.

The government discussed among dozens of its officials and lawyers whether to correct the testimony. No correction was made — not after trial, not before sentencing, not on appeal, and not in this review. Confronted with its own internal memoranda, the government now says that, well, it might have misstated the truth, but that it was Wilson's fault, it did not really matter, and it did not know what it was doing. Because the government knowingly used false evidence against him and suppressed favorable evidence, his conviction will be vacated.[109]

What had happened in the 1983 prosecution of the C-4 case was that Wilson attempted to show that he was still working for the CIA, or at least believed that he was doing so, by introducing evidence of many contacts that he had with active CIA employees in setting up the deal with Libya so that he could get on the inside with the Qaddafi regime. The CIA sought to have a high-ranking official testify pseudonymously, and ultimately the judge settled on the compromise of the affidavit mentioned above denying that he "was not asked or requested, directly or indirectly, to perform or provide any service, directly or indirectly, for [the] CIA."

The judge in the 2003 motion repeatedly took the government to task for knowingly relying on false information in the 1983 prosecution. This is not so much a CIPA case as just a case of "manufactured" or "fabricated" evidence in rebuttal to a defense claim. CIPA was involved because Wilson had sought CIA documents in discovery and was rebuffed under the procedures of CIPA. It is also likely that the Wilson experience will weigh on the minds of judges in future CIPA cases when confronted with government claims of privilege and the need for secrecy.

[B] CIPA Procedures

The Classified Information Procedures Act (CIPA)[110] stems from the proposition that government is obligated to put on its evidence and to provide the defendant with evidence in its possession that might be exculpatory, after which the defendant has the right to put on evidence in his or her own behalf. Government secrets thus could be at stake either in a discovery request or in the defendant's disclosure of evidence already in his possession. The statute allows the government to make an *ex parte, in camera*

---

[109] *Id.* at 802.

[110] 18 U.S.C. App. §§ 1-16 (2007).

disclosure to the judge of secret information asking that the information not be disclosed to the defendant.[111] If the judge agrees that the information would not be helpful to the defense, that is the end of the matter. If the information would be helpful but a substantial equivalent can be obtained by redacting the secrets or providing a summary, then the judge can order disclosure in the appropriate form.[112] Finally, if the information is necessary to the defense and the government refuses to disclose, dismissal of the prosecution would be the ultimate remedy.[113]

---

[111] 18 U.S.C. App. § 6(a) (2007): "Within the time specified by the court for the filing of a motion under this section, the United States may request the court to conduct a hearing to make all determinations concerning the use, relevance, or admissibility of classified information that would otherwise be made during the trial or pretrial proceeding. Upon such a request, the court shall conduct such a hearing. Any hearing held pursuant to this subsection (or any portion of such hearing specified in the request of the Attorney General) shall be held in camera if the Attorney General certifies to the court in such petition that a public proceeding may result in the disclosure of classified information."

[112] 18 U.S.C. App. § 4 (2007):

The court, upon a sufficient showing, may authorize the United States to delete specified items of classified information from documents to be made available to the defendant through discovery under the Federal Rules of Criminal Procedure, to substitute a summary of the information for such classified documents, or to substitute a statement admitting relevant facts that the classified information would tend to prove."

18 U.S.C. § 6(c)(1) (2007):

Upon any determination by the court authorizing the disclosure of specific classified information under the procedures established by this section, the United States may move that, in lieu of the disclosure of such specific classified information, the court order—

(A) the substitution for such classified information of a statement admitting relevant facts that the specific classified information would tend to prove; or

(B) the substitution for such classified information of a summary of the specific classified information.

The court shall grant such a motion of the United States if it finds that the statement or summary will provide the defendant with substantially the same ability to make his defense as would disclosure of the specific classified information. The court shall hold a hearing on any motion under this section. Any such hearing shall be held in camera at the request of the Attorney General.

[113] 18 U.S.C. § 6(e) (2007):

(1) Whenever the court denies a motion by the United States that it issue an order under subsection (c) and the United States files with the court an affidavit of the Attorney General objecting to disclosure of the classified information at issue, the court shall order that the defendant not disclose or cause the disclosure of such information.

(2) Whenever a defendant is prevented by an order under paragraph (1) from disclosing or causing the disclosure of classified information, the court shall dismiss the indictment or information; except that, when the court determines that the interests of justice would not be served by dismissal of the indictment or information, the court shall order such other action, in lieu of dismissing the indictment or information, as the court determines is appropriate. Such action may include, but need not be limited to—

(A) dismissing specified counts of the indictment or information;

(B) finding against the United States on any issue as to which the excluded classified information relates; or

(C) striking or precluding all or part of the testimony of a witness.

CIPA is essentially a statute of trial procedure, and the appellate courts have not been particularly receptive to claims of violations of CIPA, usually relying on the discretion of the trial court. In almost all the reported decisions, the trial court has found after *ex parte, in camera* review that the material was irrelevant or otherwise not helpful to the defense, and the reviewing court has concurred.[114] Several of the cases involve claims that the defendant had a prior relationship with the government, specifically the CIA, and that classified information would support his claim that he thought his conduct in this instance was authorized or at least would not be prosecuted.[115]

United States v. Smith[116] is the most thorough discussion of CIPA, although it involves a rather esoteric issue. Smith (real name apparently) was accused of espionage for selling government secrets to a Russian agent. Smith was employed in Army Intelligence and claims that he sold material to the Russian agent at the behest of two people whom he believed to be CIA agents. To support his defense, he wanted to introduce evidence of some specific CIA operations to show that he had reason to believe that this was part of the same pattern. The trial court ruled that the relevant evidence would be admissible, although the statutory procedure seems to contemplate a ruling first on relevance, then on admissibility in light of any proposed redactions or substitutions. The government did not come forward with suggested redactions or substitutions but instead took an immediate appeal as authorized by the statute.[117] On appeal, the initial Fourth Circuit panel held that the trial judge was correct, but the *en banc* court then held that the trial judge should have considered admissibility as a question of government privilege going beyond the mere inquiry into relevance. In the absence of proposed redactions or substitutions, the court balanced the interests in favor of the government.

The debate in *Smith* is esoteric indeed. Because Smith already had the information in question, the provisions regarding defense discovery were not applicable. So the argument was whether the government's privilege should be balanced against the defendant's right to present evidence, or whether instead the defendant's rights were to be protected by admitting all relevant evidence. A middle ground would have been to ask whether the defendant's rights could have been implemented by finding a "substantial equivalent" of the classified information. The *en banc* majority held that the government's claim of privilege was not outweighed by the defendant's claim of need to use the evidence.[118]

---

[114] *See generally* United States v. Klimavicius-Violoria, 144 F.3d 1249 (9th Cir. 1998); United States v. Wilson, 732 F.2d 404 (5th Cir. 1984).

[115] United States v. Rewald, 889 F.2d 836 (9th Cir. 1989).

[116] 780 F.2d 1102 (4th Cir. 1985) (*en banc*).

[117] 18 U.S.C. App. § 7(a) (2007): "An interlocutory appeal by the United States taken before or after the defendant has been placed in jeopardy shall lie to a court of appeals from a decision or order of a district court in a criminal case authorizing the disclosure of classified information, imposing sanctions for nondisclosure of classified information, or refusing a protective order sought by the United States to prevent the disclosure of classified information."

[118] *Smith*, 780 F.2d at 1109.

The dissent to the *en banc* holding opted for the middle ground. It insisted that the proper procedure was for the trial judge to determine relevance, then for the government to make a motion for redaction or summarization, and at that point the trial judge could rule on the "substantial equivalent" issue.[119] In the dissent's view, by allowing the immediate appeal, the court was allowing the government to do an end run around the statutory procedure, thus avoiding the need to examine whether redacted materials could have been an adequate substitute.[120] Ironically, the Fourth Circuit later decided not to allow an immediate appeal from a CIPA discovery order in *United States v. Moussaoui*.[121]

The Fourth Circuit balanced interests to dismiss a case after the government's refusal to allow introduction of classified information in *United States v. Fernandez*,[122] part of the fallout of the Iran-Contra scandal of 1984-86. Fernandez was CIA Station Chief in Costa Rica during the time that Congress prohibited use of U.S. funds for supplying the "Contras," a paramilitary organization attempting to overthrow the leftist government of Nicaragua from bases in El Salvador, Honduras, and Costa Rica. As part of the 1980 settlement with Iran of the hostage situation in that country, the U.S. sold Iran military equipment. Colonel Oliver North diverted proceeds of those sales to "private benefactors" who would help supply the Contras. When questioned about these activities, Fernandez allegedly lied and misled investigators by obfuscating the purpose of building an airstrip in Costa Rica. Fernandez wanted to introduce as part of his defense particulars of other CIA projects in the region and the U.S. objected under CIPA.

In essence, Fernandez' defense wanted to use classified items of information "because they would help paint a picture of massive CIA involvement in and knowledge of the resupply of the Contras. This picture, in turn, would support Fernandez's claim that he never made the allegedly false statements (which were never recorded or transcribed), and thus did not lie, and had no motive or intent to lie."[123] The Government offered to provide substitutes, apparently in the form of admissions about active CIA involvement in the operation, but the district court held this would not be sufficient to paint the picture that the defense wanted to present. Ultimately, the government refused to allow disclosure of the material, and the district court ordered the indictment dismissed. The Fourth Circuit affirmed on the basis that the classified material was critical to Fernandez' ability to present his case because the other projects would show that he had no reason to lie about the airstrip and that the CIA was fully knowledgeable of his activities.

---

[119] *Id.* at 1112.

[120] *Id.* at 1113.

[121] 483 F.3d 220 (4th Cir. 2007).

[122] 913 F.2d 148 (4th Cir. 1990).

[123] *Id.* at 152.

The D.C. Circuit in *Yunis* responded as follows to the argument that the defendant is handicapped in arguing materiality of classified material because he does not know what the material says: "Yunis was present during all the relevant conversations. It does not impose upon him any burden of absolute memory, omniscience, or superhuman mental capacity to expect some specificity as to what benefit he expects to gain from the evidence sought here."[124] What if in fact Yunis had not been present? How does a defendant who is the subject of a mistaken identity, and has no knowledge of the crime, defend himself? Secondly, is it proper to insist on "materiality" of the desired evidence rather than a mere "helpful to the defense" standard?

The Ninth Circuit in *Sarkissian* cited one case from the First Circuit[125] for the proposition that, in matters of discovery as opposed to disclosure of information already in the possession of the defendant, CIPA sets up a balancing of the defendant's need for the information with the government's (or public's) harm if the information were disclosed. The D.C. Circuit in *Yunis* refused to adopt a balancing approach while ruling against the defendant, and the Fourth Circuit in *Smith* claimed to be balancing while deciding against the defendant. *Fernandez* had this to say about "balancing" interests while deciding for the defendant:

> The judge emphasized that he reached this decision after weighing the interests of national security against the need to provide Fernandez with a fair trial. He concluded by emphasizing: "I believe that the identity of these *** is necessary for the defense, and would rule that your substitution would not be adequate." It was clearly within the district court's discretion to conclude that the government's vague, compressed descriptions about the CIA's general presence in the region and about its general familiarity with the resupply operations were no substitute for live testimony from witnesses and the introduction of actual documents detailing the CIA's intimate involvement with the resupply operation.[126]

This is not "balancing" so much as placing a burden on the government to justify imposition on the right to present testimony.[127] The *Smith* and *Sarkissian* approach, by contrast, seems to place the burden on the defendant to show admissibility against the government's claim of privilege. CIPA provides that the court will accept substitute material "if it finds that the statement or summary will provide the defendant with substantially the same ability to make his defense as would disclosure of the specific classified information." Because the government has sole discretion

---

[124] United States v. Yunis, 867 F.2d 617, 624 (D.C. Cir. 1989).

[125] United States v. Pringle, 751 F.2d 419 (1st Cir. 1984) (seeking information about surveillance in a marijuana smuggling case; court held information not helpful to defense).

[126] *Fernandez*, 913 F.2d at 161.

[127] A Legal Realist or Critical Legal Studies scholar might be quick to note that the only reported case dismissing a prosecution under CIPA is one in which the defendant was a CIA station chief.

whether to authorize disclosure, but the defense has constitutionally based claims at stake, then the court really need not balance but instead can decide the question of whether the substituted material is a substantial equivalent of the actual material. If it is not, and the court is persuaded that the defendant needs the information for his or her defense, then the government always has the choice of dismissing the case. This may not be as damaging to the public interest as might be thought for the simple reason that this defendant is not likely to go far without government shadows at every step.

[C] Discovery of Classified Information

Zacarias Moussaoui is the only person who has been charged in the U.S. with direct participation in the 9/11 attacks.[128] He allegedly was to have been one of the hijackers but did not make the flight because he was already in custody for violations of the immigration laws. He was charged with six conspiracy counts: to commit a terrorist act under 2332b, to commit air piracy, to destroy aircraft, to use weapons of mass destruction, to murder U.S. employees, and to destroy property. The tortured progress of attempting to bring his case to trial went on for over three years before he finally pleaded guilty.[129] The central difficulty of the case revolved around attempting to proceed with a trial when the defendant was requesting access to witnesses who were in government custody but as to whom the government claimed a national security need for secrecy.

After about a year of pretrial wrangling over secret documents, the trial judge in February 2003 began reviewing government responses to requests from the Moussaoui defense team to interview some al Qaeda members in U.S. custody to determine if they had information relevant to the defense position that Moussaoui was not part of the 9/11 plot. (It has been widely reported, and not denied, that the key witness involved was Khalid Sheikh Mohammed, the alleged mastermind of 9/11.) The government took the position that interviews would inevitably "disclose" classified information and resisted the interview while suggesting alternatives. When the judge was not satisfied with the government's suggestions and finally ordered depositions to occur, the government immediately appealed to the Fourth Circuit. The *en banc* court decided that there was no right to immediate appeal.[130]

The Fourth Circuit described the trial court's decision as follows:

> [T]he court determined that testimony from the enemy combatant witness would be relevant and material to Moussaoui's planned defense to the charges. The court also concluded that Moussaoui

---

[128] United States v. Moussaoui, 382 F.3d 453 (4th Cir. 2004) (en banc).

[129] *See* Statement of Facts in Support of Guilty Plea, United States v. Moussaoui, Crim. No. 01-455-A (E.D. Va. April 22, 2005), *available at* www.law.utah.edu/faculty/bios/mccormackw/website/Terrorism/Cases/crim_terror/moussaoui_plea_facts.pdf.

[130] United States v. Moussaoui, 333 F.3d 509 (4th Cir. 2003).

and the public's interest in a fair trial outweighed the Government's national security interest in precluding access to the enemy combatant witness. However, the court ruled that the Government's national security concerns counseled against granting unfettered pretrial access to the enemy combatant witness and against requiring that the enemy combatant witness be produced for testimony at trial. The district court therefore issued a testimonial writ directing that the Government produce the witness for a Rule 15 deposition and setting conditions for the deposition.[131]

The en banc court then decided that this was not really a CIPA order:

It is true, of course, that the district court issued the testimonial writ based in part on its assessment that the enemy combatant witness' testimony would likely be helpful to Moussaoui's defense. But, neither this conclusion, nor the fact that the purpose of the deposition is to preserve the enemy combatant witness' testimony for potential use at trial, is sufficient to establish the applicability of CIPA. At its core, the order of the district court concerned only the question of whether Moussaoui and standby counsel would be granted access to the enemy combatant witness (and if so, what form of access), not whether any particular statement of this witness would be admitted at trial. The district court was thus correct to conclude that CIPA applies here only by analogy. Because CIPA is not directly applicable, [CIPA] does not authorize an interlocutory appeal.[132]

Going back to the trial court, the government continued to resist the court's order to allow the deposition, stating that if necessary it would stand in contempt of court or suffer dismissal of the indictment as a means of obtaining appellate review of the order. Instead of doing either of these things, however, the trial judge decreed that the government would be allowed neither to introduce any evidence regarding 9/11 nor to seek the death penalty.[133]

The government appealed that ruling, which was not actually a CIPA ruling on the admissibility of classified information but was a discovery order with which the government chose not to comply. The government may refuse to divulge classified information such as the identity or location of a witness, and there is no CIPA procedure involved because that information is not what is proposed for use at trial. CIPA was involved in the case to the extent that it provided guidance for the handling of classified information.

The first panel to hear the appeal agreed with the district judge that the Government did not have to provide access to a witness whose location was classified, but the panel thought that substituted evidence would be

---

[131] *Id.* at 513.

[132] *Id.* at 514-15.

[133] United States v. Moussaoui, 282 F. Supp. 2d 480 (E.D. Va. 2003).

adequate at trial and vacated the sanctions imposed by the trial judge.[134] The full court then took the case *en banc* and modified the result.[135] The Government had suggested that it would provide summaries of the information being provided by the witnesses while under interrogation, and the panel agreed that those summaries would be adequate. The *en banc* court did not think those satisfied the defendant's rights to obtain testimony[136] but it did not think the defendant was entitled to depose classified witnesses.[137] It described instead a procedure by which the prosecution would provide summaries of witness statements to the defense, the defense could then promulgate questions to be asked of the witness, and the prosecution would come back with summaries of the responses to those questions.[138] The dissenting judge argued that the defense would not be able to probe the reliability or complete memory of a witness without direct access to the person.[139]

[D] Executive Control of Classified Information

Fernandez clearly makes the point that disclosure of classified information is completely within the control of the Government. The case was being prosecuted by an independent counsel under the Ethics in Government Act.[140] When the district court ruled that substitutions would not suffice, the Attorney General filed an affidavit that disclosure would harm the national interest of the U.S. and prohibited disclosure in any form. The Attorney General also filed an interlocutory appeal to the Fourth Circuit, which the appellate court denied because the Attorney General was not a party to the case. In the process, however, the court had these comments about the options open to the prosecution:

> What is never affected by this interpretation of CIPA is the Attorney General's constitutionally-based power to protect information important to national security. . . . The Act plainly does not

---

[134] United States v. Moussaoui, 365 F.3d 292 (4th Cir. 2004).

[135] *Moussaoui*, 382 F.3d 453.

[136] The Sixth Amendment grants a right to "compulsory process for obtaining witnesses in his favor." That right is implemented by Fed. R. Crim. P. 15, which provides for depositions of witnesses in government custody.

[137] *Moussaoui*, 382 F.3d at 456-57:

> [W]e reject the Government's claim that the district court exceeded its authority in granting Moussaoui access to the witnesses. We affirm the conclusion of the district court that the enemy combatant witnesses could provide material, favorable testimony on Moussaoui's behalf, and we agree with the district court that the Government's proposed substitutions for the witnesses' deposition testimony are inadequate. However, we reverse the district court insofar as it held that it is not possible to craft adequate substitutions, and we remand with instructions for the district court and the parties to craft substitutions under certain guidelines. Finally, we vacate the order imposing sanctions on the Government.

[138] *Id.* at 480.

[139] *Id.* at 483, 486 (Gregory, J., dissenting in part).

[140] 28 U.S.C. § 594 (2007), *expired by operation of* 28 U.S.C. § 599 (2007).

affect the Attorney General's authority to protect information important to national security by filing a section 6(e) affidavit [prohibiting disclosure]. The constitutional concerns that would be raised if the power to protect national security information were vested in a prosecutor not fully accountable to the President therefore need not engage us, for as long as the Attorney General can file a section 6(e) affidavit prohibiting absolutely the disclosure of classified information by a criminal defendant, national security cannot be compromised.[141]

The independence of Article III judges raises the question of how classified information should be handled when it is presented to the court. The Executive may not have the ability to control the behavior of an Article III judge, but it does have the ability to refuse to deliver information and Congress has legislated with respect to the handling of secret information is in the possession of a court. Under section 9 of CIPA,[142] the Chief Justice "in consultation with the Attorney General, the Director of National Intelligence, and the Secretary of Defense, shall prescribe rules establishing procedures for the protection against unauthorized disclosure of any classified information in the custody of United States" courts. Under those rules, the courts appoint security officers, who are responsible for facilities and handling of documents in cases involving classified matters, from lists approved by the Justice Department. Court personnel, other than judges, may not have access to classified materials without obtaining a security clearance from the executive branch.

One judge objected to the requirement of security clearances for his court personnel and ruled that the regulations unconstitutionally infringed on the independence of the judiciary. The Sixth Circuit reversed.[143] While acknowledging the concerns of the district judge for judicial independence,[144] the court countered that the procedures allowed sufficient independence because "any problem of security involving court personnel or persons acting for the court shall be referred to the court for appropriate action." This allows the judge to determine what to do about a potential security breach within his or her arena and precludes executive intrusion into the judicial process itself.[145] As the court in *Fernandez* pointed out, nothing

---

[141] United States v. Fernandez, 887 F.2d 465, 470-71 (4th Cir. 1989).

[142] 18 U.S.C. App. § 9 (2007).

[143] United States v. Smith, 899 F.2d 564 (6th Cir. 1990).

[144] *Id.* at 569:

[The] concerns about preserving the judiciary from unwarranted encroachment by co-equal branches are firmly rooted in the Constitution and Supreme Court precedents. Under no circumstances should the Judiciary become the handmaiden of the Executive. The independence of the Judiciary must be jealously guarded at all times against efforts by prosecutors to erode its authority.

[145] *Id.* at 570:

Such a requirement affecting law clerks, secretaries and bailiffs is not closely related to the deliberative process because these individuals do not and should not decide cases; thus it only mildly intrudes into the manner in which federal judges

in CIPA requires the Executive to relinquish classified material if it chooses not to do so.

[E] Secret Trials

One option not mentioned in the statute for dealing with classified information would be to close the trial, or portions of it, to the public. At first glance, this option would seem to fly in the face of the Sixth Amendment, but some courts have toyed with this approach.

In *United States v. Clark*,[146] the defendant was charged with possession of heroin and cocaine that were detected in his hand luggage at the boarding gate of an airport. He was searched more thoroughly than was usual under procedures in place at the time, and the reason for the thorough search was that he fit an unpublished "skyjacker profile" used by ticket agents to alert security personnel. On the defense motion to suppress fruits of the search, the trial judge conducted a hearing *in camera* without either the defendant or the public present, in response to the government's request to keep the details of the profile secret. On appeal the Second Circuit held that it would have been permissible to close the portion of the hearing that dealt with the details of the profile but that secrecy of the profile did not justify closing the entire proceeding, which dealt with far more than the profile itself.

Two Sixth Amendment rights are implicated in closed hearings. One is the defendant's right to confront witnesses and the other is the right to a public trial. Neither has been held to be absolute but the few exceptions for secret evidence have been limited to matters that present a "compelling urgency" for secrecy, do not go to the question of guilt or innocence, and are displayed to the court with counsel present and able to cross-examine.

The military courts have dealt with arguments for closed hearings more often than the civilian courts. In *United States v. Grunden*,[147] the defendant was on trial for espionage as the result of a sting operation in which he attempted to communicate secrets to government agents posing as foreign agents. Because portions of the evidence related to classified information, counsel and all members of the hearing panel (the military equivalent of a jury consists of military officers) were required to have security clearances and some portions of the proceedings were closed to the

---

conduct business. *See* In re United States Department of Justice, No. 87-1205, slip. op. at 4 (4th Cir. Apr. 7, 1988) (unpublished disposition) (in issuing writ of mandamus that required security clearances for courtroom staff in civil case, court concluded that contempt or disclosure dilemma justified "minimally intrusive" requirement of routine security clearance). Under section 4 of the Burger regulations, district courts retain sufficient power to preclude the Executive from engaging in procedures that intrude upon both the judicial function and, potentially, the privacy interests of court personnel. Proper administration of the regulations is therefore consistent with the doctrine of separation of powers.

[146] 475 F.2d 240 (2d Cir. 1973).

[147] 2 M.J. 116 (1977).

public. The Court of Military Appeals found that the trial court had gone too far in closing the proceedings:

> [T]he public was excluded from virtually the entire trial as to the espionage charges. During this portion of the trial, nine witnesses testified, only one of whom discussed classified matters at any length. Of the remaining eight witnesses one made less than 10 references to classified matters, three made only one reference, and the remaining four made no references. In excising the public from the trial, the trial judge employed an ax in place of the constitutionally required scalpel.

> The propriety or impropriety of the exclusion of the public from all or part of a trial cannot, as attempted by the government in this case, be reduced to solution by mathematical formulas. The logic and rationale governing the exclusion, not mere percentages of the total pages of the record, must be dispositive.

In several passages, the reviewing court emphasized that the defendant's right to a public trial is constitutionally based and that there is no "military exception" to the right. "Indeed, this Court has long held that an accused is, at the very least, entitled to have his friends, relatives, and counsel present regardless of the offense charged. The improper exclusion of the public has been treated as error per se in recognition that to do otherwise is to place the defendant in the ironic position of having 'to prove what the disregard of his constitutional right has made it impossible for him to learn.'" Nevertheless, "the right to a public trial is not absolute, and under exceptional circumstances, limited portions of a criminal trial may be partially closed over defense objection. In each instance the exclusion must be used sparingly with the emphasis always toward a public trial."[148]

United States v. Reynolds[149] is frequently cited in CIPA cases as establishing the governmental privilege for classified information and is also cited in *Clark* and *Grunden* as bearing on the public trial issue. *Reynolds*, however, has even more to say about the limits of the governmental privilege. The case was a damage action under the Federal Tort Claims Act stemming from a crash of a military plane in which some civilian employees were killed. The plane carried secret electronic equipment and the government sought to prevent discovery of some information about the flight. The question of whether there could be an official secrets privilege and its breadth

---

[148] Citing three law review articles, the court categorized the limited exceptions occasioned by government privileges or courtroom decorum. "See, e.g., Note, *The Accused's Right to a Public Trial*, 42 NOTRE DAME L. 499 (1967); Note, *The Right to a Public Trial in Criminal Cases*, 41 N.Y.U. L. REV. 1138 (1966); Radin, *The Right to a Public Trial*, 6 TEMP. L.Q. 381 (1932). These traditional exceptions have been broadened to include limited exclusions to protect undercover policemen or agents, to insure full and honest testimony by government witnesses, to protect airline hijacking profiles, and to preserve order." *Id.* at 121.

[149] 345 U.S. 1 (1953).

went to the Supreme Court, which acknowledged the existence of a common-law privilege and described its application this way:

> There must be a formal claim of privilege, lodged by the head of the department which has control over the matter, after actual personal consideration by that officer. The court itself must determine whether the circumstances are appropriate for the claim of privilege, and yet do so without forcing a disclosure of the very thing the privilege is designed to protect. The latter requirement is the only one which presents real difficulty. As to it, we find it helpful to draw upon judicial experience in dealing with an analogous privilege, the privilege against self-incrimination.[150]

The techniques that the Court drew from exercise of similar privileges contemplated disclosure by the claimant of the privilege of enough information to the judge for the judge to decide on the existence of the privilege and to what extent it could be overridden by the opposing party's need for the information. In *Reynolds*, the information about the electronic equipment was hardly important to the plaintiff's proof of negligence, so the privilege could be invoked with little difficulty. In the process of discussion, however, the Court referred to

> cases in the criminal field, where it has been held that the Government can invoke its evidentiary privileges only at the price of letting the defendant go free. The rationale of the criminal cases is that, since the Government which prosecutes an accused also has the duty to see that justice is done, it is unconscionable to allow it to undertake prosecution and then invoke its governmental privileges to deprive the accused of anything which might be material to his defense. Such rationale has no application in a civil forum where the Government is not the moving party, but is a defendant only on terms to which it has consented.[151]

This language from *Reynolds* should be the foundation on which all considerations of CIPA, discovery, and public trials is based. For example, the members of the "jury" in a military trial can be selected with security classifications in mind and are already under the coverage of official secrets sanctions. This is one way in which the Presidential Order attempts to justify use of military tribunals. But if the military courts are under the same obligation to provide discovery and a public trial, then what difference does this really make?

§ 7.04 CONCLUSION

Modern international terrorism operates through complex clandestine cells. The structure of these operations requires a response that is similarly clandestine and complex. It has been tempting for the U.S. with its

---

[150] *Id.* at 8.

[151] *Id.* at 12.

enormous firepower and military organization to want to muscle its way through the al Qaeda defenses. This will not happen, and we will be required to fall back to stealth and cunning. Along the way, we will be dealing with some unsavory characters, but that is another story. What this article attempts to do is to lay out the options for folding prosecutions of terrorist conspirators into the frameworks of acceptable western traditions for fair trials.

In defining a conspiracy, prosecutors will want to sweep extremely broadly and judges will need to be alert to the requirement that schemes and dreams of would-be terrorists are truly related by some link before they can be brought together for prosecution.

In dealing with clandestinely acquired information, investigators will have access to both human intelligence (often stemming from unsavory characters who will not make good witnesses) and with some extraordinarily high-tech surveillance equipment whose very existence will be classified information. This will make for some very difficult choices when deciding what cases to prosecute and with what information. Judges will need to be alert to the niceties of FISA and CIPA in dealing with clandestinely acquired information that the government would like to keep secret.

None of this is different in kind, however, from dilemmas that have faced prosecutors for centuries. The frameworks for analysis and the principles to be applied have been in operation throughout the existence of the U.S. and are being refined in prosecutions in other countries as well as in international tribunals. We may not always be happy with the results, as some criminal terrorists are released from custody (only to be closely surveilled at continuing taxpayer expense), but the price of freedom is eternal vigilance in more ways than one.

Finally, we need to look at the impact of CIPA in prosecution of alleged terrorists. One of the reasons advanced by the government for being allowed to hold alleged terrorists in military custody without hearing is the need to protect confidential sources of information, some of which may be persons informing from within terrorist cells and others which are technological devices whose use is unknown to the persons under surveillance. In a prosecution that involves information gathered in clandestine fashion or from confidential informants, government will attempt to protect its sources and methods of investigation.

There is nothing in CIPA that allows the government to produce summarized or redacted evidence in its case-in-chief against the defendant. Issues of national security interest may well affect the degree of detail that the government puts on, and may be grounds in unusual cases for partial closing of a trial to the public, but they do not justify departures from the normal rules of evidence. What CIPA deals with is the defendant's right of access to, and use of, classified information in preparing a defense. If the court finds that a summary or a proffer of admitted fact is "substantially" equivalent to the classified information, then the summary or admissions will be substituted for the classified evidence.

The courts have described the CIPA process as similar to recognition of an "informant privilege" in which government may withhold the identity of an informant unless disclosure is "relevant and helpful to the defense." A good example of the CIPA process occurred during the *Yunis* trial. The methods by which Yunis eventually was lured out of hiding and into the hands of U.S. authorities included sending a friend to spend time with him while under surveillance by U.S. agents. When Yunis sought to acquire the tapes of all the conversations with this friend, the government declined on the basis that nothing in the tapes would materially assist the defense and that disclosure could compromise secret surveillance techniques. The D.C. Circuit was persuaded that the tapes and transcripts would not assist the defense sufficiently to override the government's need for secrecy.

> Our own review of the government's affidavits and transcripts reveals that much of the government's security interest in the conversation lies not so much in the contents of the conversations, as in the time, place, and nature of the government's ability to intercept the conversations at all. Things that did not make sense to the District Judge would make all too much sense to a foreign counter-intelligence specialist who could learn much about this nation's intelligence-gathering capabilities from what these documents revealed about sources and methods. Implicit in the whole concept of an informant-type privilege is the necessity that information-gathering agencies protect from compromise "intelligence sources and methods."[152]

---

[152] *Yunis*, 867 F.2d at 623.

Chapter 8

MILITARY ACTION — LAW OF WAR

SYNOPSIS

The Bush Administration's "Global War on Terrorism" (GWOT) is a nomenclature with a number of confusing consequences:

1. First, it raises the issue of whether terrorists can be shot on sight no matter where or under what circumstances they may be found. If not, then what are the limitations on lethal military force that apply in various settings?

2. Second, it has been used to justify the imprisonment of persons with no due process and the authorization of military commissions to try alleged terrorists if they were ever to be charged with a crime. This leads to confusion over why some terrorist suspects are sent to civilian criminal processes and others not.

237

3. Third, it has been used to justify the invasion of Iraq when there
    was no credible evidence of a link between Iraq and clandestine
    terrorist attacks on other nations.

On top of these confusions, the United States has lost enormous amounts
of credibility in the world because of the use of military force as well as
the apparent abandonment of legal processes. Particularly troubling in this
regard has been the claim of unreviewable discretion to imprison persons
accused either of taking up arms against the United States or of plotting
terrorist actions. For all of these reasons, it is necessary to devote one
chapter of this book to the language and rules of the law of war.

§ 8.01 TYPES OF MILITARY ACTION

[A] The "War on Terrorism"

Terrorism may come in many forms and under many guises, but the
common theme is that of clandestine attacks on civilian populations. The
link between the law of war and response to terrorism consists of at least
these facets:

*   First, some observers treat terrorism as the use of illegal methods
    of warfare under the laws and customs of war (or "armed con-
    flict"), standards that can be enforced through appropriate tribu-
    nals. The difficulty in this approach is attempting to fit the
    terrorist into the framework of standards designed to deal with
    nation-state behavior.

*   Second, there is the question of whether acts of terrorism consti-
    tute "armed attack" on the target nation so as to justify military
    response. The principal issue in this context is the threshold at
    which non-state actors become subject to justifiable use of mili-
    tary force.

*   Third, if the target nation attempts to use the language of war
    to justify the use of military force in responding to terrorist acts,
    then international law establishes controls on the use of military
    force, particularly in dealings with non-state actors.

In traditional international terms, it would not be possible for a nation
to go to war with a group of criminals. War is a state that exists between
or among entities claiming or seeking status of nation-state, not with
individuals or even groups of individuals having no territorial objectives.
Professor Feldman argues that the matter is no longer so clear-cut, that
the identity of the actor is only one of four elements that go into the distinction between war and crime. In his construct, the other three elements are
provenance (whether the actor is within the jurisdiction of the state), intent
(whether the actor intends to challenge the very existence of the state or
its government), and scale (whether the hostile acts are sufficiently large

to justify military response).[1] We can agree that the three additional elements have a lot to do with whether an action will be punished as crime by the target state, without conceding that they are necessary elements of the conditions of war or, as more commonly labeled today, "armed conflict." These elements may influence whether the state can punish an act as crime or whether the state chooses to respond with armed conflict, but they are not part of whether the state can choose to go to war in the absence of the essential identity element. In other words, identity is an essential although not always sufficient element of the conditions of armed conflict.

Professor Paust asserts that "the United States simply cannot be at war" with any group that is not a "state, nation, belligerent, or insurgent group (as those entities are understood in international law)."[2]

> The lowest level of warfare or armed conflict to which certain laws of war apply is an insurgency. For an insurgency to occur, the insurgent group would have to have the semblance of a government, an organized military force, control of significant portions of territory as its own, and its own relatively stable population or base of support within a broader population.[3]

In the absence of these factors, a group engaged in violence is nothing more than a criminal organization, unless there is an adequate justification for the violence. The clearest example of justification is that of self-defense. The Geneva Convention on Treatment of POW's provides protection for those who engage in defense of their homeland, but imposes requirements on the defenders that vary according to the level of control that the invading forces have obtained over the territory, a distinction based on whether the territory is "occupied" or merely under attack.[4]

---

[1] Noah Feldman, *Choices of Law, Choices of War*, 25 HARV. J.L. & PUB. POL'Y 457, 458-61 (2002).

[2] Jordan J. Paust, *War and Enemy Status After 9/11: Attacks on the Law of War*, 28 YALE J. INT'L L. 325, 326 (2003).

[3] *Id.*

[4] Geneva Convention on Treatment of Prisoners of War, art. IV, Aug. 12, 1949, 74 U.N.T.S. 135:

> Prisoners of war . . . are persons belonging to one of the following categories, who have fallen into the power of the enemy:
>
> 2. Members of other militias and members of other volunteer corps, including those of organized resistance movements, belonging to a Party and operating in or outside their own territory, even if this territory is occupied, provided that such militias or volunteer corps, including such organized resistance movements, fulfill the following conditions:
>
> (a) that of being commanded by a person responsible for his subordinates;
>
> (b) that of having a fixed distinctive sign recognizable at a distance;
>
> (c) that of carrying arms openly;
>
> (d) that of conducting their operations in accordance with the laws and customs of war.
>
> 6. Inhabitants of a non-occupied territory, who on the approach of the enemy spontaneously take up arms to resist the invading forces, without having had time to form themselves into regular armed units, provided they carry arms openly and respect the laws and customs of war.

Professor de Lupis provides a further explanation of the point that Professor Paust makes: "Parties which engage in war do not have to be recognized as States by their enemy. A country, nation or group can be a belligerent in spite of non-recognition."[5] She goes on to insist that a state of "war" implies at minimum a group with a claim to governance of a "territorial unit" and then points out that international law has shown a marked movement toward the term "armed conflict" rather than "war" to deal with the variety of conditions that constitute warlike status among contending forces. She concedes that a terrorist group that wishes to create a separate State may achieve the status of belligerent but insists that the intermittent and clandestine nature of terrorist acts take them out of the category of war, although "terrorist 'tactics' may be adopted in war for the purposes of guerilla warfare."[6]

To apply the GPW provisions to familiar examples, if paragraph 6 were operative, then French citizens could have taken up arms openly during the German invasion without any further requirements than that they "respect the laws and customs of war," which refers to the methods of warfare (no poisonous weapons, no attacks on civilians, etc.). If a resistance fighter were killed in the fighting, the German forces would have committed no war crime by the killing because the resistance fighter would be treated as military personnel for that purpose. If the citizen-soldier were captured, then the Convention entitles him/her to treatment as a POW, not an out-of-uniform illegal combatant.

The Mel Gibson movie *The Patriot* makes a big point of the difference in honorable behavior between the American militia and at least one British officer who did not "play by the rules." But the American civilians did not meet paragraph 6 for two reasons. First, they had time to organize into regular armed units; second, they were contending against an occupying force, not an invading force. As a militia operating in occupied territory, they met only three of the four requirements in paragraph 2. They not only did not have a "distinctive sign recognizable at a distance," there is even one scene in the movie in which they don the uniforms of the British. Granted that the brutality of the British officer against civilians would be a clear violation of the law of war on several bases (actions which today we would call crimes against humanity or genocide), the behavior of the American militia as depicted still would be a violation of a lesser degree.

Returning to the French scenario, once the German forces occupied the territory, then the French Resistance operated illegally by not meeting the requirements of paragraph 2. The harsh reality is that these "heroes" were violating the law of war. They of course knew that they could be shot on sight but what is more harsh is that they had no rights to surrender and expect humane treatment — if captured, at that time, they could have been tortured and executed with impunity. Today, with the 1949 Geneva Conventions in place, the resistance fighter against an occupying force might expect

---

[5] Ingrid Detter De Lupis, The Law of War 16 (1987).

[6] *Id.* at 23.

somewhat more protection but still could be a criminal subject to the harshest of punishments after some form of hearing.

[B] Military Force in Response to Crime (MOOTW)

To understand how the terrorist fits into this schema, we can emphasize that war exists among recognized entities which can strike only at military targets of an opposing entity. The terrorist has no authorization from a pretense governmental source,[7] attacks civilian targets, and blends back into a civilian population. Each of the three phases of this conduct defies the rules laid down by nations for the conduct of their affairs. That makes the terrorist an international criminal, when adjudicated to be so, and it makes the use of military force to apprehend the terrorist appropriate. This is the condition known as "military operations other than war" (MOOTW).[8]

The terrorist first is a criminal, only occasionally coming anywhere close to having a sufficient organization and territorial presence to achieve insurgent or belligerent status. So can we use all our available military force to go into another nation to arrest a criminal? In theory, not without the permission of the other nation. Sending a military force into another nation is an act of war that can be justified only by consent or prior aggressive act on the part of the attacked nation. There are several examples in recent decades of the U.S. government's seizing drug lords and bringing them to trial in this country.[9] In the case of Manuel Noriega, we justified our actions by claiming that the prior government of Panama was the legitimate government and we were carrying out their wishes.[10] In the cases of a few individuals seized in Mexico and tried in the U.S., we did not have permission and the Mexican government has objected vociferously.[11]

---

[7] Keeping this distinction is why most observers place state terrorist tactics in the international humanitarian regime of law rather than under the heading of terrorism.

[8] *See generally* Defense Technical Information Center, *Overview of MOOTW, available at* www.dtic.mil/doctrine/jrm/mootw.doc (last visited Aug. 1, 2007).

[9] United States v. Alvarez-Machain, 504 U.S. 655 (1992). The proposition that prosecution of accuseds in U.S. courts is permissible following abduction from another country is known as the Ker-Frisbie doctrine. *See* Ker v. Illinois, 119 U.S. 436 (1886); Frisbie v. Collins, 342 U.S. 519 (1952). *See generally* § 3.03[A] *supra.*

[10] United States v. Noriega, 117 F.3d 1206 (11th Cir. 1997).

[11] These abductions have arisen after Mexico refused to extradite to the U.S. without an assurance that the defendant would not be subject to the death penalty. Official protests by the Mexican government over the abductions were then followed by Mexican extradition requests to send perpetrators back to Mexico for trial. The death penalty issue has become a difficulty between the U.S. and many nations.

The 1980 extradition treaty between the U.S. and Mexico allows either country to refuse to extradite its own national to the other state. The Mexico Supreme Court has ruled that life imprisonment would constitute cruel and unusual punishment and thus the extradition treaty bars extradition if the potential for a life sentence exists under U.S. law. Senator Feinstein has introduced a resolution calling for renegotiation of the U.S.-Mexico treaty. For a brief summary of the issues, see feinstein.senate.gov/04Releases/r-extradition.htm. (last visited June 21, 2007).

There are two theories under which the U.S. invaded Afghanistan. One is that Afghanistan "harbored" terrorists to the extent that the terrorists became essentially the agents of that government, thus moving from the class of mere criminal to agents of war.[12] Because these state agents violated the rules of war by taking aggression, by striking civilian targets, and by blending back into civilian populations, other nations were justified in using military force to retaliate and prevent further attack.

The second theory harkens back to the piracy and slave trading of the 18th and 19th Centuries. The phrase "to the shores of Tripoli" salutes the actions of Marines who rooted out pirate strongholds located in other nations.[13] Other nations of the world were never called on to decide whether our actions were legitimate.[14] Similarly, the European-American nations were in some discord over whether it was legitimate to strike militarily against slave depots and slave trading ships within the boundaries of other nations.[15]

It is now beyond dispute, on the basis of international conventions, that it is legal for ships on the high seas to interdict other ships engaged in piracy or slave trade,[16] but there is no apparent authority for one state to make unilateral incursions into another country to root out a pirate or slave trader. Only when the actions of "pirates" or "slave traders" have been thought to carry direct harm to the interests of a state has that state even argued for the right to use force to excise the offending facility.[17] The use of military force in dealing with international crime, regardless of the legal theories invoked, is part of MOOTW.

---

[12] Authorization for Use of Military Force Pub. L No. 107-40 (2001) [herinafter Joint Resolution]:

> [T]he President is authorized to use all necessary and appropriate force against those nations, organizations, or persons he determines planned, authorized, committed, or aided the terrorist attacks that occurred on September 11, 2001, or harbored such organizations or persons, in order to prevent any future acts of international terrorism against the United States by such nations, organizations or persons.

[13] The official history of the Marine Corps states that the "raising of the American flag over the walled city of Derna, Tripoli in April 1805 by Lieutenant Presley N. O'Bannon signaled to the world that the young republic was not reticent about defending or pursuing its national interests beyond the borders of North America." U.S. Marine Corps History Division, *available at* hqinet001.hqmc.usmc.mil/HD/Historical/Frequently_Requested/Mediterranean.htm (last visited June 21, 2007).

[14] *See, e.g.*, Douglas R. Burgess Jr., *The Dread Pirate Bin Laden*, LEGAL AFFAIRS (July/Aug 2005), *available at* www.legalaffairs.org/issues/July-August-2005/feature_burgess_julaug05.msp.

[15] U.S. forces attempted to disrupt the slave trade from Africa as early as 1820, while the question of slavery in the U.S. itself was a debate that would rage for four more decades.

[16] *See* Convention on the Law of the Sea, art. 110 (Dec. 10, 1982) *available at* www.un.org/Depts/los/convention_agreements/texts/unclos/unclos_e.pdf.

1. Except where acts of interference derive from power conferred by treaty, a warship which encounters on the high seas a foreign ship, . . . is not justified in boarding her unless there is reasonable ground for suspecting:

   (a)   That the ship is engaged in piracy;

   (b)   That the ship is engaged in the slave trade; . . . .

[17] *See* OSCAR SCHACHTER, INTERNATIONAL LAW IN THEORY AND PRACTICE 144-46 (1991).

§ 8.02 SOURCES OF THE LAW OF WAR

The British commander as portrayed in *The Patriot* expresses dismay at the tactics of the American militia and the brutality of his own subordinate, and is depicted in one scene as having a full-dress lavish party with ladies of the aristocracy at a mansion in the middle of a war, yet is undeniably an accomplished leader of a military force.

What accounts for such insistence on "playing by the rules" in a "game" that is designed to kill people? A superficial explanation could be that the British penchant for gentlemanly behavior, demanded that things be done correctly even when what was being done was violent. That thought, however, can carry only so far. War is killing and maiming people, hardly the pursuits of proper gentlemanly drawing room behavior. The explanations for "rules of war" have much more pragmatic roots. One is a straightforward self-interested expression of the Golden Rule: "Do unto others as you would have them do unto you" in this context yields the hope that humane treatment of enemies will prompt their humane treatment of you and your soldiers. A second motivation may be a more deeply rooted psychological need to place self-imposed limits on one's capacity for violence. A key factor in the early insistence on wearing of uniforms and staying in ranks was attempting to end violence against civilians. The British commander in the movie plays heavily on the theme of not targeting officers because it is through the officers that the troops would be disciplined to curb their violent natures.

A further motivation for harsh views of groups that do not play by the rules can be found in Colonel Winthrop's castigation of guerilla forces. "Irregular armed bodies or persons not forming part of the organized forces of a belligerent, or operating under the orders of its established commanders, are not in general recognized as legitimate troops or entitled, when taken, to be treated as prisoners of war but may upon capture be summarily punished even with death."[18] The image he has in mind is of undisciplined bands of marauders "killing, disabling and robbing of peaceable citizens or soldiers . . . from motives mostly of personal profit or revenge."[19] This picture of roving gangs of criminals is one of the earliest depictions in a legal treatise of what today we know as terrorism. But at that early stage of legal development, Winthrop did not distinguish between guerillas who attack civilians and those that "respect the laws and customs of war." His legal conclusion would have applied to Mel Gibson's citizen-soldiers as readily as to the roving gang of thieves and murderers.

It is also possible that some of the animus toward non-uniformed or undisciplined bands from the European point of view reflected ethnic or cultural biases prevalent during the colonial era, but there may also be a more natural tendency for violence to degenerate in the absence of social controls. Speaking of irregulars in the American Revolution, one author makes this observation:

---

[18] William Winthrop, Military Law and Precedents 783 (reprint 1920).

[19] *Id.* at 784.

On the one hand there were the standards laid down by George Washington, himself a regular soldier, who was at pains to show, by the professional behavior of the American armies, that the United States had the right to be treated as a sovereign state. On the other was the ferocious banditry into which the war degenerated at the fringes, as it is always liable to do when irregular belligerents escape professional control.[20]

International law has developed over several millennia, but the current version consists principally of rules laid down in the 18th Century by the European nations during the colonial era. These nations were running into each other in "remote" and "unsettled" places around the world. They needed rules to set limits on their conflicts to minimize the possibility that those conflicts would spill over into damage to their homelands.[21] Without being conscious of all their motivations, which included setting limits on how the "uncivilized" portions of the world should behave, they naturally drew on their existing historical backgrounds.

> Constraints on war as we have experienced them in our own societies [Western European] have been largely shaped by Christian ethic defined by leading teachers in the Catholic church of the Middle Ages and the Renaissance, an ethic transformed in the seventeenth and eighteenth centuries into something more rationalistic and utilitarian by such international lawyers as . . . Grotius and . . . de Vattel, and made increasingly specific by international agreements such as the Hague and Geneva Conventions in the nineteenth and twentieth centuries.[22]

The historical background of European-based international law stemmed from Hebrew texts through St. Augustine's elaboration of "just war" in the 6th Century to Grotius' instructions to European monarchs of the 17th Century.[23] Starting from earliest days there are two themes that have remained constant as other details have been refined. These are protection of noncombatants and protection of the means of human survival. The most significant addition to these beginnings, about 1,500 years ago, was the theme of nonaggression. And the 20th Century brought the necessity of defining and criminalizing brutality and genocide.

The "law of war" flows from self-imposed limitations on the use of force that have been promulgated by every known civilization.

> As early as the Egyptian and Sumerian wars of the second millenium B.C., there were rules defining the circumstances under which war might be initiated. Among the Hittites of the fourteenth

---

[20] Michael Howard, *Constraints on Warfare*, in THE LAWS OF WAR 2 (M. Howard, G. Andreopoulos, M. Shulman eds., 1994).

[21] *See generally* ANTONY ANGHIE, IMPERIALISM, SOVEREIGNTY, AND THE MAKING OF INTERNATIONAL LAW (2004).

[22] Howard, *supra* note 20, at 5.

[23] HUGO GROTIUS, THE LAW OF WAR AND PEACE (1625).

century B.C., a formal exchange of letters and demands generally preceded hostilities.[24]

Protection of noncombatants was the first step of societies turning from nomadic to agrarian ways of life. Nomadic tribes generally followed proscriptions against poisoning wells and water supplies, for obvious reasons, but now wars were to be fought by identified armies, leaving civilian populations to carry on the business of living. Protection of noncombatants became necessary when people settled in permanent locations, and the whole tribe was no longer involved in skirmishes with other tribes. A corollary to this proscription was the requirement of saving the "trees of the field" so that life could go on regardless of who won.[25] The importance of these rules can be seen in the mere fact that ruling autocrats imposed these limits on themselves so that each could be mutually assured that the outcome of war would not be the elimination of civilization.

In what is known as the Axial Age,[26] the First Millenium BCE produced the earliest written codes known to mankind. Some of the first written works focused on modes of behavior among warring tribes. The Hebrew Torah was written down in pieces over an extended period, but mostly during the Exile around 700 BCE. Its *Book of Deuteronomy* contains descriptions of divine proscriptions to the earlier Hebrew warlords to spare noncombatants and the "trees of the field," except that with the nearby cities of Canaan they were to "save alive nothing that breatheth."[27] This is a harsh departure from the other codes that were being written down at the time, and the explanation for its harshness may be that it was written as justification by divine instruction for past behavior many centuries earlier during the conquest of Canaan. The Babylonian Sennacherib who conquered Jerusalem in 690 said that he killed the officials and patricians, treated citizens who were guilty of minor crimes as prisoners of war, and released everyone else.[28]

Sun Tzu wrote his treatise on *The Art of War* in about 300 BCE. Although he advocated trickery and surprise in warfare, he insisted on sparing wounded and elderly. "Treat the captives well, and care for them. All the soldiers taken must be cared for with magnanimity and sincerity so that they may be used by us."

---

[24] Leon Friedman, I The Law of War: A Documentary History 3 (1972).

[25] *Deuteronomy* 20:19.

[26] The Axial Age is so designated because it is the turning point for modern civilization, producing the earliest major works of philosophy and theology in Asia, India, Persia, and parts of the Mediterranean. Some scholars wonder why the movement did not reach the desert areas of what are now most of Arabia and Egypt. One speculation is that the more ancient cultures of Egypt and Berber still held sway in those regions and so there was not fertile soil for the newer philosophies until the time of Muhammad. *See* Karen Armstrong, A History of God (1994).

[27] The Hebrew texts written in the 8th Century BCE claimed that God had instructed their ancestors to spare the women and children of "far off cities," while in those cities that were given the Hebrews "for an inheritance" nothing that breathes should be left alive. *See Deuteronomy* 20:10-20 (King James).

[28] Friedman, *supra* note 24, at 3.

The Hindu Book of Manu was written about 200 BCE and contains many elaborate exhortations having to do with what kinds of weapons may be used (prohibiting barbed, poisoned, or flaming arrows) and when to spare someone who has yielded or been injured.[29]

From examples such as the honestly self-interested motivation expressed by Sun Tzu, Leon Friedman acknowledges that many of the "rules of warfare" may have arisen as attempts to limit the behavior of one's own army so as to be treated well if "we" should happen to lose or as efforts toward a productive peacetime economy and trade with the conquered citizenry. "But many of the historical restraints on war cannot be explained solely by such strategic pragmatism." Friedman points to correspondence between Freud and Einstein regarding war in which Freud speculates that the destructive tendencies unleashed by an emotional "call to arms" will necessarily be tempered by an almost reflexive reaction to the horrors of war.[30]

Augustine is usually credited with being the origin of European criteria for "just war," although it was actually Thomas Aquinas writing much later in the 14th Century who systematized the criteria.[31] Augustine was writing in the fourth century when contending forces were scrambling to control the remnants of Rome which would become the Holy Roman Empire. He contended that war could be justified as a defensive measure so long as each military action was proportional to the threat or prior act with which a nation was faced. Thus were born the twin notions of nonaggression and military proportionality.[32] "The Christian doctors, from Augustine to Aquinas in the Middle Ages, followed by . . . de Vitoria in the sixteenth century, were above all concerned with defining the just war, jus ad bellum: wars in which Christians might fight with a clear conscience."[33]

It is important to emphasize, as so many others have already done, that the Judeo-Christian sources of European law under which the world operates today, are almost identical to the norms that have developed on parallel tracks in other parts of the world. Sun Tzu in China, the *Book of Manu* in India, and many strands of Islamic thought as well coincide. The idea of "just war" in Christian-European terms does not *require* that any war be fought, it only describes the justifications required before a war *may* be fought. Similarly, according to at least some Muslim scholars, Jihad does not require war but utilizes similar criteria to determine if a nation is

---

[29] *Id.* (quoting *Book of Manu* 90-93).

[30] *Id.* at 5.

[31] *See generally*, THOMAS AQUINAS, 3 SUMMA THEOLOGICA, 1354 (Dominican ed. 1981); R. A. McCormick, *Morality of War, 14, in* THE NEW CATHOLIC ENCYCLOPEDIA 803 (1967); John Langan, S.J., *The Elements of St. Augustine's Just War Theory*, 12 J. RELIGIOUS ETHICS, 19 (1984).

[32] The religion-based arguments against the legality of nuclear weapons are that they can never be limited effectively to military targets without extensive destruction of human life and that they will do severe damage to the environment. The legality of nuclear weapons is still under debate in the international law community.

[33] Howard, *supra* note 20, at 2.

permitted to wage war. Perhaps there is a subtle difference in that the concept of jihad may require that a believer fight when called to do so by religious authority,[34] while the Christian separation of church and state means that the individual is obligated to fight only by call from secular authority which can actually conflict with religious mandates.

§ 8.03 MODERN LAW OF ARMED CONFLICT (LOAC)

Who cares about these ivory tower constructs? Why should we be the least bit concerned about whether actions contemplated by the U.S. government are called "war" and whether they conform to the rules of international law? The U.S. Administration has said in essence that nothing is more important than the safety and security of our citizens.

First, there is the problem of using military force against non-state targets. Our forces are still constrained by the requirements of military necessity and avoiding harm to civilians. In virtually every combat operation, some civilian deaths will occur whether by mistake or simple inevitability. The difficulty of using military force against those who hide in civilian populations will give our military planners nightmares for a long time to come.[35]

Second, the use of military force opens our agents to the threat of prosecution by international tribunals and other nation states. Any nation who believed that a U.S. military action was a violation of the law of war, and who could capture a responsible U.S. official (general or key civilian) theoretically could prosecute that person for war crimes.[36]

Third, there is the pragmatic problem of fighting an "asymmetrical war." Guerilla forces learned long ago that a weak opponent can inflict damage and wage what may become a successful war of attrition against a stronger opponent through hit and run tactics. Indeed, the U.S. may have taught this strategy too well to some of the leaders of what became al Qaeda when those persons were acting as mujahadeen in the war of attrition against the Soviet Union in Afghanistan.[37] The use of military force may prompt the creation of even more terrorist cells by fostering an "asymmetrical" war.

---

[34] Douglas E. Streusand, *What Does Jihad Mean?*, MIDDLE EAST Q., Sept. 1997, *available at* www.ict.org.il/articles/jihad.htm.

[35] A related and increasingly significant problem is that of casualties from friendly fire, which military leaders say is becoming more visible as casualties from hostile fire go down.

On one night during World War II (July 9-10, 1943) 23 U.S. troop transports carrying paratroopers of the 82nd Airborne Division were shot down by American forces in Sicily who mistook the planes for German bombers. The death toll in that single friendly fire incident was 410. But about 300,000 U.S. servicemen died in World War II. Fratricide killed 35 of the 146 Americans who died in the 1991 Gulf War 24 percent. To date in Afghanistan, friendly fire has been responsible for the deaths of three or possibly four out of 14 Americans killed in action — more than 20 percent.

Richard Whittle, *Low Incidence of Other Casualties Make "Friendly Fire" More Prominent*, DALLAS MORNING NEWS, Apr. 19, 2002.

[36] *See* § 6.01[B], *supra*.

[37] *See* ROHAN GUNARATNA, INSIDE AL QAEDA 23 (2002); *see generally* JOHN COOLEY, UNHOLY WARS (2002).

Finally, and perhaps most important, using the language of war in dealing with terrorists could run some risk of legitimating their activities. The combatant in a war cannot be punished merely for participating in the war. So a member of a terrorist organization who had no connection with actions against civilian targets and limited his actions to military targets would not be punishable under the law of war.[38] Those acts might be illegal as crimes against the state, but that would be a matter of domestic law, not the law of war.

All these questions must be considered in determining whether to use military force in pursuit of terrorists. International law applies to armed conflict. In recent decades, commentators have been abandoning the term "war" because of the need to deal with undeclared conditions of combat. Some people are tempted to believe that it is also an oxymoron to speak of international "law" because the rules to be followed appear to be simply whatever the strongest wish to apply to the weaker. More prosaically, it might be said that the rules of etiquette are set by the 500 pound gorilla at the dinner table. There is some truth to this observation, but the complete picture is much more complex. Over the last 4,000 years, norms have been written down, and in the last few hundred years those norms have come to receive increasing levels of enforcement in various settings. The desires of the 500 pound gorilla become philosophy, which eventually may become rules of law.

[A] Enforcement

From Augustine and Aquinas, Europeans derived principles of nonaggression and limitations on the brutality of force. Over the course of European history, rules for the conduct of warfare became ever more elaborate. Rules of warfare during the medieval period were expressed mostly in the codes of chivalry. Then, at the dawn of the age of colonialism, as European nations came into contact with other cultures that they wished to subdue, writers began to elaborate the "laws and customs" by which these other cultures were to be approached and by which the European nations could minimize conflicts with each other. The principal architect of what is now the international law of war was Hugo Grotius. In a series of three books,[39] Grotius, a Dutch lawyer, set out the requirements for lawful use of military force and the limitations on the use of force. Throughout the 18th and 19th Centuries, European leaders came to recognize a variety of norms as *jus cogens* or customary international law, and then in the 20th Century began to elaborate these norms into conventions and treaties.

The cynical may view all these mandates, and the many departures from them over the centuries, as nothing but self-aggrandizing sentiments that could be followed or not as the military commanders and their sovereigns chose. Certainly, human history is rampant with unjustified use of force

---

[38] Paust, *supra* note 2, at 327.

[39] HUGO GROTIUS, ON THE LAW OF WAR AND PEACE (1625).

and with extreme cruelty and barbarity to both civilians and combatants. Nevertheless, there are self-interested reasons for imposing limitations. Lawrence Friedman puts the self-interest aspect quite succinctly:

> A commander does not kill his prisoners because he does not want his own men slaughtered if they fall into an enemy's hands. Civilian populations should not be eliminated after they have been conquered since they can work for, pay tribute to, or be conscripted into, the victorious army. Unrestrained warfare would jeopardize reconciliation and make later trade and peaceful intercourse impossible.[40]

In addition, Friedman points out that evolving standards of civilization (to which we might add increasing levels of globalized trade) have added levels of conscience to the human tension between violence and peace. Philosophical norms eventually do find their way into enforceable norms of law.

Fourteen separate Conventions adopted at the Hague in 1907 committed signatory nations to a variety of limitations on the use of force. Hague I (Pacific Settlement of International Disputes) stated that "the Signatory Powers agree to use their best efforts to ensure the pacific settlement of disputes" and established a system of mediation and the Permanent Court of Arbitration for international disputes. Hague II (Laws and Customs of War on Land) stated that "In the view of the High Contracting Parties, these provisions, the wording of which has been inspired by the desire to diminish the evils of war so far as military necessities permit, are destined to serve as general rules of conduct for belligerents in their relations with each other and with populations." The other Conventions established conditions for conduct of military operations in specific settings, established conditions for treatment of prisoners, and prohibited certain kinds of weapons. Although the Hague Conventions were treated with near contempt in the initiation and conduct of World War I, it was the rules of these conventions that ultimately became the bases for prosecutions after World War II for violations of the "laws and customs of war."

The most visible enforcement mechanisms of current international law can be grouped into one set of mechanisms for nations and another for individuals. The United Nations Security Council enforces rules of nonaggression by calling on member states to invoke sanctions against any state which violates the U.N. Charter's prohibition on aggression.[41] That there are obvious political dimensions to the decisions of the Security Council does not take away the facial legitimacy of those decisions. Moreover, the International Court of Justice has taken the position that the role of the Security Council is not exclusive and that courts such as itself can also provide remedies for violation of the law of armed conflict by nations.

---

[40] FRIEDMAN, *supra* note 24, at 4.

[41] All U.N. Security Council Resolutions are now available on the web at www.un.org/Docs/sc/. The reader can now review the progression of steps taken in response to international crises by scrolling through a given year with a particular country in mind.

The second set of enforcement mechanisms, applying the law of war to individuals, begins with war crimes trials following World War II. The United States tried some German spies and saboteurs in military courts.[42] The United States also conducted military trials against vanquished Japanese commanders accused of allowing their troops to violate the "laws and customs of war."[43] The highlight for international enforcement of the law of war was the Treaty of London and the resulting Nuremberg trials of high-ranking Nazi officials. The trials at Nuremberg were intended to import the processes of law onto the international scene for dealing with war crimes. Prior to that time, "victor's justice" had been meted out at the national level.[44] The Nuremberg trials have been followed in more recent times by Ad Hoc Tribunals for Rwanda & Yugoslavia.[45]

The older focus of international law on nation-state participation also has been modified by the emergence of additional organizations as world players, such as Regional Organizations (e.g., NATO, EU, OAS) and Non Governmental Organizations (e.g., Amnesty International, International Red Cross). Although these additional actors are participants in the development of international law, there are only a few instances of treaties that specifically recognize their role as legal actors.

Until recently, the world has held to a dichotomous distinction between the processes of warfare and those of the civilian criminal system. War was something that took place between nations, involved an effort to kill or capture enemy combatants, and thus provided no occasion for making considered judgments about the culpability of someone on the other side. The rules of engagement of a particular military action eliminate the soldier's need to inquire into the culpability of someone in uniform carrying arms. But those rules cannot authorize violence against noncombatants. "The State is represented in active war by its contending army, and the laws of war justify killing or disabling of members of the one army by those of the other in battle or hostile operations."[46] By contrast, those who are suspected of committing crimes against the law of a nation were treated as individuals whose culpability must be judged in an individualized proceeding.

The lines between warfare and criminal processes have blurred because of changes in approach both by the enforcers of peace and the perpetrators of violence. The peacemakers have attempted to use processes patterned from criminal law to punish violations of respected rules of warfare, while the perpetrators of violence have acted on their own outside the confines

---

[42] See Ex parte Quirin, 317 U.S. 1 (1942); see also Johnson v. Eisentrager, 339 U.S. 763 (1950).

[43] In re Yamashita, 327 U.S. 1 (1946).

[44] Gerry J. Simpson, War Crimes: A Critical Introduction, in McCORMACK & SIMPSON, THE LAW OF WAR CRIMES 5 (1997).

[45] See Christopher Blakesley, Atrocity and its Prosecution, in THE LAW OF WAR CRIMES 189 (1997).

[46] WINTHROP, supra note 18, at 778.

of government and those same rules of warfare. The world's search for a new paradigm to deal with these phenomena has produced international commissions for prosecution of war crimes and is now engaged in defining responses to terrorism.

[B] Justifying Acts of War

The starting point for international law is similar to the basic proposition regarding assault between individuals: if you use force against another, you must have a justification. U.N. Charter Article 2(4) sets out the basic rule of nonaggression: "All Members shall refrain in their international relations from the threat or use of force against the territorial integrity or political independence of any state, or in any other manner inconsistent with the Purposes of the United Nations." Articles 39-50 give the Security Council authority to determine when a nation is committing aggression and to call on Member nations to employ sanctions, ranging from diplomatic and economic sanctions to the use of military force against the aggressor.

Justifications for the use of force are implied in Article 51, which states that "Nothing in the present Charter shall impair the inherent right of individual or collective self-defense if an armed attack occurs against a Member of the United Nations." Recognition of the right of self-defense calls into play a network of doctrines regarding response to threats, proportional reprisals, protection of nationals, humanitarian intervention, and dealing with insurgents or belligerents.

First, there is the question of what constitutes aggression sufficient to justify self-defensive reaction. "Armed attack" under Article 51 seems to imply the obvious, incursion of armed invaders with full military equipment (planes, tanks, etc) in the uniforms of the invading country into the recognized borders of another nation. In this event, the invaded country can use whatever force is necessary to defend itself including, at least if it declares war, invading the offending country to take the offensive.

Short of the obvious level of armed attack, however, there are a host of lesser incursions that might trigger the right of self-defense. Blockade of a nation's ports is traditionally regarded as an act of war. An embassy is generally regarded as part of the sovereign territory of the guest nation so that an attack on the embassy is an act of war. Attacks on military ships on the high seas, and arguably attacks on merchant vessels as well, are acts of war. Minor border skirmishes may trigger rights of self-defense, and there will inevitably be questions raised as to whether the incursions were actually undertaken on behalf of the neighboring state or were instead private actions (by "irregulars" or terrorists).[47] In all these instances of "minor" acts of war, the defending nation is limited to the degree of force necessary to defend itself and in proportion to the actions of the aggressor.[48]

---

[47] The issues of "armed attack" and appropriate responses are explored in the opinions of the International Court of Justice in Nicaragua v. United States, 1986 I.C.J. 14.

[48] *See* CHRISTINE GRAY, INTERNATIONAL LAW AND THE USE OF FORCE 105-08 (2000); SCHACHTER, *supra* note 17, at 152-53.

These rules of necessity and proportionality may be more frequently observed than one might think, for the simple reason that escalation of the conflict is undertaken only at risk of triggering "total war," in which all the military-industrial apparatus of the enemy nation is arrayed in an effort to obliterate the defensive capability of the enemy.

Second, to what extent may a state strike first in response to a perceived threat from another state? The United Nations has never adopted language that specifically addresses this issue, and indeed has consciously refrained from defining the scope of self-defense. As discussed above, many observers believe that a majority of nations do not subscribe to the doctrine of anticipatory self-defense or preemptive strikes.[49]

Third, may one state invade the territory of another state to protect its nationals? The U.S. has claimed this right in its invasions of Panama (1989)[50] and Grenada (1983),[51] the hostage-rescue attempt in Iran (1980), and a few other instances. One of the most famous incidents of this type was the hostage rescue by Israeli forces at Entebbe in 1976.[52] Gray points out that the pattern of allowing incursions into other states to rescue a nation's own citizens has been accepted by silence of the invaded state in most instances but that there is not a widely accepted norm that would lead to the conclusion that this is a lawful practice. "The legal arguments of Belgium, the USA, Israel, and the UK in favour of such a wide right to self-defence have attracted few aherents."[53] The options, however, are limited if the "resident" state does not respond immediately to diplomatic demands.

Fourth, may one state or a collection of states invade another for humanitarian reasons? This rationale was probably unheard of until the late 20th Century. It has been the focus of a number of legal debates regarding the NATO intrusion into Kosovo, the most significant of which was expression of serious doubts about the matter by the International Court of Justice.[54] In justifying invasion of Iraq in 2003, the Bush Administration repeatedly referred to the "brutal dictatorship" of Saddam Hussein

---

[49] *See* GRAY, *supra* note 48, at 111-15. Schachter points out that the matter cannot be quite this clear because an "imminent" attack may leave "no moment for deliberation" and "no choice of means." *See* SCHACHTER, *supra* note 17, at 152.

[50] "On December 20, President Bush ordered the U.S. military into Panama to protect U.S. lives and property, to fulfill U.S. treaty responsibilities to operate and defend the Canal, to assist the Panamanian people in restoring democracy, and to bring Noriega to justice." U.S. State Department, www.state.gov/r/pa/ei/bgn/2030.htm#relations (last visited June 21, 2007).

[51] "Following a breakdown in civil order, a U.S.-Caribbean force landed on Grenada on October 25 in response to an appeal from the governor general and to a request for assistance from the Organization of Eastern Caribbean States. U.S. citizens were evacuated, and order was restored." U.S. State Department, www.state.gov/r/pa/ei/bgn/2335.htm (last visited June 21, 2007).

[52] The BBC account of the Entebbe raid can be found at news.bbc.co.uk/onthisday/hi/dates/stories/july/4/newsid_2786000/2786967.stm (last visited June 21, 2007).

[53] GRAY, *supra* note 48, at 109.

[54] Case Concerning Legality of Use of Force (Yugoslavia v. Belgium), 1999 I.C.J. 124, 1999 WL 1693067 (I.C.J.).

as a political justification to the American people but did not seem to be arguing for humanitarian intervention as a matter of legal justification.[55]

Fifth, and finally for our purposes, may a state invade the territory of another in pursuit of terrorists? The justification for U.S. invasion of Afghanistan in 2002 was that Afghanistan was "harboring" persons involved in the 9/11 attacks.[56] Earlier justifications for limited strikes by Israel and the U.S. may have been more in the nature of "reprisals" than defensive actions. None of those strikes was sharply limited by "necessity and proportionality" but instead seemed to be designed to punish the offending state. The U.N. Security Council in Resolution 188 stated in 1964 that it condemned reprisals in general. Perhaps the closest corollary in international custom has been the use of military force to root out piracy and slave trading centers in the 18th and 19th Centuries. It will be a matter of intense discussion in the future whether actions such as the U.S. invasion of Afghanistan comply with Articles 2(4) and 51.

There are only a handful of cases from the International Court of Justice regarding the justifications for military invasion of another country. The two most significant are *Nicaragua v. United States of America*[57] and *Yugoslavia v. Belgium.*[58]

In simplistic terms, the situation in Central America in the 1980s can be described as consisting of a leftist government in Nicaragua opposed by the United States and governments somewhat allied with the U.S. in the neighboring states of El Salvador, Honduras, and Costa Rica. Of course, the situation was further complicated by rogue elements within the three "friendly" countries as well. The U.S.-supported "Contras" used guerilla-style tactics against Nicaraguan targets from bases in the three friendly countries. Nicaragua's allegations against the United States were that it had attempted to overthrow the Sandinista regime of that country by "recruiting, training, arming, equipping, financing, supplying and otherwise encouraging, supporting, aiding, and directing military and paramilitary actions in and against Nicaragua."[59] The so-called Contras, according

---

[55] "When the Ba'ath regime refused to fully cooperate with the U.N. inspections, the Security Council employed sanctions to prevent further WMD development and compel Iraqi adherence to international obligations. Coalition forces enforced no-fly zones in southern and northern Iraq to protect Iraqi citizens from attack by the regime and a no-drive zone in southern Iraq to prevent the regime from massing forces to threaten or again invade Kuwait. A U.S.-led coalition removed the Ba'ath regime in March and April 2003, bringing an end to more than 12 years of Iraqi defiance of U.N. Security Council resolutions." U.S. State Department, www.state.gov/r/pa/ei/bgn/6804.htm (last visited June 21, 2007).

[56] *See Joint Resolution, supra* note 12, which authorized "necessary and appropriate force against those nations, organizations, or persons he determines planned, authorized, committed, or aided the terrorist attacks that occurred on September 11, 2001, or harbored such organizations or persons, in order to prevent any future acts of international terrorism against the United States by such nations, organizations or persons."

[57] 1986 I.C.J. 14.

[58] 1999 I.C.J. 124.

[59] *Nicaragua*, 1986 I.C.J. at ¶ 15 (a).

to Nicaragua, were recruited, supplied, trained and led by U.S. agents operating from bases in El Salvador, Honduras, and Costa Rica. The U.S. denied that it had official involvement with the Contras except for some limited actions that were justified because Nicaragua had violated the sovereignty of El Salvador, Honduras, and Costa Rica, with whom the U.S. sought to invoke the right of collective self-defense.[60]

The U.S. objected to the ICJ's taking jurisdiction of the dispute on the ground that it raised issues that were committed to the U.N. Security Council by the U.N. Charter. When the ICJ decided that issues of customary international law were appropriate for the court despite the role of the U.N., the U.S. informed the court that it would "not participate" in the proceedings. As a result of this procedural posture, the court received "evidence" from Nicaragua, much of which consisted of newspaper and congressional reports from U.S. sources, but had no submissions from the U.S. Government.[61]

In the view of the ICJ, the American support did not rise to the level of armed aggression by the U.S., but it did constitute illegal support of insurgents who could not claim legitimacy as the government of Nicaragua. Thus, the U.S. actions constituted illegal interference in the affairs of another state as well as invalid acts of war against a non-aggressor. The ICJ's Judgment in the case was issued two years after the litigation began. The majority held that "the United States of America, by training, arming, equipping, financing and supplying the contra forces or otherwise encouraging, supporting and aiding military and paramilitary activities in and against Nicaragua, has acted, against the Republic of Nicaragua, in breach of its obligation under customary international law not to intervene in the affairs of another State."[62] A majority also held that these and a handful of direct actions by the U.S. forces, specifically bombing raids and mining of harbors, violated customary international law by unjustified use of force against another State and violation of the sovereignty of another State.[63]

Finally, in response to a claim of self-defense by the U.S.-friendly countries, the majority also found that whatever "armed attacks" had occurred against El Salvador or its neighbors may have been the official work of the Nicaraguan regime but none of these countries had appealed to the U.S. officially for self-defense assistance.

Nicaragua exemplifies several of the rules that were mentioned above. First, the court holds that "support" of "insurgents" against their home country amounts to an "armed attack" on that country. In terms of the Geneva Conventions, this constitutes an "armed conflict not of an international character." Customary international law includes the principle that

---

[60] *Id.* at ¶ 229-234. Although the U.S. did not participate in the proceedings of the ICJ after the jurisdictional issue was decided, this line of argument was made in various submissions to the Court.

[61] *Id.* at ¶ 26-30.

[62] *Id.* at ¶ 292, conclusion 3.

[63] *Id.* at ¶ 292, conclusion 5.

if the insurgents had sufficient status to be entitled to recognition as the formal government of the country, thus becoming "belligerents" against what they deemed to be a usurper, then other nations such as the U.S. could provide support. The U.S. had already forfeited this argument by recognizing the Sandinista regime as the legitimate government of Nicaragua.

Second, there were significant questions in the case about what constitutes an armed attack. Although Nicaragua argued that the U.S. controlled the Contras to the degree that their actions would be "imputable" to the U.S., the court did not agree. It found that the Contras were a sufficiently independent force to be responsible for their own behavior,[64] but that the U.S. would be responsible for its actions in supporting them. That support itself could constitute violations of international law. The Court distinguished between mere supplying of rebels and more active participation in this way:

> 228. In the view of the Court, while the arming and training of the contras can certainly be said to involve the threat or use of force against Nicaragua, this is not necessarily so in respect of all the assistance given by the United States Government. In particular, the Court considers that the mere supply of funds to the contras, while undoubtedly an act of intervention in the internal affairs of Nicaragua . . . does not in itself amount to a use of force.

Third, if Nicaragua had been found to have supported attacks on El Salvador, would that have justified the U.S. in its support of insurgents against Nicaragua? or is this an issue of the degree of response that could be justified? In a passage that is critical to the idea of what constitutes an "armed conflict," the court stated that "while the concept of an armed attack includes the despatch by one State of armed bands into the territory of another State, the supply of arms and other support to such bands cannot be equated with armed attack."[65]

The ICJ opinions in *Nicaragua* bear heavily on our question of whether it is permissible to invade another State that is alleged to be "harboring terrorists." The Nicaraguan-backed incursions against El Salvador did not justify the U.S. in coming to the defense of El Salvador, but they certainly

---

[64] *Id.* at ¶ 116.

[65] 247. . . . So far as regards the allegations of supply of arms by Nicaragua to the armed opposition in El Salvador, the Court has indicated that while the concept of an armed attack includes the despatch by one State of armed bands into the territory of another State, the supply of arms and other support to such bands cannot be equated with armed attack. Nevertheless, such activities may well constitute a breach of the principle of the non-use of force and an intervention in the internal affairs of a State, that is, a form of conduct which is certainly wrongful, but is of lesser gravity than an armed attack. . . .

249. . . . While an armed attack would give rise to an entitlement to collective self-defence, a use of force of a lesser degree of gravity cannot . . . produce any entitlement to take collective counter-measures involving the use of force. The acts of which Nicaragua is accused, even assuming them to have been established and imputable to that State, could only have justified proportionate counter-measures on the part of the State which had been the victim of these acts, namely El Salvador, Honduras or Costa Rica.

would have justified El Salvador in taking proportionate action to defend itself. Conversely, would the U.S. violations of Nicaraguan sovereignty, while not constituting armed attack on Nicaragua, nevertheless have justified Nicaraguan attacks on U.S. soil? Again, the principle of military proportionality would limit any response to military targets with a commensurate level of force as had been directed against it.

What constitutes a proportional response to terrorism? And, for that matter, is proportional reprisal a wise response, even if its legality could be established? Israel has been roundly criticized for striking at Palestinian camps in reprisal for terrorist raids and has on occasion destroyed homes of person associated with suicide bombers. Alan Dershowitz argues that an even more effective approach would be to pick out Palestinian homes in advance and state that those will be destroyed after the next suicide bombing regardless of complicity.[66] Dershowitz argues that it is not unusual to penalize someone who fails to prevent a violent act and that even collective penalties are used in such cases as economic sanctions.[67] Even under the current policy of striking the family home, there are both pragmatic and legal difficulties. The pragmatic argument is that striking the innocent creates more terrorists, and it is a sound argument. On a legal plane, it is clearly invalid to strike at civilian targets even in reprisal for attacks on your own civilians.

The Dershowitz proposal of penalizing presumably innocent bystanders is unthinkable to a western notion of due process, but he claims that our ideas of deterrence must override notions of individual responsibility.[68] Thus far, international law limiting responses to military proportionality operates even when the terrorist has not played by the rules. The difficulty is that if future threats are represented by unknown civilians who are eager to die for their cause, then there is simply no punitive measure that will deter that behavior. This makes it appear that the choice is between two unacceptable extremes, doing nothing while the suicide bomber prepares to strike or retaliating against bystanders. In reality, there is a middle ground, difficult as it may be to employ, that is to track down and immobilize the leaders who select and instruct the suicide bombers.[69]

These exercises in armed responses to surrogate attacks illustrate part of the problems with "asymmetrical warfare." So much attention has been paid over the past 50 years to the superpowers and weapons of mass

---

[66] ALAN DERSHOWITZ, WHY TERRORISM WORKS 177 (2002).

[67] "Although collective punishment is prohibited by international law, it is widely practiced throughout the world, including by the most democratic and liberty-minded countries." *Id.* at 172.

[68] "The international community must come to accept the justice of directing proportionate, nonlethal deterrents against those who support and benefit from terrorism, rather than threatening meaningless sanctions against the suicide terrorists themselves." *Id.* at 179.

[69] The word "immobilize" begs the question of the degree of force that can be used against the leader without capture and trial. It may be possible to agree with Dershowitz that the leadership can be hunted down and killed but it would be preferable not to legitimize this behavior. Instead, it is better left to the clandestine underworld in which it now resides.

destruction that the much more common problem of small-scale violence has received little popular attention. But it is precisely small-scale violence that feeds the terrorist phenomenon. The massive arms and military machinery of a superpower are almost irrelevant to the issue of responding to terrorist attack. Even when the terrorist kills 3,000 people in one incident, the phenomenon of scale still presents difficulties in trying to respond with appropriate action against the remaining terrorist group.

The second ICJ case of note is *Yugoslavia v. Belgium* and companion cases against the other members of NATO. Following the battles between Serbian, Croatian, and Bosnian forces, the Serbian state claimed to retain the title of Yugoslavia. When its forces embarked on "pacifying" the province of Kosovo through "ethnic cleansing," most of the world was outraged at reports of atrocities. Under intense pressure to view the situation as a "European problem" to be taken care of by Europe, NATO decided to intervene for humanitarian reasons. Serbia then, in the name of Yugoslavia, brought an action in the ICJ against the European members of NATO, alleging that NATO had taken aggressive action against it and that its bombing of Bosnian targets was resulting in civilian casualties.[70]

Yugoslavia requested "provisional remedies" (similar to a preliminary injunction in Anglo-American legal systems), which the court was not prepared to grant, but the court had these comments about the use of force under these circumstances:

17. Whereas the Court is profoundly concerned with the use of force in Yugoslavia; whereas under the present circumstances such use raises very serious issues of international law;

---

[70] Yugoslavia's allegations included the following:

The subject-matter of the dispute are acts of [each member of NATO] by which it has violated its international obligation banning the use of force against another State, the obligation not to intervene in the internal affairs of another State, the obligation not to violate the sovereignty of another State, the obligation to protect the civilian population and civilian objects in wartime, the obligation to protect the environment, the obligation relating to free navigation on international rivers, the obligation regarding fundamental human rights and freedoms, the obligation not to use prohibited weapons, the obligation not to deliberately inflict conditions of life calculated to cause the physical destruction of a national group;

The Governments of Member States of NATO took part in the acts of use of force against the Federal Republic of Yugoslavia by taking part in bombing targets in the Federal Republic of Yugoslavia. In bombing the Federal Republic of Yugoslavia military and civilian targets were attacked. Great number of people were killed, including a great many civilians. Residential houses came under attack. Numerous dwellings were destroyed. Enormous damage was caused to schools, hospitals, radio and television stations, cultural and health institutions and to places of worship. A large number of bridges, roads and railway lines were destroyed. Attacks on oil refineries and chemical plants have had serious environmental effects on cities, towns and villages in the Federal Republic of Yugoslavia. The use of weapons containing depleted uranium is having far-reaching consequences for human life. The above-mentioned acts are deliberately creating conditions calculated at the physical destruction of an ethnic group, in whole or in part.

This cryptic comment is addressed in part to the issue of whether "humanitarian intervention" into the affairs of another nation can be justified. In paragraph 17, the ICJ sounds a strong warning that even multilateral action undertaken by an organization outside the processes of the United Nations Security Council will not be valid under international law. It runs against our instincts to insist that other nations must stand by while genocidal behavior within another nation occurs, but the arguments against unilateral intervention are several. For one thing, intervention opens the door to reprisals and escalation. Doing so without U.N. Security Council authority could leave other nations wondering who is in the right and undercuts the proposition that the U.N. Security Council should be the sole arbiter of authorizing intervention. There are also pragmatic difficulties involved in unilateral intervention, such as those experienced by the U.S. in Somalia. As indicated above, the weight of international scholarly authority is against the validity of intervention on humanitarian grounds without the sanction of the Security Council.

If humanitarian intervention is not authorized under international law, then a conundrum exists with the criminalization of genocide and crimes against humanity. Assume that the leaders of a government are engaged in atrocities against their own people that could be prosecuted in the International Criminal Court. How are these leaders to be apprehended without intervention by some other government? An investigation leading to prosecution can be initiated on the request of any State Party, the U.N. Security Council, or on the Prosecutor's initiative.[71] If "reasonable grounds to believe that the person has committed a crime" are shown by the Prosecutor, the Pre-Trial Chamber can issue an arrest warrant which serves as a request to a State Party to take that person into custody for surrender to the Court. There are elaborate provisions for cooperation and for setting priorities if a State receives both a request from the Court and a request for extradition from another State.

Over all of this elaborate machinery there floats the reality that a regime accused of committing atrocities is not likely to surrender its own leaders for prosecution so long as that regime remains in control of its territory. This fact leaves the Court subject to the vicissitudes of armed conflict before it can obtain effective power over an accused. If, under the prevailing views of international law, only the Security Council can authorize intervention into the internal affairs of a State, then only the Security Council can initiate armed invasion of a State to topple a regime and take its leaders into custody.

Of course, a regime that is committing atrocities against its own people may well step outside its own borders. Once it attacks the territory of another sovereign State, the attacked State can call for outside assistance and thus trigger a state of war that will result in invasion and overthrow of the abusive regime by other States. In this instance, a warrant of arrest

---

[71] Rome Statute of the International Criminal Court 183/9* (as corrected Nov. 10, 1998 and July 12, 1999), art. 15 U.N. DOC A/CONF.

from the ICC could become effective as a result of aggressive action by the regime in question. This possibility leads back to the murkiness of what is a legitimate government in this fashion: if Kosovo had been recognized as an independent State prior to "invasion" by Serbia, then collective self-defense by NATO forces would have been perfectly appropriate without Security Council authorization.

For Americans, some of these difficulties are analogous to the early days of federalism and the post-Civil War era. When the people of the American Colonies formed the United States, under the Articles of Confederation they gave the central government no coercive power over the States. But when the Constitution was framed by "We the People" with the Supremacy Clause of Article VI, there was at least the vestige of coercive power in the federal government. The Civil War and the post-war amendments settled the proposition that the federal government can intervene in the internal affairs of a State to enforce provisions of federal law. Nothing in the American experience, however, implies that California can intervene in the affairs of Nevada without federal authority. Eventually, it may become reality that the United Nations exercises the power to intervene in the affairs of a nation-state to enforce norms of international law, in a fashion similar to the federal enforcement of civil rights laws within one of the United States.

[C] The Special Case of Military Force and Terrorism

Even prior to 9/11, a few internationalists had focused on the question of whether one state could send military forces into another state for the purpose of pursuing terrorists. International law was already in a state of flux on this issue and has probably evolved further since 9/11.

Gray reviewed four U.S. and two Israeli actions against other states in response to terrorist attacks that were thought to be supported from within the other states.[72] The U.S.-Israeli position elaborated over time combines the logic of anticipatory self-defense with reprisal for deterrence purposes. In the U.N. Security Council debate over the U.S. missile attack on the Iraqi Intelligence Headquarters in Baghdad in 1993, only Russia and the UK supported the U.S. position. With regard to bombing of Libyan targets in Tripoli in 1986, the UK and France joined the U.S. in vetoing a Security Council resolution condemning the action. And when the U.S. bombed an al Qaeda training camp in Afghanistan in 1998 in response to the bombings of U.S. embassies in Kenya and Ethiopia, Russia joined most of the world in condemning the U.S. action and the UK showed only mild acceptance.[73]

The two Israeli incursions were airstrikes on Beirut in 1968 and on Tunis in 1985.[74] In both incidents, the U.S. joined in Security Council resolutions

---

[72] GRAY, *supra* note 48, at 115-19.

[73] *Id.* at 117-18.

[74] *Id.* at 116.

condemning the Israeli acts on the ground that reprisals are not allowed without reference to proportional responses to ongoing threats. The U.S. position at that time was that military action could be taken against another state as a matter of self-defense if necessary to deter or protect against future attacks. The U.S. used a self-defense rationale to justify its blockade of Cuba during the 1962 missile crisis, while also claiming that it was engaged in regional peacekeeping under Chapter VIII of the U.N. Charter. Interestingly enough, Chairman Krushchev asserted that the missiles initially were placed in Cuba to deter foreign invasion of Cuba,[75] thus illustrating the "slippery slope" problem of preemptive action in a claim of self-defense.

The U.S. specifically invoked anticipatory self-defense with regard to Iraq, first in enforcing the "no-fly" zones by targeting Iraqi installations that showed "hostile intent" and then ultimately in the 2003 invasion based on reported stockpiles of weapons of mass destruction.

Gray observed prior to the 2003 invasion of Iraq that

> reluctance to rely on anticipatory self-defence even by the USA and Israel is not conclusive that they do not believe that it is legal, as it is natural for states to choose the strongest grounds to justify their claims, but it is strong evidence of the controversial nature of this justification for the use of force, as is the deliberate avoidance of the issue of the legality of anticipatory self-defence by the International Court of Justice in the Nicaragua case. States prefer to argue for an extended interpretation of armed attack and to avoid the fundamental doctrinal debate.[76]

Gray's conclusion from the waffling of the international community in response to these major incidents is that "[f]ailure to condemn the USA should be taken to indicate sympathy and understanding rather than acceptance of a legal doctrine which destroys the distinction between reprisals and self-defense and which the USA would never contemplate being used against itself."[77]

Oscar Schachter's more elaborate analysis of military incursions into other states in pursuit of terrorists makes a distinction between the justification of self-defense and the excuse of necessity.[78] This distinction is more common in international law than in U.S. law but it is not unknown to us. The difference is that when self-defense is successfully invoked, there

---

[75] Library of Congress, *Revelations from the Russian Archives, Cold War: Cuban Missile Crisis*, *available at* www.loc.gov/exhibits/archives/colc.html (last visited Aug 1, 2007):

> According to Nikita Khrushchev's memoirs, in May 1962 he conceived the idea of placing intermediate-range nuclear missiles in Cuba as a means of countering an emerging lead of the United States in developing and deploying strategic missiles. He also presented the scheme as a means of protecting Cuba from another United States-sponsored invasion, such as the failed attempt at the Bay of Pigs in 1961.

[76] GRAY, *supra* note 48, at 115.

[77] *Id.* at 119.

[78] SCHACHTER, *supra* note 17, at 162-73.

is no wrong, whereas the excuse of necessity leaves the wrong in place but persuades the enforcing body to do nothing about it. In U.S. law, the Model Penal Code has attempted to eliminate the distinction by making all justifications involve a balancing of choices between two evils.[79] If the appropriate criteria are met, necessity will serve as justification for what would otherwise be an offense even when there is resulting damage to a person who was not responsible for the threat of harm to the defendant. For example, tying one's boat to another's dock during a storm may damage the dock without fault or liability, or destroying one building to prevent the spread of fire to others may be justified by necessity.[80] Choosing between the lives of innocent persons usually is not appropriate for humans, so the Model Penal Code recognizes the defense of necessity for deadly force only in the most extreme situations, as when the person killed will die anyway.[81]

On the international scene, the excuse of necessity for the use of deadly force is triggered when one party (in this case a state or its nationals) is threatened with imminent danger of great bodily harm and no more peaceful means of rescue are available. A useful set of terminology in this analysis is to refer to the state whose nationals allegedly have been or are likely to be attacked as the target state, and the state where the attackers are located as the resident state. At least, this avoids more inflammatory phrases such as the state "under attack" or the "harboring" state.

First, there is now widespread acceptance of the obligation of a state in which a terrorist is found, the resident state, either to prosecute or extradite.[82] Failure to do so may as a practical matter set the stage for intervention by the target state, even though that intervention itself would not be justified as self-defense without a showing of imminent threat of further violence to the target state.

Second, there is at least grudging acceptance of the permissibility of a state to employ military force to rescue its nationals who are being held hostage in another state, either as self-defense under some circumstances

---

[79] MODEL PENAL CODE § 3.02. Justification Generally: Choice of Evils.

1.   Conduct that the actor believes to be necessary to avoid a harm or evil to himself or to another is justifiable, provided that:

    (a)   the harm or evil sought to be avoided by such conduct is greater than that sought to be prevented by the law defining the offense charged; and

    (b)   neither the Code nor other law defining the offense provides exceptions or defenses dealing with the specific situation involved; and

    (c)   a legislative purpose to exclude the justification claimed does not otherwise plainly appear.

[80] For a discussion of the Model Penal Code and a more complete listing of examples, see WAYNE LAFAVE, CRIMINAL LAW § 10.1(c), 527 (2003).

[81] There are some open questions regarding such issues as whether it is appropriate for persons in a lifeboat to draw lots to see who is tossed overboard. See id. at 528-31.

[82] Some authors tie this obligation to U.N. General Assembly Resolution 40/61. See SCHACHTER, supra note 17, at 163 (citing Y. DINSTEIN, THE INTERNATIONAL LEGAL RESPONSE TO TERRORISM, 2 INTERNATIONAL LAW AT THE TIME OF ITS CODIFICATION 139 (1987)). See also J. MURPHY, PUNISHING INTERNATIONAL TERRORISTS (1985).

or excused by necessity in others. For self-defense to be invoked, the state or its nationals would have to be under attack by the resident state, at least in the sense that the resident state is accountable for the situation. If there is threat of imminent bodily harm and the threat can be imputed to the resident state, then logically there should be no requirement for the target state to exhaust peaceful solutions. The only point of doubt here is whether protecting nationals is the same as protecting the homeland of the target state. Even if the presence of hostages could not be imputed to the resident state, the excuse of necessity should be triggered by threat of imminent bodily harm and exhaustion of peaceful means of resolution. Necessity is necessity regardless of who is presenting the threat.

Third, if the resident state could be held accountable for the actions of the attackers, under the tests and logic of the *Nicaragua* case discussed below, then use of military force against the resident state for self-defense would be justified. The tests for accountability of the resident state, phrased by the ICJ as whether the acts of the terrorist can be imputed to the state, call for assessment of what level of support has been supplied by the resident state. Something more than mere tolerance of their presence (such as provision of money, arms, passports with knowledge of their activities, and the like) would be required. This means that mere failure to extradite would not be enough to trigger state accountability and the self-defense argument fails. "From the standpoint of self-defense (in contrast to retribution) the use of force must have a defensive purpose; it must be intended to prevent and deter future attacks."[83]

That brings the analysis to the situation of the resident state that has not provided support to the level of being accountable but also is failing to extradite or otherwise deal with the terrorists itself. In a few situations of drug-related violence, when the resident state has refused extradition to the U.S. because the U.S. would not waive the death penalty, the U.S. has abducted the accused to the U.S. for trial.[84] With respect to terrorists, there are only a handful of minor examples when the resident state allowed U.S. agents to seize the accused without insisting on formal extradition,[85] and then there are the post-9/11 invasions of Afghanistan and Iraq.

The word necessity plays a role in arguments both for self-defense and for excuse, but with slightly different meanings in the two contexts. The legitimate use of force in self-defense must be measured by necessity and proportionality even when the resident state is accountable. In this guise, military necessity refers to the limits on force to militarily defined targets. Of course, the terrorist camps to be attacked are not part of the uniformed services of the resident state, so military necessity refers to avoiding unnecessary collateral damage.

---

[83] SCHACHTER, *supra* note 17, at 167.

[84] *See* United States v. Alvarez-Machain, 504 U.S. 655 (1992). *See also* United States v. Noriega, 117 F.3d 1206 (11th Cir. 1997).

[85] *See* United States v. Yousef, 927 F. Supp. 673 (S.D.N.Y. 1996).

The sense in which necessity stands as an excuse refers to (1) whether there are peaceful solutions that have a reasonable chance of success and have not yet been attempted and (2) whether the target state or its nationals are in imminent danger of great bodily harm. In the case of a resident state that is not accountable for the acts of the terrorists, then both tests must be met for the excuse of necessity to justify the use of military force by the target state.

[D]   U.S. Invasions of Afghanistan and Iraq

Illustration of these principles in the U.S. response to terrorism can be explored briefly in the basic questions of whether either of those invasions was valid under international law and how to approach rules of engagement with respect to the "post-war" ongoing resistance.

[1]   Validity of the Invasions

There is little support under international law for the proposition that one nation may invade another on "humanitarian" grounds to protect the citizens of the invaded nation from their own regime. There is some greater argument for the proposition that it is permissible to invade another nation to root out terrorists that are being "harbored" within the invaded nation by analogizing to piracy and slavery. Moreover, we cannot avoid the prudential consideration of whether either one was a wise method of combating the phenomenon of terrorism. Many observers have argued that military action on this scale against Arab nations has created more terrorists than it eliminated.

The U.S. invasion of Afghanistan was premised directly on finding and "neutralizing" at least the leadership if not most components of the al Qaeda organization, although the Bush administration also made a major point of the atrocities committed by the Taliban regime against its own people.

The U.S. invasion of Iraq was premised primarily on allegations that Iraq possessed and intended to use, or allow terrorists to use, weapons of mass destruction, although the administration also made a major point of the atrocities committed by the Hussein regimes against its own people. There were some hints of possible links between Hussein and al Qaeda but it soon became apparent that there were no such connections.

The two situations turned out to be quite different on the facts. The formal government of Afghanistan certainly was more than just "harboring" international terrorists, it was actively supporting them. Following requests to arrest and extradite the al Qaeda members in Afghanistan, it is difficult to see how the United States would have been in violation of international law in taking matters into its own hands. Just as with piracy and slavery, terrorism has become a universally condemned activity that justifies "police" action with the use of military force. The U.S. was more justified under international law in taking this action than it would be in using either military force or clandestine agents to capture drug violators in Mexico or Colombia against the wishes of that country.

The government of Iraq, however, would have been a very strange bedfellow of the al Qaeda organization, which viewed that government as decadent apostates. Nor has there been produced any evidence of support by the Hussein regime for other organizations that threatened the territory or citizens of the U.S. The invasion of Iraq simply cannot be justified on the basis of self-defense.

[2] Dealing with Resistance

Earlier, we described how the French Resistance fighters during World War II acted at their complete risk because there was no international law to protect their clandestine activities toward an occupying force. "Common article 3" of the Geneva Conventions applies to "armed conflict not of an international character," such as organized resistance to an occupying force, and protects against inhumane treatment as well as punishment without "judgment pronounced by a regularly constituted court affording all the judicial guarantees which are recognized as indispensable by civilized peoples." In this scenario, the resistance fighter loses the status of prisoner of war and becomes a criminal to be dealt with according to the criminal law of the occupying forces, and international law imposes only those "indispensable" restrictions on the internal operation of a criminal justice system that are universally recognized.[86]

Now fast forward to Afghanistan and Iraq in 2003. The U.S. and allied forces in Afghanistan are there theoretically at the request of the legitimate government, one that the victorious forces installed but nonetheless a government with recognized legitimacy. In both Afghanistan and Iraq, as of mid-2007, U.S. forces are still attempting to establish dominion sufficient to quell resistance. In neither instance could civilians carrying arms reasonably expect POW treatment when captured (not even if they met the conditions of either paragraph 2 or 6, which most would not).

Might the Afghan or Iraqi resistance fighter expect to be treated as a criminal with the due process that the American system normally would provide? The Feldman distinction between war and crime is pertinent, but both models eventually lead to the same conclusion. If we follow the model of war, then the resistance fighter can be killed without warning unless trying to surrender, at which point he falls into the grey area of being an unlawful combatant. If we follow the model of crime, then he must be captured without deadly force if possible but can then be punished in criminal proceedings. Under either model, deadly force can be used against someone carrying arms in a hostile fashion and punishment would be meted out according to a civilized justice system.

---

[86] Other international treaties and conventions could also apply regardless of the state of occupation or warfare at the time. For example, the Convention Against Torture cannot be derogated under any circumstances.

There is no question of the authority of military tribunals to dispense punishment in occupied territory or in a zone of armed conflict. In these settings, the military justice system can enforce the ordinary norms of criminal law. The resistance fighter has engaged in violence without the justification of self-defense, which was lost when the invading forces became victorious occupying forces. So under the Geneva Conventions, the captured resistance fighter can hope for only humane treatment (not POW status) and can expect to be punished for the crime of insurrection against the occupying force.

§ 8.04 LAW OF WAR AND DOMESTIC MILITARY LAW

The U.S. administration argues that military commissions can be convened pursuant to the President's C-in-C powers as augmented by statutory authorization for the use of military commissions when warranted by the law of war. The argument is that members of a well-organized international terrorist group engaged in violent attack on the United States qualify as enemy combatants under international law. The counter-argument is that the customs and usages of international law permit military commissions to operate only in the actual "theater of operations" of the military or in occupied territory. We will get to the details of these arguments after developing much of the background and implications of using military commissions.

With regard to those who carry out illegal activities within this country on behalf of a foreign state, the Supreme Court was willing to allow the military to deal with them outside the setting of the normal criminal processes during World War II.[87] That incident, however, is "bookended" by Civil War cases insisting that military courts cannot operate in areas where the civilian courts are open and operating[88] and by the invalidity of using military tribunals in Hawaii during World War II.[89]

[A] The Civil War and WWII Precedents

The leading case is *Ex parte Quirin*,[90] in which eight persons were arrested early in World War II by the FBI and handed over to military authorities for trial as spies or saboteurs. They had landed in two groups of four by German submarine, one group on Long Island with targets in New York City and the other group near Jacksonville, Florida with a variety of targets. Each had undergone training in Germany, was paid by German officials, was issued a German military uniform to wear until ashore in the

---

[87] *Ex parte* Quirin, 317 U.S. 1, 35-36 (1942).

[88] *Ex parte* Milligan, 71 U.S. (4 Wall.) 2 (1866); Beckwith v. Bean, 98 U.S. 266, 293 (1878). *See* Jordan Paust, *Antiterrorism Military Commissions: Courting Illegality*, 23 Mich. J. Int'l L. 5, 9 (2001).

[89] Duncan v. Kahanamoku, 327 U.S. 304 (1946) (decided on statutory grounds but with constitutional overtones).

[90] 317 U.S. 1 (1942).

U.S., was arrested in civilian clothing, and brought a quantity of explosives ashore. With a bit of procedural maneuvering regarding whether captured spies could even have recourse to the civilian courts for a writ of habeas corpus, which the Supreme Court did not hesitate to answer affirmatively, the Court held that they were not entitled to the processes of civil courts but could be dealt with under military law for violations of the "law of war."

The Constitution has three statements regarding the place and type of trial for offenses against the United States, with one key exception for cases "arising in the land and naval forces, or in the Militia, in actual service in time of War or public danger."[91] For substantive rules of criminal behavior, Article I, § 8 grants Congress the power, in addition to the familiar power to make rules and regulations for governance of the military, "To define and punish Piracies and Felonies committed on the high Seas, and Offenses against the Law of Nations."

Taking all these provisions together, it is easy to construct an argument that it is up to Congress to define and criminalize offenses such as sabotage and war crimes, that the place of trial shall be where the offense was committed or such other place as directed by law, that the accused is entitled to trial by jury and the other rights of the Sixth Amendment, and that none of this contemplates anything other than the normal processes of the civilian courts except in cases "arising in the land or naval forces, or in the Militia, when in actual service in time of War or public danger."[92] The exception is so clearly targeted to offenses committed by U.S. personnel that it is difficult to imagine its application to foreign nationals either one way or the other.

These provisions are all so consistent with each other and with the argument for civilian courts that it is difficult to construct the counter argument. The Supreme Court in *Quirin* relied upon a minimal amount of textual analysis to point out that the Article III and Fifth Amendment provisions must be read in light of their historical understanding, which was that not all offenses give rise to a right of trial by jury. The two

---

[91] Art. III, § 2:

> The trial of all Crimes except in cases of Impeachment shall be by Jury and such Trial shall be held in the State where the said Crimes shall have been committed but when not committed within any State, the Trial shall be at such Place or Places as the Congress may by Law have directed.

The Fifth Amendment:

> No person shall be held to answer for a capital, or otherwise infamous crime, unless on a presentment or indictment of a Grand Jury, except in cases arising in the land or naval forces, or in the Militia, when in actual service in time of War or public danger . . . .

The Sixth Amendment:

> In all criminal prosecutions, the accused shall enjoy the right to a speedy and public trial, by an impartial jury of the State and district wherein the crime shall have been committed, which district shall have been previously ascertained by law, and notice of charges, confrontation of witnesses, subpoena power, and right to counsel.

[92] *See generally* Paust, *supra* note 88.

examples used for this purpose — petty offenses and criminal contempt charges — did not give rise to a jury trial but did remain in the civilian court systems.[93] The *Quirin* opinion also relied on a structural anomaly: if our own troops are subject to military tribunals, why should the alleged bad guys get better treatment by being sent to the civilian system?

Most of the opinion was historical, citing examples from the Revolutionary War and Civil War of alleged spies who were subjected to the death penalty either by commanding officer fiat or after the current version of a military proceeding. Of interest to the current situation, the Court stated in no uncertain terms that the offenders were outside the constitutional guaranty of trial by jury, not because they were aliens[94] but because they had violated the law of war by committing offenses traditionally triable by military tribunal.[95]

This approach makes the jurisdiction of military tribunals depend on the nature of the charged offense — violation of the law of war. In the case of members of terrorist groups, what law of war has been violated? *Quirin* was decided in the unquestioned context of war, a more or less easily understood term referring to conditions of hostilities between nation states. Since WWII, the international community has been defining crimes of international law that do not depend on conditions of hostility between nations. But are those offenses triable under U.S. law in military courts or in the civilian courts? In fact, the international community has been quite adamant in not defining the acts of terrorists to be acts of war, lawful or unlawful.

The argument for using civilian courts rather than military courts under U.S. domestic law hinges on *Ex parte Milligan*.[96] Milligan was arrested in Indiana during the Civil War, charged with conspiracy before a military commission, convicted and sentenced to death by hanging. His habeas

---

[93] After *Quirin* there have been further restrictions placed on both these exceptions to jury trial, defining petty offenses as those punishable by no more than six months incarceration, (*see* Baldwin v. New York, 399 U.S. 66 (1970)), and requiring a separate trial for contempt that does not threaten the continuation of the proceedings. (Frank v. United States, 395 U.S. 147 (1969); Harris v. United States, 382 U.S. 162 (1965)). Under FED. R. CRIM. P. 42(b), if the alleged contempt involves disrespect of the judge, then that judge is disqualified from hearing the contempt trial.

[94] "Citizenship in the United States of an enemy belligerent does not relieve him from the consequences of a belligerency which is unlawful because in violation of the law of war." *Quinn*, 317 U.S. at 37.

[95] The Court blended U.S. and international law regarding the rules applicable to unlawful combatants:

> Our Government, by thus defining lawful belligerents entitled to be treated as prisoners of war, has recognized that there is a class of unlawful belligerents not entitled to that privilege, including those who, though combatants, do not wear "fixed and distinctive emblems." And by [the predecessor of 10 U.S.C. § 815], Congress has made provision for their trial and punishment by military commission, according to the "law of war."

Quinn, 317 U.S. at 35.

[96] 71 U.S. 2 (4 Wall.) (1866).

corpus petition was granted by the Supreme Court unanimously, although the nine Justices disagreed over whether the defects in the proceedings were constitutional or statutory. Justice Davis, for the five-vote majority, held that Congress could not authorize the use of military commissions even for violations of the "laws and usages of war" in areas outside the "theater of operations" and in which the civilian courts were open and operating.[97] Chief Justice Chase, for the four-vote minority, believed that Congress could have authorized the use of military commissions under these circumstances but had not done so.[98]

Milligan is often read as stating emphatically that it would be unconstitutional to prosecute citizens in military commissions for crimes committed in areas in which the civilian courts are open and operating. There is even stronger language in *Beckwith v. Bean*[99] a civil case for false imprisonment under similar facts as *Milligan* but decided long after the Civil War was over. In *Beckwith*, Justice Field delivered a vigorous lecture about the

---

[97] *Id.* at 76.

It can serve no useful purpose to inquire what those laws and usages [of war] are, whence they originated, where found, and on whom they operate; they can never be applied to citizens in states which have upheld the authority of the government, and where the courts are open and their process unobstructed. This court has judicial knowledge that in Indiana the Federal authority was always unopposed, and its courts always open to hear criminal accusations and redress grievances; and no usage of war could sanction a military trial there for any offence whatever of a citizen in civil life, in nowise connected with the military service. Congress could grant no such power; and to the honor of our national legislature be it said, it has never been provoked by the state of the country even to attempt its exercise. One of the plainest constitutional provisions was, therefore, infringed when Milligan was tried by a court not ordained and established by Congress, and not composed of judges appointed during good behavior.

[98] *Id.* at 90:

The fact that the Federal courts were open was regarded by Congress as a sufficient reason for not exercising the power; but that fact could not deprive Congress of the right to exercise it. Those courts might be open and undisturbed in the execution of their functions, and yet wholly incompetent to avert threatened danger, or to punish, with adequate promptitude and certainty, the guilty conspirators.

. . . .

It was for Congress to determine the question of expediency. And Congress did determine it. That body did not see fit to authorize trials by military commission in Indiana, but by the strongest implication prohibited them.

. . . .

With that prohibition [by Congress] we are satisfied, and should have remained silent if the answers to the questions certified had been put on that ground, without denial of the existence of a power which we believe to be constitutional and important to the public safety, — a denial which, as we have already suggested, seems to draw in question the power of Congress to protect from prosecution the members of military commissions who acted in obedience to their superior officers, and whose action, whether warranted by law or not, was approved by that up-right and patriotic President under whose administration the Republic was rescued from threatened destruction.

[99] 98 U.S. 266 (1878).

inability of Congress to suspend the operation of civilian law even in war time.[100]

The Supreme Court in *Quirin* answered the *Milligan* argument rather curtly by pointing out that "Milligan, not being a part of or associated with the armed forces of the enemy, was a non-belligerent, not subject to the law of war save as — in circumstances found not there to be present, and not involved here — martial law might be constitutionally established."[101] In this statement, the *Quirin* Court observed that Congress had not established "martial law" in the U.S., but the opinion relies extensively on explaining that these saboteurs had penetrated behind military lines to reach targets that were potentially civilian support systems for the military's war effort.

The implication of these observations is that the "theater of operations," in which military commissions could act, was expanded to reach those areas behind friendly lines in which saboteurs would find it profitable to operate. From this, one could conclude that the "theater of operations" in time of armed conflict extends to any target that a saboteur desires to strike, and from this the act of a terrorist becomes the act of an "enemy combatant."

But can the President, even with the consent of Congress, authorize military detention or trial of a U.S. citizen when the civilian courts are open and operating? *Quirin* points in the direction of yes, at least when the U.S. is in the middle of a declared war and the alleged perpetrators are captured in the middle of attacking U.S. targets. *Milligan* says emphatically no, unless the context of national emergency is so great that there is military necessity for supplanting the civilian processes.

There is further guidance to be gained from *Duncan v. Kahanamoku,*[102] which struck down the use of military tribunals during a time of "martial law" in Hawaii following the attack on Pearl Harbor. Duncan was a "civilian shipfitter employed in the Navy Yard at Honolulu" who "engaged in a brawl with two armed Marine sentries at the yard." The military authorities (presumably foregoing a charge of criminal stupidity) charged him with violation of a standing military order, "assault on military or naval personnel with intent to resist or hinder them in the discharge of their duty." At the time, Hawaii was under martial law, although the civilian courts were open and operating for some purposes. Duncan was convicted and sentenced by a military tribunal, and the Supreme Court invalidated his conviction. While recognizing that Congress had authorized the declaration of martial law in the Hawaii Organic Act, the Court reviewed the history of military

---

[100] *Id.* at 293.

   No mere order or proclamation of the President for the arrest and imprisonment of a person not in the military service, in a State removed from the scene of actual hostilities, where the courts are open and in the unobstructed exercise of their jurisdiction, can constitute the due process of law, nor can it be made such by any act of Congress.

[101] *Quirin,* 317 U.S. at 45.

[102] 327 U.S. 304 (1946).

tribunals as it existed at the time of the Organic Act and concluded that it "was not intended to authorize the supplanting of courts by military tribunals."[103]

By relying on congressional intent, the Court in *Duncan* avoided constitutional grounds for its decision, but it was clear that the situation skirted on constitutional issues. Citing *Milligan*, the Court stated,

> We have always been especially concerned about the potential evils of summary criminal trials and have guarded against them by provisions embedded in the Constitution itself. Legislatures and courts are not merely cherished American institutions; they are indispensable to our Government.
>
> Military tribunals have no such standing.[104]

Indeed, in something approaching a fit of pique, Justice Black's opinion referred to the Civil War experience by pointing out that "in order to prevent this Court from passing on the constitutionality of [Reconstruction] legislation Congress found it necessary to curtail our appellate jurisdiction."

The *Duncan* Court was well aware of *Quirin*, decided just four years earlier, as well as *In re Yamashita*,[105] decided three weeks earlier. What the Court said to distinguish these cases, as well as others involving legitimate use of military tribunals was this:

> Our question does not involve the well-established power of the military to exercise jurisdiction over members of the armed forces, those directly connected with such forces, or enemy belligerents, prisoners of war, or others charged with violating the laws of war. We are not concerned with the recognized power of the military to try civilians in tribunals established as a part of a temporary military government over occupied enemy territory or territory regained from an enemy where civilian government cannot and does not function. . . . Nor need we here consider the power of the military simply to arrest and detain civilians interfering with a necessary military function at a time of turbulence and danger from insurrection or war.

In short, the Court limited the legitimate realm of military tribunals to governance of the armed forces themselves, the "theater of operations" (including occupied territory, as Winthrop argued) and "others charged with violating the laws of war." So once again we come to the question of whether a person acting without "color of state action" can violate the law of war.

[B] Non-State Actors and the "Law of War"

The Government claims statutory authority in support of the Commander-in-Chief powers from article 15 of the UCMJ,[106] which states that

---

[103] *Id.* at 324.

[104] *Id.* at 322.

[105] 327 U.S. 1 (1946).

[106] 10 U.S.C. § 821 (2007).

creation of military courts-martial by statute does not "deprive military commissions . . . of concurrent jurisdiction with respect to offenders or offenses that . . . by the law of war may be tried by military commissions." The argument from *Quirin* goes on to assert that in wartime conditions, military necessity as determined by the Commander-in-Chief can justify using military tribunals for punishment of offenses against the law of war. Because a terrorist act (wearing civilian clothing, targeting a civilian facility, and blending back into a civilian population) is against the law of war, even in the absence of an international definition of "terrorism," then the power of the military is complete.[107]

The *Quirin* opinion distinguished *Milligan* on the ground that "Milligan, not being a part of or associated with the armed forces of the enemy, was a non-belligerent." Professors Bradley and Goldsmith argue that al Qaeda is a sufficiently organized and hostile organization to be subject to the law of war. "If the September 11 attacks were committed by traditional state actors during this armed conflict, they would clearly violate international law prohibitions on attacking civilian populations and destroying their property."[108] They argue that "there is precedent for applying the laws of war to groups not directly acting on behalf of nation-states, such as guerilla groups and insurgents."

Guerrillas and insurgents, however, do not violate the law of war by the inherent nature of their mission or composition. They may violate provisions against systematically attacking populations and engaging in armed conflict without appropriate insignia. For specific violations of this type, the guerilla may be criminally responsible, but it is also possible to conduct guerilla operations in compliance with the law of war. For example, the lack of insignia may be justified by defense of home so long as they limit targets to military ones. Thus, this argument in favor of allowing military commissions to try offenses committed by terrorists boils down to equating the terrorist operation to an ongoing state of armed conflict with a "belligerent" who violates the law of war, or as often designated in government policy statements, an "illegal enemy combatant." But a belligerent is not illegal just by being a belligerent.

Professor Paust argues not just from *Milligan* but also from general international law as represented by noted scholars[109] that the authority of military commissions is limited to the "theatre of operations" or occupied territory. Moreover, he points out that granting the status of "insurgent" or "belligerent" to al Qaeda would have the unintended, and potentially disastrous, effect of giving them the option of practicing their terrorist acts in legitimate ways.[110] All they would have to do is don an appropriate

---

[107] Curtis Bradley & Jack Goldsmith, *The Constitutional Validity of Military Commissions*, 5 Green Bag 2d, at 249, 257 (2002).

[108] *Id.* at 256. Bradley and Goldsmith point out, however, that "isolated or sporadic" attacks would not violate the law of war because they would not constitute a "state of armed conflict."

[109] In the European tradition, international law is often contained in scholarly commentaries more than in legislative documents or court opinions.

[110] Paust, *supra* note 88, at 8 n.6.

insignia, limit their attacks to militarily defined targets, and they do not commit any crime against the law of war. Of course, anyone wearing such an insignia could be hunted down and killed without warning, but they could not be prosecuted for war crimes.

There are two interesting aspects of this argument. One is that there is another way of looking at *Quirin* and *Milligan*, which focuses more on the role of Congress and "martial law" in keeping with the concurrence of Chief Justice Chase in *Milligan*. The other interesting issue has to do with the terminology. We will consider them in reverse order.

There has been a great deal of sloppiness in the popular press, and even in some legal writing, around the terms "insurgent," "belligerent," and "combatant." A quick explanation of these terms will help explain why the language of war just does not fit the actions of or reactions to an organized terrorist group. Most of these terms have been designed for use in determining when it is appropriate for an outside nation to come to the aid of a group fighting with its own recognized government. Until now, it has not been necessary to have special terminology for the member of an enemy military.

The terms "rebel" and "rebellion" refer to persons or groups who are violently opposed to the existing regime within their own country. It is not legitimate for another nation to come to the aid of a rebellious force. For this purpose, rebellion "covers minor instances of internal war of a wide variety: violent protest involving a single issue . . . or an uprising that is so rapidly suppressed as to warrant no acknowledgment of its existence on an international level."[111] The second stage of internal conflict is "insurgency," which is somewhere between rebellion and belligerency. The declaration of an activity as insurgency basically protects other nations and their nationals from being accused of aiding a criminal faction if they have any contact with the insurgents, such as by doing business in nonmilitary goods. Only when a group achieves the status of "belligerent" can other nations come to their aid. A belligerent is characterized by the ability to control a segment of territory and thus require other nations either to choose sides in the conflict or to declare neutrality between them.

Because the terms "insurgent" and "belligerent" were developed for use in sorting out the rights and obligations of other nations with respect to an internal dispute in one nation, they are not suited for use in instances of open armed conflict between nations. For that purpose, international law has turned to the concepts of "combatant" and "noncombatant," along with occasional use of terms such as "camp follower" and "retainer." Combatants are expected to be in uniform or otherwise recognizably identified. Noncombatants need not carry any special insignia but certain facilities such as hospitals and schools are entitled to even greater protection when they are clearly identified, as are the medical and religious personnel who wear special symbols so long as they refrain from any military act.

---

[111] Richard Falk, *Janus Tormented: The International Law of Internal War, in* JAMES N. ROSENAV, INTERNATIONAL ASPECT OF CIVIL STRIFE 185, 198-99 (1964).

The U.S. governmental positions of the past year have attempted to brand everyone connected with al Qaeda an "unlawful enemy combatant." The potency of this term, if successful, would be enormous. It is the same as branding someone a spy or war criminal. This term places the accused squarely within the operation of military law.[112] It further triggers application of the law of war and all its defined criminal behavior, such as targeting civilian populations. It does not, however, eliminate the need to adjudicate whether the accused has in fact violated the law of war. There is nothing in this line of thought that justifies treating the whole earth as if it were a battlefield.

With the terminology more firmly in mind, let us return to the question of using military commissions in civilian territory during wartime. The concurring opinion in *Milligan* is sometimes dubbed a dissent because Chase disagreed vigorously with the constitutional analyis of the majority. The majority had said that Congress could not authorize military commissions and the suspension of habeas corpus in areas that were out of the theater of operations and in which the civilian courts were open and operating. Chase, on the other hand, argued that Congress could have done so but had affirmatively chosen not to allow those actions during the Civil War.[113] The Government now argues that *Quirin* chose the Chase formulation and that Congress has provided the necessary authorization.

Chase's opinion, however, deals with declaration of "martial law," not just with the use of military commissions when martial law has not been declared. In the absence of application of military law generally to a region, then there is no place for the use of military commissions absent military action of the type portrayed in *Quirin*. Colonel Morgan makes this point vigorously and even Colonel-Professor Winthrop may be read as having the concept of martial law in mind as a precursor to exercise of the power claimed for Congress. Certainly, even Winthrop would agree that Congress would have to declare a national emergency or be unable to act.

As a matter of pure logic, Professor Paust must have the better of the argument: that the use of military commissions is limited to the theater of operations. The government's argument that the President can apply military law and procedures to anyone who engages in "armed attack" upon the United States would have no limits. Anyone who attacks a U.S. governmental, military, or even civilian target could be branded an enemy combatant under this view of plenary military authority.

---

[112] As a matter of internal direction to the Executive Branch, the Military Order takes away the option of referring a case to the civilian courts by saying that a person subject to the order "shall be tried only" by military commissions. But the order is triggered only by a presidential finding that it is applicable to a particular person, so the option of not certifying a person for that treatment remains available.

[113] *Milligan*, 71 U.S. at 139.

[C] Application of Military Law to Alleged Terrorists

Having cast at least some doubt on the "jurisdiction" of military tribunals, we should explore the question of what law applies. Because picking the tribunal depends in part on what law applies, we need to know the sources of law that can be applied to terrorists.

Some of the Guantánamo detainees may have been members of al Qaeda or related terrorist organizations. Some may have been more or less directly implicated in specific terrorist actions. Because the language of war was used from the beginning with respect to these detainees, a widespread perception has been created that the alleged terrorist is to be dealt with in military fashion. There may even be a perception in existence that there is no criminal law to deal with the alleged wrongs of some of these people. In fact, there is a substantial body of law that applies to both citizen and noncitizen alike, to offenses committed on U.S. soil and to those committed abroad. So before we turn to the military commission, it would be profitable first to outline the law that could be applied to an alleged terrorist in the civilian courts.

[1] Citizen-Noncitizen Distinctions

For some reason, the Bush administration chose to draw a distinction between citizens and noncitizens in the Military Order authorizing the trial of al Qaeda members by military commissions.[114] The same distinction also has been drawn as a practical matter in dealing with the detainees because the only two known U.S. citizens originally confined in Cuba were transferred to Virginia, one to be tried in the civilian courts[115] and one to be detained in military isolation.[116]

Citizenship does matter in this context in one important regard. The citizen has a constitutionally protected right to enter the United States at any time,[117] whereas the noncitizen has rights of entry only so far as granted by Congress.[118] It may have been a violation of citizenship rights to have continued confinement of citizens in Cuba, whereas the noncitizens have no more right to be brought to the United States than to be taken anywhere else. Their confinement is purely a matter of international law except to the extent that there is a question of Presidential emergency power to hold people in confinement temporarily. When we look at that question below, there may well be a distinction to be drawn between citizens and noncitizens on that issue as well.

---

[114] Professor Cole sees this distinction as part of a broad attempt to isolate noncitizens for unusually harsh treatment reminiscent of Japanese internment. *See generally* David Cole, *Enemy Aliens*, 54 STAN. L. REV. 953 (2002).

[115] *See* Plea Agreement, United States v. John Walker Lindh (ED Va. July 25, 2002), *available at* news.findlaw.com/hdocs/docs/lindh/uslindh71502pleaag.pdf (last visited 1/26/03).

[116] *See* Hamdi v. Rumsfeld, 316 F.3d 450 (4th Cir. 2003).

[117] *See* Afroyim v. Rusk, 387 U.S. 253 (1967); Kennedy v. Mendoza-Martinez, 372 U.S. 144 (1963).

[118] Chae Chin Ping v. United States (Chinese Exclusion Case), 130 U.S. 581 (1889).

Oddly, the citizen-noncitizen distinction has worked the reverse with regard to persons arrested on U.S. soil. Padilla, a citizen, was sent to military custody[119] while a number of noncitizens arrested on charges of supporting terrorist activity have been prosecuted in civilian courts.[120] Again, the citizen-noncitizen distinction has no function in the context of which court system will take jurisdiction over the offender, and we are met with another example of incoherence in government responses to the terrorism phenomenon.

[2] Acts Committed Outside U.S. Territory

It might be thought that there would be a difference between criminal acts committed on U.S. soil and those committed abroad. This distinction is material only in a very limited class of cases. The U.S., like most nations, claims extra-territorial jurisdiction to apply its law and procedures in roughly five classes of cases:[121]

1. external incidents with effects in U.S. territory

2. a victim that is a U.S. national

3. a perpetrator that is a U.S. national

4. impacts on interests of the U.S.

5. "universal" jurisdiction

Unfortunately, the categories are spelled out this cleanly neither in U.S. statutes nor even in the Restatement of Foreign Relations.[122] The statute defining "special maritime and territorial jurisdiction" of the U.S.,[123] contains a long list of provisions that have accumulated over the years and includes several examples of the first four categories by referring to crimes committed by or against U.S. nationals under certain circumstances, by detailing offenses committed on the high seas on or against certain vehicles, and by referring to categories of U.S. possessions. In some instances, the statute limits application of U.S. law in extraterritorial settings "to the extent permitted by international law." This is a reference to an inherent limitation that no application of one nation's law is to interfere with the sovereignty of another nation.[124]

---

[119] See Padilla v. Bush, 233 F. Supp. 2d 564 (S.D.N.Y. 2002).

[120] See §§ 3.02 & 4.01 supra.

[121] United States v. Layton, 509 F. Supp. 212 (N.D. Cal. 1981); see also United States v. Yunis, 924 F.2d 1086 (D.C. Cir. 1991); United States v. Yousef, 927 F. Supp. 673 (S.D.N.Y. 1996).

[122] Restatement (third) Foreign Relations §§ 402-404 (1987).

[123] 18 USC § 7 (2000).

[124] See Restatement supra note 122. The Restatement expresses this principle by insisting that every application of national law be tested against the question of whether "exercise of such jurisdiction is unreasonable" with a list of factors to be considered. This formulation may work well in application of civil law but it is rather loose and vague for application of criminal penalties. Due process may well require more specificity, subject to prosecutorial discretion if a particular prosecution would offend the interests of another nation.

The federal statute detailing "acts of terrorism transcending national boundaries"[125] likewise relies on several aspects of U.S. interests, such as "interstate or foreign commerce," U.S. officials, U.S. property, along with anything with the "special maritime and territorial jurisdiction." For most crimes of terrorism there will be some offense under U.S. law that can be charged whenever the terrorism touches our shores or our overseas interests.

The fifth category, "universal jurisdiction," refers to the power of any nation to punish offenses that transgress against the universal law of nations. The Restatement describes this as the authority to "define and prescribe punishment for certain offenses recognized by the community of nations as of universal concern, such as piracy, slave trade, attacks on or hijacking of aircraft, genocide, war crimes and *perhaps certain acts of terrorism.*"[126]

Universal jurisdiction has been used as the basis for creation of international tribunals to deal with war crimes in situations when the persons or state most affected were not viewed by the international community as being up to the task, such as tribunals created for Rwanda and Yugoslavia. Virtually the only nation that has avowedly used "universal jurisdiction" as a heading for its own criminal prosecutions is Israel's use of the concept to try Nazi leaders for offenses that occurred on other territory before the State of Israel existed. Historically, universal jurisdiction could also have been part of the justification for "police actions" against pirates and slave traders. The Restatement contemplates this prospect by allowing a nation to "punish noncompliance . . . by police or other nonjudicial action."[127]

It may be noteworthy that the U.S. has not made a general claim of universal jurisdiction regarding any offenses. Given the expansive reading that can be given to U.S. interests in such matters as "foreign commerce," however, particularly in the globalized economy, the issue of universal jurisdiction may be of little consequence other than as it affects the use of military commissions for prosecution of a crime "against the law of nations."

Another important question is whether U.S. intrusion into another nation's territory to apprehend or "punish" an offender is justified under international law, which could be incorporated into domestic law. Extradition from another country is subject to whatever treaty arrangements exist between the two countries. In most instances, good politics more than law will dictate the wisdom of having either the consent of that nation or an international sanction, such as U.N. resolution, in place before any such enforcement action occurs.[128] The propriety of using military force to

---

[125] 18 U.S.C. § 2332b (1996).

[126] *See* RESTATEMENT *supra* note 122 at § 404 (emphasis added).

[127] *Id.* at § 401.

[128] The Supreme Court has upheld the "kidnapping" of criminal defendants from other countries for trial in the U.S., at least so long as existing treaties do not prohibit that action. *See* United States v. Alvarez-Machain, 504 U.S. 655 (1992). *See also* United States v. Noriega, 117 F.3d 1206 (11th Cir. 1997).

capture or kill a suspected terrorist in another country is beyond the scope of this book.

The Department of Justice Task Force on Terrorism has an informal list of 148 federal statutes that can be considered when deciding what criminal offenses to charge in a terrorism case. In addition, federal law defines a "federal crime of terrorism" as violation of any of 39 statutes when the "offense is calculated to influence or affect the conduct of government by intimidation or coercion, or to retaliate against government conduct."[129] There are also federal statutes defining offenses of providing financing for terrorism, providing material support for terrorists,[130] and providing material support for terrorist organizations.[131] The implications of these statutes are also beyond the scope of this book.

[3] Sabotage and Spying

The *Quirin* opinion relied on historical antecedents stemming from the exigencies of war-time conditions (essentially battlefield trials of alleged spies) and from a quid-pro-quo comparison of alleged saboteurs to U.S. soldiers. We should attempt to determine whether these or similar considerations apply to alleged members of terrorist organizations and also whether international law has criminalized terrorist behavior in such fashion as to indicate what sort of tribunal should conduct the trials.

The historic examples that the Supreme Court used in *Quirin* had the distinguishing characteristic of having occurred mostly under battlefield conditions. The Court cited 11 cases of persons convicted as spies by courts-martial and executed during the Revolutionary War. These proceedings were conducted under the authority of a Resolution of the Continental Congress, which was later converted to statutory form. The original resolution and statute applied to "alien spies." The Court also mentions seven cases in which there may not have even been a court martial but just summary execution by authority of the field commander.

Three persons were tried by courts-martial for spying during the War of 1812, one was hanged, one acquitted, and the third was convicted but then "released by President Madison on the ground that he was an American citizen."[132]

The statute was amended in 1862 to apply not just to aliens but to any person on the ground that almost all combatants in the Civil War (and those civilians likely to aid them) were actually U.S. citizens, and it would not make sense to subject an Englishman to military justice but not the South

---

[129] 18 U.S.C. § 2332b(g) (2006).

[130] 18 U.S.C. § 1332A. This statute depends on knowledge that funds, shelter, or goods may be used "in preparation for, or in carrying out, a violation of" specified federal crimes of terrorism.

[131] 18 U.S.C. § 1332B. This statute depends on designation of a particular organization by the Secretary of State.

[132] *Quirin*, 317 U.S. at 17, n.14.

Carolinian who was doing the same thing to the forces of the Union.[133] In other words, the enemies were citizens and the circumstances were indisputably war.

A potentially significant issue arose a year later when the 1863 Conscription Act expanded the areas to which this provision would extend. From 1775 to 1863, the scope of military jurisdiction extended to those "lurking as spies in or about the fortifications or encampments of the armies of the United States." The 1863 Act extended to "in or about any of the fortifications, posts, quarters, or encampments of any of the Armies of the United States, or elsewhere." A motion to strike the phrase "or elsewhere" failed and the language has remained since.[134]

One other change from the original versions of the spy provision was made during codification in 1912 when the phrase "shall be triable" was converted without explanation to "shall be tried." Colonel-Professor Morgan notes that the change was not even disclosed to Congress when voting on the codification and that it could remove discretion from the executive branch to take either the military course or the civilian course of trial for treason.[135]

[a] Citizen Spies and Alien Spies

Colonel-Professor Morgan argues forcefully that it is within Congress' power to subject a citizen spy to the same military authority as the alien spy. Congress has the power to raise an army, to define offenses against the law of nations, and to make rules and regulations for the governance of the military. So far as jury trial is concerned, there is pre-Constitution precedent for treating the offense of spying as "arising within the land and naval forces" so as to be exempted by the Sixth Amendment.

Morgan believed that the more important issue was the breadth of the power to subject a citizen to court-martial, the issue raised in the addition of the phrase "or elsewhere" in 1863. He was writing in 1920 with reference to the conditions of WWI and noted that much of the nation was mobilized for the war effort by making and supplying everything from munitions to food and clothing, while also keeping open channels of communication and transportation on which the military would rely along with the rest of the country. "Under such circumstances, the zone of operations in truth and in fact comprehends the entire country."

The "zone of operations" was an attempt to distinguish the act of spying from that of tourism. What is it that makes gathering information punishable by death? In the 18th and 19th Centuries, military encampments and posts were easily identifiable and there was little motivation to gather information about those encampments other than for nefarious reasons.

---

[133] Edmund Morgan, *Court-Martial Jurisdiction over Non-Military Persons Under the Articles of War*, 4 MINN. L. REV. 79, 109 (1920).

[134] *Id.* at 111.

[135] *Id.* at n.112.

Conversely, there was little motivation for anyone to attack anything else and so no proscription on gathering information about civilian establishments. In the context of WWI, when Morgan was writing, and even more so during WWII, when the entire industrial complex was mobilized for support of the war effort, the zone of operations could have been significantly blurred.

Colonel Morgan, however, remained unconvinced. He asserted that the citizen spy is engaged in treason, which must be tried in the civilian courts with a jury, unless "in the theatre of operations or any other area subject to the actual control and dominion of the military." Only in this way can the act be deemed to "arise in the land or naval forces." He conceded that modern conditions of armaments and supply were moving toward a day when the "zone of operations [could] include the entire area of a belligerent country." Referring to *Milligan*, however, he believed that the term should be limited to the "theatre of actual hostilities, the lines of communication, and the reserves and service of supply under actual military control, and that it cannot properly be enlarged to cover the farms, factories and workshops under exclusively civilian control."[136]

The counter position to Colonel-Professor Morgan was the opinion of Colonel-Professor Wambaugh, who wrote as Judge Advocate General that the civilian spy was punishable by death as a threat to military operations.[137] In fact, Colonel-Professor Wambaugh asserted that a spy is not a criminal unless a citizen. The alien spy, he claimed, might actually be engaged in a brave and honorable act but is still shot because of the threat to the military, just as a soldier in uniform would be shot without the luxury even of court martial trial. To Wambaugh, the concept of a treasonous crime which could also be the subject of a court martial noncrime was not disturbing. To Morgan, however, the crime of treason was so heavily protected by constitutional prescriptions of trial by jury and evidence, that only an act within the immediate vicinity of military control could justify abandoning those prescriptions.

The debate between Colonel-Professors Morgan and Wambaugh is instructive for the proposition that almost a century ago experts were already beginning to realize that time of war could involve most of a belligerent country. But even then, at least some voices were heard to argue for recourse to the civilian courts. The reasons advanced had to do with constitutional guarantees. The heart of the matter seems to have been that there are such significant constitutional guarantees surrounding the crime of "treason" that it would be foolhardy to bypass those guarantees by remitting the accused to military power.

In addition to constitutional guarantees, I would add the thought that it is critically important to the national psyche today to see our civilian processes as up to the task of defending our freedoms — both physical

---

[136] *Id.* at 116.

[137] The Wambaugh discussion is from a governmental memorandum as quoted by Morgan, *id.* at 113.

freedom and legal civil liberties. If the terrorist can change our ways of life, then we have lost. Moreover, the offense of spying exists under military law only in time of war. Information gathering for the purpose of destroying a building or taking life during peacetime may be an act in furtherance of a conspiracy to commit murder or other crimes, but it is not spying. Here is a clear example of the importance of deciding what it means to be at war or whether there is some other status between war and peace.

[b] Citizen Saboteurs and Suppliers of the Enemy

The prior section dealt with the phenomenon of spying, which essentially consists of gathering information. Curiously enough, it was the basis for the Court's decision in *Quirin* with regard to planned sabotage. The person who already has information on where to plant a bomb and is captured with explosives in hand may not be a spy. He may be bent on murder or destruction of property, but the principal reason that the language of spying has been borrowed is that he is moving clandestinely and out of uniform toward his target. That may make him an unlawful combatant under the international law of war, but there is a provision in the UCMJ that also should be considered.

Article 106 declares that "any person who aids . . . the enemy with arms, ammunition, supplies, money, or other things . . . shall suffer death or such other punishment as a court martial or military commission may direct."[138] If we carried the Wambaugh theory to this provision, then supplying of money to "charities" that aid a terrorist organization could subject an individual to trial by military commission.

We are not entirely without precedent for construction of this provision. In several cases in the post-Civil War era involving persons who were trading with Indian tribes, it became apparent that the principal difficulty would be in determining when a "state of war" existed with a particular tribe or band. The Attorney General declared that this section could be triggered when there were armed conflicts occurring between those tribes and U.S. military forces.[139] It might be tempting to assert that a state of hostility between the U.S. and a group of people such as al Qaeda is similar to the conditions of hostility with some Indian tribes in the late 19th Century. The analogy fails, however, on a couple of fronts. First, a particular Indian tribe would be defined by a common ethnic and cultural heritage that is vastly more homogeneous than what is likely to exist with most terrorist groups.[140] Secondly, although Indian tribes did not attempt to stake out very precise borders of their territory, they clearly had claims

---

[138] 10 U.S.C. § 906 (2006).

[139] Unlawful Traffic with Indians, 13 Op. Atty. Gen. 470 (1871); *see* WILLIAM WINTHROP, MILITARY LAW AND PRECEDENTS 86, 101, 103 (reprint 1920).

[140] Although many terrorist groups share common ethnic, religious, and cultural bonds, any particular group may also recruit from outside these bonds. Al Qaeda appears to have been extremely successful in recruiting from a number of cultures. *See* JOHN COOLEY, UNHOLY WARS 66-85 (3d ed. 2002).

of right to areas that constituted their homelands. Thirdly, a point that is of much greater significance than might be imagined, the Indian tribes can be considered similar to nation-states for the simple reason that the European settlers regarded them as at least resembling nations for purposes of international dealings, for example in treaty negotiations and cession of territory.[141]

[c] Treason and its Derivatives

The law of treason has not been widely studied in a very long time, but it may offer us some interesting insights. The Framers were so concerned about the potential misuses of treason charges that this is the only "crime" which is given special treatment in the Constitution.[142] The Treason Clause builds extremely high barricades against prosecution for this "heinous" crime, so the question becomes whether those barricades can be circumvented by creating other crimes, or by calling the traitor something else such as an "enemy combatant." To be grossly flippant, could we avoid restrictions on prosecution for treason by calling it jaywalking? and the answer turns out to be yes, we can! But there is nothing to indicate that we can avoid conducting public trials for jaywalking.

Article III's "peculiar phraseology observable in the definition of" treason, and "the equally stringent feature" requiring two eyewitness' testimony of the same overt act, have been said to flow from the Framers' discomfort with "abuses . . . under the tyrannical reigns of the Tudors and the Stuarts."[143] In particular, the Framers were reacting to the concept of "constructive treason" by which anyone who spoke in support of, or was friendly with those who expressed, resistance to policies of the Crown could be accused of treason. Indeed, it is not likely that even the Tudors and Stuarts would have had an easy time of tossing a citizen into jail indefinitely on the mere say-so of a military officer. That they did so on occasion led directly to our constitutional language preventing the possibility.

Is it possible to square this history with the "enemy combatant" concept employed by the Supreme Court in *Quirin* and leading to the Bush Military Order? The answer is "not very easily," and the lessons to be learned are not very clear. The Treason Clause creates two categories of treason: levying war against the United States, and providing aid and comfort to the enemy. In the first there must be an armed assemblage and the second requires an enemy.

---

[141] *See* United States v. Sioux Nation, 448 U.S. 371 (1980); Johnson v. M'Intosh, 21 U.S. (8 Wheat.) 543 (1823).

[142] U.S. CONST. art. 3, § 3:

Treason against the United States, shall consist only in levying War against them, or in adhering to their Enemies, giving them Aid and Comfort. No Person shall be convicted of Treason unless on the Testimony of two Witnesses to the same overt Act, or on Confession in open Court.

[143] *In re* Charge to Grand Jury, 30 F. Cas. 1034, 1035 (C.C.N.Y. 1861) (No. 18, 271).

Chief Justice Marshall gave us our first instruction in the operation of the Treason Clause in *Ex parte Bollman*,[144] dealing with some of the alleged conspirators in the Burr escapade. Some of his discussion is so pertinent that it is set out at length below.[145] Marshall distinguished strongly between treason and conspiracy: "However flagitious may be the crime of conspiring to subvert by force the government of our country, such

---

[144] 8 U.S. (4 Cranch) 75 (1807).

[145] *Id.* at 126-27:

> To constitute that specific crime for which the prisoners now before the court have been committed, war must be actually levied against the United States. However flagitious may be the crime of conspiring to subvert by force the government of our country, such conspiracy is not treason. To conspire to levy war, and actually to levy war, are distinct offences. The first must be brought into operation by the assemblage of men for a purpose treasonable in itself, or the fact of levying war cannot have been committed. So far has this principle been carried, that, in a case reported by Ventris, and mentioned in some modern treatises on criminal law, it has been determined that the actual enlistment of men to serve against the government does not amount to levying war. It is true that in that case the soldiers enlisted were to serve without the realm, but they were enlisted within it, and if the enlistment for a treasonable purpose could amount to levying war, then war had been actually levied.
>
> It is not the intention of the court to say that no individual can be guilty of this crime who has not appeared in arms against his country. On the contrary, if war be actually levied, that is, if a body of men be actually assembled for the purpose of effecting by force a treasonable purpose, all those who perform any part, however minute, or however remote from the scene of action, and who are actually leagued in the general conspiracy, are to be considered as traitors. But there must be an actual assembling of men for the treasonable purpose, to constitute a levying of war.
>
> Crimes so atrocious as those which have for their object the subversion by violence of those laws and those institutions which have been ordained in order to secure the peace and happiness of society, are not to escape punishment because they have not ripened into treason. The wisdom of the legislature is competent to provide for the case; and the framers of our constitution, who not only defined and limited the crime, but with jealous circumspection attempted to protect their limitation by providing that no person should be convicted of it, unless on the testimony of two witnesses to the same overt act, or on confession in open court, must have conceived it more safe that punishment in such cases should be ordained by general laws, formed upon deliberation, under the influence of no resentments, and without knowing on whom they were to operate, than that it should be inflicted under the influence of those passions which the occasion seldom fails to excite, and which a flexible definition of the crime, or a construction which would render it flexible, might bring into operation. It is therefore more safe as well as more consonant to the principles of our constitution, that the crime of treason should not be extended by construction to doubtful cases; and that crimes not clearly within the constitutional definition, should receive such punishment as the legislature in its wisdom may provide.
>
> To complete the crime of levying war against the United States, there must be an actual assemblage of men for the purpose of executing a treasonable design. In the case now before the court, a design to overturn the government of the United States in New Orleans by force, would have been unquestionably a design which, if carried into execution, would have been treason, and the assemblage of a body of men for the purpose of carrying it into execution would amount to levying of war against the United States; but no conspiracy for this object, no enlisting of men to effect it, would be an actual levying of war.

conspiracy is not treason." It must be remembered, however, that the Burr escapade did not involve a foreign enemy, so there was no occasion for him to deal with the offense of providing aid and comfort to the enemy.

Marshall went on to deal with our very question. Although "to complete the crime of levying war against the United States, there must be an actual assemblage of men for the purpose of executing a treasonable design," he expressed the view that the legislature could define other offenses to which the strictures of the Treason Clause would not apply. The Framers were concerned about the passions that the thought of treason would engender, but they could have been comfortable with the thought that "crimes not clearly within the constitutional definition, should receive such punishment as the legislature in its wisdom may provide."

In a number of cases stemming from the Civil War, the judges expanded Marshall's view of conspiracy to state that there could be no such concept as an accessory to treason because an act was either treason or not.[146] They consistently recognized the differences between the two kinds of treason, the first depending on whether the defendant has taken up arms,[147] the second consisting of providing material support to a recognized enemy. It is familiar ground that President Lincoln attempted to use the military courts for prosecution of Southern sympathizers, leading eventually to the opinion in *Milligan*. For the remainder of the story, we become embroiled in the tripartite struggle for power among the President (Andrew Johnson), the Court (Taney, then Chase), and Congress (Radical Republican by 1865). In *Thorington v. Smith*,[148] the Court dealt with the question of whether debts payable in Confederate currency were still valid as between two individuals (and, thus, payable in U.S. currency after the war ended). Chief Justice Chase distinguished among different levels of *de facto* governments. At one extreme would be a solidly established actual government such that "adherents to it in war against the government *de jure* do not incur the penalties of treason." The government of the Confederacy, he said, was sufficiently established that it obtained "actual supremacy, however unlawfully gained, in all matters of government within its military lines."

> That supremacy did not justify acts of hostility to the United States. How far it should excuse them must be left to the lawful government upon the re-establishment of its authority. But it made obedience to its authority, in civil and local matters, not only a necessity but a duty. Without such obedience, civil order was impossible.[149]

By this language, Chase was implying that there could be no prosecution for providing aid and comfort to the enemy by a person residing within the military control of the Confederacy. As we know, there were no such prosecutions. Moreover, when Congress attempted to punish former active

---

[146] United States v. Greathouse, 26 F. Cas. 18 (C.C.N.D. Cal. 1863) (No. 15,254).

[147] *Id.*; *see* Charges to Grand Juries *collected at* 30 F. Cas. Nos. 18,270-273 (1863).

[148] 75 U.S. (8 Wall.) 1 (1869).

[149] *Id.* at 11.

rebels by forfeiture of their property, the President decreed that a Presidential pardon worked to prevent forfeiture and the Court sided with the President. [150] There is little more that we can make of the Civil War experience with regard to the ability of Congress to decree punishment for the sympathizers and supporters of foreign enemies, so we now fast-forward to World War I.

The seminal case in First Amendment law is *Schenck v. United States*. [151] Schenck and his cohorts were convicted of conspiracy to violate the Espionage Act of 1917, which made it unlawful to "cause insubordination . . . in the military and naval forces of the United States, and to obstruct the recruiting and enlistment service of the United States." Justice Holmes' famous opinion for the Court, after using the analogy of "falsely shouting fire in a crowded theater," stated:

> The question in every case is whether the words used are used in such circumstances and are of such a nature as to create a clear and present danger that they will bring about the substantive evils that Congress has a right to prevent. It is a question of proximity and degree. When a nation is at war many things that might be said in time of peace are such a hindrance to its effort that their utterance will not be endured so long as men fight and that no Court could regard them as protected by any constitutional right. It seems to be admitted that if an actual obstruction of the recruiting service were proved, liability for words that produced that effect might be enforced. The statute of 1917 in § 4 punishes conspiracies to obstruct as well as actual obstruction. If the act (speaking, or circulating a paper), its tendency and the intent with which it is done are the same, we perceive no ground for saying that success alone warrants making the act a crime.

Before *Schenck* was decided, Congress had already responded to the emerging level of dissension regarding U.S. entry into the war in Europe by passing the 1918 amendments to the Espionage Act. Under the amendments, it was unlawful to "urge, incite, or advocate" actions that could disrupt the war effort. [152] The majority of the Court found that an intent

---

[150] United States v. Klein, 80 U.S. (13 Wall.) 128 (1872).

[151] 249 U.S. 47 (1919).

[152] *Id.* at 48-49:

> Each of the first three counts charged the defendants with conspiring, when the United States was at war with the Imperial Government of Germany, to unlawfully utter, print, write and publish: In the first count, "disloyal, scurrilous and abusive language about the form of Government of the United States;" in the second count, language "intended to bring the form of Government of the United States into contempt, scorn, contumely and disrepute;" and in the third count, language "intended to incite, provoke and encourage resistance to the United States in said war." The charge in the fourth count was that the defendants conspired "when the United States was at war with the Imperial German Government, . . . unlawfully and wilfully, by utterance, writing, printing and publication, to urge, incite and advocate curtailment of production of things and products, to wit, ordnance and ammunition, necessary and essential to the prosecution of the war." The offenses were charged in the language of the act of Congress.

to disrupt the war effort was sufficient to uphold conviction under the statute. Justice Holmes, joined by Brandeis, dissented with the famous "marketplace of ideas" analysis. The combination of opinions sounds as if the majority were treating the statute as if it were a finding by Congress of "clear and present danger." The interesting point for our purposes is that nobody questioned whether Congress could define crimes that came very close to "providing aid and comfort to the enemy" without requiring two witnesses to the same overt act. It seems that in this stage, Congress and the Court had accepted Chief Justice Marshall's invitation to Congress to define non-treason offenses.

The only World War II case in the Supreme Court on the subject of treason was *Cramer v. United States*,[153] a follow-up to *Quirin*. One of the eight German saboteurs, Thiel, had a friend in the U.S. named Cramer, who was German by birth and a naturalized U.S. citizen. Thiel contacted Cramer in New York, met with him twice in public places, and gave Cramer some money to hold for him. Cramer testified that he suspected Thiel was here as a propagandist for the German government, but there was no evidence that Cramer suspected anything of the violent intentions of the saboteurs. Cramer was convicted of treason.[154] The basic question presented to the Supreme Court was whether an overt act in furtherance of treason needed to be done with intent by the defendant of furthering enemy action against the government, or whether an innocent overt act could be treasonous because of its role in the enemy's plan.

Justice Jackson's majority opinion in *Cramer* has received surprisingly little attention.[155] He canvassed the history of treason prosecutions from English law through the colonial era, pointing out that much of the turbulence of those periods could lead to a citizen's being caught between competing loyalties and this subject to treason from two different sides. The Framers built protections against treason prosecutions to guard against two dangers: "(1) perversion by established authority to repress peaceful political opposition; and (2) conviction of the innocent as a result of perjury, passion or inadequate evidence."[156] The critical passage for definition of criminal behavior is this:

> Thus the crime of treason consists of two elements: adherence to the enemy; and rendering him aid and comfort. A citizen intellectually or emotionally may favor the enemy and harbor sympathies

---

[153] 325 U.S. 1 (1945).

[154] Former 18 U.S.C. § 1 is now codified as 18 U.S.C. § 2381 (2007):

> Whoever, owing allegiance to the United States, levies war against them or adheres to their enemies, giving them aid and comfort within the United States or elsewhere, is guilty of treason and shall suffer death, or shall be imprisoned not less than five years and fined under this title but not less than $10,000; and shall be incapable of holding any office under the United States.

[155] Shepard's lists only 20 judicial "analyses" of the opinion and only 115 "citing decisions" in the 58 years since it was issued.

[156] *Cramer*, 325 U.S. at 27.

or convictions disloyal to this country's policy or interest, but so long as he commits no act of aid and comfort to the enemy, there is no treason. On the other hand, a citizen may take actions which do aid and comfort the enemy — making a speech critical of the government or opposing its measures, profiteering, striking in defense plants or essential work, and the hundred other things which impair our cohesion and diminish our strength — but if there is no adherence to the enemy in this, if there is no intent to betray, there is no treason.[157]

Applying these thoughts to the evidence, Jackson pointed out that the prosecution had "withdrawn" the safekeeping of money as an overt act to be submitted to the jury.[158] That left only the two meetings with Thiel that were corroborated by eyewitness testimony. These could not be said to have shown either furtherance of a scheme sufficient to prove either aid or adherence to the enemy. By contrast, the money transaction, if proved by the requisite testimony, would have made "a quite different case."[159] Finally, Justice Jackson addressed the Government's arguments for relaxing the standards related to treason:

> The Government has urged that our initial interpretation of the treason clause should be less exacting, lest treason be too hard to prove and the Government disabled from adequately combating the techniques of modern warfare. But the treason offense is not the only nor can it well serve as the principal legal weapon to vindicate our national cohesion and security. In debating this provision, Rufus King observed to the Convention that the "controversy relating to Treason might be of less magnitude than was supposed; as the legislature might punish capitally under other names than Treason." His statement holds good today. Of course we do not intimate that Congress could dispense with the two-witness rule merely by giving the same offense another name. But the power of Congress is in no way limited to enact prohibitions of specified acts thought detrimental to our wartime safety.[160]

Congress, with the assistance of many subsequent administrations, has accepted this invitation by enacting many statutes that relate to providing aid and comfort to those who threaten the public safety of the United States. Perhaps the most directly relevant are those that criminalize "Providing Material Support to Terrorists"[161] and "Providing Material Support or

---

[157] *Id.* at 29.

[158] We can speculate that there were neither two eyewitnesses to this act nor a "confession in open court." Cramer's testimony described the money transaction while denying that he knew the purpose of the money or the purpose of Thiel's presence in the US. *Id.* at 5.

[159] *Id.* at 39.

[160] *Id.* at 45.

[161] 18 U.S.C. § 2339A ("knowing or intending that they are to be used in preparation for, or in carrying out, a violation of [specified federal crimes], or in preparation for, or in carrying out, the concealment or an escape from the commission of any such violation").

Resources to Designated Terrorist Organizations."[162] There are also crimes, such as what John Walker Lindh pleaded guilty to, defined as violations of Presidential directives blocking trading with, or providing services to, regimes designated in time of national emergency.[163] Given the history of the Treason Clause, and particularly Justices Marshall's and Jackson's invitations to Congress, there can be little doubt about the validity of these statutes, except insofar as they might in some situations be subject to First Amendment restrictions.

But does the ability of Congress to define crimes other than treason extend to the ability of the military to imprison either with or without trial? There is no hint in any of this that the normal processes of the civilian justice system should not apply to crimes undermining the public safety just because there are foreign connections to the crime.

[D] Terrorists as Unlawful Combatants

There will likely be disputes for some time over the degree to which the international law of war is incorporated into the domestic law of the U.S.[164] To grapple with that requires considering what the international law of warfare has to say about persons who attempt to inflict destruction on a particular nation and its inhabitants. Much of the discussion of spies and comforters of the enemy draws on the law of war as justification for treating these as military matters rather than crimes of treason or other civilly defined offenses.

Colonel Winthrop begins from the proposition that the law of war is limited to the "theatre of operations" and sets out a frame of reference for the citizens of belligerent states.[165] "[U]pon the declaration or initiation of war," he says, "not only the opposed military forces but all the inhabitants of the belligerent nations . . . become . . . the enemies both of the adverse governments and of each other."

Civilian enemies, however, are not necessarily combatants. The civilian is disempowered from trading with civilian enemies and is at risk of having his property destroyed or seized if it is useful to the enemy, but a noncombatant is not to be subjected to personal violence. Among the few reasonably consistent edicts of warfare throughout recorded history are the rules protecting noncombatants. In modern times, those rules have extended to those engaged in medical or spiritual support of combatants. It is a clear violation of the law of war to target noncombatants, although obviously civilian casualties have been heavy in some instances of bombing. The

---

[162] 18 U.S.C. § 2339B ("knowingly provides material support or resources to a foreign terrorist organization, or attempts or conspires to do so").

[163] 50 U.S.C. § 1705(b) makes it a crime to violate a presidential directive of this nature. The designation of the Taliban regime as off-limits to American citizens was effective Jan. 1, 2001 under 31 C.F.R. § 545.204.

[164] See § 9.04[B] & [C] infra.

[165] WILLIAM WINTHROP, MILITARY LAW AND PRECEDENTS 776 (reprint 1920).

justification advanced by the U.S. for civilian casualties of bombing is that it is the other side's choice of where to place military industrial targets and that if we target those structures, then the "collateral damage" to civilian populations is not our fault.

The principal gray area for noncombatants is in the category of "camp followers" or "retainers." Civilian employees of the military are subject to capture just as if they were prisoners of war and are to be treated as such, but they are not to be subjected to violence so long as they do not threaten violence themselves. Winthrop states that "[c]amp followers, although they may be made prisoners, are to be treated as noncombatants."

Winthrop deals rather cursorily with the question of "THE FORCES BY WHICH WAR IS TO BE WAGED" and states "the general rule that the operations of war on land can legally be carried on only through the recognized armies or soldiery of the State as duly enlisted or employed in its service." He has a special place for "irregulars" or "guerillas." "Irregular armed bodies or persons not forming part of the organized forces of a belligerent, or operating under the orders of its established commanders, are not in general recognized as legitimate troops or entitled, when taken, to be treated as prisoners of war but may upon capture be summarily punished even with death."[166] This is a surprisingly harsh statement in a text generally attempting to place more civilized and humane boundaries on the conduct of warfare, and the explanation can be found in the image that he portrays of marauding bands inside the enemy's borders "killing, disabling and robbing of peaceable citizens or soldiers . . . from motives mostly of personal profit or revenge."[167] The picture of undisciplined, nonuniformed persons wreaking havoc upon civilians and blending back into civilian populations is Winthrop's contribution to the earliest depiction of what today we might call a terrorist.

This depiction is significantly different from the image one has of a citizen defending his homeland against an invading force. Would we really expect summary execution of a person captured while shooting back at invaders from inside his home? The 1949 Geneva Convention dealt explicitly with this phenomenon by including within the definition of prisoners of war, and thus protected from summary punishment, both organized militias which "conduct their operations in accordance with the laws and customs of war" and those "inhabitants of a non occupied territory, who on the approach of the enemy spontaneously take up arms to resist the invading force" [emergency defense of home].[168] What evolved between the 19th Century and the end of WWII, it appears, is a sense that the treatment of a person depends more on how that person behaved during warfare than on the official status of the person.

---

[166] *Id.* at 783.

[167] *Id.* at 784.

[168] Geneva Convention Relative to the Treatment of Prisoners of War, art. 4, Oct. 21, 1950, 75 U.N.T.S. 135.

The 1949 Geneva Convention recognizes that rules are one thing and application another by providing that if there is any doubt about whether a person belongs to the protected categories, then "such persons shall enjoy the protection of the present Convention until such time as their status has been determined by a competent tribunal."[169] The companion Convention Relative to the Protection of Civilian Persons provides that there shall be no reprisals and that no "protected person may be punished for an offence he or she has not personally committed."[170]

The upshot of all this is that individuals who are captured in the course of military action in another country must be treated as prisoners of war or civilians unless they were engaged in clandestine use of arms without the excuse of emergency defense of home. According to Winthrop, who probably had a good feel for the "customs and usages" of war, a person clandestinely using arms without the emergency home defense excuse could have been summarily executed upon capture. There can be little doubt that the customs and usages have changed in the past century to the point that no summary executions are allowed under any circumstances. Indeed, the most recent statements on war crimes would make it a crime to "pass sentence or execute anyone who is *hors de combat* without previous judgement by a regularly constituted court."[171]

This is the backdrop against which the Supreme Court worked in *Hamdan*[172] when it held that the military commissions, as they existed prior to the Military Commission Act of 2006, were invalid not just under U.S. law but under international law. The incorporation of international law into domestic law was easy in that case because Congress had authorized commissions to try offenses against the "law of war,"[173] which is treaty and customary international law.[174]

§ 8.05 GLOBAL FEDERALISM, TERRORISM, AND LOAC

Under current federal law, the use of military commissions for trial of alleged terrorists depends on finding that an alleged offense constitutes a violation of the "law of war."[175] More generally, the question of whether

---

[169] *Id.* at art. 5.

[170] Convention Relative to the Protection of Civilian Persons in Time of War, art. 33, Oct. 21, 1950, 75 U.N.T.S. 287.

[171] Rome Statute of the International Criminal Court, § 8(2)(c)(4).

[172] Hamdan v. Rumsfeld, 126 S. Ct. 2749 (2006).

[173] *Id.* at 2794 ("compliance with the law of war is the condition upon which the authority set forth in [the UCMJ] is granted").

[174] *See* § 9.04[B] *infra*.

[175] The Bush Military Order, (66 Fed. Reg. 833 (Nov. 13, 2001)) cites for its statutory authority 10 U.S.C. § 821 (2002), which states that the UCMJ provisions "conferring jurisdiction upon courts-martial do not deprive military commissions, provost courts, or other military tribunals of concurrent jurisdiction with respect to offenders or offenses that *by statute or by the law of war* may be tried by military commissions, provost courts, or other military tribunals." [emphasis added]

to apply military law to terrorism implicates other questions that are important for those who wish to believe that the international arena has developed coherent norms for the conduct of warfare, questions such as with whom are we at war? what are the rules of engagement for a war that is against an ideological group rather than a national group?

It is no accident that the history of the United States is roughly contemporaneous with the development of modern international law, a development that was fueled by the Europeans' Age of Colonialism and its demise.[176] For most of that history, international law has been seen as rules or norms that pertain to relations among nations.[177] Until recently, the world has held to a dichotomous distinction between the processes of warfare and those of the civilian criminal system. War was something that took place between nations, involved an effort to kill or capture enemy combatants, and thus provided no occasion for making considered judgments about the culpability of someone on the other side.[178] By contrast, those who are suspected of committing crimes against the law of a nation were treated as individuals whose culpability must be judged in an individualized proceeding.

The lines between warfare and criminal processes have blurred because of changes in approach both by the enforcers of peace and the perpetrators of violence. The peacemakers have attempted to use processes patterned from criminal law to punish violations of respected rules of warfare,[179] while the perpetrators of violence have acted on their own outside the confines of government and those same rules of warfare. The world's search

---

[176] The rules pertaining to war can be traced almost to prehistory through Leviticus in the Middle East and Sun Tzu in the Far East. St. Augustine amplified on the Hebraic traditions with his concepts of just war, outlining rules both for entry into war and conduct of war. But the modern version, which depends on the concept of nation state, begins with Grotius and the Treaty of Westphalia in 1648. As the European nation states fanned out around the globe in search of adventure and resources, they would bump into each other in primitive locations and needed rules to govern their behavior so as not to alienate other nation states who could cause them difficulties in other locations. Thus the Age of Colonialism fueled the effort to codify the "understandings and practices of civilized nations." A concise summary of this history is contained in LEON FRIEDMAN, THE LAW OF WAR 3-15 (1972).

[177] The exclusive focus on nation-state participation in international law has been modified by the emergence of additional organizations as world players, such as Regional Organizations (*e.g.*, NATO, EU, OAS) and Non-Governmental Organizations (*e.g.*, Amnesty International, International Red Cross). Although these additional actors are participants in the development of international law, there are only a few instances of treaties that specifically recognize their role as legal actors.

[178] The rules of engagement of a particular military action eliminate the soldier's need to inquire into the culpability of someone in uniform carrying arms. But those rules cannot authorize violence against noncombatants. WINTHROP, *supra* note 18, at 778: "The State is represented in active war by its contending army, and the laws of war justify killing or disabling of members of the one army by those of the other in battle or hostile operations."

[179] The trials at Nuremberg were intended to import the processes of law onto the international scene for dealing with war crimes. Prior to that time, "victor's justice" had been meted out at the national level. Gerry J. Simpson, *War Crimes: A Critical Introduction, in* MCCORMACK & SIMPSON, THE LAW OF WAR CRIMES 5 (1997).

for a new paradigm to deal with these phenomena has produced international commissions for prosecution of war crimes[180] and is now engaged in defining responses to terrorism.[181]

The United States and Israel disagreed over whether the Egyptian expatriate who shot three people at the El Al counter in LAX was a terrorist.[182] The nations of the world have been at odds for decades over the definition of terrorist and whether it constitutes a crime under international law.

The familiar theme of "one person's terrorist is another's freedom fighter" has muddled the issue enormously.[183] As numerous authors have pointed out, this is an almost silly argument because universal law criminalizes attacks on civilian populations without regard to the political motivations of the actor.[184] The difficulty is not whether there could be justification for an attack on civilians because legally there cannot be. The difficulty is in determining by what process to respond to such an attack depending on the degree of affiliation by the actor with a nation-state.

What distinguishes the "terrorist" from the ordinary street criminal with ties to an international criminal organization? Take, for instance, a murder committed on the streets of an American city by a drug dealer who knows in some vague way that his livelihood is linked to a well-organized and well-funded cartel in Colombia or Afghanistan. Is this an act of terrorism? Is it an act of war? Is the U.S. justified in invading Colombia because there are organized criminals there who carry out violence on U.S. civilians? This has been the theme of at least two movies,[185] both carrying the message that U.S. involvement in Colombia would be permissible only with the permission of the Colombian government, certainly the correct answer under international law. Meanwhile, international law is creating

---

[180] For a specific discussion of the significance of the Ad Hoc Tribunals for Rwanda & Yugoslavia, see Christopher Blakesley, *Atrocity and its Prosecution*, *in* McCormack & Simpson, The Law of War Crimes 189 (1997).

[181] U.N. Convention of Financing of Terrorism, U.N. Convention on Hostage Taking, U.N. Convention on Air Piracy.

[182] "American and Israeli officials initially appeared to disagree on Thursday about whether Mr. Hadayet's rampage should be called a terrorist attack. But it became clear today that the difference was really over what constitutes terrorism. Yuval Rotem, Israel's consul general in Los Angeles, said that even a lone individual attacking an Israeli target like the El Al ticket counter should be considered a terrorist. But F.B.I. officials said that only if Mr. Hadayet was linked to a terrorist organization would American investigators call it that, rather than a hate crime." N.Y. Times, July 6, 2002, *available at* query.nytimes.com/search/article-printpage.html?res=9800E2DE1E31F935A35754C0A9649C8B63 (last visited July 10, 2007).

[183] The argument alludes to the difficulties of small dissident groups in fighting against repressive regimes and attempts to lend legitimacy to the use of violence by persons who operate clandestinely. The key distinction between freedom fighters and terrorists is the targeting of civilian populations.

[184] Christopher Harmon, Terrorism Today 188-196 (2000). As Harmon also points out, the habit of inflicting violence on civilians is not easy for a group to break and terrorist organizations gaining control of political power often continue their patterns of abuse.

[185] Clear and Present Danger (Paramount Pictures 1994) and Collateral Damage (Warner Bros. 2002).

cooperative efforts to deal with the transborder aspects of large criminal organizations without promoting intrusion into the internal affairs of any one nation.[186]

On the global stage, what distinguishes José Padilla from Terry McVeigh? Assuming the facts as disclosed in press releases about Padilla, both were motivated by extreme hatred for the U.S. government, both were planning mass civilian casualties at governmental centers. Padilla was in league with foreign citizens, but what does this signify? How do we distinguish him from alleged Mafiosi, or drug dealers in league with Colombian cartels?

The difficulty in remitting Padilla, or even Hamdi, to the military is not just that the Supreme Court has expressed distrust of military tribunals, which it certainly has, but also that the law abhors incoherence. If there is no rational distinguishing principle among these examples, and if the choice of military or civilian trial is pure executive whim, then we are left with unbridled executive discretion that is more than just uncomfortable — it at least verges on a level of incoherence that due process itself would prevent.

The post-Civil War federalism experience of the U.S. offers some very sensible guidance at this point. Indeed, for this author, the current situation on a global scale makes the concerns of that era much more readily understandable than they had been to this point. For 150 years, the federal courts have struggled with criminal, civil rights, and conspiracy statutes that make federal jurisdiction over an incident turn on whether the actor acted "under color of state law." In some instances, the KKK or related miscreants were sufficiently aligned with local governmental officials to make this finding, while in others the "private citizen" could escape federal jurisdiction for lack of any connection to a governmental official or agency. Given the power of racial discrimination, particularly in the South through at least the 1960s, it was very difficult for many to understand why the governmental connection needed to be made. Now I for one can see the point.

The Reconstruction statutes created two classes of federal crimes for interference with "any right or privilege secured to him by the Constitution or laws of the United States:" those committed "under color of law"[187] and

---

[186] The United Nations' Office of Drug Control and Crime Prevention is charged with coordinating efforts with respect to organized crime as well as terrorism. Its principal mandate is the Convention Against Transnational Organized Crime. "In the new global age, borders have opened up, trade barriers have fallen and information speeds around the world at the touch of a button. Business is booming — and so is transnational organized crime. Fortunes are being made from drug trafficking, prostitution, illegal firearms and a host of other cross-border crimes. Every year, organized crime groups launder huge amounts of money in illegal proceeds. These large criminal groups often mimic legitimate business by forming multinational alliances to extend their reach and push up profits." UNODC, *Organized Crime, available at* www.odccp.org/odccp/organized_crime.html?id = 11704 (last visited July 10, 2007).

[187] 18 U.S.C. § 242 (1996):

　　Whoever, under color of any law, statute, ordinance, regulation, or custom, willfully

those committed by combination of two or more persons.[188]

The "color of law" provision came safely within the "state action" requirement of the Fourteenth Amendment, which was in turn an expression that the federal government operated on the states and not directly on the citizenry at large.[189] The conspiracy statute, however, presented a bit of a conundrum. If the Fourteenth Amendment operated only against the states, how could Congress criminalize private behavior? The few cases actually using this criminal provision thus far have found either that the perpetrators were acting "in concert" with state officials or acted in direct contravention of defined federal interests, such as federal instrumentalities of commerce.[190]

Many commentators, and some Justices of the Supreme Court, have thought that these limitations were unduly restrictive of federal power. In particular, because the statutes arose out of widespread concern over the lack of state enforcement against the Ku Klux Klan, it could be argued that the federal government should be able to criminalize any behavior that has an impact on racial minorities.[191]

With the international experience with terrorism in mind, perhaps it makes more sense to realize that the difficulty with federalizing crime is essentially one of line-drawing. Without some "color of state law" or a federally-defined right at stake, how does one distinguish the KKK "terrorist" from the ordinary street criminal who also carries racial animosity for his victims?

The primary federal interest in the post-Civil War Era was the unwillingness of state governments to take steps to enforce the law against the KKK or similar groups. The resulting violence against U.S. citizens (newly defined as such by the Fourteenth Amendment) gave rise to a collective interest among other states to enforce legal controls against state-sanctioned violence. The primary federal interest in the KKK or similar

---

subjects any person in any State, Territory, Commonwealth, Possession, or District to the deprivation of any rights, privileges, or immunities secured or protected by the Constitution or laws of the United States, or to different punishments, pains, or penalties, on account of such person being an alien, or by reason of his color, or race, than are prescribed for the punishment of citizens . . . .

[188] 18 U.S.C. § 241 (1996):

If two or more persons conspire to injure, oppress, threaten, or intimidate any person in any State, Territory, Commonwealth, Possession, or District in the free exercise or enjoyment of any right or privilege secured to him by the Constitution or laws of the United States, or because of his having so exercised the same; or

If two or more persons go in disguise on the highway, or on the premises of another, with intent to prevent or hinder his free exercise or enjoyment of any right or privilege so secured

[189] *Civil Rights Cases*, 109 U.S. 3 (1883).

[190] United States v. Guest, 383 U.S. 745 (1966) (concerted action through defendants' "causing arrests" plus private interference with federal right to travel); United States v. Price, 383 U.S. 787 (1966) (state officials were defendants); Screws v. United States, 325 U.S. 91 (1945) (state officials).

[191] *See Guest*, 383 U.S. at 774-86 (Brennan, J., concurring and dissenting).

groups today lies in the greater psychological (as well as physical) impact of a large, concerted, organized group with common means of carrying out their hostility.

Identical statements can be made with regard to terrorism. The international interest in terrorism lies in the greater psychological (as well as physical) impact of a large, concerted, organized group with common means of carrying out their hostility. The international community is based in a respect for the individual sovereignty of nations that is even greater than that of the federal respect for state sovereignty in the U.S. Given that respect, the international law does not need to intrude into the internal affairs of a nation to deal with ordinary street criminals. It is when a large, organized and well-funded group appears on the scene with the means to wreak widespread psychological and physical harm that the international interest is triggered. This leads to the international corollary of federalist-defined offenses: either when the actor is clothed with some semblance of "state authority" or the conspiracy is sufficiently large to be a concern of the international community.

Under this view, an act may be an act of "terrorism" (as in the Israeli view of the LAX shooter) without triggering the international concern of "terrorism" for lack of a well-organized group identity. This is the position taken by the FBI in the case of the LAX shooter and it makes a great deal of sense from the international perspective.

To carry out the analogy, consider the case of John Paul Franklin, who acted alone in shooting two white men who were in the company of two African-American women and who also engaged in other racially-motivated behavior.[192] Should he have been charged with a federal crime or left to the state criminal justice system? This is a very close case in U.S. law. For the federal government to intervene might imply an unhealthy lack of respect for state justice, but for the federal government to ignore the situation could be seen as expressing a lack of concern for the racial issues of the country. In the end, it may have been the flamboyance of Franklin's racial attitudes that tipped the scales to federal prosecution because of the potential contagion of his racism, but the federal nexus of authority was the "use of public facilities" by the victims.

Crimes of violence often carry racial overtones. It is often impossible to say that any one motivation is the sole force in driving a person to violence. Any ordinary street crime may have an element of racial hostility buried within it. For the federal government to pick and choose those that it will prosecute, without any guiding principle for its decisions, would be contrary to the rationality that we demand of our criminal justice system. Thus, distinctions in American civil rights law that depend on "state action" (state sponsorship would be the analogy in terrorism) or "conspiracy" (a large terrorist organization) make sense from the point of view of importing rationality into what might otherwise become decisions based on whim, or the identity of the victim, or even the color of the defendant's skin.

---

[192] United States v. Franklin, 704 F.2d 1183 (10th Cir. 1983).

This line of analogy leads in the field of terrorism to considering a terrorist act to be a violation of the "law of war" only if carried out with state sanction. It might also be a violation of international law (the "law of nations") but that only serves to provide universal jurisdiction for the courts of any nation; it does not indicate which court system within the U.S. structure should take jurisdiction. For that, we need a rational distinction such as state sponsorship.

Now the use of the "color of state law" requirement in the post-Civil War legislation begins to make more sense. The limitation of federal power to actors who were in league with governmental agents was a very rational way of confining the operation of law. Similarly, limiting application of military authority to actors who are in league with foreign governmental agents is a rational limiting principle, one that courts can apply with confidence.

There is another limiting principle available, but we must wonder whether the courts can apply it with the requisite level of confidence. The most likely limit is that of "member of a terrorist organization," which imports criteria of political motivation, organized group behavior, and funding capabilities to reach international targets. If Congress plainly authorized military tribunals for actors who meet these criteria, and if the government were willing to show to a court in habeas corpus that an individual meets these criteria, it is likely that the court will accede to the government's demand for military authority. To claim that the courts have no review power over these criteria is utterly disingenuous. Even in *Quirin* the courts received evidence of the behavior of the German saboteurs showing that they were acting under direction and in the service of a foreign enemy.

Thus, by foregoing the claim of immunity from habeas corpus review, the government can construct an argument that an individual falls within the modern definition of pirate — i.e., a terrorist. We should not, however, confuse the subject by using the language of war. These people are not combatants in armed conflict between nations. They are in a category of criminal that arguably places them within the domain of the military, but they are also criminals who could be referred to the ordinary processes of the civilian justice system.

At the time of *Hamdan*, the only statutory basis for military tribunals was "violation of the law of war." And just as the KKK did not violate federal law if not acting "under color of state law," on the world stage a terrorist does not violate the law of war unless acting "under color of state authority." How else can we distinguish the terrorist from the mafiosi? Congress has now provided in the MCA a list of "war crimes" and provided for commission jurisdiction over "any offense made punishable by this chapter or the law of war."[193]

The U.S. is promoting in many ways the proposition that democratic processes are better than a mere show of force. A critical factor in being

---

[193] 10 U.S.C. § 948d (2007).

"better" is the rationality by which different handling of different cases can be explained by public policies. Another factor is the transparent fairness of civilian systems of justice with attendant due process. With regard to the alleged al Qaeda confederates at Guantánamo, they could be transferred to the civilian criminal system with attendant difficulties of the disclosure of classified intelligence information. Perhaps they could be extradited to another country for trial, but that presents issues of whether the requesting country provides adequate safeguards for rights of the defendant.

The law abhors incoherence. The lack of coherence in this setting results from making the defining characteristic for recourse to a military commission to be violation of the "law of war," and the international community has not defined terrorist acts as violations of the law of war. One approach worth exploring is that definition of international terrorism for this purpose should be limited to those who act "under color of state authorization" in a fashion similar to the U.S. definition of civil rights violations committed "under color of state law."

If there is any general thought that comes to mind about terrorism and the processes of American law, it is this. Terrorism is not subject to a war to be won with brute force, it is a battle for the hearts and minds of a very large disaffected portion of the world population. To win that battle, we must be better than we want to be. One beginning point is building coherence into our legal responses, and the history of our own country should be useful.

Chapter 9

MILITARY DETENTIONS

SYNOPSIS

The heart of the Bush Administration's "war on terrorism" — and some would say its assault on civil liberties[1] — has been the imprisonment of alleged terrorist collaborators without trial. This practice stemmed from the reasonably innocuous proposition that persons violating the law of war should be tried by military tribunals, but the written Order[2] embodying that policy swept in accused terrorist supporters regardless of the place or circumstances of their activity. And as the policy went into practice, it even extended to a U.S. citizen arrested by civilian agents on U.S. soil for an alleged conspiracy to do damage to civilian property on U.S. soil.

Designating an accused as an enemy combatant subject to permanent military detention without judicial review is a radical shift that does not comport with modern notions of due process and the rule of law. In essence, the Bush Administration has argued that terrorist sympathizers have become so dangerous that we should allow the executive to operate as if the whole world were a battlefield free from judicial oversight.

---

[1] *See, e.g.,* DAVID COLE & JAMES X. DEMPSEY, TERRORISM AND THE CONSTITUTION (2002); RANETA LAWSON MACK & MICHAEL J. KELLY, EQUAL JUSTICE IN THE BALANCE (2004); MARK SIDEL, MORE SECURE LESS FREE (2004).

[2] Detention, Treatment, and Trial of Certain Non-Citizens in the War Against Terrorism, 66 Fed. Reg. 57,833 (Nov. 13, 2001).

This chapter proceeds by looking at the background for military involvement on the home front, then turning to the first wave of Supreme Court cases that dealt with detentions, then moving to the follow-up cases triggered by congressional action to authorize executive detentions. As a legend for this road map, there are three lines of cases and two recent statutes involved. The three lines of cases deal with persons detained in military prisons on the U.S. mainland, those charged with crimes before a military commission, and those detained at Guantánamo without expectation of trial before a military commission. The two recent statutes are the Detainee Treatment Act of 2005 and the Military Commission Act of 2006. These are in addition to the 1971 anti-detention statute, the statutory provisions on Habeas Corpus, and the Authorization for Use of Military Force following 9/11.

§ 9.01 THE MILITARY DETENTIONS IN BRIEF

The administration's challenge to judicial review lies at the heart of its so-called "war" on terrorism because it reflects the idea that civilian courts cannot second-guess the decisions of the executive branch. It is important to the rule of law that courts not cede unreviewable authority to the military on our own soil.[3]

Military detention of civilians on domestic soil is far from a new idea in the United States. The War of 1812 produced a few examples,[4] the Civil War saw Lincoln's use of military tribunals for Southern sympathizers,[5] and World War II produced Japanese internment.[6] For the most part, these experiences have produced a pattern of judicial tolerance and deference to the Executive during the initial stages of emergency followed by a sober rethinking of power when passions have cooled and fear has receded.[7]

Early reaction to the Bush administration's claims of executive power focused on the plan for use of military commissions to try accused

---

[3] Much of the same ground has been covered by others with different emphases. *See* Laura Dickinson, *Using Legal Process to Fight Terrorism: Detentions, Military Commissions, International Tribunals, and the Rule of Law*, 75 S. CAL. L. REV. 1407 (2002); Carl Tobias, *Detentions, Military Commissions, and Domestic Case Precedent*, 76 S. CAL. L. REV. 1371 (2003).

[4] Apparently, President Madison acquiesced in holdings of state and lower federal courts to the effect that neither military commanders nor courts-martial had power to detain or prosecute civilian citizens for spying or treason. Ingrid Brunk Wuerth, *The President's Power to Detain "Enemy Combatants:" Modern Lessons from Mr. Madison's Forgotten War*, 98 NW. U. L. REV. 1567 (2004); *see also In re* Stacy, 10 Johns. 328, 333 (N.Y. 1813) (granting habeas corpus for citizen held "without any color of authority in any military tribunal to try a citizen for" treason).

[5] *Ex parte* Milligan, 4 Wall. 2 (1866); *see generally* WILLIAM H. REHNQUIST, ALL THE LAWS BUT ONE (1998).

[6] Korematsu v. United States, 323 U.S. 214 (1944); *see generally* PERSONAL JUSTICE DENIED, REPORT OF THE COMMISSION ON WARTIME RELOCATION AND INTERNMENT OF CIVILIANS (1997).

[7] Oren Gross, *Chaos and Rules: Should Responses to Violent Crises Always Be Constitutional?*, 112 YALE L.J. 1011, 1019-20 (2003).

terrorists.[8] Professor Paust, a former faculty member of the Army JAG School, took the position that the President's power to establish military commissions, whether derived from constitutional or statutory sources,[9] applied only within a combat zone or war-related occupied territory and that the authority would end when peace was finalized.[10] Professors Bradley and Goldsmith, however, argued that President Bush had statutory authority to issue the Order, and probably also had independent constitutional authority to do so as Commander in Chief.[11]

As events have unfolded, the proposed military commissions are only a part of the story. A variety of persons captured not only in Afghanistan but in various countries have been imprisoned in Guantánamo, U.S. citizens have been placed in military jails in the U.S. without any hearing, and unknown persons have been held in undisclosed locations around the world. The military detentions, both at Guantánamo and in the U.S., are the subject of this chapter.

The military detention cases involve three lines of cases and two recent statutes. In brief, the sequence of judicial and congressional action on the subject has been as follows. Habeas corpus petitions resulted in three cases before the Supreme Court in June 2004. Those cases held that a person could be detained in military custody in the U.S. upon a showing before a "neutral decisionmaker" that the individual was an "enemy combatant" and thus within the realm of military authority.[12] In addition, the Court at least implied that those persons held at Guantánamo stated a claim for relief, presumably on the basis that they were entitled to determination by a competent tribunal regarding their potential POW status, thus allowing detainees access to a federal court for habeas corpus review of the basis of that detention.[13]

---

[8] Detention, Treatment, and Trial of Certain Non Citizens in the War Against Terrorism, 66 Fed. Reg. 57, 834 (Nov. 13, 2001).

[9] The power as Commander-in-Chief under Art. II arguably could be implemented without statutory authority, but Congress has power to "make Rules for the Government and Regulation of the [armed] forces." The authority for military commissions found in the Uniform Code of Military Justice is now codified at 10 U.S.C. § 821 (2006).

[10] Jordan J. Paust, *Antiterrorism Military Commissions: Courting Illegality*, 23 Mich. J. Int'l Law 1, 5, 9 (2001). Professor Paust argues that even Guantánamo Bay is not a "war-related occupied territory." *Id.* at 25 n.70. The word "finalized" is an important qualifier on the statement because the power can extend throughout occupation of conquered territory or even beyond occupation with the consent of a new government. *See also* Neal Kaytal & Laurence Tribe, *Waging War, Deciding Guilt: Trying the Military Tribunals*, 111 Yale L.J. 1259 (2002).

[11] Curtis A. Bradley & Jack L. Goldsmith, *The Constitutional Validity of Military Commissions*, 5 Green Bag 2d 249 (2002). "Although the Order was not preceded by a congressional declaration of war, such a declaration is not constitutionally required in order for the President to exercise his constitutional or statutory war powers, including his power to establish military commissions. We also argue that the September 11 terrorist attacks, to which the Order was a response, violate the laws of war and therefore fall within the jurisdiction of military commissions."

[12] Hamdi v. Rumsfeld, 542 U.S. 507 (2004).

[13] *Id.* at 531.

Following the 2004 cases, the military created Combatant Status Review Tribunals to determine whether any detainee met the qualifications for POW status, while six detainees were charged with crimes against the law of war before military commissions.

Those detainees who were not before military commissions continued their habeas corpus proceedings. Most cases were consolidated before Judge Green in D.C. and she ruled in January 2005 that the Combatant Status Review Tribunals (CSRT) procedures did not provide adequate due process because of secret evidence while another group of cases before Judge Leon were dismissed pursuant to his conclusion that the procedures were adequate. Congress responded in December 2005 with the Detainee Treatment Act (DTA),[14] which purported to withdraw habeas corpus jurisdiction over the Gitmo detainees but provided for review of the CSRT determinations by the D.C. Circuit.

Meanwhile, the military authorities charged six persons with crimes before military commissions and those persons pursued separate challenges through the federal courts. The Supreme Court decided in June 2006 that the DTA did not withdraw habeas jurisdiction over cases pending at the time of its enactment.[15] The Court then held that the commissions were invalidly constituted because they did not comply with either U.S. law or the customary international law of war that Congress had incorporated into U.S. law. The essential problems identified by the Court were (1) the potential use of summaries of classified evidence or evidence from which the defendant was excluded entirely, and (2) conspiracy is not a crime triable by military commission under the law of war. Congress then came back with the Military Commission Act of 2006 (MCA)[16] which authorized the military commissions to consider any evidence that "would have probative value to a reasonable person" and provided a list of crimes triable by the commissions along with the offense of conspiracy to commit such a crime.

The MCA became relevant to the appeal of the Guantánamo detainee cases because it reinforced the withdrawal of habeas corpus jurisdiction and made it clear that the withdrawal applied to cases already pending.

On appeal, the D.C. Circuit held that the DTA and MCA precluded judicial review of the CSRT procedures except in the context of specific cases as provided in the statute.[17] That case was first rejected by the Supreme Court but on the last day of the Term in June 2007 the Court voted to grant certiorari.[18]

Under the MCA, commissions have jurisdiction over crimes committed by an "alien unlawful enemy combatant." In a peculiar twist, the two

---

[14] Pub. L. No. 109-148, 119 Stat. 2680 (2005).

[15] Hamdan v. Rumsfeld, 126 S. Ct. 2749 (2006).

[16] Pub. L. 109-366 (2006).

[17] Boumediene v. Bush, 476 F.3d 981 (D.C. Cir. 2007), *cert. granted*, 2007 U.S. LEXIS 8757 (June 29, 2007).

[18] *Id., cert. granted*, 2007 U.S. LEXIS 8757 (June 29, 2007).

military judges appointed to preside over the trials of Hamdan and Omar Khadr dismissed the charges against both on the ground that the CSRT had only decided that the defendant was an enemy combatant and had not gone the next step to decide that the defendant was an "unlawful" enemy combatant.[19] This ruling is a bit mystifying. Ordinarily, a jurisdictional fact is decided by the court whose jurisdiction is invoked. Thus, for the term "unlawful enemy combatant" to serve as a jurisdictional fact, it should be established it in the trial before the military commission.[20] The Pentagon is appealing the judges' rulings.

§ 9.02   *POSSE COMITATUS* AND MARTIAL LAW

Before turning to the current military detentions, it should be helpful to have some background from the history of military operations in the domestic setting. This section will explore concepts of martial law and limitations on domestic military operations in U.S. law.

[A]   *Posse Comitatus*

The federal "*posse comitatus*" statute[21] prohibits use of the military in civil law enforcement. The statute was first adopted in 1875 as part of the end of Reconstruction, the immediate impetus being the presence of military troops as election monitors when civil authority had been restored. Although the sweep of the statute could be read as building a wall between military and civilian authorities, it has not been given that effect by subsequent Congresses. Indeed, Congress has authorized a wide array of military assistance to federal, state, or local authorities in pursuit of maintaining order or law enforcement, so long as military personnel are not directly engaged in searches or arrests. As will be spelled out below, courts have routinely upheld "passive" engagement of military personnel in support of civilian criminal investigations and have upheld "active"

---

[19] *See* Sgt. Sara Wood, *Charges Dismissed Against Canadian at Guantánamo, available at* www.defenselink.mil/news/newsarticle.aspx?id = 46281 (June 4, 2007) (last visited Aug. 1, 2007).

[20] Judge Brownback's response to that argument in the *Khadr* case was that "a person has a right to be tried only by a court which he knows has jurisdiction over him. If the military commission were to make the determination, a person could be facing trial for months, without knowing if the court, in fact and in law, had jurisdiction." www.nimj.com/documents/ Khadr%20Order%20on%20Jurisdiction.pdf.

[21] 18 U.S.C. § 1385 (2003):

> Whoever, except in cases and under circumstances expressly authorized by the Constitution or Act of Congress, willfully uses any part of the Army or the Air Force as a *posse comitatus* or otherwise to execute the laws shall be fined under this title or imprisoned not more than two years, or both.

These provisions were extended to the Navy and Marines by 10 U.S.C. § 375 (2007), which also provides for the Secretary of Defense to promulgate regulations "to ensure that any [assistance to state and local authorities] does not include or permit direct participation . . . in a search, seizure, arrest, or other similar activity."

participation of military personnel in criminal enforcement when the offense concerns a military facility or activity.

The use of federal troops,[22] or even Presidential call-up of State National Guard units,[23] to aid civilian authorities in response to insurrection is specifically provided by statute. Use of these forces to protect against violence or looting during the recovery period of natural disasters has never been seriously questioned. President Eisenhower used federal troops and overrode the Governor's authority with the State National Guard to enforce court orders dealing with school desegregation.[24] The principal Supreme Court precedent for use of military force in this situation unfortunately came from a federal court injunction against labor organizing activities and socialist campaigning by Eugene Debs,[25] but the point of using federal military force in aid of court orders is nevertheless well-established. Attorney General Brownell advised President Eisenhower that the *posse comitatus* statute was not intended to limit the President's authority to deal with mob violence or similar threats to enforcement of federal law.[26]

The most extensive analysis of the *posse comitatus* statute came in a series of cases arising out of the three-week occupation of Wounded Knee by members of the American Indian Movement in 1973. Various defendants were prosecuted for offenses such as trespass, assault, and interference with federal officers in the discharge of their duties. The defendants pointed to the involvement of military units in what could have been viewed as an ordinary law enforcement operation and asserted that this involvement violated the *posse comitatus* statute. This defense was relevant at least to the question of whether the federal officers were "lawfully engaged in the discharge of their duties."

The FBI and Bureau of Indian Affairs had closed off the town to prevent additional sympathizers from joining those dissidents already on the scene. As part of the control operation, military units assisted with advice, aerial reconnaissance and the loan of equipment. The district judges dealing with the defense of *posse comitatus* violation reached different conclusions with

---

[22] 10 U.S.C. § 332 (2007).

[23] 10 U.S.C. § 331 (2007).

[24] Attorney General Herbert Brownell delivered a formal opinion to President Eisenhower dealing with a range of issues regarding the desegregation of the Little Rock schools. 41 Op. Att'y Gen. 313 (1957). The federal court had issued an order requiring desegregation of Central High School, but Governor Faubus mobilized the state militia and highway patrol with orders to "place off limits to colored students those schools heretofore operated and recently set up for white students."

[25] *In re* Debs, 158 U.S. 564, 582 (1894): "The entire strength of the nation may be used to enforce in any part of the land the full and free exercise of all national powers and the security of all rights entrusted by the Constitution to its care. . . . If the emergency arises, the army of the Nation, and all its militia, are at the service of the Nation to compel obedience to its laws."

[26] Indeed, the Brownell opinion expressed "grave doubts as to the authority of the Congress to limit the constitutional powers of the President to enforce the laws and preserve the peace under circumstances which he deems appropriate." 41 Op. Att'y Gen. 313 (1957).

different standards for testing the validity of military involvement.[27] To Judge Urbom, the statute would be violated if military personnel influenced the decisions of the civilian officers or actively maintained and operated the equipment provided.[28] Judge Nichol went "one step further" than Judge Ubrom and held that there was no evidence justifying submission of issues to the jury regarding the nature of the military involvement.[29] Judge Bogue provided a more nuanced analysis by concentrating on whether military personnel were "actively engaged in law enforcement."[30]

> Based upon the clear intent of Congress, this Court holds that the clause "to execute the laws" makes unlawful the use of federal military troops in an active role of direct law enforcement by civil law enforcement officers. Activities which constitute an active role in direct law enforcement are: arrest; seizure of evidence; search of a person; search of a building; investigation of crime; interviewing witnesses; pursuit of an escaped civilian prisoner; search of an area for a suspect and other like activities. Such use of federal military troops to "execute the laws," or as the Court has defined the clause, in "an active role of direct law enforcement," is unlawful under 18 U.S.C. § 1385.

> Activities which constitute a *passive* role which might *indirectly* aid law enforcement are: mere presence of military personnel under orders to report on the necessity for military intervention; preparation of contingency plans to be used if military intervention is ordered; advice or recommendations given to civilian law enforcement officers by military personnel on tactics or logistics; presence of military personnel to deliver military materiel, equipment or supplies, to train local law enforcement officials on the proper use and care of such material or equipment, and to maintain such materiel or equipment; aerial photographic reconnaissance flights and other like activities.[31]

For Judge Van Sickle, the opinions of the prior judges were not sufficient.[32] He assessed the history and purposes of the statutes and concluded that Americans are suspicious of military involvement because the military training is not designed to take into account civilian rights but also that

---

[27] United States v. McArthur, 419 F. Supp. 186 (D.N.D. 1975); United States v. Red Feather, 392 F. Supp. 916 (D.S.D. 1975); United States v. Banks, 383 F. Supp. 368, 374-77 (D.S.D. 1974); United States v. Jaramillo, 380 F. Supp. 1375 (D. Neb. 1974).

[28] *Jaramillo*, 380 F. Supp. 1375.

[29] *Banks*, 383 F. Supp. 368.

[30] *Red Feather*, 392 F. Supp. 916 ("the phrase 'uses any part of the Army or the Air Force as a *posse comitatus* or otherwise' means the direct active use of Army or Air Force personnel and does not mean the use of Army or Air Force equipment or material").

[31] *Id.* at 925.

[32] *McArthur*, 419 F. Supp. 186. "[M]y concern with Judge Urbom's analysis is that I feel his rule requires a judgment be made from too vague a standard. At the same time, my concern with Judge Bogue's analysis is that it is too mechanical, and inevitably when the rule is applied to borderline cases, it will crumble at the edges." *Id.* at 194.

military specialization could be useful in unusual situations of civil disturbance. To sum up his conclusions, he stated that "the feared use which is
prohibited by the *posse comitatus* statute is that which is regulatory,
proscriptive or compulsory in nature, and causes the citizens to be presently
or prospectively subject to regulations, proscriptions, or compulsions imposed by military authority."

In this sequence of cases, the judges took varying approaches to interpret-
ing the phrase "use [military] forces . . . to execute the laws." Although
there were constitutional concerns lurking in the background of the analyses, the focus was on whether Congress had authorized or prohibited the
use of military force in domestic disturbances. The constitutional issues are
more forcefully stated in the next section.

[B] Martial Law

The effect of the *posse comitatus* statute on the question of declaring
martial law essentially is to preserve the power to make such a declaration
in Congress. The military can be used to assist directly in civil law
enforcement only when authorized by statute. This approach codifies, with
some clarification, the results reached following the Civil War and Reconstruction. Prior to that time, the Judiciary Act of 1789 had authorized
federal marshals to call on the military to serve as a posse whenever it was
useful for execution of the law.[33]

In *Texas v. White*,[34] the Supreme Court validated the occupation of
Southern states by federal military force following the Civil War. In *Ex
parte Milligan*,[35] the Court invalidated the trial of civilians by military
tribunals in areas in which the civilian courts were open and operating.
The combination of these cases could be read as permitting martial law in
areas that are in a state of war but not allowing it elsewhere. As Colonel
Winthrop points out, this is an oversimplification.[36]

Through these cases runs the distinction between military government
and martial law. The former is the result of occupation of hostile territory,
whether foreign or rebellious. The latter is a condition that provides a
military complement to the civil authorities on home soil because of an
emergency. Military government completely supplants civil government
while martial law provides a type of self-defensive use of force commensurate with the necessity. The Supreme Court adopted this view in *Duncan
v. Kahanamoku*[37] when it overturned a conviction by military tribunal in
Hawaii during a time of declared martial law because the civilian courts
were open and operating. Thus, martial law can allow the military commander to override some of the normal operations of the civil authorities,

---

[33] *See* WILLIAM WINTHROP, MILITARY LAW & PRECEDENTS 866-67 (1920).

[34] 74 U.S. 700 (1868).

[35] 71 U.S. 2 (1866).

[36] WINTHROP, *supra* note 33, at 799.

[37] 327 U.S. 304 (1946).

to provide for law enforcement and maintenance of order, without supplanting the civil judicial function.

The most significant aspect of *Duncan*, however, is that it was a statutorily based rather than constitutionally based decision. Before getting to that point, however, Justice Black's opinion for the Court pointed out what the case *did not concern*:

> Our question does not involve the well-established power of the military to exercise jurisdiction over members of the armed forces, those directly connected with such forces, or enemy belligerents, prisoners of war, or others charged with violating the laws of war. We are not concerned with the recognized power of the military to try civilians in tribunals established as a part of a temporary military government over occupied enemy territory or territory regained from an enemy where civilian government cannot and does not function. . . . Nor need we here consider the power of the military simply to arrest and detain civilians interfering with a necessary military function at a time of turbulence and danger from insurrection or war.[38]

Thus, in *Duncan*, the Court recognized the basic distinction between military government and martial law, the former having to do with enemy territory and the latter with home turf. The Court then went on to decide only whether the Hawaii Organic Act authorized martial law to the point of excluding the civilian courts. "These petitioners were tried before tribunals set up under a military program which took over all government and superseded all civil laws and courts."[39]

After canvassing the history, admittedly a bit checkered but stabilizing in the direction of allowing military force to be used without supplanting civil authority, the Court declared:

> We believe that when Congress passed the Hawaiian Organic Act and authorized the establishment of "martial law" it had in mind and did not wish to exceed the boundaries between military and civilian power, in which our people have always believed, which responsible military and executive officers had heeded, and which had become part of our political philosophy and institutions prior to the time Congress passed the Organic Act. The phrase "martial law" as employed in that Act, therefore, while intended to authorize the military to act vigorously for the maintenance of an orderly civil government and for the defense of the Islands against actual or threatened rebellion or invasion, was not intended to authorize the supplanting of courts by military tribunals.[40]

Justice Black may have been a bit overly enthusiastic about what "our people have always believed"[41] or about what "responsible military and

---

[38] *Duncan*, 327 U.S. at 313-14.

[39] *Id.* at 314.

[40] *Id.* at 324.

[41] *Id.*

executive officers had heeded,"[42] but his message is clearly stated that martial law does not itself close the civilian courts nor authorize diversion of civilian defendants to military tribunals. Referring to the Court's martial law opinion in *Sterling v. Constantin*,[43] Justice Black stated that "this Court 'has knocked out the prop'" on which earlier lower court approvals of military tribunals had been based.[44]

Justice Murphy was even more emphatic and did not rest on statutory grounds. "Equally obvious, as I see it, is the fact that these trials were forbidden by the Bill of Rights of the Constitution of the United States . . . . Indeed, the unconstitutionality of the usurpation of civil power by the military is so great in this instance as to warrant this Court's complete and outright repudiation of the action."[45] Justice Murphy referred to criticism of the "so-called 'open court' rule of the *Milligan* case" and responded vigorously:

> The argument thus advanced is as untenable today as it was when cast in the language of the Plantagenets, the Tudors and the Stuarts. It is a rank appeal to abandon the fate of all our liberties to the reasonableness of the judgment of those who are trained primarily for war. It seeks to justify military usurpation of civilian authority to punish crime without regard to the potency of the Bill of Rights. It deserves repudiation.
>
> From time immemorial despots have used real or imagined threats to the public welfare as an excuse for needlessly abrogating human rights. That excuse is no less unworthy of our traditions when used in this day of atomic warfare or at a future time when some other type of warfare may be devised.[46]

Duncan does not deny the possibility of using military presence to supplement or even replace some functions of civilian government in time of actual emergency. The examples cited in *Duncan* of martial law to quell civil disturbances stemming principally from labor disputes do not seem to have taken into account the *posse comitatus* statute. Given the tacit approval of the use of troops in those cases, so long as crimes were tried in the civilian courts, it is not clear how the Court would deal with this statutory argument. Some further insight might be gleaned from *Youngstown Sheet & Tube v. Sawyer*,[47] in which the Court struck down President Truman's attempt to seize the steel mills to avert labor strife during the Korean War. Only the three dissenting Justices were impressed by the argument that there was any level of national emergency justifying unilateral seizure without congressional authorization.

---

[42] *Id.*

[43] 287 U.S. 378 (1932).

[44] *Duncan*, 327 U.S. at 321 n.18.

[45] *Id.* at 325.

[46] *Id.* at 329-30.

[47] 343 U.S. 579 (1952).

In his classic concurrence analyzing separation of powers, Justice Jackson pointed out that the President is on strongest ground when he acts with congressional authorization, may or may not have constitutional powers when acting in congressional silence, and must have strong independent constitutional grounds when going against the will of Congress.[48] To justify military force to perform civil law enforcement after passage of the *posse comitatus* legislation, the President would have to persuade a majority of the court that a genuine emergency existed sufficient to justify departure from specific congressional direction. After the experience of *Korematsu*, *Duncan*, and *Youngstown*, it is doubtful that anything short of imminent invasion could justify unilateral action.

This is not to say that Congress could not be persuaded to authorize martial law under threat of war-time conditions. That it did not do so under the extreme stress of the early stages of World War II is highly instructive. Again, it is worth pointing out that declaring martial law does not require supplanting the normal processes of the civilian courts. Whether *Milligan* and *Duncan* express constitutional norms as well as statutory decisions may ultimately have to be faced if the courts continue to view loosely worded statutes as authorizing military tribunals whenever the President chooses.

Quirin[49] was a wartime decision, made after the fact of military trials, and probably should not be repeated, at least not in the absence of a real war with real saboteurs. How do we know if it is a real war with real saboteurs? By judicial review, of course. Before we reach that stage, however, we really should ask why the ordinary civilian courts are not fully equipped to handle a trial of this type.

Justice Murphy in *Duncan* addressed seven different arguments in favor of military courts over civilian courts in time of war and rejected each of them.[50] Several of the arguments he dismissed as smacking of racism, despotism, viciousness, or just petty military carping about the civil justice system.[51] The only argument that appears to have any facial validity today is that the civilian courts are likely to take longer in reaching judgment than would a military tribunal.[52] If anything, the intervening half-century has brought the military judicial system closer to the civil system and made it more difficult to justify diverting cases to it. With regard to the delay argument, Justice Murphy said: "Civil liberties and military expediency are often irreconcilable. . . . The swift trial and punishment which the military desires is precisely what the Bill of Rights outlaws."[53]

Perhaps the best way to approach the issue of martial law within the borders of the U.S. is with utter pragmatism. If a national emergency is

---

[48] *Id.* at 634-39.

[49] 317 U.S. 1 (1942).

[50] *Duncan*, 327 U.S. at 329-34.

[51] *Id.*

[52] *Id.* at 330-31.

[53] *Id.* at 331.

so severe that the civilian courts are not able to meet and enjoin the declaration of martial law, then probably the emergency justifies the declaration. Anything short of that eventuality will give rise to a justiciable controversy of the type seen in *Youngstown Sheet & Tube*.

In this pragmatic vein, comparing *Korematsu* and *Endo* with *Milligan* and *Duncan* is particularly instructive. The majority in *Korematsu* pretended that it was not ruling on detention of anyone because it was only dealing with exclusion of a particular ethnic group from militarily sensitive areas. By this rubric, it could decide in the companion case of *Endo*[54] that detention was unauthorized by Congress or Presidential order.[55] In scathing opinions in both cases, Justice Murphy blistered the Court for ducking the constitutional questions of racism and failing to examine the public record for facts that would belied the military judgment to which the Court purported to give deference.[56] Justice Jackson provided the pragmatic notion that the Court should not even rule on *Korematsu* if it were going to give such great deference because now the Court had written into posterity its approval of an unreviewed race-based internment.[57]

If the War Relocation effort truly had emergency behind it, the Supreme Court would have been able to look at the record and make that determination readily. To hide behind deference is the worst affront to the judicial authority and constitutional strictures.

By contrast, *Milligan* (whether on constitutional or statutory grounds) and *Duncan* both emphatically embrace the "open court" rule to insist on civilian judicial processes when available. The only imaginable reason that *Quirin* allowed departure from this approach is that the military prosecution had already occurred and the political fallout of setting that conviction aside was too fearsome for the Court to bear.

The most pragmatic approach to martial law is to recognize that it is always a possibility. If there is a future attempt to supplant civilian courts with military tribunals in derogation of the principles of *Milligan* and *Duncan*, it should be hoped that the courts will stand firmly against their derogation. As Chief Justice Taney and Justice Jackson both noted, however, the courts are powerless against the "superior force" of the military and must look "to the political judgments of their contemporaries and to the moral judgments of history."[58]

Other than martial law as an emergency measure, some use of the military to assist civilian authorities in times of civil disturbance or emergency is also possible. Statutes providing for assistance to state governments in time of insurrection and providing for military involvement in radiological emergencies are considered in the next chapter. These

---

[54] 323 U.S. 283 (1944).

[55] *Id.* at 302.

[56] *Id.* at 307-08; *see also* Korematsu v. United States, 323 U.S. 214 (1944).

[57] *Korematsu*, 323 U.S. at 244-45.

[58] *Id.* at 248.

statutes are limited by their own terms and do not affect the basic principles of the *posse comitatus* statute or the principles controlling martial law.

§ 9.03 DETENTION WITHOUT TRIAL

If the detainees were alien combatants in a war against the U.S., then there would be no crime in their taking up arms against the U.S. except to the extent that they violated the rules of *jus in bello* as those rules exist in the law of armed conflict (LOAC) (failing to wear a uniform, targeting civilians, etc). Customary international law, codified in some degree in convention law, has solidified the idea of a trial for alleged violations of LOAC. On the other hand, citizens who are alleged to have taken up arms against the U.S. may be accused of treason or related crimes, which may also be punishable by military law if the appropriate jurisdictional elements are met.

There is nothing in either LOAC or domestic criminal law that provides for preventive detention or executive detention in the absence of a cognizable state of armed conflict. The only rationale for detention without trial is to prevent enemy combatants from rejoining the war effort for the duration of hostilities. The Bush Administration has tried to have its cake and eat it too by declaring that alleged terrorists are not prisoners of war but that they are "unlawful enemy combatants," a term that did not exist prior to its usage in this context and which does not provide any basis for declaring a person to be in violation of law without a trial.

Granted, there are practical arguments for allowing the military to detain a person indefinitely without trial, such as preventive detention, detention to assist interrogation, or avoiding disclosure of classified information. Although some of these approach justification of military detention of "enemy combatants," none is sufficiently persuasive to undermine the fundamental bedrock of Anglo-American concepts of due process or customary international law entitling an accused to a hearing on specified charges before a competent tribunal.

[A] Indeterminate Duration of Hostilities

One argument for detention without trial could track closely the analogy of war. Because the suspected terrorist is part of a group that has promised continuing hostile action, the members of the group can hardly be turned loose to help carry out that promise. Prisoners of war are detained for the duration of hostilities because it would be foolish to send them back to have another chance to kill people on our side. This is a compelling argument if we can be sure that the person to whom it applies is in fact committed to taking violent action.

Criminology has put substantial effort into the predictability of the violent offender, or at least of identifying the factors that tend toward anti-social behavior. Young males are far more likely to commit violent crimes than any other group.[59] Perhaps violence would be reduced dramatically if we could just warehouse all males between the ages of 16 and 30. In a more serious vein, the "idea of *incapacitation* is simply that offenders separated from society will not be able to inflict harms on innocent people during the period of their incarceration."[60] There are many observers who argue against repeat offender laws on the basis that they tend to apply only to those offenders who are already nearing the end of their criminal careers.[61]

There are two problems with the incapacitation model in criminal law. One is that the predictive factors are still just too uncertain to allow anyone to make more than just an educated guess about whether a particular person is likely to commit a violent crime. Even the principles of rehabilitation and parole have fallen on hard times in recent decades. The second problem is that the very idea of predictive incapacitation conflicts with our deeply held values of free will. We want desperately to believe that even the most likely offender can have a change of heart before harming innocent persons.

Indeed, it is this emphasis on free will that lies at the heart of conspiracy law. We don't punish for joining groups or even for planning a criminal act. We insist on an overt act in furtherance of the plan for the very reason that we do not want to punish evil intent or proclivities without providing the opportunity for the potential miscreant to "wise up."

Suppose we decided to lock up a person just for being a member of a terrorist organization. The task is daunting and the problems multiply rapidly. First of all, there are too many to be all-inclusive so the effort will be highly select and arbitrary. Secondly, for each one that we treat in this fashion, we persuade two or more fellow travelers to convert to the cause. Next, we cut off some of the most promising sources of information about the plans of terrorist organizations. Lastly, although we could probably go on and on, this action would undercut the whole notion of free will and persuasion to peaceful dispute resolution.

All of this just relates to the question of whether we want to pursue the prospect of indefinite detention without trial. The very idea is anathema to western notions of law and justice, but it has to be mentioned. With regard to a person who has been proven guilty of active participation in a conspiracy, whether in military or civilian trial, a very lengthy sentence may be appropriate. After all, the conspiracy of terrorism is conspiracy to commit murder (and probably on a broad scale and probably of unknown persons), so the prospect of near life imprisonment is not out of bounds. The emphasis here is on the need to have a trial for an act — the question of sentence is another matter entirely.

---

[59] R.J. Herrnstein, *Criminogenic Traits*, *in* JAMES WILSON & JOAN PETERSILIA, CRIME 40-43 (1995).

[60] Brian Forst, *Prosecution and Sentencing*, *in* WILSON & PETERSILIA, *supra* note 59, at 376.

[61] The Supreme Court upheld these laws in *Ewing v. California*, 538 U.S. 11 (2003).

[B]　Detention as Incentive To Talk

In one explanation of the Government's position with respect to both Hamdi and Padilla, the Government has argued that they should be detained in isolation to promote their talking about their knowledge of the al Qaeda organization and its future plans. Deal brokering with organized crime members is certainly not unknown, but it usually takes place in the context of criminal trials. It can also lead to abuses in which government officials end up protecting ongoing criminal activity to obtain information on other criminal activity.[62]

The major problem with indefinite detention to obtain information is that it flies in the face of basic notions of due process, at least in the American system if not internationally. At the domestic level, it has been said repeatedly that government cannot incarcerate someone without due process, meaning at least a decision by a competent tribunal.

Although we can use incarceration as a method of coercing information from an individual in American law, it is accomplished only by court order and then almost never carried out. In civil litigation, for example, refusal to provide information in discovery can become the basis of a court order under Rule 37. Refusal to comply with the order can then be punished by contempt. Although in theory a court can order a contumacious witness to be incarcerated until he or she complies,[63] in practice this power is rarely, if ever, exercised because the courts have other less intrusive remedies available and because incarceration is surrounded by heavy procedural safeguards.[64] If an individual can be shown to have information to which a government agency has a right, then a court will order the individual to divulge that information,[65] and refusal to obey that court order could result in imprisonment for contempt of court.[66] Contempt may also be used to coerce a witness to testify before a grand jury.[67] But "the justification for

---

[62] Some particularly heinous abuses of the criminal justice system have been alleged recently in the context of protected Mafia informants in the Boston area. The allegations include the proposition that government informants were allowed to perjure themselves to obtain convictions of their enemies for crimes actually committed by the informants themselves.

[63] See Fremont Energy Corp. v. Seattle Post-Intelligencer, 688 F.2d 1285 (9th Cir. 1982).

[64] See Mertsching v. United States, 704 F.2d 505 (10th Cir. 1983) (dismissal of lawsuit for failure to answer questions).

[65] The appropriate procedure is for the agency to file a lawsuit for enforcement of an administrative subpoena. See Smith v. United States, 289 F.3d 843 (6th Cir. 2001); NLRB v. G. Rabine & Sons, 2001 U.S. Dist. Lexis 14090 (ND Ill. 2001).

[66] Courts will go to extreme lengths to avoid using incarceration as a method of coercing disclosure of information. "In the case of administrative subpoenas, parties may immediately appeal district court orders enforcing these subpoenas, as the Supreme Court has deemed them to be 'self-contained, so far as the judiciary is concerned[.]' " Cobbledick v. United States, 309 U.S. 323, 330 (1940)." Doe v. United States, 253 F.3d 256 (6th Cir. 2001).

[67] Shillitani v. United States, 384 U.S. 364, 370 (1966): "Where contempt consists of a refusal to obey a court order to testify at any stage in judicial proceedings, the witness may be confined until compliance." (citing McCrone v. United States, 307 U.S. 61 (1939)).

coercive imprisonment as applied to civil contempt depends upon the ability of the contemnor to comply with the court's order" and "a court must exercise 'the least possible power adequate to the end proposed.' "[68] In all of these examples, the requirement of a court order at least ensures a judicial check against governmental abuse in the quest for information, and in addition the courts are adamant that incarceration be circumspectly applied if at all.

At the international level, there are a number of provisions that need to be considered. One is the provision from the Geneva Convention that prisoners of war cannot be punished for wrongdoing without a determination of wrongdoing by a competent tribunal. Another is the proscription on hostage taking that has been built into several international treaties and conventions. Is the detainee essentially being held hostage for information? The common sense idea of hostage taking is that the detained person is being held until someone else is given up. But it could be argued that holding someone until he gives up information in his own possession is no different.

The Supreme Court of Israel dealt with two levels of this argument in *Anonymous v. Minister of Defence*.[69] The unnamed petitioners were being held under the Israeli Emergency Powers (Administrative Detention) Law of 1979, which has been in effect for over 30 years as an "emergency" measure. It authorizes detention of persons as to whom "the Minister of Defence has reasonable cause to believe that reasons of State security or public security require that a particular person be detained." The order of detention can be renewed every six months so long as the same findings are made. In the *Anonymous* case, the government conceded that the individuals in custody no longer represented a threat themselves (how this could be known is a mystery) but that they could be held as bargaining chips to obtain information from terrorist groups about a missing Israeli soldier.

In its initial decision in this case, the Israeli Court held that there was nothing in Israeli law to counter the grant of power to the Minister of Defence. With regard to basic human rights principles, the Court merely said that it is the legislature's job to create a "balance between freedom and dignity on one hand and security on the other." After severe criticism from a number of quarters, the Court granted a rehearing and reversed itself. Noting that international law prohibits hostage-taking, the Court said that using a detainee as a bargaining chip "comprises a serious infringement of human dignity." The Court pointed out that the detainees could not provide the desired information themselves and thus "detention of the appellants is nothing other than a situation in which the key to a person's prison is not held by him but by others."

---

68 *Id.* (citing Maggio v. Zeitz, 333 U.S. 56 (1948), Anderson v. Dunn, (6 Wheat.) 204 (1821)).

69 Cv.A. 7048-97, Anonymous v. Minister of Def., 54(1) P.D. 721 (Sup. Ct. Israel 1997); *see* Emanuel Gross, *Human Rights, Terrorism and the Problem of Administrative Detention in Israel*, 18 ARIZ. J. INT'L & COMP. L. 721 (2001).

But what if the information in fact were in the person's own head? Would detention to persuade him to talk still constitute an illegal hostage situation? This may be an interesting question in international law, but it is virtually irrelevant to American law because the concept of administrative detention without court order has been unknown until now.

[C] Detention To Prevent Violent Acts

Another argument for detention could be that the individual can be held because he represents a danger to public safety, that if released he would be likely to commit an act of violence. Other than civil commitment, the only detentions without conviction that American law has acknowledged have been those for purposes of pre-trial proceedings or based on some judicial mechanism for preventing administrative abuse. During the 1960s and 1970s, there was some thought given to the notion of "preventive detention," in which persons who were a threat to society could be incarcerated, but this idea mostly died out under political pressure. The portion that remained is the presence in a few states of civil commitment proceedings for violent sexual offenders. These persons are thought to be in a special category because evidence shows that they tend not to "age out" of their aggressive behavior.[70] These statues differentiate little from those that authorize civil commitment for a person who is "a danger to himself or others."

When the Kansas sexual offender statute was challenged, the Supreme Court stated, "We have consistently upheld such involuntary commitment statutes provided the confinement takes place pursuant to proper procedures and evidentiary standards."[71]

> Although freedom from physical restraint has "always been at the core of the liberty protected by the Due Process Clause from arbitrary governmental action," that liberty interest is not absolute. The Court has recognized that an individual's constitutionally protected interest in avoiding physical restraint may be overridden even in the civil context.[72]

Now that Britain and Israel have adopted emergency detention provisions, is the United States likely to follow suit? Perhaps more incidents such as 9/11 could persuade the populace to go along with such a severe imposition on basic liberties, but the courts are not likely to play along.

[D] Problems With the Civilian Criminal System

Finally, what is wrong with use of the civilian court system for trial of those Guantánamo detainees who are accused of being al Qaeda

---

[70] Indeed, evidence exists to show that a sexual offender will still engage in physical abuse even after chemical castration eliminates the sexual urge.

[71] Kansas v. Hendricks, 521 U.S. 346, 357 (1997).

[72] *Id.* at 356 (quoting Foucha v. Louisiana, 504 U.S. 71, 80 (1992)).

confederates? or of additional persons arrested and accused of being part of a terrorist cell, such as the Lackawanna Six or the Portland Five? or José Padilla?

One problem with use of the criminal process for alleged terrorists is in defining a crime. Clandestine use of arms may well constitute a crime under international law. There are ample crimes that can be charged in the civilian system under the heading of universal jurisdiction. Crimes against air piracy, hostage taking, destruction of life or property, are all criminalized by U.S. statute as well as by international conventions. The only thing lacking in international law is a proscription against terrorism generally.

The U.S. has attempted to fill the terrorism definitional void by defining the crime of providing material support to a terrorist or a designated terrorist organization.[73] These statutes are being employed against those who may be supportive of others who have committed or planned to commit violent acts. In a sense, the statute defines a conspiracy without calling it a conspiracy. Even under the relaxed standards of conspiracy law, the criminal defendant is not usually accountable absent knowledge of the general nature of a crime that is to be committed. Generalized knowledge that a group is likely to carry out violent action when the occasion arises is not enough for conviction of conspiracy to commit the crime.

Under the most relaxed view of due process, reflected in the anti-labor and anti-communist legislation of the early 20th Century, the Supreme Court did uphold legislation that made it a crime merely to belong to an organization with unlawful objectives.[74] When the red baiting of the 1950s subsided, the Court then stated that these holdings had been thoroughly discredited and that constitutional guarantees of free speech and free press do not permit a State to forbid or proscribe advocacy of the use of force or of law violation except where such advocacy is directed to inciting or producing imminent lawless action and is likely to incite or produce such actions.[75]

If an individual were subjected to prosecution for belonging to a terrorist organization, U.S. constitutional guarantees would require proof that the individual knew of the imminence of violence. This is the type of evidence that may be extremely difficult to marshal with regard to someone whose role in a foreign organization took place clandestinely in various foreign arenas.

Perhaps the most salient argument against the civilian justice system is the military courts' ability to "provide for in a manner consistent with

---

[73] There are two statutes, 18 U.S.C. § 2339A for providing material support or resources knowing or intending that they be used in violent acts, and § 2339B for providing material support or resources to a designated organization.

[74] Whitney v. California, 274 U.S. 357 (1927). Interestingly, Justices Brandeis and Holmes in concurrence described "advocacy of criminal syndicalism" as a crime "very unlike the old felony of conspiracy because it creates guilt although the society may not contemplate immediate promulgation of the doctrine." See also Herndon v. Lowry, 301 U.S. 242 (1937) (prosecution for speech must show a "reasonable apprehension of danger").

[75] Brandenburg v. Ohio, 395 U.S. 444 (1970).

the protection of information classified or classifiable . . . the handling of, admission into evidence of, and access to materials and information." The civilian courts similarly can hear claims of privilege that would prevent disclosure of classified information, but because criminal proceedings must be open to the public, the civilian courts could not receive that evidence without making it known to the public. Indeed, the U.S. Court of Military Appeals has held that the right of public trial applies to courts-martial, so it will be interesting to see if military commissions may operate any differently.[76]

The administration does not want a public trial with disclosure of evidence because it does not want public disclosure of the sources of its information. Moreover, in many instances that information might be sufficient to justify a reasonable person's acting on it but fall short of proof beyond a reasonable doubt.[77] Again, it is worth pointing out what the criminal defendant would be entitled to receive: a speedy and fair public trial, a terminable sentence commensurate with the evidence, proof beyond a reasonable doubt that this individual participated in conduct constituting a crime.

The heart of the problem with open trials for alleged terrorists is that thwarting well-organized, well-disciplined, fanatical groups will require intelligence work premised on infiltration. This means placing informants into, or buying the cooperation of informants within, the heart of the organizations. We will be doing business with some very nasty people, and we will need to protect those people by not revealing the nature of the information we have about those we capture. Revealing that information necessarily would demonstrate the source of the information, thus jeopardizing the informants or methods which provided it.[78]

These problems have been addressed by Congress in the Classified Information Procedures Act.[79] In essence, the statute permits the trial judge in a criminal prosecution to review government claims for secrecy of evidence *in camera*, to order use of redacted disclosures or summaries, and to exclude classified information from introduction at trial.[80]

The extent to which the classified information procedures can be applied consistently with the defendant's rights to confrontation and due process remains to be seen. Certainly, judges could be presented with some excruciatingly difficult choices, in the extreme being faced with the prospect

---

[76] United States v. Grunden, 2 M.J. 116 (U.S.C.M.A. 1972).

[77] The Military Order authorizing commissions for trial of alleged al Qaeda members uses a reasonableness standard rather than beyond a reasonable doubt.

[78] In some instances, the source of the information may be a person who is still entrenched in the organization and providing further information. Disclosing the identity of an in-place informant is obviously detrimental to the health of that person. In other instances, the source may be highly sophisticated technology and disclosure of its operation would give the organization clues about how to avoid detection.

[79] 18 U.S.C. App. §§ 1-16 (1980).

[80] *See* § 7.03 *supra*.

of releasing a very nasty terrorist to prevent disclosure of information in a public trial. One consolation is that the terrorist is not likely to have committed only one crime; there may be other offenses that can be charged without the need for disclosure of classified information. Another consolation is that the government would not likely let that person wander loose in public without constant surveillance. This will be expensive, yes, but perhaps not that much more expensive than life-time confinement in a secure facility.

§ 9.04 JUDICIAL REVIEW OF MILITARY DETENTIONS

The Bush Administration first claimed authority for unreviewable detentions from inherent presidential powers as well as from implicit congressional authorization in the 2001 Authorization to Use Military Force.[81] After Supreme Court cases cast doubt on some aspects of these positions, Congress moved in two statutes, the Detainee Treatment Act of 2005[82] and the Military Commission Act of 2006,[83] to provide more authority and to insulate detentions from judicial review.

[A] The 2004 Cases

In June 2004, the Supreme Court decided three cases dealing with military detentions. Two of the cases involved U.S. citizens detained within the 50 States while the third involved the alien detainees at Guantánamo. Although it is possible to view the results as being hostile to the Bush Administration's detention program, the Court actually gave the Government more than might have been expected under traditional legal principles. One case of domestic executive detention (*Padilla*)[84] resulted in a jurisdictional dismissal, the case involving a U.S. citizen captured in a battle zone (*Hamdi*)[85] resulted in a qualified type of judicial review of the detention, while the Guantánamo case (*Rasul*)[86] provided merely a remand for further proceedings regarding the legality of the detentions. Thus the Government came away with what amounts to a series of holding patterns or delaying actions pending further review.

In all three instances, the Government claimed that it could detain these persons as "enemy combatants" pursuant to the war powers of the President. The clearest example of departure from peacetime norms in the "war on terrorism" is that of Padilla, the military detention without trial of a U.S. citizen arrested by the FBI on U.S. soil and accused of planning to engage in a terrorist act on U.S. soil. But the others are also clear

---

[81] S.J. Res. 23, 107th Cong. (2001); Pub. L. 107-40, 115 stat. 224.

[82] H.R. 2863, 109th Cong. (2005).

[83] Pub. L. No. 109-366 (2006).

[84] Rumsfeld v. Padilla, 542 U.S. 426 (2004).

[85] Hamdi v. Rumsfeld, 542 U.S. 507 (2004).

[86] Rasul v. Bush, 542 U.S. 466 (2004).

departures from established law. Under the law of war, a combatant in an international armed conflict possesses combat immunity for acts that do not violate the law of war, while a civilian would have no combat immunity unless he or she can fall within the definitions of eligibility for POW status under article 4 of Geneva III (GPW). And the law of war generally would not require recognition of combat immunity for violent acts during a period of insurrection or internal armed conflict. These concepts form part of the background for the question of how to deal with violent actors who are not connected with any entity claiming the status of a nation or state.

Yaser Esam Hamdi and José Padilla were held in the Navy brig at Charleston, South Carolina for over two years before their habeas corpus cases reached the Supreme Court. Hamdi is a U.S. citizen who was captured in military action (unquestionably during wartime) in Afghanistan. The Government first chose not to disclose the circumstances of his capture, whether he was actively engaged in carrying arms against U.S. troops or what he was doing. Under pressure from the district court, the Government produced an affidavit containing very summary statements about the circumstances of his capture. Padilla was arrested by civilian authorities when deplaning in Chicago after a trip to Pakistan, during which he allegedly made plans to detonate a "dirty bomb" in the District of Columbia. In both cases, the Justice Department took the position that the Government was not required to disclose to a court the basis for the detention beyond the conclusion that each was an "enemy combatant."

[1] *Hamdi*

Understanding what the Supreme Court held in *Hamdi* is aided by understanding what the Government argued in the lower courts. The Government first took the position that Hamdi could be held without review by the courts. "Especially in a time of active conflict, a court considering a properly filed habeas action generally should accept the military's determination that a detainee is an enemy combatant."[87] Even granting the wiggle room of the word "generally," this is at best an astonishing statement. If made by the government of any number of third-world countries over the last half century, it would bring instant rebuke from both left and right political allegiances. The United States Government, apparently recognizing the enormity of the statement, immediately asserted that its position "does not nullify the writ."

The Government suggested two checks on the power to detain. First, a court could insist on a statement of the detainee's status, and second, the courts should be assured of the efficacy of political checks on the executive branch. The first argument threw into doubt the extent of judicial review authority to determine whether the detainee is an "enemy combatant." The *Hamdi* brief attempted reassurance by stating that

> [A]lthough a court should accept the military's determination that an individual is an enemy combatant, a court may evaluate the legal

---

[87] Hamdi v. Rumsfeld, Brief of Respondents-Appellants at 31 (No. 02-6895 (4th Cir. 2004).

consequences of that determination. For example, a court might evaluate whether the military's determination that an individual is an enemy combatant is sufficient as a matter of law to justify his detention even if the combatant has a claim to American citizenship. In doing so, however, a court may not second guess the military's determination that the detainee is an enemy combatant, and therefore no evidentiary proceedings concerning such determination are necessary.[88]

But the Government also took the position that the executive determination was "sufficient as a matter of law to justify his detention." If a court were to decide as the Government wished, then the executive determination effectively isolates the detainee from any judicial oversight whatsoever. The Supreme Court never hesitated in either *Quirin* or *Eisentrager* to assert its authority to make the basic determination of the prisoner's status. Anything less would undercut the entire structure on which this nation's jurisprudence is built. If there were any need for specific authority for this proposition, we need look no further than the essentials of due process in the Fifth Amendment, seizure and arrest requirements in the Fourth Amendment, and place of trial requirements in the Sixth Amendment.

The Supreme Court held that "due process demands that a citizen held in the United States as an enemy combatant be given a meaningful opportunity to contest the factual basis for that detention before a neutral decisionmaker."[89] That statement hardly ends the matter, however, because now the Government must decide what its next step should be. It can turn either to proof of combatant status in the habeas proceeding or to another course such as trial for specific criminal conduct. Pursuing the first course requires asking what sort of evidence would be required for the United States to justify its holding a citizen without trial. If the Government seeks to show that he was bearing arms against the U.S., the Supreme Court insisted that Hamdi have an opportunity to rebut the Government's evidence. Because bearing arms against the U.S. by a citizen violates any number of statutes, it is difficult to see why the Government's evidence and Hamdi's rebuttal should not take place in a full-blown trial, either in the civilian criminal justice system (a la John Walker Lindh) or in the military system. In the latter instance, a person captured bearing arms in the "theater of operations" should rather clearly be subject to the jurisdiction of a military commission.

The Government tried to make two arguments against the need for a trial. First, an argument regarding the desirability of detention for interrogation was answered by the plurality with the flat statement that "indefinite detention for interrogation is not authorized." The Government's second argument was that combatants could be held to prevent their rejoining the fray. The plurality's partial agreement with this argument

---

[88] *Id.*

[89] *Hamdi*, 542 U.S. at 509.

stated its "understanding" that Congress had authorized military detention without trial only

> . . . for the duration of the relevant conflict, and our understanding is based on longstanding law-of-war principles. If the practical circumstances of a given conflict are entirely unlike those of the conflicts that informed the development of the law of war, that understanding may unravel. But that is not the situation we face as of this date. Active combat operations against Taliban fighters apparently are ongoing in Afghanistan. The United States may detain, for the duration of these hostilities, individuals legitimately determined to be Taliban combatants who "engaged in an armed conflict against the United States."[90]

By contrast, Justice Scalia said that there was nothing in Anglo-American law since Magna Carta to authorize executive detention of a citizen without trial.[91] He distinguished *Quirin* on the ground that "in *Quirin* it was uncontested that the petitioners were members of enemy forces,"[92] to which the plurality responded that Hamdi was picked up on a foreign battlefield and the proof of enemy status would be forthcoming in the hearing envisioned on remand.[93] With all due respect, this dialogue between Justice Scalia and Justice O'Connor misses the point that Hamdi is being held *without trial* and will still be so even after the hearing contemplated by the plurality. In *Quirin*, there was a trial, albeit a military one because of the status as a member of "enemy forces." Justice Scalia surely has the better of the argument that indefinite detention without trial is alien to our constitutional underpinnings.[94]

The plurality's position carried the day only because Justice Souter, joined by Justice Ginsburg, would have preferred to reach a similar position to Justice Scalia on statutory rather than constitutional grounds but relented to vote with the plurality because otherwise there would have been no resolution of the case.[95] It would have been an extremely odd situation for eight Justices to reject the lower court's acceptance of the Government's position and yet the Court not be able to reverse the lower court for failure to agree on a disposition.

The second reassurance offered by the Government in *Hamdi* was the usual fallback for executive discretion, basically consisting of "trust us."

---

[90] *Id.* at 521.

[91] *Id.* at 557-58.

[92] *Id.* at 571.

[93] *Id.* at 523-24.

[94] The plurality at this point also accuses Justice Scalia of creating a "perverse incentive" to hold citizens abroad rather than bringing them back to the U.S., because Scalia would deny U.S. courts jurisdiction to issue habeas corpus to persons held abroad. But this ignores the one critical feature of citizenship that remains in the modern world — a citizen cannot be held in exile. The right of a citizen to enter his country of nationality would be the only apparent reason why Hamdi was brought to Virginia and then South Carolina. *Id.* at 524.

[95] *See generally id.* at 542-58.

Coupling two different statements from the Federalist Papers together, the Government asserts that the courts have no role in "reviewing military decisions or operations." The first statement from the Federalist is said to be that, with regard to military affairs, "if the majority should be really disposed to exceed the proper limits, the community will be warned of the danger [by the minority], and [the community] will have an opportunity of taking measures to guard against it."[96] Looking at this language in context leads almost to the conclusion that the Government is playing cynical games. The passage is by Hamilton and concerns assurances that Congress will have control of the military by virtue of its inability "to vest permanent funds for the support of an army" and by action of the "party in opposition." When the entire objective of the executive is to hide information from the other branches and the public, as in *Hamdi*, it is difficult to place much reliance on the power of the Loyal Opposition. The

---

[96] THE FEDERALIST NO. 26 (Alexander Hamilton). The language chosen by the Government is italicized:

> The legislature of the United States will be OBLIGED, by this provision, once at least in every two, years, to deliberate upon the propriety of keeping a military force on foot to come to a new resolution on the point and to declare their sense of the matter, by a formal vote in the face of their constituents. They are not AT LIBERTY to vest in the executive department permanent funds for the support of an army, if they were even incautious enough to be willing to repose in it so improper a confidence. As the spirit of party, in different degrees, must be expected to infect all political bodies, there will be, no doubt, persons in the national legislature willing enough to arraign the measures and criminate the views of the majority. The provision for the support of a military force will always be a favorable topic for declamation. As often as the question comes forward, the public attention will be roused and attracted to the subject, by the party in opposition and *if the majority should be really disposed to exceed the proper limits, the community will be warned of the danger, and will have an opportunity of taking measures to guard against it.* Independent of parties in the national legislature itself, as often as the period of discussion arrived, the State legislatures, who will always be not only vigilant but suspicious and jealous guardians of the rights of the citizens against encroachments from the federal government, will constantly have their attention awake to the conduct of the national rulers, and will be ready enough, if any thing improper appears, to sound the alarm to the people, and not only to be the VOICE, but, if necessary, the ARM of their discontent.

> Schemes to subvert the liberties of a great community REQUIRE TIME to mature them for execution. An army, so large as seriously to menace those liberties, could only be formed by progressive augmentations which would suppose, not merely a temporary combination between the legislature and executive, but a continued conspiracy for a series of time. Is it probable that it would be persevered in, and transmitted along through all the successive variations in a representative body, which biennial elections would naturally produce in both houses? Is it presumable, that every man, the instant he took his seat in the national Senate or House of Representatives, would commence a traitor to his constituents and to his country? Can it be supposed that there would not be found one man, discerning enough to detect so atrocious a conspiracy, or bold or honest enough to apprise his constituents of their danger? If such presumptions can fairly be made, there ought at once to be an end of all delegated authority. The people should resolve to recall all the powers they have heretofore parted with out of their own hands, and to divide themselves into as many States as there are counties, in order that they may be able to t manage their own concerns in person.

second quote, regarding the judiciary's lack of influence over either sword or purse, related to assurances that the judiciary would not be able to rule by fiat.[97]

Using these quotes to support plenary military authority is far from fair to the authors of the Federalist Papers, who could hardly have been arguing in favor of rule by military fiat. They had just fought a war against a runaway monarch, had drafted a Constitution full of checks on executive power, and were consistently reminding the public of the need to be vigilant against the abuses of a standing army.

The Fourth Circuit's response to these arguments[98] was to straddle both sides of the fence, an uncomfortable if not downright painful position. After reciting the reasons for judicial deference to executive military decisions and praising American reliance on the Bill of Rights and habeas corpus, the court held that Hamdi could be detained because in fact he had been captured bearing arms against the U.S. in an active combat zone. "We shall, in fact, go no further in this case than the specific context before us — that of the undisputed detention of a citizen during a combat operation undertaken in a foreign country and a determination by the executive that the citizen was allied with enemy forces."[99]

The Fourth Circuit seemed to hold that a court must accept the factual determinations of the military without judicial review because of the difficulty of conducting a trial away from the battlefield[100] but it backed off the most extreme implications of this position by gratefully accepting the Government's "voluntary" submission of some factual information.[101]

---

[97] THE FEDERALIST No. 78 (Alexander Hamilton).

[98] Hamdi v. Rumsfeld, 316 F.3d 450 (4th Cir. 2003).

[99] Id. at 465.

[100] Id. at 471:

> The factual inquiry upon which Hamdi would lead us, if it did not entail disclosure of sensitive intelligence, might require an excavation of facts buried under the rubble of war. The cost of such an inquiry in terms of the efficiency and morale of American forces cannot be disregarded. Some of those with knowledge of Hamdi's detention may have been slain or injured in battle. Others might have to be diverted from active and ongoing military duties of their own. The logistical effort to acquire evidence from far away battle zones might be substantial. And these efforts would profoundly unsettle the constitutional balance.

[101] Id. at 472:

> This deferential posture, however, only comes into play after we ascertain that the challenged decision is one legitimately made pursuant to the war powers. It does not preclude us from determining in the first instance whether the factual assertions set forth by the government would, if accurate, provide a legally valid basis for Hamdi's detention under that power. Otherwise, we would be deferring to a decision made without any inquiry into whether such deference is due. For these reasons, it is appropriate, upon a citizen's presentation of a habeas petition alleging that he is being unlawfully detained by his own government, to ask that the government provide the legal authority upon which it relies for that detention and the basic facts relied upon to support a legitimate exercise of that authority. Indeed, in this case, the government has voluntarily submitted — and urged us to review — an affidavit

A fair reading of the Fourth Circuit's opinion is that the judiciary must defer to the military and that the military must defer to the judiciary, which shows the extraordinarily difficult position in which the court found itself.

The Supreme Court rejected this argument, 8-1. In neither military law nor civilian law is there any justification for indefinite detention of an American citizen once he is removed from the theater of operations. Accepting the Government's position in *Hamdi*, that civilian courts may not inquire into the bases of classifying a person as an enemy combatant, would have constituted a radical change in the American way of doing government business. The argument about the difficulty of conducting a trial is unpersuasive in light of modern communications and transportation, especially a year after the military operation had reached 90% of its objectives and consisted of an occupation more than active engagement, and ultimately it is the government's choice whether to attempt imprisonment for criminal charges away from the theater of operations. As Justice Souter stated,

> Whether insisting on the careful scrutiny of emergency claims or on a vigorous reading of § 4001(a), we are heirs to a tradition given voice 800 years ago by Magna Carta, which, on the barons' insistence, confined executive power by "the law of the land."[102]

[2] *Padilla*

Unfortunately, the Court stopped short of the logical implications of its *Hamdi* position when it turned to the case of José Padilla.[103] Padilla is a U.S. citizen, arrested on U.S. soil, carrying no weapons (he just stepped off a commercial airplane), but allegedly hoping to carry out an attack on U.S. soil at an undisclosed date in the future. The Government first held him as a "material witness" before a grand jury in New York but then transferred him to military custody as an "enemy combatant." A habeas corpus petition in the Southern District of New York was met with claims by the U.S. that isolation of Padilla is necessary "to bring psychological pressure to bear on him for interrogation," and that the court should accept the factual conclusions of the Defense Intelligence Agency that Padilla was engaged on a mission for a terrorist network.

Whatever the facts that may have been disclosed to the court *in camera*, neither of these arguments even comes close to justifying placing a U.S. citizen in military detention without court action. Moreover, the Government's argument would not work even to justify a military tribunal as in *Quirin* because the terrorist network is not the same as a foreign enemy state.

---

from Michael Mobbs, Special Advisor to the Under Secretary of Defense for Policy, describing what the government contends were the circumstances leading to Hamdi's designation as an enemy combatant under Article II's war power.

[102] *Hamdi*, 542 U.S. at 552.

[103] *Padilla*, 542 U.S. 426.

The precedent for the Government's argument that Padilla can be classified as an "enemy combatant" and thus exempted from civilian judicial processes is *Ex parte Quirin*. Although it could be argued that *Quirin* was as much a mistake as *Korematsu* and should be overruled, there is a glaring distinction between Padilla and the *Quirin* defendants. The *Quirin* group was acting under the orders of an enemy nation-state during a declared war. By contrast, al Qaeda is not a nation-state and there is no "law of war" for a military court to apply.

On the merits, following *Hamdi*, the *Padilla* habeas petition should be a slam dunk. Unfortunately, the Court ducked the implications of its holding in *Hamdi* by holding that Padilla's petition should have been filed in South Carolina rather than in New York.[104] In a routine case, this would be an appropriate result. But this was no ordinary case. As Justice Stevens pointed out in dissent, Padilla was already represented by counsel when he was held in New York pursuant to a material witness warrant.[105] When the New York court ruled that his status under that warrant gave have rights to meet with counsel, the Attorney General transferred him to the Secretary of Defense, who then authorized his transfer from New York to South Carolina. The habeas corpus petition was filed promptly on his behalf in New York by New York counsel. If the petition had been filed in New York before his transfer to South Carolina, then the New York court could have retained jurisdiction over the custodian. Allowing the Government to escape the jurisdiction of the court by a quick move of the prisoner is uncomfortable at best, especially when the merits of the petition seem so obviously to call for his release or charge in a criminal proceeding.

The most likely explanation for the Court's ducking of Padilla's petition is that the Justices had already dealt the administration's policies significant blows in *Hamdi* and *Rasul*, and so did not want to make it a 3-0 result on one day for the whole program of military detentions.

It is interesting that the Government made a point of trying to persuade the district court that Padilla could be held in indefinite detention without trial, when the information provided to the court apparently is very similar, if not the same, as what might be provided at a civilian trial given the requirements of the Classified Information Act procedures. Perhaps this point can be understood best by imagining three ways of dealing with Padilla. First, he could be tried in civilian court for conspiracy to commit any number of crimes by exploding a bomb. Second, he could be tried in military court for violation of the law of war. Is there really any difference between trial in a civilian court and a military court? The U.S. Court of Military Appeals has applied the same standards of public trial requirements in dealing with classified materials as would a civilian court. The problem is that without a nation-state sponsor or principal, there is no provision of the law of war that Padilla has violated, and the military courts

---

[104] *Id.* at 446.
[105] *Id.* at 458-59.

are not statutorily authorized to try offenses that do not have a military connection.

Third, the Government argues that Padilla could be held in indefinite military detention without any trial process at all. The minimum thrust of due process, from Magna Carta forward, has been to prevent unreviewed executive incarceration. Even with the precedent of *Quirin*, there is no justification for allowing the military to hold a U.S. citizen arrested on U.S. soil without trial. The defendants in *Quirin* at least received a prompt (very prompt) military trial.

The District Court in *Padilla* issued two opinions, the first rather scholarly and deferential, and the second approaching testiness with the Government. As in *Hamdi*, the Government argued that the President was entitled to classify Padilla as an enemy combatant under the precedent of *Quirin* and that the determination was entitled to deference from the courts. When pressed by the court as to why this should be the case, the Government proferred basically two justifications for detention without trial: to "prevent him from rejoining the enemy" and to allow investigators to maintain "psychological pressure" to obtain information from him.[106] Despite the court's impatience with the Government's behavior in the case, it accepted both arguments as valid and required only that "some evidence" be offered to show that he was "engaged in a mission against the United States on behalf of an enemy with whom the United States is at war."[107]

With all due respect, neither of the proferred justifications is persuasive. The argument of preventing Padilla from rejoining the enemy calls for nothing more than a trial, conviction, and sentence. He should no more be allowed to rejoin his al Qaeda buddies than should a drug lord be allowed to rejoin his cohorts. What distinguishes Padilla from the common street criminal with ties to a Colombian drug cartel? The wantonness of his desire to kill and maim? Is he more like a serial killer or mass murder? Neither the drug lord nor the serial killer can be imprisoned without judicial process; the concept of preventive detention has been considered and rejected in any number of settings. The court commented that prisoners of war could be detained "for the duration of the hostilities," but there is not likely to be a duration of hostilities with al Qaeda for the simple reason that there is no political structure with which to negotiate terms and conditions of peace. The object of war is peace, al Qaeda has no peaceful objectives, and the conflict with al Qaeda cannot plausibly be considered a war.

The psychological pressure argument flies in the face of due process and all its related themes. It is difficult even to imagine cases dealing with this kind of argument. Do we look at cases granting immunity as the Government argued? Nothing in those cases even hint at isolated confinement without judicial process. Court orders for immunity or to compel testimony

---

[106] Padilla rel. Newman v. Bush, 233 F. Supp. 2d 564, 593 (S.D.N.Y. 2002).

[107] *Id.* at 608.

before a grand jury are court orders in which the witness knows exactly what is demanded and knows the consequences of refusing to divulge.

There is one glaring distinction between Padilla and the *Quirin* defendants. The *Quirin* group was acting under the orders of an enemy nation-state during a declared war. By contrast, al Qaeda is not a nation-state and there is no "law of war" for a military court to apply. There are basically three ways of dealing with Padilla. First, he could be tried in civilian court for conspiracy to commit any number of crimes by exploding a bomb. Second, he could be tried in military court for violation of the law of war. Is there really any difference between trial in a civilian court and a military court? The U.S. Court of Military Appeals has applied the same standards of public trial requirements in dealing with classified materials as would a civilian court. The problem is that without a nation-state sponsor or principal, there is no provision of the law of war that Padilla has violated, and the military courts are not statutorily authorized to try offenses that do not have a military connection.

Third, the Government argued that Padilla could be held in indefinite military detention without any trial process at all. The minimum thrust of due process, from Magna Carta forward, has been to prevent unreviewed executive incarceration. Even with the precedent of *Quirin*, it is not easy to construct a justification for allowing the military to hold a U.S. citizen arrested on U.S. soil without trial. The defendants in *Quirin* at least received a prompt (very prompt) military trial.

Finally, for the same reasons that there is not an enemy with whom to negotiate a cessation of hostilities, there is no entity as to which to apply the court's "some evidence" standard. Who is the "enemy with whom the United States is at war?" Is al Qaeda different from ETA? from any number of other para-military organizations that use violence against civilians either to make political points or to carry out their own frustrations?

Now, instead of José Padilla, let us hypothesize the arrest of a U.S. citizen alleged to be acting as an agent of the Iraqi government during time of war. In this context, the Government arguments make more sense. There is an identified enemy nation, an identified battlefield, and the prospect of a cessation of hostilities that would carry repatriation. But even then, the "unlawful" combatant (i.e., spy or saboteur) would be punishable only after a "determination by a competent tribunal" not by mere executive fiat. Battlefield torture and executions of unlawful combatants, such as soldiers masquerading as civilians, certainly occur but they are violations of international law and conventions. Even incarceration outside the rules of POW status would likewise be a violation of those same provisions, and it would be terrible for the courts to sanction a practice that violates international obligations. If the military holds this person in POW status, there is no need for judicial review. If it subjects this person to military trial for violation of the law of war, then *Quirin* is ample precedent. What is happening in *Padilla* is not either of these situations.

As the Supreme Court stated in response to an apparently fraudulent effort on the part of the Governor of Texas to declare martial law to limit production from oil wells:

> What are the allowable limits of military discretion, and whether or not they have been overstepped in a particular case, are judicial questions. Thus, in the theatre of actual war, there are occasions in which private property may be taken or destroyed to prevent it from falling into the hands of the enemy or may be impressed into the public service and the officer may show the necessity in defending an action for trespass. "But we are clearly of opinion," said the Court speaking through Chief Justice Taney, "that in all of these cases the danger must be immediate and impending; or the necessity urgent for the public service, such as will not admit of delay, and where the action of the civil authority would be too late in providing the means which the occasion calls for. . . . Every case must depend on its own circumstances. It is the emergency that gives the right, and the emergency must be shown to exist before the taking can be justified."[108]

Accepting the Government's position in *Hamdi*, that civilian courts may not inquire into the bases of classifying a person as an enemy combatant, would constitute a radical change in the American way of doing government business. That position in the context of Padilla, who was not captured within any theater of operations, is quite simply unsupportable.

Following the Supreme Court opinion in *Padilla*, his attorneys filed a habeas corpus petition in South Carolina. The District Court held that the AUMF did not authorize detention of Padilla, who was not captured on the battlefield (unlike Hamdi) and who was not charged with any violation of the law of war or any other crime but was merely held in preventive detention.[109]

The Fourth Circuit disagreed. "Like Haupt [the U.S. citizen involved in *Quirin*], Padilla associated with the military arm of the enemy, and with its aid, guidance, and direction entered this country bent on committing hostile acts on American soil. Padilla thus falls within *Quirin*'s definition of enemy belligerent, as well as within the definition of the equivalent term accepted by the plurality in *Hamdi*."[110]

Padilla then petitioned for certiorari, at which point the Government decided to transfer him to civilian custody to face charges in federal court. Supreme Court Rules required a court order to allow transfer of custody, which the Fourth Circuit refused but the Supreme Court then granted.

---

[108] Sterling v. Constantin, 287 U.S. 378, 401 (1932) (citing Mitchell v. Harmony, 54 U.S. 115 (1851)).

[109] Padilla v. Hanft, 389 F. Supp. 2d 678 (D.S.C. 2005).

[110] Padilla v. Hanft, 423 F.3d 386 (4th Cir. 2005).

Ultimately, the Court denied certiorari[111] and Padilla is on trial for conspiracy charges.[112]

Justice Kennedy, for himself and two others, concurred in the denial of certiorari with these comments:

> In light of the previous changes in his custody status and the fact that nearly four years have passed since he first was detained, Padilla, it must be acknowledged, has a continuing concern that his status might be altered again. That concern, however, can be addressed if the necessity arises. Padilla is now being held pursuant to the control and supervision of the United States District Court for the Southern District of Florida, pending trial of the criminal case. In the course of its supervision over Padilla's custody and trial the District Court will be obliged to afford him the protection, including the right to a speedy trial, guaranteed to all federal criminal defendants. Were the Government to seek to change the status or conditions of Padilla's custody, that court would be in a position to rule quickly on any responsive filings submitted by Padilla. In such an event, the District Court, as well as other courts of competent jurisdiction, should act promptly to ensure that the office and purposes of the writ of habeas corpus are not compromised. Padilla, moreover, retains the option of seeking a writ of habeas corpus in this Court.[113]

Justice Ginsburg dissented from the denial of certiorari on the ground that the case was one "capable of repetition yet evading review."[114]

[3] *Rasul* — The Guantánamo Detainees

As of July 2003, approximately 660 persons were being held at Guantánamo Bay, Cuba after being captured in Afghanistan, and facilities were being constructed to hold as many as 2,000 prisoners. The initial detainees were captured in Afghanistan and alleged to be members of the Taliban militia. Over the intervening two years, some persons have been released to their countries of nationality while other alleged "enemy combatants" have been brought to Guantánamo, some apparently having been captured in various countries as alleged members of terrorist cells.

The Taliban detainees include nationals from a number of countries, notably Britain, Australia, and Sweden, which have been demanding that their citizens either be repatriated or accused of a crime.[115] It is possible

---

[111] 547 U.S. 1062 (2006).

[112] The indictment that charges Padilla along with three others can be found at fl1.findlaw.com/news.findlaw.com/hdocs/docs/padilla/uspad111705ind.pdf. It charges them with conspiracy to commit murder and kidnaping along with material support for terrorists. The indictment does not sound anything like the "dirty bomb" plot to which the Government referred at the time of his arrest.

[113] *Padilla*, 547 U.S. at 1650.

[114] *Id.* at 1651.

[115] On Nov. 25, 2003, Australia agreed to U.S. military trials for its nationals.

that some of the detainees from the original Afghan captures could be charged with terrorist acts in league with organizations such as al Qaeda, but Government press releases and court filings indicated only that they were being held for their involvement as functionaries of the Taliban regime.[116] The first releases from Guantánamo Bay occurred in October 2002 when three Afghanis were repatriated to that country pursuant to a finding that they were connected to neither the Taliban regime nor al Qaeda.[117]

As time has gone along, additional captives from a variety of sites, including notorious figures such as Khalid Sheikh Muhammed, have been sent to Guantánamo and the character of the institution has changed. The Department of Defense on June 19, 2007 provided this update with the announcement of transfer six detainees from Guantánamo Bay to other countries:

> Two detainees were transferred to Tunisia and four detainees were transferred to Yemen. . . . Approximately 80 detainees remain at Guantánamo who the U.S. government has determined eligible for transfer or release. Departure of these remaining detainees is subject to ongoing discussions between the United States and other nations.

> Since 2002, approximately 405 detainees have departed Guantánamo for other countries.

Approximately 375 detainees remain at Guantánamo.[118]

The United States administration will not likely prosecute any of the Taliban in the U.S. criminal justice system for the simple reason that most of them cannot be accused of crimes cognizable under U.S. law. There are some, undoubtedly, who could be brought to task for "crimes against humanity" on the basis of the human rights violations that occurred in

---

> The United States and Australian governments announced today that they agree the military commission process provides for a full and fair trial for any charged Australian detainees held at Guantánamo Bay Naval Station. Following discussions between the two governments concerning the military commission process, and specifics of the Australian detainees' cases, the U.S. government provided significant assurances, clarifications and modifications that benefitted the military commission process.

Press Release, Dep't. Of Defense, U.S. & Australia Announce Arguments on Guantánamo Detainees, *available at* www.defenselink.mil/releases/2003/nr20031125-0702.html (last visited July 17, 2007).

[116] Professor Paust dealt with the POW issue in the context of whether the detainees have the international version of due process rights under the GPW. Jordan Paust, *Antiterrorism Military Commissions: Courting Illegality*, 23 MICH. J. INT'L. 5-8, n.15 & 16 (2001); Jordan Paust, *War and Enemy Status After 9/11: Attacks on the Laws of War*, 28 YALE J. INT'L. L. 325, 328-34 (2003).

[117] CNN.com, *Three detainees leave Guantánamo for Afghanistan, available at* www.cnn.com/2002/WORLD/asiapcf/central/10/28/afghans.returned/index.html (last visited July 17, 2007).

[118] Press Release, Dep't. Of Defense, Detainee Transfer Anounced, *available at* www.defenselink.mil/Releases/Release.aspx?ReleaseID = 11030 (last visited July 17, 2007).

Afghanistan while the Taliban regime was in place. Torture, dismember-ment, and execution may be crimes cognizable in universal jurisdiction, but only if they were either part of an "armed conflict"[119] or "committed as part of a widespread or systematic attack against any civilian population"[120] and only if the individual had a culpable level of knowledge or intent.[121] Universal jurisdiction over acts of brutality generally does not apply to the internal actions of a state against its own citizens until those acts rise to the level of systematic torture.[122] Although it might be worthwhile to prosecute some of the Taliban leadership for their most egregious violations of human rights, there is no indication that the persons held by the U.S. military fall into the leadership category. Moreover, in its position opposing the International Criminal Court, the United States has expressed grave concern about the concept of universal jurisdiction by which persons could be tried outside their home countries for offenses committed against their own population.

The Government position with regard to all detainees denies any role for judicial review over their status under the premise that *Johnson v. Eisen-trager* precludes habeas corpus for foreign nationals held outside the United States. The United States initially stated that the Guantánamo detainees were not to be considered prisoners of war.[123] President Bush has extended that thought to allow the CIA to capture and imprison persons in foreign locations without application of the Geneva Conventions.[124]

The status of detainees under the Geneva Convention on Prisoners of War (GPW) is not particularly relevant to questions of treatment. First, however, we should be clear that if one is neither arrested in the civilian system nor classified as a prisoner of war, that person still cannot be treated with impunity and subjected to brutal treatment. The universal rules of law, as

---

[119] Rome Statute of the International Criminal Court [hereinafter Rome Statute] art. 8(2); *see Prosecutor v. Furundzija*, No. IT-95-17 (Dec. 10, 1998), Int'l Criminal Tribunal for the Former Yugoslavia.

[120] Rome Statute art. 7, *see supra* note 119.

[121] Rome Statute art. 25, *see supra* note 119.

[122] The extradition of Augusto Pinochet from England to Spain was sought on the basis of "state torture" committed "by or with the acquiescence of a public official or other person acting in an official capacity." Regina v. Bow Street Magistrate, 1 App. Cas. 147, 2 All Eng. Rep. 97 (HL 2000).

[123] *See supra* note 2. The statement distinguished between Taliban detainees and al Qaeda detainees. With respect to the former, because the Taliban government was never recognized as the legitimate government of Afghanistan, its troops would not be POWs of a nation. With respect to the al Qaeda members, the statement declares that they are members of a foreign terrorist group and not entitled to POW status. The statement declared that although the detainees are not entitled to POW privileges, they will be provided many POW privileges as a matter of policy. The statement delineated some aspects of humane treatment that would be available to the detainees and some that would not. In general, they would be given food, clothing, and shelter, but would not be provided access to money or purchasable goods.

[124] *Executive Order: Interpretation of the Geneva Conventions Common Article 3 as Applied to a Program of Detention and Interrogation Operated by the Central Intelligence Agency* (July 20, 2007), *available at* www.whitehouse.gov/news/releases/2007/07/20070720-4.html (last visited Aug 1, 2007).

well as various treaties and conventions, prevent murder, torture, starvation, or holding of hostages.[125]

Several habeas corpus and related petitions were presented to federal courts in the District of Columbia[126] and Ninth Circuit.[127] All these petitions were brought on behalf of nationals of nations other than Afghanistan,[128] and all essentially challenged the authority of the United States to hold the detainees without due process. The D.C. Circuit held that habeas corpus is not available to aliens held outside the "sovereign territory" of the United States for the simple reason that those persons have no constitutional rights under U.S. law. The Ninth Circuit disagreed, holding that Guantánamo is subject to U.S. control and jurisdiction, and that the rights of the detainees would need to be determined after consideration of the Government's response to the habeas petitions. The Ninth Circuit expressed astonishment at what it considered the Government's "extreme position."[129]

Under the heading of *Rasul v. Bush*,[130] the Supreme Court essentially agreed with the Ninth Circuit.[131] It distinguished *Padilla* on the basis that

---

[125] *See* Rome Statute art. 8(2)(a), *supra* note 119.

[126] Al Odah v. United States, 321 F.3d 1134 (D.C. Cir. 2003).

[127] Gherebi v. Bush, 352 F.3d 1278 (9th Cir. 2003).

[128] The named individuals on whose behalf relief was sought in D.C. were 12 Kuwaitis, two Australians, and two Britons, all of whom were alleged to be in Afghanistan for various personal or humanitarian reasons, to have been kidnapped by locals, and to have ended up in the hands of U.S. military forces without having taken up arms against the U.S. The Ninth Circuit did not indicate the nationality of Gherebi.

[129] *Gherebi*, 352 F.3d at 1299:

Unlike the petitioners in *Johnson*, and even in *Yamashita* and *Quirin*, Gherebi has not been subjected to a military trial. . . . [U]nder the government's theory, it is free to imprison Gherebi indefinitely along with hundreds of other citizens of foreign countries, friendly nations among them, and to do with Gherebi and these detainees as it will, when it pleases, without any compliance with any rule of law of any kind, without permitting him to consult counsel, and without acknowledging any judicial forum in which its actions may be challenged. Indeed, at oral argument, the government advised us that its position would be the same even if the claims were that it was engaging in acts of torture or that it was summarily executing the detainees. To our knowledge, prior to the current detention of prisoners at Guantánamo, the U.S. government has never before asserted such a grave and startling proposition. Accordingly, we view Guantánamo as unique not only because the United States' territorial relationship with the Base is without parallel today, but also because it is the first time that the government has announced such an extraordinary set of principles — a position so extreme that it raises the gravest concerns under both American and international law.

[130] 542 U.S. 466 (2004).

[131] *Id.* at 476:

Petitioners in these cases differ from the *Eisentrager* detainees in important respects: They are not nationals of countries at war with the United States, and they deny that they have engaged in or plotted acts of aggression against the United States; they have never been afforded access to any tribunal, much less charged with and convicted of wrongdoing; and for more than two years they have been imprisoned in territory over which the United States exercises exclusive jurisdiction and control.

these detainees were being held outside the U.S. but under federal custody. Thus the "immediate custodian" rule would not apply, the Secretary of Defense would be an adequate defendant, and the District Court for the District of Columbia could exercise jurisdiction. The Supreme Court went about as far as the Ninth Circuit in expressing an opinion on the merits of the petitions, but in a slightly different direction. In a mere footnote, the Supreme Court stated

> Petitioners' allegations — that, although they have engaged neither in combat nor in acts of terrorism against the United States, they have been held in Executive detention for more than two years in territory subject to the long-term, exclusive jurisdiction and control of the United States, without access to counsel and without being charged with any wrongdoing — unquestionably describe "custody in violation of the Constitution or laws or treaties of the United States."[132]

Unfortunately, the Supreme Court did not go on to delineate what law applies to the Guantánamo detainees. There are issues to be considered with each of the possibilities:

1.   constitutional rights — It is doubtful that an alien held in federal custody outside the U.S. would have constitutional rights[133] other than perhaps some rights regarding conditions of confinement. An alien held within the U.S. has at least the due process right to a determination of status accorded to Hamdi, so the status of Guantánamo could become critical.

2.   statutory rights — An alien seeking admission to the U.S. may have claims to statutory rights under the immigration laws but unless Congress legislates directly on the question, there are no statutes applicable to Guantánamo.

3.   treaty rights — It is not resolved whether the Geneva Conventions are self-executing to create rights on behalf of individuals or even what the impact of those conventions would be in this situation.

4.   customary international law — The strongest argument is that both treaties and customary international law entitle a person to freedom from "arbitrary" detention, which implies some level of judicial review over the propriety of detention.[134]

---

[132] *Id.* at 483 n.15.

[133] In one of the cases reviewed in *Rasul*, the D.C. Circuit stated: "We cannot see why, or how, the writ may be made available to aliens abroad when basic constitutional protections are not. This much is at the heart of *Eisentrager*. If the Constitution does not entitle the detainees to due process, and it does not, they cannot invoke the jurisdiction of our courts to test the constitutionality or the legality of restraints on their liberty." Al Odah v. United States, 355 U.S. App. D.C. 189 (D.C. Cir. 2003).

[134] *See* Jordan J. Paust, *Judicial Power to Determine the Status and Rights of Persons Detained Without Trial*, 44 HARV. INT'L L.J. 503 (2003).

[B] *Hamdan* and Military Commissions

Following the decision in *Rasul*, the handling of detainees at Guantánamo split into two tracks: six persons were charged with crimes under
the law of war before military commissions while the rest (about 600) were
sent before panels known as Combatant Status Review Tribunals (CSRT).
Those who were not charged with crimes were represented in habeas corpus
actions that were filed in or transferred to the District Court for the District
of Columbia.[135] Of those were charged before military commissions, the
first one to reach a court was Salim Ahmed Hamdan, alleged to have been
Osama bin Laden's driver and thus knowledgeable of all or virtually all
al Qaeda actions.

Hamdan was charged with "conspiracy to commit . . . offenses triable
by military commission."[136] Before his trial commenced, his attorneys
brought a habeas corpus petition in the District Court for D.C. That court
held that he was being deprived of rights guaranteed by military law and
international law, such as the right to confront witnesses and be present
at all stages of the trial.[137] The D.C. Circuit reversed,[138] holding that the
President could constitute military commissions to meet emergency circumstances under the law of war.

The Supreme Court held that the military commissions violated both U.S.
law and international law because they were not immune from command
influence and because the procedures contemplated introduction of hearsay
evidence as well as secret evidence that the accused would not be able to
confront.[139] In addition, four members of the Court held that conspiracy
is not an offense cognizable under the law of war.

The specific objections to the procedures of the commissions were based
on a provision in the Uniform Code of Military Justice stating that the
procedures of commissions, when used, may not be "contrary to or inconsistent with" the requirements of the UCMJ and shall be identical to those
of military courts "insofar as practicable."[140] The commission procedures
allowed for exclusion of the accused and his chosen counsel from hearing
classified evidence in the discretion of the hearing officer and also allowed
admission of "reasonably probative" evidence. Both these provisions differed
from the requirements of the UCMJ without any showing that it would be
impracticable to apply the procedures of ordinary courts-martial.[141]

---

[135] *See* § 9.04[C] *infra.*

[136] 415 F.3d 33, 34 (D.C. Cir. 2005).

[137] *See generally* 344 F. Supp. 2d 152 (D.D.C. 2004).

[138] 415 F.3d at 43.

[139] Hamdan v. Rumsfeld, 126 S. Ct. 2749 (2006).

[140] UCMJ art. 36, 10 U.S.C. § 836 (2007).

[141] "Nothing in the record before us demonstrates that it would be impracticable to apply
court-martial rules in this case. There is no suggestion, for example, of any logistical difficulty
in securing properly sworn and authenticated evidence or in applying the usual principles of
relevance and admissibility." *Hamdan,* 126 S. Ct. at 2792. Referring to public statements by
administration officials, the Court observed that

In addition to these difficulties under the UCMJ, the majority pointed to a violation of the Geneva Conventions. The Government argued that the Geneva Conventions conferred no individual rights and were enforceable only by diplomatic action. This was the apparent holding of *Eisentrager*. [142] The majority, however, pointed out that the rights of the Conventions were part of the law of war and it was the law of war on which Congress based the military commissions. [143] Once the Court looked at the Geneva Convention, it found that the military commissions were not a "regularly constituted court affording all the judicial guarantees which are recognized as indispensable by civilized peoples."

The plurality's discussion of the validity of the charges against Hamdan cast doubt on the entire construct of the "Global War on Terror."

> Neither the purported agreement with Osama bin Laden and others to commit war crimes, nor a single overt act, is alleged to have occurred in a theater of war or on any specified date after September 11, 2001. None of the overt acts that Hamdan is alleged to have committed violates the law of war.

> These facts alone cast doubt on the legality of the charge and, hence, the commission; as Winthrop makes plain, the offense alleged must have been committed both in a theater of war and during, not before, the relevant conflict. But the deficiencies in the time and place allegations also underscore — indeed are symptomatic of — the most serious defect of this charge: The offense it alleges is not triable by law-of-war military commission. [144]

The plurality went on to discuss the international law of war and concluded that nothing Hamdan was alleged to have done could be considered to have occurred in a theater of war. [145] This discussion incorporates

---

the only additional reason the comments provide — aside from the general danger posed by international terrorism — for departures from court-martial procedures is the need to protect classified information. As we explain in the text, and as Justice Kennedy elaborates in his separate opinion, the structural and procedural defects of Hamdan's commission extend far beyond rules preventing access to classified information.

Id. at n.52.

[142] 393 U.S. 763 (1950).

[143] "[R]egardless of the nature of the rights conferred on Hamdan, they are, as the Government does not dispute, part of the law of war. And compliance with the law of war is the condition upon which the authority set forth in Art. 21 is granted." *Hamdan*, 126 S. Ct. at 2794.

[144] *Hamdan*, 126 S. Ct. at 2778-79.

[145] *Id.* at 2786:

The charge's shortcomings are not merely formal, but are indicative of a broader inability on the Executive's part here to satisfy the most basic precondition — at least in the absence of specific congressional authorization — for establishment of military commissions: military necessity. Hamdan's tribunal was appointed not by a military commander in the field of battle, but by a retired major general stationed away from any active hostilities. Hamdan is charged not with an overt act for which

international law into domestic law, but that is primarily because Congress had incorporated the law of war into the statement of jurisdiction of military commissions.

Thus, *Hamdan* incorporated international law into the controls on military commissions in several different ways:

1. the crime of conspiracy is not part of the law of war, at least not outside the theater of war (plurality holding),

2. exclusion of the accused from hearing evidence is not permitted by the law of war,

3. and trial by ad hoc procedures failing to provide confrontation of the evidence is a violation of the law of war and the Geneva Conventions.

Incorporation of international law into constitutional requirements would mean that Congress could not authorize the commissions to try conspiracies or to consider secret evidence. The *Hamdan* approach, however, relied on incorporation of international law into the UCMJ by Congress' reliance on the law of war, a result that Congress could nullify by further legislation. That was the next step in the drama as Congress got into the act.

The Military Commissions Act of 2006 (MCA), in essence, does the following:

1. authorizes "the use of military commissions to try alien unlawful enemy combatants engaged in hostilities against the United States for violations of the law of war and other offenses triable by military commission"

2. defines an "unlawful enemy combatant" as "a person who has engaged in hostilities or who has purposefully and materially supported hostilities against the United States or its co-belligerents who is not a lawful enemy combatant"

3. provides a specific list of "war crimes" that may be tried by military commission, including conspiracy, torture, "cruel or inhuman treatment" (not degrading treatment or outrages upon personal dignity); performing biological experiments; murder; mutilation or maiming; intentionally causing great suffering or bodily injury; rape; sexual assault or abuse; and taking hostages

---

he was caught redhanded in a theater of war and which military efficiency demands be tried expeditiously, but with an agreement the inception of which long predated the attacks of September 11, 2001 and the AUMF. That may well be a crime, but it is not an offense that "by the law of war may be tried by military commission." None of the overt acts alleged to have been committed in furtherance of the agreement is itself a war crime, or even necessarily occurred during time of, or in a theater of, war. Any urgent need for imposition or execution of judgment is utterly belied by the record; Hamdan was arrested in November 2001 and he was not charged until mid-2004. These simply are not the circumstances in which, by any stretch of the historical evidence or this Court's precedents, a military commission established by Executive Order under the authority of Art. 21 of the UCMJ may lawfully try a person and subject him to punishment.

4.   precludes habeas corpus review on behalf of any detainee classified as an "unlawful enemy combatant" (not just Guantánamo) and allows only D.C. Circuit review of the determinations by Combatant Status Review Tribunals (CSRT)

5.   provides that "no person in any habeas action or any other action may invoke the Geneva Conventions or any protocols thereto as a source of rights, whether directly or indirectly, for any purpose in any court of the United States"

Three cases were charged before reconstituted military commissions, at which point two of the military judges dismissed the charges against Hamdan and Omar Khadr on the grounds that they had not been found by a Combatant Status Review Tribunal (CSRT) to be an "unlawful enemy combatant" but had merely been found to be an "enemy combatant."[146] The prosecution is appealing to the Military Commission Appeals Court. The rulings are rather odd because the facts forming the basis of the tribunal's jurisdiction (unlawful status) ordinarily would be part of the case to be proved at trial, not something to be found beforehand. The military judges, however, responded to this argument by pointing out that the statute seems to contemplate a prior determination.[147]

The MCA has one feature that could dramatically affect the approach taken by the Court in *Hamdan*. The Court held that the military commissions, as they existed prior to the MCA, were invalid not just under U.S. law but under international law. The incorporation of international law into domestic law was easy in that case because Congress had authorized commissions to try offenses against the "law of war,"[148] which is treaty and customary international law. But now Congress has spelled out a list of crimes that are triable by the commissions. When a commission case comes back to the Court, the arguments will involve the question of whether international treaty and customary law are part of the domestic law of the U.S.

At the time of *Hamdan*, the only statutory basis for military tribunals was "violation of the law of war." Congress has now provided in the MCA a list of "war crimes" and provided for commission jurisdiction over "any offense made punishable by this chapter or the law of war."[149] Thus, the commissions still have jurisdiction over crimes under the "law of war," which still seems to incorporate international law under the theory of *Hamdan*. The counter-argument will be that if only a crime under the statute is charged, then international law does not enter the picture for that particular offense.

---

[146] Sgt. Sara Wood, *Judge Dismisses Charges Against Second Guantánamo Detainee, American Forces Press Service*, (June 4, 2007), *available at* www.defenselink.mil/news/newsarticle.aspx?id=46288.

[147] *See supra* note 20.

[148] *Hamdan*, 126 S. Ct. at 2794 ("compliance with the law of war is the condition upon which the authority set forth in [the UCMJ] is granted").

[149] MCA § 948d.

[C] Judicial Review Under the DTA and MCA

Following the 2004 opinions, the Guantánamo detainees were provided reviews by Combatant Status Review Tribunals (CSRTs) and Congress enacted the Detainee Treatment Act of 2005 (DTA). The DTA withdrew habeas corpus jurisdiction for any person who was the subject of a CSRT or waiting for a CSRT review. In return, the CSRT reviews themselves were subject to judicial review in the D.C. Circuit for issues of law. The DTA was passed shortly before the Supreme Court took up the *Hamdan* case, so the first issue in that case was whether the DTA insulated the commissions from habeas corpus review.

The Court held that the DTA did not apply to cases pending at the time of its passage. Although the legislation applied to "claims" pending on or after the date of the act that were governed by the provisions related to CSRTs or commissions, the Court pointed out that the paragraph withdrawing habeas corpus jurisdiction was not specifically mentioned in the provisions on effective date. Therefore, ordinary principles of statutory construction operated to mean that Congress would not have intended to withdraw important rights without saying so.[150]

As the D.C. Circuit would later say, Congress came back to the judicial review issue in the MCA by saying that habeas corpus jurisdiction was withdrawn for pending cases "and we really mean it."[151] The cases that were heard by the Supreme Court under the name of *Rasul* were back in the district courts under a couple of different headings. Judge Leon had a group of cases known as *Khalid v. Bush*[152] while Judge Green had the bulk of the cases and labeled them *In re Guantánamo Detainee Cases*.[153] Judge Leon ruled that the AUMF authorized the President to take all appropriate action with regard to terrorism, that the war powers of Article II included military detention of alien enemy combatants, and that there were no federal rights accruing to persons so detained. Judge Green disagreed and held that, pursuant to Rasul, the detainees had acquired due process rights by being held in territory subject to the exclusive control of the U.S. and that allowing them some due process would not threaten the security of the U.S.

Both these sets of cases went to the D.C. Circuit under the heading of *Boumediene v. Bush*.[154] The D.C. Circuit did not adopt the rationale of either of the district judges; Congress in the meantime had passed the Military Commission Act, which the D.C. Circuit applied to dismiss all the petitions. Because Congress had been unequivocal about applying its "no habeas" mandate to pending cases, the only significant issue before the

---

[150] *Hamdan*, 126 S. Ct. at 2765.

[151] "It is almost as if the proponents of these words were slamming their fists on the table shouting 'When we say 'all,' we mean all — **without exception!**'" Boumediene v. Bush, 476 F.3d 981, 987 (D.C. Cir. 2007).

[152] 355 F. Supp. 2d 311 (D.D.C. 2005).

[153] 355 F. Supp. 2d 443 (D.D.C. 2005).

[154] 476 F.3d 981 (D.C. Cir. 2007).

court was whether that action amounted to a suspension of the writ that would have to be justified by "rebellion or invasion." As the court recognized, neither rebellion nor invasion applies neatly in a foreign military operation, but the court also pointed out that the nature of the writ in 1789 would have had no application to aliens detained outside the sovereign territory of the nation. Therefore, there was no right to habeas corpus and no claim of an invalid suspension. Moreover, the court held that the detainees could state no constitutional claim because "the Constitution does not confer rights on aliens without property or presence within the United States."

The D.C. Circuit's holding that the detainees failed to state a constitutional claim flies in the face of the *Rasul* holding. The court dealt with that apparent anomaly with a mere footnote:

> The *Rasul* decision, resting as it did on statutory interpretation, could not possibly have affected the constitutional holding of *Eisentrager*. Even if *Rasul* somehow calls *Eisentrager*'s constitutional holding into question, as the detainees suppose, we would be bound to follow *Eisentrager*.[155]

Thus the Administration, Congress, and the D.C. Circuit have challenged the Supreme Court's holding in *Rasul* that the Guantánamo detainees state a claim to relief on federal constitutional, or maybe international law, grounds. The Supreme Court initially denied certiorari in *Boumediene*.[156] Then, on the last day of the Term in June 2007, the Court reversed itself and granted certiorari.[157]

Most of the political pundits assumed this meant that five votes exist to reverse because otherwise the Court would let the D.C. Circuit's opinion stand. Another possible scenario stems from the emergence in June 2007 of a solid 5-vote conservative majority including Justice Kennedy. These five could go forward with affirmation of the D.C. Circuit and validation of a program of executive detentions.

---

[155] *Boudediene*, 476 F.3d at 992 n.10.

[156] 127 S. Ct. 1478 (2007).

[157] 2007 U.S. LEXIS 8757 (June 29, 2007).

Chapter 10

CIVIL LIBERTIES AND EMERGENCY POWERS

SYNOPSIS

> *There is danger that, if the Court does not temper its doctrinaire logic with a little practical wisdom, it will convert the constitutional Bill of Rights into a suicide pact.*
>
>   —Justice Jackson, dissenting in Terminiello v. Chicago, 337 U.S. 1, 37 (1949).

> *The moral strength, vitality and commitment proudly enunciated in the Constitution is best tested at a time when forceful, emotionally moving arguments to ignore or trivialize its provisions seek a subordination of time honored constitutional protections.*
>
>   —Judge Takasugi, in United States v. Rahmani, 209 F. Supp. 2d 1045 (C.D. Cal. 2002).

> *If the people ever let command of the war power fall into irresponsible and unscrupulous hands, the courts wield no power equal to its restraint. The chief restraint upon those who command the physical forces of the country, in the future as in the past, must be their responsibility to the political judgments of their contemporaries and to the moral judgments of history.*
>
>   —Justice Jackson, dissenting in Korematsu v. United States, 323 U.S. 214, 248 (1944).

It may seem strange in the quotes above to set the now-famous words of a noted Supreme Court Justice warning of a "suicide pact" against the words of one District Court Judge counseling forbearance in time of crisis.

But Justice Jackson in the first quote was not writing at a time of national emergency; his "suicide pact" rhetorical flourish came in dissent from a case of only mild significance in the law of civil liberties.[1] By contrast, his counsel to a vigilant populace came in the watershed war-time decision of *Korematsu* and Judge Takasugi's words arose in the heat of the so-called "war on terrorism."

There are four central policies that have been launched under the rhetoric of "war on terrorism" and each of which has produced consternation among civil liberties advocates:

1. executive nonjudicial detentions (at Guantánamo and in the U.S.),

2. electronic surveillance outside the confines of FISA,

3. "extraordinary renditions" of suspects to other countries,

4. detention and interrogation of aliens on the basis of ethnicity,

5. "harsh interrogation" methods (the torture issue).

The first three have been dealt with in prior chapters. This chapter will address detentions and interrogation methods. In different ways, each of these practices has been justified by reference to what some authors call a "state of exception."[2] Some even argue that the exceptional is rapidly becoming the norm, not just in the United States, as executives use the idea of emergency to justify semi-permanent extraordinary powers.[3]

§ 10.01 THE BASIC ISSUES

The phrase "war on terrorism" is unfortunate for several reasons, the most obvious of which is that there is no entity with whom to be at war.[4] The Bush Administration has used the phrase to justify some of its activities as "war" while trying to apply the rules of war in selective fashion to justify indefinite detentions and harsh interrogation methods.

If war and civil liberties make strange bedfellows, what can we say about a "war" without a defined enemy or a defined end? The rhetorical flourish

---

[1] Justice Goldberg, even more noted as a defender of civil liberties, borrowed Justice Jackson's phrase in another case during the Cold War and on the verge of Vietnam: "[W]hile the Constitution protects against invasions of individual rights, it is not a suicide pact." Kennedy v. Mendoza-Martinez, 372 U.S. 144, 159-60 (1963) (Goldberg, J., dissenting).

[2] A "state of exception" is a condition in which normal rules are "suspended temporarily and extraordinary powers given to a strong executive or even a dictator in order to protect the republic." MICHAEL HARDT AND ANTONIO NEGRI. MULTITUDE: WAR AND DEMOCRACY IN THE AGE OF EMPIRE 7 (2005).

[3] GIORGIO AGAMBEN, STATE OF EXCEPTION (2005); Mark Danner, *Into the Light of Day: Torture, Human Rights, and the New State of Exception* (Nov. 16, 2006) (lecture at the Salt Lake City Library, sometimes available on the internet at www.markdanner.com/speaking/).

[4] *See* Wayne McCormack, *Military Detention and the Judiciary,: Al Qaeda, the KKK, and Supra-State Law*, 5 SAN DIEGO INT'L L.J. 7 (2004); Jordan J. Paust, *War and Enemy Status After 9/11: Attacks on the Law of War*, 28 YALE J. INT'L L. 325, 327-28 (2003). For the view that the distinction between war and crime is more nuanced, see Noah Feldman, *Choices of Law, Choices of War*, 25 HARV. J.L. & PUB. POL'Y 457 (2002).

of "War on Terrorism" has its historical roots in some loose use of language beginning with the "War on Poverty" followed by the "War on Drugs."[5] Maybe the "War on Poverty" did not do much to civil rights (although some conservatives would differ strongly), but the "War on Drugs" has certainly pushed the envelope.[6] Now enhanced powers of law enforcement, legislated in response to the "terrorism" threat, are being deployed in pursuit of drug dealers and other "ordinary" criminals.[7]

The headlines of two early Op Ed pieces on succeeding days capture one element of the potential issues nicely: *Success in War Requires the Violation of Some Civil Liberties*,[8] and *War on Terror Has Turned Into War on Constitution*.[9] There are many questions involved in the broad scope of civil liberties and times of crisis. The first step of the lawyer is to separate the questions into manageable pieces.

There is nothing unusual or particularly threatening about heightened security and decreased mobility during time of war. Much has changed in several areas of law since World War II, and much of our First Amendment lore comes out of Vietnam times. American attitudes toward a time of national crisis provide an opportunity to explore concepts of civil liberties in a time of difficulty, looking ahead to think of proper responses in future engagements.

Concretely, the disclosure of prisoner abuses in Abu Ghraib Prison presents rather stark questions of the extent to which we as a community are willing to tolerate gross violations of both domestic and international law, apparently condoned if not sanctioned by the upper echelons of the executive branch. Meanwhile, the 9/11 Commission Report highlights some of the difficulties in anti-terrorism, namely obtaining information about a

---

[5] As one Navy Commander quipped to me, "What were we supposed to do, shoot a homeless person?" He went on to point out that the Navy did what was requested in interdicting drugs at sea but would like to turn the job over to law enforcement agencies.

[6] Judge Posner takes the interesting view that this is a good time to recognize that the "war on drugs has been a big flop" and to "redirect law-enforcement resources from the investigation and apprehension of drug offenders to the investigation and apprehension of international terrorists." Richard A. Posner, *Security Versus Civil Liberties*, ATLANTIC MONTHLY, Dec. 2001. Meanwhile, Senator Hatch has suggested conflating the two wars into a war on "narco-terrorism." Press release, Orrin Hatch, Judiciary Statement, *Narco-Terrorism: Int'l Drug Trafficking & Terrorism — A Dangerous Mix* (May 20, 2003), *available at* hatch.senate.gov/index.cfm?FuseAction = PressReleases.Detail&PressRelease_id = 784&Month = 5&Year = 2003. Senator Hatch was widely reported to have floated a draft bill entitled "Vital Interdiction of Criminal Terrorist Organizations" or VICTORY Act, but the measure never was introduced. *See, e.g.*, Dean Shabner, *Draft Bill Seeks Braod Power in "Narco-Terror" Fight*, Aug. 20, 2003, *available at* abcnews.go.com/US/story?id = 90316&page = 1.

[7] David Caruso, *Use of Patriot Act Widens*, ASSOCIATED PRESS, Sept. 15, 2003. According to this story, a county prosecutor in North Carolina is charging a methamphetamine manufacturer with making chemical weapons in violation of the state's terrorism statute. The "Serial Sniper" was prosecuted in Virginia under that state's terrorism statute.

[8] Michael Kelly, *Success in War Requires the Violation of Some Civil Liberties*, SALT LAKE TRIB., June 13, 2002, at A19.

[9] Robyn Blumner, *War on Terror Has Turned Into War on Constitution*, SALT LAKE TRIB., June 14, 2002, at A25.

planned attack in time and with resources to forestall it. The Commission's recommendations raise further issues, such as consolidation of intelligence gathering, that could affect civil liberties and which will be debated in the political arena.

It has been over 50 years since U.S. courts dealt with these issues in a time of recognized "national emergency," and many observers note that the American judiciary has not exactly been aggressive in response to government actions in times of crisis.[10] As noted judges such as Learned Hand[11] and Robert Jackson[12] have pointed out, the judiciary is not the final bulwark against government repression. We the People ultimately must decide to what extent we are willing to sacrifice freedom for security.[13] Much of the discussion inevitably will involve political judgments. How well We the People respond to these challenges is up to Us.

Each generation's emergency tends to become the fuel for the next generation's resistance to encroachments on civil liberties, perhaps because we happily live through each emergency and realize that extreme encroachments were not necessary.[14] As war is too important to be left to the generals,[15] so also are civil liberties too important to be left to the courts.[16] Most of the issues ultimately are not about the law so much as they are about the people, both those enforcing the law and those involved in the political process.

Professor Oren Gross asserts emphatically that emergency powers suspend civil liberties, whether we like it or not:

> Experience shows that when grave national crises are upon us, democratic nations tend to race to the bottom as far as the protection of human rights and civil liberties, indeed of basic and fundamental legal principles, is concerned. Emergencies suspend, or at

---

[10] William J. Brennan, Jr., *The Quest To Develop a Jurisprudence of Civil Liberties in Times of Security Crises*, 18 ISRAEL Y.B. ON H.R. 11 (1988).

[11] LEARNED HAND, THE SPIRIT OF LIBERTY: PAPERS AND ADDRESSES OF LEARNED HAND 189-90 (Irving Dilliard ed., 3d ed. 1960).

[12] Korematsu v. United States, 323 U.S. 214, 248 (1984) (Jackson, J., dissenting): "If the people ever let command of the war power fall into irresponsible and unscrupulous hands, the courts wield no power equal to its restraint. The chief restraint upon those who command the physical forces of the country, in the future as in the past, must be their responsibility to the political judgments of their contemporaries and to the moral judgments of history."

[13] This is not to say that courts shouldn't be expected to protect minority interests against the "tyranny of the majority," but just to recognize that the rest of us have an obligation in this regard as well.

[14] Jack Goldsmith & Cass Sunstein, *Military Tribunals and Legal Culture: What a Difference Sixty Years Makes*, 19 CONST. COMMENT. 261 (2002); *see also* Brennan, *supra* note 10, at 11.

[15] "War is much too serious a business to be entrusted to the military." *Attributed to* Charles Maurice de Talleyrand-Perigord, BARTLETT'S FAMILIAR QUOTATIONS 354:9 (16th ed. 1992).

[16] The extreme version of this view, to which I do not subscribe, is that the courts should stay out of the fray and that "redress must be achieved politically if it is to be effective." George J. Alexander, *The Illusory Protection of Human Rights by National Courts During Periods of Emergency*, 5 HUM. RTS. L.J. 1, 27, 65 (1984).

least redefine, de facto, if not de jure, much of our cherished freedoms and rights.[17]

Gross goes on to point out that, so far at least, the ship of State tends to right itself as the emergency passes, but in the meantime the response threatens the very democratic values for which the State intends to stand. It is tempting to sit back, take the "longer view" of history, and assume that as the crisis eases, protection for civil liberties will regenerate in both political and judicial settings. Or it might be tempting to take the opposite view, that this is a crisis for civil liberties that must be fought with every tool in every forum lest even a minute erosion of our freedoms become a landslide. Either approach could be tied to an assumption that the judiciary eventually will take care of any serious problems that emerge.

The judiciary, however, will struggle with the potential impact of its rulings on public safety. Similarly to Professor Gross, Chief Justice Rehnquist has written:

> It is neither desirable nor is it remotely likely that civil liberty will occupy as favored a position in wartime as it does in peacetime. But it is both desirable and likely that more careful attention will be paid by the courts to the basis for the government's claims of necessity as a basis for curtailing civil liberty. The laws will thus not be silent in time of war, but they will speak with a somewhat different voice.[18]

The Gross and Rehnquist views are within the mainstream of thought on this topic, which is that as a practical matter, the courts will lessen the rigor of civil liberties requirements during time of *extremis*. Then, as the crisis fades, some governmental actions will be determined to have been excessive, so that there is some limiting precedent for the next crisis.

Several authors have pointed out that the American judiciary has been hesitant to enforce civil rights in response to government actions in time of crisis, but in truth only a small handful of emergency actions have been upheld and those mostly as authorized by established law in wartime. Lincoln's blockade of Southern ports was upheld as an ordinary incident of civil war in the *Prize Cases*,[19] the World War II expulsion of Japanese from the West Coast was upheld in *Korematsu*[20] (hardly a precedent on which to place much reliance), and use of military tribunals for saboteurs in the service of a foreign enemy was upheld in *Quirin*[21] (more an application of traditional military law in wartime than an exercise of emergency power). By contrast, executive actions were struck down in major cases such

---

[17] Oren Gross, *Chaos and Rules: Should Responses to Violent Crises Always Be Constitutional?*, 112 YALE L.J. 1011 (2003).

[18] WILLIAM H. REHNQUIST, ALL THE LAWS BUT ONE 224-25 (1998).

[19] The Prize Cases, 67 U.S. 635 (1862).

[20] *Korematsu*, 323 U.S. 214.

[21] *Ex parte* Quirin, 317 U.S. 1 (1942).

as *Milligan*,[22] *Youngstown*,[23] and *Endo*[24] (attempting to limit the impact of *Korematsu*).

It is surely tempting to answer the question of the existence of emergency powers by either "Yes, they exist" or "No, they don't." In constitutional terms, the question is framed as whether constitutional protections of civil liberties can be set aside, at least temporarily, during the emergency. *Inter arma, silent leges* translates roughly as "During war, the laws are silent." Setting the issue as a stark contrast of suspending the constitution or not, however, creates a false dichotomy.

There are at least three potential approaches to answering the question, two of which further subdivide into additional choices. First is the "no special rules" answer: under no circumstances does the law countenance departures from established norms. Second is the "it's in there" answer: the law includes, or at least should include, circumstances that allow departure from otherwise applicable norms. Third, is the "permitted violations" answer: in times of extreme danger, the executive is allowed to violate otherwise applicable law.

The "no special rules" answer further subdivides by the question of discretionary enforcement. Some people would insist that the law be applied with no attention to the pressures that a perpetrator faced.[25] Others would

---

[22] *Ex parte* Milligan, 71 U.S. 2 (1866).

[23] Youngstown Sheet & Tube v. Sawyer, 343 U.S. 579 (1952).

[24] *Ex parte* Endo, 323 U.S. 283 (1944). Justice Douglas' opinion in *Endo* is worth particular note:

> Broad powers frequently granted to the President or other executive officers by Congress so that they may deal with the exigencies of wartime problems have been sustained. And the Constitution when it committed to the Executive and to Congress the exercise of the war power necessarily gave them wide scope for the exercise of judgment and discretion so that war might be waged effectively and successfully. At the same time, however, the Constitution is as specific in its enumeration of many of the civil rights of the individual as it is in its enumeration of the powers of his government.

> We mention these constitutional provisions not to stir the constitutional issues which have been argued at the bar but to indicate the approach which we think should be made to an Act of Congress or an order of the Chief Executive that touches the sensitive area of rights specifically guaranteed by the Constitution. This Court has quite consistently given a narrower scope for the operation of the presumption of constitutionality when legislation appeared on its face to violate a specific prohibition of the Constitution. . . . In interpreting a wartime measure we must assume that their purpose was to allow for the greatest possible accommodation between those liberties and the exigencies of war. We must assume, when asked to find implied powers in a grant of legislative or executive authority, that the law makers intended to place no greater restraint on the citizen than was clearly and unmistakably indicated by the language they used.

Id. at 299-300.

[25] Professor Gross refers to this as the "absolutist" position, but his own argument leads to insisting that conduct be considered illegal no matter what the circumstances while still acknowledging that some circumstances will lead to a lack of enforcement. Oren Gross, *Are Torture Warrants Warranted?*, 88 MINN. L. REV. 1481 (2004). In this view of "absolutism," there need not be absolute enforcement.

insist in some situations that discretionary decisions be made not to prosecute or not to convict a perpetrator who acted in the best interests of the community. In this approach, the behavior still remains illegal although sanctions are not applied in all settings.

The "it's in there" answer also subdivides into two parts. A rule limiting power could be stated with exceptions for extreme circumstances, or at least allow for the inference of exceptions under criteria outlining when the exception would be necessary and desirable. As an alternative, a rule granting power could be stated as being applicable only in the exceptional case. For example, rules of search and seizure under the Fourth Amendment carry the built-in allowance for exigent circumstances when seizure of an item is necessary for public safety, and it really doesn't matter whether the rule requiring a warrant is limited to non-exigent situations or whether the exigency is considered an exception to the normal rule. Professor Schauer points out that a law prohibiting Nazi propaganda can be pictured as either an exception to usual laws protecting free expression or as a limitation built into the law of free expression.[26] He then argues that the proper way to view the matter is context-specific. In Germany, Nazi propaganda could be defined out of the operation of the law protecting free expression without raising significant concerns because expression simply should not include Nazi propaganda. In the United States, that approach does not carry the same contextualized justification; meanwhile, any proposal to create an exception to free expression so as to disallow certain content leads to fears of a "slippery slope" on which there are no sensible stopping points.

The "permitted violations" answer seems to be commonly perceived as part of the Realpolitik of the modern world. It is a very dangerous answer, however, and should be rejected at least with regard to any rules that have already contemplated the presence of emergencies in the formulation of the rule. A Realpolitik approach can lead to the utterly outlandish statement that the President of the United States could authorize violations of domestic and international law and that Congress and the courts would be constitutionally disenfranchised from applying legal norms to the President while acting as Commander-in-Chief. There is really no "slippery slope" problem here; there is only the question of whether the king is above the law, a question that was answered hundreds of years ago and should not be rethought in the nuclear age. To the extent that exigent circumstances require action for the public good, then the question of legality should be faced head-on. Either the absolutist approach will say that the behavior is illegal (with or without room for prosecutorial discretion) or the built-in approach will say that the limits of power have already been stated (either contained within the statement of the rule or as exceptions).

The prisoner abuse scandal highlights the problem nicely. Professor Dershowitz has received a lot of publicity for his advocacy of judicially authorized torture in the "ticking bomb" scenario. The hypothetical is that

---

[26] Frederick Schauer, *Exceptions*, 58 U. Chi. L. Rev. 871 (1991).

a person in custody admits to knowing where a bomb is planted, claims that it will explode in the next two hours, but refuses to divulge where it is located. The interrogator, Dershowitz argues, should be able to apply for a judicial torture warrant to force the information from the suspect, a variation of the "it's in there" approach. Gross argues that this approach will lead to a "slippery slope" in which the legality of torture under a warrant will lead to torture without warrants in situations that are thought to present "exigent circumstances" with no time to go before a judge, and then a climate of officially sanctioned torture will have been created. Gross first took an approach that seemed to countenance "extra-legal" behavior if the actor could persuade the public after the fact that the action was justified,[27] but in dealing with torture specifically Gross has adhered to the absolutist approach with discretion for non-enforcement.[28]

Dershowitz insists that torture will occur whatever legal approach we take and that it would be better controlled by judicial authority than by *post hoc* evaluation. By contrast, journalist Mark Bowden, in a very thorough review of interrogation techniques that forecast the Abu Ghraib debacle, argues that because torture will occur regardless of the legal posture, it is better to say that torture is criminal under all circumstances, but that prosecutorial discretion can appropriately allow some offenses to go unpunished.[29]

Dershowitz, Gross, and Bowden all agree that the slippery slope is something to be avoided, but they differ over how best to avoid it. The most

---

[27] Gross, *supra* note 25, at 1536.

[28] *Id*. at 1522:

> The officials must assume the risks involved in acting extralegally. Rather than recognize ex ante the possibility of a lawful override of the general prohibition on torture, as suggested by the presumptive approach, official disobedience focuses on the absolute nature of the ban while accepting the possibility that an official who deviates from the rule may escape sanctions in exceptional circumstances.

[29] Mark Bowden, *The Dark Art of Interrogation*, ATLANTIC MONTHLY, Oct. 2003:

> Candor and consistency are not always public virtues. Torture is a crime against humanity, but coercion is an issue that is rightly handled with a wink, or even a touch of hypocrisy; it should be banned but also quietly practiced. Those who protest coercive methods will exaggerate their horrors, which is good: it generates a useful climate of fear. It is wise of the President to reiterate U.S. support for international agreements banning torture, and it is wise for American interrogators to employ whatever coercive methods work. It is also smart not to discuss the matter with anyone.
>
> If interrogators step over the line from coercion to outright torture, they should be held personally responsible. But no interrogator is ever going to be prosecuted for keeping Khalid Sheikh Mohammed awake, cold, alone, and uncomfortable. Nor should he be.

Bowden was writing before the revelations following Abu Ghraib. In the aftermath of the prison disclosures, memoranda surfaced arguing that torture could be justified and even legal. Other memoranda approving various "aggressive interrogation techniques" have been leaked to the press. Bowden stated that "The Bush Administration has adopted exactly the right posture on the matter." That statement would have to be reconsidered in light of what has since surfaced about the actual posture of the Bush Administration.

probable reality is that no approach will avoid it entirely. But the prospect of illegal behavior does not mean that we throw up our hands. All of criminal law is based on the realization that illegal conduct will occur. Our responses to emergencies similarly should be premised on the realization that officials will do what they think necessary in an emergency situation. The criminal law deals with this phenomenon by creating only minimal exceptions for duress and the excuse of necessity. In dealing with the actions of those low in the chain of command, criminal and military law typically exclude the defense of superior orders to the extent that the defendant should have known that an order was illegal.

In the first place, there are constitutional norms that relate to separation of powers and those that relate to individual liberties, although the two types of limitations often overlap. Whether the Executive is encroaching on the powers that the Legislature would normally exercise may be a very different question from whether either or both is exceeding limits that are explicitly crafted for protection of the individual. For example, in ordinary times private property is not subject to use restrictions except as established by law subject to the due process clause. Absent an emergency or threat to public safety, the executive could not unilaterally declare a facility closed to the public without legislative action, and even with legislative action individual rights to use and access of the facility are likely to prevail.[30] During an emergency, however, law enforcement might declare a certain facility off limits for the purpose of clearing away dangerous conditions. The executive in this situation has not encroached on legislative powers if the existing organic law allows unilateral executive action to meet emergencies. With regard to individual rights, the executive action would be tested by the doctrine of necessity to determine whether it was legal and, even if legal, the "takings" doctrine might require compensation for a lawful taking.[31] The question of emergency powers is much more complex that a simple yes or no question.

The titles, if not the substance, of some treatments of these issues suggest that responses to crises need not always be constitutional.[32] Sorry, but that is impossible. At the outer limits of valid governmental action, the Constitution stands as an impermeable barrier. If an action is unconstitutional, then it is unconstitutional. Short of that, however, a world of options exist and they need not all be treated as equally. To say that something is within constitutional powers does not mean it is the only option that is constitutional. The Justice Department response to many critics of its post-9/11 policies has been to point out that particular techniques have been upheld by the courts as being constitutional. This "constitutional therefore valid" argument says only that a particular practice has not been found to be

---

[30] Denying an owner "all beneficial use" of a property will in most circumstances constitute a "taking" that would require compensation. *See, e.g.*, Lucas v. S.C. Coastal Council, 505 U.S. 1003 (1992).

[31] *See* § 10.02[A] *infra*.

[32] *See* Gross, *supra* note 17; *see also* REHNQUIST, *supra* note 18.

beyond the pale, not that it is a good idea. It is unresponsive to the political concern of whether a practice has encroached on liberty to a point that the populace finds unacceptable.

With regard to unusual exercises of power, activities that would not be legal under ordinary circumstances, might they be constitutional in an emergency? Clearly so, and the Constitution can be interpreted easily to authorize them. It is very difficult to dispute the propriety of Justice Jackson's analysis in *Youngstown* that there are areas of executive discretion in which the President's powers standing alone will be sufficient, at least when Congress has been silent on the subject. Certainly one of those is to preserve the nation from attack, and even the "radical" War Powers Resolution recognizes this responsibility. Because this responsibility is within constitutional limits, there is no need for extra-constitutional measures to carry it out ("it's in there").

In Justice Jackson's framework, however, there are two areas in which Congress has addressed the particular exercise of power in question. One is when Congress has explicitly rejected a claimed power. In this instance, Justice Jackson's approach says that the President's power must be found within Article II or implied from the nature of the Executive.[33] Of course, once past that hurdle of lack-of-power, the President would still face a challenge from the direction of individual liberty.[34] The obverse situation occurs when Congress has authorized the action. In this instance, both Congress and the President still must face the challenge of individual liberty. Either way, the challenge of claims of individual liberty do not go away because of the emergency. They may change and morph to meet the times, but they do not disappear just because there is authority for the action.

It is true that the pressures to modify the demands of liberty in time of emergency will be very strong. The Constitution makes many of the demands of liberty contextual by using phrases such as "due" process, or "unreasonable" searches and seizures. Virtually all Supreme Court expressions of liberty in the past half-century have been contextualized by asking whether governmental justifications for an action serve a compelling or important governmental interest. Surely, a genuine emergency will present a strong case for a compelling governmental interest, such as in the example of racial segregation to quell a prison race riot.[35]

Because emergencies generate strong demands for "erosion" of civil liberties, there is a rhetorical gap to bridge so that we can speak a common language. Take the familiar example of not being allowed to publish ship sailing times during time of war. Assuming the validity of the proscription

---

[33] *Youngstown*, 343 U.S. at 637.

[34] *Id.* at 629-633, where Justice Douglas implied that the Executive could never exercise unilateral seizure power because only the legislature has the authority to pay compensation for the taking. Reid v. Covert, 354 U.S. 1 (1957) seems to yield the proposition that an authorized military action could still be a violation of constitutional rights.

[35] Richmond v. J. A. Croson Co., 488 U.S. 469, 521 (1989) (Scalia, J., concurring).

so that my expectations of free expression are diminished, does that mean that my First Amendment liberties have been curtailed or does it mean that my First Amendment liberties are different depending on the context? The "it's in there" approach avoids saying that government is allowed to do something unconstitutional. Therefore, what we must always be seeking is a way to read the constitutional language, history, and structure in light of the emergency involved.

Again, it must be remembered that a contextualized statement that an action is not unconstitutional is hardly a ringing endorsement of its wisdom or even validity. Holding that a measure is constitutional simply refers the matter back to the political process in which We the People must decide what We choose to allow.

§ 10.02 EXISTING LAW RELATED TO EMERGENCIES

Terrorism incidents may create an emergency. Emergencies can be classified as "natural," "technologic," or "complex." Natural emergencies include weather, earthquake, and the like. Technologic emergencies include destruction or immobilization of facilities or infrastructure, whether intentional or not. Complex emergencies have been described as "situations in which the capacity to sustain livelihood and life is threatened primarily by political factors, and in particular, by high levels of violence."[36] Terrorism thus fits within the rubric of a complex emergency.

It would be a serious mistake to forget that there are centuries of experience in Anglo-American law in dealing with emergencies, at least of the natural or technologic kind. Emergency power to deal with disasters of the natural or technologic variety is fully recognized in U.S. law and has been exercised on numbers of occasions. In response to "complex emergencies," Congress has explicitly authorized military involvement in domestic affairs at least when the civilian courts are incapacitated.[37] Moreover, doctrines of necessity have developed to excuse governmental actions taken in time of complex emergencies such as wartime. The important point to remember, however, is that these doctrines all carry within them stated, or inferrable, limitations on the scope of the emergency power.

---

[36] Thomas Ditzler, *Malevolent Minds: the Teleogy of Terrorism, in* FATHALI MOGHADDAM & ANTHONY MARSELLA, UNDERSTANDING TERRORISM 189 (2004) (quoting London School of Health and Tropical Medicine).

[37] 10 U.S.C. § 332 (2007):

Whenever the President considers that unlawful obstructions, combinations, or assemblages, or rebellion against the authority of the United States, make it impracticable to enforce the laws of the United States in any State or Territory by the ordinary course of judicial proceedings, he may call into Federal service such of the militia of any State, and use such of the armed forces, as he considers necessary to enforce those laws or to suppress the rebellion.

[A] The Doctrine of Necessity

We have a complete federal agency devoted to civil emergency response. The Federal Emergency Management Agency traces its history in much the same fashion as the accretion of federal power in many areas, particularly fueled by the Depression and New Deal.[38] The current version was created by Executive Order in 1979, amalgamating the activities of over 100 federal agencies that were engaged in some form of "disaster relief,"[39] and then transferred to the Department of Homeland Security in 2002. Disaster relief encompasses coordinating disaster recovery and mitigation in conjunction with other federal agencies and state government.[40] FEMA is not specifically authorized to commandeer resources from unwilling owners, but it does have authority to incur obligations for use of resources such as vehicles, food, clothing, and facilities for shelter.[41]

So what happens if a federal agency believes that it must have something that the owner is not willing to provide? Not surprisingly, the majority of cases dealing with this phenomenon occur in the context of claims for compensation for private property that was used, damaged, or destroyed in the course of governmental response to an emergency.

---

[38] Congress had provided relief for natural disasters by ad hoc legislation beginning as early as 1803. "By the 1930s, when the federal approach to problems became popular, the Reconstruction Finance Corporation was given authority to make disaster loans for repair and reconstruction of certain public facilities following an earthquake, and later, other types of disasters. In 1934, the Bureau of Public Roads was given authority to provide funding for highways and bridges damaged by natural disasters. The Flood Control Act, which gave the U.S. Army Corps of Engineers greater authority to implement flood control projects, was also passed. This piecemeal approach to disaster assistance was problematic and it prompted legislation that required greater cooperation between federal agencies and authorized the President to coordinate these activities." www.fema.gov/about/history.shtm.

[39] FEMA, *FEMA History, available at* www.fema.gov/about/history.shtm (last visited July 17, 2007).

[40] 42 U.S.C. § 5149(a):

In carrying out the purposes of this Act, any Federal agency is authorized to accept and utilize the services or facilities of any State or local government, or of any agency, office, or employee thereof, with the consent of such government.

42 U.S.C. § 5143(a):

Immediately upon his declaration of a major disaster or emergency, the President shall appoint a Federal coordinating officer to operate in the affected area.

42 U.S.C. § 5143(c):

When the President determines assistance under this Act is necessary, he shall request that the Governor of the affected State designate a State coordinating officer for the purpose of coordinating State and local disaster assistance efforts with those of the Federal Government.

[41] Any federal agency involved in disaster relief is authorized "to incur obligations on behalf of the United States by contract or otherwise for the acquisition, rental, or hire of equipment, services, materials, and supplies for shipping, drayage, travel, and communications, and for the supervision and administration of such activities. Such obligations, including obligations arising out of the temporary employment of additional personnel, may be incurred by an agency in such amount as may be made available to it by the President." 42 U.S.C. § 5149(b)(3).

Executive takings of private property for a public use in British practice occurred in the early stages mostly as responses to emergencies. The privilege to damage or destroy private property to prevent a greater harm was recognized in early British cases so that there was no tort when the Crown dug saltpeter from the plaintiff's land to make gunpowder[42] or tossed articles overboard to save a ship.[43] The British cases seem to make the necessity a complete defense regardless of whether the property damaged was itself threatened by the emergency.[44]

The American version of the defense of necessity has taken a slightly different turn from the British experience. When the property itself is reasonably believed to be threatened as part of the emergency, as when the house stands in the way of the fire, then there is no reason to compensate the owner for its destruction. When the property is not itself threatened by the emergency, there is a split of opinion. The Restatement takes the position that the privilege is complete so long as the actor acts reasonably.[45] Several commentators, however, take the position that the owner should be compensated by the public on whose behalf the property was used.[46]

The Supreme Court cases are inconclusive. In a number of cases involving wartime destruction of property, the Court has simply dictated that citizens take the risk of property loss due to war.[47] The emergency is still sufficient justification even if the officers involved had the opportunity to make a calculated choice about the matter.[48] On the other hand, the government has often "requisitioned" supplies and materials and acted as if compensation were required. For example, in evacuating the Phillipines the Army paid for those petroleum products that it used but not for those that were destroyed to prevent their capture by the Japanese.[49] Benefit to the public is probably not the basis for the distinction. The distinction could be simply that the products used were not subject to capture by the enemy while those destroyed were. In the case of something that is subject to capture, destruction is not any greater loss to the owner. It might also be that consumables are more likely to be the subject of a bargained exchange than

---

[42] King's Prerogative in Saltpetre, 12 Co. Rep. 12, 77 Eng. Rep. 1294 (1607).

[43] Mouse's Case, 12 Co. Rep. 63, 77 Eng. Rep. 1341 (1609).

[44] *See* Hall & Wigmore, *Compensation for Property Destroyed to Stop the Spread of a Conflagration*, 1 ILL. L. REV. 501, 525 (1907). The doctrine was sufficiently ill-defined that the Mayor of London is said to have allowed the city to burn to the ground in 1666 rather than risk a trespass action for destroying forty houses that might have prevented spread of the fire. Hall & Wigmore doubt the significance of this claim. *Id.* at 502 n.2.

[45] RESTATEMENT (SECOND) TORTS §§ 196, 262 (1974).

[46] The public in this view substitutes for the administrative problem of finding those persons who have benefitted and adjudicating their collective liability. W. PROSSER & P. KEETON, TORTS 146-47 (5th ed. 1984); Hall & Wigmore, *supra* note 44.

[47] Juragua Iron Co. v. United States, 212 U.S. 297 (1909) (destruction of factory to prevent spread of smallpox); United States v. Pacific RR, 120 U.S. 227 (1887) (destruction of bridges by retreating Union Army).

[48] United States v. Caltex Inc., 344 U.S. 149 (1952); Castro v. United States, 500 F.2d 436, 205 Ct. Cl. 534 (1974).

[49] *Caltex*, 344 U.S. at 151.

capital goods, although this distinction would not support payment of rent for occupied premises.

The notion of public necessity takes on more dimension in the opinions of the Court of Claims. This court frequently awards compensation in cases of military use or occupation of property while refusing compensation for wartime destruction of property. The difference seems to lie mostly in the degree of urgency or compulsion from outside sources. For example, in another case from the wartime South Pacific,[50] owners were kept away from their land because ammunition dumps were based there, then later because some live ammunition remained in the area. When they were finally allowed back on the land some 22 years after the war ended, they were awarded the fair market rental value of the land for the duration of their exclusion, but they were denied compensation for the destruction of coconut trees during the invasion of the island. It seems that military necessity existed as much with respect to the occupation as with the destruction of the coconut trees; what is more likely the distinction is the degree of likelihood that some third party, the enemy, would have destroyed or taken the trees or that the destruction was an inadvertent happenstance of war.

These cases on military necessity seem to reject the Restatement position of absolute privilege and to adopt the commentators' view of a privilege to destroy only property that is itself threatened. With respect to property that would not otherwise be lost, the public representatives have the power to take the use of the property but must compensate for its use. This is a pragmatic adjustment reflecting notions of causation and carries no hint of the impropriety of executive response to emergency.

[B]   Military Assistance to Civilian Authorities

The concepts of posse comitatus limits and martial law were explored in Chapter 9. Other than martial law as an emergency measure, some use of the military to assist civilian authorities in times of civil disturbance is also possible and its limits are found in the statutes that prevent use of the military in direct search and arrest of offenders. Although the *posse comitatus* statute seems to imply that the military can have no involvement in civilian law enforcement, another federal statute offers assistance to state governments in time of "insurrection."[51] The "insurrection" statute amounts to a standing delegation from Congress of the power to make an exception to the posse comitatus statute when a state government requests assistance and the President finds that there is a need for military force

---

[50] *Castro*, 500 F.2d 436, 205 Ct. Cl. 534.

[51] 10 U.S.C. § 331:

> Whenever there is an insurrection in any State against its government, the President may, upon the request of its legislature or of its governor if the legislature cannot be convened, call into Federal service such of the militia of the other States, in the number requested by that State, and use such of the armed forces, as he considers necessary to suppress the insurrection.

to "suppress the insurrection." It is not, however, a standing delegation of the power to declare martial law. That power remains implicitly within Congress unless Congress cannot meet.

The authority of the President under the insurrection statute has come before the Supreme Court on only two occasions, and one of those did not involve insurrection.[52] In *Martin v. Mott*,[53] a member of the New York militia had refused to answer the President's call to arms during the War of 1812. He was fined, his belongings were seized, and he brought a replevin action claiming that the President was without authority to order him into service prior to an actual invasion of the territory of the U.S. His first argument was that the fact of a military emergency should have been shown to the court, to which the Supreme Court seemed to respond that the President's determination was conclusive on the courts as well as on military personnel.[54] The only reason to hedge with the phrase "seemed to respond" is that all the arguments put forth by the Court were addressed to the need for immediate unquestioning obedience by military personnel. Whether those same arguments would hold when a court was faced with a more doubtful situation, one in which the presence of a military threat was less clear, could be a slightly different matter as we will see with *Youngstown Sheet & Tube*.

The *Prize Cases*[55] similarly contained language seeming to grant the President unreviewable discretion to engage in acts of war.[56] Several ships

---

[52] One other insurrection case did not involve validity of a military call-out. With regard to Shea's Rebellion, the Court held that it had no power to determine which of the contending parties was the legitimate government of a state, that this is a question for the political branches. Luther v. Borden, 48 U.S. (7 How.) 1 (1849).

[53] 25 U.S. (12 Wheat.) 19 (1827).

[54] *Id.* at 32-33:

> [T]he authority to decide whether the exigency has arisen, belongs exclusively to the President, and that his decision is conclusive upon all other persons. We think that this construction necessarily results from the nature of the power itself, and from the manifest object contemplated by the act of Congress. The power itself is to be exercised upon sudden emergencies, upon great occasions of state, and under circumstances which may be vital to the existence of the Union.
>
> The argument is, that the power confided to the President is a limited power, and can be exercised only in the cases pointed out in the statute, and therefore it is necessary to aver the fact which bring the exercise within the purview of the statute. . . . When the President exercises an authority confided to him by law, the presumption that it is exercised in pursuance of law. Every public officer is presumed to act in obedience to his duty, until the contrary is shown; and, a fortiori, this presumption ought to be favourably applied to the chief magistrate of the Union. It is not necessary to aver, that the act which he may rightfully do, was so done. If the fact of the existence of the exigency were averred, it would be traversable, and of course might be passed upon by a jury; and thus the legality of the orders of the President would depend, not on his own judgment of the facts, but upon the finding of those facts upon the proofs submitted to a jury.

[55] 67 U.S. 635 (1863).

[56] *Id.* at 670:

owned by foreign nationals and flagged by neutral countries had been seized while running a blockade against the Confederate states. The owners argued that the President lacked authority to enforce a blockade against neutrals. Again the word "seeming" is used in describing the Court's deference to the President to emphasize that there was no question about the state of armed conflict between the Union and Confederacy, and that the only significant arguments in the case had to do with the status of the contending sides under international law. Whether the President needed deference regarding the fact of armed conflict was hardly in issue.

The only 20th Century case citing the assistance statute is a federal court case dealing with property damage in D.C. during the riots following the 1968 assassination of Dr. Martin Luther King.[57] Insurers who had paid out damage claims brought suit against the U.S. alleging that the government had been negligent in failing to call out the militia or use military force to suppress the riots. The district court simply pointed out that "the decision whether to use troops or the militia (National Guard) in quelling a civil disorder is exclusively within the province of the President. The Courts also have made it clear that presidential discretion in exercising those powers granted in the Constitution and in the implementing statutes is not subject to judicial review."[58]

It is one thing to say that there is no constitutional duty on the part of the President to call out military force, at least not a duty enforceable by judicial damage action, but it is quite another to say that there is no judicially enforceable limit on the President's ability to call out military force when no state of insurrection justifies it. The limiting case would be one in which the President was alleged to be resorting to despotic measures to subdue the populace for whatever nefarious reasons may be motivating him or her. This is the case to which Justice Jackson's language in *Korematsu* is addressed: "The chief restraint upon those who command the physical forces of the country, in the future as in the past, must be their responsibility to the political judgments of their contemporaries and to the moral judgments of history."[59]

As a lecture in civic responsibility, Justice Jackson surely has a salient point. As a limit on the constitutional role of the courts, however, it is much more doubtful. How does this language fit with the basic premise of

---

Whether the President in fulfilling his duties, as Commander in-chief, in suppressing an insurrection, has met with such armed hostile resistance, and a civil war of such alarming proportions as will compel him to accord to them the character of belligerents, is a question to be decided by him, and this Court must be governed by the decisions and acts of the political department of the Government to which this power was entrusted. "He must determine what degree of force the crisis demands." The proclamation of blockade is itself official and conclusive evidence to the Court that a state of war existed which demanded and authorized a recourse to such a measure, under the circumstances peculiar to the case.

[57] Monarch Ins. Co. of Ohio v. Dist. of Columbia, 353 F. Supp. 1249 (D.D.C. 1973).

[58] *Id.* at 1254-55.

[59] *Korematsu*, 323 U.S. at 248.

Marbury that the courts have an obligation to apply constitutional limitations wherever they exist? Surely if the power of the President is limited to times of genuine emergency, then the courts must be willing to state whether such an emergency exists. To state the proposition in more mealy-mouthed justiciability terms, if the power of the President is limited *by a judicially enforceable constitutional principle* to times of genuine emergency, then the courts must be willing to state whether such an emergency exists. To be true to the rationale of *Marbury*, recognizing an unfettered discretion in the President to use military force on the domestic arena is to say that there is no constitutional *law* constraining that discretion. Maybe there is a constitutional exhortation, but it is not a matter of law.

Justice Jackson's statement also carries a familiar pragmatic warning it its reference to "the physical forces of the country." Federalist No. 78 spoke of the courts as the "Least Dangerous Branch," a phrase key to Professor Bickel's insistence that courts should be careful in husbanding their limited "power."[60] Indeed, President Lincoln did ignore Chief Justice Taney's decree in *Merryman*, and Jefferson ignored Marshall's decree in *Cherokee Nation*. But when President Nixon's lawyers hinted that he might not obey an order to deliver the tapes from his office, the public outcry caused an almost immediate reversal and promise to obey a Supreme Court decision.[61]

As a practical matter, certainly if there is *any level* of threatened violence to the community, then the courts will accept the executive's decision to involve the military. Stated this way, the proposition preserves the rule of law and simply states an evidentiary standard that should be perfectly satisfactory for any President acting in good faith. Putting forward some evidence of a threat of violence should not be difficult in any situation that calls for military force. Justice Grier's concern in *Martin v. Mott* that even a "some evidence" standard could jeopardize military secrets[62] is quite simply implausible. The presence of an emergency can be shown factually with very little effort, and if the only action contemplated is calling out the military to patrol the streets, then the courts can leave that judgment to the executive because at that point there is no clear countervailing threat to individual liberty.

But what if the action taken by the executive involves isolation of persons by race, or detention of alleged conspirators without hearing? As soon as military action threatens values protected by equal protection or due process, then surely more is required of the courts. *Korematsu* has been roundly criticized, and as the Supreme Court has now made clear, executive detentions will be tested by due process standards.[63] So why are we so chary about saying that the courts must review executive determinations

---

[60] ALEXANDER BICKEL, THE LEAST DANGEROUS BRANCH (1986).

[61] United States v. Nixon, 418 U.S. 683 (1974).

[62] 25 U.S. 19 (1827).

[63] *See* § 9.04 *supra*.

of emergency? Perhaps the answer lies in the very real sense that judges are not mythic creatures.

Imagine a scenario in which terrorists have unleashed botulin into the water supply of New York City. There is no way of knowing what city the cadres may strike next and no way that domestic police forces can patrol all the vulnerable locations of water supplies in the country. When the President calls out the military to patrol the water supplies of the nation, there can be little prospect of judicial intervention. Carry the scenario to the next level. Military orders are issued creating a 200 meter perimeter around every access point to municipal water supplies. Any unauthorized person entering that perimeter is to be arrested immediately and incarcerated until it can be determined what he or she was up to. For at least some period of time, the President would not even need to suspend the writ of habeas corpus to make these orders effective. A court presented with a habeas petition during the first few weeks or even months after the initial attack could not be expected to turn the defense of the entire populace on its ear by releasing persons who had violated the perimeter ban. But notice that the violation of the perimeter would need to be shown to the satisfaction of the judge before this proposition kicks in.

The point of this scenario is simply that the overblown hyperbole of unreviewable military discretion is unnecessary as a matter of law. Good faith executive-military decisions in any genuine emergency are not going to be overturned by any sensible judge. But what if the claim of emergency drags on for many months, maybe years, with no further threat of violence? Now is a judge to accept a claim of emergency without being persuaded with hard evidence that a person violating the perimeter ban was actually engaged in at least a conspiracy to commit an observable crime? It would not take Herculean courage to exercise the judicial function when there is no plausible threat to the populace of the country.

Why did Chief Justice Taney not pursue the *Merryman* case? He said it was because his "power has been resisted by a force too strong for me to overcome."[64] At the time, there was active fighting in Baltimore, Merryman was almost certainly involved in sabotage with others who were still at large, the seat of government in D.C. was virtually cut off from its loyal states, and there was no hope of enforcing an order to release Merryman.[65] But wait until after the war is over and it becomes safe for the Court to issue its opinion in *Milligan*. If the government had made a return to the habeas petition in *Merryman* stating its evidence of his involvement in blowing up railroad bridges, and asserting an intent to conduct a trial (even a military trial in an active theater of combat might have been acceptable), then there would have been no violation. The suspension of the writ by the President was really overkill. There was no need for it because the judges and the people would have willingly accepted military law enforcement in the face of a genuine emergency and the

---

[64] *Ex parte* Merryman, 17 F. Cas. 144, 153 (D. Md. 1861).

[65] REHNQUIST, *supra* note 18, at 18-25.

government could easily have made satisfactory returns to habeas corpus petitions until the emergency passed.

Merryman never faced a trial, neither by military tribunal nor civilian court. He was released on bail some months after the Taney opinion and never brought to trial, allegedly because Taney himself stalled any potential trial in the civilian courts.[66] The implication may be that Lincoln and his advisors accepted Taney's belief that Merryman could only be tried in civilian courts or it may be that they simply lost interest when public pressure in Merryman's favor failed to dissipate as more urgent matters of warfare occupied the attention of the administration.

[C] Japanese "Exclusion" as an "Emergency"

A consideration of emergencies in the context of war must include consideration of the use of race, including "detain and query" practices directed to groups defined on the basis of national origin. And the question of race must begin with the Japanese cases of World War II. While the most notorious of the three Supreme Court cases is *Korematsu v. United States*,[67] *Hirabayashi v. United States*[68] may be a closer precedent to what could happen again. Justice Jackson's dissent in *Korematsu* forecast the concern (while perhaps foreshadowing his role as chief prosecutor at Nuremberg) when he bemoaned the Court's war-time review of military judgments:

> [T]he Court for all time has validated the principle of racial discrimination in criminal procedure and of transplanting American citizens. The principle then lies about like a loaded weapon ready for the hand of any authority that can bring forward a plausible claim of an urgent need.[69]

Japanese exclusion came in three steps. First, there was a Presidential directive broadly authorizing military commanders to exclude persons from certain areas, primarily Hawaii and the Pacific Coast. The second step was an Act of Congress criminalizing violation of military orders issued under the President's authorization. Then the military commanders issued orders setting curfews, authorizing detention, and establishing relocation camps.

Hirabayashi upheld a curfew by which all persons of Japanese ancestry in certain areas were required to be in their residences from 8 p.m. to 6 a.m. The order was challenged on the grounds that it was beyond the war powers as well as racial discrimination, to which the Court responded that

> we cannot reject as unfounded the judgment of the military authorities and of Congress that there were disloyal members of that population, whose number and strength could not be precisely and

---

[66] Rehnquist, *supra* note 18, at 39 (citing Walker Lewis, Without Fear or Favor: A Biography of Chief Justice Roger Brooke Taney 453 (1965)).

[67] 323 U.S. 214 (1944).

[68] 320 U.S. 81 (1943).

[69] *Korematsu*, 323 U.S. at 246.

quickly ascertained. We cannot say that the war-making branches of the Government did not have ground for believing that in a critical hour such persons could not readily be isolated and separately dealt with, and constituted a menace to the national defense and safety, which demanded that prompt and adequate measures be taken to guard against it.[70]

Moving from curfew to detention, the Court upheld "temporary" relocation of thousands of persons of Japanese ancestry while recognizing that relocation carried a much greater impact than curfew:

Compulsory exclusion of large groups of citizens from their homes, except under circumstances of direst emergency and peril, is inconsistent with our basic governmental institutions. But when under conditions of modern warfare our shores are threatened by hostile forces, the power to protect must be commensurate with the threatened danger.[71]

Justice Black's opinion insisted that the Court was addressing only exclusion from the West Coast and was not concerned with "relocation centers" (refusing to call them "concentration camps") because that was all that Korematsu was charged with violating. Then, when the validity of continued detention was considered in *Ex parte Endo*,[72] the Court construed the EO and statute narrowly to find that detention would be authorized only by the exigencies of separating the loyal from the disloyal or as a voluntary measure of humanitarian aid to those excluded from coastal areas:

The authority to detain a citizen or to grant him a conditional release as protection against espionage or sabotage is exhausted at least when his loyalty is conceded. If we held that the authority to detain continued thereafter, we would transform an espionage or sabotage measure into something else. That was not done by Executive Order No. 9066 or by the Act of March 21, 1942, which ratified it. What they did not do we cannot do. Detention which furthered the campaign against espionage and sabotage would be one thing. But detention which has no relationship to that campaign is of a distinct character.[73]

Although the combination of *Korematsu* and *Endo* technically was to authorize exclusion while invalidating detention, as a practical matter one carried implication of the other. First, the burden was on the applicant to prove loyalty and, moreover, it was not clear where this person was to go when excluded from the home and community in which he or she had been born and raised. Even long after the military justification had ceased, inertia delayed the end of detention. The effect was that over 100,000

---

[70] *Hirabayashi*, 320 U.S. at 99.

[71] *Korematsu*, 323 U.S. at 220-21.

[72] 323 U.S. 283 (1944).

[73] *Id.* at 302.

presumably loyal citizens spent the war years behind barbed wire in mostly desert encampments, and lost their jobs and homes in the process.

The aftermath of the program eventually led to a congressionally mandated Commission on Wartime Relocation and Internment of Civilians. The CWRIC described the subsequent remorse of many of the participants in the program[74] and summarized its own findings this way:

> The promulgation of Executive Order 9066 was not justified by military necessity, and the decisions which followed from it — detention, ending detention, and ending exclusion — were not driven by analysis of military conditions. The broad historical causes which shaped these decisions were race prejudice, war hysteria and a failure of political leadership. Widespread ignorance of Japanese Americans contributed to a policy conceived in haste and executed in an atmosphere of fear and anger at Japan. A grave injustice was done to American citizens and resident aliens of Japanese ancestry who, without individual review or any probative evidence against them, were excluded, removed and detained by the United States during World War II.[75]

To what extent does *Korematsu* stand as precedent today? As thoroughly regretted and discredited as the Japanese exclusion program itself may be, the opinion has never been overruled and indeed is cited as the beginning of reviewing racial discrimination by government with strict scrutiny. The most that a rigorous proponent of equal protection, Jacobus tenBroek, has said of the precedent is that one may concede the necessity of waging war successfully while still insisting that "the war power, when exerted in the military government of citizen civilians within the country, does not exist in the absence of a grave military peril, does not exceed measures reasonably appropriate to cope with that peril, and does not comprehend violations of civil and individual guarantees of the Constitution in the presence of a militarily adequate alternative." Nevertheless, it is quite possible that racial or ethnic differentiations among the populace in time of war would pass judicial muster so long as the consequences were not wholesale internment of people on the basis of race or ethnicity alone.

§ 10.03 POST 9/11 EMERGENCY

The ongoing claim of national emergency and reliance on executive power under the commander-in-chief clause rings rather hollow six years after 9/11. To some observers it seemed highly questionable at the time. Reviewing some of the elements of the emergency argument may provide some guidance for the future.

---

[74] Among those expressing regret or stating that the program was a mistake were William Douglas (who voted with the majority in *Korematsu*), Francis Biddle (Attorney General), Henry Stimson (Secretary of War), Earl Warren (supported exclusion as Attorney General), and Tom Clark (liaison between Depts. of Justice and Defense). CWRIC at 18.

[75] *Id.*

[A] Ethnic Profiling

Two early responses to 9/11 by the Justice Department had ethnic overtones. One was to interview many U.S. citizens or resident aliens who came from countries with terrorist ties in an effort to obtain information that could be assembled and analyzed to discern patterns related either to 9/11 itself or to future plots. The second initiative was to detain many aliens from those same countries who had overstayed their visas or otherwise violated immigration laws, some of whom eventually might be deportable. As a number of advocacy groups observed, most of the countries considered to be linked to terrorist planning were Arab nations and most of those detained were young Arab males. While not explicitly based on ethnicity, the practice resulted in a clearly disparate impact on Arab aliens.

Ironically, the 9/11 investigations that focused on initial interviews of thousands of young Arab males occurred as a number of states were considering or passing legislation to outlaw "racial profiling" by law enforcement and the Justice Department itself was studying the issue. Critics charge that the offense of DWB ("driving while black") is the basis for so many traffic stops leading to severe questioning that the phenomenon ultimately is harmful to law enforcement. It is on this basis that a few courts have moved in the direction of requiring police forces to adopt policies regarding ethnic profiling.

Ethnic profiling has been a target of significant scrutiny in the past decade.[76] In the 9/11 setting, public opinion swung suddenly and visibly to acceptance of racial or ethnic profiling. One survey conducted in Detroit reported that 61% of Arab Americans believed that "extra scrutiny of people with Middle Eastern features or accents by law enforcement officials" was justified.[77] Academic commentary immediately after 9/11 showed a similar swing in emphasis. Noting that as of September 10, 2001, a strong consensus against racial profiling had been accepted by everyone from Jesse Jackson to John Ashcroft, Professors Gross and Livingston argued that harsh realities prompted a rethinking of the issues:

> The September 11 attacks and the threat of future terrorism clearly require an intensive investigation. Given the extremity of the threat and identity of the known terrorists, the government is justified in focusing that investigation on Middle Eastern men despite the fact that the public decision to do so has caused

---

[76] See DAVID COLE, NO EQUAL JUSTICE: RACE AND CLASS IN THE AMERICAN CRIMINAL JUSTICE SYSTEM (1999); RANDALL KENNEDY, RACE, CRIME, AND THE LAW 149 (1997) ("It is not surprising that virtually all the riots we have experienced in this country since World War II have been sparked by racially charged police-citizen encounters."); David Cole, *Race, Policing, and the Future of Criminal Law*, 26 HUM. RTS. 2 (1999); David A. Harris, *The Stories, The Statistics, and the Law: Why "Driving While Black" Matters*, 84 MINN. L. REV. 265 (1999); Dorothy E. Roberts, *Foreword: Race, Vagueness, and the Social Meaning of Order-Maintenance Policing*, 89 J. CRIM. L. & CRIMINOLOGY 775 (1999).

[77] *Arab Americans Expect Scrutiny, Feel Sting of Bias*, DETROIT FREE PRESS, Oct. 1, 2001, *available at* www.freep.com/news/nw/terror2001/poll1_20011001.htm.

understandable pain and anxiety for many Arab Americans. But that should be only the beginning of our inquiry. In the end, what the Department of Justice does to those it seeks to interview, for what reasons and on what basis, are more important than the fact that they may have been initially selected for interviews in part because of their ethnicity or national origin.[78]

Professor Harris now thinks that the earlier unacceptability of racial profiling should be reinstated, although he believes that a sophisticated form of "behavioral profiling" could be more effective without the stigma.[79]

It is exceedingly difficult to prove racial bias in an individual stop or arrest situation because the defendant must show that the officer acted from a discriminatory motive.[80] The Supreme Court has held that a defendant alleging racial bias in prosecutions may not even have discovery of prosecutorial decisions without a preliminary showing of reason to believe that "similarly situated individuals of a different race were not prosecuted."[81] Courts generally have cautiously allowed claims of racial profiling to go forward[82] and have dealt with established patterns of racial disparities in "stop and frisk" situations by setting out guidelines for education and control of police discretion.[83] One reason given for a reluctance to find discrimination from mere arrest patterns is fear that the police response would be to decrease law enforcement efforts in low-income, high-crime, predominantly minority neighborhoods.[84]

The classic example of permissible racial segregation is that of separating prison inmates by race during a race riot.[85] When the Supreme Court has cited this example, it has never had reason to speculate about the degree

---

[78] Samuel R. Gross & Debra Livingston, *Racial Profiling Under Attack*, 102 COLUM. L. REV. 1413, 1437 (2002).

[79] David A. Harris, *New Risks, New Tactics: An Assessment of the Re-Assessment of Racial Profiling in the Wake of September 11, 2001*, 2004 UTAH L. REV. 913.

[80] Farm Labor Org. Comm. v. Ohio State Highway Patrol, 308 F.3d 523, 533 (6th Cir. 2002); Chavez v. Illinois State Police, 251 F.3d 612, 635 (7th Cir. 2001).

[81] United States v. Armstrong, 517 U.S. 456, 465 (1996); *see also* Wade v. United States, 504 U.S. 181 (1992).

[82] Price v. Kramer, 200 F.3d 1237 (2d Cir. 2000) (damage award); Rodriguez v. Cal. Highway Patrol, 89 F. Supp. 2d 1131 (N.D. Cal. 2000) (denying defendants' motions to dismiss Fourth Amendment and equal protections claims for targeting African American and Latino drivers); National Congress of Puerto Rican Rights v. City of New York, 191 F.R.D. 52 (S.D.N.Y. 1999) (concluding that Black and Latino plaintiffs stated an equal protection claim by alleging police targeted them for Terry stops because of their race and national origin); Wilson v. Tinicum Township, 1993 U.S. Dist. LEXIS 9971, No. 92-6617, 1993 WL 280205 (E.D. Pa. 1993) (certifying class action against officers for violating Fourth and Fourteenth Amendments by profiling).

[83] White v. Williams, 179 F. Supp. 2d 405 (D.N.J. 2002); Martinez v. Village of Mt. Prospect, 92 F. Supp. 2d 780 (N.D. Ill. 2000).

[84] Marshall v. Columbia Lea Regional Hospital, 345 F.3d 1157, 1167 (10th Cir. 2003) (independent case-specific evidence corroborated racial bias of arresting officer); *see generally* RANDALL KENNEDY, RACE, CRIME AND THE LAW (1997).

[85] Richmond v. J. A. Croson Co., 488 U.S. 469, 521 (1989) (Scalia, J., concurring).

of evidence that would be required to support the conclusion of an emergency for this purpose. Perhaps it is safe to assume that in the context of a prison riot, we would know an emergency when we see it, but more troubling is whether we know a national emergency when we see it. The reason for the difficulty is that the greater the intrusion into personal liberties, the greater the showing of emergency that should be expected. And, as Justice Jackson intimated, and as we all feel instinctively, at the extremes the courts may be powerless to curtail governmental abuse.

In June 2003, the Department of Justice announced new Guidelines dealing with racial profiling.[86] The policy broadly prohibits racial or ethnic profiling in investigations with some pertinent exceptions. For example, ethnic information can be provided in describing a suspect when a crime has already been committed and reliable evidence makes ethnicity part of a description. The DOJ Guidelines as well as most state statutes allow racial or ethnic descriptions as part of the description of a known suspect. Superficially, this seems only common sense. But if a description of a suspect characterizes him as a "Hispanic male," the police are likely to stop and question a disproportionate number of Hispanic males as compared to Asian or White males in the same vicinity.

More problematic is an exception for "national security and border integrity" although the policy itself only restates that law enforcement officers are bound by the "Constitution and laws of the United States."[87]

> The policy makes a clear distinction between routine law enforcement work and that involving national security or border security. Although reliance on racial and ethnic stereotypes is broadly forbidden, the guidelines say that authorities can subject certain ethnic or racial groups to greater scrutiny if there is specific information that such people are preparing to mount a terrorist attack.[88]

Critics pounced on the terrorism and immigration exceptions, some even claiming that concentrating on Arab or Muslim males in pursuit of terrorist cells could create more problems than it solved.[89] The argument is that focused questioning of Arab and Muslim males could serve the recruiting objectives of the radicals in much the same way that invading Iraq is argued to have produced more terrorists for the anti-American cause. Critics also

---

[86] *See* www.usdoj.gov/crt/split/documents/guidance_on_race.htm (last visited July 25, 2007).

[87] "In investigating or preventing threats to national security or other catastrophic events (including the performance of duties related to air transportation security), or in enforcing laws protecting the integrity of the Nation's borders, Federal law enforcement officers may not consider race or ethnicity except to the extent permitted by the Constitution and laws of the United States."

[88] Curt Anderson, *Federal Agencies Get Racial Profiling Ban*, ASSOCIATED PRESS, June 18, 2003.

[89] American-Arab Anti-Discrimination Committee, *DOJ Racial Profiling Guidelines Not Sufficient*, *available at* adc.org/index.php?id = 1948.

pointed out that racial profiling could be a highly inefficient method of identifying suspects for further scrutiny. [90]

The DOJ Guidelines set out two extremes without expressing an opinion in the grey area between. The Guidelines state that if investigators acquire specific reliable information involving a specific plot by persons of a specific ethnic group, then more aggressive domestic investigation or screening of members of that group at border entry points would be permissible. At the opposite extreme, more aggressive screening of entrants to a federal courthouse on the basis of ethnicity not tied to a specific threat would not be permissible. In between these extremes is the more likely scenario in which there is some reason to believe that members of a particular ethnic group are planning some unidentified violent activity.

In this middle ground, the question is whether a heightened level of concern during a time of "emergency" is warranted. The validity of a disparate treatment on the basis of race or ethnicity should depend on the degree of harm foreseen versus the degree of harm caused by the profiling practice. At minimum, a conscientious investigatory policy would recognize the harmful potential of focusing unduly on a particular ethnic or cultural group.

[B] The Torture Debacle

The interrogation of prisoners poses the problem of emergency powers starkly. In the famous "ticking bomb" hypothetical, the question is presented of whether it should be legal to torture the person who knows the location of the bomb. As a result of the far-from-hypothetical display of abuse by U.S. prison guards and interrogators, the U.S. public must now face the question of whether it wants to hold military or civilian public officials accountable for clear violations of both domestic and international law. [91]

Abu Ghraib is a paradigm of the proverbial slippery slope. What began as marginal levels of improper interrogation for those who might have had some knowledge of terrorist organizations expanded outward until it became policy at rather high levels. Memoranda from the Pentagon and Justice Department make it clear that a climate of emergency excuse existed during 2002 and 2003, [92] during which it became increasingly

---

[90] Sherry F. Colb, *The New Face of Racial Profiling: How Terrorism Affects The Debate*, Oct. 10, 2001, *available at* writ.news.findlaw.com/colb/20011010.html:

> Unlike the drug trade, in which very large numbers of people — of every race — are involved, there is reason to think that relatively few individuals here are engaged in planning terrorist attacks on the United States. Therefore, any criteria police use to identify or "profile" terrorists, whether or not those criteria rely on suspect classifications such as race, ethnicity, or national origin, will yield many more false positives than they will disclose true conspiring murderers.

[91] Under military tradition, the Generals, Secretary of Defense, and even President could be held responsible for what was essentially policy. After all, the U.S. executed General Yamashita for failure to control his troops during the Japanese occupation of the Phillipines.

[92] A catalogue of the memoranda addressed to methods of interrogation can be found at www.washingtonpost.com/wp-dyn/articles/A62516-2004Jun22.html.

acceptable to treat prisoners in ways that had no justification under either domestic or international law.[93]

One memorandum from the Justice Department to White House Counsel, the "Bybee Memorandum,"[94] attempted to legitimate abusive interrogation techniques at two levels. At the first level, the Memorandum argued that some techniques constituting "cruel, inhuman or degrading treatment" would not violate the Convention against Torture or its implementing statutes. At the second level, arguments were made that even torture could be excused either because military actions in wartime are not subject to the requirements of law or that "necessity or self-defense" could justify what would otherwise be illegal conduct. These arguments are so outrageous that commentators have had a bit of a field day with their implications.[95]

It is true that some of the interrogation techniques authorized by Secretary Rumsfeld were labeled by the European Court of Human Rights as constituting not torture but "cruel, inhuman or degrading treatment."[96] That does not make them legal, however. It leaves them illegal under provisions of both domestic[97] and international law[98] other than the Torture Convention and its statutes. The Bybee Memorandum emphasized that both the Executive and Congress had endorsed an "understanding" when ratifying the Convention that "torture" was an "extreme form of cruel, inhuman or degrading treatment" and further stating that "cruel, inhuman or degrading treatment" would be considered limited to those acts that would be unconstitutional under the U.S. Eighth Amendment. The Convention states that Parties "undertake to prevent" the lesser category of "cruel, inhuman or degrading." So far, the Bybee Memorandum is on solid ground in distinguishing between torture and other acts, the first category to be criminalized and the other to be prevented by other means.

But the Bybee Memorandum stops there. It fails to point out that "cruel, inhuman or degrading treatment" would violate not only the Eighth

---

"Given the known facts, the notion that the photographed outrages at Abu Ghraib were just the actions of a few sick men and women, as President Bush has repeatedly argued, is beyond belief." Anthony Lewis, *Making Torture Legal*, 51 N.Y. REV. OF BOOKS, July 15, 2004.

[93] General Taguba's report in March 2004 specifically found "That between October and December 2003, at the Abu Ghraib Confinement Facility (BCCF), numerous incidents of sadistic, blatant, and wanton criminal abuses were inflicted on several detainees. This systemic and illegal abuse of detainees was intentionally perpetrated by several members of the military police guard force." Taguba Report, Part I, ¶ 5, *available at* news.findlaw.com/hdocs/docs/iraq/tagubarpt.html.

[94] *See* news.findlaw.com/hdocs/docs/torture/bybee20702mem.html.

[95] "The memos read like the advice of a mob lawyer to a mafia don on how to skirt the law and stay out of prison." Lewis, *supra* note 92.

[96] Republic of Ireland v. United Kingdom (Series A, No. 25), 2 EHRR 25 (1979-80).

[97] There are a host of statutes, including the Uniform Code of Military Justice, that criminalize excessive use of force by federal officers charged with custody of prisoners.

[98] The United States is a signatory to the Covenant on Civil and Political Rights, which condemns both torture and "cruel, inhuman, or degrading treatment or punishment" in the same language as the European Convention on Human Rights which was interpreted by the ECHR in the *Ireland* case.

Amendment but also the obligation under the Convention to "prevent" those acts. In other words, the United States has obligated itself as a matter of law to prevent an array of actions in addition to those that are criminalized under the Torture Statute. One of the worst "lawyer tricks" is to answer only the question asked, knowing that the answer should lead to another pertinent question that has not been asked.

At the second level, the Bybee Memorandum makes the rather unexceptional point that the Constitution vests the President with the Commander-in-Chief power and that the Supreme Court has recognized that the Executive has a "unity in purpose and energy in action" that makes it better suited to conduct the strategy and tactics of warfare.[99] The military has the obligation to capture, detain, and interrogate enemy combatants (and, we could add, criminals such as terrorists) to obtain valuable information to prevent further harm. Again, so far so good. But then the Memorandum makes this astonishing leap:

> Any effort by Congress to regulate the interrogation of battlefield combatants would violate the Constitution's sole vesting of the Commander-in-Chief authority in the President. . . . Just as statutes that order the President to conduct warfare in a certain manner or for specific goals would be unconstitutional, so too are laws that seek to prevent the President from gaining the intelligence he believes necessary to prevent attacks upon the United States.[100]

This statement is astonishing. It could render the Uniform Code of Military Justice unconstitutional or make it unconstitutional for Congress to ratify treaties prohibiting war crimes and cruel, inhuman or degrading treatment of prisoners. And it was even unconstitutional for Congress to authorize and set goals for the invasion of Iraq? If the Memorandum had suggested any limits on its sweeping statement of Presidential autonomy, then it might be possible to address it seriously. As it stands, however, it is impossible to imagine what the limits might be and thus impossible to describe these conclusions as anything but ludicrous.

The final level at which the Bybee Memorandum operates is to put forward potential defenses of necessity or "defense of others" that could be raised in criminal prosecutions under the torture statutes. The Memorandum recognizes the argument that the defense of necessity is not available with regard to any offense in which the legislative body has already made the decision that there shall be no defense. The Torture Convention contains the provision that "no exceptional circumstances whatsoever, whether a state of war or a threat of war, internal political instability or

---

[99] Bybee Memorandum at 37. For this proposition, the Memorandum cites a number of cases with dicta to the effect that the President is better suited than Congress to conduct military operations. The Memorandum does not cite cases such as *Youngstown* or *Milligan* that place restraints on the Presidential powers.

[100] *Id*. at 39.

any other public emergency, may be invoked as a justification of torture."[101] The Memorandum responds to this by pointing out that this provision was not enacted into the U.S. Code, so because "Congress omitted CAT's effort to bar a necessity or wartime defense, we read Section 2340 as permitting the defense."[102] It is just as plausible to believe that Congress did not enact it because it was already part of the framework of the statute. Moreover, just because a defense might be allowed under domestic law does not make that defense available in any setting other than domestic courts.[103] The Memorandum opens a U.S. interrogator to prosecution by another signatory nation, or possibly by any nation under the doctrine of universal jurisdiction,[104] in which the defense clearly would be unavailable. This seems irresponsible lawyering at best.

In addition to its sweeping rejection of Congress' role in lawmaking, the Memorandum's general tone ignores treaty law and *jus cogens* as limits on U.S. military or executive action. It is almost as if the authors of the memorandum were unaware that treaty obligations and *jus cogens* could be operative over and above domestic law.[105] The Bush Administration has attempted to distance itself from the memorandum by stating that no decisions were ever made to implement its conclusions.[106] But the existence

---

[101] CAT art. 2.2.

[102] Bybee Memorandum at 41 n.23.

[103] U.S. courts typically take the view that Congress' statutory law stands on a higher footing than a treaty where the two conflict. Although some treaties are self-executing, most will require some legislative action to put their provisions into effect as domestic law. When Congress does act, it can decide to modify the terms of international law. "Our duty is to enforce the Constitution, laws, and treaties of the United States, not to conform the law of the land to norms of customary international law. 'Statutes inconsistent with principles of customary international law may well lead to international law violations. But within the domestic legal realm, that inconsistent statute simply modifies or supersedes customary international law to the extent of the inconsistency.'" United States v. Yunis, 288 U.S. App. D.C. 129; 924 F.2d 1086 (D.C. Cir. 1991), (quoting Committee of U.S. Citizens Living in Nicaragua v. Reagan, 859 F.2d 929 (D.C. Cir. 1988)).

[104] *See generally Ex parte* Pinochet Ugarte (No. 3), [2000] 1 AC 147, [1999] 2 All ER 97 (House of Lords 1999).

[105] *See* lawofwar.org/Torture_Memos_analysis.htm:

This argument presents an interesting question of domestic law as to whether a Commander in Chief can order a violation of international law by making a factual finding unsupported by independent evidence. Could one charged under the War Crimes Act (18 U.S.C. 2441) assert as a defense that as a matter of domestic law there was no grave breach, even though it was clearly a violation of international law? The answer to that proposition is beyond the scope of this discussion, although it appears questionable. What the argument does not do, however, . . . is present any defense to charges by any other Geneva III signatory charged to prosecute perpetrators of grave breaches wherever they may be found.

[106] White House Counsel Alberto R. Gonzales said in a May 21 interview with *The Washington Post*:

> Anytime a discussion came up about interrogations with the president, . . . the directive was, "Make sure it is lawful. Make sure it meets all of our obligations under the Constitution, U.S. federal statutes and applicable treaties."

Memo on Torture Draws Focus to Bush, WASHINGTON POST, June 9, 2004.

of the memorandum, unless it were clearly and firmly repudiated by higher levels than its authors, must have contributed to the climate of "emergency powers" that toppled the traditional constraints on prisoner treatment like dominos from "undisclosed locations" to Guantánamo to Abu Ghraib.[107]

The Dershowitz proposal for a torture warrant at least provides for judicial review of each claim of necessity, but it has not been enacted and would be impossible to get through the international bodies. The counter view that is more likely to prevail is that it is better to state and hold to the legal principle that torture is criminal conduct, while recognizing the inevitable place of discretion in the functions of prosecutor, judge, and jury. Discretion necessarily will dispense a rough sort of justice without promoting the idea of a legal excuse. With regard to those interrogations that we "know" are taking place in "undisclosed locations" around the world, some degree of "see no evil, hear no evil" also is inevitable in this arena. That we can tolerate a generalized knowledge of the existence of illegal behavior, however, does not mean that we should condone it.

Finally, there is nothing in this whole line of thought to suggest that the policy makers ought to be immune from all consequences of clandestine authorization of illegal conduct. What that leaves is the ultimate type of prosecutorial discretion, namely the response of the voters at the next election.

Dershowitz' principal point is that torture is most certainly going to occur clandestinely if we do not provide for it, and that it would be better to provide an official mechanism to see that it does not get out of hand. One clear difficulty with his argument is that it would violate many international legal provisions. The counter-argument seems much more persuasive. If torture will occur clandestinely regardless of our best efforts to curtail it, then better not to give it the sanction of approval but attempt to restrain it. We may recognize that some instances of abuse will occur and that "prosecutorial discretion" will be exercised to avoid punishment of the interrogator without giving moral sanction to the practice through judicial approval.[108] Emergency situations will be dealt with by emergency

---

[107] *See, e.g.,* Reed Brody, Human Rights Watch, *Prison Abuse Calls for 9/11-Type Probe,* Aug. 1, 2004, *available at* hrw.org/english/docs/2004/08/02/usint9172.htm:

> The photos were followed by revelations that the use of illegal, coercive interrogation methods on detainees had been approved at the highest levels of government, and by evidence that abuse of detainees was widespread in both Iraq and Afghanistan. Yet only a few low-ranking soldiers have been called to account, and the administration is sticking to its line that the Abu Ghraib crimes were the work of a few "bad apples."

[108] Bowden, *supra* note 29:

> In other words, when the ban is lifted, there is no restraining lazy, incompetent, or sadistic interrogators. As long as it remains illegal to torture, the interrogator who employs coercion must accept the risk. He must be prepared to stand up in court, if necessary, and defend his actions. Interrogators will still use coercion because in some cases they will deem it worth the consequences. This does not mean they will necessarily be punished. In any nation the decision to prosecute a crime is an

measures, prosecutors will examine the worst abuses for possible criminal sanction, and ultimately it will be the judgment of peers and history that determines whether government agents over-reacted.[109]

It is easy to sit in my "ivory tower" office and insist that U.S. agents should be held at least to some minimal standard of decency in their treatment of persons in their custody. Spy novels and political rhetoric are replete with criticisms of those of us who would "hamstring" or "shackle" our representatives in their fight against unreasoning terror. But several factors motivate my belief that courts should enforce a rule such as *Toscanino* envisions:

1.   The U.S. is a Party to the Torture Convention. Torture is thus illegal by the terms of our own international commitments.

2.   Torture for the sake of obtaining information or confessions can easily result in mistakes and inaccuracies. Granted that some reliable information can be obtained, it is risky because the mistakes can be very costly.

3.   If we stoop to official torture, then we lose the moral high ground that promotes our system of government to be the model for the rest of the world.

4.   Behaving as the bully that many disaffected people believe us to be may push those disaffected persons to respond in violence. Acting as the terrorists claim we act will create more terrorists.

§ 10.04 BRITISH AND CANADIAN DETENTION CASES

The British House of Lords dealt with executive detentions of aliens in a fashion very similar to the U.S. Supreme Court's opinion in *Zadvydas*

---

executive one. A prosecutor, a grand jury, or a judge must decide to press charges, and the chances that an interrogator in a genuine ticking-bomb case would be prosecuted, much less convicted, is very small.

The Bush Administration has adopted exactly the right posture on the matter. Candor and consistency are not always public virtues. Torture is a crime against humanity, but coercion is an issue that is rightly handled with a wink, or even a touch of hypocrisy; it should be banned but also quietly practiced. Those who protest coercive methods will exaggerate their horrors, which is good: it generates a useful climate of fear. It is wise of the President to reiterate U.S. support for international agreements banning torture, and it is wise for American interrogators to employ whatever coercive methods work. It is also smart not to discuss the matter with anyone.

If interrogators step over the line from coercion to outright torture, they should be held personally responsible. But no interrogator is ever going to be prosecuted for keeping Khalid Sheikh Mohammed awake, cold, alone, and uncomfortable. Nor should he be.

[109] "The chief restraint upon those who command the physical forces of the country, in the future as in the past, must be their responsibility to the political judgments of their contemporaries and to the moral judgments of history." *Korematsu*, 323 U.S. at 248 (Jackson, J., dissenting).

v. Davis[110] despite the British Government's invocation of a national emergency claim.

In *A. v. Home Secretary*,[111] the House of Lords was presented with a petition on behalf of several aliens who were being detained under statutory authorization because they were suspected of ties to terrorist organizations and were unwilling to be deported to their country of origin. Parliament had responded to a request from the government to allow certification of a person as a terrorist based on "links to an international terrorist organization," which in turn required that "he supports or assists it."[112] Once certified, an alien who could not be deported could be detained indefinitely.[113] This mechanism was challenged as being in violation of European Convention on Human Rights (ECHR), article 5, which protects "liberty and security of person" except in circumstances such as detention "with a view to deportation." Because the plaintiffs could not be deported against their will, they argued that the detention was not undertaken with a view to deportation.

The government argued that Article 5 was subject to the "derogation" principle of ECHR article 15, which allows departure from ECHR requirements in "time of war or other public emergency threatening the life of the nation . . . to the extent strictly required by the exigencies of the situation."

Lord Bingham took the lead for the House of Lords and held that there was no sufficient explanation for why aliens should be treated differently from anyone else for this purpose — the alien was no more likely to be a threat to the public peace and security than a citizen, and the government had not chosen to imprison citizens under the same conditions.[114]

The only opinion speaking directly to whether there was an emergency was that of Lord Hoffmann. Although he noted that the failure to imprison suspected terrorist citizens was relevant, he insisted that the real question was whether there was an emergency that "threatened the life of the nation." On this point, he was adamant that there was not:

> There may be some nations too fragile or fissiparous to withstand a serious act of violence. But that is not the case in the United Kingdom. When Milton urged the government of his day not to censor the press even in time of civil war, he said: "Lords and Commons of England, consider what nation it is whereof ye are, and whereof ye are the governours."
>
> This is a nation which has been tested in adversity, which has survived physical destruction and catastrophic loss of life. I do not underestimate the ability of fanatical groups of terrorists to kill and

---

[110] 533 U.S. 678 (2001). *See* § 2.02[A] *supra*.

[111] 3 All E.R. 169 (2005).

[112] Anti-Terrorism Act of 2001 § 23.

[113] *Id*. In the British scheme, the alien could "end his detention at any time by agreeing to leave the United Kingdom." CLIVE WALKER, THE ANTI-TERRORISM LEGISLATION 224 (2002).

[114] 3 All Eng. Rep. 169 at ¶ 43.

destroy, but they do not threaten the life of the nation. Whether we would survive Hitler hung in the balance, but there is no doubt that we shall survive al-Qaeda. The Spanish people have not said that what happened in Madrid, hideous crime as it was, threatened the life of their nation. Their legendary pride would not allow it. Terrorist violence, serious as it is, does not threaten our institutions of government or our existence as a civil community.[115]

Only one member of the panel was willing to accord full deference to the judgment of the political branches.

Following the opinion in *A v. Home Secretary*, the British Parliament adopted statutory measures allowing for a form of "house arrest" through "control orders" that could be issued by the Secretary. In a case consolidating challenges to several control orders, the appellate division of Queen's Bench ruled that the control orders amounted to a "deprivation of liberty" under the ECHR and thus were invalid executive detentions.[116]

The court recognized a distinction between a "restriction on movement" and a "deprivation of liberty." In some instances, government may be able to prevent a person from entering certain locations (restriction) without confining that person to a certain location (deprivation). In this instance, the Government argued that restricting a person to a state-provided one-room apartment for 18 hours per day, allowing him out for six hours during the work day, was merely a restriction on movement. The appellate bench agreed with the trial judge's assessment of this argument:

> I have considered the cumulative impact of the obligations and therefore the extent to which they restrict the respondents' liberty in the six hours when they are allowed out of their residences, as well as the effect of the 18 hour curfew and the obligations imposed on the respondents whilst they have to remain within their residences during that period. If I had to assess the impact of the obligations individually, I would consider that house arrest for 18 hours each day, even if it was the only obligation (apart from obligations such as reporting and tagging to ensure that it was strictly observed) would be more realistically described as deprivation of liberty, and not as a restriction on liberty, if it prevented the individual from pursuing a normal "in at home/out at work" life cycle.[117]

The Canadian Supreme Court also reached a similar result in a case challenging detention of an alien deemed to be a threat to national security.[118] The Canadian provisions required periodic judicial review but did not allow the detainee to see classified evidence on which the Government was relying. The Court held that there were alternatives by which

---

[115] *Id.* at ¶ 95-96.

[116] Secretary of State v. JJ, KK, et al. (QB 2007).

[117] *Id.* at ¶ 10.

[118] Charkaoui v. Minister of Citizenship and Immigration, 2007 SCC 9 (Sup. Ct. Canada 2007).

more protection for the individual could be obtained, such as appointment of a special counsel to review the classified evidence on behalf of the detainee.

§ 10.05   FREE EXPRESSION AND SECURITY

In addition to privacy concerns, many advocacy groups confronted with government surveillance or investigations have raised First Amendment concerns. The difference between a "due process" or "privacy" argument and a "freedom of expression" argument may be fuzzy and indeed the arguments will often overlap. The two sets of interests, however, express some slightly different concerns. In due process and privacy, the concerns are mostly with information that the individual does not want government to have. In First Amendment arguments, the concern is with the individual's ability to obtain information and express opinions. Obviously, some collection of private information can have a dampening or "chilling" effect on the individual's willingness to engage in expressive activities, and conversely some expressive activities can be effective only if undertaken in private. Even with the so-called "intimate relationships" branch of the concept of "liberty," we find the necessary mingling of privacy and free expression.

Perhaps an easy way to understand the division of analysis is to see that each branch of doctrine starts from a different perspective, although each may include elements of the other before the analysis is complete. So for this section of the book, we will be starting from the perspective of the First Amendment, which includes freedom of assembly, freedom of speech and press, and matters of conscience as well. In the course of the discussion, some privacy concerns will arise.

One of the core principles of the First Amendment is that speech in places known as public fora can be subjected only to "time, place, and manner" regulations. The impact of this is that in traditional open spaces such as parks and sidewalks, government can regulate the time of activities in certain places for valid governmental reasons. For example, a parade on a busy street would not be allowed during rush hour. Speeches in a park could be banned during night-time hours to avoid disturbing the neighbors. The keys to time, place, and manner regulations are whether the regulations fit the legitimate interests of the public and whether there are reasonable alternatives available for the speaker's message to reach its intended audience.

There are two lines of cases directly raising issues of security and First Amendment protection. One is from the Nixon era and involves official attempts to limit expression during appearances of the President. The other is more recent and deals with demonstrations at national political conventions.

In 1971, the city of Charlotte declared a "Billy Graham Day" to be celebrated with (among other events) an appearance of President Nixon at the Charlotte Coliseum. The Secret Service performed its customary role of coordinating security for the President with the cooperation of local and state law enforcement and the FBI. Although the event was open to the public and "free tickets were widely distributed," a number of people were excluded from the event on bases that were not completely clear at the time of litigation but allegedly included such criteria as their appearance, being on a name list, or carrying signs critical of the President. The district court granted a preliminary injunction preventing the Secret Service from "discriminatorily arresting or detaining, or keeping from the general public presence of the President, plaintiffs and others similarly situated, on account of their mode of dress or hair style, life style, peaceable expression of political (including dissenting) views, exercise of constitutional rights of free speech, petition for redress of grievances or right of association, without prior judicial authorization or without probable cause, or for any other cause not rationally necessary for the personal safety of the President." On appeal, the Government made several arguments regarding official immunity and discovery issues but apparently did not even question the proposition that excluding people from a public event on the basis of their political expression would be unconstitutional.[119]

The almost obvious proposition that people cannot be excluded from a "public" event on the basis of their "expression" leads directly to two limitations with which security planners must deal. One is the degree to which demonstrators must be allowed to approach the attendees at a "private" event while they are arriving or leaving the event, as well as to gain proximity to the event on adjacent public fora. The second is the extent to which "expression" may lead to the likelihood of prohibitable violence or other unlawful activity. The former is a concern with "security" and terrorism only in the sense to which it could lead to the latter.

It is clear that demonstrators can be prevented from blocking ingress and egress for those using the facility. Government also can impose a sufficient buffer zone to allow activities inside the facility to go on undisturbed. But how close is too close? Or, asked the other way around, how far is too far? In *United States v. Baugh*,[120] a group wanted to protest the Defense Department's decision to privatize the land and buildings of the Presidio in San Francisco rather than using the premises to provide shelter for homeless persons. The group's desired location was the entrance to the Visitors' Center operated by the National Park Service. The NPS established a zone of 150 yards away from the entrance, and the Ninth Circuit said this was too far away for the protesters to capture the attention of their intended audience. In the language of TPM, the government was denying access to a forum without providing an adequate alternative, or in the

---

119 The Fourth Circuit also noted a similar case out of Hawaii involving military security at Hickham Field air base when the President made a visit there. *Butler v. United States*, 365 F. Supp. 1035 (D. Hawaii 1973).

120 187 F.3d 1037 (9th Cir. 1999) . Quoting from its own prior case in which a 75-yard buffer zone was held too far away from a naval facility, the court stated, "an alternative is not ample if the speaker is not permitted to reach the 'intended audience.'" Bay Area Peace Navy v. United States, 914 F.2d 1224, 1226 (9th Cir. 1990).

language of more classic First Amendment analysis, the government was imposing a prior restraint on speech without an emergency justification.[121]

One of the most widely-cited permit demonstration cases involved the 2000 Republican National Convention at the Staples Center in Los Angeles.[122] For security reasons, the Secret Service and local law enforcement agencies had established a fenced and ticketed perimeter of several blocks around the convention center but had provided a "First Amendment zone" near this perimeter. The district court granted an injunction against this arrangement because it did not allow protesters sufficient opportunity to reach their intended audience, the media and delegates attending the convention.

The D.C. District Court similarly struck down a ban on demonstrations at the U.S. Capitol Building on the ground that the appropriate mechanism for protecting against disruption of government business inside the building is to punish disruptive behavior when it occurs.[123] On the other hand, the Second Circuit upheld a ban on amplified sound near a city hall during business hours, except during ticker-tape parades, because unamplified alternatives would allow protesters to reach patrons entering or leaving the building.[124]

The Supreme Court's most notable foray into this arena was *Madsen v. Women's Health Center*,[125] the principal abortion demonstration case. The Court upheld restrictions imposed by a state court on noise levels outside the clinic and a 36-foot buffer zone to allow unimpeded ingress, and egress to the clinic but struck down other provisions of the state court's order such as restrictions on personal contact with patrons and prohibition of "observable images." The Court's opinion was deferential to the state courts and their knowledge of the facts, pointing out that "[t]here are obvious differences . . . between an injunction and a generally applicable ordinance."[126] The differences cut both ways because the legislative judgment contained in an ordinance is entitled to deference on policy grounds while the closer observation of specific fact settings warrants deference to a court-ordered injunction in the specific context. Conversely, the specificity of an injunction makes it a tool that could make unwarranted inroads on rights of expression, so an appellate court will be alert to that potential as well.

These cases establish some basic principles for TPM regulations. Government can designate certain premises for certain uses and can adopt regulations designed to serve those purposes. It can protect ingress and

---

[121] The Ninth Circuit acknowledged NPS' concern that demonstrators would, if allowed to gather at the Visitors' Center, encroach on closed areas and commit trespass violations. The court was emphatic that the proper method of dealing with this concern should be to punish offenses after they occur, not to prohibit otherwise lawful speech. *Id.* at 1044.

[122] Service Employees Local 660 v. City of Los Angeles, 114 F. Supp. 2d 966 (C.D. Cal. 2000).

[123] Bynum v. U.S. Capitol Police Bd., 93 F. Supp. 2d 50 (D.D.C. 2000).

[124] Housing Works v. Kerik, 283 F.3d 471 (2d Cir. 2002).

[125] 512 U.S. 753 (1994).

[126] *Id.* at 764.

egress for those using a facility. But it must provide a reasonable opportunity for assemblages to reach their intended audience.

This line of analysis has produced the concept of "free speech zones" that is now familiar to special event planners. Demonstrators at an event may be confined to certain zones for the purposes of crowd control and avoidance of violent confrontation so long as the assigned zones are designed to provide reasonable access to the intended audience. The language of "reasonableness" is unfortunately loose in the context of delicate rights of free expression, but the concept is familiar to judges and nothing better has suggested itself as yet. The balancing required in planning free speech zones for a special event will usually proceed in roughly the following steps:

1. event organizer obtains exclusive use of a facility (whether private or public),

2. event organizer requests public services, such as police protection to maintain crowd control,

3. public agencies decide which streets and walkways will be closed to provide ingress and egress to the facility,

4. protestors object to the closures and demand access to promote their messages,

5. supplied with information from both groups, public agencies then engage in balancing the needs of the event against the needs of the protestors to reach their audience, crafting a plan that includes designated free speech zones as well as designated "restricted" zones for ingress and egress.

Eventually, the results of this process are likely to be challenged in court. Of course, a judicial challenge may be forestalled if the public officials have obtained formal agreements to the plan from the groups known to have an interest in demonstrating at the event. If there is a judicial challenge, the court will need to assure itself that the needs of the protestors have been addressed in reasonable fashion, that they have been given a reasonable opportunity of reaching their intended audience. If the analysis and designation of free speech zones has been performed in an openly public process, then the reviewing court will be much more likely to give its results a high degree of deference than would be true if the process were undertaken behind closed doors.

§ 10.06 CONCLUSION

The counter-terrorism measures of the Bush administration have produced a great deal of dialogue about the existence and scope of emergency powers. Emergency powers surely exist in some parts of the constitutional framework. They are not to be found in authority to violate the law but in the very statement of the law itself. The whole point of statutes and treaties setting out the rules of law to govern use of force and conduct of war are to prevent claims of necessity or emergency from overriding the dictates of law.

As Justice Jackson said, if the electorate hands over unrestrained power, then it is likely that the courts would be powerless to prevent tyranny. When a set of laws are designed specifically to restrain governmental power, then courts are capable of making those limits clear in specific situations. When the limits are to be inferred from the interstices of constitutional provisions, as in the clash of military authority and due process, it is again the traditional role of the judiciary to say what the law is. And, finally, in those situations in which the Constitution itself does not set limits against what Government is doing, the electorate must exercise independent review of governmental action and make its voice heard.

APPENDIX — DOCUMENTS

I. U.S. STATUTES, RESOLUTIONS, AND ORDERS

1. General Federal Criminal Law

18 U.S.C. § 1111. Murder

(a)   Murder is the unlawful killing of a human being with malice aforethought. Every murder perpetrated by poison, lying in wait, or any other kind of willful, deliberate, malicious, and premeditated killing; or committed in the perpetration of, or attempt to perpetrate, any arson, escape, murder, kidnaping, treason, espionage, sabotage, aggravated sexual abuse or sexual abuse, child abuse, burglary, or robbery; or perpetrated as part of a pattern or practice of assault or torture against a child or children; or perpetrated from a premeditated design unlawfully and maliciously to effect the death of any human being other than him who is killed, is murder in the first degree.

Any other murder is murder in the second degree.

(b)   Within the special maritime and territorial jurisdiction of the United States,

Whoever is guilty of murder in the first degree shall be punished by death or by imprisonment for life;

Whoever is guilty of murder in the second degree, shall be imprisoned for any term of years or for life.

18 U.S.C. § 1114. Protection of officers and employees of the United States

Whoever kills or attempts to kill any officer or employee of the United States or of any agency in any branch of the United States Government (including any member of the uniformed services) while such officer or employee is engaged in or on account of the performance of official duties, or any person assisting such an officer or employee in the performance of such duties or on account of that assistance, shall be punished

(1) in the case of murder, as provided under section 1111;

(2) in the case of manslaughter, as provided under section 1112; or

(3) in the case of attempted murder or manslaughter, as provided in section 1113.

18 U.S.C. § 1119.   Foreign murder of United States nationals

(a) Definition. In this section, "national of the United States" has the meaning stated in section 101(a)(22) of the Immigration and Nationality Act (8 U.S.C. 1101(a)(22)).

(b) Offense. A person who, being a national of the United States, kills or attempts to kill a national of the United States while such national is outside the United States but within the jurisdiction of another country shall be punished as provided under sections 1111, 1112, and 1113.

(c) Limitations on prosecution.

     (1) No prosecution may be instituted against any person under this section except upon the written approval of the Attorney General, the Deputy Attorney General, or an Assistant Attorney General, which function of approving prosecutions may not be delegated. No prosecution shall be approved if prosecution has been previously undertaken by a foreign country for the same conduct.

     (2) No prosecution shall be approved under this section unless the Attorney General, in consultation with the Secretary of State, determines that the conduct took place in a country in which the person is no longer present, and the country lacks the ability to lawfully secure the person's return. A determination by the Attorney General under this paragraph is not subject to judicial review.

18 U.S.C. § 844.   [Penalties for unlawful use of explosive materials]

     (d)   Whoever transports or receives, or attempts to transport or receive, in interstate or foreign commerce any explosive with the knowledge or intent that it will be used to kill, injure, or intimidate any individual or unlawfully to damage or destroy any building, vehicle, or other real or personal property, shall be imprisoned for not more than ten years, or fined under this title, or both; and if personal injury results to any person, including any public safety officer performing duties as a direct or proximate result of conduct prohibited by this subsection, shall be imprisoned for not more than twenty years or fined under this title, or both; and if death results to any person, including any public safety officer performing duties as a direct or proximate result of conduct prohibited by this subsection, shall be subject to imprisonment for any term of years, or to the death penalty or to life imprisonment.

     (e)   Whoever, through the use of the mail, telephone, telegraph, or other instrument of interstate or foreign commerce, or in or affecting interstate or foreign commerce, willfully makes any threat, or maliciously conveys false information knowing the same to be false, concerning an attempt or alleged attempt being made, or to be made, to kill, injure, or intimidate any individual or unlawfully to damage or destroy any building, vehicle, or other real or personal property by means of fire or an explosive shall be imprisoned for not more than 10 years or fined under this title, or both.

     (f) (1)   Whoever maliciously damages or destroys, or attempts to damage or destroy, by means of fire or an explosive, any building, vehicle, or other personal or real property in whole or in part owned or possessed by, or leased to, the United States, or any department or agency thereof, or any institution or organization receiving Federal financial assistance, shall be imprisoned for not less than 5 years and not more than 20 years, fined under this title, or both.

(2) Whoever engages in conduct prohibited by this subsection, and as a result of such conduct, directly or proximately causes personal injury or creates a substantial risk of injury to any person, including any public safety officer performing duties, shall be imprisoned for not less than 7 years and not more than 40 years, fined under this title, or both.

(3) Whoever engages in conduct prohibited by this subsection, and as a result of such conduct directly or proximately causes the death of any person, including any public safety officer performing duties, shall be subject to the death penalty, or imprisoned for not less than 20 years or for life, fined under this title, or both.

2. Federal Civil Rights Statutes

18 U.S.C. § 241. Conspiracy against rights

If two or more persons conspire to injure, oppress, threaten, or intimidate any person in any State, Territory, Commonwealth, Possession, or District in the free exercise or enjoyment of any right or privilege secured to him by the Constitution or laws of the United States, or because of his having so exercised the same; or

If two or more persons go in disguise on the highway, or on the premises of another, with intent to prevent or hinder his free exercise or enjoyment of any right or privilege so secured;

They shall be fined under this title or imprisoned not more than ten years, or both; and if death results from the acts committed in violation of this section or if such acts include kidnaping or an attempt to kidnap, aggravated sexual abuse or an attempt to commit aggravated sexual abuse, or an attempt to kill, they shall be fined under this title or imprisoned for any term of years or for life, or both, or may be sentenced to death.

18 U.S.C. § 242. Deprivation of rights under color of law

Whoever, under color of any law, statute, ordinance, regulation, or custom, willfully subjects any person in [U.S. territory] to the deprivation of any rights, privileges, or immunities secured or protected by the Constitution or laws of the United States, . . . shall be fined under this title or imprisoned not more than one year, or both; and if bodily injury results from the acts committed in violation of this section or if such acts include the use, attempted use, or threatened use of a dangerous weapon, explosives, or fire, shall be fined under this title or imprisoned not more than ten years, or both; and if death results from the acts committed in violation of this section or if such acts include kidnaping or an attempt to kidnap, aggravated sexual abuse, or an attempt to commit aggravated sexual abuse, or an attempt to kill, shall be fined under this title, or imprisoned for any term of years or for life, or both, or may be sentenced to death.

18 U.S.C. § 245.   Federally Protected Activities

(b)   Whoever, whether or not acting under color of law, by force or threat of force willfully injures, intimidates or interferes with, or attempts to injure, intimidate or interfere with

(1) any person because he is or has been, or in order to intimidate such person or any other person or any class of persons from

(A) voting or qualifying to vote, qualifying or campaigning as a candidate for elective office, or qualifying or acting as a poll watcher, or any legally authorized election official, in any primary, special, or general election;

(B) participating in or enjoying any benefit, service, privilege, program, facility, or activity provided or administered by the United States; . . . or

(2) any person because of his race, color, religion or national origin and because he is or has been

(A) enrolling in or attending any public school or public college;

(B) participating in or enjoying any benefit, service, privilege, program, facility or activity provided or administered by any State or subdivision thereof; . . . .

(E) traveling in or using any facility of interstate commerce, or using any vehicle, terminal, or facility of any common carrier by motor, rail, water, or air;

(F) enjoying the goods, services, facilities, privileges, advantages, or accommodations of any inn, hotel, motel, or other establishment which provides lodging to transient guests, or of any restaurant, cafeteria, lunchroom, lunch counter, soda fountain, or other facility which serves the public . . . .

shall be fined under this title, or imprisoned not more than one year, or both; and if bodily injury results from the acts committed in violation of this section or if such acts include the use, attempted use, or threatened use of a dangerous weapon, explosives, or fire shall be fined under this title, or imprisoned not more than ten years, or both; and if death results from the acts committed in violation of this section or if such acts include kidnapping or an attempt to kidnap, aggravated sexual abuse or an attempt to commit aggravated sexual abuse, or an attempt to kill, shall be fined under this title or imprisoned for any term of years or for life, or both, or may be sentenced to death.

3.   U.S. Statutes Based on Extraterritoriality

18 U.S.C. § 7.   Special maritime and territorial jurisdiction of the United States defined

The term "special maritime and territorial jurisdiction of the United States", as used in this title, includes:

(1)   The high seas, any other waters within the admiralty and maritime jurisdiction of the United States and out of the jurisdiction of any particular State, and any vessel belonging in whole or in part to the United States or any citizen thereof, or to any corporation created by or under the laws of the United States, or of any State, Territory, District, or possession thereof, when such vessel is within the admiralty and maritime jurisdiction of the United States and out of the jurisdiction of any particular State.

(2)   Any vessel registered, licensed, or enrolled under the laws of the United States, and being on a voyage upon the waters of any of the Great Lakes, or any of the waters connecting them, or upon the Saint Lawrence River where the same constitutes the International Boundary Line.

(3)   Any lands reserved or acquired for the use of the United States, and under the exclusive or concurrent jurisdiction thereof, or any place purchased or otherwise acquired by the United States by consent of the legislature of the State in which the same shall be, for the erection of a fort, magazine, arsenal, dockyard, or other needful building.

(4)   Any island, rock, or key containing deposits of guano, which may, at the discretion of the President, be considered as appertaining to the United States.

(5)   Any aircraft belonging in whole or in part to the United States, or any citizen thereof, or to any corporation created by or under the laws of the United States, or any State, Territory, district, or possession thereof, while such aircraft is in flight over the high seas, or over any other waters within the admiralty and maritime jurisdiction of the United States and out of the jurisdiction of any particular State.

(6)   Any vehicle used or designed for flight or navigation in space and on the registry of the United States pursuant to the Treaty on Principles Governing the Activities of States in the Exploration and Use of Outer Space, Including the Moon and Other Celestial Bodies and the Convention on Registration of Objects Launched into Outer Space, while that vehicle is in flight, which is from the moment when all external doors are closed on Earth following embarkation until the moment when one such door is opened on Earth for disembarkation or in the case of a forced landing, until the competent authorities take over the responsibility for the vehicle and for persons and property aboard.

(7)   Any place outside the jurisdiction of any nation with respect to an offense by or against a national of the United States.

(8)   To the extent permitted by international law, any foreign vessel during a voyage having a scheduled departure from or arrival in the United States with respect to an offense committed by or against a national of the United States.

(9)   With respect to offenses committed by or against a national of the United States as that term is used in section 101 of the Immigration and Nationality Act

(A) the premises of United States diplomatic, consular, military or other United States Government missions or entities in foreign States, including the buildings, parts of buildings, and land appurtenant or ancillary thereto or used for purposes of those missions or entities, irrespective of ownership; and

(B) residences in foreign States and the land appurtenant or ancillary thereto, irrespective of ownership, used for purposes of those missions or entities or used by United States personnel assigned to those missions or entities.

Nothing in this paragraph shall be deemed to supersede any treaty or international agreement with which this paragraph conflicts. This paragraph does not apply with respect to an offense committed by a person described in section 3261(a) of this title.

18 U.S.C. § 32.   Destruction of aircraft or aircraft facilities

(a)   Whoever willfully

(1) sets fire to, damages, destroys, disables, or wrecks any aircraft in the special aircraft jurisdiction of the United States or any civil aircraft used, operated, or employed in interstate, overseas, or foreign air commerce;

(2) places or causes to be placed a destructive device or substance in, upon, or in proximity to, or otherwise makes or causes to be made unworkable or unusable or hazardous to work or use, any such aircraft, or any part or other materials used or intended to be used in connection with the operation of such aircraft, if such placing or causing to be placed or such making or causing to be made is likely to endanger the safety of any such aircraft;

(3) sets fire to, damages, destroys, or disables any air navigation facility, or interferes by force or violence with the operation of such facility, if such fire, damaging, destroying, disabling, or interfering is likely to endanger the safety of any such aircraft in flight;

(4) with the intent to damage, destroy, or disable any such aircraft, sets fire to, damages, destroys, or disables or places a destructive device or substance in, upon, or in proximity to, any appliance or structure, ramp, landing area, property, machine, or apparatus, or any facility or other material used, or intended to be used, in connection with the operation, maintenance, loading, unloading or storage of any such aircraft or any cargo carried or intended to be carried on any such aircraft;

(5) performs an act of violence against or incapacitates any individual on any such aircraft, if such act of violence or incapacitation is likely to endanger the safety of such aircraft;

(6) communicates information, knowing the information to be false and under circumstances in which such information may reasonably be believed, thereby endangering the safety of any such aircraft in flight; or

(7) attempts or conspires to do anything prohibited under paragraphs (1) through (6) of this subsection;

shall be fined under this title or imprisoned not more than twenty years or both.

(b)   Whoever willfully

(1) performs an act of violence against any individual on board any civil aircraft registered in a country other than the United States while such aircraft is in flight, if such act is likely to endanger the safety of that aircraft;

(2) destroys a civil aircraft registered in a country other than the United States while such aircraft is in service or causes damage to such an aircraft which renders that aircraft incapable of flight or which is likely to endanger that aircraft's safety in flight;

(3) places or causes to be placed on a civil aircraft registered in a country other than the United States while such aircraft is in service, a device or substance which is likely to destroy that aircraft, or to cause damage to that aircraft which renders that aircraft incapable of flight or which is likely to endanger that aircraft's safety in flight; or

(4) attempts or conspires to commit an offense described in paragraphs (1) through (3) of this subsection;

shall be fined under this title or imprisoned not more than twenty years, or both. There is jurisdiction over an offense under this subsection if a national of the United States was on board, or would have been on board, the aircraft; an offender is a national of the United States; or an offender is afterwards found in the United States. For purposes of this subsection, the term "national of the United States" has the meaning prescribed in section 101(a)(22) of the Immigration and Nationality Act [8 U.S.C. § 1101(a)(22)].

(c)   Whoever willfully imparts or conveys any threat to do an act which would violate any of paragraphs (1) through (5) of subsection (a) or any of paragraphs (1) through (3) of subsection (b) of this section, with an apparent determination and will to carry the threat into execution shall be fined under this title or imprisoned not more than five years, or both.

18 U.S.C. § 2340.   [Torture Act] Definitions

As used in this chapter

(1)   "torture" means an act committed by a person acting under the color of law specifically intended to inflict severe physical or mental pain or suffering (other than pain or suffering incidental to lawful sanctions) upon another person within his custody or physical control;

(2)   "severe mental pain or suffering" means the prolonged mental harm caused by or resulting from

(A) the intentional infliction or threatened infliction of severe physical pain or suffering;

(B) the administration or application, or threatened administration or application, of mind-altering substances or other procedures calculated to disrupt profoundly the senses or the personality;

(C) the threat of imminent death; or

(D) the threat that another person will imminently be subjected to death, severe physical pain or suffering, or the administration or application of mind-altering substances or other procedures calculated to disrupt profoundly the senses or personality; and

(3) "United States" includes all areas under the jurisdiction of the United States including any of the places described in sections 5 and 7 of this title and section 46501(2) of title 49.

18 U.S.C. § 2340A.   Torture

(a) Offense. Whoever outside the United States commits or attempts to commit torture shall be fined under this title or imprisoned not more than 20 years, or both, and if death results to any person from conduct prohibited by this subsection, shall be punished by death or imprisoned for any term of years or for life.

(b) Jurisdiction. There is jurisdiction over the activity prohibited in subsection (a) if

(1) the alleged offender is a national of the United States; or

(2) the alleged offender is present in the United States, irrespective of the nationality of the victim or alleged offender.

49 U.S.C. § 46502.   Aircraft Piracy

(a)   In special aircraft jurisdiction.

(1) In this subsection—

(A) "aircraft piracy" means seizing or exercising control of an aircraft in the special aircraft jurisdiction of the United States by force, violence, threat of force or violence, or any form of intimidation, and with wrongful intent.

(B) an attempt to commit aircraft piracy is in the special aircraft jurisdiction of the United States although the aircraft is not in flight at the time of the attempt if the aircraft would have been in the special aircraft jurisdiction of the United States had the aircraft piracy been completed.

(2) An individual committing or attempting or conspiring to commit aircraft piracy—

(A)   shall be imprisoned for at least 20 years; or

(B)   notwithstanding section 3559(b) of title 18, if the death of another individual results from the commission or attempt, shall be put to death or imprisoned for life.

(b)   Outside special aircraft jurisdiction.

(1) An individual committing or conspiring to commit an offense (as defined in the Convention for the Suppression of Unlawful Seizure of Aircraft) on an aircraft in flight outside the special aircraft jurisdiction of the United States—

(A) shall be imprisoned for at least 20 years; or

(B) notwithstanding section 3559(b) of title 18, if the death of another individual results from the commission or attempt, shall be put to death or imprisoned for life.

(2) There is jurisdiction over the offense in paragraph (1) if—

(A) a national of the United States was aboard the aircraft;

(B) an offender is a national of the United States; or

(C) an offender is afterwards found in the United States.

18 U.S.C. § 1203. Hostage Taking

(a) Except as provided in subsection (b) of this section, whoever, whether inside or outside the United States, seizes or detains and threatens to kill, to injury, or to continue to detain another person in order to compel a third person or a governmental organization to do or abstain from doing any act as an explicit or implicit condition for the release of the person detained, or attempts or conspires to do so, shall be punished by imprisonment for any term of years or for life and, if the death of any person results, shall be punished by death or life imprisonment.

(b) (1) It is not an offense under this section if the conduct required for the offense occurred outside the United States unless—

(A) the offender or the person seized or detained is a national of the United States;

(B) the offender is found in the United States; or

(C) the governmental organization sought to be compelled is the Government of the United States.

(2) It is not an offense under this section if the conduct required for the offense occurred inside the United States, each alleged offender and each person seized or detained are nationals of the United States, and each alleged offender is found in the United States, unless the governmental organization sought to be compelled is the Government of the United States.

4.   U.S. Statutes Referring to "Terrorism"
A.   Designation of Organizations by State Department

8 U.S.C. § 1189.   Designation of foreign terrorist organizations

(a) Designation.

(1) In general. The Secretary is authorized to designate an organization as a foreign terrorist organization in accordance with this subsection if the Secretary finds that

(A)   the organization is a foreign organization;

(B)   the organization engages in terrorist activity (as defined in [8 U.S.C. § 1182(a)(3)(B)]) or terrorism (as defined in [22 U.S.C. § 2656f(d)(2)]), or retains the capability and intent to engage in terrorist activity or terrorism; and

(C)   the terrorist activity or terrorism of the organization threatens the security of United States nationals or the national security of the United States.

(2) Procedure.

(A) Notice.

(i) To congressional leaders. Seven days before making a designation under this subsection, the Secretary shall, by classified communication, notify the Speaker and Minority Leader of the House of Representatives, the President pro tempore, Majority Leader, and Minority Leader of the Senate, and the members of the relevant committees of the House of Representatives and the Senate, in writing, of the intent to designate an organization under this subsection, together with the findings made under paragraph (1) with respect to that organization, and the factual basis therefor.

(ii) Publication in Federal Register. The Secretary shall publish the designation in the Federal Register seven days after providing the notification under clause (i).

(B) Effect of designation.

(i)   For purposes of section 2339B of title 18, United States Code, a designation under this subsection shall take effect upon publication under subparagraph (A)(ii).

(ii)   Any designation under this subsection shall cease to have effect upon an Act of Congress disapproving such designation.

(C) Freezing of assets. Upon notification under paragraph (2)(A)(i), the Secretary of the Treasury may require United States financial institutions possessing or controlling any assets of any foreign organization included in the notification to block all financial transactions involving those assets until further directive from either the Secretary of the Treasury, Act of Congress, or order of court.

(3) Record.

(A) In general. In making a designation under this subsection, the Secretary shall create an administrative record.

(B) Classified information. The Secretary may consider classified information in making a designation under this subsection. Classified information shall not be subject to disclosure for such time as it remains classified, except that such information may be disclosed to a court ex parte and in camera for purposes of judicial review under subsection (b).

(4) Period of designation.

(A) In general. Subject to paragraphs (5) and (6), a designation under this subsection shall be effective for all purposes for a period of 2 years beginning on the effective date of the designation under paragraph (2)(B).

(B) Redesignation. The Secretary may redesignate a foreign organization as a foreign terrorist organization for an additional 2-year period at the end of [any] 2-year period.

(b) Judicial review of designation.

(1) In general. Not later than 30 days after publication of the designation in the Federal Register, an organization designated as a foreign terrorist organization may seek judicial review of the designation in the United States Court of Appeals for the District of Columbia Circuit.

(2) Basis of review. Review under this subsection shall be based solely upon the administrative record, except that the Government may submit, for *ex parte* and *in camera* review, classified information used in making the designation.

(3) Scope of review. The Court shall hold unlawful and set aside a designation the court finds to be

(A) arbitrary, capricious, an abuse of discretion, or otherwise not in accordance with law;

(B) contrary to constitutional right, power, privilege, or immunity;

(C) in excess of statutory jurisdiction, authority, or limitation, or short of statutory right;

(D) lacking substantial support in the administrative record taken as a whole or in classified information submitted to the court under paragraph (2), or

(E) not in accord with the procedures required by law.

(4) Judicial review invoked. The pendency of an action for judicial review of a designation shall not affect the application of this section, unless the court issues a final order setting aside the designation.

8 U.S.C. § 1182(a)(3). Terrorist activity defined.

As used in [§ 1189], the term "terrorist activity" means any activity which is unlawful under the laws of the place where it is committed (or which, if it had been committed in the United States, would be unlawful under the laws of the United States or any State) and which involves any of the following:

(I)   The highjacking or sabotage of any conveyance (including an aircraft, vessel, or vehicle).

(II)   The seizing or detaining, and threatening to kill, injure, or continue to detain, another individual in order to compel a third person (including a governmental organization) to do or abstain from doing any act as an explicit or implicit condition for the release of the individual seized or detained.

(III)   A violent attack upon an internationally protected person (as defined in 18 U.S.C. § 1116(b)(4)) or upon the liberty of such a person.

(IV)   An assassination.

(V)   The use of any

(a) biological agent, chemical agent, or nuclear weapon or device, or

(b) explosive, firearm, or other weapon or dangerous device (other than for mere personal monetary gain),

with intent to endanger, directly or indirectly, the safety of one or more individuals or to cause substantial damage to property.

(VI)   A threat, attempt, or conspiracy to do any of the foregoing.

22 U.S.C. § 2256f(d). [definition of terrorism for purposes of designations]

(2)   the term "terrorism" means premeditated, politically motivated violence perpetrated against noncombatant targets by subnational groups or clandestine agents.

B.   Criminal Statutes Referring to Terrorism

18 U.S.C. § 2331. Definitions

As used in this chapter [18 U.S.C. §§ 2331 et seq.]

(1)   the term "international terrorism" means activities that

(A) involve violent acts or acts dangerous to human life that are a violation of the criminal laws of the United States or of any State, or that would be a criminal violation if committed within the jurisdiction of the United States or of any State;

(B) appear to be intended

(i) to intimidate or coerce a civilian population;

(ii) to influence the policy of a government by intimidation or coercion; or

(iii) to affect the conduct of a government by mass destruction, assassination or kidnapping; and

(C) occur primarily outside the territorial jurisdiction of the United States, or transcend national boundaries in terms of the means by which they are accomplished, the persons they appear intended to intimidate or coerce, or the locale in which their perpetrators operate or seek asylum;

(2)   the term "national of the United States" has the meaning given such term in section 101(a)(22) of the Immigration and Nationality Act [8 U.S.C.S. § 1101(a)(22)];

(3)   the term "person" means any individual or entity capable of holding a legal or beneficial interest in property;

(4)   the term "act of war" means any act occurring in the course of

(A) declared war;

(B) armed conflict, whether or not war has been declared, between two or more nations; or

(C) armed conflict between military forces of any origin; and

(5)   the term "domestic terrorism" means activities that

(A) involve acts dangerous to human life that are a violation of the criminal laws of the United States or of any State;

(B) appear to be intended

(i) to intimidate or coerce a civilian population;

(ii) to influence the policy of a government by intimidation or coercion; or

(iii) to affect the conduct of a government by mass destruction, assassination, or kidnapping; and

(C) occur primarily within the territorial jurisdiction of the United States.

18 U.S.C. § 2332.   Criminal penalties

(a) *Homicide.* Whoever kills a national of the United States, while such national is outside the United States, shall,

    (1) if the killing is murder (as defined in section 1111(a)), be fined under this title, punished by death or imprisonment for any term of years or for life, or both;

    (2) if the killing is a voluntary manslaughter as defined in section 1112(a) of this title, be fined under this title or imprisoned not more than ten years, or both; and (3) if the killing is an involuntary manslaughter as defined in section 1112(a) of this title, be fined under this title or imprisoned not more than three years, or both.

(b) *Attempt or conspiracy with respect to homicide.* Whoever outside the United States attempts to kill, or engages in a conspiracy to kill, a national of the United States shall

    (1) in the case of an attempt to commit a killing that is a murder as defined in this chapter be fined under this title or imprisoned not more than 20 years, or both; and

    (2) in the case of a conspiracy by two or more persons to commit a killing that is a murder as defined in section 1111(a) of this title, if one or more of such persons do any overt act to effect the object of the conspiracy, be fined under this title or imprisoned for any term of years or for life, or both so fined and so imprisoned.

(c) *Other conduct.* Whoever outside the United States engages in physical violence

    (1) with intent to cause serious bodily injury to a national of the United States; or

    (2) with the result that serious bodily injury is caused to a national of the United States;

shall be fined under this title or imprisoned not more than ten years, or both.

(d) *Limitation on prosecution.* No prosecution for any offense described in this section shall be undertaken by the United States except on written certification of the Attorney General or the highest ranking subordinate of the Attorney General with responsibility for criminal prosecutions that, in the judgment of the certifying official, such offense was intended to coerce, intimidate, or retaliate against a government or a civilian population.

18 U.S.C. § 2332b.   Acts of terrorism transcending national boundaries

(a) Prohibited acts.

    (1) Offenses. Whoever, involving conduct transcending national boundaries and in a circumstance described in subsection (b)

(A)   kills, kidnaps, maims, commits an assault resulting in serious bodily injury, or assaults with a dangerous weapon any person within the United States; or

(B)   creates a substantial risk of serious bodily injury to any other person by destroying or damaging any structure, conveyance, or other real or personal property within the United States or by attempting or conspiring to destroy or damage any structure, conveyance, or other real or personal property within the United States;

in violation of the laws of any State, or the United States, shall be punished as prescribed in subsection (c).

(2) Treatment of threats, attempts and conspiracies. Whoever threatens to commit an offense under paragraph (1), or attempts or conspires to do so, shall be punished under subsection (c).

(b) Jurisdictional bases.

(1) Circumstances. The circumstances referred to in subsection (a) are

(A)   the mail or any facility of interstate or foreign commerce is used in furtherance of the offense;

(B)   the offense obstructs, delays, or affects interstate or foreign commerce, or would have so obstructed, delayed, or affected interstate or foreign commerce if the offense had been consummated;

(C)   the victim, or intended victim, is the United States Government, a member of the uniformed services, or any official, officer, employee, or agent of the legislative, executive, or judicial branches, or of any department or agency, of the United States;

(D)   the structure, conveyance, or other real or personal property is, in whole or in part, owned, possessed, or leased to the United States, or any department or agency of the United States;

(E)   the offense is committed in the territorial sea (including the airspace above and the seabed and subsoil below, and artificial islands and fixed structures erected thereon) of the United States; or

(F)   the offense is committed within the special maritime and territorial jurisdiction of the United States.

(2) Co-conspirators and accessories after the fact. Jurisdiction shall exist over all principals and co-conspirators of an offense under this section, and accessories after the fact to any offense under this section, if at least one of the circumstances described in subparagraphs (A) through (F) of paragraph (1) is applicable to at least one offender.

(c) Penalties.

(1) Penalties. Whoever violates this section shall be punished

(A) for a killing, or if death results to any person from any other conduct prohibited by this section, by death, or by imprisonment for any term of years or for life;

(B) for kidnapping, by imprisonment for any term of years or for life;

(C) for maiming, by imprisonment for not more than 35 years;

(D) for assault with a dangerous weapon or assault resulting in serious bodily injury, by imprisonment for not more than 30 years;

(E) for destroying or damaging any structure, conveyance, or other real or personal property, by imprisonment for not more than 25 years;

(F) for attempting or conspiring to commit an offense, for any term of years up to the maximum punishment that would have applied had the offense been completed; and

(G) for threatening to commit an offense under this section, by imprisonment for not more than 10 years.

(2) Consecutive sentence. Notwithstanding any other provision of law, the court shall not place on probation any person convicted of a violation of this section; nor shall the term of imprisonment imposed under this section run concurrently with any other term of imprisonment.

(d) Proof requirements. The following shall apply to prosecutions under this section:

(1) Knowledge. The prosecution is not required to prove knowledge by any defendant of a jurisdictional base alleged in the indictment.

(2) State law. In a prosecution under this section that is based upon the adoption of State law, only the elements of the offense under State law, and not any provisions pertaining to criminal procedure or evidence, are adopted.

(e) Extraterritorial jurisdiction. There is extraterritorial Federal jurisdiction

(1) over any offense under subsection (a), including any threat, attempt, or conspiracy to commit such offense; and

(2) over conduct which, under section 3, renders any person an accessory after the fact to an offense under subsection (a).

(f) Investigative authority. In addition to any other investigative authority with respect to violations of this title, the Attorney General shall have primary investigative responsibility for all Federal crimes of terrorism, and any violation of section 351(e), 844(e), 844(f)(1), 956(b), 1361, 1366(b), 1366(c), 1751(e), 2152, or 2156 of this title, and the Secretary of the Treasury shall assist the Attorney General at the request of the Attorney General. Nothing in this section shall be construed to interfere with the authority of the United States Secret Service under section 3056.

(g) Definitions. As used in this section

(1) the term "conduct transcending national boundaries" means conduct occurring outside of the United States in addition to the conduct occurring in the United States;

(2) the term "facility of interstate or foreign commerce" has the meaning given that term in section 1958(b)(2);

(3) the term "serious bodily injury" has the meaning given that term in section 1365(g)(3);

(4) the term "territorial sea of the United States" means all waters extending seaward to 12 nautical miles from the baselines of the United States, determined in accordance with international law; and

(5) the term "Federal crime of terrorism" means an offense that

(A) is calculated to influence or affect the conduct of government by intimidation or coercion, or to retaliate against government conduct; and

(B) is a violation of

(i) section 32 (relating to destruction of aircraft or aircraft facilities), 37 (relating to violence at international airports), 81 (relating to arson within special maritime and territorial jurisdiction), 175 or 175b (relating to biological weapons), 229 (relating to chemical weapons), subsection (a), (b), (c), or (d) of section 351 (relating to congressional, cabinet, and Supreme Court assassination and kidnaping), 831 (relating to nuclear materials), 842(m) or (n) (relating to plastic explosives), 844(f)(2) or (3) (relating to arson and bombing of Government property risking or causing death), 844(i) (relating to arson and bombing of property used in interstate commerce), 930(c) (relating to killing or attempted killing during an attack on a Federal facility with a dangerous weapon), 956(a)(1) (relating to conspiracy to murder, kidnap, or maim persons abroad), 1030(a)(1) (relating to protection of computers), 1030(a)(5)(A)(i) resulting in damage as defined in 1030(a)(5)(B)(ii) through (v) (relating to protection of computers), 1114 (relating to killing or attempted killing of officers and employees of the United States), 1116 (relating to murder or manslaughter of foreign officials, official guests, or internationally protected persons), 1203 (relating to hostage taking), 1362 (relating to destruction of communication lines, stations, or systems), 1363 (relating to injury to buildings or property within special maritime and territorial jurisdiction of the United

States), 1366(a) (relating to destruction of an energy facility), 1751(a), (b), (c), or (d) (relating to Presidential and Presidential staff assassination and kidnaping), 1992 (relating to wrecking trains), 1993 (relating to terrorist attacks and other acts of violence against mass transportation systems), 2155 (relating to destruction of national defense materials, premises, or utilities), 2280 (relating to violence against maritime navigation), 2281 (relating to violence against maritime fixed platforms), 2332 (relating to certain homicides and other violence against United States nationals occurring outside of the United States), 2332a (relating to use of weapons of mass destruction), 2332b (relating to acts of terrorism transcending national boundaries), 2332f (relating to bombing of public places and facilities), 2339 (relating to harboring terrorists), 2339A (relating to providing material support to terrorists), 2339B (relating to providing material support to terrorist organizations), 2339C (relating to financing of terrorism, or 2340A (relating to torture) of this title;

(ii)   section 236 (relating to sabotage of nuclear facilities or fuel) of the Atomic Energy Act of 1954 *(42 U.S.C. 2284);* or

(iii)   section 46502 (relating to aircraft piracy), the second sentence of section 46504 (relating to assault on a flight crew with a dangerous weapon), section 46505(b)(3) or (c) (relating to explosive or incendiary devices, or endangerment of human life by means of weapons, on aircraft), section 46506 if homicide or attempted homicide is involved (relating to application of certain criminal laws to acts on aircraft), or section 60123(b) (relating to destruction of interstate gas or hazardous liquid pipeline facility) of title 49.

18 U.S.C. § 2332f.   Bombings of places of public use, government facilities, public transportation systems and infrastructure facilities

(a) Offenses.

(1) In general. Whoever unlawfully delivers, places, discharges, or detonates an explosive or other lethal device in, into, or against a place of public use, a state or government facility, a public transportation system, or an infrastructure facility

(A)   with the intent to cause death or serious bodily injury, or

(B)   with the intent to cause extensive destruction of such a place, facility, or system, where such destruction results in or is likely to result in major economic loss,

shall be punished as prescribed in subsection (c).

(2) Attempts and conspiracies. Whoever attempts or conspires to commit an offense under paragraph (1) shall be punished as prescribed in subsection (c).

(b) Jurisdiction. There is jurisdiction over the offenses in subsection (a) if

    (1) the offense takes place in the United States and

        (A) the offense is committed against another state or a government facility of such state, including its embassy or other diplomatic or consular premises of that state;

        (B) the offense is committed in an attempt to compel another state or the United States to do or abstain from doing any act;

        (C) at the time the offense is committed, it is committed

            (i) on board a vessel flying the flag of another state;

            (ii) on board an aircraft which is registered under the laws of another state; or

            (iii) on board an aircraft which is operated by the government of another state;

        (D) a perpetrator is found outside the United States;

        (E) a perpetrator is a national of another state or a stateless person; or

        (F) a victim is a national of another state or a stateless person;

    (2) the offense takes place outside the United States and

        (A) a perpetrator is a national of the United States or is a stateless person whose habitual residence is in the United States;

        (B) a victim is a national of the United States;

        (C) a perpetrator is found in the United States;

        (D) the offense is committed in an attempt to compel the United States to do or abstain from doing any act;

        (E) the offense is committed against a state or government facility of the United States, including an embassy or other diplomatic or consular premises of the United States;

        (F) the offense is committed on board a vessel flying the flag of the United States or an aircraft which is registered under the laws of the United States at the time the offense is committed; or

        (G) the offense is committed on board an aircraft which is operated by the United States.

(c) Penalties. Whoever violates this section shall be punished as provided under section 2332a(a) of this title.

(d) Exemptions to jurisdiction. This section does not apply to

(1) the activities of armed forces during an armed conflict, as those terms are understood under the law of war, which are governed by that law,

(2) activities undertaken by military forces of a state in the exercise of their official duties; or

(3) offenses committed within the United States, where the alleged offender and the victims are United States citizens and the alleged offender is found in the United States, or where jurisdiction is predicated solely on the nationality of the victims or the alleged offender and the offense has no substantial effect on interstate or foreign commerce.

18 U.S.C. § 2339A.   Providing material support to terrorists

(a) Offense. Whoever, within the United States, provides material support or resources or conceals or disguises the nature, location, source, or ownership of material support or resources, knowing or intending that they are to be used in preparation for, or in carrying out, a violation of [specified federal crimes], or in preparation for, or in carrying out, the concealment or an escape from the commission of any such violation, shall be fined under this title, imprisoned not more than 10 years, or both.

(b) Definitions. As used in this section

(1) the term "material support or resources" means any property, tangible or intangible, or service, including currency or monetary instruments or financial securities, financial services, lodging, training, expert advice or assistance, safehouses, false documentation or identification, communications equipment, facilities, weapons, lethal substances, explosives, personnel (1 or more individuals who may be or include oneself), and transportation, except medicine or religious materials;

(2) the term "training" means instruction or teaching designed to impart a specific skill, as opposed to general knowledge; and

(3) the term "expert advice or assistance" means advice or assistance derived from scientific, technical or other specialized knowledge.

[Prior to Dec. 17, 2004, subsection (b) read: In this section, the term "material support or resources" means currency or other financial securities, financial services, lodging, training, safehouses, false documentation or identification, communications equipment, facilities, weapons, lethal substances, explosives, personnel, transportation, and other physical assets, except medicine or religious materials.]

18 U.S.C. § 2339B. Providing material support or resources to designated foreign terrorist organizations

(a) Prohibited Activities.

(1) Unlawful conduct. Whoever knowingly provides material support or resources to a foreign terrorist organization, or attempts or conspires to do so, shall be fined under this title or imprisoned not more than 10 years, or both. To violate this paragraph, a person must have knowledge that the organization is a designated terrorist organization (as defined in subsection (g)(6)), that the organization has engaged or engages in terrorist activity (as defined in 8 U.S.C. § 1182(a)(3)), or that the organization has engaged or engages in terrorism (as defined in 8 U.S.C. 2656f). [The last sentence was added by Pub. L. 108-458 Dec. 17, 2004]

(2) Financial institutions. Except as authorized by the Secretary, any financial institution that becomes aware that it has possession of, or control over, any funds in which a foreign terrorist organization, or its agent, has an interest, shall

(A) retain possession of, or maintain control over, such funds; and

(B) report to the Secretary the existence of such funds in accordance with regulations issued by the Secretary

(b) Civil Penalty. Any financial institution that knowingly fails to comply with subsection (a)(2) shall be subject to a civil penalty in an amount that is the greater of

(A) $50,000 per violation; or

(B) twice the amount of which the financial institution was required under subsection (a)(2) to retain possession or control.

(c) Injunction. Whenever it appears to the Secretary or the Attorney General that any person is engaged in, or is about to engage in, any act that constitutes, or would constitute, a violation of this section, the Attorney General may initiate civil action in a district court of the United States to enjoin such violation.

(d) Extraterritorial Jurisdiction.

(1) In general. There is jurisdiction over an offense under subsection (a) if

(A) an offender is a national of the United States or an alien lawfully admitted for permanent residence in the United States;

(B) an offender is a stateless person whose habitual residence is in the United States;

(C) after the conduct required for the offense occurs an offender is brought into or found in the United States, even if the conduct required for the offense occurs outside the United States;

(D)   the offense occurs in whole or in part within the United States;

(E)   the offense occurs in or affects interstate or foreign commerce; or

(F)   an offender aids or abets any person over whom jurisdiction exists under this paragraph in committing an offense under subsection (a) or conspires with any person over whom jurisdiction exists under this paragraph to commit an offense under subsection (a).

(2) Extraterritorial jurisdiction. There is extraterritorial Federal jurisdiction over an offense under this section.

(e) Investigations.

(1) In general. The Attorney General shall conduct any investigation of a possible violation of this section, or of any license, order, or regulation issued pursuant to this section.

(2) Coordination with the department of the treasury. The Attorney General shall work in coordination with the Secretary in investigations relating to

(A)   the compliance or noncompliance by a financial institution with the requirements of subsection (a)(2); and

(B)   civil penalty proceedings authorized under subsection (b).

(3) Referral. Any evidence of a criminal violation of this section arising in the course of an investigation by the Secretary or any other Federal agency shall be referred immediately to the Attorney General for further investigation. The Attorney General shall timely notify the Secretary of any action taken on referrals from the Secretary, and may refer investigations to the Secretary for remedial licensing or civil penalty action.

(f)   Classified Information in Civil Proceedings Brought by the United States.

(1) Discovery of classified information by defendants.

(A) Request by united states. -In any civil proceeding under this section, upon request made ex parte and in writing by the United States, a court, upon a sufficient showing, may authorize the United States to

(i)   redact specified items of classified information from documents to be introduced into evidence or made available to the defendant through discovery under the Federal Rules of Civil Procedure;

(ii)   substitute a summary of the information for such classified documents; or

(iii)   substitute a statement admitting relevant facts that the classified information would tend to prove.

[omitted details on introduction of redacted classified information and interlocutory appeals]

(g) Definitions. As used in this section

(4) the term "material support or resources" has the same meaning as in section 2339A;

(6) the term "terrorist organization" means an organization designated as a terrorist organization under [8 U.S.C. § 1189].

(h) Provision of Personnel. No person may be prosecuted under this section in connection with the term "personnel" unless that person has knowingly provided, attempted to provide, or conspired to provide a foreign terrorist organization with 1 or more individuals (who may be or include himself) to work under that terrorist organization's direction or control or to organize, manage, supervise, or otherwise direct the operation of that organization. Individuals who act entirely independently of the foreign terrorist organization to advance its goals or objectives shall not be considered to be working under the foreign terrorist organization's direction and control. [added by Pub. L. 108-458, Dec. 17, 2004]

(i) Rule of Construction. Nothing in this section shall be construed or applied so as to abridge the exercise of rights guaranteed under the First Amendment to the Constitution of the United States.

(j) Exception. No person may be prosecuted under this section in connection with the term "personnel", "training", or "expert advice or assistance" if the provision of that material support or resources to a foreign terrorist organization was approved by the Secretary of State with the concurrence of the Attorney General.

18 U.S.C. § 2339D.   Receiving military-type training from a foreign terrorist organization

[added by Pub. L. 108-458, Dec. 17, 2004]

(a) Offense. Whoever knowingly receives military-type training from or on behalf of any organization designated at the time of the training by the Secretary of State under section 219(a)(1) of the Immigration and Nationality Act as a foreign terrorist organization shall be fined under this title or imprisoned for ten years, or both. To violate this subsection, a person must have knowledge that the organization is a designated terrorist organization (as defined in subsection (c)(4)), that the organization has engaged or engages in terrorist activity (as defined in section 212 of the Immigration and Nationality Act), or that the organization has engaged or engages in terrorism (as defined in section 140(d)(2) of the Foreign Relations Authorization Act, Fiscal Years 1988 and 1989).

(b) Extraterritorial Jurisdiction. There is extraterritorial Federal jurisdiction over an offense under this section. There is jurisdiction over an offense under subsection (a) if

(1) an offender is a national of the United States (as defined in 101(a)(22) of the Immigration and Nationality Act) or an alien lawfully admitted for permanent residence in the United States (as defined in section 101(a)(20) of the Immigration and Nationality Act);

(2) an offender is a stateless person whose habitual residence is in the United States;

(3) after the conduct required for the offense occurs an offender is brought into or found in the United States, even if the conduct required for the offense occurs outside the United States;

(4) the offense occurs in whole or in part within the United States;

(5) the offense occurs in or affects interstate or foreign commerce; or

(6) an offender aids or abets any person over whom jurisdiction exists under this paragraph in committing an offense under subsection (a) or conspires with any person over whom jurisdiction exists under this paragraph to commit an offense under subsection (a).

(c) Definitions. As used in this section

(1) the term "military-type training" includes training in means or methods that can cause death or serious bodily injury, destroy or damage property, or disrupt services to critical infrastructure, or training on the use, storage, production, or assembly of any explosive, firearm or other weapon, including any weapon of mass destruction.

5. Statutes Providing for Civil Actions

18 U.S.C. § 2333. Civil remedies

(a) Action and jurisdiction. Any national of the United States injured in his or her person, property, or business by reason of an act of international terrorism, or his or her estate, survivors, or heirs, may sue therefor in any appropriate district court of the United States and shall recover threefold the damages he or she sustains and the cost of the suit, including attorney's fees.

(b) Estoppel under United States law. A final judgment or decree rendered in favor of the United States in any criminal proceeding under [designated statutes] shall estop the defendant from denying the essential allegations of the criminal offense in any subsequent civil proceeding under this section.

(c) Estoppel under foreign law. A final judgment or decree rendered in favor of any foreign state in any criminal proceeding shall, to the extent that such judgment or decree may be accorded full faith and credit under the law of the United States, estop the defendant from denying the essential allegations of the criminal offense in any subsequent civil proceeding under this section.

A. Alien Tort Act and Torture Victim Prevention Act

28 U.S.C. § 1350. Alien's action for tort

The district courts shall have original jurisdiction of any civil action by an alien for a tort only, committed in violation of the law of nations or a treaty of the United States.

[The Torture Prevention Act is not codified. It appears as a "Note" to § 1350.]

Note

Sec. 2. Establishment of civil action

(a) Liability. An individual who, under actual or apparent authority, or color of law, of any foreign nation

(1) subjects an individual to torture shall, in a civil action, be liable for damages to that individual; or

(2) subjects an individual to extrajudicial killing shall, in a civil action, be liable for damages to the individual's legal representative, or to any person who may be a claimant in an action for wrongful death.

Sec. 3. Definitions

(a) Extrajudicial killing. For the purposes of this Act, the term "extrajudicial killing" means a deliberated killing not authorized by a previous judgment pronounced by a regularly constituted court affording all the judicial guarantees which are recognized as indispensable by civilized peoples. Such term, however, does not include any such killing that, under international law, is lawfully carried out under the authority of a foreign nation.

(b) Torture. For the purposes of this Act

(1) the term "torture" means any act, directed against an individual in the offender's custody or physical control, by which severe pain or suffering (other than pain or suffering arising only from or inherent in, or incidental to, lawful sanctions), whether physical or mental, is intentionally inflicted on that individual for such purposes as obtaining from that individual or a third person information or a confession, punishing that individual for an act that individual or a third person has committed or is suspected of having committed, intimidating or coercing that individual or a third person, or for any reason based on discrimination of any kind; and

(2) mental pain or suffering refers to prolonged mental harm caused by or resulting from

(A) the intentional infliction or threatened infliction of severe physical pain or suffering;

(B) the administration or application, or threatened administration or application, of mind altering substances or other procedures calculated to disrupt profoundly the senses or the personality;

(C) the threat of imminent death; or

(D) the threat that another individual will imminently be subjected to death, severe physical pain or suffering, or the administration or application of mind altering substances or other procedures calculated to disrupt profoundly the senses or personality.

B.   Foreign Sovereign Immunities Act

28 U.S.C. § 1603.   Definitions

For purposes of this chapter

(a)   A "foreign state", except as used in section 1608 of this title, includes a political subdivision of a foreign state or an agency or instrumentality of a foreign state as defined in subsection (b).

(b)   An "agency or instrumentality of a foreign state" means any entity

(1) which is a separate legal person, corporate or otherwise, and

(2) which is an organ of a foreign state or political subdivision thereof, or a majority of whose shares or other ownership interest is owned by a foreign state or political subdivision thereof, and

(3) which is neither a citizen of a State of the United States . . . nor created under the laws of any third country.

(c)   The "United States" includes all territory and waters, continental or insular, subject to the jurisdiction of the United States.

(d)   A "commercial activity" means either a regular course of commercial conduct or a particular commercial transaction or act. The commercial character of an activity shall be determined by reference to the nature of the course of conduct or particular transaction or act, rather than by reference to its purpose.

(e)   A "commercial activity carried on in the United States by a foreign state" means commercial activity carried on by such state and having substantial contact with the United States.

28 U.S.C. § 1605.   General exceptions to the jurisdictional immunity of a foreign state

(a)   A foreign state shall not be immune from the jurisdiction of courts of the United States or of the States in any case

(1) in which the foreign state has waived its immunity either explicitly or by implication, notwithstanding any withdrawal of the waiver which the foreign state may purport to effect except in accordance with the terms of the waiver;

(2) in which the action is based upon a commercial activity carried on in the United States by the foreign state; or upon an act performed in the United States

in connection with a commercial activity of the foreign state elsewhere; or upon an act outside the territory of the United States in connection with a commercial activity of the foreign state elsewhere and that act causes a direct effect in the United States;

(3) in which rights in property taken in violation of international law are in issue and that property or any property exchanged for such property is present in the United States in connection with a commercial activity carried on in the United States by the foreign state; or that property or any property exchanged for such property is owned or operated by an agency or instrumentality of the foreign state and that agency or instrumentality is engaged in a commercial activity in the United States;

(4) in which rights in property in the United States acquired by succession or gift or rights in immovable property situated in the United States are in issue;

(5) not otherwise encompassed in paragraph (2) above, in which money damages are sought against a foreign state for personal injury or death, or damage to or loss of property, occurring in the United States and caused by the tortious act or omission of that foreign state or of any official or employee of that foreign state while acting within the scope of his office or employment; except this paragraph shall not apply to

(A) any claim based upon the exercise or performance or the failure to exercise or perform a discretionary function regardless of whether the discretion be abused, or

(B) any claim arising out of malicious prosecution, abuse of process, libel, slander, misrepresentation, deceit, or interference with contract rights;

(6) in which the action is brought, either to enforce an agreement made by the foreign state with or for the benefit of a private party to submit to arbitration all or any differences which have arisen or which may arise between the parties with respect to a defined legal relationship, or

(7) not otherwise covered by paragraph (2), in which money damages are sought against a foreign state for personal injury or death that was caused by an act of torture, extrajudicial killing, aircraft sabotage, hostage taking, or the provision of material support or resources (as defined in section 2339A of title 18) for such an act if such act or provision of material support is engaged in by an official, employee, or agent of such foreign state while acting within the scope of his or her office, employment, or agency, except that the court shall decline to hear a claim under this paragraph.

(A) if the foreign state was not designated as a state sponsor of terrorism . . . at the time the act occurred, unless later so designated as a result of such act or the act is related to Case Number 1:00CV03110(EGS) in the United States District Court for the District of Columbia; and

(B) even if the foreign state is or was so designated, if

(i)   the act occurred in the foreign state against which the claim has been brought and the claimant has not afforded the foreign state a reasonable opportunity to arbitrate the claim in accordance with accepted international rules of arbitration; or

(ii)   neither the claimant nor the victim was a national of the United States (as that term is defined in [8 U.S.C. § 1101(a)(22)]) when the act upon which the claim is based occurred.

(e)   For purposes of paragraph (7) of subsection (a)

(1) the terms "torture" and "extrajudicial killing" have the meaning given those terms in section 3 of the Torture Victim Protection Act of 1991 [28 U.S.C. § 1350 note];

(2) the term "hostage taking" has the meaning given that term in Article 1 of the International Convention Against the Taking of Hostages; and

(3) the term "aircraft sabotage" has the meaning given that term in Article 1 of the Convention for the Suppression of Unlawful Acts Against the Safety of Civil Aviation.

6.   Statutes Relating to Information and Investigations

18 U.S.C. § 793.   Gathering, transmitting, or losing defense information

(a)   Whoever, for the purpose of obtaining information respecting the national defense with intent or reason to believe that the information is to be used to the injury of the United States, or to the advantage of any foreign nation, goes upon, enters, flies over, or otherwise obtains information concerning any vessel, aircraft, . . . canal, railroad, . . . factory, mine, ... telephone, wireless, . . . building, office, . . . or other place connected with the national defense owned . . . or under the control of the United States, . . . or any prohibited place so designated by the President by proclamation in time of war or in case of national emergency; or

(b)   Whoever, for the purpose aforesaid, and with like intent or reason to believe, copies, takes, makes, or obtains, . . . any sketch, photograph, . . . plan, map, . . . writing, or note of anything connected with the national defense; or

(f)   Whoever, being entrusted with or having lawful possession or control of any document . . . or information, relating to the national defense, (1) through gross negligence permits the same to be removed from its proper place of custody or delivered to anyone in violation of his trust, or to be lost, stolen, abstracted, or destroyed, or (2) having knowledge that the same has been illegally removed from its proper place of custody or delivered to anyone in violation of his trust, or lost, or stolen, abstracted, or destroyed, and fails to make prompt report of such loss, theft, abstraction, or destruction to his superior officer

Shall be fined under this title or imprisoned not more than ten years, or both.

18 U.S.C. § 794. Gathering or delivering defense information to aid foreign government

(a)   Whoever, with intent or reason to believe that it is to be used to the injury of the United States or to the advantage of a foreign nation, communicates, delivers, or transmits, or attempts to communicate, deliver, or transmit, to any foreign government, or to any faction or party or military or naval force within a foreign country, whether recognized or unrecognized by the United States, or to any representative, officer, agent, employee, subject, or citizen thereof, either directly or indirectly, any document, writing, code book, signal book, sketch, photograph, photographic negative, blueprint, plan, map, model, note, instrument, appliance, or information relating to the national defense, shall be punished by death or by imprisonment for any term of years or for life, except that the sentence of death shall not be imposed unless the jury or, if there is no jury, the court, further finds that the offense resulted in the identification by a foreign power (as defined in section 101(a) of the Foreign Intelligence Surveillance Act of 1978) of an individual acting as an agent of the United States and consequently in the death of that individual, or directly concerned nuclear weaponry, military spacecraft or satellites, early warning systems, or other means of defense or retaliation against large-scale attack; war plans; communications intelligence or cryptographic information; or any other major weapons system or major element of defense strategy.

(b)   Whoever, in time of war, with intent that the same shall be communicated to the enemy, collects, records, publishes, or communicates, or attempts to elicit any information with respect to the movement, numbers, description, condition, or disposition of any of the Armed Forces, ships, aircraft, or war materials of the United States, or with respect to the plans or conduct, or supposed plans or conduct of any naval or military operations, or with respect to any works or measures undertaken for or connected with, or intended for the fortification or defense of any place, or any other information relating to the public defense, which might be useful to the enemy, shall be punished by death or by imprisonment for any term of years or for life.

18 U.S.C. § 798. Disclosure of classified information

(a)   Whoever knowingly and willfully communicates, furnishes, transmits, or otherwise makes available to an unauthorized person, or publishes, or uses in any manner prejudicial to the safety or interest of the United States or for the benefit of any foreign government to the detriment of the United States any classified information

(1) concerning the nature, preparation, or use of any code, cipher, or cryptographic system of the United States or any foreign government; or

(2) concerning the design, construction, use, maintenance, or repair of any device, apparatus, or appliance used or prepared or planned for use by the United States or any foreign government for cryptographic or communication intelligence purposes; or

(3) concerning the communication intelligence activities of the United States or any foreign government; or

(4) obtained by the processes of communication intelligence from the communications of any foreign government, knowing the same to have been obtained by such processes

Shall be fined under this title or imprisoned not more than ten years, or both.

(b)   As used in subsection (a) of this section

The term "classified information" means information which, at the time of a violation of this section, is, for reasons of national security, specifically designated by a United States Government Agency for limited or restricted dissemination or distribution;

The term "foreign government" includes in its meaning any person or persons acting or purporting to act for or on behalf of any faction, party, department, agency, bureau, or military force of or within a foreign country, . . . whether or not such government is recognized by the United States;

The term "communication intelligence" means all procedures and methods used in the interception of communications and the obtaining of information from such communications by other than the intended recipients;

The term "unauthorized person" means any person who, or agency which, is not authorized to receive information of the categories set forth in subsection (a) of this section, by the President, or by the head of a department or agency of the United States Government which is expressly designated by the President to engage in communication intelligence activities for the United States.

A.   Classified Information Procedures Act, 18 U.S.C. App

§ 1.   Definitions

(a)   "Classified information", as used in this Act, means any information or material that has been determined by the United States Government pursuant to an Executive order, statute, or regulation, to require protection against unauthorized disclosure for reasons of national security and any restricted data, as defined in paragraph r. of section 11 of the Atomic Energy Act of 1954.

(b)   "National security", as used in this Act, means the national defense and foreign relations of the United States.

§ 3.   Protective orders

Upon motion of the United States, the court shall issue an order to protect against the disclosure of any classified information disclosed by the United States to any defendant in any criminal case in a district court of the United States.

§ 4.   Discovery of classified information by defendant

The court, upon a sufficient showing, may authorize the United States to delete specified items of classified information from documents to be made available to the defendant through discovery under the Federal Rules of Criminal Procedure, to substitute a summary of the information for such classified documents, or to substitute a statement admitting relevant facts that the classified information would tend to prove. The court may permit the United States to make a request for such authorization in the form of a written statement to be inspected by the court alone. If the court enters an order granting relief following such an ex parte showing, the entire text of the statement of the United States shall be sealed and preserved in the records of the court to be made available to the appellate court in the event of an appeal.

§ 5.   Notice of defendant's intention to disclose classified information

(a) Notice by defendant. If a defendant reasonably expects to disclose or to cause the disclosure of classified information in any manner in connection with any trial or pretrial proceeding involving the criminal prosecution of such defendant, the defendant shall, within the time specified by the court or, where no time is specified, within thirty days prior to trial, notify the attorney for the United States and the court in writing. Such notice shall include a brief description of the classified information. Whenever a defendant learns of additional classified information he reasonably expects to disclose at any such proceeding, he shall notify the attorney for the United States and the court in writing as soon as possible thereafter and shall include a brief description of the classified information. No defendant shall disclose any information known or believed to be classified in connection with a trial or pretrial proceeding until notice has been given under this subsection and until the United States has been afforded a reasonable opportunity to seek a determination pursuant to the procedure set forth in section 6 of this Act, and until the time for the United States to appeal such determination under section 7 has expired or any appeal under section 7 by the United States is decided.

(b) Failure to comply. If the defendant fails to comply with the requirements of subsection (a) the court may preclude disclosure of any classified information not made the subject of notification and may prohibit the examination by the defendant of any witness with respect to any such information.

§ 6.   Procedure for cases involving classified information

(a) Motion for hearing. Within the time specified by the court for the filing of a motion under this section, the United States may request the court to conduct a hearing to make all determinations concerning the use, relevance, or admissibility of classified information that would otherwise be made during the trial or pretrial proceeding. Upon such a request, the court shall conduct such a hearing. Any hearing held pursuant to this subsection (or any portion of such hearing specified in the request of the Attorney General) shall be held in camera if the Attorney General certifies to the court in such petition that a public proceeding may result in the disclosure of classified information. As to each item of classified information, the court shall set forth in writing the basis for its determination. Where the United States' motion under this subsection is filed prior to the trial or pretrial proceeding, the court shall rule prior to the commencement of the relevant proceeding.

(b) Notice.

(1) Before any hearing is conducted pursuant to a request by the United States under subsection (a), the United States shall provide the defendant with notice of the classified information that is at issue. Such notice shall identify the specific classified information at issue whenever that information previously has been made available to the defendant by the United States. When the United States has not previously made the information available to the defendant in connection with the case, the information may be described by generic category, in such form as the court may approve, rather than by identification of the specific information of concern to the United States.

(2) Whenever the United States requests a hearing under subsection (a), the court, upon request of the defendant, may order the United States to provide the defendant, prior to trial, such details as to the portion of the indictment or information at issue in the hearing as are needed to give the defendant fair notice to prepare for the hearing.

(c)   Alternative procedure for disclosure of classified information.

(1) Upon any determination by the court authorizing the disclosure of specific classified information under the procedures established by this section, the United States may move that, in lieu of the disclosure of such specific classified information, the court order

(A) the substitution for such classified information of a statement admitting relevant facts that the specific classified information would tend to prove; or

(B) the substitution for such classified information of a summary of the specific classified information.

The court shall grant such a motion of the United States if it finds that the statement or summary will provide the defendant with substantially the same ability to make his defense as would disclosure of the specific classified information. The court shall hold a hearing on any motion under this section. Any such hearing shall be held in camera at the request of the Attorney General.

(2) The United States may, in connection with a motion under paragraph (1), submit to the court an affidavit of the Attorney General certifying that disclosure of classified information would cause identifiable damage to the national security of the United States and explaining the basis for the classification of such information. If so requested by the United States, the court shall examine such affidavit in camera and ex parte.

(d)   Sealing of records of in camera hearings. If at the close of an in camera hearing under this Act (or any portion of a hearing under this Act that is held in camera) the court determines that the classified information at issue may not be disclosed or elicited at the trial or pretrial proceeding, the record of such in camera hearing shall be sealed and preserved by the court for use in the event of an appeal. The defendant may seek reconsideration of the court's determination prior to or during trial.

(e)   Prohibition on disclosure of classified information by defendant, relief for defendant when United States opposes disclosure.

(1) Whenever the court denies a motion by the United States that it issue an order under subsection (c) and the United States files with the court an affidavit of the Attorney General objecting to disclosure of the classified information at issue, the court shall order that the defendant not disclose or cause the disclosure of such information.

(2) Whenever a defendant is prevented by an order under paragraph (1) from disclosing or causing the disclosure of classified information, the court shall dismiss the indictment or information; except that, when the court determines that the interests of justice would not be served by dismissal of the indictment or information, the court shall order such other action, in lieu of dismissing the indictment or information, as the court determines is appropriate. Such action may include, but need not be limited to

(A)   dismissing specified counts of the indictment or information;

(B)   finding against the United States on any issue as to which the excluded classified information relates; or

(C)   striking or precluding all or part of the testimony of a witness.

An order under this paragraph shall not take effect until the court has afforded the United States an opportunity to appeal such order under section 7, and thereafter to withdraw its objection to the disclosure of the classified information at issue.

(f) Reciprocity. Whenever the court determines pursuant to subsection (a) that classified information may be disclosed in connection with a trial or pretrial proceeding, the court shall, unless the interests of fairness do not so require, order the United States to provide the defendant with the information it expects to use to rebut the classified information. The court may place the United States under a continuing duty to disclose such rebuttal information. If the United States fails to comply with its obligation under this subsection, the court may exclude any evidence not made the subject of a required disclosure and may prohibit the examination by the United States of any witness with respect to such information.

§ 7. Interlocutory appeal

(a)   An interlocutory appeal by the United States taken before or after the defendant has been placed in jeopardy shall lie to a court of appeals from a decision or order of a district court in a criminal case authorizing the disclosure of classified information, imposing sanctions for nondisclosure of classified information, or refusing a protective order sought by the United States to prevent the disclosure of classified information.

(b)   An appeal taken pursuant to this section either before or during trial shall be expedited by the court of appeals. Prior to trial, an appeal shall be taken within ten days after the decision or order appealed from and the trial shall not commence until the appeal is resolved. If an appeal is taken during trial, the trial court shall adjourn the trial until the appeal is resolved and the court of appeals (1) shall hear argument on such appeal within four days of the adjournment of the trial, (2) may dispense with written briefs other than the supporting materials previously submitted to the trial court, (3) shall render its decision within four days of argument on appeal, and (4) may dispense with the issuance of a written opinion in rendering its decision. Such appeal and decision shall not affect the right of the defendant, in a subsequent appeal from a judgment of conviction, to claim as error reversal by the trial court on remand of a ruling appealed from during trial.

B.   Foreign Intelligence Surveillance Act

[50 U.S.C. §§ 1801-1862, as amended by USA PATRIOT Act]

50 U.S.C. § 1801.   Definitions

As used in this title:

(a)   "Foreign power" means

(1) a foreign government or any component thereof whether or not recognized by the United States;

(2) a faction of a foreign nation or nations, not substantially composed of United States persons;

(3) an entity that is openly acknowledged by a foreign government or governments to be directed and controlled by such foreign government or governments;

(4) a group engaged in international terrorism or activities in preparation therefor;

(5) a foreign-based political organization, not substantially composed of United States persons; or

(6) an entity that is directed and controlled by a foreign government or governments.

(b)   "Agent of a foreign power" means

(1) any person other than a United States person, who

(A)   acts in the United States as an officer or employee of a foreign power, or as a member of a foreign power as defined in subsection (a)(4);

(B)   acts for or on behalf of a foreign power which engages in clandestine intelligence activities in the United States contrary to the interests of the United States, when the circumstances of such person's presence in the United States indicate that such person may engage in such activities in the United States, or when such person knowingly aids or abets any person in the conduct of such activities or knowingly conspires with any person to engage in such activities; or

 (C) engages in international terrorism or activities in preparation therefor [paragraph (C) was added on Dec. 17, 2004 and is scheduled to "sunset" on Dec. 31, 2005]; or

 (2) any person who

 (A) knowingly engages in clandestine intelligence gathering activities for or on behalf of a foreign power, which activities involve or may involve a violation of the criminal statutes of the United States;

 (B) pursuant to the direction of an intelligence service or network of a foreign power, knowingly engages in any other clandestine intelligence activities for or on behalf of such foreign power, which activities involve or are about to involve a violation of the criminal statues of the United States;

 (C) knowingly engages in sabotage or international terrorism, or activities that are in preparation therefor, for or on behalf of a foreign power;

 (D) knowingly enters the United States under a false or fraudulent identity for or on behalf of a foreign power or, while in the United States, knowingly assumes a false or fraudulent identity for or on behalf of a foreign power; or

 (E) knowingly aids or abets any person in the conduct of activities described in subparagraph (A), (B), or (C) or knowingly conspires with any person to engage in activities described in subparagraph (A), (B), or (C).

(c) "International terrorism" means activities that

 (1) involve violent acts or acts dangerous to human life that are a violation of the criminal laws of the United States or of any State, or that would be a criminal violation if committed within the jurisdiction of the United States or any State;

 (2) appear to be intended

 (A) to intimidate or coerce a civilian population;

 (B) to influence the policy of a government by intimidation or coercion; or

 (C) to affect the conduct of a government by assassination or kidnapping; and

 (3) occur totally outside the United States or transcend national boundaries in terms of the means by which they are accomplished, the persons they appear intended to coerce or intimidate, or the locale in which their perpetrators operate or seek asylum.

(d)   "Sabotage" means activities that involve a violation of [18 U.S.C. §§ 2151 *et seq.*], or that would involve such a violation if committed against the United States.

(e)   "Foreign intelligence information" means

(1) information that relates to, and if concerning a United States person is necessary to, the ability of the United States to protect against—

(A)   actual or potential attack or other grave hostile acts of a foreign power or an agent of a foreign power;

(B)   sabotage or international terrorism by a foreign power or an agent of a foreign power; or

(C)   clandestine intelligence activities by an intelligence service or network of a foreign power or by an agent of a foreign power; or

(2) information with respect to a foreign power or foreign territory that relates to, and if concerning a United States person is necessary to

(A)   the national defense or the security of the United States; or

(B)   the conduct of the foreign affairs of the United States.

(i)   "United States person" means a citizen of the United States, an alien lawfully admitted for permanent residence, an unincorporated association a substantial number of members of which are citizens of the United States or aliens lawfully admitted for permanent residence, or a corporation which is incorporated in the United States, but does not include a corporation or an association which is a foreign power, as defined in subsection (a)(1), (2), or (3).

50 U.S.C. § 1804.   Applications for court orders [for electronic surveillance — essentially the same procedures apply to searches under § 1823 by substituting "premises" for "target"]

(a)   Submission by Federal officer; approval of Attorney General; contents. Each application for an order approving electronic surveillance under this title shall be made by a Federal officer in writing upon oath or affirmation to a judge having jurisdiction under section 1803. Each application shall require the approval of the Attorney General based upon his finding that it satisfies the criteria and requirements of such application as set forth in this title. It shall include

(1) the identity of the Federal officer making the application;

(2) the authority conferred on the Attorney General by the President of the United States and the approval of the Attorney General to make the application;

(3) the identity, if known, or a description of the target of the electronic surveillance;

(4) a statement of the facts and circumstances relied upon by the applicant to justify his belief that—

(A) the target of the electronic surveillance is a foreign power or an agent of a foreign power; and

(B) each of the facilities or places at which the electronic surveillance is directed is being used, or is about to be used, by a foreign power or an agent of a foreign power;

(5) a statement of the proposed minimization procedures;

(6) a detailed description of the nature of the information sought and the type of communications or activities to be subjected to the surveillance;

(7) a certification or certifications by the Assistant to the President for National Security Affairs or an executive branch official or officials designated by the President from among those executive officers employed in the area of national security or defense and appointed by the President with the advice and consent of the Senate—

(A) that the certifying official deems the information sought to be foreign intelligence information;

(B) that a significant purpose of the surveillance is to obtain foreign intelligence information;

(C) that such information cannot reasonably be obtained by normal investigative techniques;

(D) that designates the type of foreign intelligence information being sought according to the categories described in section 1801(e); and

(E) including a statement of the basis for the certification that

(i) the information sought is the type of foreign intelligence information designated; and

(ii) such information cannot reasonably be obtained by normal investigative techniques;

(8) a statement of the means by which the surveillance will be effected and a statement whether physical entry is required to effect the surveillance;

50 U.S.C. § 1805. Issuance of order

(a) Necessary findings. Upon an application made pursuant to section 1804, the judge shall enter an ex parte order as requested or as modified approving the electronic surveillance if he finds that—

(3) on the basis of the facts submitted by the applicant there is probable cause to believe that—

(A)   the target of the electronic surveillance is a foreign power or agent of a foreign power: Provided, That no United States person may be considered a foreign power or an agent of a foreign power solely upon the basis of activities protected by the first amendment to the Constitution of the United States; and

(B)   each of the facilities or places at which the electronic surveillance is directed is being used, or is about to be used, by a foreign power or an agent of a foreign power;

(4) the proposed minimization procedures meet the definition of minimization procedures under section 1804(h); and

(5) the application which has been filed contains all statements and certifications required by section 1804 and, if the target is a United States person, the certification or certifications are not clearly erroneous on the basis of the statement made under section 1804(a)(7)(E) and any other information furnished under section 1804(d).

50 U.S.C. § 1806.   Use of information

(a) *Compliance with minimization procedures; privileged communications; lawful purposes.* Information acquired from an electronic surveillance conducted pursuant to this title concerning any United States person may be used and disclosed by Federal officers and employees without the consent of the United States person only in accordance with the minimization procedures required by this title. No otherwise privileged communication obtained in accordance with, or in violation of, the provisions of this title shall lose its privileged character. No information acquired from an electronic surveillance pursuant to this title may be used or disclosed by Federal officers or employees except for lawful purposes.

(b) *Statement for disclosure.* No information acquired pursuant to this title shall be disclosed for law enforcement purposes unless such disclosure is accompanied by a statement that such information, or any information derived therefrom, may only be used in a criminal proceeding with the advance authorization of the Attorney General.

(c) *Notification by United States.* Whenever the Government intends to enter into evidence or otherwise use or disclose in any trial, hearing, or other proceeding in or before any court, department, officer, agency, regulatory body, or other authority of the United States, against an aggrieved person, any information obtained or derived from an electronic surveillance of that aggrieved person pursuant to the authority of this title, the Government shall, prior to the trial, hearing, or other proceeding or at a reasonable time prior to an effort to so disclose or so use that information or submit it in evidence, notify the aggrieved person and the court or other authority in which the information is to be disclosed or used that the Government intends to so disclose or so use such information.

(e) *Motion to suppress.* Any person against whom evidence obtained or derived from an electronic surveillance to which he is an aggrieved person is to be, or has been, introduced or otherwise used or disclosed in any trial, hearing, or other proceeding in or before any court, department, officer, agency, regulatory body, or other authority of the United States, a State, or a political subdivision thereof, may move to suppress the evidence obtained or derived from such electronic surveillance on the grounds that

(1) the information was unlawfully acquired; or

(2) the surveillance was not made in conformity with an order of authorization or approval.

Such a motion shall be made before the trial, hearing, or other proceeding unless there was no opportunity to make such a motion or the person was not aware of the grounds of the motion.

(f) *In camera and ex parte review by district court.* Whenever a court or other authority is notified pursuant to subsection (c) or (d), or whenever a motion is made pursuant to subsection (e), or whenever any motion or request is made by an aggrieved person pursuant to any other statute or rule of the United States of any State before any court or other authority of the United States or any state to discover or obtain applications or orders or other materials relating to electronic surveillance or to discover, obtain, or suppress evidence or information obtained or derived from electronic surveillance under this Act, the United States district court or, where the motion is made before another authority, the United States district court in the same district as the authority, shall, notwithstanding any other law, if the Attorney General files an affidavit under oath that disclosure or an adversary hearing would harm the national security of the United States, review in camera and ex parte the application, order, and such other materials relating to the surveillance as may be necessary to determine whether the surveillance of the aggrieved person was lawfully authorized and conducted. In making this determination, the court may disclose to the aggrieved person, under appropriate security procedures and protective orders, portions of the application, order, or other materials relating to the surveillance only where such disclosure is necessary to make an accurate determination of the legality of the surveillance.

(k) *Coordination with law enforcement.*

(1) Federal officers who conduct electronic surveillance to acquire foreign intelligence information under this title may consult with Federal law enforcement officers or law enforcement personnel of a State or political subdivision of a State (including the chief executive officer of that State or political subdivision who has the authority to appoint or direct the chief law enforcement officer of that State or political subdivision) to coordinate efforts to investigate or protect against

(A) actual or potential attack or other grave hostile acts of a foreign power or an agent of a foreign power;

(B)   sabotage or international terrorism by a foreign power or an agent of a foreign power; or

(C)   clandestine intelligence activities by an intelligence service or network of a foreign power or by an agent of a foreign power.

(2) Coordination authorized under paragraph (1) shall not preclude the certification required by section 1804(a)(7)(B) or the entry of an order under section 1805.

50 U.S.C. § 1861.   Access to certain business records for foreign intelligence and international terrorism investigations

(a) (1)   The Director of the Federal Bureau of Investigation or a designee of the Director (whose rank shall be no lower than Assistant Special Agent in Charge) may make an application for an order requiring the production of any tangible things (including books, records, papers, documents, and other items) for an investigation to obtain foreign intelligence information not concerning a United States person or to protect against international terrorism or clandestine intelligence activities, provided that such investigation of a United States person is not conducted solely upon the basis of activities protected by the first amendment to the Constitution.

(2) An investigation conducted under this section shall

(A)   be conducted under guidelines approved by the Attorney General under Executive Order 12333 [50 U.S.C. § 401 note] (or a successor order); and

(B)   not be conducted of a United States person solely upon the basis of activities protected by the first amendment to the Constitution of the United States.

(b)   Each application under this section

(1) shall be made to

(A)   a judge of the [FISA] court; or

(B)   a United States Magistrate Judge who is publicly designated by the Chief Justice of the United States to have the power to hear applications and grant orders for the production of tangible things under this section on behalf of a judge of that court; and

(2) shall specify that the records concerned are sought for an authorized investigation conducted in accordance with subsection (a)(2) to obtain foreign intelligence information not concerning a United States person or to protect against international terrorism or clandestine intelligence activities.

(c) (1)   Upon an application made pursuant to this section, the judge shall enter an ex parte order as requested, or as modified, approving the release of records if the judge finds that the application meets the requirements of this section.

(2) An order under this subsection shall not disclose that it is issued for purposes of an investigation described in subsection (a).

(d)   No person shall disclose to any other person (other than those persons necessary to produce the tangible things under this section) that the Federal Bureau of Investigation has sought or obtained tangible things under this section.

(e)   A person who, in good faith, produces tangible things under an order pursuant to this section shall not be liable to any other person for such production. Such production shall not be deemed to constitute a waiver of any privilege in any other proceeding or context.

7.   Military Provisions

A.   Uniform Code of Military Justice

10 U.S.C. § 821.   Jurisdiction of courts-martial not exclusive

The provisions of this chapter [10 U.S.C. §§ 801 *et seq.*] conferring jurisdiction upon courts-martial do not deprive military commissions, provost courts, or other military tribunals of concurrent jurisdiction with respect to offenders or offenses that by statute or by the law of war may be tried by military commissions, provost courts, or other military tribunals.

10 U.S.C. § 836.   President may prescribe rules

(a)   Pretrial, trial, and post-trial procedures, including modes of proof, for cases arising under this chapter [10 U.S.C. §§ 801 *et seq.*] triable in courts-martial, military commissions and other military tribunals, and procedures for courts of inquiry, may be prescribed by the President by regulations which shall, so far as he considers practicable, apply the principles of law and the rules of evidence generally recognized in the trial of criminal cases in the United States district courts, but which may not be contrary to or inconsistent with this chapter.

(b)   All rules and regulations made under this article shall be uniform insofar as practicable.

B.   Resolutions and Orders

MILITARY ORDER #1
PUBLIC PAPERS OF THE PRESIDENTS
(Vol 37 — Number 46, Nov. 19, 2001)
(Fed. Reg. Nov. 16, 2001)
November 13, 2001

By the authority vested in me as President and as Commander in Chief of the Armed Forces of the United States by the Constitution and the laws of the United States of America, including the Authorization for Use of Military Force Joint Resolution (Public Law 107-40, 115 Stat. 224) and sections 821 and 836 of title 10, United States Code, it is hereby ordered as follows:

Sec. 1.   Findings.

(a)   International terrorists, including members of al Qaida, have carried out attacks on United States diplomatic and military personnel and facilities abroad and on citizens and property within the United States on a scale that has created a state of armed conflict that requires the use of the United States Armed Forces.

(b)   In light of grave acts of terrorism and threats of terrorism, including the terrorist attacks on September 11, 2001, on the headquarters of the United States Department of Defense in the national capital region, on the World Trade Center in New York, and on civilian aircraft such as in Pennsylvania, I proclaimed a national emergency on September 14, 2001 (Proc. 7463, Declaration of National Emergency by Reason of Certain Terrorist Attacks).

(e)   To protect the United States and its citizens, and for the effective conduct of military operations and prevention of terrorist attacks, it is necessary for individuals subject to this order pursuant to section 2 hereof to be detained, and, when tried, to be tried for violations of the laws of war and other applicable laws by military tribunals.

(f)   Given the danger to the safety of the United States and the nature of international terrorism, and to the extent provided by and under this order, I find consistent with section 836 of title 10, United States Code, that it is not practicable to apply in military commissions under this order the principles of law and the rules of evidence generally recognized in the trial of criminal cases in the United States district courts.

Sec. 2.   Definition and Policy.

(a)   The term "individual subject to this order" shall mean any individual who is not a United States citizen with respect to whom I determine from time to time in writing that:

    (1) there is reason to believe that such individual, at the relevant times,

        (i)   is or was a member of the organization known as al Qaida;

        (ii)   has engaged in, aided or abetted, or conspired to commit, acts of international terrorism, or acts in preparation therefor, that have caused, threaten to cause, or have as their aim to cause, injury to or adverse effects on the United States, its citizens, national security, foreign policy, or economy; or

        (iii)   has knowingly harbored one or more individuals described in subparagraphs (i) or (ii) of subsection 2(a)(1) of this order; and

    (2) it is in the interest of the United States that such individual be subject to this order.

(b)   It is the policy of the United States that the Secretary of Defense shall take all necessary measures to ensure that any individual subject to this order is detained in accordance with section 3, and, if the individual is to be tried, that such individual is tried only in accordance with section 4.

(c)   It is further the policy of the United States that any individual subject to this order who is not already under the control of the Secretary of Defense but who is under the control of any other officer or agent of the United States or any State shall, upon delivery of a copy of such written determination to such officer or agent, forthwith be placed under the control of the Secretary of Defense.

Sec. 3. Detention Authority of the Secretary of Defense. Any individual subject to this order shall be

(a)   detained at an appropriate location designated by the Secretary of Defense outside or within the United States;

(b)   treated humanely, without any adverse distinction based on race, color, religion, gender, birth, wealth, or any similar criteria;

(c)   afforded adequate food, drinking water, shelter, clothing, and medical treatment;

(d)   allowed the free exercise of religion consistent with the requirements of such detention; and

(e)   detained in accordance with such other conditions as the Secretary of Defense may prescribe.

Sec. 4. Authority of the Secretary of Defense Regarding Trials of Individuals Subject to this Order.

(a)   Any individual subject to this order shall, when tried, be tried by military commission for any and all offenses triable by military commission that such individual is alleged to have committed, and may be punished in accordance with the penalties provided under applicable law, including life imprisonment or death.

(b)   As a military function and in light of the findings in section 1, including subsection (f) thereof, the Secretary of Defense shall issue such orders and regulations, including orders for the appointment of one or more military commissions, as may be necessary to carry out subsection (a) of this section.

(c)   Orders and regulations issued under subsection (b) of this section shall include, but not be limited to, rules for the conduct of the proceedings of military commissions, including pretrial, trial, and post-trial procedures, modes of proof, issuance of process, and qualifications of attorneys, which shall at a minimum provide for

(1) military commissions to sit at any time and any place, consistent with such guidance regarding time and place as the Secretary of Defense may provide;

(2) a full and fair trial, with the military commission sitting as the triers of both fact and law;

(3) admission of such evidence as would, in the opinion of the presiding officer of the military commission (or instead, if any other member of the commission so requests at the time the presiding officer renders that opinion, the opinion of the commission rendered at that time by a majority of the commission), have probative value to a reasonable person;

(4) in a manner consistent with the protection of information classified or classifiable under Executive Order 12958 of April 17, 1995, as amended, or any successor Executive Order, protected by statute or rule from unauthorized disclosure, or otherwise protected by law, (A) the handling of, admission into evidence of, and access to materials and information, and (B) the conduct, closure of, and access to proceedings;

(5) conduct of the prosecution by one or more attorneys designated by the Secretary of Defense and conduct of the defense by attorneys for the individual subject to this order;

(6) conviction only upon the concurrence of two-thirds of the members of the commission present at the time of the vote, a majority being present;

(7) sentencing only upon the concurrence of two-thirds of the members of the commission present at the time of the vote, a majority being present; and

(8) submission of the record of the trial, including any conviction or sentence, for review and final decision by me or by the Secretary of Defense if so designated by me for that purpose.

Joint Resolution to authorize the use of United States Armed Forces against those responsible for the recent attacks launched against the United States Pub. L. 107-40 [S.J. Res. 23] (Sept. 18, 2001)

Whereas, on September 11, 2001, acts of treacherous violence were committed against the United States and its citizens; and

Whereas, such acts render it both necessary and appropriate that the United States exercise its rights to self-defense and to protect United States citizens both at home and abroad; and

Whereas, in light of the threat to the national security and foreign policy of the United States posed by these grave acts of violence; and

Whereas, such acts continue to pose an unusual and extraordinary threat to the national security and foreign policy of the United States; and

Whereas, the President has authority under the Constitution to take action to deter and prevent acts of international terrorism against the United States: Now, therefore, be it

Resolved by the Senate and House of Representatives of the United States of America in Congress assembled,

Sec. 1. SHORT TITLE.

This joint resolution may be cited as the "Authorization for Use of Military Force."

Sec. 2. AUTHORIZATION FOR USE OF UNITED STATES ARMED FORCES.

(a) In General. That the President is authorized to use all necessary and appropriate force against those nations, organizations, or persons he determines planned, authorized, committed, or aided the terrorist attacks that occurred on September 11, 2001, or harbored such organizations or persons, in order to prevent any future acts of international terrorism against the United States by such nations, organizations or persons.

(b) War Powers Resolution Requirements

(1) Specific statutory authorization. Consistent with section 8(a)(1) of the War Powers Resolution, the Congress declares that this section is intended to constitute specific statutory authorization within the meaning of section 5(b) of the War Powers Resolution.

(2) Applicability of other requirements. Nothing in this resolution supercedes any requirement of the War Powers Resolution.

Joint Resolution to authorize the use of United States Armed Forces against Iraq
Pub. L. 107-243 [H.J. Res. 114] (Oct. 16, 2002).

Whereas in 1990 in response to Iraq's war of aggression against and illegal occupation of Kuwait, the United States forged a coalition of nations to liberate Kuwait and its people in order to defend the national security of the United States and enforce United Nations Security Council resolutions relating to Iraq;

Whereas after the liberation of Kuwait in 1991, Iraq entered into a United Nations sponsored cease-fire agreement pursuant to which Iraq unequivocally agreed, among other things, to eliminate its nuclear, biological, and chemical weapons programs and the means to deliver and develop them, and to end its support for international terrorism;

Whereas the efforts of international weapons inspectors, United States intelligence agencies, and Iraqi defectors led to the discovery that Iraq had large stockpiles of chemical weapons and a large scale biological weapons program, and that Iraq had an advanced nuclear weapons development program that was much closer to producing a nuclear weapon than intelligence reporting had previously indicated;

Whereas Iraq, in direct and flagrant violation of the cease-fire, attempted to thwart the efforts of weapons inspectors to identify and destroy Iraq's weapons of mass destruction stockpiles and development capabilities, which finally resulted in the withdrawal of inspectors from Iraq on October 31, 1998;

. . . .

Whereas United Nations Security Council Resolution 678 (1990) authorizes the use of all necessary means to enforce United Nations Security Council Resolution 660

(1990) and subsequent relevant resolutions and to compel Iraq to cease certain activities that threaten international peace and security, including the development of weapons of mass destruction and refusal or obstruction of United Nations weapons inspections in violation of United Nations Security Council Resolution 687 (1991), repression of its civilian population in violation of United Nations Security Council Resolution 688 (1991), and threatening its neighbors or United Nations operations in Iraq in violation of United Nations Security Council Resolution 949 (1994);

. . . .

Sec. 3. AUTHORIZATION FOR USE OF UNITED STATES ARMED FORCES.

(a) Authorization. The President is authorized to use the Armed Forces of the United States as he determines to be necessary and appropriate in order to

(1) defend the national security of the United States against the continuing threat posed by Iraq; and

(2) enforce all relevant United Nations Security Council resolutions regarding Iraq.

(b) Presidential Determination. In connection with the exercise of the authority granted in subsection (a) to use force the President shall, prior to such exercise or as soon thereafter as may be feasible, but no later than 48 hours after exercising such authority, make available to the Speaker of the House of Representatives and the President pro tempore of the Senate his determination that

(1) reliance by the United States on further diplomatic or other peaceful means alone either (A) will not adequately protect the national security of the United States against the continuing threat posed by Iraq or (B) is not likely to lead to enforcement of all relevant United Nations Security Council resolutions regarding Iraq; and

(2) acting pursuant to this joint resolution is consistent with the United States and other countries continuing to take the necessary actions against international terrorist and terrorist organizations, including those nations, organizations, or persons who planned, authorized, committed or aided the terrorist attacks that occurred on September 11, 2001.

(c) War Powers Resolution Requirements.

(1) Specific statutory authorization. Consistent with section 8(a)(1) of the War Powers Resolution, the Congress declares that this section is intended to constitute specific statutory authorization within the meaning of section 5(b) of the War Powers Resolution.

(2) Applicability of other requirements. Nothing in this joint resolution supersedes any requirement of the War Powers Resolution.

Sec. 4. REPORTS TO CONGRESS.

(a) Reports. The President shall, at least once every 60 days, submit to the Congress a report on matters relevant to this joint resolution, including actions taken pursuant to the exercise of authority granted in section 3 and the status of planning for efforts that are expected to be required after such actions are completed, including those actions described in section 7 of the Iraq Liberation Act of 1998 (Public Law 105-338).

(b) Single Consolidated Report. To the extent that the submission of any report described in subsection (a) coincides with the submission of any other report on matters relevant to this joint resolution otherwise required to be submitted to Congress pursuant to the reporting requirements of the War Powers Resolution (Public Law 93-148), all such reports may be submitted as a single consolidated report to the Congress.

(c) Rule of Construction. To the extent that the information required by section 3 of the Authorization for Use of Military Force Against Iraq Resolution (Public Law 102-1) is included in the report required by this section, such report shall be considered as meeting the requirements of section 3 of such resolution.

C.   Detention Statutes and Orders

Detainee Treatment Act of 2005

§ 1005(e).   Judicial Review of Detention of Enemy Combatants

(1) In general. 28 U.S.C. § 2241 is amended by adding at the end the following:

(e) Except as provided in section 1005 of the Detainee Treatment Act of 2005, no court, justice, or judge shall have jurisdiction to hear or consider

(1) an application for a writ of habeas corpus filed by or on behalf of an alien detained by the Department of Defense at Guantanamo Bay, Cuba; or

(2) any other action against the United States or its agents relating to any aspect of the detention by the Department of Defense of an alien at Guantanamo Bay, Cuba, who

(A) is currently in military custody; or

(B) has been determined by the United States Court of Appeals for the District of Columbia Circuit in accordance with the procedures set forth in section 1005(e) of the Detainee Treatment Act of 2005 to have been properly detained as an enemy combatant.

(2) Review of decisions of combatant status review tribunals of propriety of detention.

(A) In general. —Subject to subparagraphs (B), (C), and (D), the United States Court of Appeals for the District of Columbia Circuit shall have exclusive jurisdiction to determine the validity of any final decision of a Combatant Status Review Tribunal that an alien is properly detained as an enemy combatant.

(B) Limitation on claims. —The jurisdiction of the United States Court of Appeals for the District of Columbia Circuit under this paragraph shall be limited to claims brought by or on behalf of an alien—

(i) who is, at the time a request for review by such court is filed, detained by the Department of Defense at Guantanamo Bay, Cuba; and

(ii) for whom a Combatant Status Review Tribunal has been conducted, pursuant to applicable procedures specified by the Secretary of Defense.

(C) Scope of review. —The jurisdiction of the United States Court of Appeals for the District of Columbia Circuit on any claims with respect to an alien under this paragraph shall be limited to the consideration of

(i) whether the status determination of the Combatant Status Review Tribunal with regard to such alien was consistent with the standards and procedures specified by the Secretary of Defense for Combatant Status Review Tribunals (including the requirement that the conclusion of the Tribunal be supported by a preponderance of the evidence and allowing a rebuttable presumption in favor of the Government's evidence); and

(ii) to the extent the Constitution and laws of the United States are applicable, whether the use of such standards and procedures to make the determination is consistent with the Constitution and laws of the United States.

(3) Review of final decisions of military commissions.

(A) In general. —Subject to subparagraphs (B), (C), and (D), the United States Court of Appeals for the District of Columbia Circuit shall have exclusive jurisdiction to determine the validity of any final decision rendered pursuant to Military Commission Order No. 1, dated August 31, 2005 (or any successor military order).

(D) Scope of review. —The jurisdiction of the United States Court of Appeals for the District of Columbia Circuit on an appeal of a final decision with respect to an alien under this paragraph shall be limited to the consideration of

(i) whether the final decision was consistent with the standards and procedures specified in the military order referred to in subparagraph (A); and

(ii) to the extent the Constitution and laws of the United States are applicable, whether the use of such standards and procedures to reach the final decision is consistent with the Constitution and laws of the United States.

(h) Effective Date.

(1) In general. —This section shall take effect on the date of the enactment of this Act.

(2) Review of combatant status tribunal and military commission decisions. —Paragraphs (2) and (3) of subsection (e) shall apply with respect to any claim whose review is governed by one of such paragraphs and that is pending on or after the date of the enactment of this Act.

§ 1006. Training of Iraqi Forces Regarding Treatment of Detainees

(a) Required Policies.

(1) In general. —The Secretary of Defense shall ensure that policies are prescribed . . . to ensure that all personnel receive training regarding the international obligations and laws applicable to the humane detention of detainees, including protections afforded under the Geneva Conventions and the Convention Against Torture.

Military Commission Act of 2006

10 U.S.C. § 948a. Definitions

(1) Unlawful enemy combatant.

(A) The term "unlawful enemy combatant" means

(i) a person who has engaged in hostilities or who has purposefully and materially supported hostilities against the United States or its co-belligerents who is not a lawful enemy combatant (including a person who is part of the Taliban, al Qaeda, or associated forces); or

(ii) a person who . . . has been determined to be an unlawful enemy combatant by a Combatant Status Review Tribunal or another competent tribunal established under the authority of the President or the Secretary of Defense.

(2) Lawful enemy combatant. The term "lawful enemy combatant" means a person who is

(A) a member of the regular forces of a State party engaged in hostilities against the United States;

(B) a member of a militia, volunteer corps, or organized resistance movement belonging to a State party engaged in such hostilities, which are under responsible command, wear a fixed distinctive sign recognizable at a distance, carry their arms openly, and abide by the law of war; or

(C) a member of a regular armed force who professes allegiance to a government engaged in such hostilities, but not recognized by the United States.

10 U.S.C. § 948c.   Persons subject to military commissions

Any alien unlawful enemy combatant is subject to trial by military commission.

10 U.S.C. § 948d.   Jurisdiction of military commissions

(a) Jurisdiction. A military commission shall have jurisdiction to try any offense made punishable by this chapter or the law of war when committed by an alien unlawful enemy combatant before, on, or after September 11, 2001.

(b) Lawful enemy combatants. Military commissions under this chapter shall not have jurisdiction over lawful enemy combatants. Lawful enemy combatants who violate the law of war are subject to chapter 47 of this title [UCMJ, 10 U.S.C. §§ 801 et seq.]. Courts-martial established under that chapter shall have jurisdiction to try a lawful enemy combatant for any offense made punishable under this chapter.

(c) Determination of unlawful enemy combatant status dispositive. A finding, whether before, on, or after the date of the enactment of the Military Commissions Act of 2006 [enacted Oct. 17, 2006], by a Combatant Status Review Tribunal or another competent tribunal established under the authority of the President or the Secretary of Defense that a person is an unlawful enemy combatant is dispositive for purposes of jurisdiction for trial by military commission.

Executive Order: Interpretation of the Geneva Conventions Common Article 3 as Applied to a Program of Detention and Interrogation Operated by the Central Intelligence Agency
(July 20, 2007)

By the authority vested in me as President and Commander in Chief of the Armed Forces . . . it is hereby ordered as follows:

Sec. 1.   General Determinations.

(a)   The United States is engaged in an armed conflict with al Qaeda, the Taliban, and associated forces. These forces continue to fight the United States and its allies in Afghanistan, Iraq, and elsewhere, and they continue to plan additional acts of terror throughout the world. On February 7, 2002, I determined for the United States that members of al Qaeda, the Taliban, and associated forces are unlawful enemy combatants who are not entitled to the protections that the Third Geneva Convention provides to prisoners of war. I hereby reaffirm that determination.

(b)   The Military Commissions Act defines certain prohibitions of Common Article 3 for United States law, and it reaffirms and reinforces the authority of the President to interpret the meaning and application of the Geneva Conventions.

Sec. 2. Definitions. As used in this order:

(a)   "Common Article 3" means Article 3 of the Geneva Conventions.

(c)   "Cruel, inhuman, or degrading treatment or punishment" means the cruel, unusual, and inhumane treatment or punishment prohibited by the Fifth, Eighth, and Fourteenth Amendments to the Constitution of the United States.

Sec. 3. Compliance of a Central Intelligence Agency Detention and Interrogation Program with Common Article 3.

(a)   Pursuant to the authority of the President under the Constitution and the laws of the United States, including the Military Commissions Act of 2006, this order interprets the meaning and application of the text of Common Article 3 with respect to certain detentions and interrogations, and shall be treated as authoritative for all purposes as a matter of United States law, including satisfaction of the international obligations of the United States. I hereby determine that Common Article 3 shall apply to a program of detention and interrogation operated by the Central Intelligence Agency as set forth in this section. The requirements set forth in this section shall be applied with respect to detainees in such program without adverse distinction as to their race, color, religion or faith, sex, birth, or wealth.

(b)   I hereby determine that a program of detention and interrogation approved by the Director of the Central Intelligence Agency fully complies with the obligations of the United States under Common Article 3, provided that:

(i) the conditions of confinement and interrogation practices of the program do not include:

(A)   torture, as defined in section 2340 of title 18, United States Code;

(B)   any of the acts prohibited by section 2441(d) of title 18, United States Code, including murder, torture, cruel or inhuman treatment, mutilation or maiming, intentionally causing serious bodily injury, rape, sexual assault or abuse, taking of hostages, or performing of biological experiments;

(C)   other acts of violence serious enough to be considered comparable to murder, torture, mutilation, and cruel or inhuman treatment, as defined in section 2441(d) of title 18, United States Code;

(D)   any other acts of cruel, inhuman, or degrading treatment or punishment [as defined by the DTA or MCA];

(E)   willful and outrageous acts of personal abuse done for the purpose of humiliating or degrading the individual in a manner so serious that any reasonable person, considering the circumstances, would deem the acts to be beyond the bounds of human decency, such as sexual or sexually indecent acts undertaken for the purpose of humiliation, forcing the individual to perform sexual acts or to pose sexually, threatening the individual with sexual mutilation, or using the individual as a human shield; or

(F)   acts intended to denigrate the religion, religious practices, or religious objects of the individual;

(ii) the conditions of confinement and interrogation practices are to be used with an alien detainee who is determined by the Director of the Central Intelligence Agency:

(A)   to be a member or part of or supporting al Qaeda, the Taliban, or associated organizations; and

(B)   likely to be in possession of information that:

(1)   could assist in detecting, mitigating, or preventing terrorist attacks, such as attacks within the United States or against its Armed Forces or other personnel, citizens, or facilities, or against allies or other countries cooperating in the war on terror with the United States, or their armed forces or other personnel, citizens, or facilities; or

(2)   could assist in locating the senior leadership of al Qaeda, the Taliban, or associated forces;

(iii) the interrogation practices are determined by the Director of the Central Intelligence Agency, based upon professional advice, to be safe for use with each detainee with whom they are used; and

(iv) detainees in the program receive the basic necessities of life, including adequate food and water, shelter from the elements, necessary clothing, protection from extremes of heat and cold, and essential medical care.

II. INTERNATIONAL CONVENTIONS

1. Geneva Conventions (1949)

[Note: There are four 1949 Geneva Conventions. Convention I deals with "Wounded and Sick Members of Armed Forces in the Field," II with "Wounded, Sick and Shipwrecked Members of Armed Forces at Sea," and IV with "Protection of Civilian Persons in Time of War." Convention IV is "Relative to the Treatment of Prisoners of War." Article 3 is identical in all four conventions and is known as "Common Article 3."]

III. Convention Relative to the Treatment of Prisoners of War

Article 2

In addition to the provisions which shall be implemented in peace time, the present Convention shall apply to all cases of declared war or of any other armed conflict which may arise between two or more of the High Contracting Parties, even if the state of war is not recognized by one of them.

The Convention shall also apply to all cases of partial or total occupation of the territory of a High Contracting Party, even if the said occupation meets with no armed resistance.

Although one of the Powers in conflict may not be a party to the present Convention, the Powers who are parties thereto shall remain bound by it in their mutual relations. They shall furthermore be bound by the Convention in relation to the said Power, if the latter accepts and applies the provisions thereof.

Article 3

In the case of armed conflict not of an international character occurring in the territory of one of the High Contracting Parties, each party to the conflict shall be bound to apply, as a minimum, the following provisions:

1.   Persons taking no active part in the hostilities, including members of armed forces who have laid down their arms and those placed hors de combat by sickness, wounds, detention, or any other cause, shall in all circumstances be treated humanely, without any adverse distinction founded on race, colour, religion or faith, sex, birth or wealth, or any other similar criteria.

To this end the following acts are and shall remain prohibited at any time and in any place whatsoever with respect to the above-mentioned persons:

(a) Violence to life and person, in particular murder of all kinds, mutilation, cruel treatment and torture;

(b) Taking of hostages;

(c) Outrages upon personal dignity, in particular, humiliating and degrading treatment;

(d) The passing of sentences and the carrying out of executions without previous judgment pronounced by a regularly constituted court affording all the judicial guarantees which are recognized as indispensable by civilized peoples.

2.   The wounded and sick shall be collected and cared for.

An impartial humanitarian body, such as the International Committee of the Red Cross, may offer its services to the Parties to the conflict.

The Parties to the conflict should further endeavour to bring into force, by means of special agreements, all or part of the other provisions of the present Convention.

The application of the preceding provisions shall not affect the legal status of the Parties to the conflict.

Article 4

A.   Prisoners of war, in the sense of the present Convention, are persons belonging to one of the following categories, who have fallen into the power of the enemy:

1. Members of the armed forces of a Party to the conflict as well as members of militias or volunteer corps forming part of such armed forces.

2. Members of other militias and members of other volunteer corps, including those of organized resistance movements, belonging to a Party to the conflict and operating in or outside their own territory, even if this territory is occupied, provided that such militias or volunteer corps, including such organized resistance movements, fulfil the following conditions:

(a)   That of being commanded by a person responsible for his subordinates;

(b)   That of having a fixed distinctive sign recognizable at a distance;

(c)   That of carrying arms openly;

(d)   That of conducting their operations in accordance with the laws and customs of war.

3. Members of regular armed forces who profess allegiance to a government or an authority not recognized by the Detaining Power.

4. Persons who accompany the armed forces without actually being members thereof, such as civilian members of military aircraft crews, war correspondents, supply contractors, members of labour units or of services responsible for the welfare of the armed forces, provided that they have received authorization from

the armed forces which they accompany, who shall provide them for that purpose with an identity card similar to the annexed model.

5. Members of crews, including masters, pilots and apprentices, of the merchant marine and the crews of civil aircraft of the Parties to the conflict, who do not benefit by more favourable treatment under any other provisions of international law.

6. Inhabitants of a non-occupied territory, who on the approach of the enemy spontaneously take up arms to resist the invading forces, without having had time to form themselves into regular armed units, provided they carry arms openly and respect the laws and customs of war.

B.   The following shall likewise be treated as prisoners of war under the present Convention:

1. Persons belonging, or having belonged, to the armed forces of the occupied country, if the occupying Power considers it necessary by reason of such allegiance to intern them, even though it has originally liberated them while hostilities were going on outside the territory it occupies, in particular where such persons have made an unsuccessful attempt to rejoin the armed forces to which they belong and which are engaged in combat, or where they fail to comply with a summons made to them with a view to internment.

2. The persons belonging to one of the categories enumerated in the present Article, who have been received by neutral or non-belligerent Powers on their territory and whom these Powers are required to intern under international law, without prejudice to any more favourable treatment which these Powers may choose to give and with the exception of Articles 8, 10, 15, 30, fifth paragraph, 58-67, 92, 126 and, where diplomatic relations exist between the Parties to the conflict and the neutral or non-belligerent Power concerned, those Articles concerning the Protecting Power. Where such diplomatic relations exist, the Parties to a conflict on whom these persons depend shall be allowed to perform towards them the functions of a Protecting Power as provided in the present Convention, without prejudice to the functions which these Parties normally exercise in conformity with diplomatic and consular usage and treaties.

C.   This Article shall in no way affect the status of medical personnel and chaplains as provided for in Article 33 of the present Convention.

Article 5

The present Convention shall apply to the persons referred to in Article 4 from the time they fall into the power of the enemy and until their final release and repatriation.

Should any doubt arise as to whether persons, having committed a belligerent act and having fallen into the hands of the enemy, belong to any of the categories enumerated in Article 4, such persons shall enjoy the protection of the present Convention until such time as their status has been determined by a competent tribunal.

Article 99

No prisoner of war may be tried or sentenced for an act which is not forbidden by the law of the Detaining Power or by international law, in force at the time the said act was committed.

No moral or physical coercion may be exerted on a prisoner of war in order to induce him to admit himself guilty of the act of which he is accused.

No prisoner of war may be convicted without having had an opportunity to present his defence and the assistance of a qualified advocate or counsel.

Article 100

Prisoners of war and the Protecting Powers shall be informed as soon as possible of the offences which are punishable by the death sentence under the laws of the Detaining Power.

Other offences shall not thereafter be made punishable by the death penalty without the concurrence of the Power upon which the prisoners of war depend.

The death sentence cannot be pronounced on a prisoner of war unless the attention of the court has, in accordance with Article 87, second paragraph, been particularly called to the fact that since the accused is not a national of the Detaining Power, he is not bound to it by any duty of allegiance, and that he is in its power as the result of circumstances independent of his own will.

Article 102

A prisoner of war can be validly sentenced only if the sentence has been pronounced by the same courts according to the same procedure as in the case of members of the armed forces of the Detaining Power, and if, furthermore, the provisions of the present Chapter have been observed.

Article 105

The prisoner of war shall be entitled to assistance by one of his prisoner comrades, to defence by a qualified advocate or counsel of his own choice, to the calling of witnesses and, if he deems necessary, to the services of a competent interpreter. He shall be advised of these rights by the Detaining Power in due time before the trial.

Failing a choice by the prisoner of war, the Protecting Power shall find him an advocate or counsel, and shall have at least one week at its disposal for the purpose. The Detaining Power shall deliver to the said Power, on request, a list of persons qualified to present the defence. Failing a choice of an advocate or counsel by the prisoner of war or the Protecting Power, the Detaining Power shall appoint a competent advocate or counsel to conduct the defence.

Article 118

Prisoners of war shall be released and repatriated without delay after the cessation of active hostilities.

IV. Convention Relative to the Protection of Civilian Persons in Time of War

Article 2

In addition to the provisions which shall be implemented in peace-time, the present Convention shall apply to all cases of declared war or of any other armed conflict which may arise between two or more of the High Contracting Parties, even if the state of war is not recognized by one of them.

The Convention shall also apply to all cases of partial or total occupation of the territory of a High Contracting Party, even if the said occupation meets with no armed resistance.

Article 3

In the case of armed conflict not of an international character occurring in the territory of one of the High Contracting Parties, each Party to the conflict shall be bound to apply, as a minimum, the following provisions:

(1)   Persons taking no active part in the hostilities, including members of armed forces who have laid down their arms and those placed hors de combat by sickness, wounds, detention, or any other cause, shall in all circumstances be treated humanely, without any adverse distinction founded on race, colour, religion or faith, sex, birth or wealth, or any other similar criteria.

To this end the following acts are and shall remain prohibited at any time and in any place whatsoever with respect to the above-mentioned persons:

(a) violence to life and person, in particular murder of all kinds, mutilation, cruel treatment and torture;

(b) taking of hostages;

(c) outrages upon personal dignity, in particular humiliating and degrading treatment;

(d) the passing of sentences and the carrying out of executions without previous judgment pronounced by a regularly constituted court, affording all the judicial guarantees which are recognized as indispensable by civilized peoples.

Article 4

Persons protected by the Convention are those who, at a given moment and in any manner whatsoever, find themselves, in case of a conflict or occupation, in the hands of a Party to the conflict or Occupying Power of which they are not nationals.

Nationals of a State which is not bound by the Convention are not protected by it. Nationals of a neutral State who find themselves in the territory of a belligerent State, and nationals of a co-belligerent State, shall not be regarded as protected persons while the State of which they are nationals has normal diplomatic representation in the State in whose hands they are.

Article 5

Where in the territory of a Party to the conflict, the latter is satisfied that an individual protected person is definitely suspected of or engaged in activities hostile to the security of the State, such individual person shall not be entitled to claim such rights and privileges under the present Convention as would, if exercised in the favour of such individual person, be prejudicial to the security of such State.

Where in occupied territory an individual protected person is detained as a spy or saboteur, or as a person under definite suspicion of activity hostile to the security of the Occupying Power, such person shall, in those cases where absolute military security so requires, be regarded as having forfeited rights of communication under the present Convention.

In each case, such persons shall nevertheless be treated with humanity and, in case of trial, shall not be deprived of the rights of fair and regular trial prescribed by the present Convention. They shall also be granted the full rights and privileges of a protected person under the present Convention at the earliest date consistent with the security of the State or Occupying Power, as the case may be.

Section III. Occupied territories

Article 64

The penal laws of the occupied territory shall remain in force, with the exception that they may be repealed or suspended by the Occupying Power in cases where they constitute a threat to its security or an obstacle to the application of the present Convention.

Subject to the latter consideration and to the necessity for ensuring the effective administration of justice, the tribunals of the occupied territory shall continue to function in respect of all offences covered by the said laws.

The Occupying Power may, however, subject the population of the occupied territory to provisions which are essential to enable the Occupying Power to fulfil its obligations under the present Convention, to maintain the orderly government of the territory, and to ensure the security of the Occupying Power, of the members and property of the occupying forces or administration, and likewise of the establishments and lines of communication used by them.

Article 72

Accused persons shall have the right to present evidence necessary to their defence and may, in particular, call witnesses. They shall have the right to be assisted by a qualified advocate or counsel of their own choice, who shall be able to visit them freely and shall enjoy the necessary facilities for preparing the defence.

Failing a choice by the accused, the Protecting Power may provide him with an advocate or counsel. When an accused person has to meet a serious charge and the Protecting Power is not functioning, the Occupying Power, subject to the consent of the accused, shall provide an advocate or counsel.

2. Statutes of the International Criminal Tribunals

[Note: The two ICT's were established for slightly different circumstances. The assumption at the time seems to have been that Yugoslavia presented an "international armed conflict" while Rwanda was an "armed conflict not of an international character," thus producing slightly different statements of substantive law to be applied with respect to the Geneva Conventions. The substantive law portions of the two statutes are rearranged for ease of comparison.]

STATUTE OF THE INTERNATIONAL CRIMINAL TRIBUNAL FOR YUGOSLAVIA

Article 1   Competence of the International Tribunal

The International Tribunal shall have the power to prosecute persons responsible for serious violations of international humanitarian law committed in the territory of the former Yugoslavia since 1991 in accordance with the provisions of the present Statute.

Article 2   Grave breaches of the Geneva Conventions of 1949

The International Tribunal shall have the power to prosecute persons committing or ordering to be committed grave breaches of the Geneva Conventions of 12 August 1949, namely the following acts against persons or property protected under the provisions of the relevant Geneva Convention:

    (a)   wilful killing;

    (b)   torture or inhuman treatment, including biological experiments;

    (c)   wilfully causing great suffering or serious injury to body or health;

    (d)   extensive destruction and

appropriation of property, not justified by military necessity and carried out unlawfully and wantonly;

    (e)   compelling a prisoner of war or a civilian to serve in the forces of a hostile power;

    (f)   wilfully depriving a prisoner of war or a civilian of the rights of fair and regular trial;

    (g)   unlawful deportation or transfer or unlawful confinement of a civilian;

    (h)   taking civilians as hostages.

Article 4   Genocide

    1.   The International Tribunal shall have the power to prosecute persons committing genocide as defined in paragraph 2 of this article or of committing any of the other acts enumerated in paragraph 3 of this article.

    2.   Genocide means any of the following acts committed with intent to destroy, in whole or in part, a national, ethnical, racial or religious group, as such:

(a) killing members of the group;

(b) causing serious bodily or mental harm to members of the group;

(c) deliberately inflicting on the group conditions of life calculated to bring about its physical destruction in whole or in part;

(d) imposing measures intended to prevent births within the group;

(e) forcibly transferring children of the group to another group.

3. The following acts shall be punishable:

(a) genocide;

(b) conspiracy to commit genocide;

(c) direct and public incitement to commit genocide;

(d) attempt to commit genocide;

(e) complicity in genocide.

Article 5 Crimes against humanity

The International Tribunal shall have the power to prosecute persons responsible for the following crimes when committed in armed conflict, whether international or internal in character, and directed against any civilian population:

(a) murder;

(b) extermination;

(c) enslavement;

(d) deportation;

(e) imprisonment;

(f) torture;

(g) rape;

(h) persecutions on political, racial and religious grounds;

(i) other inhumane acts.

Article 3 Violations of the laws or customs of war

The International Tribunal shall have the power to prosecute persons violating the laws or customs of war. Such violations shall include, but not be limited to:

(a) employment of poisonous weapons or other weapons calculated to cause unnecessary suffering;

(b)   wanton destruction of cities, towns or villages, or devastation not justified by military necessity;

(c)   attack, or bombardment, by whatever means, of undefended towns, villages, dwellings, or buildings;

(d)   seizure of, destruction or wilful damage done to institutions dedicated to religion, charity and education, the arts and sciences, historic monuments and works of art and science;

(e)   plunder of public or private property.

STATUTE OF THE INTERNATIONAL CRIMINAL TRIBUNAL FOR RWANDA

Article 1:   Competence of the International Tribunal for Rwanda

The International Tribunal for Rwanda shall have the power to prosecute persons responsible for serious violations of international humanitarian law committed in the territory of Rwanda and Rwandan citizens responsible for such violations committed in the territory of neighbouring States between 1 January 1994 and 31 December 1994, in accordance with the provisions of the present Statute.

Article 4:   Violations of Article 3 Common to the Geneva Conventions and of Additional Protocol II

The International Tribunal for Rwanda shall have the power to prosecute persons committing or ordering to be committed serious violations of Article 3 common to the Geneva Conventions of 12 August 1949 for the Protection of War Victims, and of Additional Protocol II thereto of 8 June 1977. These violations shall include, but shall not be limited to:

(a)   Violence to life, health and physical or mental well-being of persons, in particular murder as well as cruel treatment such as torture, mutilation or any form of corporal punishment;

(b)   Collective punishments;

(c)   Taking of hostages;

(d)   Acts of terrorism;

(e)   Outrages upon personal dignity, in particular humiliating and degrading treatment, rape, enforced prostitution and any form of indecent assault;

(f)   Pillage;

(g)   The passing of sentences and the carrying out of executions without previous judgement pronounced by a regularly constituted court, affording all the judicial guarantees which are recognized as indispensable by civilised peoples;

(h)   Threats to commit any of the foregoing acts.

Article 2   Genocide

1.   The International Tribunal for Rwanda shall have the power to prosecute persons committing genocide as defined in paragraph 2 of this Article or of committing any of the other acts enumerated in paragraph 3 of this Article.

2.   Genocide means any of the following acts committed with intent to destroy, in whole or in part, a national, ethnical, racial or religious group, such as:

(a) Killing members of the group;

(b) Causing serious bodily or mental harm to members of the group;

(c) Deliberately inflicting on the group conditions of life calculated to bring about its physical destruction in whole or in part;

(d) Imposing measures intended to prevent births within the group;

(e) Forcibly transferring children of the group to another group.

3.   The following acts shall be punishable:

(a) Genocide;

(b) Conspiracy to commit genocide;

(c) Direct and public incitement to commit genocide;

(d) Attempt to commit genocide;

(e) Complicity in genocide.

Article 3   Crimes against Humanity

The International Tribunal for Rwanda shall have the power to prosecute persons responsible for the following crimes when committed as part of a widespread or systematic attack against any civilian population on national, political, ethnic, racial or religious grounds:

(a)   Murder;

(b)   Extermination;

(c)   Enslavement;

(d)   Deportation;

(e)   Imprisonment;

(f)   Torture;

(g)   Rape;

(h)   Persecutions on political, racial and religious grounds;

(i)   Other inhumane acts.

3. Convention Against Torture and Other Cruel, Inhuman or Degrading Treatment or Punishment

Article 1

1.   For the purposes of this Convention, torture means any act by which severe pain or suffering, whether physical or mental, is intentionally inflicted on a person for such purposes as obtaining from him or a third person information or a confession, punishing him for an act he or a third person has committed or is suspected of having committed, or intimidating or coercing him or a third person, or for any reason based on discrimination of any kind, when such pain or suffering is inflicted by or at the instigation of or with the consent or acquiescence of a public official or other person acting in an official capacity. It does not include pain or suffering arising only from, inherent in or incidental to lawful sanctions.

2.   This article is without prejudice to any international instrument or national legislation which does or may contain provisions of wider application.

Article 2

1.   Each State Party shall take effective legislative, administrative, judicial or other measures to prevent acts of torture in any territory under its jurisdiction.

2.   No exceptional circumstances whatsoever, whether a state of war or a threat or war, internal political instability or any other public emergency, may be invoked as a justification of torture.

3.   An order from a superior officer or a public authority may not be invoked as a justification of torture.

Article 3

1.   No State Party shall expel, return ("refouler") or extradite a person to another State where there are substantial grounds for believing that he would be in danger of being subjected to torture.

2.   For the purpose of determining whether there are such grounds, the competent authorities shall take into account all relevant considerations including, where applicable, the existence in the State concerned of a consistent pattern of gross, flagrant or mass violations of human rights.

Article 4

1.   Each State Party shall ensure that all acts of torture are offences under its criminal law. The same shall apply to an attempt to commit torture and to an act by any person which constitutes complicity or participation in torture.

2.   Each State Party shall make these offences punishable by appropriate penalties which take into account their grave nature.

Article 5

1.   Each State Party shall take such measures as may be necessary to establish its jurisdiction over the offences referred to in article 4 in the following cases:

When the offences are committed in any territory under its jurisdiction or on board a ship or aircraft registered in that State;

When the alleged offender is a national of that State;

When the victim was a national of that State if that State considers it appropriate.

2.   Each State Party shall likewise take such measures as may be necessary to establish its jurisdiction over such offences in cases where the alleged offender is present in any territory under its jurisdiction and it does not extradite him pursuant to article 8 to any of the States mentioned in Paragraph 1 of this article.

3.   This Convention does not exclude any criminal jurisdiction exercised in accordance with internal law.

Article 6

1.   Upon being satisfied, after an examination of information available to it, that the circumstances so warrant, any State Party in whose territory a person alleged to have committed any offence referred to in article 4 is present, shall take him into custody or take other legal measures to ensure his presence. The custody and other legal measures shall be as provided in the law of that State but may be continued only for such time as is necessary to enable any criminal or extradition proceedings to be instituted.

Article 7

1.   The State Party in territory under whose jurisdiction a person alleged to have committed any offence referred to in article 4 is found, shall in the cases contemplated in article 5, if it does not extradite him, submit the case to its competent authorities for the purpose of prosecution.

Article 8

1.   The offences referred to in article 4 shall be deemed to be included as extraditable offences in any extradition treaty existing between States Parties. States Parties undertake to include such offences as extraditable offences in every extradition treaty to be concluded between them.

4.   Such offences shall be treated, for the purpose of extradition between States Parties, as if they had been committed not only in the place in which they occurred but also in the territories of the States required to establish their jurisdiction in accordance with article 5, paragraph 1.

4. Convention for Suppression of the Financing of Terrorism

Article 2

1. Any person commits an offence within the meaning of this Convention if that person by any means, directly or indirectly, unlawfully and wilfully, provides or collects funds with the intention that they should be used or in the knowledge that they are to be used, in full or in part, in order to carry out:

(a) An act which constitutes an offence within the scope of and as defined in one of the treaties listed in the annex; or

(b) Any other act intended to cause death or serious bodily injury to a civilian, or to any other person not taking an active part in the hostilities in a situation of armed conflict, when the purpose of such act, by its nature or context, is to intimidate a population, or to compel a government or an international organization to do or to abstain from doing any act.

3. For an act to constitute an offence set forth in paragraph 1, it shall not be necessary that the funds were actually used to carry out an offence referred to in paragraph 1.

4. Any person also commits an offence if that person attempts to commit an offence as set forth in paragraph 1 of this article.

5. Any person also commits an offence if that person:

(a) Participates as an accomplice in an offence as set forth in paragraph 1 or 4 of this article;

(b) Organizes or directs others to commit an offence as set forth in paragraph 1 or 4of this article;

(c) Contributes to the commission of one or more offences as set forth in paragraphs 1 or 4 of this article by a group of persons acting with a common purpose. Such contribution shall be intentional and shall either:

(i) Be made with the aim of furthering the criminal activity or criminal purpose of the group, where such activity or purpose involves the commission of an offence as set forth in paragraph 1 of this article; or

(ii) Be made in the knowledge of the intention of the group to commit an offence as set forth in paragraph 1 of this article.

Article 3

This Convention shall not apply where the offence is committed within a single State, the alleged offender is a national of that State and is present in the territory of that State and no other State has a basis under article 7, paragraph 1, or article 7, paragraph

2, to exercise jurisdiction, except that the provisions of articles 12 to 18 shall, as appropriate, apply in those cases.

Article 4

Each State Party shall adopt such measures as may be necessary:

(a) To establish as criminal offences under its domestic law the offences set forth in article 2;

(b) To make those offences punishable by appropriate penalties which take into account the grave nature of the offences.

Article 5

1. Each State Party, in accordance with its domestic legal principles, shall take the necessary measures to enable a legal entity located in its territory or organized under its laws to be held liable when a person responsible for the management or control of that legal entity has, in that capacity, committed an offence set forth in article 2. Such liability may be criminal, civil or administrative.

2. Such liability is incurred without prejudice to the criminal liability of individuals having committed the offences.

3. Each State Party shall ensure, in particular, that legal entities liable in accordance with paragraph 1 above are subject to effective, proportionate and dissuasive criminal, civil or administrative sanctions. Such sanctions may include monetary sanctions.

Article 6

Each State Party shall adopt such measures as may be necessary, including, where appropriate, domestic legislation, to ensure that criminal acts within the scope of this Convention are under no circumstances justifiable by considerations of a political, philosophical, ideological, racial, ethnic, religious or other similar nature.

Article 7

1. Each State Party shall take such measures as may be necessary to establish its jurisdiction over the offences set forth in article 2 when:

(a) The offence is committed in the territory of that State;

(b) The offence is committed on board a vessel flying the flag of that State or an aircraft registered under the laws of that State at the time the offence is committed;

(c) The offence is committed by a national of that State.

2. A State Party may also establish its jurisdiction over any such offence when:

(a) The offence was directed towards or resulted in the carrying out of an offence referred to in article 2, paragraph 1, subparagraph (a) or (b), in the territory of or against a national of that State;

(b) The offence was directed towards or resulted in the carrying out of an offence referred to in article 2, paragraph 1, subparagraph (a) or (b), against a State or government facility of that State abroad, including diplomatic or consular premises of that State;

(c) The offence was directed towards or resulted in an offence referred to in article 2, paragraph 1, subparagraph (a) or (b), committed in an attempt to compel that State to do or abstain from doing any act;

(d) The offence is committed by a stateless person who has his or her habitual residence in the territory of that State;

(e) The offence is committed on board an aircraft which is operated by the Government of that State.

[The "prosecute or extradite" provisions are essentially the same as in other Conventions, such as the Torture Convention.]

5. UN Security Council Resolution 1373

Sept. 28, 2001

The Security Council,

Reaffirming its resolutions 1269 (1999) of 19 October 1999 and 1368 (2001) of 12 September 2001,

Reaffirming also its unequivocal condemnation of the terrorist attacks which took place in New York, Washington, D.C. and Pennsylvania on 11 September 2001, and expressing its determination to prevent all such acts,

Reaffirming further that such acts, like any act of international terrorism, constitute a threat to international peace and security,

Reaffirming the inherent right of individual or collective self-defence as recognized by the Charter of the United Nations as reiterated in resolution 1368 (2001),

Reaffirming the need to combat by all means, in accordance with the Charter of the United Nations, threats to international peace and security caused by terrorist acts,

Deeply concerned by the increase, in various regions of the world, of acts of terrorism motivated by intolerance or extremism,

Calling on States to work together urgently to prevent and suppress terrorist acts, including through increased cooperation and full implementation of the relevant international conventions relating to terrorism,

Recognizing the need for States to complement international cooperation by taking additional measures to prevent and suppress, in their territories through all lawful means, the financing and preparation of any acts of terrorism,

Reaffirming the principle established by the General Assembly in its declaration of October 1970 (resolution 2625 (XXV)) and reiterated by the Security Council in its resolution 1189 (1998) of 13 August 1998, namely that every State has the duty to refrain from organizing, instigating, assisting or participating in terrorist acts in another State or acquiescing in organized activities within its territory directed towards the commission of such acts,

Acting under Chapter VII of the Charter of the United Nations,

1.   *Decides* that all States shall:

(a) Prevent and suppress the financing of terrorist acts;

(b) Criminalize the wilful provision or collection, by any means, directly or indirectly, of funds by their nationals or in their territories with the intention that the funds should be used, or in the knowledge that they are to be used, in order to carry out terrorist acts;

(c) Freeze without delay funds and other financial assets or economic resources of persons who commit, or attempt to commit, terrorist acts or participate in or facilitate the commission of terrorist acts; of entities owned or controlled directly or indirectly by such persons; and of persons and entities acting on behalf of, or at the direction of such persons and entities, including funds derived or generated from property owned or controlled directly or indirectly by such persons and associated persons and entities;

(d) Prohibit their nationals or any persons and entities within their territories from making any funds, financial assets or economic resources or financial or other related services available, directly or indirectly, for the benefit of persons who commit or attempt to commit or facilitate or participate in the commission of terrorist acts, of entities owned or controlled, directly or indirectly, by such persons and of persons and entities acting on behalf of or at the direction of such persons;

2.   *Decides also* that all States shall:

(a) Refrain from providing any form of support, active or passive, to entities or persons involved in terrorist acts, including by suppressing recruitment of members of terrorist groups and eliminating the supply of weapons to terrorists;

(b) Take the necessary steps to prevent the commission of terrorist acts, including by provision of early warning to other States by exchange of information;

(c) Deny safe haven to those who finance, plan, support, or commit terrorist acts, or provide safe havens;

(d) Prevent those who finance, plan, facilitate or commit terrorist acts from using their respective territories for those purposes against other States or their citizens;

(e) Ensure that any person who participates in the financing, planning, preparation or perpetration of terrorist acts or in supporting terrorist acts is brought to justice and ensure that, in addition to any other measures against them, such terrorist acts are established as serious criminal offences in domestic laws and regulations and that the punishment duly reflects the seriousness of such terrorist acts;

(f) Afford one another the greatest measure of assistance in connection with criminal investigations or criminal proceedings relating to the financing or support of terrorist acts, including assistance in obtaining evidence in their possession necessary for the proceedings;

(g) Prevent the movement of terrorists or terrorist groups by effective border controls and controls on issuance of identity papers and travel documents, and through measures for preventing counterfeiting, forgery or fraudulent use of identity papers and travel documents;

3.   *Calls* upon all States to:

(a) Find ways of intensifying and accelerating the exchange of operational information, especially regarding actions or movements of terrorist persons or networks; forged or falsified travel documents; traffic in arms, explosives or sensitive materials; use of communications technologies by terrorist groups; and the threat posed by the possession of weapons of mass destruction by terrorist groups;

(b) Exchange information in accordance with international and domestic law and cooperate on administrative and judicial matters to prevent the commission of terrorist acts;

(c) Cooperate, particularly through bilateral and multilateral arrangements and agreements, to prevent and suppress terrorist attacks and take action against perpetrators of such acts;

(d) Become parties as soon as possible to the relevant international conventions and protocols relating to terrorism, including the International Convention for the Suppression of the Financing of Terrorism of 9 December 1999;

(e) Increase cooperation and fully implement the relevant international conventions and protocols relating to terrorism and Security Council resolutions 1269 (1999) and 1368 (2001);

(f) Take appropriate measures in conformity with the relevant provisions of national and international law, including international standards of human rights, before granting refugee status, for the purpose of ensuring that the asylum-seeker has not planned, facilitated or participated in the commission of terrorist acts;

(g) Ensure, in conformity with international law, that refugee status is not abused by the perpetrators, organizers or facilitators of terrorist acts, and that claims of political motivation are not recognized as grounds for refusing requests for the extradition of alleged terrorists;

4.   *Notes* with concern the close connection between international terrorism and transnational organized crime, illicit drugs, money-laundering, illegal armstrafficking,

and illegal movement of nuclear, chemical, biological and other potentially deadly materials, and in this regard emphasizes the need to enhance coordination of efforts on national, subregional, regional and international levels in order to strengthen a global response to this serious challenge and threat to international security;

5.   *Declares* that acts, methods, and practices of terrorism are contrary to the purposes and principles of the United Nations and that knowingly financing, planning and inciting terrorist acts are also contrary to the purposes and principles of the United Nations;

6.   *Decides* to establish, in accordance with rule 28 of its provisional rules of procedure, a Committee of the Security Council, consisting of all the members of the Council, to monitor implementation of this resolution, with the assistance of appropriate expertise, and calls upon all States to report to the Committee, no later than 90 days from the date of adoption of this resolution and thereafter according to a timetable to be proposed by the Committee, on the steps they have taken to implement this resolution;

7.   *Directs* the Committee to delineate its tasks, submit a work programme within 30 days of the adoption of this resolution, and to consider the support it requires, in consultation with the Secretary-General;

8.   *Expresses* its determination to take all necessary steps in order to ensure the full implementation of this resolution, in accordance with its responsibilities under the Charter;

9.   *Decides* to remain seized of this matter.

6. Draft Comprehensive Convention on International Terrorism

Article I

For the purposes of this Convention:

1.   "State or government facility" includes any permanent or temporary facility or conveyance that is used or occupied by representatives of a State, members of Government, the legislature or the judiciary or by officials or employees of a State or any other public authority or entity or by employees or officials of an intergovernmental organization in connection with their official duties.

2.   "Military forces of a State" means the armed forces of a State which are organized, trained and equipped under its internal law for the primary purpose of national defence or security, and persons acting in support of those armed forces who are under their formal command, control and responsibility.

3.   "Infrastructure facility" means any publicly or privately owned facility providing or distributing services for the benefit of the public, such as water, sewerage, energy, fuel or communications, and banking services, telecommunications and information networks.

4. "Place of public use" means those parts of any building, land, street, waterway or other location that are accessible or open to members of the public, whether continuously, periodically or occasionally, and encompasses any commercial, business, cultural, historical, educational, religious, governmental, entertainment, recreational or similar place that is so accessible or open to the public.

5. "Public transportation system" means all facilities, conveyances and instrumentalities, whether publicly or privately owned, that are used in or for publicly available services for the transportation of persons or cargo.

Article 2

1. Any person commits an offence within the meaning of this Convention if that person, by any means, unlawfully and intentionally, does an act intended to cause:

(a) Death or serious bodily injury to any person; or

(b) Serious damage to a State or government facility, a public transportation system, communication system or infrastructure facility with the intent to cause extensive destruction of such a place, facility or system, or where such destruction results or is likely to result in major economic loss;

when the purpose of such act, by its nature or context, is to intimidate a population, or to compel a Government or an international organization to do or abstain from doing any act. [In some versions of the draft, this last clause is printed at the end of, as if part of, subsection (b). If placed there, then (a) would stand alone without a requirement of political motivation and thus cover virtually any act of violence.]

2. Any person also commits an offence if that person attempts to commit an offence or participates as an accomplice in an offence as set forth in paragraph 1.

3. Any person also commits an offence if that person:

(a) Organizes, directs or instigates others to commit an offence as set forth in paragraph 1 or 2; or

(b) Aids, abets, facilitates or counsels the commission of such an offence; or

(c) In any other way contributes to the commission of one or more offences referred to in paragraphs 1, 2 or 3(a) by a group of persons acting with a common purpose; such contribution shall be intentional and either be made with the aim of furthering the general criminal activity or purpose of the group or be made in the knowledge of the intention of the group to commit the offence or offences concerned.

Article 3

This Convention shall not apply where the offence is committed within a single State, the alleged offender is a national of that State and is present in the territory of that State and no other State has a basis under article 6, paragraph 1, or article 6, paragraph

2, to exercise jurisdiction, except that the provisions of articles 10 to 22 shall, as appropriate, apply in those cases.

Article 4

Each State Party shall adopt such measures as may be necessary:

(a)   To establish as criminal offences under its domestic law the offences set forth in article 2;

(b)   To make those offences punishable by appropriate penalties which take into account the grave nature of those offences.

Article 5

Each State Party shall adopt such measures as may be necessary, including, where appropriate, domestic legislation, to ensure that criminal acts within the scope of this Convention are under no circumstances justifiable by considerations of a political, philosophical, ideological, racial, ethnic, religious or other similar nature.

Article 6

1.   Each State Party shall take such measures as may be necessary to establish its jurisdiction over the offences referred to in article 2 in the following cases.

(a) When the offence is committed in the territory of that State or on board a ship or aircraft registered in that State;

(b) When the alleged offender is a national of that State or is a person who has his or her habitual residence in its territory;

(c) When the offence is committed wholly or partially outside its territory, if the effects of the conduct or its intended effects constitute or result, within its territory, in the commission of an offence referred to in article 2.

2.   A State may also establish its jurisdiction over any such offence when it is committed:

(a) By a stateless person whose habitual residence is in that State; or

(b) With respect to a national of that State; or

(c) Against a State or government facility of that State abroad, including an embassy or other diplomatic or consular premises of that State; or

(d) In an attempt to compel that State to do or to abstain from doing any act;

(e) On board a ship or aircraft which is operated by the Government of that State.

3.   Each State Party shall take such measures as may be necessary to establish its jurisdiction over the offences referred to in article 2 in cases where the alleged

offender is present in its territory and where it does not extradite such person to any of the States Parties that have established their jurisdiction in accordance with paragraphs 1 or 2.

4.   When more than one State Party claims jurisdiction over the offences set forth in article 2, the relevant States Parties shall strive to coordinate their actions appropriately, in particular concerning the conditions for prosecution and the modalities for mutual legal assistance.

5.   This Convention does not exclude any criminal jurisdiction exercised in accordance with national law.

Article 7

States Parties shall take appropriate measures, before granting asylum, for the purpose of ensuring that asylum is not granted to any person in respect of whom there are reasonable grounds indicating his involvement in any offence referred to in article 2.

Article 8

States Parties shall cooperate in the prevention of the offences set forth in article 2, particularly:

(a)   By taking all practicable measures, including, if necessary, adapting their domestic legislation, to prevent and counter preparations in their respective territories for the commission, by whomsoever and in whatever manner, of those offences within or outside their territories, including:

(i) Measures to prohibit in their territories the establishment and operation of installations and training camps for the commission, within or outside their territories, of offences referred to in article 2; and

(ii) Measures to prohibit the illegal activities of persons, groups and organizations that encourage, instigate, organize, knowingly finance or engage in the commission, within or outside their territories, of offences referred to in article 2;

(b)   By exchanging accurate and verified information in accordance with their national law, and coordinating administrative and other measures taken as appropriate to prevent the commission of offences as referred to in article 2.

Article 9

1.   Each State Party, in accordance with its domestic legal principles, shall take the necessary measures to enable a legal entity located in its territory or organized under its laws to be held liable when a person responsible for the management or control of that legal entity has, in that capacity, committed an offence referred to in article 2. Such liability may be criminal, civil or administrative.

2.   Such liability is incurred without prejudice to the criminal liability of individuals having committed the offences.

3.   Each State Party shall ensure, in particular, that legal entities liable in accordance with paragraph (i) above are subject to effective, proportionate and dissuasive criminal, civil or administrative sanctions. Such sanctions may include monetary sanctions.

Article 10

1.   Upon receiving information that a person who has committed or who is alleged to have committed an offence referred to in article 2 may be present in its territory, the State Party concerned shall take such measures as may be necessary under its domestic law to investigate the facts contained in the information.

2.   Upon being satisfied that the circumstances so warrant, the State Party in whose territory the offender or alleged offender is present shall take the appropriate measures under its domestic law so as to ensure that person's presence for the purpose of prosecution or extradition.

6.   When a State Party, pursuant to the present article, has taken a person into custody, it shall immediately notify, directly or through the Secretary-General of the United Nations, the States Parties which have established jurisdiction in accordance with article 6, paragraph 1 or 2, and if it considers it advisable, any other interested States Parties, of the fact that such person is in custody and of the circumstances which warrant that person's detention. The State which makes the investigation contemplated in paragraph 1 shall promptly inform the said States Parties of its findings and shall indicate whether it intends to exercise jurisdiction.

Article 11

1.   The State Party in whose territory the alleged offender is found shall, if it does not extradite the person, be obliged, without exception whatsoever and whether or not the offence was committed in its territory, to submit the case to its competent authorities for the purpose of prosecution through proceedings in accordance with the laws of that State. Those authorities shall take their decision in the same manner as in the case of any ordinary offence of a grave nature under the law of that State.

2.   Whenever a State Party is permitted under its domestic law to extradite or otherwise surrender one of its nationals only upon the condition that the person will be returned to that State to serve the sentence imposed as a result of the trial or proceeding for which the extradition or surrender of the person was sought, and that State and the State seeking the extradition of the person agree with this option and other terms they may deem appropriate, such a conditional extradition or surrender shall be sufficient to discharge the obligation set forth in paragraph 1.

TABLE OF CASES

[References are to pages.]

[References are to pages.]

[References are to pages.]

[References are to pages.]

INDEX

A

AFGHANISTAN INVASION
Generally . . . 263
Dealing with resistance . . . 264

ALIEN TORT CLAIMS
Alien Tort Act and Torture Victim Prevention Act
. . . App-27
International law . . . 76

C

CIVIL LIBERTIES AND EMERGENCY POWERS
Generally . . . 339; 340; 374
Association of rights . . . 87; 102; 105; 106
British detention cases . . . 368
Canadian detention cases . . . 368
Ethnic profiling . . . 360
Existing law related to emergencies
    Generally . . . 349
    Japanese "exclusion" as an "emergency"
    . . . 357
    Military assistance to civilian authorities
    . . . 352
    Necessity doctrine . . . 350
Free expression and security . . . 371
Other states, violence in . . . 25
Post 9/11 emergency
    Generally . . . 359
    Ethnic profiling . . . 360
    Torture . . . 363
Torture . . . 363

CLASSIFIED INFORMATION PROCEDURES ACT (CIPA)
Generally . . . 221
CIPA procedures . . . 223
Discovery of classified information . . . 228
Executive control of classified information . . . 230
Secret evidence . . . 222
Secret trials . . . 232
Text of . . . App-32

CONSPIRACIES AND INCITEMENT
Generally . . . 83-84; 106; 114
Communist conspiracy and right of association
. . . 102

CONSPIRACIES AND INCITEMENT—Cont.
Defining the terrorist conspiracy . . . 87
Imminent threat . . . 106
International standards of incitement . . . 107
Intervening in . . . 90
Other nations
    Generally . . . 110
    Australia . . . 113
    France . . . 113
    Germany . . . 111
    Netherlands . . . 112
    United Kingdom . . . 110
Prosecution examples . . . 92
Treason, association, and conspiracy
    Generally . . . 96
    Communist conspiracy and right of association . . . 102
    Political freedom and . . . 97
    Sabotage and spying . . . 281
U.S. threats and incitements . . . 106
World Trade Center I and embassy bombings
. . . 84

D

DEFINITIONS (See STRUCTURES AND DEFINITIONS)

DESCRIBING TERRORIST GROUPS
Generally . . . 9
Funding . . . 12
Organization . . . 13
Religious motivations . . . 10
Separatism, revolution, and political motivations
. . . 11

DETENTIONS
British detention cases . . . 368
Canadian detention cases . . . 368
Convention Against Torture and Other Cruel, Inhuman or Degrading Treatment or Punishment . . . App-65
Military detentions (See MILITARY DETENTIONS)
Treatment of Prisoners of War, Convention Relative to . . . App-55
Without trial
    Generally . . . 50
    Aliens and visa violations . . . 50

[References are to page numbers]

[References are to page numbers]

[References are to page numbers]

[References are to page numbers]